# LibreOffice

# LibreOffice 5.4 Writer Guide

*Word Processing with Style*

*by*
*LibreOffice Documentation Team*

# Copyright

This document is Copyright © 2017 by the LibreOffice Documentation Team. Contributors are listed below. You may distribute it and/or modify it under the terms of either the GNU General Public License (http://www.gnu.org/licenses/gpl.html), version 3 or later, or the Creative Commons Attribution License (http://creativecommons.org/licenses/by/4.0/), version 4.0 or later.

All trademarks within this guide belong to their legitimate owners.

## Contributors

Jean Hollis Weber          Cathy Crumbley

## Acknowledgments

This book is updated from the *LibreOffice 4.2 Writer Guide*, which was adapted from the *OpenOffice.org 3.3 Writer Guide*. Contributors to those books are listed on page 21.

## Feedback

Please direct any comments or suggestions about this document to the Documentation Team's mailing list: documentation@global.libreoffice.org

**Note:** Everything you send to a mailing list, including your email address and any other personal information that is written in the message, is publicly archived and cannot be deleted.

## Publisher

Friends of OpenDocument, Inc.
544/60 Beck Drive North
Condon, QLD 4815, Australia
ISBN 978-1-921320-55-2

## Publication date and software version

Published 28 January 2018. Based on LibreOffice 5.4.

# Contents

# LibreOffice

*Preface*

# Who is this book for?

Anyone who wants to get up to speed quickly with LibreOffice Writer will find this book valuable. You may be new to word processing software, or you may be familiar with another office suite.

# What's in this book?

This book introduces some of the main features of Writer, the word processor component of LibreOffice, and provide instructions for their use.

**Part 1: Essentials**

**Part 2: Extras**

# Minimum requirements for using LibreOffice 5.4

For a detailed list of requirements and operating systems supported, see the LibreOffice website, https://www.libreoffice.org/get-help/system-requirements/

# How to get LibreOffice

Versions of LibreOffice for Windows, Linux, and MacOS can be downloaded free from https://www.libreoffice.org/download. Linux users will also find LibreOffice included free in many of the latest distributions. MacOS users can also purchase LibreOffice Vanilla from the App Store.

Portable and other versions of LibreOffice are listed on the download page. Linux, Vanilla, and other versions may differ in a few features from the descriptions in this book.

# Installing LibreOffice

Information on installing and setting up LibreOffice on the various supported operating systems is given here: https://www.libreoffice.org/get-help/install-howto/

# Setting up and customizing LibreOffice

You can change the default settings (options) in LibreOffice to suit your preferences. To change settings, go to **Tools > Options** on the Menu bar. Settings are described in the Help and in Chapter 2, Setting up LibreOffice, in the *Getting Started Guide*. Some settings of particular interest to users of Writer are covered in Chapter 20, Setting up Writer, in this book.

> ### Tip
>
> Many settings are intended for power users and programmers. If you don't understand what an option does, we recommend leaving it on the default setting unless instructions in this book recommend changing the setting.

You can customize menus, toolbars, and keyboard shortcuts in LibreOffice, add new menus and toolbars, and assign macros to events. See Chapter 21, Customizing Writer, for details.

# Extensions and add-ons

You can add functionality to LibreOffice with extensions and add-ons. Several extensions are installed with the program and you can get others from the official extensions repository, https://extensions.libreoffice.org/ and from other sources. See Chapter 21, Customizing Writer, for more information on installing extensions and add-ons.

# Where to get more help

This book, the other LibreOffice user guides, the built-in Help system, and user support systems assume that you are familiar with your computer and basic functions such as starting a program, opening and saving files.

## Help system

LibreOffice comes with an extensive Help system. This is your first line of support. The Help is available both online and offline. Windows and Linux users can choose to download and install the offline Help for use when not connected to the Internet; the offline Help is installed with the program on MacOS.

To display the Help system, press *F1* or select **LibreOffice Help** from the Help menu. If you do not have the offline help installed on your computer, your default browser will open a page on the LibreOffice wiki.

For quick tips, place the mouse pointer over any of the icons to see a small box ("tooltip") with a brief explanation of the icon's function. For a more detailed explanation, select **Help > What's This?** and hold the pointer over the icon. In addition, you can activate Extended Tips using **Tools > Options > LibreOffice > General**.

## Free online support

The LibreOffice community not only develops software, but provides free, volunteer-based support. See Table 1 and this web page: https://www.libreoffice.org/get-help/

For comprehensive online support from the community, look at mailing lists and the Ask LibreOffice website, https://ask.libreoffice.org/en/questions/. Other websites run by users also offer free tips and tutorials.

Table 1: Free support for LibreOffice users

| Free LibreOffice support | |
| --- | --- |
| Ask LibreOffice | Questions and answers from the LibreOffice community<br>https://ask.libreoffice.org/en/questions/ |
| Documentation | User guides, how-tos, and other documentation.<br>https://www.libreoffice.org/get-help/documentation/<br>https://wiki.documentfoundation.org/Documentation/Publications |
| FAQs | Answers to frequently asked questions<br>https://wiki.documentfoundation.org/Faq |
| Mailing lists | Free community support is provided by a network of experienced users<br>https://www.libreoffice.org/get-help/mailing-lists/ |
| Native language support | The LibreOffice website in various languages<br>https://www.libreoffice.org/community/nlc/<br>Mailing lists for native languages<br>https://wiki.documentfoundation.org/Local_Mailing_Lists<br>Information about social networking<br>https://wiki.documentfoundation.org/Website/Web_Sites_services |
| Accessibility options | Information about available accessibility options.<br>https://www.libreoffice.org/get-help/accessibility/ |

## Paid support and training

You can also pay for support through service contracts from a vendor or consulting firm specializing in LibreOffice. For information about certified professional support, see The Document Foundation's website: https://www.documentfoundation.org/gethelp/support/

# What you see may be different

## Illustrations

LibreOffice runs on Windows, Linux, and MacOS operating systems, each of which has several versions and can be customized by users (fonts, colors, themes, window managers). The illustrations in this guide were taken from a variety of computers and operating systems. Therefore, some illustrations will not look exactly like what you see on your computer display.

Also, some of the dialogs may be different because of the settings selected in LibreOffice. You can use dialogs either from your computer's operating system or from LibreOffice. The differences affect mainly Open, Save, and Print dialogs. To change which dialogs are used, go to **Tools > Options > LibreOffice > General** and select or deselect the option **Use LibreOffice dialogs**.

## Icons

The LibreOffice community has created icons for several icon sets: Breeze, Galaxy, High Contrast, Oxygen, Sifr, and Tango. Each user can select a preferred set. The icons in this guide have been taken from a variety of LibreOffice installations that use different sets of icons. The icons for some of the many tools available in LibreOffice may then differ from the ones used in this guide.

To change the icon set used, go to **Tools > Options > LibreOffice > View**. In the **User Interface** section, choose from the drop-down lists under **Icon size and style.**

**Note**

Some Linux distributions, for example Ubuntu, include LibreOffice as part of the installation and may not include all the icon sets mentioned above. You should be able to download other icon sets from the software repository for your Linux distribution if you wish to use them.

## Using LibreOffice on a Mac

Some keystrokes and menu items are different on a Mac from those used in Windows and Linux. The table below gives some common substitutions for the instructions in this chapter. For a more detailed list, see the application Help.

| Windows or Linux | Mac equivalent | Effect |
|---|---|---|
| Tools > Options menu selection | LibreOffice > Preferences | Access setup options |
| Right-click | Control+click and/or right-click depending on computer setup | Opens a context menu |
| Ctrl (Control) | ⌘ (Command) | Used with other keys |
| F5 | Shift+⌘+F5 | Open the Navigator |
| F11 | ⌘+T | Open the Styles and Formatting window |

## What are all these things called?

The terms used in LibreOffice for most parts of the user interface (the parts of the program you see and use, in contrast to the behind-the-scenes code that actually makes it work) are the same as for most other programs.

A dialog is a special type of window. Its purpose is to inform you of something, or request input from you, or both. It provides controls for you to specify how to carry out an action. The technical names for common controls are shown in Figure 1. In most cases the technical terms are not used in this book, but the Help and other sources of information often use them.

1) Tabbed page (not strictly speaking a control).
2) Radio buttons (only one can be selected at a time).
3) Checkbox (more than one can be selected at a time).
4) Spin box (click the up and down arrows to change the number shown in the text box next to it, or type in the text box).
5) Thumbnail or preview.
6) Drop-down list from which to select an item.
7) Push buttons.

In most cases, you can interact only with the dialog (not the document itself) as long as the dialog remains open. When you close the dialog (usually, clicking **OK** or a similar button saves your changes and closes the dialog; clicking **Cancel** closes the dialog without saving any changes), then you can again work with the document.

Some dialogs can be left open as you work, so you can switch back and forth between the dialog and your document. An example of this type is the Find & Replace dialog.

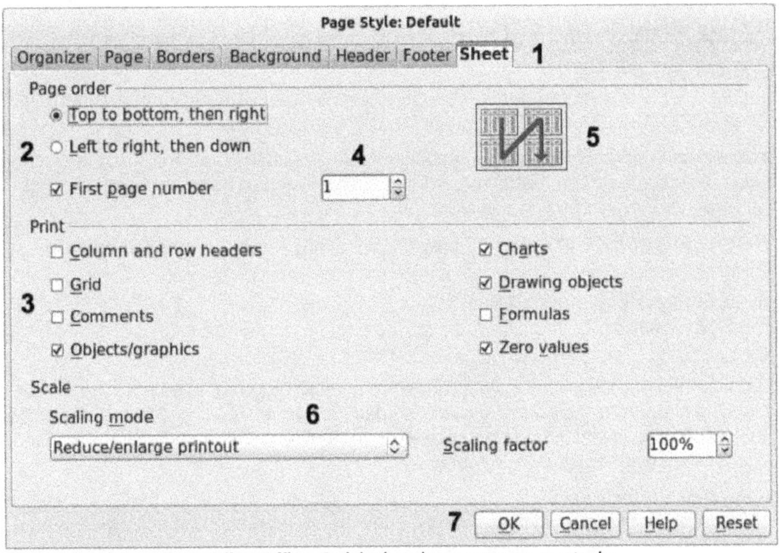

Figure 1: Dialog (from LibreOffice Calc) showing common controls

# Who wrote this book?

This book was written by volunteers from the LibreOffice community. You can contribute to writing this and other guides. Profits from sales of the printed edition will be used to benefit the community.

# Acknowledgements

This book is updated from previous versions of the *LibreOffice Writer Guide*. Contributors to the earlier versions are:

John A Smith
Hazel Russman
Jeremy Cartwright
Jamie Eby
Klaus-Jürgen Weghorn

Jean Hollis Weber
Leo Moons
John M. Długosz
Ron Faile Jr.
Rafael Atias

Peter Schofield
David Blymire
Barbara Duprey
Gary Schnabl
Preston Manning Bernstein

This book was adapted from the *OpenOffice.org 3.3 Writer Guide*. Contributors to that book were:

Jean Hollis Weber
Agnes Belzunce
Dick Detwiler
Katharina Greif
John Kane
Michael Kotsarinis
Alan Madden
Carol Roberts
Janet M. Swisher
Bob Wickham

Michele Zarri
Ken Byars
Alexander Noël Dunne
Tara Hess
Rachel Kartch
Sigrid Kronenberger
Paul Miller
Iain Roberts
Barbara M. Tobias
Claire Wood

Gary Schnabl
Bruce Byfield
Laurent Duperval
Peter Hillier-Brook
Stefan A. Keel
Peter Kupfer
Vincenzo Ponzi
Joe Sellman
Catherine Waterman
Linda Worthington

Magnus Adielsson
Daniel Carrera
Martin Fox
Lou Iorio
Jared Kobos
Ian Laurenson
Scott Rhoades
Robert Scott
Sharon Whiston

# Frequently asked questions

**How is LibreOffice licensed?**

LibreOffice 5.2 is distributed under the Open Source Initiative (OSI) approved Mozilla Public License (MPL). See https://www.libreoffice.org/about-us/licenses/

It is based on code from Apache OpenOffice made available under the Apache License 2.0 but also includes software that differs from version to version under a variety of other Open Source licenses. New code is available under LGPL 3.0 and MPL 2.0.

**May I distribute LibreOffice to anyone? May I sell it? May I use it in my business?**

Yes.

**How many computers may I install it on?**

As many as you like.

**Is LibreOffice available in my language?**

LibreOffice has been translated (localized) into over 40 languages, so your language probably is supported. Additionally, over 70 *spelling, hyphenation*, and *thesaurus* dictionaries for languages and dialects that do not have a localized program interface are available from the LibreOffice website at www.libreoffice.org.

**How can you make it for free?**

LibreOffice is developed and maintained by volunteers and has the backing of several organizations.

**How can I contribute to LibreOffice?**

You can help with the development and user support of LibreOffice in many ways, and you do not need to be a programmer. To start, check out this web page: https://www.libreoffice.org/community/get-involved/

**May I distribute the PDF of this book, or print and sell copies?**

Yes, as long as you meet the requirements of one of the licenses in the copyright statement at the beginning of this book. You do not have to request special permission. We request that you share with the project some of the profits you make from sales of books, in consideration of all the work we have put into producing them.

# LibreOffice

# Chapter 1
# Introducing Writer

# What is Writer?

Writer is the word processor component of LibreOffice. In addition to the usual features of a word processor (spelling checker, thesaurus, hyphenation, autocorrect, find and replace, and others), Writer provides these important features:

- Text entry, editing, and formatting (Chapter 2, 3, and 4)
- Change tracking during revisions (Chapter 4)
- Page layout methods, including styles, frames, columns, and tables (Chapters 5 and 6)
- Export to PDF, including bookmarks (Chapter 7)
- Document digital signatures (Chapter 7)
- Templates and styles (Chapters 8, 9, and 10)
- Images and drawing tools (Chapter 11)
- Lists (Chapter 12)
- Tables of data (Chapter 13)
- Mail merge (Chapter 14)
- Automated tables of contents and indexes (Chapter 15)
- Master documents, to group a collection of files into a single document (Chapter 16)
- Fields and forms (Chapters 17 and 18)
- Database integration, including a bibliography database (Chapters 14, 15, and 18)
- Embedding or linking of spreadsheets, equations, and other objects (Chapter 19)
- And many more

# Parts of the main Writer window

The main Writer window is shown in Figure 2. Its features are described in this section.

## Title bar

The Title bar is located at the top of the Writer window. It shows the file name of the current document. When the document is not yet named, the document name will appear as Untitled X, where X is a number.

## Menu bar

The Menu bar is located just below the Title bar in Windows and Linux and at the top of the screen in MacOS. When you select one of the menus, a submenu drops down to show further options, including:

- Commands that directly cause an action, such as **Close** or **Save**, in the **File** menu.
- Commands that open dialogs. These are indicated by an ellipsis (…) following a command, such as **Find** or **Paste Special,** in the **Edit** menu.
- Commands that open further submenus. These are indicated by a right-pointing arrow following a command, such as **Toolbars** and **Zoom,** in the **View** menu. Moving the cursor onto one of these items causes its submenu to open.

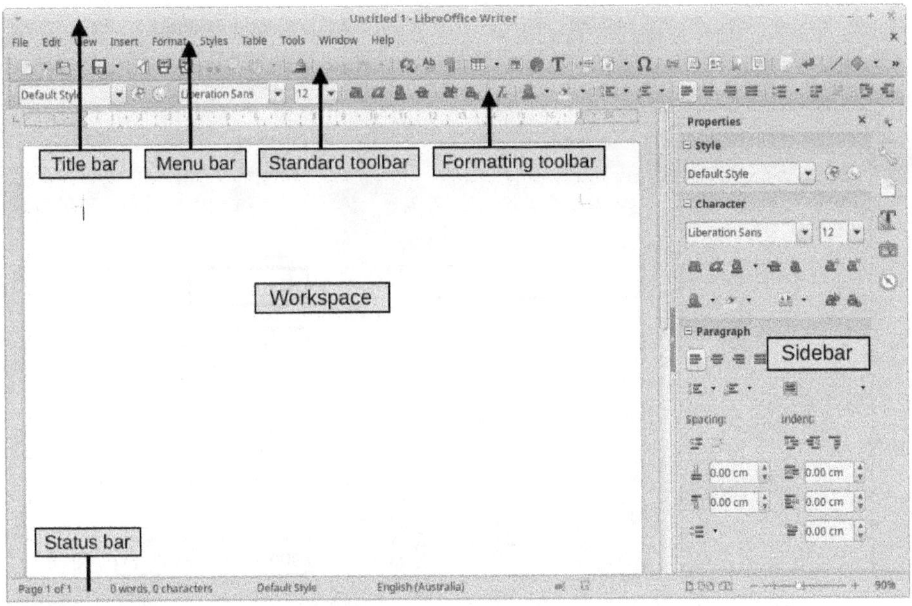

Figure 2: Parts of the main Writer window

## Sidebar

The Sidebar is normally open by default on the right side of the Writer window, as shown in Figure 2. If necessary, select **View > Sidebar** from the Menu bar to display it. The Sidebar also has a Hide/Show button, as shown in Figure 3. When the Sidebar is closed, it can be opened by clicking this button, which will be on the far right side of the window.

The Writer Sidebar contains four decks by default: *Properties*, *Styles and Formatting*, *Gallery*, and *Navigator*. Each deck can be opened by clicking its corresponding icon on the Tab bar to the right of the sidebar.

Two additional decks are available: *Manage Changes* and *Design*. By default, they are not enabled. See further information below.

Each deck consists of a title bar and one or more content panels. A panel is like a combination of toolbar and dialog. Toolbars and Sidebar panels share many functions. For example, the buttons for making text bold or italic exist in both the Formatting toolbar in the main Writer window and the Character panel of the Properties deck.

Some panels contain a **More Options** button, which opens a dialog with additional editing controls. When the dialog is open, the document is locked for other editing.

To adjust the width of the Sidebar, place the cursor on its left edge. When a double-headed arrow appears, click and drag to right or left. When the *Properties*, *Manage Changes*, or *Design* decks are open, you cannot make the Sidebar smaller than a certain width. When any of the other decks are open, the Sidebar can be collapsed to the width of its Tab bar.

To undock the Sidebar and make it floating, and to dock a floating Sidebar, use the drop-down list in the Sidebar Settings above the Tab bar (see Figure 3). From the same list, you can choose which items to include in the Sidebar.

Figure 3: Properties deck of Sidebar

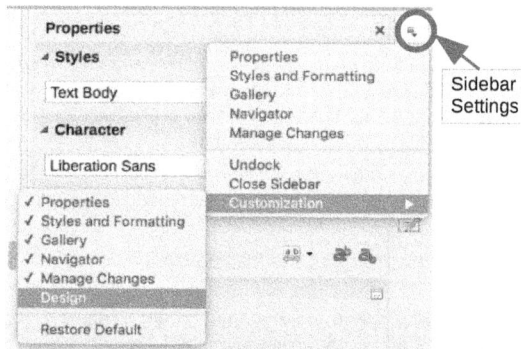

Figure 4: Sidebar Settings menu

### Sidebar decks

The decks contained in the Sidebar are described below.

**Properties deck:** Contains tools for directly formatting content.

When *text* is selected, these panels appear:

- *Styles:* Apply, create, or update a paragraph style.
- *Character:* Modify text by the font type, size, color, weight, or spacing.
- *Paragraph:* Modify a paragraph by alignment, lists or bullets, background color, indent, or spacing.
- *Page:* Format the page by orientation, margin, size, or number of columns.

## Caution

Be aware that by changing the options on the Page panel, you will change the page style in use, modifying not only the current page but all pages using the same page style in this document.

When a *graphic* is selected, these panels appear:

- *Area:* Modify the fill mode and transparency of the background.
- *Graphic:* Modify the graphic's brightness, contrast, color mode, or transparency.
- *Position:* Modify width and height.
- *Wrap:* Modify the position of the graphic relative to surrounding text, where these modifications are available.

When a *drawing object* is selected, these panels appear:

- *Area:* Modify the fill mode and transparency of the background.
- *Line:* Modify line style, width, color, or arrows.
- *Position and Size:* Modify width, height, rotation, or flip.

When a *frame* is selected, the wrap panel opens but may be grayed out if frame wrap is not available.

**Styles and Formatting deck:** Manage the styles used in the document, apply existing styles, create new styles, or modify them. For more information, see Chapter 9, Introduction to Styles, and Chapter 10, Working with Styles.

**Gallery deck:** Add images and diagrams included in the Gallery themes. The Gallery has two sections: the first lists the themes by name (Arrows, Background, Diagrams, etc.) and the second displays the images in the selected theme. Select the **New Theme** button to create new themes. To insert an image into a file, or add a new image to the Gallery, drag and drop the selected image. For more information, see Chapter 13, Images and Graphics, in *Writer Guide Part 2*.

**Navigator deck:** Browse the document and reorganize its content by selecting content categories, such as headings, tables, frames, graphics, and so on. For more information, see "Using the Navigator" on page 41.

**Manage Changes deck:** When changes have been recorded in a document, you can view, accept, or reject them in this deck. It provides the same functions as the floating Manage Changes window. This deck is available only when Experimental Features is enabled in **Tools > Options > LibreOffice > Advanced**. For more information, see Chapter 3, Working with Text: Basics.

**Design deck:** Provides quick access to document design themes (fonts and colors) and style presets. This deck is available only when Experimental Features is enabled.

## Toolbars

LibreOffice has two types of toolbar locations: docked (fixed in place) or floating. Docked toolbars can be moved to different locations (for example, top, bottom, or side of the workspace) or made to float, and floating toolbars can be docked.

### Displaying or hiding toolbars

To display or hide toolbars, go to **View > Toolbars** on the Menu bar, then click on the name of a toolbar in the drop-down list. An active toolbar shows a checkmark beside its name. Note that toolbars created from tool palettes are not listed in the View menu.

To hide a toolbar, go to **View > Toolbars** on the Menu bar and deselect the toolbar, or right-click in an empty space between the icons on a toolbar and select **Close toolbar** from the context menu.

### Most-used toolbars

In a default LibreOffice installation (see Figure 2), the top toolbar, just under the Menu bar, is called the *Standard* toolbar. It is consistent across the LibreOffice applications (Writer, Calc, Draw, Impress).

The second toolbar at the top is the *Formatting* toolbar. It is context-sensitive; that is, it shows the tools relevant to the current position of the cursor or the selected object. For example, when the cursor is in text, the Formatting toolbar provides tools for formatting text. When the cursor is on a graphic (image), the tools are for formatting images.

In some cases, it is convenient to reduce the number of toolbars displayed to free more space for the document workspace. LibreOffice provides a single-toolbar alternative to the default double-toolbar setup. It contains the most-used commands. To activate it, enable **View > Toolbars > Standard (Single Mode)** and also disable **View > Toolbars > Standard** and **View > Toolbars > Formatting**.

Other toolbars are available at **View > Toolbars.** These include commonly used toolbars such as Find, Drawing, Changes, and Bullets and Numbering. These and others are discussed in the relevant chapters of this book.

### Sub-menus and tool palettes

Toolbar icons with a small triangle to their right will display *sub-menus*, *tool palettes*, or other methods of selecting items, depending on the icon.

A tool palette is a pop-up collection of tools attached to a single tool in a toolbar. The palette can be made into a floating toolbar, as shown in Figure 5. Once removed from the parent toolbar, it displays a Title bar. Tool palettes can be floating or docked along an edge of the screen or in one of the existing toolbar areas.

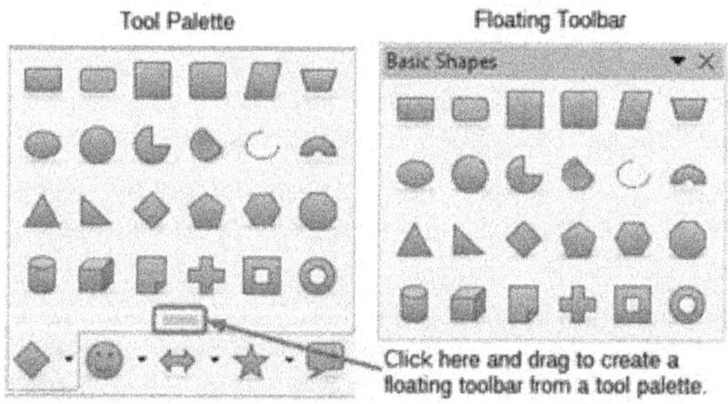

*Figure 5: Example of tearing off a tool palette*

### Moving toolbars

Docked toolbars can be undocked and either moved to a new docked position or left as a floating toolbar.

To undock a toolbar:

1) Move the mouse cursor over the toolbar handle, which is the small vertical bar to the left of a docked toolbar and highlighted in Figure 6.

2) Hold down the left mouse button and drag the toolbar to the new location.

3) Release the mouse button.

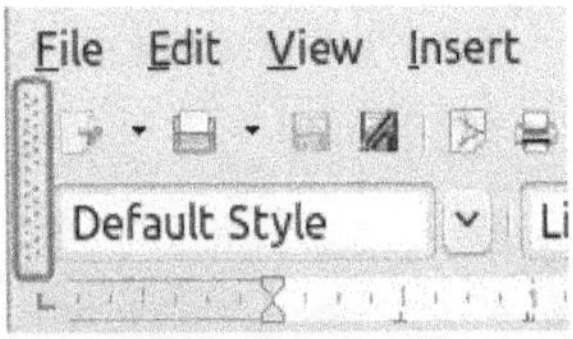

*Figure 6: Toolbar handles*

To move a floating toolbar, click on its title bar and drag it to a new floating location or dock the toolbar at the top or bottom of the main window.

### Note

You can also dock a floating toolbar by holding down the *Ctrl* key and double-clicking in the title bar of the toolbar.

## Floating toolbars

Writer includes several toolbars, whose default settings are floating in response to the current position of the cursor or selection. For example, when the cursor is in a table, a Table toolbar appears, and when the cursor is in a numbered or bullet list, the Bullets and Numbering toolbar appears. You can reposition or dock these toolbars as described in "Moving toolbars" above.

## Customizing toolbars

You can customize toolbars in several ways, including choosing which buttons are visible and locking the position of a docked toolbar. You can also add buttons and create new toolbars, as described in Chapter 19, Customizing Writer, in *Writer Guide Part 2*.

To position the toolbar:

- Click **Dock Toolbar** to dock the selected floating toolbar. By default, a toolbar will dock at the top of the workspace. You can reposition the toolbar to a different docked position. See "Moving toolbars" on page 28.

- Click **Dock All Toolbars** to dock all floating toolbars.

- Click **Lock Toolbar Position** to lock a docked toolbar into its docked position. Locking maintains the toolbar's position even when other toolbars on the same bar change location.

- Click **Close Toolbar** to close the selected toolbar.

Access a toolbar's customization options by right-clicking in an empty space between the buttons on the toolbar to open a context menu. Then choose among the following options:

- To show or hide icons defined for the selected toolbar, click **Visible Buttons** on the Context menu. Visible icons on a toolbar are indicated by an outline around the icon (Figure 7) or by a check mark beside the icon, depending on your operating system. Select or deselect icons to hide or show them on the toolbar.

- Click **Customize Toolbar** to open the Customize dialog. See Chapter 19, Customizing Writer, in *Writer Guide Part 2* for more information.

Figure 7: Toolbar Context menu and selection of visible toolbar icons

## Rulers

The horizontal ruler across the top of the workspace is visible by default but the vertical ruler on the left is hidden by default. To enable the vertical ruler, choose **View > Rulers > Vertical Ruler** from the Menu bar, or choose **Tools > Options > LibreOffice Writer > View**. To quickly show or hide both rulers, use the key combination *Ctrl+Shift+R*.

### Tip

The horizontal ruler has a comments button on its right end; click this to quickly show or hide any comments.

## Status bar

The Writer status bar is located at the bottom of the workspace. It provides information about the document and convenient ways to quickly change some document features. It can be hidden by deselecting it in the View menu.

Figure 8: Left end of Status bar

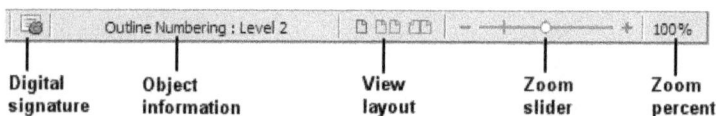

Figure 9: Right end of Status bar

**Page number**

Shows the the sequence number of the current page, the total number of pages in the document, and the current page number (if different from the sequence number). For example, if page numbering is restarted at 1 on the third page of a 6-page document, the sequence number is 3, the total number of pages is 6, and page number is 1—as shown in Figure 8.

If any bookmarks have been defined in the document, a right-click on this field pops up a list of bookmarks. Click on a bookmark to be taken to that location in the document.

To jump to a specific page in the document, click on this field. The Navigator opens (see "Using the Navigator" on page 41). Click in the **Page Number** field in the Navigator, type the sequence number of the required page, and press *Enter*.

**Word and character count**

The word and character counts of the document are shown in the status bar, and are updated as you edit. If specific text is selected, the count for that selection will replace the document total count.

What now?
Docking a boat.

11 words, 50 characters

What now?
Docking a boat.

3 words, 8 characters selected

By default, the character count includes spaces. To display the character count excluding spaces, double-click the word count in the status bar, or choose **Tools > Word Count.**

You can also see the number of words and characters (and other information including the number of pages, tables, and graphics) in the entire document in **File > Properties > Statistics**.

**Page style**

Shows the page style of the current page. To change the page style, right-click on this field. A list of page styles pops up. Click on one to select a different style. To edit the attributes of the current page style, double-click on this field. The Page Style dialog opens.

**Caution**

Changing the page style here may affect the styles of following pages, depending on how the page styles are set up. See Chapters 9 and 10 for details about styles.

**Language**

Shows the language used for spelling, hyphenation, and the thesaurus. It is based on the position of the cursor or the selected text.

Click to open a menu where you can choose another language for the selected text or for the paragraph where the cursor is located. You can also choose **None (Do not check spelling)** to exclude the text from a spelling check or **Reset to default language.** Choosing **More...** opens the Character dialog. See Chapter 3, Working with Text: Basics, for more information.

**Insert mode**

This area is blank when in Insert mode. Click to change to Overwrite mode; click again to return to Insert mode. In Insert mode, any text after the cursor position moves forward to make room for the text you type; in Overwrite mode, text after the cursor position is replaced by the text you type. This feature is disabled when using **Record Changes** mode.

**Selection mode**

Click to choose different selection modes. The icon does not change, but when you hover the mouse pointer over this field, a tooltip indicates which mode is active.

When you click in the field, a context menu displays the available options. See Chapter 3, Working with text: Basic, for details.

**Document changes status**

This icon ☑ shows when the document has no unsaved changes. This icon ☐* shows when it has been edited and the changes have not been saved.

**Digital signature**

If the document has been digitally signed, an icon is displayed here; otherwise, it is blank. Click here to sign the document or to view the existing certificate. See Chapter 8, Printing, Exporting, E-Mailing, for more information.

**Section or object information**

When the cursor is in a section, heading, or list item, or when an object (such as a picture or table) is selected, information about that item appears in this field. Double-clicking in this area opens a relevant dialog.

| Object | Information shown | Dialog opened |
|--------|-------------------|---------------|
| Image | Size and position | Image |
| List item | Level and list style | Bullets and Numbering[1] |
| Heading | Outline numbering level | Bullets and Numbering[1] |
| Table | Name or number and cell reference of cursor | Table Format |
| Section | Name of section | Edit Sections |
| Other | (Blank) | Fields |

**View layout**

Click the corresponding icon to change between single page, side-by-side, and book layout views (see Figure 10). You can edit the document in any view. Zoom settings interact with the selected view layout and the window width to determine how many pages are visible in the document window.

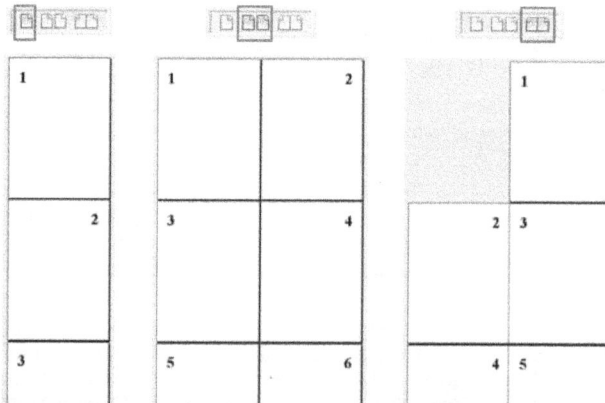

*Figure 10: View layouts: single, side-by-side, book*

---

1   If a *list style* was used with a list item or heading, no dialog appears.

**Zoom**

To change the view magnification, drag the Zoom slider, or click on the + and − signs, or right-click on the zoom level percent to pop up a list of magnification values from which to choose. Zoom interacts with the selected view layout to determine how many pages are visible in the document window.

# Context (right-click) menus

Context menus provide quick access to many menu functions. They are opened by right-clicking on a paragraph, graphic, or other object. When a context menu opens, the functions or options available will depend on the object that has been selected. This can be the easiest way to reach a function, especially if you are not sure where the function is located in the menus or toolbars.

# Document views

Writer has three ways to view a document: *Normal, Web,* and *Full Screen.* To change the view, go to the **View** menu and click on the required view.

You can also choose **View > Zoom > Zoom** from the Menu bar to display the Zoom & View Layout dialog, where you can set the same options as on the Status bar.

## Normal view

Normal view is the default view in Writer. It shows how the document will look when you print it or create a PDF. In this view, you can use the Zoom slider and the View Layout icons on the Status bar to change the magnification.

In Normal view, you can hide or show the headers and footers and the gap between pages. To hide them, choose **View > Hide Whitespace** from the Menu bar. A check mark will appear next to the option. When this option is activated, white space, headers, and footers are also hidden in Full Screen view.

## Web view

Web view shows how the document will look if viewed in a Web browser; this is useful when you create HTML documents. In Web view, you can use only the Zoom slider. The View Layout buttons on the Status bar are disabled, and most of the choices on the Zoom & View Layout dialog are not available.

## Full Screen view

In this view, no toolbars or sidebar are displayed; the document takes up the full area available, using the zoom and layout settings previously selected. To exit Full Screen view and return to either Normal or Web view, press the *Esc* key or click the **Full Screen** button on the floating toolbar in the top left-hand corner. You can also use *Ctrl+Shift+J* to enter or exit Full Screen view.

# Starting a new document

You can start a new, blank document in Writer in several ways. If a document is already open in LibreOffice, the new document opens in a new window.

## From the Start Center

When LibreOffice is open but no document is open, the Start Center is shown. Click the **Create: Writer Document** button to create a new text document, or click the **Templates** button to start a new document using a template other than the default template.

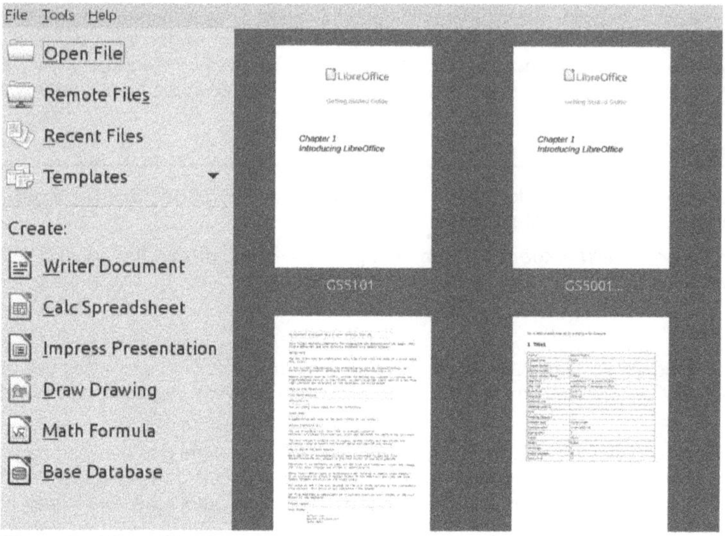

*Figure 11: LibreOffice Start Center*

## From the Quickstarter

When LibreOffice is installed on computers running Windows or Linux, a Quickstarter feature may also be installed. When Quickstarter is activated, the necessary library files are loaded when the computer system is started, resulting in a shorter startup time for LibreOffice components. Computers with a Mac operating system do not have a Quickstarter.

The default installation of LibreOffice does not set the Quickstarter to load automatically. To activate it, go to **Tools > Options > LibreOffice > Memory** on the Menu bar and select *Load LibreOffice during system start-up* (if using Windows) or *Enable systray Quickstarter* (if using Linux). Close and restart LibreOffice to have Quickstarter appear.

To use Quickstarter, right-click its icon in the system tray to open a pop-up menu (Figure 12). From here, you can create a new document or open the Template Manager dialog. You can also double-click the **Quickstarter** icon to display the Template Manager dialog. See Chapter 1, Introducing LibreOffice, in the *Getting Started* guide for more information.

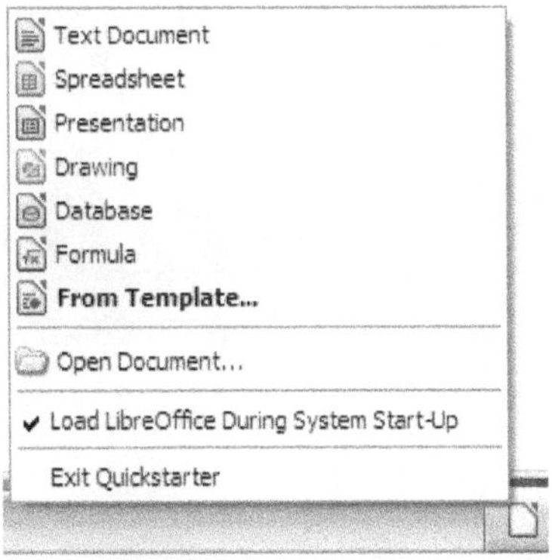

*Figure 12: Quickstarter pop-up menu*

## From the operating system menu

You can open the LibreOffice Start Center or the Writer component from the operating system menu in the same way that you start other programs. When LibreOffice was installed on your computer, in most cases a menu entry for each component was added to your system menu. If you are using a Mac, you should see the LibreOffice icon in the Applications folder. When you double-click this icon, LibreOffice opens at the Start Center (Figure 11).

## From the menu bar, toolbar, or keyboard

When LibreOffice is open, you can also start a new Writer document in one of the following ways.

* Press the *Ctrl+N* keys.
* Use **File > New > Text Document**.
* Click the **New** button on the Standard toolbar.

## From a template

A template is a set of predefined styles and settings that is used to create a new document. Templates enable the easy creation of multiple documents with the same default settings. For example, all the chapters of the *Writer Guide* are based on the same template. As a result, all the chapters look alike; they have the same headers and footers, use the same fonts, and so on.

A new LibreOffice installation contains only a few templates, but you can create your own or download more from http://templates.libreoffice.org/ and other websites. See Chapter 11, Working with Templates.

To open the Template dialog, where you can choose the template you want to use for creating your document, select one of the following:

* Press *Ctrl+Shift+N*
* **File > Templates > Manage**
* **File > New > Templates**
* Click the arrow button next to the **New** button on the Standard toolbar and select **Templates** from the drop-down list.

The example shown in Figure 13 highlights a template in the **Documents > My Templates** folder. Double-click on the desired template to create a new document based on the that template.

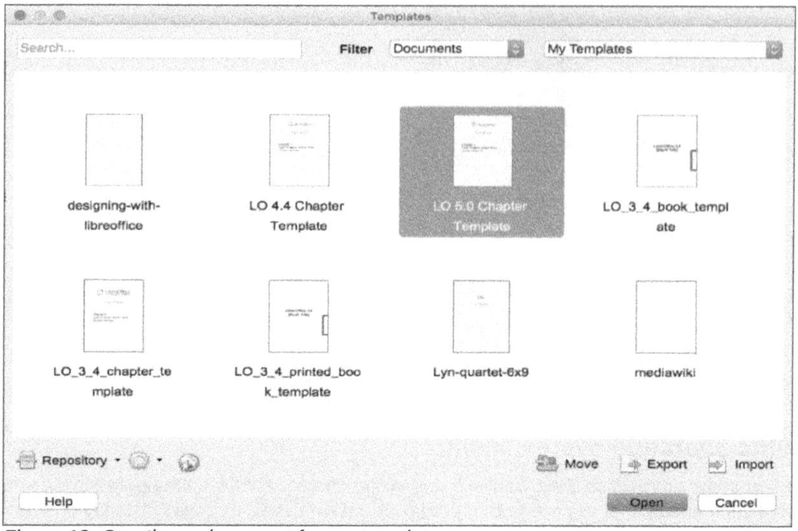

*Figure 13: Creating a document from a template*

# Opening an existing document

You can open an existing document in several ways.

When no document is open:

- Click **Open File** or **Remote files** in the Start Center.
- Choose **File > Open** or **File > Open Remote File** on the Menu bar.
- Press *Ctrl+O* on the keyboard.
- Click the **Open** button on the Standard toolbar.
- Double-click on a thumbnail of recently opened documents displayed in the Start Center. You can scroll up or down in the Start Center to locate a recently opened document.

If a document is already open:

- Click the **Open** button on the Standard toolbar and select the additional document to be opened from the Open dialog.
- Click the small triangle to the right of the **Open** button and select from a list of recently opened documents.
- Use **File > Recent Documents** to make a selection.
- Use **Open Document** on the Quickstarter.

When using the Open dialog, navigate to the folder you want, select the file you want, then click **Open**. If a document is already open in LibreOffice, the second document opens in a new window.

You can reduce the list of files in the Open dialog by selecting the type of file you are looking for. For example, if you choose **Text documents** as the file type, you will only see documents Writer can open (including .odt, .doc, .txt). This method opens Word (.doc and .docx) files as well as LibreOffice files and other formats.

You can also open an existing Writer document using the same methods you would use to open any document in your operating system.

If you have associated Microsoft Office file formats with LibreOffice, you can also open these files by double-clicking on them. See the Help for more about file associations.

# Saving a document

You can save a documents using either the Save commands or the Save as command.

## Save commands

### Save a new file or a previously-saved file

Do one of the following:

- Press *Ctrl+S*.
- Choose **File > Save** on the Menu bar.
- Click the **Save** button on the Standard toolbar.

If the file has not been saved previously, a Save As dialog appears after selecting one of the above options. Enter the file name, verify the file type and location, and click **Save**.

If a previously-saved file is being saved with the same file name, file type, and location, nothing else needs to be done.

### Save to a remote server

Use if your document is already stored on a remote server or you want to store it on a remote server. Choose **File > Save to Remote Server.** When the Save As dialog appears, enter or verify the name, type, and location, then click **Save**.

See "Opening and saving files on remote servers" on page 40 for more information.

### Save a copy

Use if you want to keep the document open for more editing and also save a separate copy of the current version.

Choose **File > Save a Copy.** When the Save As dialog appears, enter or verify the name, type, and location, then click **Save**. The copy is not opened and the original file remains open and active.

### Save all

Use to save all files open in the current session.

Choose **File > Save All.** All open files will be saved without changes to name, type, or location.

## Save As command

Use if you want to save the current version as a new document by changing the file name or file type, or by saving the file in a different location on your computer.

Choose **File > Save As**, or use *Ctrl+Shift+S* to open a **Save As** dialog where you can change the file name, type, or location, and click **Save**.

If you want to preserve the original file, first save a copy as described above.

## Saving a document automatically

You can choose to have Writer save your document automatically in a temporary file at regular intervals. To set up automatic file saving:

1) Select **Tools > Options > Load/Save > General**. (See also Chapter 20, Setting up Writer.)

2) Click on **Save AutoRecovery information every** and set the time interval. The default value is 15 minutes. Enter the value you want by typing it or by pressing the up or down arrow keys.

3) You may also wish to select **Always create backup copy**.

4) Click **OK** to save the changes.

## Saving as a Microsoft Word document

If you need to exchange files with users of Microsoft Word who are unwilling or unable to receive Open Document Format (ODF) files, you can save a document as a Microsoft Word file.

1) Important—First save your document in the file format used by LibreOffice Writer, .odt. If you do not, any changes you made since the last time you saved will only appear in the Microsoft Word version of the document.

2) Then click **File > Save As**.

3) On the Save As dialog, in the **File type** (or **Save as type**) drop-down menu, select the type of Word format you need. You may also choose to change the file name.

4) Click **Save**.

From this point on, all changes you make to the document will occur only in the new (Microsoft Word) document. If you want to go back to working with the .odt version of your document, you must open it again.

> ▶ **Tip**
>
> To have Writer save documents by default in the Microsoft Word file format, go to **Tools > Options > Load/Save > General**. In the section named Default File Format and ODF Settings, under **Document type**, select **Text document,** then under Always save as, select your preferred file format.

## Password protection

Writer provides two levels of document protection: read-protect (file cannot be viewed without a password) and write-protect (file can be viewed in read-only mode but cannot be changed without a password). Thus you can make the content available for reading by one group of people and for reading and editing by a different group. This behavior is compatible with Microsoft Word file protection.

To protect a document with passwords:

1) Use **File > Save As** when saving the document. (You can also use **File > Save** the first time you save a new document.)

2) On the Save As dialog, select the **Save with password** option in the lower left corner, and then click **Save**.

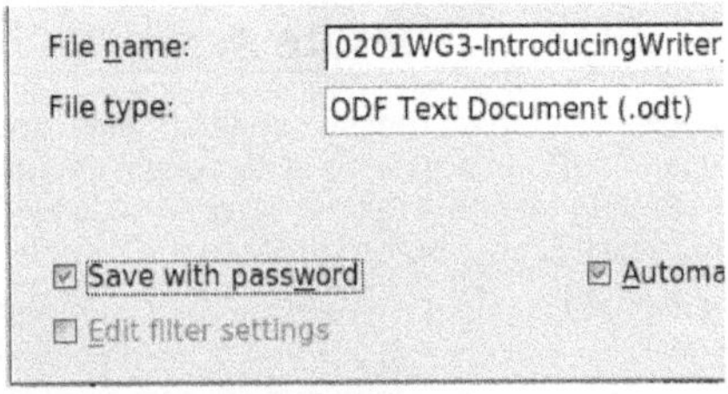

| File name: | 0201WG3-IntroducingWriter |
| File type: | ODF Text Document (.odt) |

☑ Save with password     ☑ Automa
☐ Edit filter settings

3) The Set Password dialog opens (Figure 14).

Figure 14: Two levels of password protection

Here you have several choices:

- To read-protect the document, type a password in the two fields at the top of the dialog.

- To write-protect the document, click the **Options** button and select **Open file read-only** in the File Sharing Password section.

- To write-protect the document but allow selected people to edit it, select **Open file read-only** and type a password in the two boxes at the bottom of the dialog.

4) Click **OK** to save the file. If either pair of passwords does not match, you receive an error message. Close the message box to return to the Set Password dialog and enter the password again.

### Caution

LibreOffice uses a very strong encryption mechanism that makes it almost impossible to recover the contents of a document if you lose the password.

### Changing the password for a document

When a document is password-protected, you can change the password while the document is open. Choose **File > Properties > General** and click the **Change Password** button.

# Opening and saving files on remote servers

LibreOffice can open and save files stored on remote servers (that is, not on your computer or local area network). This feature enables you to work on a document in the office and still have access to it from home or elsewhere. Storing files on a remote server also backs up documents, saving data from computer loss or hard disk failure. Some servers are also able to check files in and out, thus controlling their usage and access.

LibreOffice supports many document servers that use well-known network protocols such as FTP, WebDav, Windows share, and SSH. It also supports popular services like Google Drive and Microsoft OneNote, as well as commercial and open source servers that implement the OASIS CMIS standard.

**Note**

> To access remote servers, you must use the LibreOffice Open and Save dialogs (see Preface). If you use your operating system dialogs for saving and opening files, go to **Tools > Options > LibreOffice > General** and check the option **Use LibreOffice dialogs**.

To enable a remote server connection, use one of these methods:

- Click on the **Remote Files** button in the Start Center.
- Select **File > Open Remote File.**
- Select **File > Save to Remote Server.**

Then click on the **Add Service** button (Figure 16) in the Remote Files dialog to open the File Services dialog.

Depending on the type of file service you choose in the **Type** listbox, different parameters are necessary to fully qualify the connection to the remote server (Figure 15). These must be obtained from the service provider.

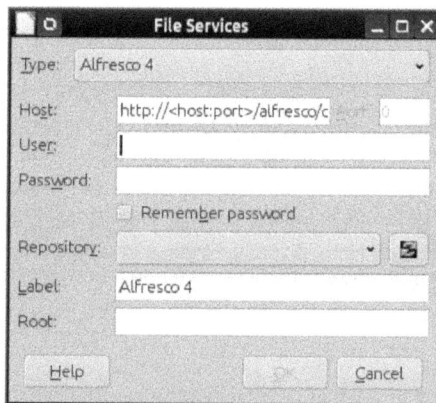

*Figure 15: Remote server configuration*

Once the connection is defined, click **OK** to connect. The dialog will dim until the connection is established with the server. A dialog asking for the user name and the password may pop up to let you log into the server. Proceed entering your credentials.

The Remote Files dialog (Figure 16) which then appears has many parts. The Service list box contains the list of remote servers you have previously defined. The line below the list box shows the path to access the folder. On the left is the folder structure of the user space in the server. The main pane displays the files in the remote folder. Click the **Open** or **Save** button to proceed.

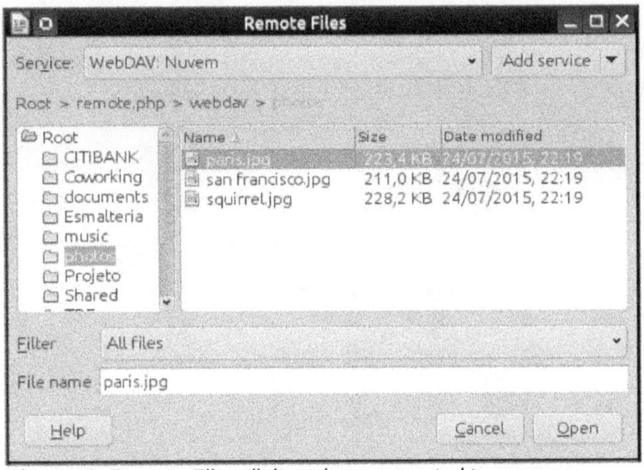

*Figure 16: Remote Files dialog when connected to a server*

## Renaming and deleting files

You can rename or delete files within the LibreOffice dialogs, just as you can in a file manager. Select a file and then right-click to open a context menu. Select either **Delete** or **Rename**, as appropriate. However, you cannot copy or paste files within the dialogs as you can in a file manager.

## Using the Navigator

Writer provides ways to move quickly through a document and find specific items by using the many features of the Navigator, the Navigation toolbar, and related buttons.

In the default installation of LibreOffice, the Navigator is part of the Sidebar. It lists all of the headings, tables, text frames, graphics, bookmarks, and other objects contained in a document.

To open the Navigator, do one of the following;

- Click the **Navigator** tab in the Tab bar on the right of the Sidebar.
- Double-click the **Page number** field on the status bar.
- Click the **Navigator** button (if visible) on the Standard toolbar.
- Press *F5*.
- Choose **View > Navigator** on the Menu bar.

Click the + sign or triangle to the left of a category or subcategory to display the contents.

Table 2 summarizes the functions of the buttons at the top of the Navigator.

**Note**

In a master document, the Navigator has different functions. See Chapter 17, Master Documents, in *Writer Guide Part 2*.

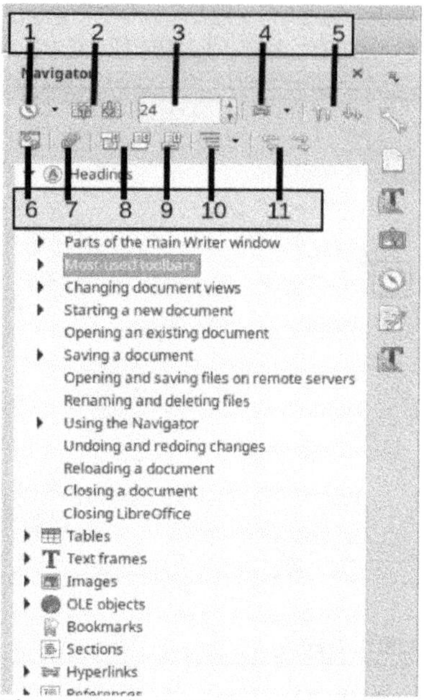

*Figure 17: The Navigator in the Sidebar*

Table 2: Function of buttons in the Navigator

| 1 | Navigation | Opens the Navigation toolbar (see page 43). |
|---|---|---|
| 2 | Previous, Next | Jumps to the previous or next item in the selected category (page, graphic, hyperlink, comment, and so on). To select the category of items, see "Using the Navigation toolbar" on page 43. |
| 3 | Page number | Jumps to the page sequence number shown in the box. Type the required page number or select it using the up and down arrows. |
| 4 | Drag Mode | Select Insert as Hyperlink, Link, or Copy. See "Choosing drag modes" on page 45. |
| 5 | Promote/Demote Chapter | Move headings and text in the document. See "Rearranging headings and text using the Navigator" on page 44. |
| 6 | Content Navigation View | Switches between showing all categories and showing only the selected category. |
| 7 | Set Reminder | Inserts a reminder. See "Setting reminders" on page 44. |
| 8 | Header/Footer | Jumps between the text area and the header or footer area (if the page has them). |
| 9 | Anchor <–> Text | Jumps between a footnote anchor and the corresponding footnote text. |
| 10 | Heading Levels Shown | Choose the number of heading levels to be shown. |
| 11 | Promote/Demote Level | Quickly change heading levels in the document. See "Rearranging headings and text using the Navigator" on page 44. |

## Moving quickly through a document

The Navigator provides several convenient ways to move around a document and find items in it:

- To jump to a specific page in the document, type its *sequence* number in the box at the top of the Navigator and press *Enter*. The sequence number may be different from the page number if you have restarted numbering at any point.
- When a category is opened to show the list of items in it, double-click on an item to jump directly to that item's location in the document. For example, you can jump directly to a selected heading, graphic, or comment by using this method.
- To see the content in only one category, highlight that category and click the Content View button. Click the button again to display all the categories. You can also change the number of heading levels shown when viewing Headings.
- Use the Previous and Next buttons to jump to other objects of the type selected in the Navigation toolbar. (See next page for details.)

### Note

A hidden section (or other hidden object) in a document appears gray in the Navigator, and displays the word "hidden" as a tooltip. For more about hidden sections, see Chapter 7, Formatting Pages: Advanced.

### Tip

Objects are much easier to find if you give them identifying names when creating them. By default, LibreOffice gives objects names such as Image1, Image2, Table1, Table2, and so on—which may not correspond to the position of the object in the document.

You can also rename objects after inserting them. For example, to rename an image, right-click on its name in the Navigator, choose Image from the context menu, then choose **Rename**. The view jumps to the image (so you can see which one it is) and a small dialog pops up. Type a new name for the image and click **OK** to save.

You can also right-click on the image and select **Properties**. In the Image dialog, go to the Options page, edit the name, and click **OK**.

## Using the Navigation toolbar

To display the Navigation toolbar (Figure 18), click the **Navigation** button (top left button on the Navigator, Figure 17) or the **Navigate by** button on the Find toolbar.

The Navigation toolbar has buttons for all the object types shown in the Navigator, plus some extras (for example, the results of a Find command). See Table 3.

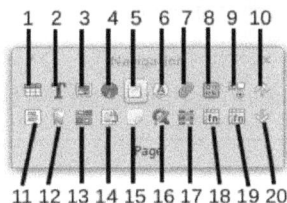

*Figure 18: Navigation toolbar*

*Table 3: Buttons in Navigation toolbar*

| 1 | Table | 6 | Headings | 11 | Section | 16 | Repeat search |
|---|---|---|---|---|---|---|---|
| 2 | Text Frame | 7 | Reminder | 12 | Bookmark | 17 | Index entry |
| 3 | Graphics | 8 | Drawing | 13 | Selection | 18 | Table formula |
| 4 | OLE Object | 9 | [Form] Control | 14 | Footnote | 19 | Wrong table formula |
| 5 | Page | 10 | Previous [Object] | 15 | Comment | 20 | Next [Object] |

Click a button to select that category of object (such as an image). Now the **Previous** and **Next** buttons (in the Navigator itself, in the Navigation toolbar, and on the Find toolbar) will jump to the previous or next occurrence of the selected type of object. This is particularly helpful for finding items like index entries, which can be difficult to see in the text. The names of the Previous and Next buttons (shown in the tooltips) change to match the selected category; for example, Next Graphic, Next Bookmark, or Continue search forward.

## Rearranging headings and text using the Navigator

You can move headings and their associated text to another location in the document by doing the following:

1) If necessary, click the expansion symbol (+ sign or arrow) to the left of a heading to expand the list of subheadings.

2) (Optional) If you have several subheading levels, you can more easily find the headings you want by changing the Heading Levels Shown selection to show only 1 or 2 levels of headings.

3) Click on the heading of the block of text that you want to move and drag the heading to a new location on the Navigator. Or, click the heading in the Navigator list, and then click either the **Promote Chapter** or **Demote Chapter** button. All of the text and subsections under the selected heading with it move up or down in the document .

To move only the selected heading and not the text associated with the heading, hold down *Ctrl*, and then click the **Promote Chapter** or **Demote Chapter** button.

### Tip

The names **Promote Chapter** and **Demote Chapter** can be misleading. They might be better described as Move Up or Move Down (within the document, without changing the heading level) to distinguish them more clearly from **Promote Level** and **Demote Level**, which change the heading level—from Level 1 to Level 2, for example.

To quickly change the *outline level* of a heading:

• To change the outline level of a heading and its associated subheadings, select the heading in the Navigator, then click either the **Promote Level** or **Demote Level** button. This action does not change the location of the headings, only their levels.

• To change the outline level of only the selected heading, but not its associated subheadings, hold down *Ctrl*, and then click the **Promote Level** or **Demote Level** button.

### Note

Users of Microsoft Word will notice the similarity between this functionality and Word's Outline View.

## Setting reminders

Reminders are one of the little-known features of Writer that you may find useful. Reminders let you mark places in your document that you want to return to later on, for example to add or correct information or simply mark where you finished editing. The possible uses of reminders are limited only by your imagination.

To set a reminder at the cursor's current location, click on the **Set Reminder** button in the Navigator. You can set up to 5 reminders in a document; setting a sixth causes the first to be deleted.

Reminders are not highlighted in any way in the document, nor are they listed in the Navigator, so you cannot see where they are, except when you jump from one to the next—the location of the cursor then shows the location of the reminder.

To jump between reminders, first select the **Reminder** button on the Navigation toolbar. Then click the Previous and Next buttons. Reminders are not saved with the document.

## Choosing drag modes

You can insert items such as other documents and images using the Navigator's drag and drop modes. Choose one of the following from the drop-down menu of the **Drag Mode** button. Then select the item and move it to where it should be inserted.

**Insert As Hyperlink**
Hyperlinks the entire item.

**Insert As Link**
Links the copied item to the original item so that when the original item is changed, that change will be reflected in the current document. By contrast, the copied item is protected and cannot be changed directly in the document. Note that you cannot create links for graphics, OLE objects, references, or indexes using this method.

**Insert As Copy**
Inserts a copy of the selected item.

# Undoing and redoing changes

To undo the most recent change in a document, press *Ctrl+Z*, choose **Edit > Undo** on the Menu bar, or click the **Undo** button on the Standard toolbar. To get a list of all the changes that can be undone, click the small triangle to the right of the **Undo** icon on the Standard toolbar. You can select several sequential changes on the list and undo them at the same time.

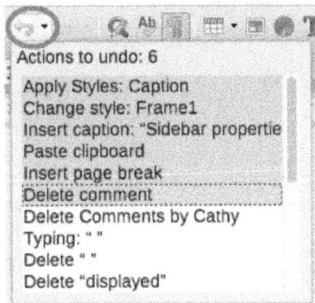

*Figure 19: List of actions that can be undone*

After changes have been undone, **Redo** becomes active. To redo a change, select **Edit > Redo**, or press *Ctrl+Y* or click on the **Redo** button ⟳ ▾ on the Standard toolbar. As with **Undo**, click on the down arrow button of the combination button to get a list of the changes that can be restored.

# Reloading a document

You may want to discard all the changes made in an editing session since the last time you saved it. But undoing each change or remembering where the changes took place can be difficult. If you are sure you do not want to keep the changes from the last time you saved the document, you can reload the document.

To reload a document, go to **File > Reload** on the menu bar. A confirmation dialog asks if you want to cancel all changes; choose Yes to return the document to the version that was last saved.

# Closing a document

If only one document is open and you want to close that document, go to **File > Close** on the Menu bar or click on the X on the Title bar. The X may be located on either the right or left end of the Title bar.

If more than one document is open and you want to close one of them, go to **File > Close** on the Menu bar or click on the X on the Menu bar of that document's window. When only the last document is open, the X on the Menu bar disappears.

If the document has not been saved since the last change, a message box is displayed. Choose whether to save or discard your changes.

# Closing LibreOffice

To close LibreOffice completely, go to **File > Exit** on the menu bar in Windows and Linux operating systems. In a Mac operating system, go to **LibreOffice > Quit LibreOffice** on the menu bar.

When you close the last document using the X on the Title bar of the window, then LibreOffice will close completely. A Mac operating system does not have this function; instead, you need to go to **LibreOffice > Quit LibreOffice** on the menu bar.

You can also use a keyboard shortcut:

- In Windows and Linux – Ctrl+Q
- In MacOS – Command ⌘+Q

If any documents have not been saved since the last change, a message box is displayed. Choose whether to save or discard your changes.

# LibreOffice

Chapter 2
*Working with Text: Basics*

# Introduction

This chapter covers the basics of working with text in Writer, the word-processing component of LibreOffice. It assumes that you are familiar with the use of a mouse and keyboard and that you have read about Writer's menus and toolbars and other topics covered in Chapter 1, Introducing Writer.

We recommend that you also display formatting aids, such as end-of-paragraph marks, tabs, breaks, and other items in **Tools > Options > LibreOffice Writer > Formatting Aids**.

When you have read this chapter, you should know how to:

- Select, cut, copy, paste, and move text
- Find and replace text
- Insert special characters
- Check spelling and grammar, use the thesaurus, and choose hyphenation options
- Use the autocorrection, word completion, autotext, and line numbering features

See Chapter 3 for more tools and techniques for working with text and Chapter 4 for methods of formatting text.

# Selecting text

Before you can do anything with text (other than typing in new text), you need to select it. Selecting text in Writer is similar to selecting text in other applications. You can swipe the mouse cursor over text or use multiple clicks to select a word (double-click), sentence (triple-click), or paragraph (quadruple-click).

You can also click in the text, press *F8* to enter "Extending selection" mode, and then use the arrow keys on your keyboard to select a contiguous block of text.

In addition to selecting blocks of text, you can select items that are not consecutive, and columns (vertical blocks) of text.

One way to change selection modes is to use the icon on the Status bar (see Chapter 1). When you click on the icon, a context menu displays the available options: Standard selection, Extending selection (*F8*), Adding selection (*Shift+F8*), and Block selection (*Ctrl+Shift+F8*).

## Selecting items that are not consecutive

To select nonconsecutive items (as shown in Figure 20) using the mouse:

1) Select the first piece of text.
2) Hold down the *Ctrl* key and use the mouse to select the next piece of text.
3) Repeat as often as needed.

To select nonconsecutive items using the keyboard:

1) Select the first piece of text. (For more information about keyboard selection of text, see the topic "Navigating and Selecting with the Keyboard" in the LibreOffice Help (*F1*).)
2) Press *Shift+F8*. This puts Writer in "Adding selection" mode.
3) Use the arrow keys to move to the start of the next piece of text to be selected. Hold down the *Shift* key and select the next piece of text.
4) Repeat as often as required.

Now you can work with the selected text.

Press *Esc* to exit from this mode.

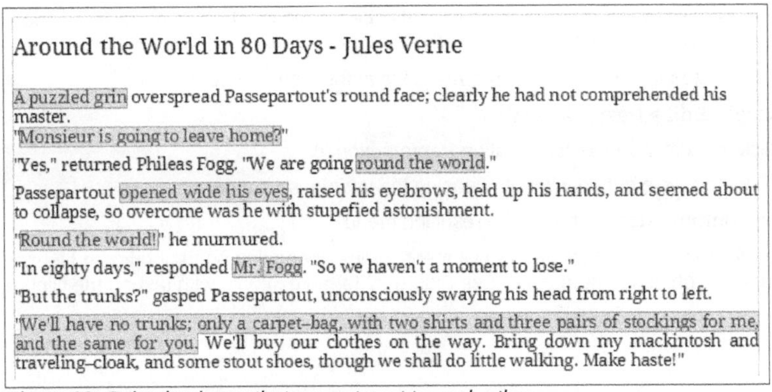

> Around the World in 80 Days - Jules Verne
>
> A puzzled grin overspread Passepartout's round face; clearly he had not comprehended his master.
> "Monsieur is going to leave home?"
> "Yes," returned Phileas Fogg. "We are going round the world."
> Passepartout opened wide his eyes, raised his eyebrows, held up his hands, and seemed about to collapse, so overcome was he with stupefied astonishment.
> "Round the world!" he murmured.
> "In eighty days," responded Mr. Fogg. "So we haven't a moment to lose."
> "But the trunks?" gasped Passepartout, unconsciously swaying his head from right to left.
> "We'll have no trunks; only a carpet-bag, with two shirts and three pairs of stockings for me, and the same for you. We'll buy our clothes on the way. Bring down my mackintosh and traveling–cloak, and some stout shoes, though we shall do little walking. Make haste!"

*Figure 20: Selecting items that are not next to each other*

## Selecting a vertical block of text

You can select a vertical block or "column" of text that is separated by spaces or tabs (as you might see in text pasted from e-mails, program listings, or other sources), using LibreOffice's block selection mode. To change to block selection mode, use **Edit > Selection Mode > Block Area**, or press *Ctrl+F8*, or click on the **Selection** icon in the status bar and select **Block selection** from the list.

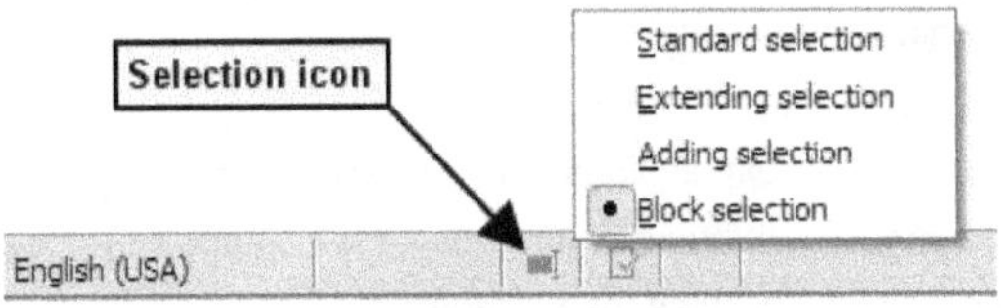

Now you can highlight the selection, using mouse or keyboard, as shown in Figure 21.

| January | February | March |
|---------|----------|-----------|
| April | May | June |
| July | August | September |
| October | November | December |

*Figure 21: Selecting a vertical block of text*

# Cutting, copying, and pasting text

Cutting and copying text in Writer is similar to cutting and copying text in other applications. You can copy or move text within a document, or between documents, by dragging or by using menu selections, icons, or keyboard shortcuts. You can also copy text from other sources such as Web pages and paste it into a Writer document.

To move (drag and drop) selected text using the mouse, drag it to the new location and release it. To copy selected text, hold down the *Ctrl* key while dragging. The text retains the formatting it had before dragging.

To move (cut and paste) selected text, use *Ctrl+X* to cut the text, insert the cursor at the paste-in point and use *Ctrl+V* to paste. Alternatively, use the buttons on the Standard toolbar.

When you paste text, the result depends on the source of the text and how you paste it. If you click on the **Paste** button, then the pasted text keeps its original formatting (such as bold or italics). Text pasted from Web sites and other sources may also be placed into frames or tables. If you do not like the results, click the **Undo** button or press *Ctrl+Z*.

To make the pasted text inherit the paragraph style at the insertion point:

- Choose **Edit > Paste Special**, or
- Click the arrow on the combination **Paste** button, or
- Click the **Paste** button without releasing the left mouse button.

Then select **Unformatted text** from the resulting menu.

The range of choices on the Paste Special menu varies depending on the origin and formatting of the text (or other object) to be pasted. See Figure 22 for an example with text on the clipboard.

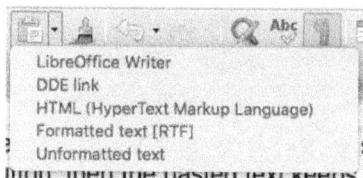

*Figure 22: Paste Special menu*

# Finding and replacing text

Writer has two ways to find text within a document: the Find toolbar for fast searching and the Find & Replace dialog. In the dialog, you can:

- Find and replace words and phrases
- Use wildcards and regular expressions to fine-tune a search (see Chapter 3)
- Find and replace specific attributes or formatting (see Chapter 3)
- Find and replace paragraph styles (see Chapter 3)

## Using the Find toolbar

By default, the Find toolbar is shown docked at the bottom of the LibreOffice window (just above the Status Bar) in Figure 23, but you can float it or dock it in another location. For more information on floating and docking toolbars, see Chapter 1, Introducing Writer. If the Find toolbar is not visible, you can display it by choosing **View > Toolbars > Find** from the Menu bar or by pressing *Ctrl+F*.

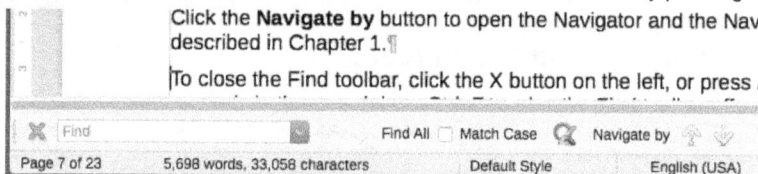

*Figure 23: Docked position of Find toolbar*

To use the Find toolbar, click in the text input box and type your search text, then press *Enter* to find the next occurrence of that term from the current cursor position. Click the **Find Next** or **Find Previous** buttons as needed.

Click the **Find All** button to select all instances of the search term within the document. Select **Match Case** to find only the instances that exactly match the search term. Click the button next to Match Case (  ) to open the Find & Replace dialog.

Click the **Navigate by** button to open the Navigator and the Navigation toolbar, which are described in Chapter 1.

To close the Find toolbar, click the X button on the left, or press *Esc* on the keyboard when the text cursor is in the search box. *Ctrl+F* toggles the Find toolbar off and on.

## Using the Find & Replace dialog

To display the Find & Replace dialog, use the keyboard shortcut *Ctrl+H*, or choose **Edit > Find & Replace** from the Menu bar, or click the Find & Replace button ( 🔍 ) on the Find toolbar. When the dialog is open, optionally click **Other Options** to expand it (see Figure 24). Extra options are shown when CTL or Asian languages have been selected in **Tools > Options > Language Settings > Languages**.

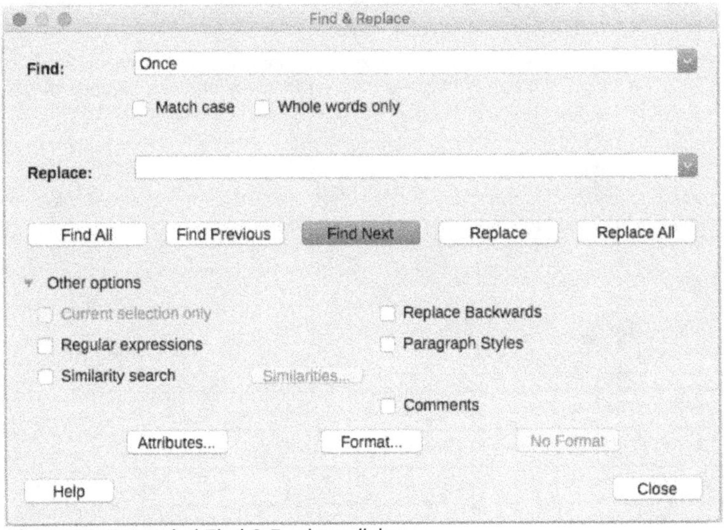

*Figure 24: Expanded Find & Replace dialog*

To use the Find & Replace dialog:

1) Type the text you want to find in the **Find** box.

2) To replace the text with different text, type the new text in the **Replace** box.

3) You can select various options, such as matching the case or matching whole words only.

   The other options include searching only in selected text, searching from the current cursor position backwards toward the beginning of the file, searching for similar words, and searching in comments.

   The use of other options choices is described in Chapter 3.

4) When you have set up your search, click **Find Next**. As the document view moves to each found instance, replace the text by clicking **Replace**.

▶ **Tip**

If you click **Find All**, Writer selects all instances of the search text in the document. Similarly, if you click **Replace All**, Writer replaces all matches, without stopping for you to accept each instance.

## Caution

Use **Replace All** with caution; otherwise, you may end up with some highly embarrassing (and hilarious) mistakes. A mistake with **Replace All** might require a manual, word-by-word, search to fix.

# Inserting special characters

A special character is one not found on a standard English keyboard. For example, © ¾ æ ç Ł ñ ö ø ¢ are all special characters. To insert a special character:

1) Place the cursor in the document where you want the character to appear.
2) Click **Insert > Special Character** or click on the Special Character icon in the main toolbar to open the Special Characters dialog (Figure 25).
3) Select the characters (from any font or mixture of fonts) you wish to insert, in order; then click **OK**. The selected characters are shown in the lower left of the dialog. As you select each character, it is shown on the right, along with the numerical code for that character.

## Tip

Different fonts include different special characters. If you do not find a particular special character you want, try changing the *Font* selection.

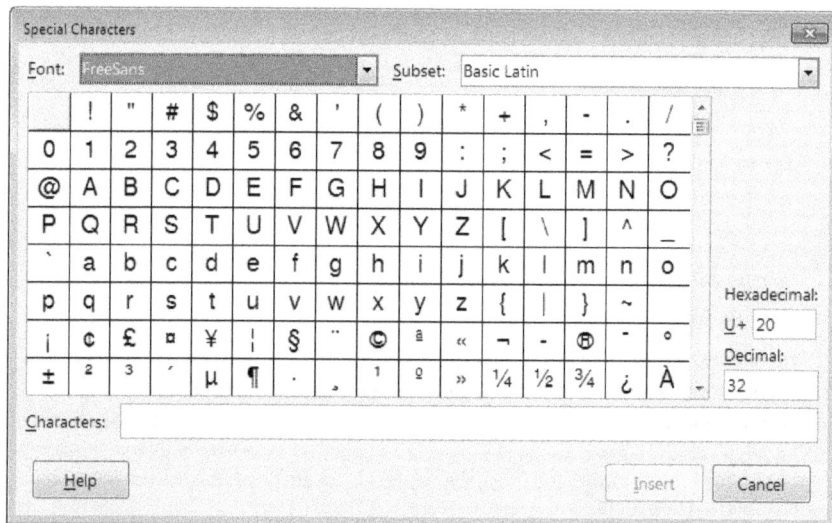

*Figure 25: The Special Characters dialog, where you can insert special characters*

## Inserting non-breaking spaces and hyphens

### Non-breaking spaces

To prevent two words from being separated at the end of a line, press *Ctrl+Shift* when you type the space between the two words.

**Non-breaking hyphen**

You can use a non-breaking hyphen in cases where you do not want the hyphen to appear at the end of a line, for example in a number such as 123-4567. To insert a non-breaking hyphen, press *Shift+Ctrl+minus sign*.

These are also available through **Insert > Formatting Mark.**

## Inserting en and em dashes

To enter en and em dashes as you type, you can use the *Replace dashes* option on the Options tab under **Tools > AutoCorrect > AutoCorrect Options**. This option replaces two hyphens, under certain conditions, with the corresponding dash.

– is an en-dash; that is, a dash the width of the letter "n" in the font you are using. Type at least one character, a space, one or two hyphens, another space, and at least one more letter. The one or two hyphens will be replaced by an en-dash.

— is an em-dash; that is, a dash the width of the letter "m" in the font you are using. Type at least one character, two hyphens, and at least one more character. The two hyphens will be replaced by an em-dash. Exception: if the characters are numbers, as in a date or time range, the two hyphens are replaced by an en-dash.

In Table 4, the A and B represent text consisting of letters A to z or digits 0 to 9.

*Table 4: Inserting dashes*

| Text that you type | Result |
|---|---|
| A - B (A, space, hyphen, space, B) | A – B (A, space, en dash, space, B) |
| A -- B (A, space, hyphen, hyphen, space, B) | A – B (A, space, en dash, space, B) |
| A--B (A, hyphen, hyphen, B) | A—B (A, em dash, B) |
| 1--2 (number, hyphen, hyphen, number) | 1–2 (number, en dash, number) |
| A-B (A, hyphen, B) | A-B (unchanged) |
| A -B (A, space, hyphen, B) | A -B (unchanged) |
| A --B (A, space, hyphen, hyphen, B) | A –B (A, space, en dash, B) |

Another means of inserting en and em dashes is through the **Insert > Special Characters** menu. Select the **U+2013** or **U+2014** character (found in the *General punctuation* subset), respectively.

A third method uses keyboard shortcuts. These shortcuts vary depending on your operating system, as described below.

▶ **Tip**

You can also record macros to insert en and em dashes and assign those macros to unused key combinations, for example *Ctrl+Shift+N* and *Ctrl+Shift+M*. For more information, see Chapter 21, Customizing Writer.

**Mac OS X**

For an en dash, hold down the *Option* (*Alt*) key and type a hyphen. For an em dash, the combination is *Shift+Option+Hyphen*.

**Windows**

On most non-Asian installations of Windows, hold down one of the *Alt* keys and type on the numeric keypad: 0150 for an en dash or 0151 for an em dash. The dash appears when you release the *Alt* key.

► **Tip**

On a keyboard with no numeric keypad, use a *Fn* (*Function*) key combination to type the numbers. (The *Fn* key is usually to the right of the left-hand *Ctrl* key on the keyboard.)

For example, on a US keyboard layout, the combination for an en dash should be *Alt+Fn+mjim* and for an em dash it should be *Alt+Fn+mjij*.

**Linux**

Hold down the *Compose* key and type two hyphens and a period for an en dash, or three hyphens for an em dash. The dash appears when you release the *Compose* key.

► **Tip**

The key that operates as a *Compose* key varies with the Linux distribution. It is usually one of the *Alt* or *Win* keys, but may be another key, and should be user-selectable.

# Checking spelling and grammar

## Spelling

Writer provides a spelling checker, which checks to see if each word in the document is in the installed dictionary. Also provided is a grammar checker, which can be used separately or in combination with the spelling checker.

**Automatic Spell Checking** checks each word as it is typed and displays a wavy red line under any unrecognized words. Right-click on an unrecognized word to open a context menu (Figure 26). You can click on one of the suggested words to replace the underlined word with the one selected. If the list does not contain the word you want, click **Spelling and Grammar** to open a dialog. When the word is corrected, the line disappears.

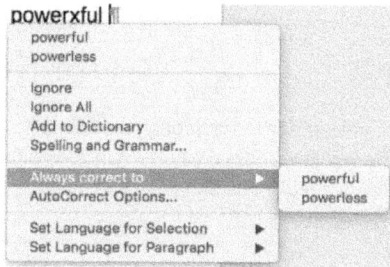

*Figure 26: Spelling context menu*

To enable automatic checking, go to **Tools** on the Menu bar and select **Automatic Spell Checking**. It can also be enabled from the Standard Toolbar by clicking the Automatic Spell Checking button (which may not be displayed on a default toolbar), or from **Tools > Options > Language Settings > Writing Aids** and selecting **Check spelling as you type** in the *Options* list.

If the document has change tracking enabled, then the context menu contains extra options relating to changes in the text.

The choices in the second and third sections of the menu are:

**Ignore**

This one instance of the underlined word will be ignored while the document is open. Other instances, if they exist, will still be underlined. This setting is not stored with the document.

**Ignore All**

All instances of the word in the document will be ignored, and the word will be added to the **IgnoreAllList** user-defined dictionary.

**Add to Dictionary**

The word is added by default to the **Standard** dictionary.

**Spelling and Grammar**

This opens the **Spelling and Grammar** checker. See the explanations for this below.

**Always correct to**

Selecting this opens the submenu, which repeats the suggestions for the word from the top section listing. Selecting a replacement word here stores the word pair in the replacement table under **Tools > AutoCorrect > AutoCorrect Options > Replacement**. The underlined word is replaced with the selected word.

**AutoCorrect Options**

Opens the AutoCorrect Options dialog (see page 62), where you can add your own corrections or change those supplied with LibreOffice.

In the fourth section of the context menu, you can set language settings for the text. These settings can be applied to the selection, or to the paragraph containing the selection.

## Spelling and grammar

To perform a combined spelling and grammar check on the document (or a text selection), select **Tools > Spelling and Grammar**, or click the **Spelling and Grammar** button on the Standard toolbar, or press *F7*. In order to use this feature, the appropriate dictionaries must be installed. By default, four dictionaries are installed: a spelling checker, a grammar checker, a hyphenation dictionary, and a thesaurus.

The Spelling and Grammar tool checks either the document from the cursor point onwards, or the text selection. It opens the Spelling and Grammar dialog (Figure 27) if any unrecognized words are found, or if any of the built-in grammar rules are broken. You can choose to restart from the beginning of the document when the check reaches the end of the document.

The elements of the Spelling and Grammar dialog are as follows.

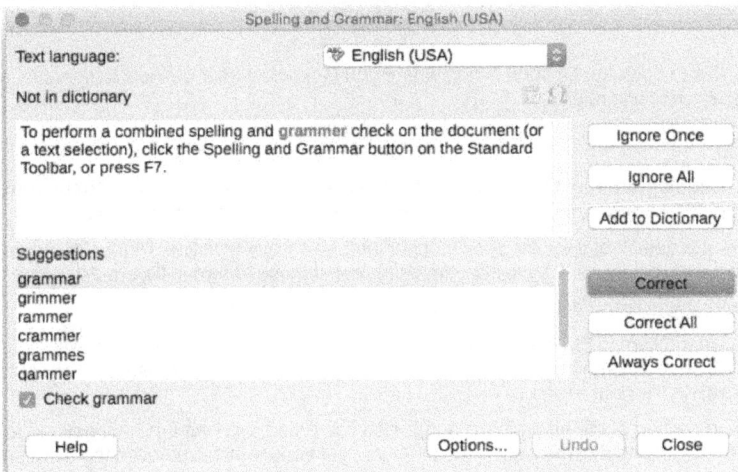

*Figure 27: Spelling alert using the Spelling and Grammar dialog*

**Text language**

The language to be used for the spelling and grammar checking can be selected from this list. If the spell check is enabled for this language, a check mark is displayed in front of it.

**Not in dictionary**

The sentence containing the error is displayed in the pane. If an unrecognized word is found, it is highlighted.

If the error is grammatical, then it is indicated in a pale colored bar below the **Text language** setting (Figure 29). The sentence or the word can be edited in the pane.

**Suggestions**

The box contains suggested replacements for the highlighted word. Select a word and then select **Correct** or **Correct All** to replace it.

For grammatical errors there is no multiple choice. Select **Change** to accept the suggestion.

**Ignore Once, Ignore All, and Add to Dictionary**

Clicking one of these buttons has the same effect as the item in the context menu described above.

**Ignore Rule**

When checking grammar, you can choose to ignore the suggested change.

**Correct**

Replaces the unknown word with the suggested word. If the sentence was edited, the whole sentence is changed.

For grammar, the suggested replacement is used to correct the text.

**Correct All**

This replaces all instances of the word with the selected replacement word. Not available for grammar checking.

**Always Correct**

This behaves in a similar fashion to **AutoCorrect** described above.

**Undo**

This button is enabled when a change has been made to the sentence, so you can reverse the change. The button is not available if you use a **Correct** button to replace a word.

**Options**

Click this to open the Options dialog where you can select user-defined dictionaries and set the spell checking rules.

## Grammar

By default, **Check grammar as you type** is enabled in **Tools > Options > Language Settings > Writing Aids > Options**. Automatic Spell Checking must be enabled for this to work.

If any errors are detected, they are shown underlined by a wavy blue line. Right-clicking on this line brings up a context menu which may be similar to one of those shown in Figure 28.

The first entry in the menu describes the suspected broken grammatical rule.

The second menu item in the left example is **Explanations**, which opens your browser to a web page offering more information about the error. This entry is not always present in the context menu, as seen in the right example.

In the second section of the menu is the suggested correction. Clicking this changes the text to the suggestion. The example to the right appears blank, but clicking here removes the extra space causing the error.

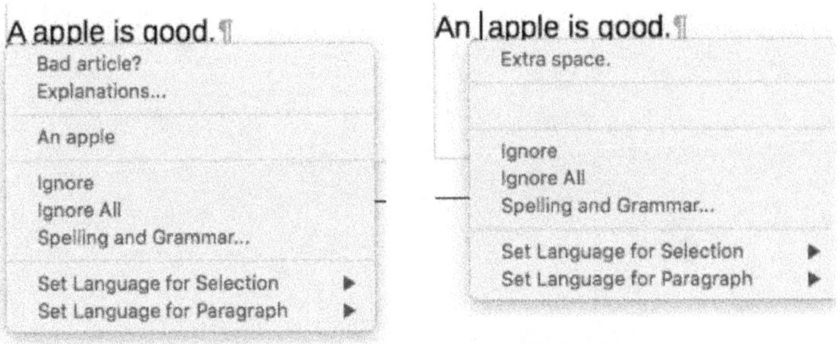

Figure 28: Typical context menus for suspected grammar errors

In the third section of the menu you can choose to ignore the indicated error, or to open the Spelling and Grammar checker, shown in Figure 29. The example displays the URL that will take you to more information on the error indicated.

In the final section of the menu, you can set the language for the selection or the paragraph.

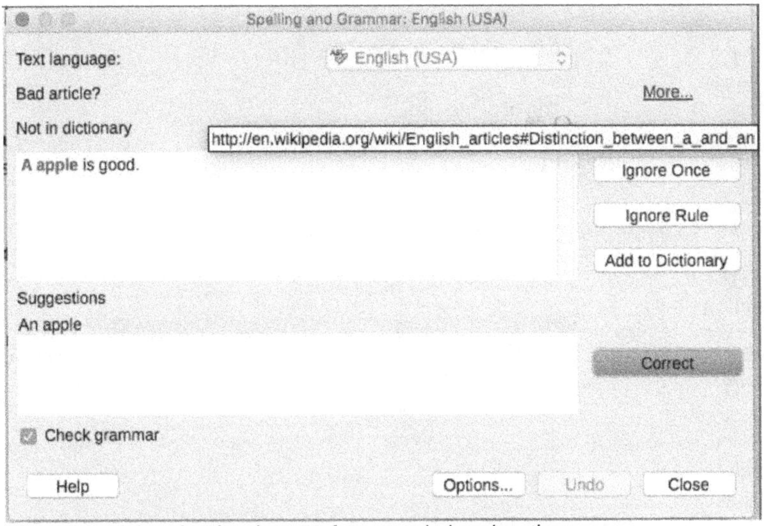

Figure 29: Dialog showing the URL for expanded explanation

## English sentence checking

Additional grammar checking rules can be selected through **Tools > Options > Language Settings > English sentence checking**, or through **Tools > Extension Manager > English spelling dictionaries > Options**.

On the **Language Settings > English sentence checking** page, you can choose which items are checked for, reported to you, or converted automatically. Select which of the optional features you wish to check.

After selecting the additional grammar checks, you must restart LibreOffice, or reload the document, for them to take effect.

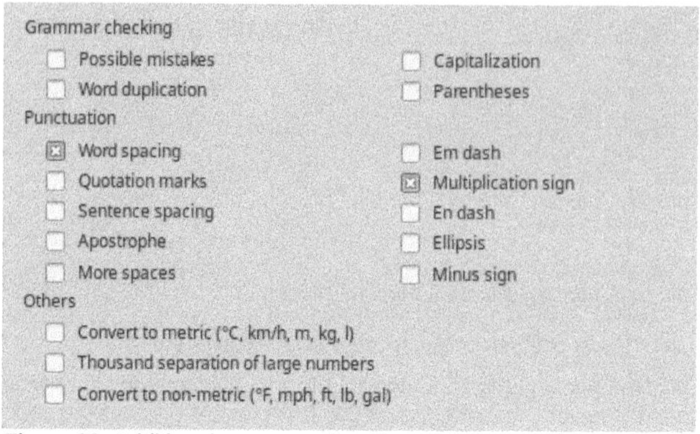

*Figure 30: Additional grammar checking options*

## Grammar checking

**Possible mistakes**
Check this for things such as; *with it's, he don't, this things* and so on.

**Capitalization**
Checks for the capitalization of sentences.

**Word duplication**
Checks for all word duplication, rather than just the default words 'and', 'or', 'for' and 'the'.

**Parentheses**
Checks for correct pairing of parentheses and quotation marks.

## Punctuation

**Word spacing**
This option is selected by default. It checks for single spaces between words, indicating instances of double or triple spaces, but not of more than that. To find and correct longer groups of spaces, you need to run the checker more than once.

**Sentence spacing**
Checks for a single space between sentences, indicating when one or two extra spaces are found.

**More spaces**
Checks word and sentence spacing for more than two extra spaces.

**Em dash; En dash**
These options force a non-spaced em dash to replace a spaced en dash, or force a spaced en dash to replace a non-spaced em dash, respectively. This feature provides for different punctuation conventions.

**Quotation marks**
This checks that double quotation marks are typographically correct—that is, beginning ["] and ending ["] quotation marks curve in the correct directions.

**Multiplication sign**
This option is selected by default. It replaces an 'x' used as a multiplication symbol with the correct typographical symbol.

**Apostrophe**
Replaces an apostrophe with the correct (curved) typographical character.

**Ellipsis**
> Replaces three consecutive periods (full stops) with the correct typographical symbol.

**Minus sign**
> Replaces a hyphen with the correct minus typographical character.

### Others

**Convert to metric; Convert to non-metric**
> Converts quantities in a given type of unit to quantities in the other type of unit.

**Thousands separation of large numbers**
> Depending on the locale setting for the document, converts a number with five or more significant digits to either use a comma as a thousands separator or the ISO format, which uses a narrow space as a separator.

# Using synonyms and the thesaurus

You can access a short list of synonyms from a context menu (Figure 31).

1) Right-click on a word and point to **Synonyms** on the context menu. A submenu of alternative words and phrases is displayed.

2) Click on a word or phrase in the submenu to have it replace the highlighted word or phrase in the document.

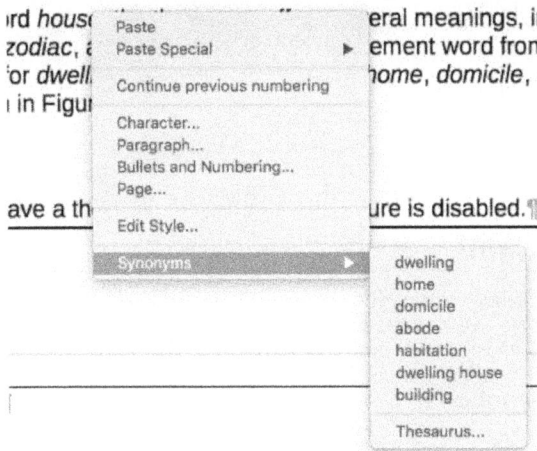

*Figure 31: Synonyms on the context menu*

The thesaurus gives a more extensive list of alternative words and phrases. To use the thesaurus:

1) Right-click on a word, point to **Synonyms** in the content menu, then click on **Thesaurus** from the Synonyms submenu.

2) In the Thesaurus dialog (shown in Figure 32), click on a word or phrase n the list of meanings to select it.

3) Click **Replace** to make the substitution.

For example, when given the word *house*, the thesaurus offers several meanings, including *dwelling, legislature, sign of the zodiac*, and others. Select a replacement word from the list under the relevant meaning, so for *dwelling*, you will see *dwelling, home, domicile*, abode, and other alternatives.

**Note**

If the current language does not have a thesaurus installed, this feature is disabled.

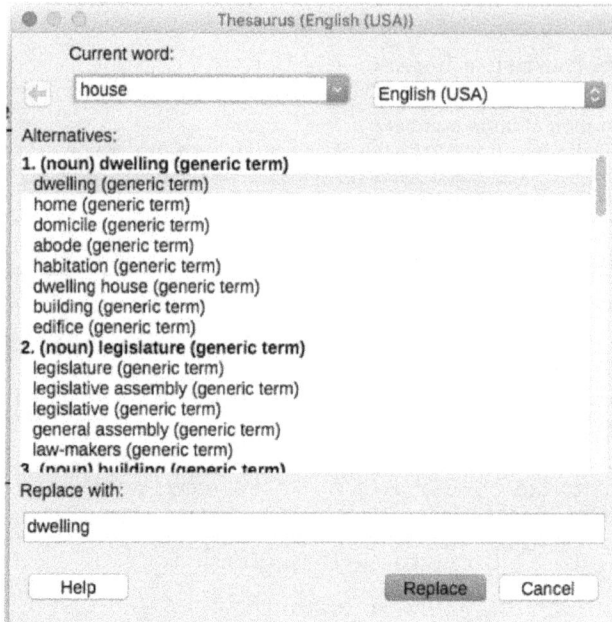

*Figure 32: The thesaurus offers alternatives to words*

# Hyphenating words

You have several choices regarding hyphenation: let Writer do it automatically (using its hyphenation dictionaries), insert conditional hyphens manually where necessary, or don't hyphenate at all. Each choice has its pros and cons.

## Automatic hyphenation

To turn automatic hyphenation of words on or off:

1)  Click on the **Styles and Formatting** tab in the Sidebar to open the Styles and Formatting deck. On the *Paragraph Styles* page, right-click on **Default Style** and select **Modify**.

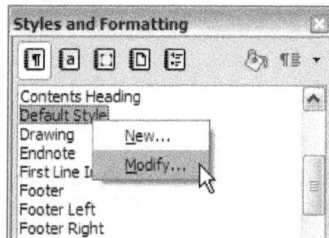

*Figure 33: Modifying a paragraph style*

2) On the Paragraph Style dialog, select the *Text Flow* tab.

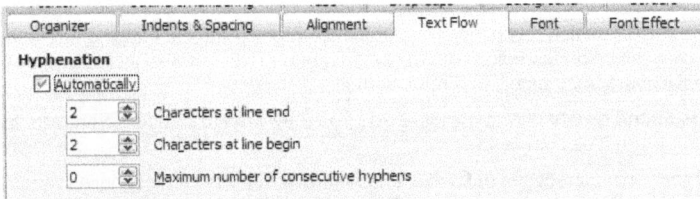

*Figure 34: Turning on automatic hyphenation*

3) Under *Hyphenation*, select or deselect the **Automatically** option.
4) Click **OK** to save.

> **Note**
>
> Turning on hyphenation for the *Default Style* paragraph style affects all other paragraph styles that are based on *Default Style*. You can individually change other styles so that hyphenation is not active; for example, you might not want headings to be hyphenated. Any styles that are not based on *Default Style* are not affected. For more on paragraph styles, see Chapters 8 and 9 in this book.

You can also set hyphenation choices through **Tools > Options > Language Settings > Writing Aids**. In *Options*, near the bottom of the dialog, scroll down to find the hyphenation settings.

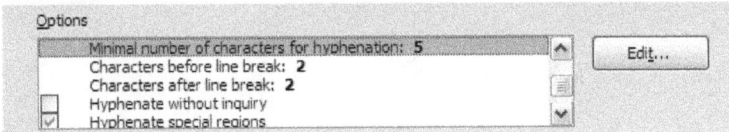

*Figure 35: Setting hyphenation options*

To change the minimum number of characters for hyphenation, or the minimum number of characters before or after a line break, select the item, and then click the **Edit** button in the Options section.

**Hyphenate without inquiry**
Specifies that you will never be asked to manually hyphenate words that the hyphenation dictionary does not recognize. If this box is not selected, when a word is not recognized, a dialog will open where you can manually enter hyphens.

**Hyphenate special regions**
Specifies that hyphenation will also be carried out in footnotes, headers, and footers.

Hyphenation options set in the **Writing Aids** dialog are effective only if hyphenation is turned on through paragraph styles.

## Manual hyphenation

To manually hyphenate words, *do not* use a normal hyphen, which will remain visible even if the word is no longer at the end of a line when you add or delete text or change margins or font size. Instead, use a *conditional hyphen*, which is visible only when required.

To insert a conditional hyphen inside a word, click where you want the hyphen to appear and press *Ctrl+hyphen* or use **Insert > Formatting Mark > Optional hyphen**. The word will be hyphenated at this position when it is at the end of the line, even if automatic hyphenation for this paragraph is switched off.

# Using AutoCorrect

Writer's AutoCorrect function has a long list of common misspellings and typing errors, which it corrects automatically. For example, "hte" will be changed to "the". It also includes codes for inserting special characters, emoji, and other symbols..

AutoCorrect is turned on when Writer is installed. You may wish to disable some of its features, modify others, or turn it off completely.

You can add your own corrections or special characters or change those supplied with LibreOffice. Select **Tools > AutoCorrect > AutoCorrect Options** to open the AutoCorrect dialog. On the *Replace* tab, you can define what strings of text are corrected and how.

To stop Writer replacing a specific spelling, go to the *Replace* tab, highlight the word pair, and click **Delete**. To add a new spelling to the list, type it into the *Replace* and *With* boxes on the *Replace* tab, and click **New**.

To turn AutoCorrect off, uncheck **Tools > AutoCorrect > While Typing**.

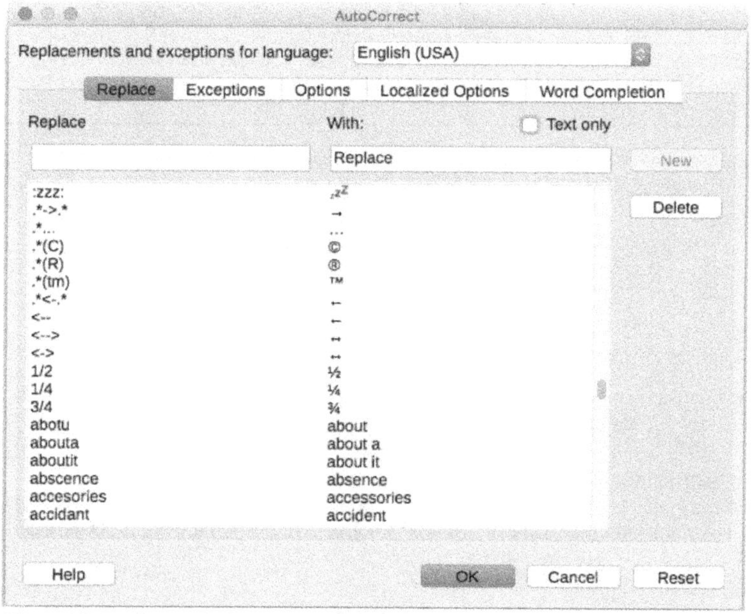

*Figure 36: Replace tab of AutoCorrect dialog*

See Chapter 4, Formatting Text: Basics, for discussion of the *Options* and *Localized Options* pages of the dialog.

# Using Word Completion

If Word Completion is enabled, Writer tries to guess which word you are typing and offers to complete the word for you. To accept the suggestion, press *Enter*. Otherwise, continue typing.

To turn off Word Completion, select **Tools > AutoCorrect > AutoCorrect Options > Word Completion** and deselect **Enable word completion**.

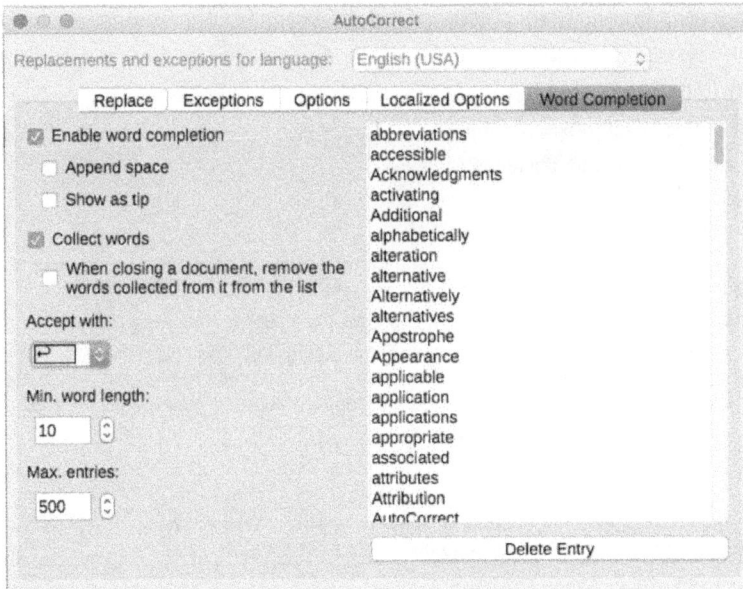

*Figure 37: Customizing word completion*

You can customize word completion from the *Word Completion* page of the AutoCorrect dialog (Figure 37).

- Add (append) a space automatically after an accepted word.
- Show the suggested word as a tip (hovering over the word) rather than completing the text as you type.
- Collect words when working on a document, and then either save them for later use in other documents or select the option to remove them from the list when closing the document.
- Change the maximum number of words remembered for word completion and the length of the smallest words to be remembered.
- Delete specific entries from the word completion list.
- Change the key that accepts a suggested entry—the options are *right arrow*, *End* key, *Enter* (*Return*), *Space bar*, and *Tab*.

**Note**

Automatic word completion occurs only after you type a word for the second time in a document.

# Using AutoText

Use AutoText to store text, tables, fields, and other items for reuse and assign them to a key combination for easy retrieval. For example, rather than typing "Senior Management" every time you use that phrase, you can set up an AutoText entry to insert those words when you type "sm" and press *F3*.

AutoText is especially powerful when assigned to fields. For more information, see Chapter 17, Fields.

## Creating AutoText

To store some text as AutoText:

1) Type the text into your document.

2) Select the text.

3) Go to **Tools > AutoText** (or press *Ctrl+F3*).

4) In the AutoText dialog (Figure 38), type a name for the AutoText in the *Name* box. Writer will suggest a one-letter shortcut, which you can change.

5) Choose the category for the AutoText entry, for example *My AutoText*.

6) Click the **AutoText** button at the bottom of the dialog and select from the menu either **New** (to have the AutoText retain specific formatting, no matter where it is inserted) or **New (text only)** (to have the AutoText take on the existing formatting around the insertion point).

7) Click **Close** to return to your document.

> ▶ **Tip**
>
> If the only option under the **AutoText** button is **Import**, either you have not entered a name for your AutoText or there is no text selected in the document.

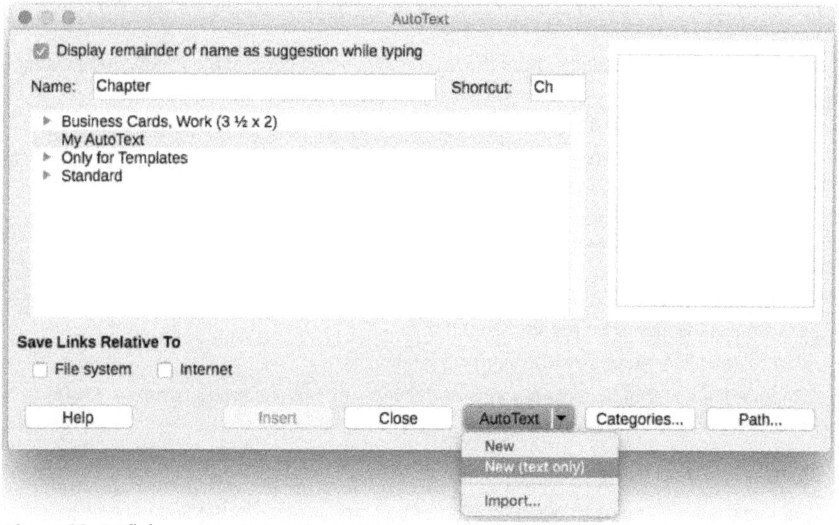

*Figure 38: Defining a new AutoText entry*

To save a table as AutoText:

1) Create a table and format it the way you want.

2) Select the table.

3) Go to **Tools > AutoText** (or press *Ctrl+F3*).

4) Type a name for the AutoText, optionally amend the suggested shortcut, and choose the category for the AutoText entry.

5) Click the **AutoText** button and select **New** (because you want the formatting of the table preserved).

6) Click **Close** to return to your document.

## Inserting AutoText

To insert AutoText, type the shortcut and press *F3*.

## Printing a list of AutoText entries

To print a list of AutoText entries:

1) Choose **Tools > Macros > Organize Macros > LibreOffice Basic**.

2) In the *Macro from* list, expand **Gimmicks**.

3) Select **AutoText** and then click **Run**. A list of the current AutoText entries is generated in a separate text document. You can then print this document.

# Changing the case of selected text

To quickly change the case of text, select it, choose **Format > Text** from the Menu bar, and then choose one of the following:

- UPPER CASE, where all letters are capitalized
- lower case, where no words (except proper nouns) are capitalized
- Cycle Case, which cycles the selected words through upper case, lower case, and capitalize every word.
- Sentence case, where only the first word is capitalized (together with any proper nouns)
- Capitalize Every Word, where every word is capitalized
- tOGGLE cASE, which changes every letter to the opposite case

There are also several options that are used with Asian text. These are not strictly "case" changes, but are lumped together in the broader sense of replacing characters with different forms of the same letter. These options are hidden when Asian language support is not enabled.

Writer does not have an automated way to do Title Case, where all words are capitalized except for certain subsets defined by rules that are not universally standardized. To achieve this affect, you can use *Capitalize Every Word* and then restore those words that were incorrectly capitalized.

You can also change the case of text using the Character dialog or a character style. Choose **Format > Character**, click the *Font Effects* tab, then select the type of capitalization in the Effects box. **Capitals** capitalizes all letters. **Title** capitalizes the first letter of each word. **Small capitals** capitalizes all letters, but in a reduced font size.

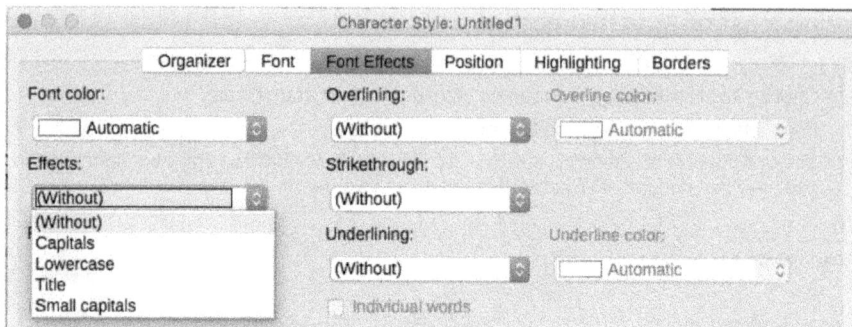

# LibreOffice

*Chapter 3*
*Working with Text: Advanced*

# Introduction

This chapter covers the more advanced tools for working with text in Writer:

- The built-in language tools
- Advanced find-and-replace techniques, including wildcards
- Track changes and insert comments
- Footnotes and endnotes
- Linking to other parts of a document
- Line numbering

This chapter assumes that you are familiar with the basic text techniques described in Chapter 2, Working with Text: Basics. We recommend that you also display formatting aids, such as end-of-paragraph marks, tabs, breaks, and other items in **Tools > Options > LibreOffice Writer > Formatting Aids**.

For information on formatting text (characters, paragraphs, lists), see Chapter 4.

# Using built-in language tools

Writer provides some tools that make your work easier if you mix multiple languages within the same document or if you write documents in various languages:

- Paragraph and character styles
- The functions in **Tools > Language**
- Language settings in Options
- The functions available on the status bar

The main advantage of changing the language for a text selection is that you can then use the correct dictionaries to check spelling and apply the localized versions of AutoCorrect replacement tables, thesaurus, and hyphenation rules. A grammar checking dictionary may be available for the selected language.

You can also set the language for a paragraph or a group of characters as **None (Do not check spelling)**. This option is especially useful when you insert text such as web addresses or programming language snippets that you do not want to check for spelling.

## Using paragraph and character styles

Specifying the language in character and paragraph styles can be problematic unless you use different styles for each language. Changing the Language on the Font tab of the Paragraph Styles dialog (Figure 39) will change the language for all paragraphs that use that paragraph style.

You can also set certain paragraphs to be checked in a language that is different from the language of the rest of the document by putting the cursor in the paragraph and changing the language on the Task Bar.

See Chapter 9, Working with Styles, for information on how to manage the language settings of a style.

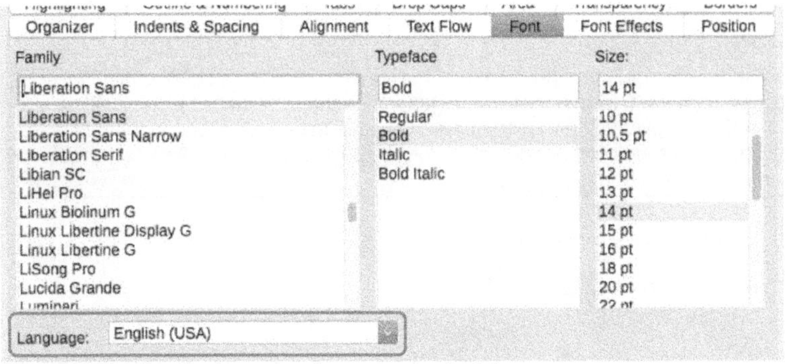

*Figure 39: Setting the language for a paragraph style*

## Using Tools > Language

You can set the language for the whole document, for individual paragraphs, or even for individual words and characters, from **Tools > Language** on the Menu bar.

- **For Selection** applies a specified language to the selected text. If the language you wish to apply is not listed in the submenu, choose **More...**
- **For Paragraph** applies the specified language to the paragraph where the cursor is located. If the language you wish to apply is not listed in the submenu, choose **More...**
- **For all Text** applies the specified language to all of the document, including text inserted after making the change. If the language you wish to apply is not listed in the submenu, choose **More...**
- **More...** opens the Character dialog, where you can select the required language on the Font tab. After a language has been applied to a selection or paragraph in the document, that language appears on the submenus for selections, paragraphs, and all text.

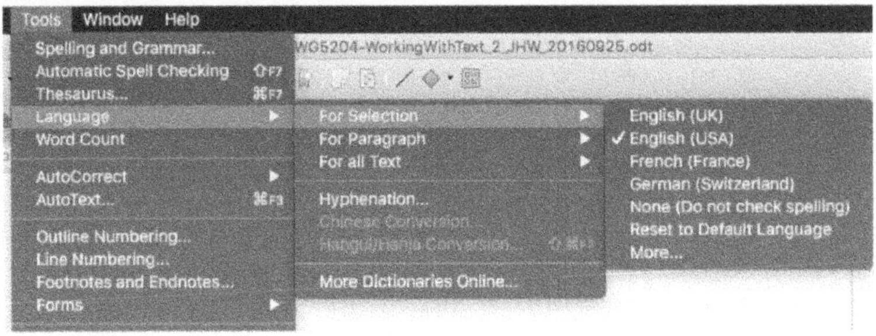

Notice the *Reset to Default Language* option on the submenu. This is the fastest way to return a selection, paragraph, or all text to the default language set in **Tools > Options** (described below).

## Using language settings in Options

Another way to change the language of a whole document is to use **Tools > Options > Language Settings > Languages**. In the *Default languages for documents* section (Figure 40), you can choose a different language for all the text that is not explicitly marked as a different language.

---

## Caution

Unlike the menu tool that applies to the individual document, a change in the default language from the **Options** dialog is a general change of settings of LibreOffice and will therefore apply to all the documents created in the future. If you want to change the language for the current document only, be sure to select the *For the current document only* option (see Figure 40).

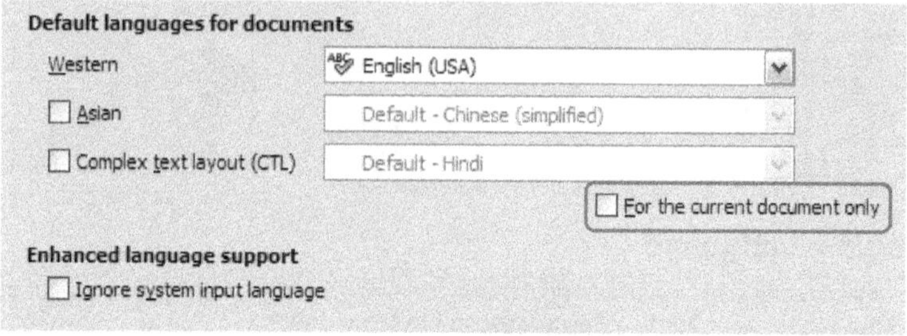

*Figure 40: Options available in the Languages settings*

## Note

The spelling checker works only for those languages in the list which have the symbol

next to them. If you do not see this symbol next to your preferred language, you can install the dictionary using **Tools > Language > More dictionaries online**.

## Using the status bar

The language used for checking spelling is also shown in the status bar, next to the page style in use. You can change the language for the paragraph or the entire document; click on the language in the status bar to pop up a menu of choices.

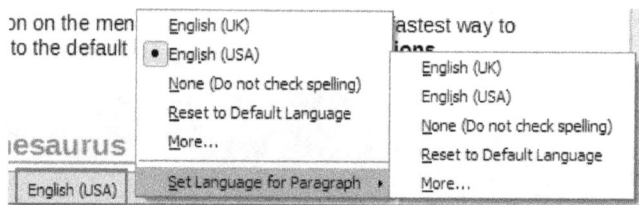

*Figure 41: Language choices on the status bar*

Notice the *Reset to Default Language* option on the menu and submenu. This is the fastest way to return a paragraph or the entire document to the default language set in **Tools > Options** (described above).

# Advanced find and replace techniques

In addition to finding and replacing words and phrases (described in Chapter 2), you can use Writer's Find & Replace dialog to find and replace text attributes, formatting, and paragraph styles. With the Alternative Find & Replace extension, you can also find and replace character styles and perform other advanced searches.

## Find and replace text attributes and formatting

To find specific *text attributes* such as alignment, background, font color, line spacing that have been changed from the default. All text that has a directly coded font attribute, and all text where a style switches the font attribute, are found.

1) On the Find & Replace dialog (with **Other Options** displayed), click the **Attributes** button.

2) Select the attribute you wish to search for from the list in the Attributes dialog and click **OK**. The names of the selected attributes appear under the *Find:* box. For example, to search for text that has been changed from the default font color, select the **Font Color** attribute.

3) Click **Find Next** or **Find All** to search the document.

To find specific *formatting* such as bold, italic, font size, open the Find & Replace dialog with **Other Options** displayed.

1) To find text with specific formatting, enter the text in the *Find:* box. To search for specific formatting only, delete any text in the *Find:* box.

2) Click **Format** to display the Text Format (Search) dialog. The tabs on this dialog are similar to those on the Paragraph and Paragraph Style dialogs.

3) Choose the formats you want to search for and then click **OK**. The names of the selected formats appear under the *Find:* box. For example, you might search for all text in 14-point bold Times New Roman. The option **Paragraph Styles** changes to **Including Styles**.

4) To replace the format, click in the *Replace:* box, choose the format to use, and then click **OK**. The format selected will be displayed below this text box. To replace text as well as formatting, type the replacement text in the *Replace:* box.

To search for specific text with specific formatting (for example, the word **hello** in bold), specify the formatting, type the text in the *Find:* box and leave the *Replace:* box blank.

To remove specific character formatting, click **Format**, select the **Font** tab, then select the opposite format (for example, No Bold). The **No Format** button on the Find & Replace dialog clears all previously selected formats.

5) Click **Find Next, Find All, Replace**, or **Replace All.**

> ▶ **Tip**
>
> Unless you plan to search for other text using those same attributes, click **No Format** to remove the attributes after completing your search. If you forget to do this, you may wonder why your next search fails to find words you know are in the document.

## Find and replace paragraph styles

If you combine material from several sources, you may discover that lots of unwanted paragraph styles have suddenly shown up in your document. To quickly change all the paragraphs from one (unwanted) style to another (preferred) style:

1) On the expanded Find & Replace dialog, select **Paragraph Styles**. The *Find:* and *Replace:* boxes now contain a list of styles in use in the document.

   If you have attributes specified, this option is labeled *Including Styles*. Select No Format to remove any attributes and return the option to *Paragraph Styles*.

2) Select the styles you want to search for and replace.

3) Click **Find, Find All**, **Replace**, or **Replace All**.

Repeat steps 2 and 3 for each style that you want to replace.

## Find and replace character styles

The Find & Replace dialog does not provide a convenient way to find and replace character styles. You may wish to consider installing the Alternative dialog Find & Replace extension, which includes this feature and others as described on this page:
http://extensions.libreoffice.org/extension-center/alternative-dialog-find-replace-for-writer

After installing the extension, you need to close LibreOffice and reopen it before it appears in the Edit menu in Writer. Instructions for use are given in the extension itself (click the ? button).

## Find and replace special characters

To enter special characters into the *Search for* and *Replace with* text input boxes, select the text box and press *Ctrl+Shift+S*. Select the required character from the Special Characters dialog and click **OK**. This version of the Special Characters dialog permits only a single character to be selected and does not allow the font family to be selected.

## Use similarity search

Find terms that are similar to the *Find:* text. For example, a similarity search can find words that differ from the *Find:* text by two characters.

Select *Similarity search* and click the **Similarities** button to open a dialog in which you can modify the text search by length and number of characters different from the search term (see Figure 42).

**Exchange characters**
Enter the number of characters in the search term that can be exchanged. For example, if you specify 2 exchanged characters, "black" and "crack" are considered similar.

**Add characters**
Enter the maximum number of characters by which a word can exceed the number of characters in the search term.

**Remove characters**
Enter the number of characters by which a word can be shorter than the search term.

**Combine**
Searches for a term that matches any combination of the similarity search settings.

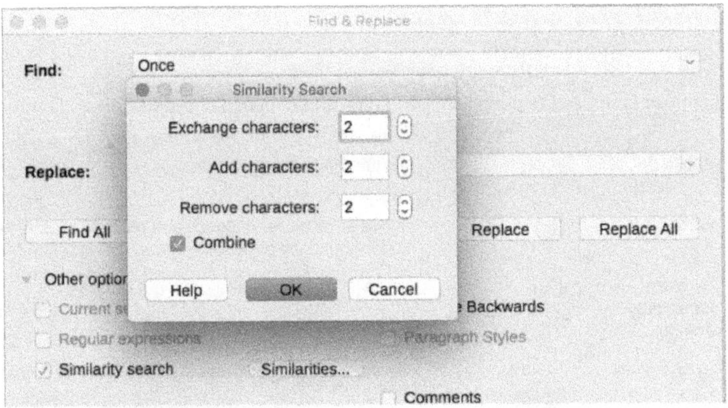

*Figure 42: Similarity search dialog*

## Use wildcards and regular expressions

Most users will be familiar with the concept of a *wildcard*—a special character that represents one or more unspecified characters. Wildcards make text searches more powerful but often less specific. LibreOffice enables you to use combinations of characters known as *regular expressions* which are more specific than simple wildcards but less so than a literal string. Regular expressions are very powerful but not very intuitive. They can save time and effort by combining multiple finds into one.

Table 5 shows a few of the regular expressions used by LibreOffice.

> ▶ **Tip**
>
> The online help describes many more regular expressions and their uses.

To use wildcards and regular expressions when searching and replacing:

1) On the Find & Replace dialog, click **Other Options** to see more choices. On this expanded dialog, select the **Regular expressions** option.

2) Type the search text, including the wildcards, in the *Search for* box and the replacement text (if any) in the *Replace with* box. Not all regular expressions work as replacement characters; the line break (\n) is one that does work.

3) Click **Find, Find All**, **Replace**, or **Replace All** (not recommended).

> ● **Note**
>
> To search for a character that is defined as a wildcard, type a backslash (\) before the character to indicate that you are using it literally. For example, to find the text $5.00, you would conduct a search using \$5\.00.

*Table 5: Examples of search wildcards (regular expressions)*

| To find | Use this expression | Examples and comments |
|---|---|---|
| Any single character | . (a period or full stop) | b.d finds *bad*, *bud*, *bid*, and *bed*. |
| One of the specified characters | [xyz] | b[iu]n finds *bin* and *bun*. |
| Any single character in this range | [x-y] | [r-t]eed finds *reed*, *seed*, and *teed*; ranges must be in alphabetically ascending order. |
| Any single character except the characters inside the brackets | [^x] | p[^a]st finds *post* and *pest*, but not past. |
| The beginning of a word | \<start | \<log finds *logbook* and *logistics*, but not *catalog*. |
| The end of a word | end\> | log\> finds *catalog*, but not *logistics*. |
| A paragraph marker | $ | Does not work as a replacement character. Use \n instead. |
| A line break | \n | Finds a line break that was inserted with *Shift+Enter*. When used as a replacement character, it inserts a paragraph marker. |

# Tracking changes to a document

You can use several methods to keep track of changes made to a document.

- Make your changes to a copy of the document (stored in a different folder, under a different name, or both), then use Writer to compare the two files and show the changes you made. This technique is particularly useful if you are the only person working on the document, as it avoids the increase in file size and complexity caused by the other methods.

- Save versions that are stored as part of the original file. However, this method can cause problems with documents of nontrivial size or complexity, especially if you save a lot of versions. Avoid this method if you can.

- Use Writer's change marks (often called "redlines" or "revision marks") to show where you have added or deleted material or changed formatting. Later, you or another person can use one of Writer's many convenient methods to review and accept or reject each change.

**Note**

Not all changes are recorded. For example, changing a tab stop from align left to align right and changes in formulas (equations) or linked graphics are not recorded.

## Preparing a document for review

When you send a document to someone else to review or edit, you may want to prepare it first so that the editor or reviewer does not have to remember to turn on the revision marks. After you have protected the document, any user must enter the correct password in order to turn off the function or accept or reject changes.

1) Open the document. To check whether it contains multiple versions, click **File > Versions**. If multiple versions are listed, save the current version as a separate document with a different name and use this new document as the review copy.

2) With the review copy open, make sure that change recording is turned on. The **Edit > Track Changes > Record Changes** menu item has a check mark next to it when recording is turned on.

3) Click **Edit > Track Changes > Protect Changes**. On the Enter Password dialog, type a password (twice) and click **OK**.

▶ **Tip**

An alternative to steps 2 and 3 above is to choose **File > Properties > Security** tab, select the **Record changes** option, then click **Protect** and enter the password.

## Recording changes

See Chapter 20, Setting up Writer, for instructions on setting up how your changes will be displayed, if you don't like the default settings.

1) To begin tracking (recording) changes, choose **Edit > Track Changes > Record Changes**. To show or hide the display of changes, click **Edit > Track Changes > Show Changes**.

▶ **Tip**

Hold the mouse pointer over a marked change; you will see a *Help Tip* showing the type of change, the author, date, and time of day for the change. If *Extended Tips* are enabled, you will also see any comments recorded for this change.

2) To enter a comment on a marked change, place the cursor in the area of the change and then click **Edit > Track Changes > Comment on Change**.

In addition to being displayed as an extended tip, the comment is also shown in the list in the Manage Changes dialog (Figure 44).

To move from one marked change to the next, use the arrow buttons. If no comment has been recorded for a change, the *Text* field is blank.

3) To stop recording changes, click **Edit > Track Changes > Record Changes** again.

▶ **Tip**

See also "Adding other comments" on page 77 for a way to annotate text that is not associated with a recorded change.

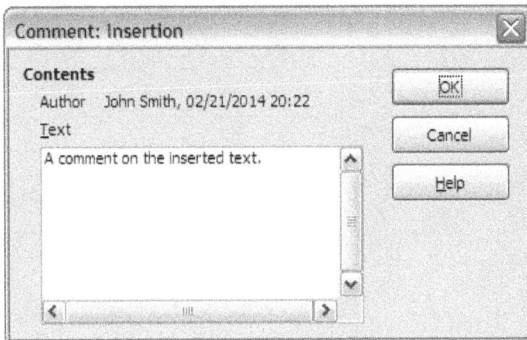

*Figure 43: Inserting a comment during change recording*

## Accepting or rejecting changes

To accept or reject recorded changes, use any of these methods:

- Changes toolbar
- Right-click (context) menu
- Manage Changes dialog
- Manage Changes pane in the Sidebar

The results of accepting or rejecting a change are as follows:

- Accepting a change incorporates the alteration into the document and removes the change indication marking.
- Rejecting a change reverts the document to its original state and removes the change indication marking.

### Changes toolbar

For quick and easy accepting and rejecting of changes, you can use the Changes toolbar, which includes buttons for the same functions as appear on the **Edit > Track Changes** submenu. To enable the Changes toolbar, click **View > Toolbars > Changes** on the Menu bar. You can dock this toolbar in a convenient place or leave it floating.

### Right-click (context) menu

1) If recorded changes are not showing, click **Edit > Track Changes > Show Changes**.
2) Hover the mouse pointer over a recorded change. A box appears with information about the type of change, who made it, and the date and time.
3) Right-click on the changed text. In the context menu, choose **Accept Change** or **Reject Change**.

### Manage Changes dialog

1) Click **Edit > Track Changes > Manage Changes**. The Manage Changes dialog (Figure 44) opens, showing changes that have not yet been accepted or rejected.
2) When you select a change in the dialog, the change itself is highlighted in the document, so you can see what the editor changed.
3) Click **Accept** or **Reject** to accept or reject the selected change. You can also click **Accept All** or **Reject All** if you do not want to review the changes individually.

To show only the changes of certain people or only the changes on specific days or various other restrictions, use the *Filter* page (Figure 45) on the Accept or Reject Changes dialog. After specifying the filter criteria, return to the *List* page to see those changes that meet your criteria.

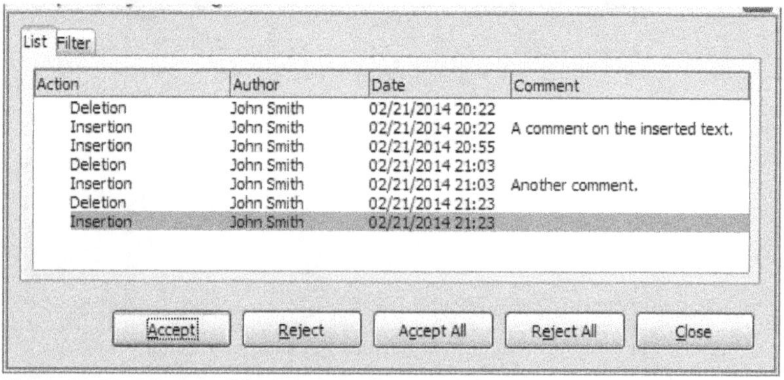

| Action | Author | Date | Comment |
|---|---|---|---|
| Deletion | John Smith | 02/21/2014 20:22 | |
| Insertion | John Smith | 02/21/2014 20:22 | A comment on the inserted text. |
| Insertion | John Smith | 02/21/2014 20:55 | |
| Deletion | John Smith | 02/21/2014 21:03 | |
| Insertion | John Smith | 02/21/2014 21:03 | Another comment. |
| Deletion | John Smith | 02/21/2014 21:23 | |
| Insertion | John Smith | 02/21/2014 21:23 | |

List Filter

Accept    Reject    Accept All    Reject All    Close

*Figure 44: The List tab of the Manage Changes dialog*

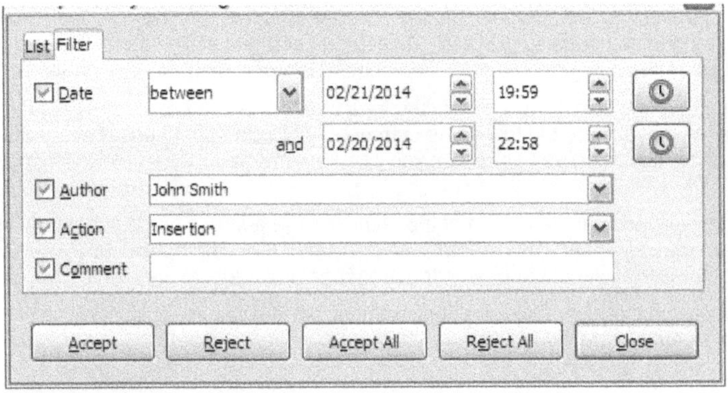

*Figure 45: The Filter page of the Manage Changes dialog*

**Manage Changes pane in the Sidebar**
The Manage Changes pane in the Sidebar shows the same information as in the Manage Changes dialog described above.

## Comparing documents

Sometimes reviewers may forget to record the changes they make. You can find the changes if you compare the original document and the one that is edited. To compare them:

1) Open the edited document. Select **Edit > Track Changes > Compare Document**.

2) The Insert dialog appears. Select the original document and click **Insert**.

Writer finds and marks the changes and displays the Manage Changes dialog. From this point, you can go through and accept or reject changes procedure as described earlier.

## Merging modified documents

The processes discussed to this point are effective when you have one reviewer at a time. Sometimes, however, multiple reviewers all return edited versions of a document. In this case, it may be quicker to review all of these changes at once, rather than one review at a time. For this purpose, you can merge documents in Writer.

To merge documents, all of the edited documents need to have recorded changes in them.

1) Open one copy.

2) Click **Edit > Track Changes > Merge Document** and select and insert another copy of the document to be merged with the first.

3) After the documents merge, the Manage Changes dialog opens, as in Figure 44, showing changes by more than one reviewer. If you want to merge more documents, close the dialog and then repeat step 2.

4) Repeat until all copies are merged.

All recorded changes are now included in the open copy. Save this file under another name.

# Adding other comments

Writer provides another type of comments, which authors and reviewers often use to exchange ideas, ask for suggestions, or mark items needing attention.

You can select a block of text, including multiple paragraphs, to be highlighted for a comment, or you can insert a comment at a single point. To insert a comment, select the text, or place the cursor in the place the comment refers to, and choose **Insert > Comment** or press *Ctrl+Alt+C*.

The anchor point of the comment is connected by a dotted line to a box on the right-hand side of the page where you can type the text of the comment. A Comments button is also added to the right of the horizontal ruler (see Figure 46); you can click this button to toggle the display of the comments.

Writer automatically adds at the bottom of the comment the author's name and a time stamp indicating when the comment was created. Select **Tools > Options > LibreOffice > User Data** to configure the name you want to appear in the Author field of the comment, or to change it.

Click somewhere on the page to finish your comment. Otherwise, you will not be able to move away from this location.

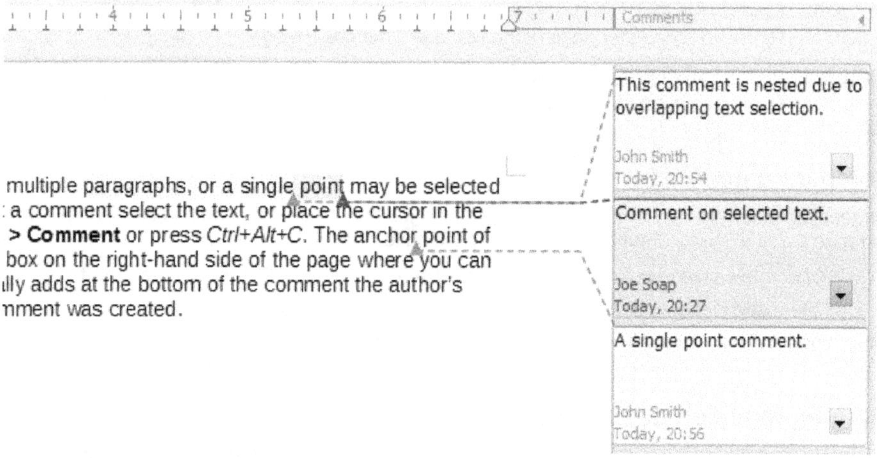

*Figure 46: Comments in LibreOffice*

If more than one person edits the document, each author is automatically allocated a different background color. Figure 46 shows an example of text with comments from two different authors. If an author selects text that overlaps another author's comments, then the comments from the second author are nested with those of the first author.

Right-click on a comment to open a context menu where you can delete the current comment, all the comments from the same author, or all the comments in the document. From this menu, you can also open a dialog to apply some basic formatting to the text of the comment. You can also change font type, size, and alignment from the Menu bar.

To navigate from one comment to another, open the Navigator (*F5*), expand the Comments section, and click on the comment text to move the cursor to the anchor point of the comment in the document. Right-click on the comment to quickly edit or delete it.

You can also navigate the comments using the keyboard. Use *Ctrl+Alt+Page Down* to move to the next comment and *Ctrl+Alt+Page Up* to move to the previous comment.

Comments can be printed next to the text in the right margin as they appear on screen. Each page is scaled down in order to make space for the comments to fit on the underlying paper size.

# Using footnotes and endnotes

Footnotes appear at the bottom of the page on which they are referenced. Endnotes are collected at the end of a document.

To work effectively with footnotes and endnotes, you need to:

- Insert footnotes and define their format
- Define the location of footnotes on the page, and the color and line styles for separator lines, if the defaults do not meet your needs (see Chapter 5, Formatting Pages: Basics).

## Inserting footnotes and endnotes

To insert a footnote or an endnote, put the cursor where you want the footnote or endnote marker to appear. Then select **Insert > Footnote and Endnote** from the Menu bar and choose **Footnote** or **Endnote**, or click the **Insert Footnote** or **Insert Endnote** button on the Standard toolbar.

A footnote or endnote marker is inserted in the text and, depending on your choice, the cursor is relocated either to the footnote area at the bottom of the page or to the endnote area at the end of the document. Type the footnote or endnote content in this area.

You can also choose use **Insert > Footnote and Endnote > Footnote or Endnote** to open the Insert Footnote/Endnote dialog (Figure 47), where you can choose whether to use the automatic numbering sequence specified in the footnote settings and whether to insert the item as a footnote or an endnote.

If you use **Insert Footnote** or **Insert Endnote**, the footnote or endnote automatically takes on the attributes previously defined in the Footnote Settings dialog.

You can edit an existing footnote or endnote the same way you edit any other text.

To delete a footnote or endnote, delete the footnote marker. The contents of the footnote or endnote are deleted automatically, and the numbering of other footnotes or endnotes is adjusted automatically.

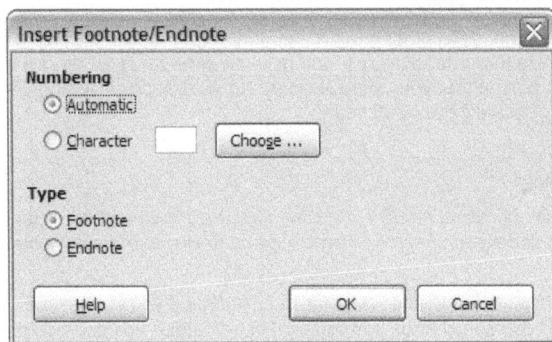

*Figure 47: Inserting a footnote/endnote*

## Defining the format of footnotes/endnotes

To format the footnotes themselves, click **Tools > Footnotes and Endnotes**. On the Footnotes/Endnotes Settings dialog (Figure 48), choose settings as required.

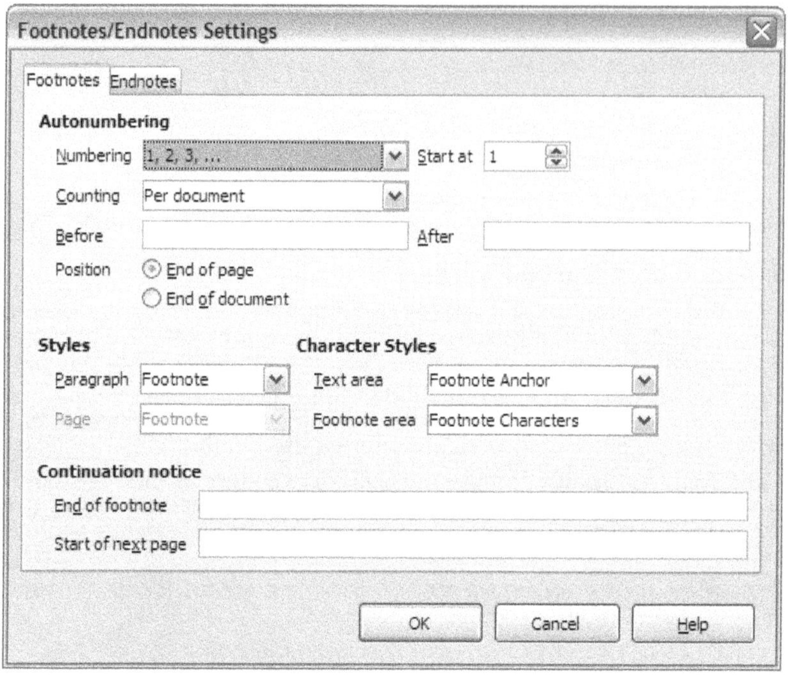

*Figure 48: Defining footnote formatting*

# Linking to another part of a document

If you type in cross-references to other parts of the document, those references can easily get out of date if you reorganize the order of topics, add or remove material, or reword a heading, Writer provides two ways to ensure that your references are up to date, by inserting links to other parts of the same document or to a different document:

- Hyperlinks
- Cross-references

The two methods have the same result if you *Ctrl+click* the link when the document is open in Writer: you are taken directly to the cross-referenced item. However, they also have major differences:

- The text in a hyperlink does **not** automatically update if you change the text of the linked item (although you can change it manually), but changed text does automatically update in a cross-reference.
- When using a hyperlink, you do not have a choice of the content of the link (for example text or page number), but when using a cross-reference, you have several choices, including bookmarks.
- To hyperlink to an object such as a graphic, and have the hyperlink show useful text such as *Figure 6*, you need to either give such an object a useful name instead of leaving it as the default name ("Graphics6"), or you need to use the Hyperlink dialog to modify the visible text. In contrast, cross-references to figures with captions automatically show useful text, and you have a choice of several variations of the name.

- If you save a Writer document to HTML, hyperlinks remain active but cross-references do not. (Both remain active when the document is exported to PDF.)

## Using cross-references

To ensure that references update if you reword a heading, caption, or other linked item, use automatic cross-references. For details, see "Using automatic cross-references" in Chapter 17, Fields.

## Using bookmarks

Bookmarks are listed in the Navigator and can be accessed directly from there with a single mouse click. In HTML documents, bookmarks are converted to anchors that you can jump to by hyperlink. For more about bookmarks, see "Using bookmarks" in Chapter 17, Fields.

## Using hyperlinks

When you type text (such as website addresses or URL) that can be used as a hyperlink, and then press the spacebar or the *Enter* key, Writer automatically creates the hyperlink and applies formatting to the text (usually a color and underlining).

If this does not happen, you can enable this feature using **Tools > AutoCorrect Options > Options** and selecting the **URL Recognition** option.

If you do not want Writer to convert a specific URL to a hyperlink, choose **Edit > Undo Insert** from the Menu bar or press *Ctrl+Z* immediately after the formatting has been applied.

You can also insert hyperlinks using the Navigator and the Hyperlink dialog, and you can modify all hyperlinks using the Hyperlink dialog, as described in this section.

### Note

Hyperlinks between documents can be set as relative or absolute, using the **Save URLs relative to** option in **Tools > Options > Load/Save > General**.

Relative linking is only possible when the document you are working on and the link destination are on the same drive, and you need to create the same directory structure on your hard disk as will apply on the destination website.

LibreOffice uses absolute path names internally, so when you move your mouse cursor over a hyperlink, the tooltip displays the absolute reference even when it is set to be a relative link.

### Inserting hyperlinks using the Navigator

The easiest way to insert a hyperlink to another part of the same document is by using the Navigator:

1) Open the document containing the items you want to cross-reference.
2) Open the Navigator (by clicking its icon, choosing **View > Navigator**, pressing *F5*, or selecting the Navigator Tab on the open Sidebar).
3) Click the arrow next to the **Drag Mode** icon, and select **Insert as Hyperlink**.
4) In the list at the bottom of the **Navigator**, select the document containing the item that you want to cross-reference.
5) In the **Navigator** list, select the item that you want to insert as a hyperlink.
6) Drag the item to where you want to insert the hyperlink in the document. The name of the item is inserted in the document as an active hyperlink.

*Figure 49: Inserting a hyperlink using the Navigator*

### Inserting hyperlinks using a dialog

To display the Hyperlink dialog (Figure 50), click the **Hyperlink** icon on the Standard Toolbar or choose **Insert > Hyperlink** from the Menu bar. To turn existing text into a link, select it before opening the dialog.

On the left hand side, select one of the four types of hyperlink:

- **Internet**: a web address, normally starting with http://
- **Mail**: an email address.
- **Document**: another document or to another place in the presentation.
- **New document**: the hyperlink creates a new document.www.libreoffice.org

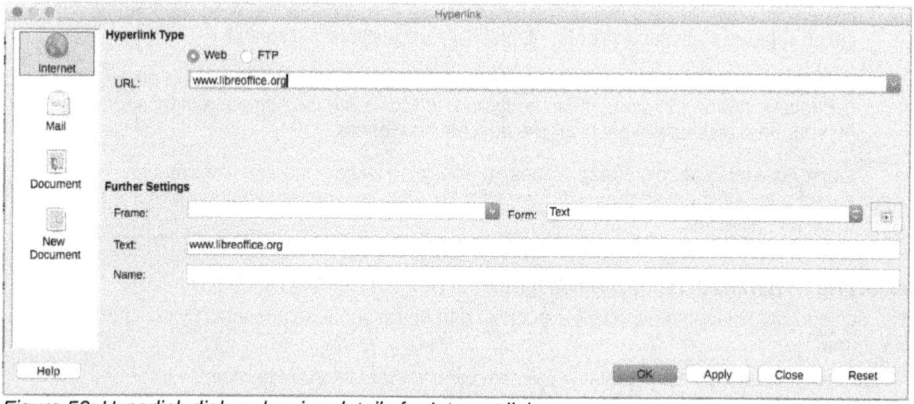

*Figure 50: Hyperlink dialog showing details for Internet links*

The top right part of the dialog changes according to your choice for the hyperlink type. A full description of all the choices, and their interactions, is beyond the scope of this chapter. Here is a summary of the most common choices used in presentations.

For an *Internet* hyperlink, choose the type of hyperlink (choose between Web, FTP or Telnet), and enter the required web address (URL).

For a *Mail* hyperlink, specify the receiver address and the subject.

---

For a *Document* hyperlink, specify the document path (the **Open File** button opens a file browser); leave this blank if you want to link to a target in the same presentation. Optionally specify the target in the document (for example a specific slide). Click on the **Target** icon to open the Navigator where you can select the target, or if you know the name of the target, you can type it into the box.

For a *New Document* hyperlink, specify whether to edit the newly created document immediately or just create it (**Edit later**) and the type of document to create (text, spreadsheet, and so on). For a text document, **Edit now** is the more likely choice. The **Select Path** button opens a directory picker.

The *Further settings* section in the bottom right part of the dialog is common to all the hyperlink types, although some choices are more relevant to some types of links.

- Set the value of **Frame** to determine how the hyperlink will open. This applies to documents that open in a Web browser.
- **Form** specifies if the link is to be presented as text or as a button.
- **Text** specifies the text that will be visible to the user.
- **Name** is applicable to HTML documents. It specifies text that will be added as a NAME attribute in the HTML code behind the hyperlink.
- **Event** button: this button will be activated to allow LibreOffice to react to events for which the user has written some code (macro). This function is not covered in this book.

### Editing hyperlinks

To edit a hyperlink, click anywhere in the link text and then open the Hyperlink dialog by clicking the **Hyperlink** icon on the Standard Toolbar or choosing **Edit > Hyperlink** from the Menu bar. Make your changes and click Apply. If you need to edit several hyperlinks, you can leave the Hyperlink dialog open until you have edited all of them. Be sure to click **Apply** after each one. When you are finished, click **Close**.

The standard (default) behavior for activating hyperlinks within LibreOffice is to use *Ctrl+click*. This behavior can be changed in **Tools > Options > LibreOffice > Security > Options**, by deselecting the option **Ctrl-click required to follow hyperlinks**. If clicking in your links activates them, check that page to see if the option has been deselected.

To change the color of hyperlinks, go to **Tools > Options > LibreOffice > Appearance**, scroll to *Unvisited links* and/or *Visited links*, select those options, pick the new colors and click **OK**. Caution: this will change the color for *all* hyperlinks in *all* components of LibreOffice—this may not be what you want.

In Writer and Calc (but not Draw or Impress), you can also change the *Internet link* character style or define and apply new styles to selected links.

# Line numbering

Line numbering puts line numbers in the margin. LibreOffice can insert line numbers in an entire document or in selected paragraphs. Line numbers are included when you print the document. You can also add a separator between line numbers. Figure 51 shows an example with numbering on every line.

You can choose how many lines are numbered (for example, every line or every tenth line), the numbering type, and whether numbers restart on each page. In addition, a text separator (any text you choose) can be set on a different numbering scheme (one every 12 lines, for example).

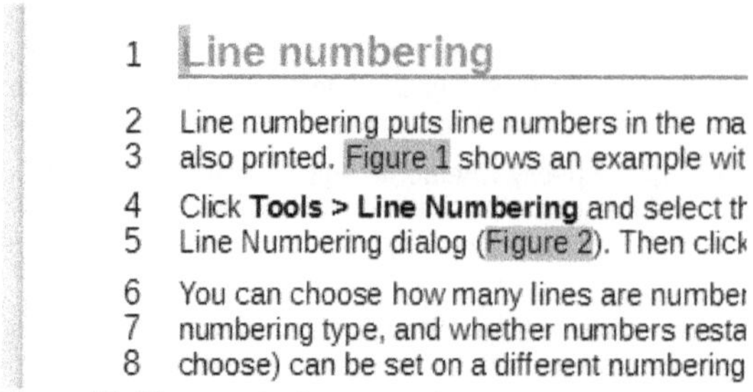

# 1 Line numbering

2 Line numbering puts line numbers in the ma
3 also printed. Figure 1 shows an example wit

4 Click **Tools > Line Numbering** and select th
5 Line Numbering dialog (Figure 2). Then click

6 You can choose how many lines are number
7 numbering type, and whether numbers resta
8 choose) can be set on a different numbering

*Figure 51: Line numbering example*

To add line numbers to an entire document:

1) Click **Tools > Line Numbering** and select the **Show numbering** option in the top left corner of the Line Numbering dialog (Figure 52).

2) Then select any options you want and click **OK**.

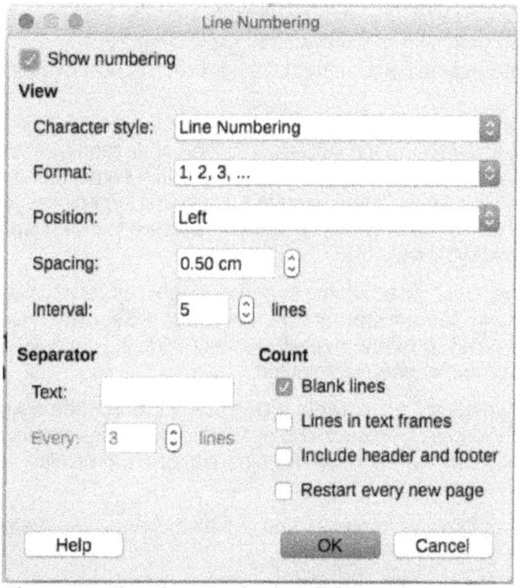

**Line Numbering**

☑ Show numbering

**View**

| | |
|---|---|
| Character style: | Line Numbering |
| Format: | 1, 2, 3, ... |
| Position: | Left |
| Spacing: | 0.50 cm |
| Interval: | 5 lines |

**Separator**

Text:

Every: 3 lines

**Count**

☑ Blank lines
☐ Lines in text frames
☐ Include header and footer
☐ Restart every new page

Help     OK     Cancel

*Figure 52: The Line Numbering dialog*

To add line numbers to specific paragraphs, you need to first disable the feature for the document and then enable it for specific paragraphs or paragraph styles.

To disable line numbering for the document, edit the *Default Style* paragraph style (because all paragraph styles are based on the Default Style):

1) In the Sidebar, go to the Styles and Formatting pane and click the **Paragraph Styles** icon.

2) Right-click the *Default Style* paragraph style and choose **Modify**.

3) Click the *Outline & Numbering* tab (see Figure 53).

4) In the *Line Numbering* area, clear the **Include this paragraph in line numbering** checkbox.

5) Click **OK**.

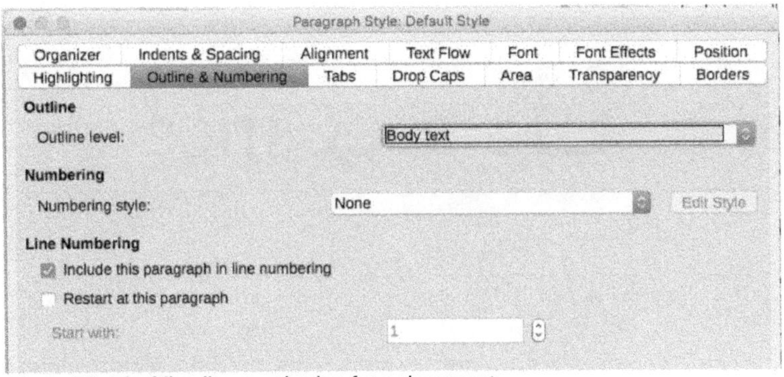

*Figure 53: Disabling line numbering for a document*

To enable line numbering for specific paragraphs:

1) Select the paragraphs where you want to add the line numbers.
2) Choose **Format > Paragraph**, and then click the *Outline & Numbering* tab.
3) Select **Include this paragraph in line numbering**.
4) Click **OK**.

You can also create a paragraph style that includes line numbering, and apply it to the paragraphs that you want to add line numbers to. For example, you might want to number the lines of example code in a document; for code, you will probably want to use a font or indentation that is different from normal text.

To specify the starting line number:

1) Click in the paragraph and choose **Format > Paragraph**.
2) On the Outline & Numbering tab, make sure the **Include this paragraph in line numbering** checkbox is selected.
3) Select the **Restart at this paragraph** checkbox and enter a line number in the **Start with** box.
4) Click **OK**.

# LibreOffice

*Chapter 4*
*Formatting Text*

# Introduction

This chapter covers the basics of formatting text in Writer, the word-processing component of LibreOffice:

- Formatting paragraphs and characters
- Using autoformatting
- Creating bulleted, numbered, and outline lists

It assumes that you are familiar with the text techniques described in Chapter 2, Working with Text: Basics and Chapter 3, Working with Text: Advanced.

We recommend that you also follow the suggestions in Chapter 20, Setting up Writer, about displaying formatting aids, such as end-of-paragraph marks, and selecting other setup options.

Page formatting is covered in Chapters 5 and 6.

# Using styles is recommended

Styles are central to using Writer. Styles enable you to easily format your documents consistently, and to change the format with minimal effort. A style is a named set of formatting options. When you apply a style, you apply a whole group of formats at the same time.

In addition, styles are used by LibreOffice for many processes, even if you are not aware of them. For example, Writer relies on heading styles (or other styles you specify) when it compiles a table of contents. Therefore, the use of paragraph styles is highly recommended as an alternative to manually formatting paragraphs, especially for long or standardized documents. The use of character styles instead of manually formatting individual words is also highly recommended.

For information on styles and how to use them, see Chapters 8 and 9 in this book.

Applying styles is quick and easy using the Styles and Formatting deck of the Sidebar.

> **Caution**
>
> Manual formatting (also called *direct formatting*) overrides styles, and you cannot get rid of the manual formatting by applying a style to it.

## Removing manual formatting

To remove manual formatting, select the text and choose **Format > Clear Direct Formatting** from the Menu bar, or click the **Clear Direct Formatting** button on the Formatting toolbar, or use *Ctrl+M* from the keyboard.

> **Note**
>
> When clearing direct formatting, the text format returns to the applied paragraph style and not the default paragraph style.

# Formatting paragraphs

You can apply many formats to paragraphs using the buttons on the Formatting toolbar and on the Paragraph panel of the Sidebar's Properties deck (**View > Sidebar**). Not all toolbar buttons are visible in a standard installation, but you can customize the toolbar to include those you use regularly (see Chapter 1, Introducing Writer). Other formatting options are provided in the Paragraph dialog (see page 91).

On the Formatting toolbar, the buttons and formats include:

- Apply Paragraph Style (Styles drop-down on the Properties deck of the Sidebar)
- Bullets On/Off (with a palette of bullet styles) —see page 102
- Numbering On/Off (with a palette of numbering styles) —see page 102
- Align Left, Center Horizontally, Align Right, or Justified
- Align Top, Center Vertically, Align Bottom
- Line Spacing (choose from 1, 1.15, 1.5, 2, or custom spacing
- Increase Paragraph Spacing, Decrease Paragraph Spacing
- Increase Indent, Decrease Indent
- Paragraph (to open the Paragraph dialog)

The Sidebar opens with the Properties deck selected by default. Click the expansion symbol (+ or triangle) to open the panels if necessary.

The Paragraph panel of the Properties deck (Figure 54) contains most of the formatting controls, including several that are not found on the Formatting toolbar. Clicking the down-arrow by a button opens the control for further choices, such as fixed line spacing or color palette.

Click the **More Options** button to open the Paragraph dialog, where other settings are available (see page 91). Changing the values of any of these settings affects only the paragraph where the insertion point (cursor) is located, or several paragraphs if more than one are selected. If you wish to change the values for many paragraphs of that type, you should use a paragraph style.

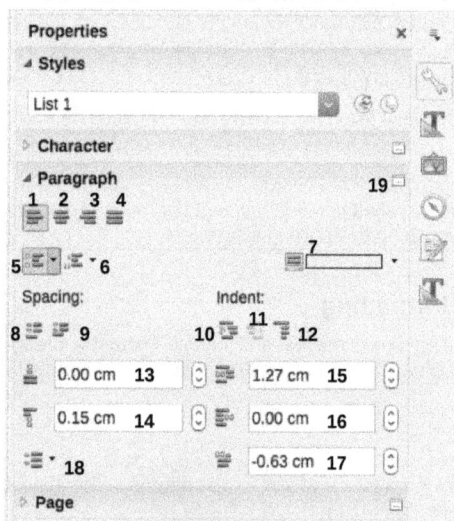

| 1 | Align Left | 8 | Increase Spacing | 15 | Indent From Left |
| 2 | Align Center | 9 | Decrease Spacing | 16 | Indent From Right |
| 3 | Align Right | 10 | Increase Indent | 17 | Indent First Line |
| 4 | Align Justified | 11 | Decrease Indent | 18 | Line Spacing |
| 5 | Bullets | 12 | Hanging Indent | 19 | More Options – opens |
| 6 | Numbering | 13 | Above Paragraph Spacing | | Paragraph dialog |
| 7 | Background Color | 14 | Below Paragraph Spacing | | |

Figure 54: Paragraph panel of the Properties deck in the Sidebar

# Alignment options

You can use the buttons labelled **1–4** in Figure 54 to choose the alignment of a paragraph: Left, Right, Centered, or Justified. Figure 55 shows examples of the alignment options applied to text.

Left aligned text.

Center aligned text.

Right aligned text.

Justified text inserts spacing between words to force the text to reach from margin to margin, if the text is longer than a single line.

*Figure 55: Text alignment options*

When using justified text, the last line is by default aligned to the left. However, you can also align the last line to the center of the paragraph area or justify it so that spaces are inserted between the words in order to fill the whole line. If you select the **Expand single word** option, then whenever the last line of a justified paragraph consists of a single word, this word is stretched by inserting spaces between characters so that it occupies the full length of the line.

Figure 56 shows an example of the effect obtained when choosing each of these options for a typical text font. In most cases, you would leave the setting on the default (left-aligned)' but for some dramatic purposes (such as a very large font on a poster), you might prefer one of the other choices.

Three options are available for the alignment of the last line of a justified paragraph. This is an example of a **left-aligned** last line.

Three options are available for the alignment of the last line of a justified paragraph. This is an example of a **centered** last line.

Three options are available for the alignment of the last line of a justified paragraph. This is      an      example      of      a      **justified**      last      line.

When the last line of a justified paragraph contains a single word, you can stretch the word to fill the entire line. This is an example with the **Expand single word** option
s            e            l            e            c            t            e            d            .

*Figure 56: Examples of choices for the last line of a justified paragraph*

These options are controlled in the *Alignment* page of the Paragraph dialog (Figure 57), reached by choosing **Format > Paragraph** from the Menu bar, or by right-clicking in the paragraph and selecting **Paragraph** from the context menu, or by clicking the **More Options** button on the Paragraph panel in the Properties deck of the Sidebar.

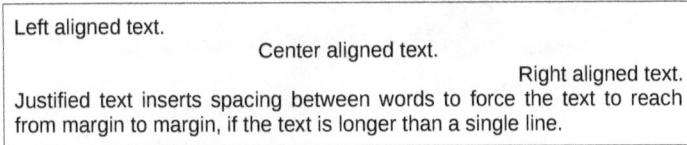

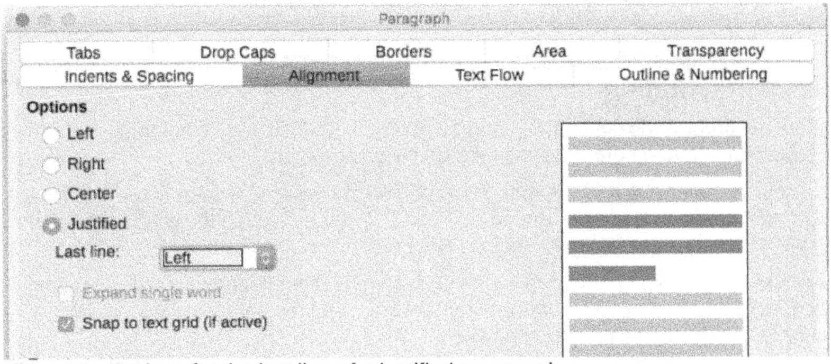

*Figure 57: Options for the last line of a justified paragraph*

## Line and paragraph spacing

*Line spacing* (button **18**, Figure 54) refers to the distance from one baseline (the imaginary line at the bottom of a letter like "n" or "m") to the next baseline. It is determined by the size of the font.

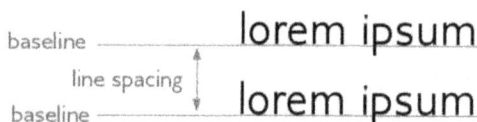

baseline ——————— lorem ipsum

line spacing

baseline ——————— lorem ipsum

*Figure 58: Line spacing is the distance between two baselines*

The Line Spacing submenu is shown in Figure 59. Here you can choose among standard spacings or define a custom value: *Proportional* (for example, 110%), *At least* (the amount specified in the *Value* box), *Leading*, or *Fixed*. To see the differences between these choices, do a few sample paragraphs and change the selections.

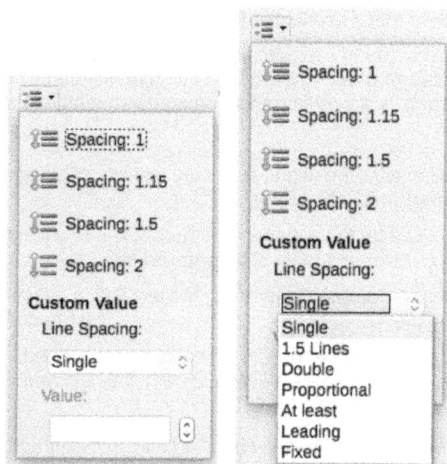

*Figure 59: Line spacing submenu*

*Paragraph spacing* refers to the vertical spacing between one paragraph and the paragraphs above and below it. As shown in Figure 54, the current values are shown in the *Above Paragraph Spacing* box (**13**) and the *Below Paragraph Spacing* box (**14**). You can change either or both of these settings independently.

## Paragraph indentation

You can use the buttons labelled **10**, **11**, and **12** in Figure 54 to increase the amount of space to leave between the left and right page margins and the paragraph.

The distances are determined by settings **15** (*Before Text Indent*; that is, from the left margin), **16** (*After Text Indent*; that is, from the right margin), and **17** (*First Line Indent*, which indents the first line from the left margin, or from the specified indentation from the margin).

Button **12**, *Switch to Hanging Indent*, leaves the first line at the left margin (or the specified indentation from the margin) and indents all the other lines of the paragraph by the amount specified by button **17** or in the Paragraph dialog.

> This paragraph is an example of a paragraph with a *first line indent*. It is typical of paragraphs in books.
>
> This paragraph is an example of a paragraph with a *hanging indent*. It is often used for numbered paragraphs or those with an icon or other image on the left.

**Note**

In right-to-left languages, the behavior of the Before Text and After Text indents is the opposite: "before" is on the right margin; "after" is on the left margin.

## Paragraph background color

Click the button labelled **7** in Figure 54 to open a palette from which you can choose a color for the background of the paragraph. From this palette, you can also click **Custom Color** to open the Pick a Color dialog, where you can define new colors to be added to the palette.

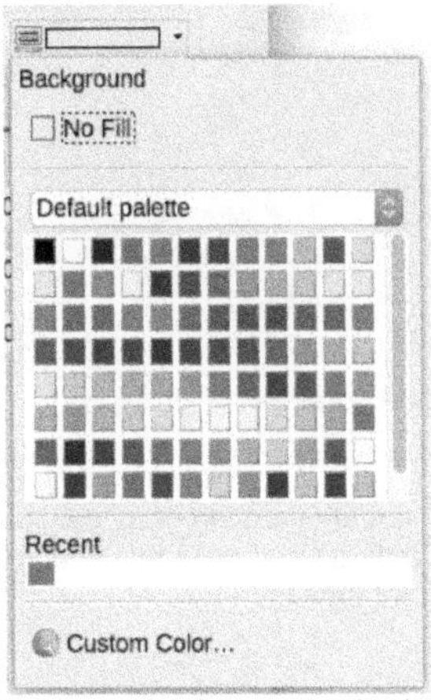

*Figure 60: Selecting a background color for a paragraph*

**Note**

If the paragraph has been indented from the right or left margin, the background color is not applied to the area of the indent. If you wish to extend the color to the margin, you will need to use a frame, table, or other method; see Chapter 6, Formatting Pages: Advanced.

## Settings on the Paragraph dialog

The paragraph dialog includes several more pages: Tabs (covered in next section, "Setting tab stops and indents"), Borders, Drop Caps, Area (more choices than just color), Transparency, Text Flow, and Outline & Numbering. For more information, see Chapter 8, Introduction to Styles, and Chapter 9, Working with Styles.

### Borders

You can add borders to any combination of top, bottom, and sides of paragraphs. You can choose the style (solid, dotted, dashed, doubled), width, and color of the lines; these choices apply to all borders on a paragraph. The spacing from each line to the paragraph's contents can be set individually for the top, bottom, left, and right.

On this dialog you can also choose to apply a shadow to a paragraph; "distance" refers to the width of the shadow.

Select the **Merge with next paragraph** option to suppress top or bottom lines when the indent, border, and shadow styles of the next paragraph are the same as the current paragraph.

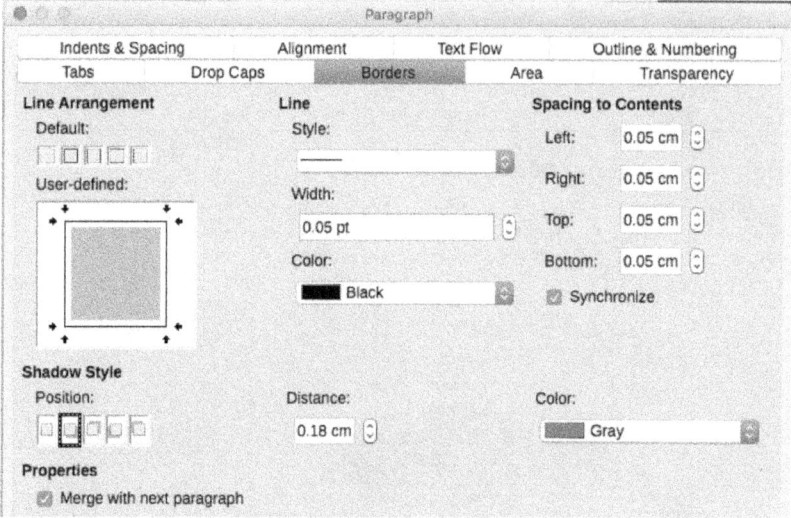

*Figure 61: Options for paragraph borders*

## Drop caps

*Drop capitals* are enlarged letters that mark the start of a new chapter or section. To improve consistency, they are best set up in a paragraph style that you apply to the relevant paragraphs. See Chapter 9, Working with Styles, for details.

## Area

*Area* (also called "fill" and "background" in some parts of LibreOffice) includes five types of fill (background): color, gradient, bitmap, pattern, and hatching. Select a fill type to display the choices available for that type. These choices are covered in more detail in Chapter 5, Formatting Pages: Basics. You can also create your own fills.

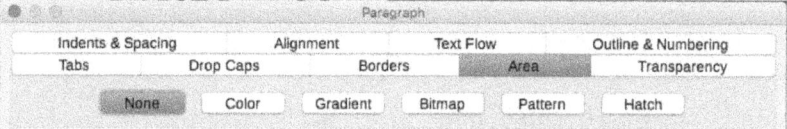

*Figure 62: Types of fill for paragraph backgrounds*

## Transparency

*Transparency* affects the paragraph's background. It is useful for creating watermarks and making colors or images more pale (for more contrast with the text). The available choices are shown in Chapter 5, Formatting Pages: Basics, and are covered in detail in the *Draw Guide*.

## Text Flow

The*Text Flow* page (Figure 63) has several sections. Hyphenation is covered in Chapter 2, Working with Text: Basics, and breaks are covered in Chapter 5, Formatting Pages: Basics.

In the *Options* section, you can specify how paragraphs are treated at the bottom of a page. *Do not split paragraph* and *Keep with next paragraph* should be self-explanatory. The other options allow you to avoid a single line at the bottom of a page (called an *orphan*) or a single line at the top of a page (a *widow*).

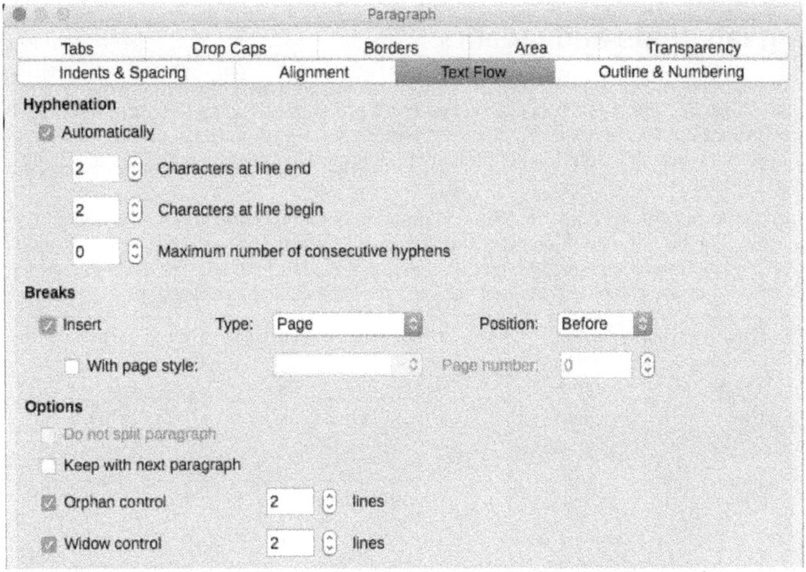

*Figure 63: Options for text flow: hyphenation, breaks, and keeping text together*

## Outline & Numbering

The *Outline & Numbering* page on the Paragraph dialog provides options for choosing the outline level of the paragraph and its numbering style. If the paragraph is part of a numbered list, you can specify that list numbering restarts at the paragraph, and what number to restart with.

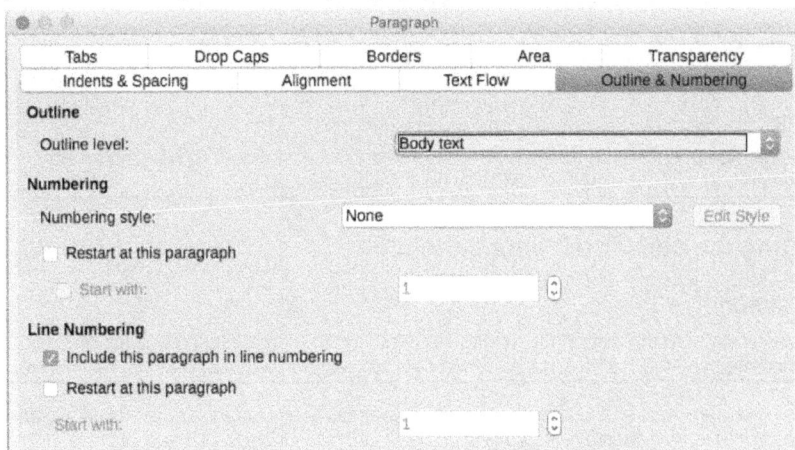

*Figure 64: Selecting outline level, paragraph numbering, and line numbering*

This page does not cover the same functions as the Outline Numbering dialog (**Tools > Outline Numbering**), but the Outline level selected here is related to the outline defined there. See Chapter 8, Introduction to Styles, and Chapter 9, Working with Styles, for a discussion of these features. Line numbering is discussed in Chapter 3, Working with Text: Advanced.

# Setting tab stops and indents

The horizontal ruler shows the tab stops. Any tab stops that you have defined will overwrite the default tab stops. Tab settings affect indentation of full paragraphs (using the **Increase Indent** and **Decrease Indent** buttons on the Formatting toolbar or the Paragraph panel of the Properties deck in the Sidebar) as well as indentation of parts of a paragraph (by pressing the *Tab* key on the keyboard).

Changing the default tab spacing can cause formatting problems if you share documents with other people. If you use the default tab spacing and then send the document to someone else who has chosen a different default tab spacing, tabbed material will change to use the other person's settings. Instead of using the defaults, define your own tab settings, as described in this section.

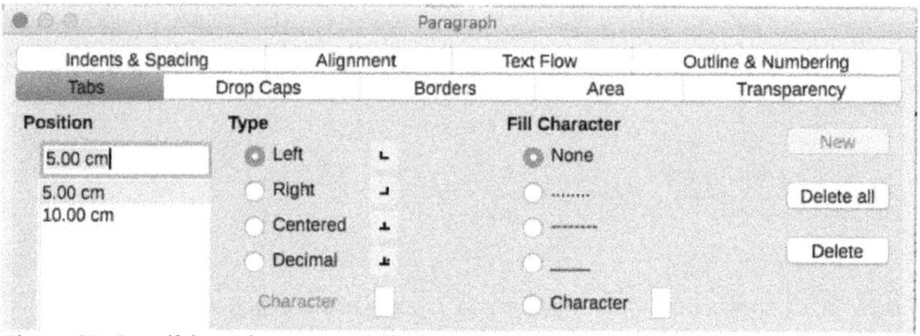

*Figure 65: Specifying tab stops and fill characters*

To define indents and tab settings for one or more selected paragraphs, right-click on a paragraph and choose **Paragraph...** to open the Paragraph dialog; then select either the *Tabs* page (Figure 65) or the *Indents & Spacing* page of the dialog. Alternatively, you can double-click on the horizontal ruler to open the *Indents & Spacing* page of the Paragraph dialog.

A better strategy is to define tabs for the paragraph style. Refer to Chapters 8 and 9 for more about paragraph styles.

▶ **Tip**

Using tabs to space out material on a page is not recommended. Depending on what you are trying to accomplish, a table is usually a better choice.

## Changing the default tab stop interval

**Caution**

Any changes to the default tab setting will affect the existing default tab stops in any document you open afterward, as well as tab stops you insert after making the change.

To set the measurement unit and the spacing of default tab stop intervals, go to **Tools > Options > LibreOffice Writer > General**.

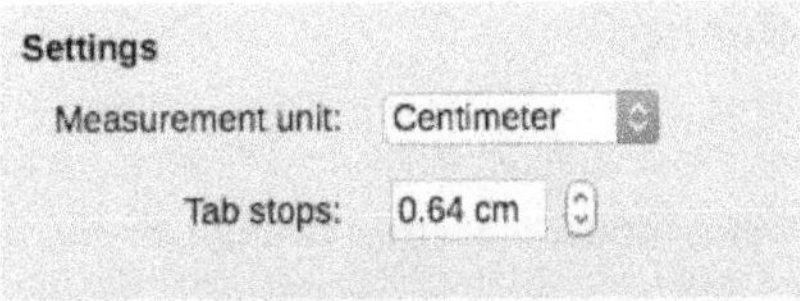

**Settings**

Measurement unit:   Centimeter

Tab stops:   0.64 cm

*Figure 66: Selecting a default tab stop interval*

You can also set or change the measurement unit for rulers in the current document by right-clicking on the ruler to open a list of units, as shown in Figure 67 for the horizontal ruler. Click on one of them to change the ruler to that unit. The selected setting applies only to that ruler.

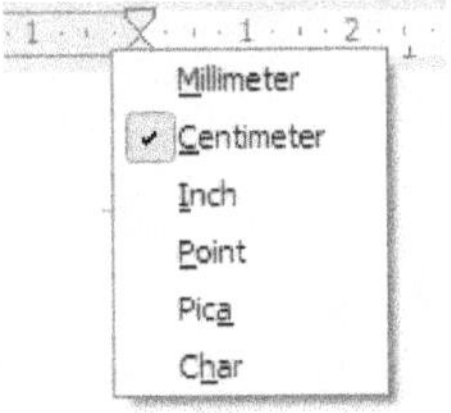

Millimeter

✓ Centimeter

Inch

Point

Pica

Char

*Figure 67: Changing the measurement unit for a ruler*

# Formatting characters

You can apply many formats to characters using the buttons on the Formatting toolbar and by using the Characters panel of the Properties deck of the Sidebar. Not all toolbar buttons are visible in a standard installation, but you can customize the toolbar to include those you use regularly; see Chapter 1, Introducing Writer. These formats include:

- Font Name, Font Size (in points)
- Bold, Italic, Underline, Double Underline, Overline, Strikethrough, Outline
- Superscript, Subscript
- Uppercase, Lowercase
- Increase Font Size, Decrease Font Size
- Font Color (with a palette of colors)
- Background Color (with a palette of colors)
- Highlighting (with a palette of colors)
- Character (to open the Character dialog)

To change the characteristics of an entire paragraph (for example the font name, size, or color), and for many other purposes, it is highly recommended that you use styles rather than manually formatting characters. For information on styles and how to use them, see Chapters 8 and 9. Applying styles is quick and easy using the Styles and Formatting deck of the Sidebar.

Figure 68 shows the Character panel in the Properties deck of the Sidebar. Clicking the down-arrow next to a button opens the control for further choices, such as font color or character spacing. The appearance of the buttons may vary with your operating system and the selection of icon size and style in **Tools > Options > LibreOffice > View**.

Click the **More Options** button (**15**) to open the Character dialog, which includes more choices than are available through the Formatting toolbar or the Sidebar.

## Font name, size, and effects

To change the **font name and size** used for selected characters, you can use the drop-down menus on the Formatting toolbar, the Character panel in the Sidebar, or the Character dialog.

Similarly, you can apply **bold**, **italics**, **underline**, **strikethrough**, or **shadow effects** to selected characters from the Formatting toolbar, the Character panel in the Sidebar, or the Character dialog. The Underline effect has a drop-down menu of line types (Figure 69). The Formatting toolbar includes other effects that are not in the Sidebar: **overline** and **double underline**; these buttons may not be visible in a default installation.

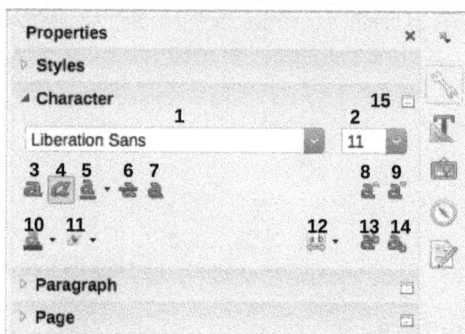

| | | | |
|---|---|---|---|
| 1 | Font Name | 6 | Strikethrough |
| 2 | Font Size | 7 | Shadow |
| 3 | Bold | 8 | Increase Font Size |
| 4 | Italic | 9 | Decrease Font Size |
| 5 | Underline | 10 | Font Color |

| | |
|---|---|
| 11 | Highlight Color |
| 12 | Character Spacing |
| 13 | Superscript |
| 14 | Subscript |
| 15 | More Options – opens Character dialog |

*Figure 68: Character panel in the Properties deck of the Sidebar*

*Figure 69: Selecting the line style for the Underline effect*

To choose the **color of the font or its highlighting**, open the appropriate color palette (**10** or **11**; similar to the one shown in Figure 60). The highlighting selection over-rides any background color that has been applied to the paragraph.

To quickly **increase or decrease the font size** of selected characters, you can click the relevant buttons on the Formatting toolbar or the Character panel in the Sidebar; however, you have no control over the amount of the increase or decrease, which is usually 2 points. For finer control, use the Font Size drop-down list instead.

To change characters into **subscripts or superscripts** (using the default values for size and position), select them and click the relevant buttons on the Formatting toolbar or the Character panel in the Sidebar. For more control, use the Character dialog.

To quickly change the **spacing between characters**, select them and choose from the Character Spacing drop-down menu in the Sidebar (Figure 70).

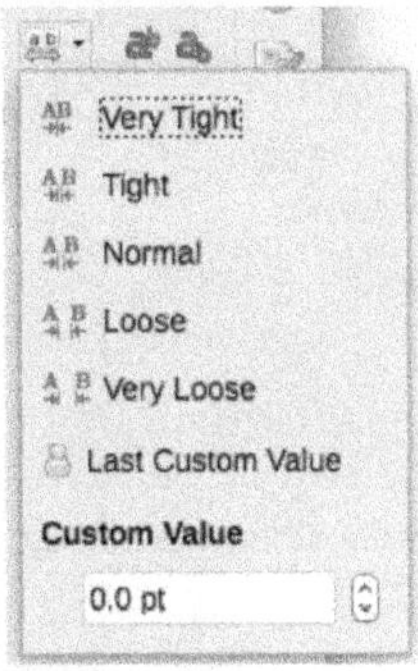

*Figure 70: Changing character spacing*

## Settings on the Character dialog

The Character dialog has six pages, shown in this section. Most of these pages are the same as the pages on the Character Style dialog (see Chapter 9, Working with Styles).

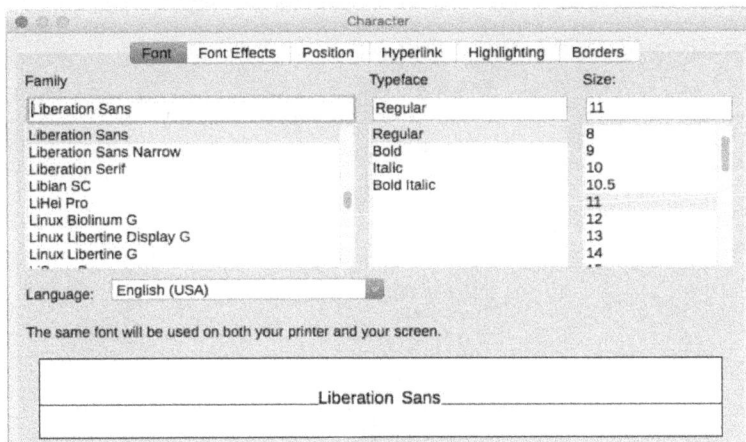

*Figure 71: Font page of the Character dialog*

### Font and Font Effects

On the *Font* page (Figure 71), you can specify the font's family, typeface (choices vary with the font, but typically include regular, bold, and italic), and size; and the language for the paragraph, if it differs from the language for the document. The box at the bottom shows a preview of the selections.

On the *Font Effects* page (Figure 72), you can choose the color of the font and a range of effects, many of which are not suitable for formal documents. Figures 73 and 74 show the choices in some of the drop-down lists.

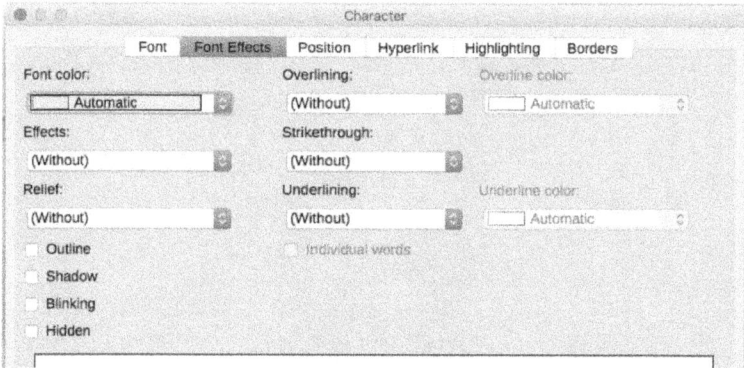

Figure 72: Font Effects page of the Character dialog

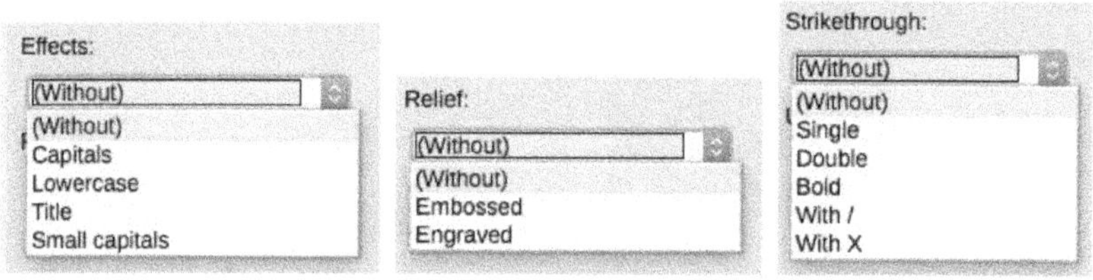

Figure 73:Choices for capitalization, relief, and strikethrough effects

Figure 74: Choices for overlining and underlining are the same

## Position

The *Position* page collects the options that affect the position of text on the page. This page is divided into three sections: *Position*, *Rotation/Scaling*, and *Spacing*.

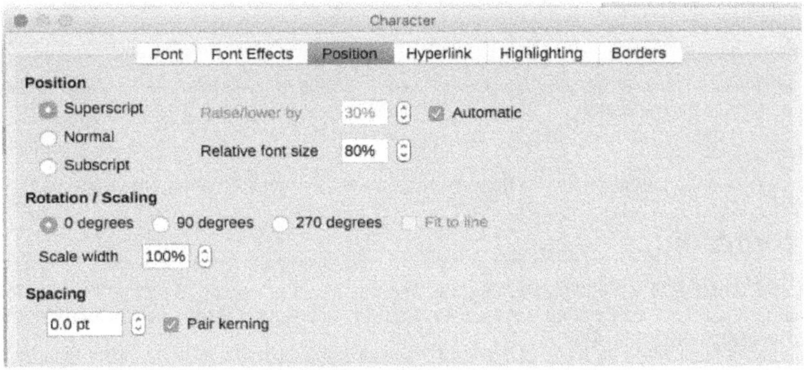

*Figure 75: Position page of the Character dialog*

The *Position* section controls the appearance of superscripts and subscripts.

The *Rotation/Scaling* section controls the rotation of the characters. The Scale width box controls the percentage of the font width by which to compress or stretch the rotated text.

The *Spacing* section controls the spacing between individual characters. The **Pair Kerning** option (selected by default) automatically adjusts the character spacing for specific letter combinations. Kerning is only available for certain font types and, for printed documents, works only if your printer supports it.

## Hyperlink

The *Hyperlink* page of the Character dialog is an alternative to using the Hyperlink dialog (**Insert > Hyperlink**). It includes fewer choices and is specifically for text (not button) links. Hyperlinks can be to other parts of the same document, to other documents, or to web pages.

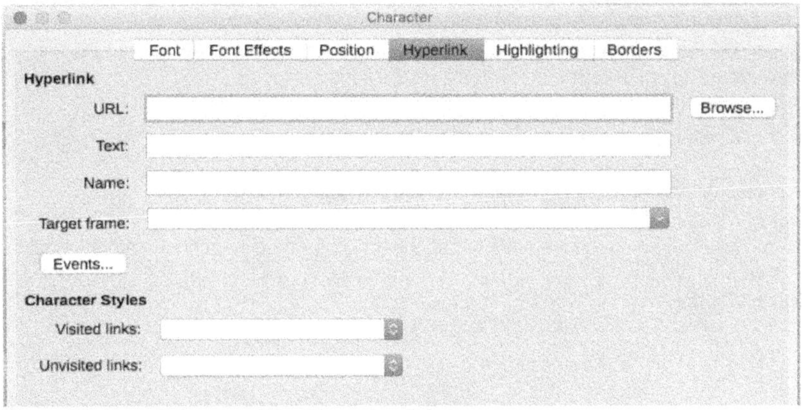

*Figure 76: Hyperlink page of the Character dialog*

When LibreOffice recognizes a string of characters that may be a URL (internet address), it replaces the characters with a hyperlink and formats the hyperlink as specified in the Internet Link character style. On this dialog you can choose a different character style (if the style has been defined previously) or replace the URL with other text. To turn off this feature, choose **Tools > AutoCorrect > AutoCorrect Options > Options** page and deselect **URL Recognition**.

For more about creating and editing hyperlinks, see the Help system or Chapter 12 in the *Getting Started Guide*.

### Highlighting

The *Highlighting* page controls the background color for selected characters. It is similar to the Highlighting drop-down palette.

### Borders

The *Borders* page is the same as the Borders page on the Paragraph dialog; see page 91.

# Autoformatting

You can set Writer to automatically format parts of a document according to the choices made on the *Options* and *Localized Options* pages of the AutoCorrect dialog (**Tools > AutoCorrect > AutoCorrect Options**).

> ### ▶ Tip
>
> If you notice unexpected formatting changes occurring in your document, this is the first place to look for the cause.

The Help describes each of these choices and how to activate the autoformats. Some common unwanted or unexpected formatting changes include:

- Horizontal lines. If you type three or more hyphens (---), underscores (_ _ _) or equal signs (===) on a line and then press Enter the paragraph is replaced by a horizontal line as wide as the page. The line is actually the lower border of the preceding paragraph.
- Bulleted and numbered lists. A bulleted list is created when you type a hyphen (-), asterisk (*), or plus sign (+), followed by a space or tab at the beginning of a paragraph. A numbered list is created when you type a number followed by a period (.), followed by a space or tab at the beginning of a paragraph. Automatic numbering is only applied to paragraphs formatted with the Default, Text body or Text body indent paragraph styles.

To automatically format the file according to the options you have set, choose **Tools > AutoCorrect** and select or deselect the items on the submenu.

**While Typing**
Automatically formats the document while you type.

**Apply**
Automatically formats the document.

**Apply and Edit Changes**
Automatically formats the file and then opens a dialog where you can accept or reject the changes.

**AutoCorrect Options**
Opens the AutoCorrect dialog (Figures 77 and 78).

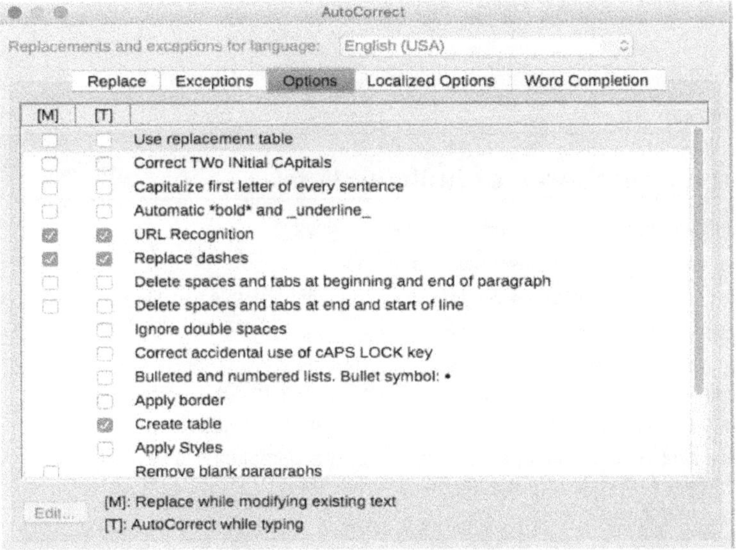

*Figure 77: Autoformat choices on the Options page of the AutoCorrect dialog*

The *Localized Options* page (Figure 78) controls the formatting of quotation marks and apostrophes (which look like a closing single quote). Most fonts include curly quotation marks (also known as "smart quotes"), but for some purposes (such as marking minutes and seconds of latitude and longitude) you may wish to format them as straight quotes.

**Straight quotes**     **Smart quotes**

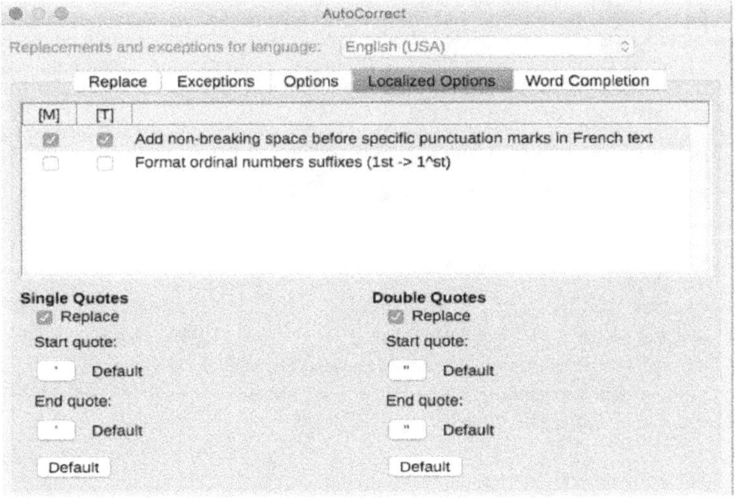

' '  " "          ' '  " "

*Figure 78: Autoformatting quotation marks*

> ▶ **Tip**
>
> Most people keep the AutoCorrect setting for smart quotes and use the Special Characters dialog to insert straight quotes when needed. See Chapter 2, Working with Text: Basics.

## Formatting numbered or bulleted lists

You can format numbered or bulleted lists in several ways:

- Use autoformatting, as described above.
- Use list (numbering) styles, as described in Chapters 8, 9, and 12 in this book.
- Use the Bullets and Numbering toolbar (see Figure 79).
- Use the Numbering and Bullets buttons on the Formatting toolbar or on the Paragraph panel of the Properties deck of the Sidebar (see Figure 80).
- Use the Bullets and Numbering dialog (see Figures 81 and 82).

To produce a simple numbered or bulleted list, select the paragraphs in the list and then click on the appropriate button on the Paragraph panel on the toolbar.

> ● **Notes**
>
> It is a matter of personal preference whether you type your information first, then apply numbering/bullets or apply these as you type.
>
> If numbering or bullets are being applied automatically in a way that you find inappropriate, you can switch them off temporarily by unchecking **Format > AutoCorrect > While Typing**.

### Using the Bullets and Numbering toolbar

You can create a nested list (where one or more list items has a sub-list under it, as in an outline) by using the buttons on the Bullets and Numbering toolbar (Figure 79). You can move items up or down the list, create subpoints, change the style of bullets, add paragraphs without numbers or bullets (for list items that include more than one paragraph), and access the Bullets and Numbering dialog, which contains more detailed controls.

Use **View > Toolbars > Bullets and Numbering** to display the toolbar.

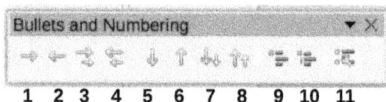

| 1 Demote One Level | 5 Move Down | 9 Insert Unnumbered Entry |
| 2 Promote One Level | 6 Move Up | 10 Restart Numbering |
| 3 Demote One Level with Subpoints | 7 Move Down with Subpoints | 11 Open the Bullets and |
| 4 Promote One Level with Subpoints | 8 Move Up with Subpoints | Numbering dialog |

*Figure 79: Bullets and Numbering toolbar*

> **Tip**
>
> You can use keyboard shortcuts to move paragraphs up or down the outline levels. Place the cursor at the beginning of the numbered paragraph and press:
>
> *Tab* = Down a level
> *Shift+Tab* = Up a level
>
> To insert a tab stop at the beginning of a numbered paragraph (that is, after the number but before the text), press *Ctrl+Tab*.

If you create a nested list using the buttons on the Bullets and Numbering toolbar, all the levels of the list (up to 10) initially apply the same numbering (or bullet) format. However, often you will want to use a combination of numbering formats and bullets when creating nested lists. Such lists can be configured in these ways:

- Click in each list item and then select one of the choices in the drop-down palettes under the Bullets and Numbering buttons on the Formatting toolbar or the Properties deck of the Sidebar, as described in "Using the Bullets and Numbering palettes on the Sidebar" below.
- Use the Bullets and Numbering dialog, as described in "Using the Bullets and Numbering dialog" below.

However, a much better strategy is to define and apply a list style, as discussed in Chapter 12, Lists.

## Using the Bullets and Numbering palettes on the Sidebar

The Bullets and Numbering palettes on the Paragraph panel on the Properties deck of the Sidebar can be used to create nested lists and access the Bullets and Numbering dialog. The Sidebar does not include tools for promoting and demoting items in the list, as found on the Bullets and Numbering toolbar.

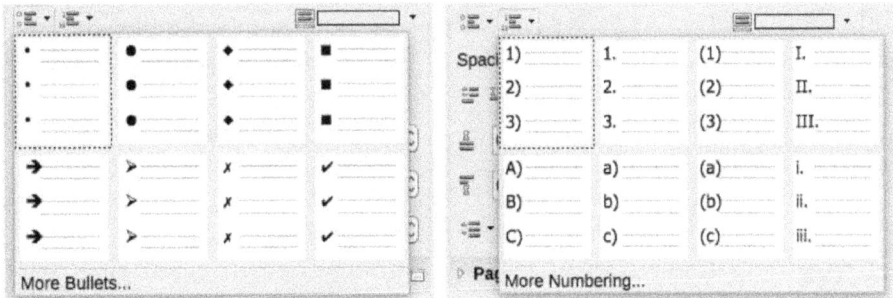

*Figure 80: Bullets and Numbering choices on the Properties deck of the Sidebar*

## Using the Bullets and Numbering dialog

The Bullets and Numbering dialog has six pages. Four pages provide pre-defined symbols and sequences to choose from: Bullets, Numbering Type, Outline (choose from eight standard outline sequences), and Image (choose a bullet image). Two pages provide detailed options for defining your own lists: *Position* (Figure 81) and *Options* (Figure 82). These are the same as the pages provided for list styles, discussed in Chapter 12, Lists.

# More information

For more information about topics in this chapter and the next chapter, you may find this book useful: *Designing with LibreOffice*, by Bruce Byfield. You can download a PDF free from http://designingwithlibreoffice.com or buy a printed copy.

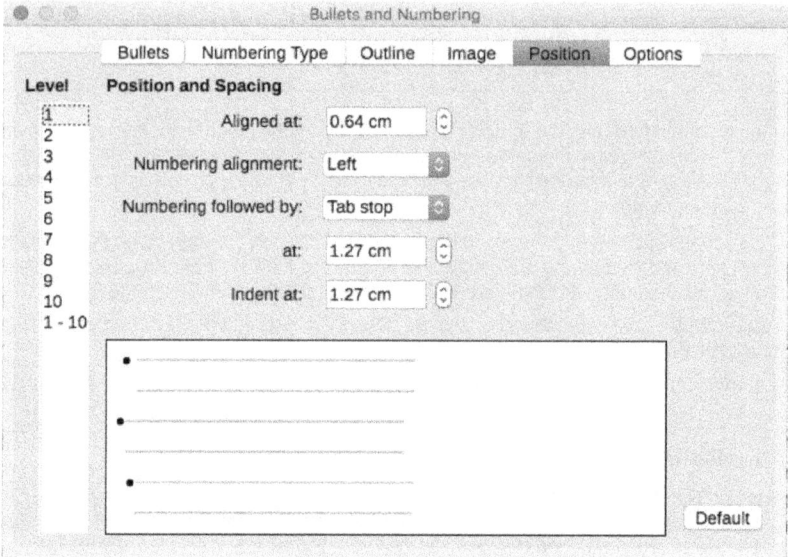

*Figure 81: Position page of the Bullets and Numbering dialog*

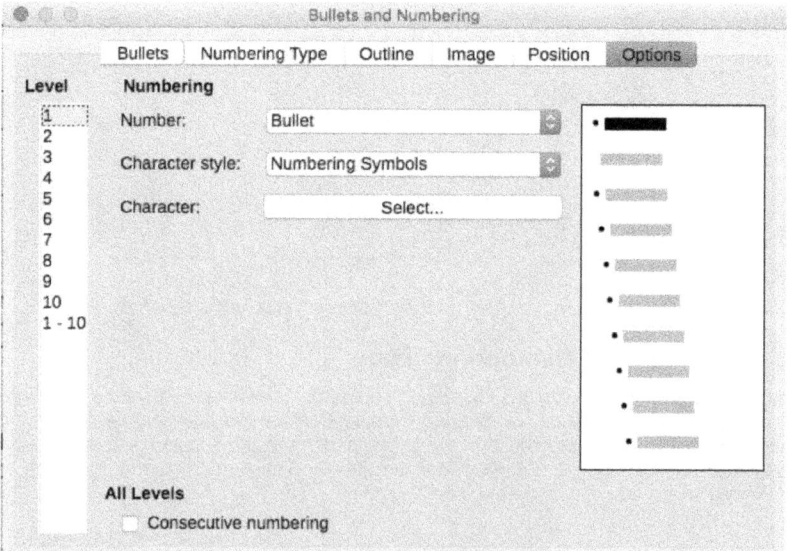

*Figure 82: Options page of the Bullets and Numbering dialog*

# LibreOffice

# Chapter 5
# Formatting Pages: Basics

*Page styles and related features*

# Introduction

Writer provides several ways for you to control page layouts.

This chapter describes the use of page styles and some associated functions:

- Headers and footers
- Page numbering
- Title pages
- Footnotes and endnotes
- Borders and backgrounds

Chapter 6 covers the use of columns, frames, tables, and sections, as well as changing page orientation within a document.

> **Note**
>
> **All pages in a Writer document are based on page styles.** The other layout methods (described in Chapter 6) build upon the underlying page style.

> **Tip**
>
> Page layout is usually easier if you select the options to show text, object, table, and section boundaries in **Tools > Options > LibreOffice > Application Colors** and the options for paragraph ends, tabs, breaks, and other items in **Tools > Options > LibreOffice Writer > Formatting Aids**.

## Setting up basic page layout using styles

In Writer, page styles define the basic layout of all pages, including page size, margins, the placement of headers and footers, borders and backgrounds, number of columns, and so on.

Writer comes with several page styles, which you can build on or modify, and you can define new (custom) page styles. You can have one or many page styles in a single document. If you do not specify a page style, Writer uses the *Default Style*.

To change the layout of individual pages, either define a new page style or use one of the techniques (sections, frames, or tables) described later in this chapter.

> **Note**
>
> Some layout changes (such as the position of page numbers and other elements in a header or footer on facing pages) can be defined in a single page style.

This chapter describes some uses of page styles. Some other uses are discussed in Chapter 8, Introduction to Styles. The Page Style dialog is covered in detail in Chapter 9, Working with Styles.

> **Tip**
>
> Any modifications of page styles, including the Default page style, apply only to the document you are working on. If you want the changes to be the default for all documents, you need to put the changes into a template and make that template the default template. See Chapter 10, Working with Templates, for details.

# Inserting a page break without changing the page style

In many documents (for example, a multi-page report), you want the text to flow from one page to the next as you add or delete information. Writer does this automatically, unless you override the text flow using one of the techniques described in this chapter.

If you want a page break in a particular place—for example, to put a heading at the top of a new page—you can position the cursor at the point where you want to start the new page and select **Insert > Page Break** from the Menu bar.

However, there are other methods to put a heading at the top of a page. For example, you can define the paragraph style for a heading to include a page break; see "Text flow options for paragraph styles" in Chapter 9, Working with Styles, for more information.

# Inserting a page break and changing to a new page style

If you want the new page to have a different page style—for example, to change from a Default page style to a First Page style—use either of these methods.

**Method 1**

1) Position the cursor at the point you want to start the next page. Select **Insert > Manual Break**.

2) In the Type section of the Insert Break dialog (Figure 83), Page break is preselected, and Style is set at [None]. From the **Style** drop-down list, select the page style for the next page. Click **OK**.

**Method 2**

1) Position the cursor in the paragraph you want to be at the start of the next page. Right-click and choose Paragraph in the context menu.

2) On the Text Flow page of the Paragraph dialog (Figure 84), in the Breaks section, select Insert and With page style. From the **Style** drop-down list, select the page style for the next page. Click **OK**.

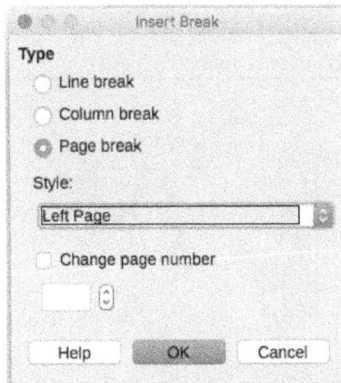

*Figure 83: Inserting a manual page break and changing the page style*

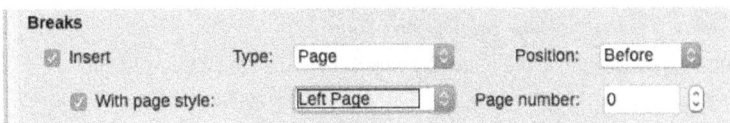

*Figure 84: Inserting a manual page break using the Paragraph dialog*

▶ **Tip**

See "Restarting page numbering" on page 116 for information on the use of the page number fields in these dialogs.

## Changing page margins

You can change page margins in these ways:

- Using the page rulers—quick and easy, but does not have fine control.
- Using the Page Style dialog—can specify margins to two (fractional) decimal places.
- Using the Page panel of the Properties deck in the Sidebar.

● **Note**

If you change the margins using the rulers or the Sidebar, the new margins affect the page style and all pages that use that style. The new margins will be shown in the Page Style dialog the next time you open it.

If you want to change the margins on some pages, but not others, you must use a different page style.

To change margins using the rulers:

1) The shaded sections of the rulers are the margins (see Figure 85). Put the mouse cursor over the line between the gray and white sections. The pointer turns into a double-headed arrow and displays the current setting in a tooltip.

2) Hold down the left mouse button and drag the mouse to move the margin.

▨ **Caution**

The small arrows on the ruler are used for indenting paragraphs. They are often in the same place as the page margins, so you need to be careful to move the margin marker, not the arrows. The double-headed arrows shown in Figure 85 are actual mouse cursors placed in the correct position.

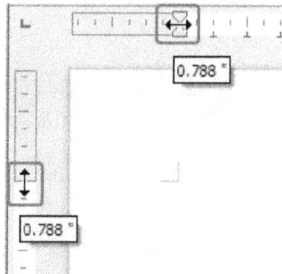

*Figure 85: Moving the margins*

To change margins using the Page Style dialog (Figure 97):

1) Right-click anywhere on the page and select Page from the context menu.

2) On the Page page of the dialog, type the required distances in the Margins boxes.

To change margins using the Page panel of the Properties deck of the Sidebar:

1) On the open Sidebar (**View > Sidebar**) select the Properties tab.

2) Open the Page panel if is not open by clicking the plus (+) symbol in the panel title.

3) Click the Margin button to open the sub-panel and enter the required dimensions in the Custom size boxes (clicking the **More Options** button will open the Page Style dialog).

# Creating headers and footers

Headers are portions of a document that appear at the top of every page; footers appear at the bottom of a page. In LibreOffice, headers and footers are specified by page styles; therefore, all the pages with the same page style will display the same header and footer, although the contents of the header/footer may vary. For example, the header/footer on the first page of a section, chapter, or document may contain different information, even though the page style be the same.

Chapter 9 describes how to format a header as part of the page style formatting. For the purpose of this example, we will insert a header in the Default pages using manual formatting.

▶ **Terminology**

A *heading* is a paragraph that introduces a chapter or section of a document, for example "Creating headers and footers" above. A *header* (also known as a *running header*) appears on each page and typically displays information about the document.

There are two ways to insert a header. The simplest method is to click above the top of the text area, then when the Header marker appears, click on the +. (To insert a footer, click below the bottom of the text area to display the Footer marker, and then click on the +.)

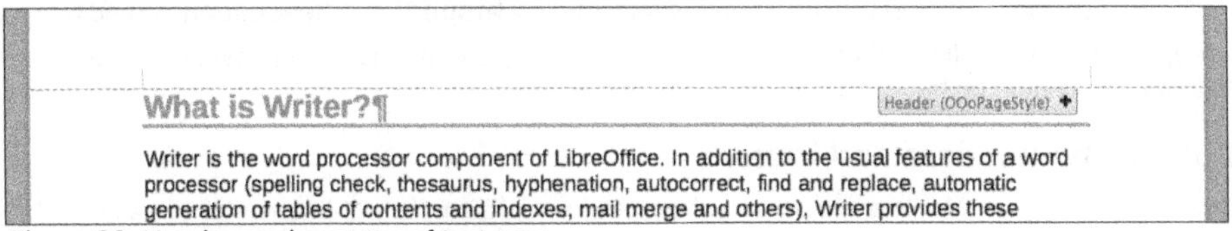

What is Writer?¶

Header (OOoPageStyle) +

Writer is the word processor component of LibreOffice. In addition to the usual features of a word processor (spelling check, thesaurus, hyphenation, autocorrect, find and replace, automatic generation of tables of contents and indexes, mail merge and others), Writer provides these

*Figure 86: Header marker at top of text area*

Headers can also be inserted from the Menu bar by selecting **Insert > Header and Footer > Header > [Page Style]**. The submenu lists the page styles used in your document. In addition, the submenu includes the entry All, which activates headers on all the pages of the document regardless of their page style. Similarly, to insert a footer, choose **Insert > Header and Footer > Footer > [Page Style]**.

● **Note**

The Insert menu can also be used for deleting a preexisting header or footer for a page style. If that page style has a check mark in front of it, it contains a header/footer, and clicking on it opens a message box warning about deletion and asks whether you want to delete the header or footer for that particular page style.

For our example, select the Default menu item to activate the headers only on the pages that use the Default page style. An area will appear at the top or bottom of the page (Figure 87).

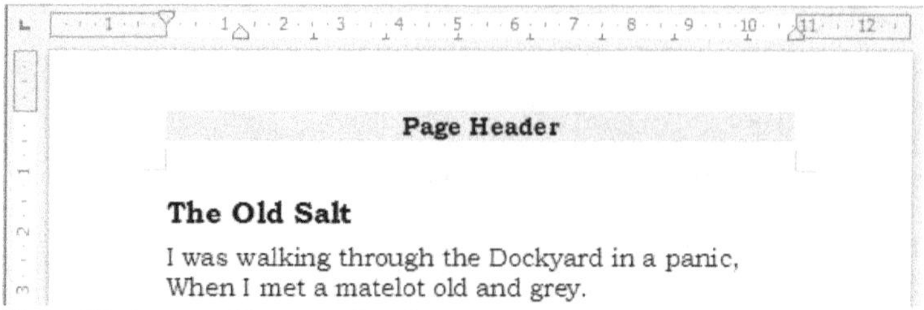

*Figure 87: A page with a page header*

## Using fields in headers and footers

You can type information into headers and footers, but some items such as document titles and chapter titles are best added as fields. That way, if something changes, the headers and footers are all updated automatically.

Fields are covered in Chapter 17, Fields, but one example here may be useful. To insert the document title into the header on a Default page style:

1) Select **File > Properties > Description**, enter a title for your document in the Title area, and click **OK** to close the dialog.

2) Add a header (**Insert > Header > Default**).

3) Place the cursor in the header part of the page.

4) Select **Insert > Fields > Title**. The title should appear on a gray background (which does not show when printed and can be turned off).

5) To change the title of the document, reselect **File > Properties > Description** and edit.

Also, you must use a field for the page number so it changes from one page to the next. See "Numbering pages" on page 111.

## Formatting headers and footers

In Writer, headers and footers are paragraphs; therefore, you can format the header or footer text using the same techniques you use for formatting text in the main body of the document. See Chapter 4, Formatting Text.

You can also add images to headers and footers using any of the techniques described in Chapter 11, Images and Graphics, and you can line up information using tables as described in Chapter 6.

> ▶ **Tip**
>
> Writer provides paragraph styles for headers and footers, which you can modify and use in the same way as other paragraph styles. See Chapters 8 and 9.

To format the layout of headers and footers manually:

1) Use any of these methods to open the relevant page style dialog:
   - Click anywhere on the page and choose **Format > Page** from the Menu bar.
   - Right-click anywhere on the page and choose **Page** from the context menu.
   - Click the top of the page. When the Header marker appears, click the plus sign or down arrow and select **Format Header**.

2) On the Header or Footer tab of the page style dialog (Figure 88), you can change the margins, spacing, and height.

3) Click **More** to open the Border/Background dialog (Figure 89), where you can add borders, background colors, and background images to the header or footer.

## Caution

Do not attempt to use the Area or Borders tabs on the Page Style dialog itself to format headers or footers. Style choices selected from those tabs apply to the entire page.

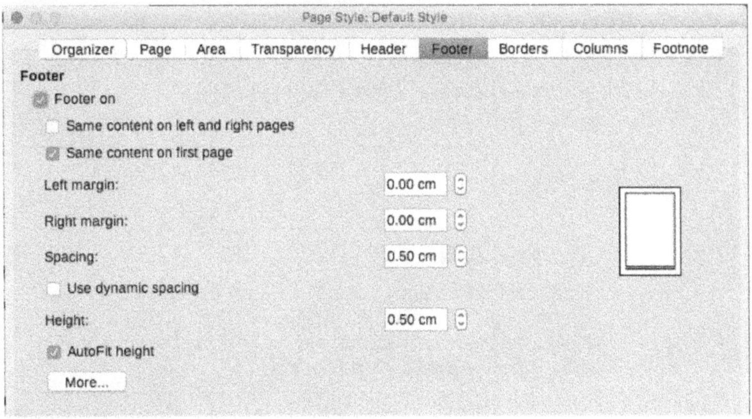

*Figure 88: Footer tab of Page Style dialog*

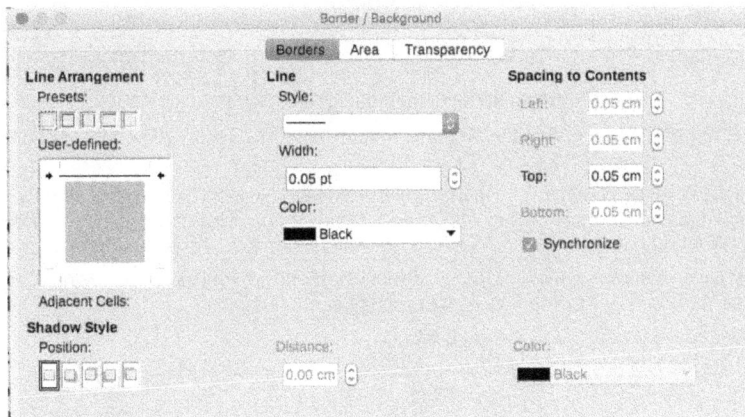

*Figure 89: Border / Background page for header or footer*

# Numbering pages

This section describes techniques to insert page numbers and related information in headers or footers of a document.

You must place a page number field in a header or footer so the number appears on every page and changes from one page to the next. The page number appears with a gray background. This gray background denotes a field; although it is visible on screen, it is not printed.

## Tips

If you wish to turn off the gray background, choose **View > Field Shadings** (or press *Ctrl+F8*).

If you see the words "Page number" instead of a number, press *Ctrl+F9*. This shortcut key toggles Writer between displaying the Field Name and the actual page number.

## Simple page numbering

The simplest case is to have the page number at the top of every page and nothing more. To do this, put the cursor on the header and choose **Insert > Page Number**.

*Figure 90: Page number inserted in the header*

## Combining header text and page number

You can apply a lot of interesting variations without further knowledge of page styles. Here are some suggestions:

- Right-align the header to make the page number appear on the top-right.
- Type the word page before the page number field so the header reads page 1, page 2, and so on.
- Add the document title so the header reads, for example: Peter's Favourite Poems, left justified, and page x with right justification, where x is the value of the Page Number field. Consider using a (right-aligned) tab to separate the title from the page number.
- LibreOffice also has a Page Count field (**Insert > Fields > Page Count**). Using it, you could, for example, have a header that reads page 2 of 12.

These variations are all illustrated in Figure 91.

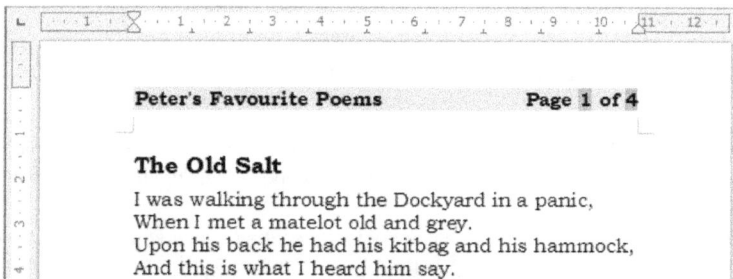

*Figure 91: Variations on the simple page numbering method*

# Changing the number format

Many more variations are possible. For example, you can set the page number to display in Roman numerals. To do that, you can double-click on the page number and select the desired format; however, a better choice is to specify the format of numbers in the page style as explained here.

Right-click in the text area of the page and select **Page** from the context menu.

On the Page page of the Page Style dialog, in the Layout settings section, select i, ii, iii, .... from the Format drop-down list to use lowercase numerals.

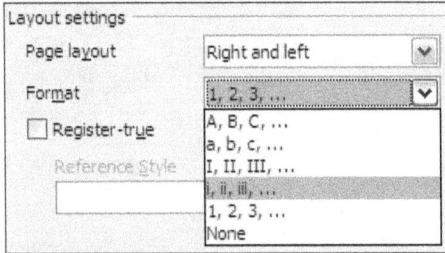

*Figure 92: Changing format of page numbers*

Remember, any change in the number format affects the page numbers on *all* pages using that page style, regardless of the method used to change the format.

# Numbering pages by chapter

Technical documents often include the chapter number with the page number in the header or footer. For example, 1-1, 1-2, 1-3, ...; 2-1, 2-2, 2-3, ... To set up this type of page numbering in Writer, you need to do three things:

1) Ensure that your chapter titles are all identified by the same paragraph style, for example, the Heading 1 style.

2) Use **Tools > Outline Numbering** to tell Writer what paragraph style you are using for Level 1 in your outline, and specify "1,2,3" in the Number box.

*Figure 93: Specifying paragraph style and numbering for chapter titles*

3) Insert the chapter number in the document. To do this:

    a) Place the cursor in the header or footer just before the page number you inserted earlier, and choose **Insert > Field > More Fields** from the Menu bar.

    b) On the Fields dialog (Figure 94), go to the Document page. Select **Chapter** in the *Type* list, **Chapter number** in the *Format* list, and **1** in the *Level* box. Click **Insert**.

    c) Type a hyphen or other punctuation between the chapter number and the page number.

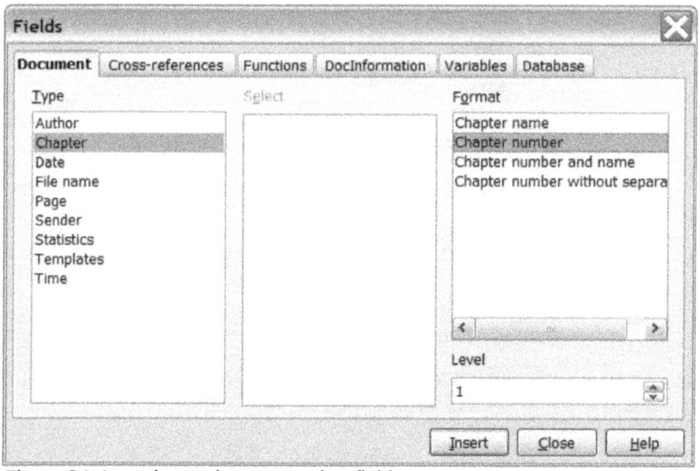

*Figure 94: Inserting a chapter number field*

## Numbering the first page something other than 1

Sometimes you may want to start a document with a page number greater than 1. Follow these instructions to do that. (These instructions are for a page number in a footer, but you could use a header instead.)

1) Click in the footer. To insert the page number, choose **Insert > Fields > Page Number**. The page number will be 1.

2) Click in the first paragraph in the text area. Choose **Format > Paragraph** (or right-click and choose **Paragraph** from the context menu), to display the Paragraph dialog.

3) On the Text Flow page, in the *Breaks* section (Figure 95), select **Insert** and select **Page** in the *Type* drop-down list. Select **With Page Style** and the page style you are using for the first page of the document.

4) Select **Page number** to make the field active. Type the page number you want to start with. Click **OK** to close the Paragraph dialog.

*Figure 95: The Breaks section of the Text Flow page of the Page Style dialog*

> ## Tip
>
> If you set a starting page number that is an even number, you will end up with a blank page before the first page. However, you can suppress this blank page when you print the file or export it as a PDF. See Chapter 7, Printing, Exporting, Emailing, for more information.

## Defining a different first page for a document

Many documents, such as letters and memos, have a first page that is different from the other pages in the document. For example, the first page of a letterhead typically has a different header, as shown in Figure 96, or the first page of a report might have no header or footer, while the other pages do.

Using the Default (or any other) page style for your document, you can add a header/footer as you wish to the first page by deselecting the **Same content on first page** option on the header/footer pages in the Page Style dialog, and then adding the header/footer. You can then add a different header/footer to the other pages of the document. See "Creating headers and footers" on page 109 for more information.

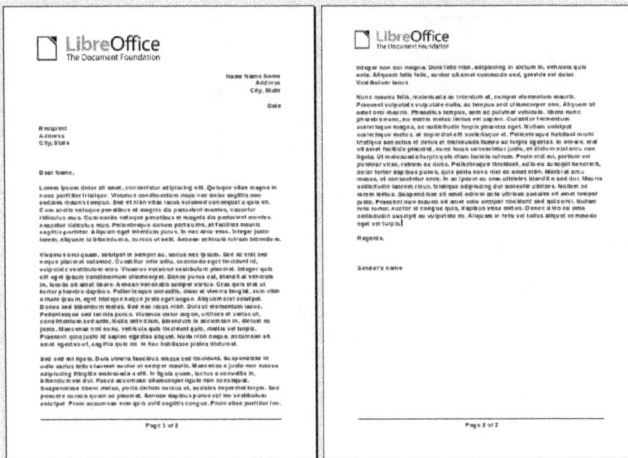

*Figure 96: Letterhead with different headers for first and following pages*

## Adding title pages

Writer provides a fast and convenient way to add one or more title pages to a document and optionally to restart the page number at 1 for the body of the document.

To begin, choose **Format > Title Page** from the Menu bar. On the Title Page dialog (Figure 97), you can make the following choices:

- Convert existing pages to title pages, or insert new title pages.
- How many pages to convert or insert.
- Where those pages are located.
- If and where to restart page numbering, and what number to start with.
- What page style to use for the title page.

Using this technique, you can insert several "title pages" at different points in your document, for example to add decorative pages between chapters as well as title, copyright, and other pages at the beginning of a book.

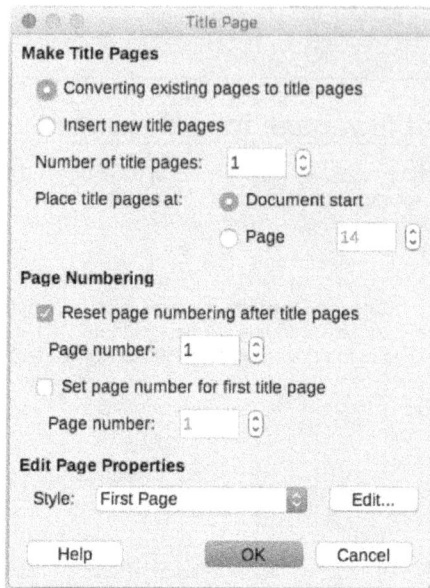

*Figure 97: Adding title pages to a document*

## Restarting page numbering

Often you will want to restart the page numbering at 1, for example, on the page following a title page or a table of contents. In addition, many documents have the front matter (such as the table of contents) numbered with Roman numerals and the main body of the document numbered in Arabic numerals, starting with 1.

If you chose not to add title pages as described above, you can restart page numbering in two ways.

**Method 1:**

1) Place the cursor in the first paragraph of the new page (a heading is a paragraph).
2) Choose **Format > Paragraph**.
3) On the Text Flow page of the Paragraph dialog, select **Insert** in the Breaks area (Figure 95 on page 114).
4) In the Type drop-down list, select **Page**.
5) In the Position drop-down list, select **Before** or **After** to position where you want to insert the page numbering break.
6) Select **With Page Style** and specify the page style to use.
7) Specify the page number to start from and then click **OK**. This does not insert a new page.

**Method 2:**

1) Place the cursor in the first paragraph of the new page.
2) Choose **Insert > Manual break**.

3) **Page break** is the default selected on the Insert Break dialog (Figure 98).

4) Choose the required page in the *Style* drop-down list.

5) Select **Change page number**.

6) Specify the page number to start from and then click **OK**. This does insert a new page.

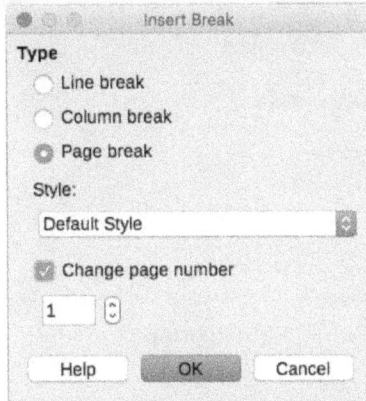

Figure 98: Restarting page numbering after a manual page break

### Example: Restart page numbering: a preface

A standard preface has the following properties:

- Page numbers are displayed in Roman numerals (i, ii, iii, iv, ...).
- After the preface, the document starts on a Default page.
- The page number resets to 1, and the number format becomes Arabic (1, 2, 3, 4, ...).

Resetting the page number requires page breaks.

First, do the preliminary work for the Preface style:

1) Create a new page style and name it Preface.

2) Set its Next Style to Preface because a preface could span multiple pages.

3) Add a header to Preface and insert the Page Number field. Make the page numbers display as Roman numerals (i, ii, iii, iv, ...):

4) Open the page style window for Preface (if not already open) and click the Header tab. Select **Header on** under Header.

5) Click the Page tab (Figure 99). Under Layout settings, in the Format drop-down list, set the format to **i, ii, iii, ...**. Click **OK** to close the dialog.

After the preface is written, we are ready to restart the page numbering in the main body of the document to Arabic numerals. Follow these steps:

1) Make an empty paragraph at the very end of the preface.

2) Put the cursor on the blank line.

3) Choose **Insert > Manual Break**.

4) Select **Page break** and choose the Default Style.

5) Select the **Change page number** option and set the new value to 1. Click **OK** to close the dialog.

These settings are shown in Figure 98.

**Note**

You cannot assign an odd page number to a left page or an even page number to a right page. LibreOffice strongly adheres to the convention that odd page numbers go on right-hand pages and even page numbers on left-hand pages.

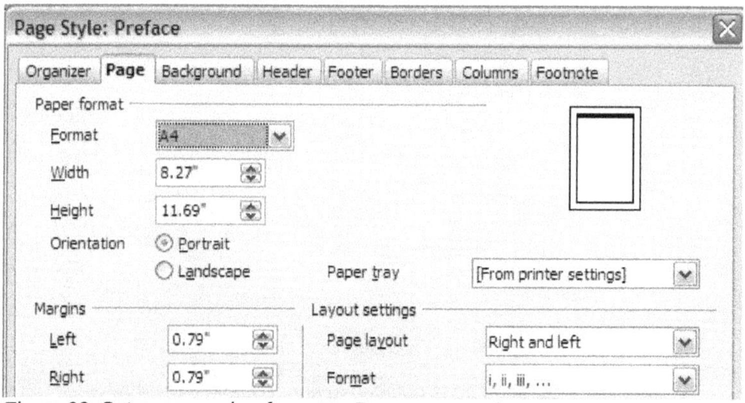

*Figure 99: Set page number format to Roman numerals*

# Formatting footnotes and endnotes

Footnotes appear at the bottom of the page on which they are referenced. Endnotes are collected at the end of a document.

To work effectively with footnotes and endnotes, you need to:

- Insert footnotes and define their format, if the default does not meet your needs (see Chapter 3, Working with Text: Advanced).
- Define the location of footnotes on the page, and the color and line styles for separator lines, if the defaults do not meet your needs.

## Defining footnote location and separator line

The location of footnotes on the page, and the color and style of the line that separates the footnotes from the text, are defined in the page style. If you are using several page styles, and may have footnotes on any of them, you need to define the footnote location and separator line on each of the page styles.

Choose **Format > Page** from the Menu bar or right-click on a page and choose **Page** from the context menu, to display the Page Style dialog. Go to the *Footnote* tab (Figure 100) and make your selections, then click **OK** to save the changes.

Keeping the default setting **Not larger than page area**, the footnotes area is calculated automatically on the basis of the number of footnotes. If you prefer to control manually the maximum space that footnotes can take, select the **Maximum footnote height** option and enter the value in the preferred unit of measurement. Use the second section of the page to customize the separator between the footnotes and the main text area.

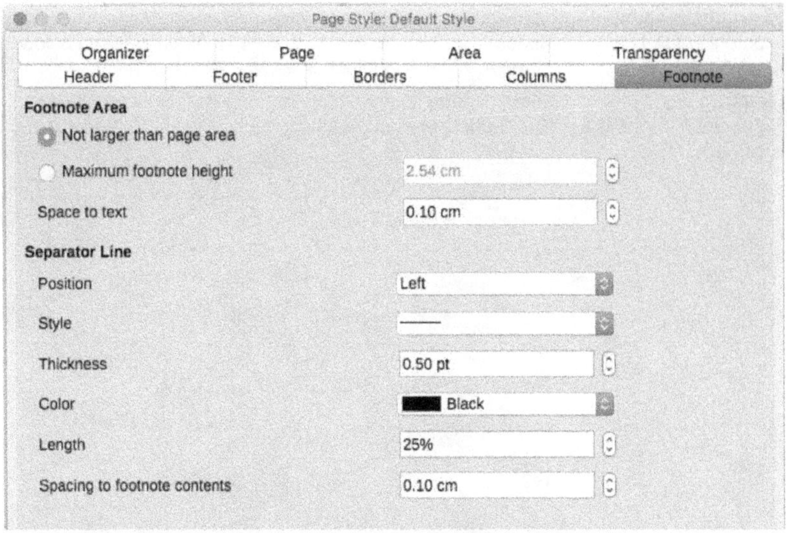

| Organizer | | Page | | Area | | Transparency |
|---|---|---|---|---|---|---|
| Header | Footer | | Borders | | Columns | Footnote |

**Footnote Area**

- Not larger than page area
- Maximum footnote height `2.54 cm`

Space to text `0.10 cm`

**Separator Line**

Position `Left`

Style `————`

Thickness `0.50 pt`

Color `▇ Black`

Length `25%`

Spacing to footnote contents `0.10 cm`

*Figure 100: Defining footnote location and separator line*

# Defining borders and backgrounds

You can apply borders and backgrounds to many elements in Writer. Paragraphs, pages, frames, sections, page styles, paragraph styles, character styles, and frame styles can include both borders and backgrounds; tables of contents and indexes can include backgrounds only. Text can have a border applied, either to individual characters or to selected text.

The dialog pages for borders and backgrounds are similar in each case. To illustrate their use, we will define a border and background for a frame.

▶ **Tip**

Page backgrounds fill only the area within the margins, including the header or footer (if any). To extend the background color or graphic into the margins, define a frame of appropriate size and position, anchor it to the page or to a paragraph, and send it to the background. For more about frames, see Chapter 6.

## Adding a border

To begin, select the frame, right-click, and choose **Object** from the context menu. Select the Borders tab (Figure 101).

Borders have three components: where they go, what they look like, and how much space is left around them.

- **Line Arrangement** specifies where the borders go. Writer provides five default arrangements but you can click on the line you want to customize in the User-defined area to get exactly what you want. Each line can be individually formatted.

- **Line** specifies what the border looks like: the style, width, and color. Each parameter has a number of attributes to choose from. The attributes selected will apply to those borders highlighted by a pair of black arrows in the *User-defined* thumbnail on the left side of the dialog.

- **Spacing to Contents** specifies how much space to leave between the border and the contents of the element. Spaces can be specified to the left, right, above, and below. Check Synchronize to have the same spacing for all four sides.
- **Shadow Style** properties always apply to the whole element. A shadow has three components: where it is (Position), how far from the element it is cast (Distance), and what color it is.

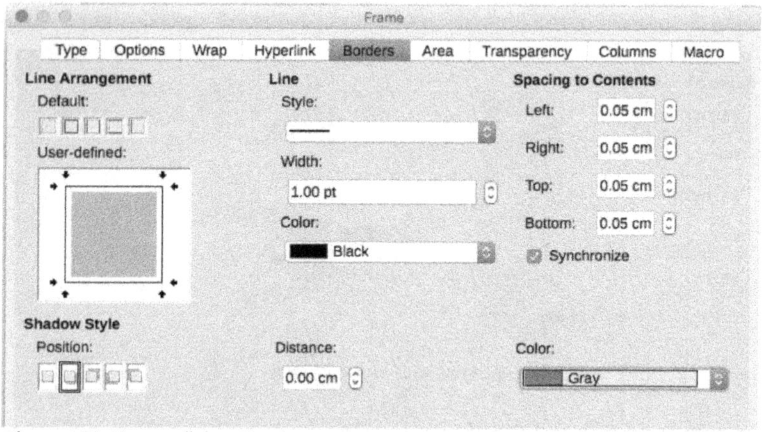

*Figure 101: Frame dialog: Borders page*

## Adding a color to the background

To begin, select the frame, right-click, and choose **Object** from the context menu. In the Frame dialog, select the *Area* tab (Figure 102), then choose **Color**. Select from the color grid or create a new color to use for this frame, and then click **OK** to apply it to the background.

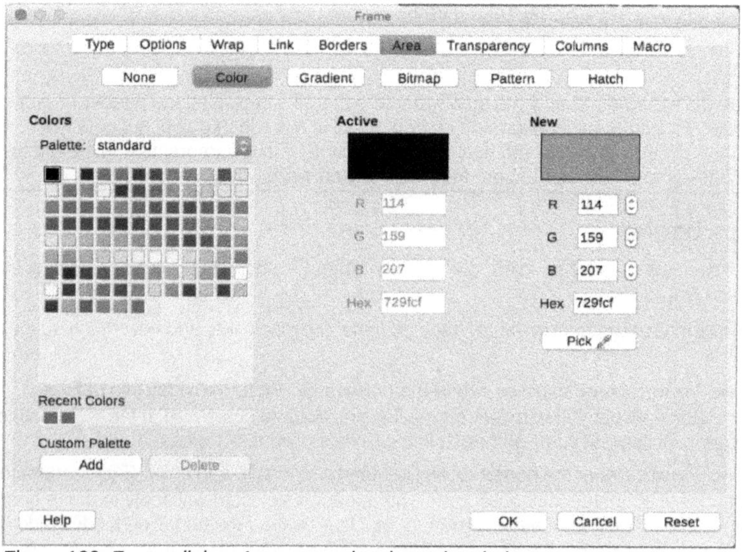

*Figure 102: Frame dialog: Area page showing color choices*

# Adding a gradient to the background

To add a gradient to the background, choose the *Area* page, then choose **Gradient**. The page now displays the gradient options (Figure 103), with an example in the preview pane to the right. Select the required gradient from the list or create a new gradient to use for this frame. Click **OK** to apply it to the background.

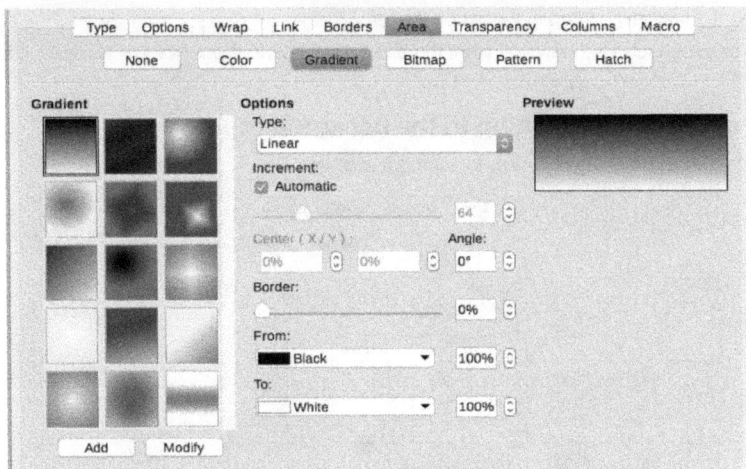

*Figure 103: Frame dialog: Area page showing gradient choices*

# Adding a bitmap (graphic) to the background

"Bitmap" is a term that covers photos and other graphics that are made up of dots of color. To add a bitmap to the background, choose the *Area* page, then choose **Bitmap**. The page now displays the bitmap options, as shown in Figure 104.

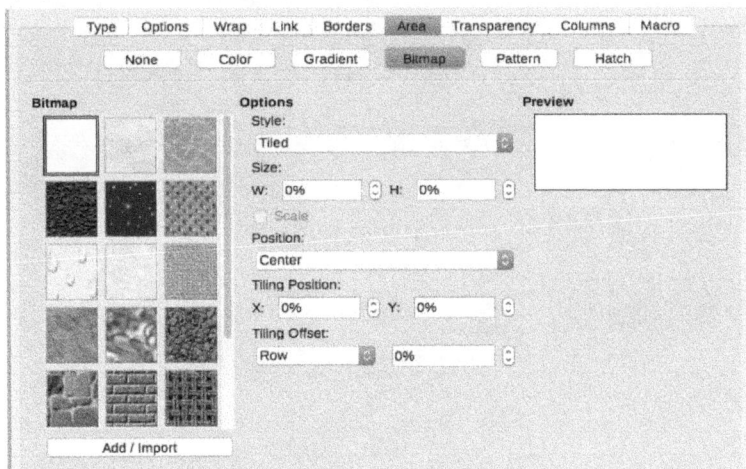

*Figure 104: Frame dialog: Area page showing bitmap choices*

You can choose one of the supplied bitmaps from the list on the left, or you can add your own.

To add a bitmap:

1) Click the **Add/Import** button. The Import dialog opens.

2) Find the file you want and then click the **Open** button. The Import dialog closes, and the selected bitmap appears in the list of thumbnails on the left and in the preview box on the right of the *Area* page.

3) Choose the new bitmap in the list on the left.

In the Options area, choose how you want the bitmap to appear, then click **OK** to apply it to the background.

## Adding a pattern or hatching to the background

Adding a pattern or hatching is similar to adding a gradient.

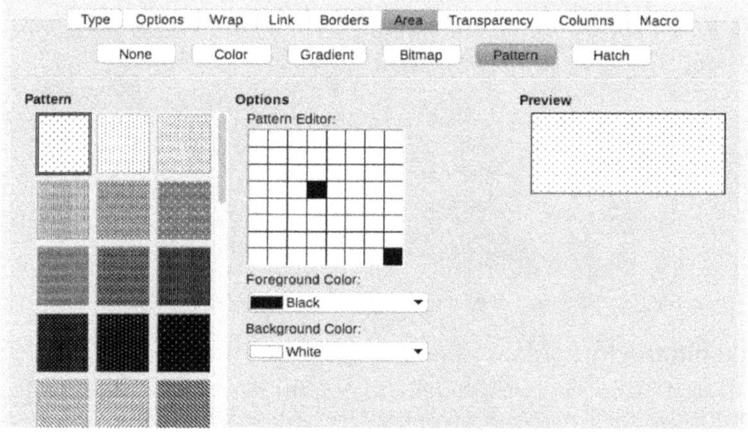

*Figure 105: Frame dialog: Area page showing pattern choices*

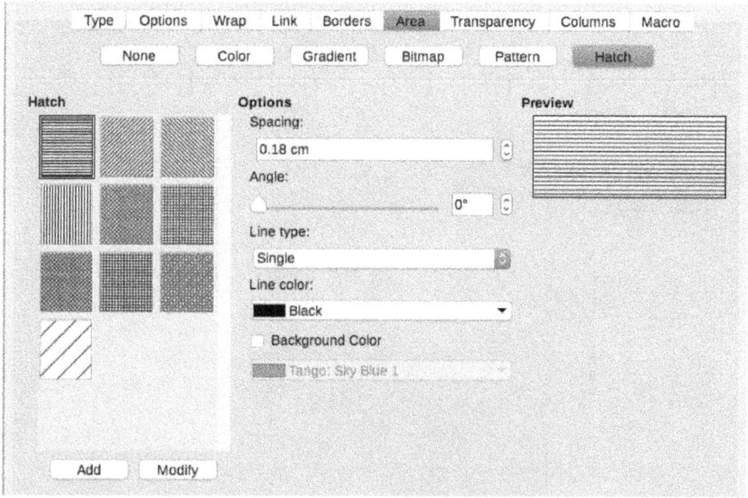

*Figure 106: Frame dialog: Area page showing pattern choices*

## Deleting a color, gradient, bitmap, or other background

To delete a color, gradient, bitmap, or other background, select **None** near the top of the *Area* page of the Frame dialog.

## Adjusting the transparency of the background

Transparency is useful for creating watermarks and making colors or images more pale (for more contrast with the text). The available choices are covered in detail in the *Draw Guide*.

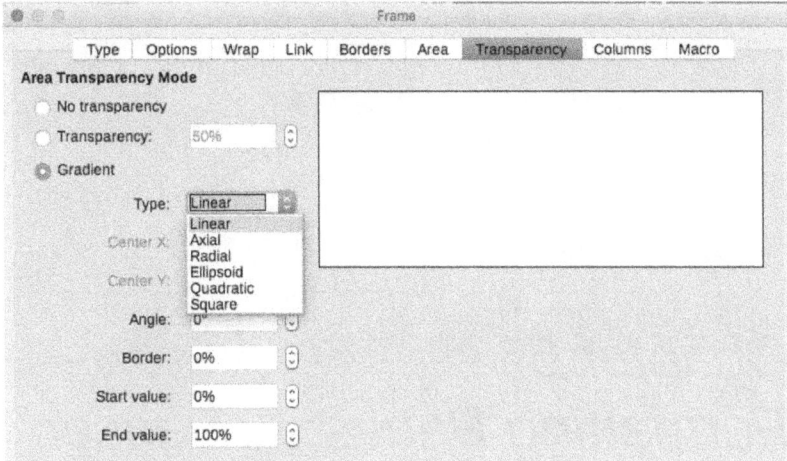

*Figure 107: Transparency options*

# LibreOffice

# Chapter 6
# Formatting Pages: Advanced

Using columns, frames, tables, and sections

# Introduction

Writer provides several ways for you to control page layouts. This chapter covers the use of:

- Columns
- Frames
- Tables
- Sections
- Changing page orientation within a document

Chapter 5 described the use of page styles and some associated functions.

**Note**

**All pages in a Writer document are based on page styles.** The other layout methods described in this chapter build upon the underlying page style.

**Tip**

Page layout is usually easier if you select the options to show text, object, table, and section boundaries in **Tools > Options > LibreOffice > Application Colors** and the options for paragraph ends, tabs, breaks, and other items in **Tools > Options > LibreOffice Writer > Formatting Aids**.

# Choosing a layout method

The best layout method depends on what the final document should look like and what sort of information will be in the document. Here are some examples. The techniques mentioned are all described in this chapter.

For a book similar to this user guide with one column of text, some figures without text beside them, and some other figures with descriptive text, use page styles for basic layout, and use tables to place figures beside descriptive text, where necessary.

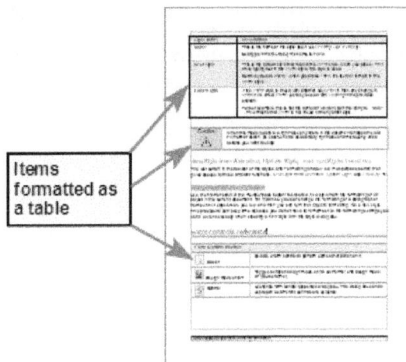

Items formatted as a table

Use page styles (with two columns) for an index or other document with two columns of text where the text continues from the left-hand column to the right-hand column and then to the next page, all in sequence (also known as snaking columns of text). If the title of the document (on the first page) is full-page width, put it in a single-column section.

Title is in a single column section

Basic layout is in two columns

For a newsletter with a complex layout, two or three columns on the page, and some articles that continue from one page to some place several pages later, use page styles for basic layout. Place articles in linked frames and anchor graphics to fixed positions on the page, if necessary.

This is a header on the first page only

This frame is linked to a frame on another page

These frames are not linked to other frames

For a document with terms and translations to appear side-by-side, use a table to keep items lined up.

This is a borderless table. Each pair of words is in a separate row, and each word is in a cell of the table.

# Using columns to define the page layout

You can use columns for page layout in these ways:

- By defining the number of columns and their layout on a page, using page styles.
- By changing the number of columns for existing text.

## Defining the columns on a page

It is a good idea to define your basic page style (such as Default) with the most common layout to be used in your document, either single-column or multiple-column. You can then either define extra page styles for pages with different numbers of columns or use sections (described in "Using sections for page layout" starting on page 137) for pages or parts of pages with different numbers of columns.

To define the number of columns on a page:

1) Choose **Format > Columns** to go to the Columns dialog (see Figure 108), or go to the *Columns* page of the Page Style dialog, or click the **More Options** button on the Page panel of the Properties deck of the Sidebar.

2) In the *Settings* section, choose the number of columns and specify any spacing between the columns and whether you want a vertical separator line to appear between the columns. You can use one of Writer's predefined column layouts, or you can create a customized column layout. The preview pane on the right of the *Settings* section shows how the column layout will look.

   Notice the **Apply to** box in the dialog of Figure 108. In this instance, the changes are being applied to the Default page style.

3) Click **OK** to save the changes.

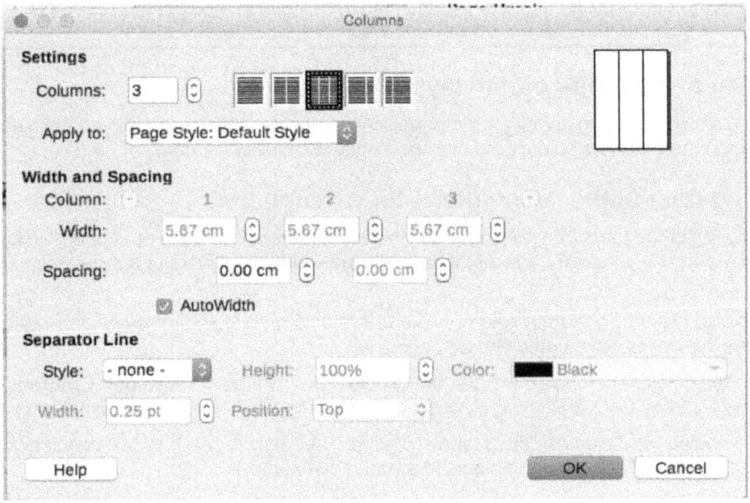

*Figure 108: Defining the number of columns on a page*

### Specifying the number of columns

In the *Settings* section, enter the number of columns into the Columns selection box, or select one of the column layout icons.

### Formatting column width and spacing

Select the **AutoWidth** option in the Width and spacing section to create columns of equal width.

To customize the width and spacing of the columns:

1) In the *Width and spacing* section, deselect the AutoWidth option.
2) In the *Width* selection boxes, enter a width for each column.
3) On the *Spacing* line, enter the amount of space that you want between each pair of columns.

If you specify more than three columns, use the arrow keys on the *Column* line to scroll among the columns.

### Formatting separator lines

To display separator lines between the columns:

1) Using the Style drop-down list, select the line style from the three styles available.
2) Using the Width control, select the width of line to use, settable from 0.25pt to 9.0pt. (1 pt = 1 point = 1/12 pica = 1/72 inch = 127/360 mm = 0.3527 mm.)
3) Using the Height control, select the height of line required, as a percentage of the column height. Variable from 25% to 100%.
4) If you entered a height of less than 100%, use the Position drop-down list to select a vertical alignment for the separator lines. The vertical-positioning options are Top, Centered, or Bottom.
5) The line color can be selected from the Color drop-down list.

> **Tip**
>
> To quickly input the maximum or minimum allowed value in an input box, click the current value and press *Page Up* or *Page Down* respectively.

## Reverting to a single-column layout

To revert to a single-column layout for the page style, go to the *Settings* section and either reset the number in the Columns box to 1 or click the single-column layout icon.

## Changing the number of columns for existing text

You might want some parts of a page to have one column and other parts of the page to have two or more columns. For example, you might have a page-width headline over a three-column news story.

You can create columns and then type or paste text into them, or you can select some existing text and change the number of columns for displaying it.

When you select text and change the number of columns for that text (**Format > Columns**), Writer turns the selected text into a section, as described in "Using sections for page layout" on page 137.

Figure 109 shows the Columns dialog for a selection. The Apply to box has Selection selected and an extra option (Evenly distribute contents to all columns) appears.

> **Tip**
>
> You cannot select text on a two-column formatted page and change it to a single column using this method. Instead, you need to define a single-column page and then select the text you want to be in a two-column section on that page.

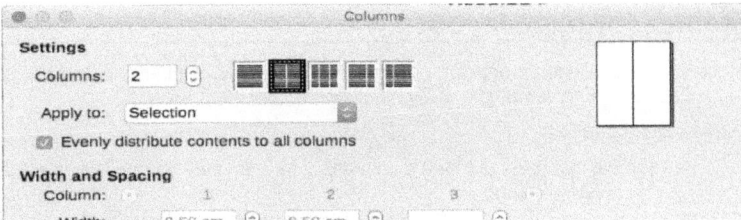

*Figure 109: Specifying columns for a selection*

## Distributing text across columns

As you add text to the section, you will see that the text flows from one column to the next. You can distribute text across the columns in one of two ways, as shown in Figure 110:

Evenly—Writer adjusts the length of the columns to the amount of text, so that all the columns are approximately the same height. As you add or delete text, the columns readjust.

Newspaper-style—Writer fills the columns one at a time, beginning with the first column. The last column may be shorter than the others.

To distribute text evenly, select the Evenly distribute contents to all columns option in the Settings area (Figure 109). Deselect this option if you want to distribute text newspaper-style.

*Figure 110: (Left) Evenly distributed columns; (Right) Newspaper-style columns.*

▶ **Tip**

Choose **View > Nonprinting Characters** (or press *Ctrl+F10*) to display end of paragraph markers (¶). Often, unexpected behavior of columns is due to extra paragraphs that are normally invisible but are taking up space.

# Using frames for page layout

Frames can be very useful when producing newsletters or other layout-intensive documents. Frames can contain text, tables, multiple columns, pictures, and other objects.

Use frames when you need to:

- Position something in a particular place on a page, for example, a logo or a "stop press" news box in one corner of a page.
- Allow text on one page to continue on another page, somewhere more distant than the next one, by linking the content of one frame to another so the contents flow between them as you edit the text.
- Wrap text around an object, such as a photograph.

Because LibreOffice does not allow you to define page styles with recurring frames, consider doing some quick sketches of the basic page layouts you need, indicating the approximate positions of different frames and their purposes. Try to keep the number of different page layouts as low as possible in order to avoid chaos in your design.

Pay special attention to the positioning of frames. Many of the predefined styles default to a center alignment. Although centering all frames looks reasonably good in most cases, it is rarely the best choice.

One of the most visually effective ways to position a frame is to align its left margin with that of the paragraph above it. To achieve this effect, the frame is inserted in a blank paragraph of the same style as the paragraph above. Select **Insert > Frame**; in the *Position* section of the *Type* page, select **From Left** in the Horizontal selection box to position the frame exactly where you want it.

Also, think about the type of wrap and the spacing between the frame and text. Instead of placing a frame close to the text, use the *Wrap* page to place some white space between them.

You can format frames individually or define and apply frame styles; see Chapter 9, Working with Styles.

**Example: Using a frame to center text on a page**

Although you can center text horizontally as part of a paragraph style or by using manual formatting, those methods do not work for vertical centering. To center text vertically, you need to place the text in a frame, anchor the frame to a page or a paragraph, and then center the frame vertically on the page. See "Anchoring frames" on page 132.

## Creating frames

You can create a frame in several ways, depending on your needs.

- Choose **Insert > Frame > Frame...** to create an empty frame. The Frame dialog (Figure 111) appears. You can click **OK** and come back to customize it later, or you can set the frame's characteristics at this stage.
- Select text and choose **Insert > Frame > Frame...** to open the Frame dialog. Customize the frame (for example, to add space between the frame and the text) and click **OK**. The selected text is removed from the normal text flow and inserted into the frame.
- Select **Insert > Frame > Interactively**. The mouse cursor changes to a plus (+) symbol. Click and drag the mouse to draw an empty frame.
- Insert a formula or OLE object by selecting **Insert > Object > [type of object]**. The item is inserted and appears in a frame, but the Frame dialog does not open.
- Use the **Insert Frame Interactively** button on the Insert toolbar to quickly draw an empty frame with several columns.

To add content to a frame, first deselect the frame by clicking somewhere else on the page. Then, click inside the frame to place the text cursor there. Now add content just like you would on the main page. When you are done, deselect the frame.

### Note

The menu item **Insert > Frame > Floating Frame** is for use with HTML documents.

## Moving, resizing, and changing frame attributes

When an object is added to Writer, it is automatically enclosed in a frame of a predetermined type. The frame sets how the object is placed on the page, as well as how it interacts with other elements in the document. You can edit the frame by modifying the frame style it uses or by manually formatting it when you add it to the document. Frame styles are discussed in Chapter 9, Working with Styles.

To change the size or location of a frame, first select the frame, then use either the mouse or the Frame dialog (Figure 111). Using the mouse is quicker but less accurate. You might want to use the mouse for gross layout and the dialog for fine-tuning.

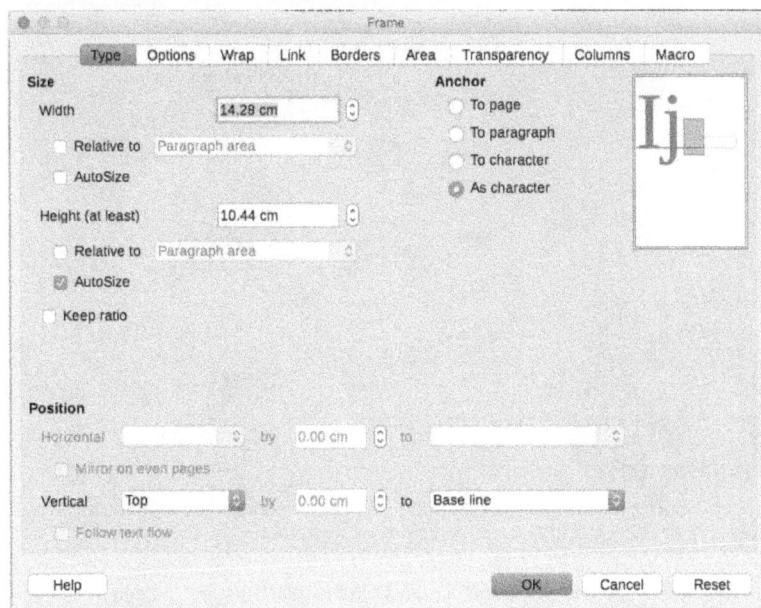

*Figure 111: Frame dialog*

You can re-size the frame manually by clicking on the green squares (sizing handles) and dragging to the appropriate size, or start adding content to it (the frame will re-size automatically if, for example, you add a large picture to it), or go back to the Frame dialog and set the size and other characteristics.

To change the location of the frame using the mouse, drag and drop one of the edges or put the cursor anywhere within the frame. (The I-bar cursor changes to a four-headed arrow when properly positioned for a drag-and-drop move.)

To change the size of the frame, drag one of the sizing handles. Drag a handle on one of the sides to enlarge or reduce the text frame in one dimension only; drag a corner handle to enlarge or reduce it in both dimensions.

These resizing actions distort the proportions of the frame. Holding down the *Shift* key while dragging one of the handles makes the frame keep the same proportions.

You can open the Frame dialog at any time by selecting the frame, right-clicking, and choosing Frame from the context menu.

To remove the default border on a newly created frame, open the Frame dialog, go to the Borders page (Figure 112), and in the Line arrangement box, select the first Present (None). Alternatively, you can assign a borderless style to the frame; see Chapter 9, Working with Styles, for information on frame styles.

● **Note**

> Do not confuse a frame's border with the text boundaries that are made visible using the View menu (by selecting **View > Text Boundaries**).

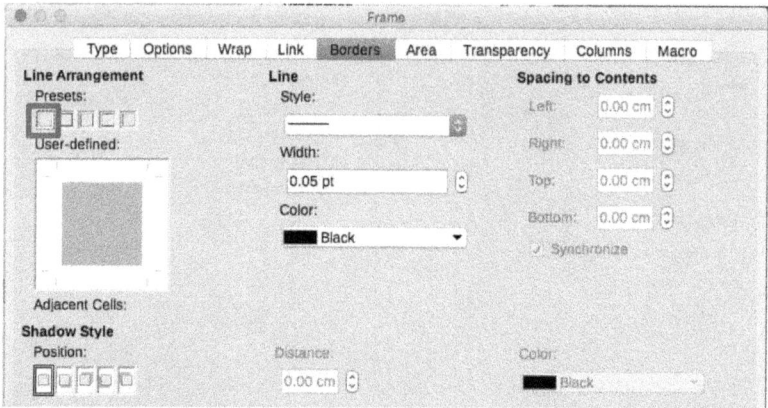

*Figure 112: Removing the border from a frame*

## Anchoring frames

Using the Frame dialog (or by right-clicking and pointing to **Anchor**), you can anchor a frame to a page, paragraph, or character, or you can anchor it as a character.

**To Page**
> The frame keeps the same position in relation to the page margins. It does not move as you add or delete text. This method is useful when the frame does not need to be visually associated with a particular piece of text. It is often used when producing newsletters or other documents that are very layout-intensive. This method is also used to center text on a page.

**To Paragraph**
> The frame is associated with a paragraph and moves with the paragraph. It may be placed in the margin or another location. This method is useful as an alternative to a table for placing icons beside paragraphs. It is also used to center text on a page in documents which will be used in a master document (frames anchored to pages will disappear from the master document).

**To Character**

> The frame is associated with a character but is not in the text sequence. It moves with the paragraph but may be placed in the margin or another location. This method is similar to anchoring to a paragraph.

**As Character**

> The frame is placed in the document like any other character and, therefore, affects the height of the text line and the line break. The frame moves with the paragraph as you add or delete text before the paragraph. This method is useful for adding a small icon in sequence in a sentence. It is also the best method for anchoring a graphic to an empty paragraph so it does not move around the page in unexpected ways.

## Linking frames

You can link frames to each other even when they are on different pages of a document. The contents will automatically flow from one to the next. This technique is very useful when designing newsletters, where articles may need to be continued on a different page.

**Note**

> You cannot link from a frame to more than one other frame.

To link one frame to another:

1) Select the frame to be linked from.

2) Click the **Link Frames** button ( 🖊 ) on the Frames toolbar.

3) Click the next frame in the series (which must be empty).

When a linked frame is selected, any existing links are indicated by a faint connecting line, as shown in Figure 113. Frames can be unlinked by selecting the **Unlink Frames** button ( 🖊 ) on the Frames toolbar.

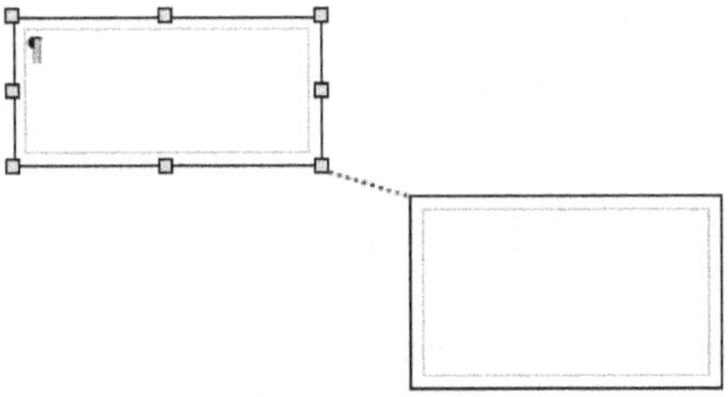

Figure 113: Linked frames

The height of a frame that is being linked from is fixed; you can change this height manually or by using the Frame dialog, but it does not automatically adjust to the size of the contents (that is, the AutoHeight attribute is disabled). Only the last frame of a chain can adapt its height to the content.

The *Options* page of the Frame dialog (Figure 114) shows the names of the selected frame and any frames it is linked to or from. You can change this information here. On this page, you can also select options to protect the contents, position, and size of the frame.

The *Wrap*, *Borders*, *Area*, *Columns*, *Transparency*, and *Macro* pages of the Frame dialog are the same as those for frame styles. Refer to the Chapter 9, Working with Styles, for details.

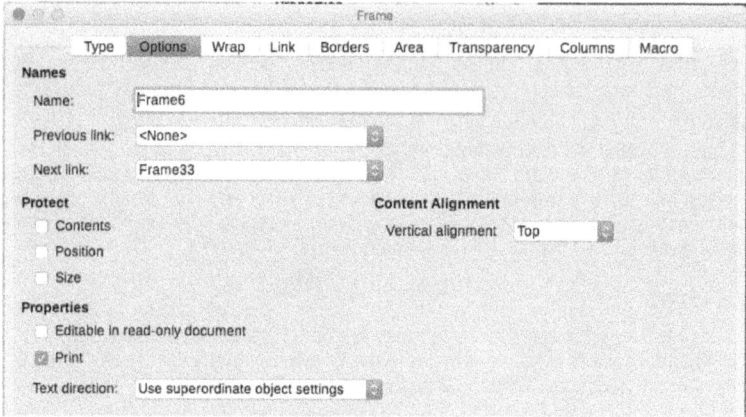

*Figure 114: Options page of the Frame dialog*

# Using tables for page layout

Writer's tables can serve several purposes, such as holding data as you might see it in a spreadsheet, lining up material, and creating more complex page layouts. For information about using tables of data, see Chapter 13, Tables.

This topic describes how to achieve some common layouts by using tables.

## Positioning information in headers or footers

Instead of using tabs, you can use a table in a header or footer to position different elements such as a page number, document title, author, and so on. These elements are often inserted using fields, as described in Chapter 17, Fields.

## Creating sideheads using tables

Sideheads and marginal notes are commonly used in documents from resumes to computer user guides. The main body of the text is offset to leave white space (usually on the left-hand side) in which the sideheads or notes are placed. The first paragraph is aligned beside the sidehead, as in Figure 115.

| **Example of a sidehead** | In some cases you may want to put only one or two paragraphs in the table itself and the rest of the text and graphics in ordinary paragraphs (formatted to line up with the paragraphs in the table) so that text and graphics will flow more easily from one page to another when you add or delete material. |
| --- | --- |
| | In other cases, you might put each paragraph in a separate row of the table and allow the table to break between pages. |

*Figure 115: Example of a sidehead*

## Note

Sideheads can also be created by placing text in a frame using the Marginalia frame style, as described in Chapter 9, Working with Styles.

### *Example*

To create a table for use with a sidehead:

1) Place the cursor where you want the table to appear and choose **Table > Insert Table** (*Ctrl+F12*).

2) In the Insert Table dialog, define a one-row, two-column table with no border and no heading. Click **Insert** to create the table.

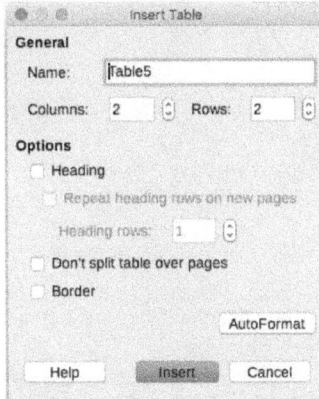

*Figure 116: Defining a two-column borderless table with no header*

3) Right-click on the table and choose **Table Properties** from the context menu. On the *Columns* page of the Table Properties dialog, make the columns the required width.

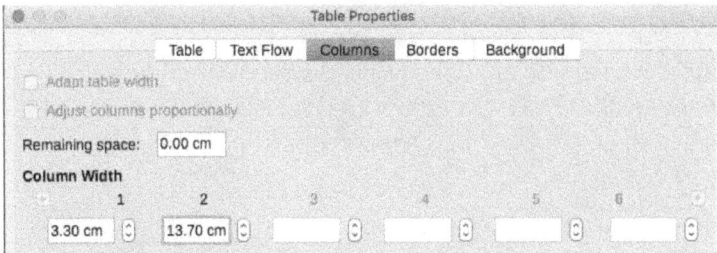

*Figure 117: Defining a two-column table to line up with text offset at 3.3cm*

4) On the *Table* page of the Table Format dialog (Figure 118), in the *Spacing* section, make the Above and Below values the same as the Top and Bottom spacing you have defined for ordinary paragraphs of text. In the Properties section, optionally give this table a name. Click **OK** to save your settings.

*Figure 118: Defining the space above and below a table*

▶ **Tip**

To check the top and bottom spacing for ordinary paragraphs:

1. Position the cursor in a paragraph and press *F11* (unless the Styles and Formatting window is already open). Check that the Styles and Formatting window shows paragraph styles (top left button).

2. The current style should be highlighted. If no paragraph style is highlighted, select All Styles in the bottom drop-down list. Right-click on it and select **Modify** from the pop-up list.

3. Go to the Indents & Spacing page and look in the *Spacing* section for the values in Above paragraph and Below paragraph.

You may also want to turn off number recognition so that Writer will not try to format numbers if you want them to be plain text. To turn number recognition off:

1) Right-click in the table and then click **Number Format** on the context menu.

2) On the Format Number dialog, make sure the *Category* is set to **Text**. Click **OK**.

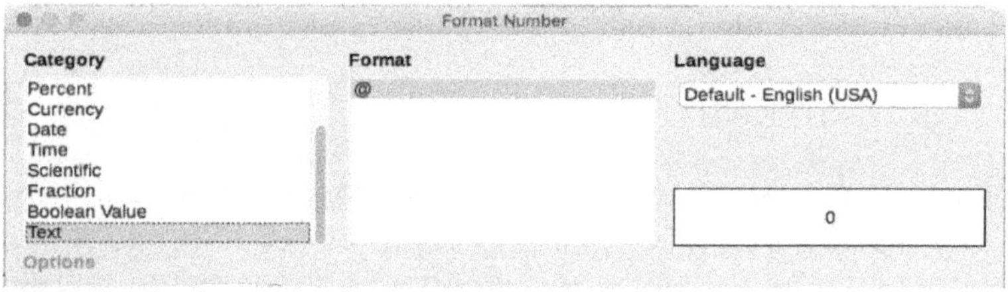

*Figure 119: Setting number format to Text*

▶ **Tip**

If you use this table format often, you may want to save it as AutoText, as described in Chapter 2, Working with Text: Basics. Select the table (not just the contents) to assign the shortcut.

# Using sections for page layout

A section is a block of text that has special attributes and formatting. You can use sections to:

- Write-protect text
- Hide text
- Dynamically insert the contents of another document
- Add columns, margin indents, a background color, or a background graphic to a portion of your document
- Customize the footnotes and endnotes for a portion of your document

## Creating sections

To create a section:

1) Place the cursor at the point in your document where you want to insert the new section. Or, select the text that you want to place in the new section.
2) From the Menu bar, choose **Insert > Section**. The Insert Section dialog (Figure 120) opens.
3) Choose settings for each page of the dialog as required.
4) Click **Insert**.

The Insert Section dialog has five tabbed pages.

- Use the *Section* page to set the section's attributes.
- Use the *Columns* page to format the section into columns.
- Use the *Indents* page to set indents from the right and left margins of the section.
- Use the *Background* page to add color or a graphic to the section's background.
- Use the *Footnotes/Endnotes* page to customize the section's footnotes and endnotes.

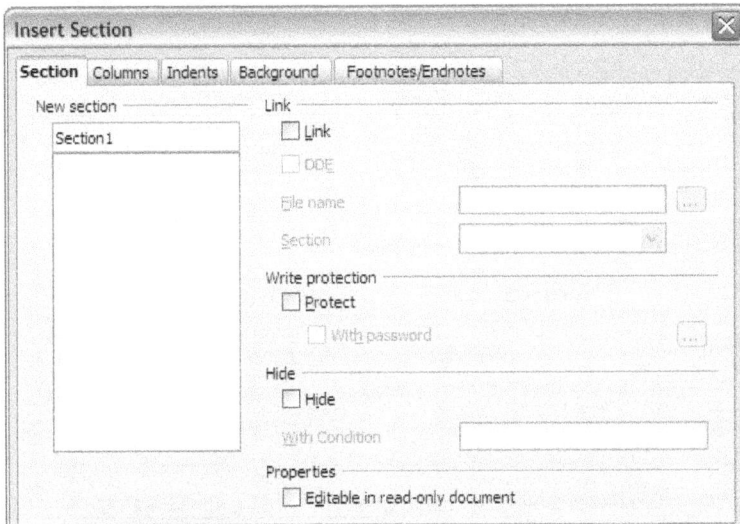

*Figure 120: Inserting a section using the Insert Section dialog*

At any time before closing the dialog, you can reset a tabbed page to its default settings by clicking the **Reset** button. (Note, however, that you cannot reset the *Section* page. If you wish to undo changes to the Section page, you must do so manually).

### Naming sections

Writer automatically enters a name for the section in the name box of the New section list box. To change the name, select it and type over it. The name is displayed in the Sections category of the Navigator window. If you give your sections meaningful names, you can navigate to them more easily.

### Linking sections

You can insert the contents of another document into the section and then have Writer update it whenever the other document is updated. This is called linking the section to the other document.

To link the section to another document, follow these steps:

1)  In the Link section of the dialog, select the Link option.

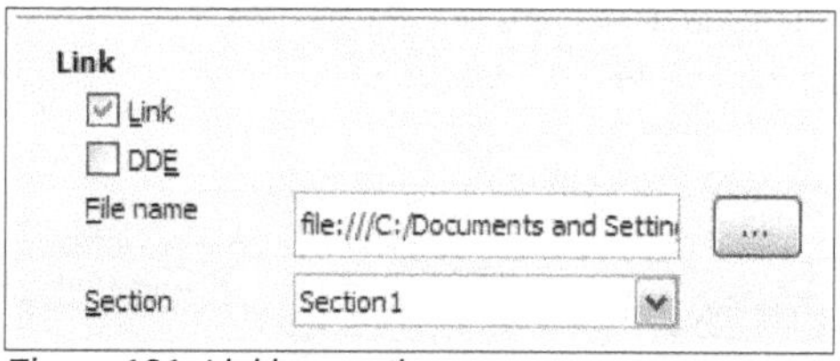

*Figure 121: Linking sections*

2)  Click the (...) button to the right of the **File name** field. The Insert dialog opens.

3)  Find and select the document you want to insert and then click the **Insert** button. The Insert dialog closes and the name of the selected document appears in the File name field.

4)  If you want to insert only a section of the selected document, select the desired section from the **Section** drop-down list.

> **Note**
>
> The section must already exist in the selected document. You cannot create a section in the selected document at this point.

You can update links automatically or manually. See "Updating links" on page 142.

### Write-protecting sections

To write-protect the section so that its contents cannot be edited, select the **Protect** option in the *Write protection* area.

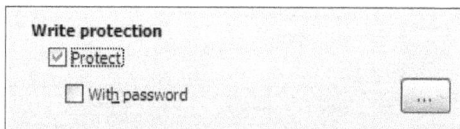

*Figure 122: Write-protecting sections*

> **Note**
>
> Write-protection protects only the section's contents, not its attributes or format.

### Password-protecting sections

To prevent others from editing the section's attributes or format, additionally protect the section with a password, as follows:

1) Select the **With password** option. The Enter Password dialog opens.

2) Type a password in the Password field and then confirm the password by typing it again in the Confirm field.

3) Click **OK**. The Enter Password dialog closes. Anyone who tries to edit the section's attributes or format will be prompted to enter the password.

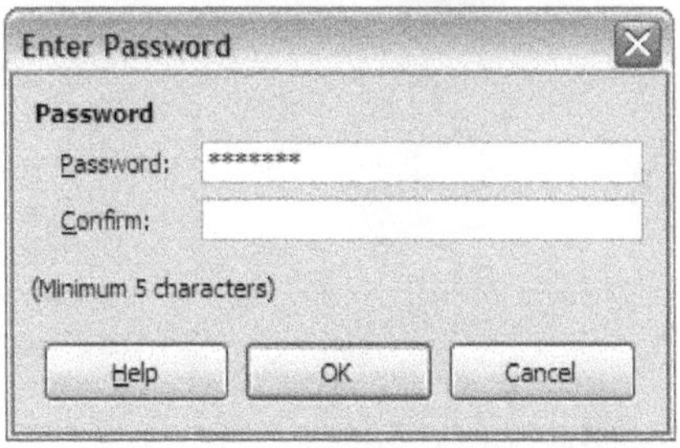

*Figure 123: Password-protecting a section*

### Hiding sections

You can hide the section so that it will not be displayed on the screen or printed. You can also specify conditions for hiding the section. For example, you can hide the section only from certain users.

**Note**

You cannot hide a section if it is the only content on the page or if the section is in a header, footer, footnote, endnote, frame, or table cell.

To hide a section, select the **Hide** option in the *Hide* section of the dialog.

*Figure 124: Hiding sections*

To hide the section only under certain conditions, enter the desired conditions in the With Condition field. The syntax and operators that you use to enter conditions are the same ones that you use to enter formulas. For syntax and a list of operators, see Writer's Help under *Conditions*. See also Chapter 17, Fields.

If the section is write-protected with a password, the password must be entered to hide or reveal the text.

**Note**

Hiding text is not a secure way to stop someone else reading it. It will stop the casual reader but will not prevent someone who actively wants to find out what you have hidden—even if it is password protected.

### Formatting a section into columns

Use the Columns page of the Insert Section dialog to format the section into columns. This page is similar to the Columns dialog shown in Figure 109 on page 129. Please refer to that topic for details.

### Indenting the section from margins

Use the Indents page (Figure 125), to set indents from the right and left margins of the section.

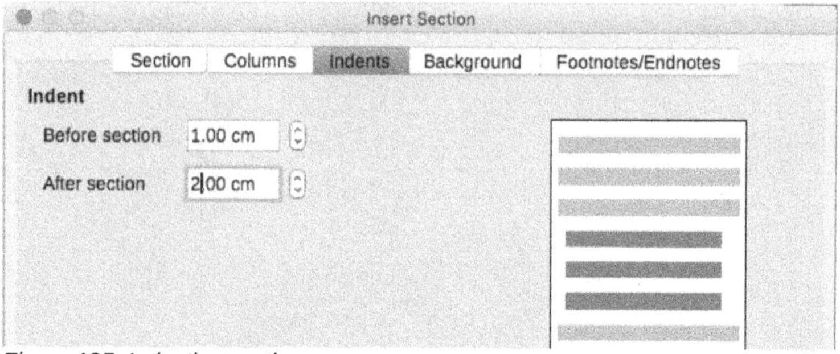

*Figure 125: Indenting sections*

Enter the desired left-margin indent in the Before section box. Enter the desired right-margin indent in the After section box. The preview box on the right-hand side of the page shows you how the section will look with the indents applied.

### Changing the background of the section

Use the *Background* page to add color or a graphic to the background of the current section. This page is similar to the Background pages for paragraphs, frames, tables, and other objects in LibreOffice. For more information, refer to Chapter 9, Working with Styles.

### Customizing footnotes and endnotes in a section

Use the *Footnotes/Endnotes* page to customize the current section's footnotes and endnotes.

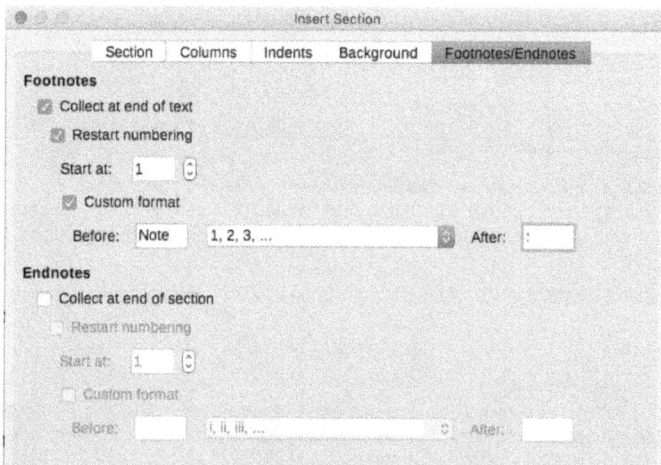

*Figure 126: Setting footnotes and endnotes for sections*

### Customizing footnotes

If you want the section's footnotes to appear separately from the other footnotes in the document, select the Collect at end of text option in the Footnotes area.

To number the section's footnotes separately from the other footnotes in the document, and format the numbering, follow these steps:

1) In the *Footnotes* section of the page, make sure that **Collect at end of text** is selected.

2) Select **Restart numbering**.

3) If you want the section's footnotes to start at a number other than 1, enter the desired starting number in the **Start at number** box.

4) Select the **Custom format** option.

5) From the drop-down list of the Custom format option, select a numbering format for the footnotes.

To add text to the selected numbering format, use the **Before** and **After** text input boxes. For example, if you want the footnote numbers to be preceded by the word "Note" and followed by a colon, fill the **Before** and **After** fields as shown in Figure 126.

### Customizing endnotes

If you want the section's endnotes to appear at the end of the section rather than at the end of the document, select the **Collect at end of section** option in the *Endnotes* area.

To number the current section's endnotes separately from the other endnotes in the document, and format the numbering, apply the procedures described above to the *Endnotes* settings.

## Saving a new section

To save a new section so that it appears in your document, click the **Insert** button. The Insert Section dialog closes and the new section appears in your document.

## Editing and deleting sections

To edit a section, follow these steps:

1) From the Menu bar, choose **Format > Sections**. The Edit Sections dialog (Figure 127) opens.

2) Select the section you want to edit by clicking its name in the list box.

### Editing section attributes

To rename the selected section, simply type over its name in the Section name box.

From the Edit Sections dialog, you can also edit the selected section's link, write-protect, and hide attributes. To learn how to edit these attributes, see:

"Linking sections" on page 138

"Write-protecting sections" on page 138

"Hiding sections" on page 139

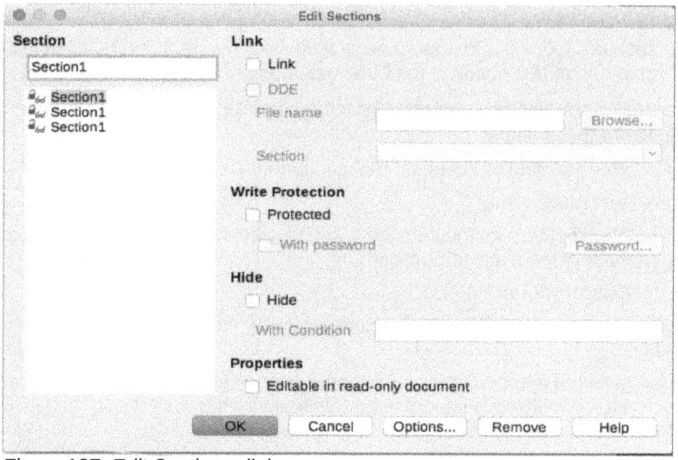

Figure 127: Edit Sections dialog

### Editing the format of a section

To edit the format of the selected section, click the **Options** button.

The Options dialog has four pages: *Columns*, *Indents*, *Background*, and *Footnotes/Endnotes*. The use of these pages is described earlier in this topic.

To reset a page to the conditions in place when the dialog opened, click the **Reset** button.

To save your Options settings and return to the Edit Sections dialog, click **OK**.

### Deleting sections

To delete the selected section, click the **Remove** button. This does **not** delete the contents of the section; the contents become part of the main document. If the contents were linked, they are now embedded.

**Note**

> Writer will not prompt you to confirm the deletion.

## Updating links

You can set Writer to update linked sections automatically, and you can also update links manually.

### Updating links automatically

To set Writer to update links without prompting you, or to turn off automatic updating, follow these steps:

1) Choose **Tools > Options > LibreOffice Writer > General**. The dialog displays general text document settings.

2) In the *Update* section of the dialog, under *Update links when loading*, select one of the following three options:

   – **Always** if you want Writer to update links automatically, without prompting you, whenever you open a document that contains links.

   – **On request** if you want Writer to prompt you before updating links.

- **Never** if you do not want Writer to update links.

3) Click **OK** to save your settings.

### Updating links manually

A protected section cannot be updated manually. It must first be unprotected.

To update a link manually:

1) Open the document that contains the link.

2) Choose **Edit > Links**. The Edit Links dialog (Figure 128) opens.

3) The list in the Edit Links dialog displays the names of all the files that are linked to the current document. Click the file that corresponds to the link that you want to update.

4) Click the **Update** button. The most recently saved contents of the linked file appear in the current document.

5) To close the Edit Links dialog, click **Close**.

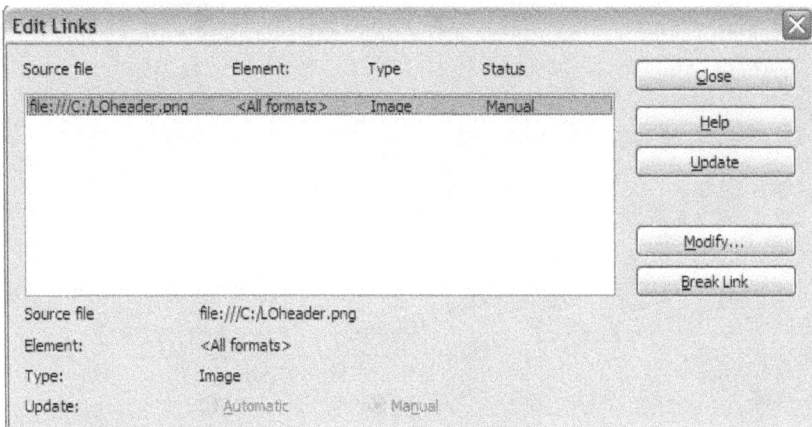

*Figure 128: Edit Links dialog*

### Removing links

To remove a linked file, go to the Edit Links dialog (see above), click the file that corresponds to the link you want to remove, and click the **Break Link** button. This action embeds the contents of the linked file.

# Changing page orientation within a document

A document can contain pages in more than one orientation. A common scenario is to have a landscape page in the middle of a document, whereas the other pages are in a portrait orientation. Here are the steps to achieve it.

## Setting up a landscape page style

1) If you wish to keep the margins the same as on other pages, then note the margin settings of the current page style. (You can find the margin settings on the Page Style dialog, by selecting the Page tab as shown in Figure 130.)

2) In the Styles and Formatting window, right-click on **Landscape** in the list of page styles and choose **Modify** from the pop-up menu.

3) On the *Organizer* page of the Page Style dialog (Figure 129), make sure the Next Style property is set to **Landscape** (to allow for having more than one sequential landscape page).

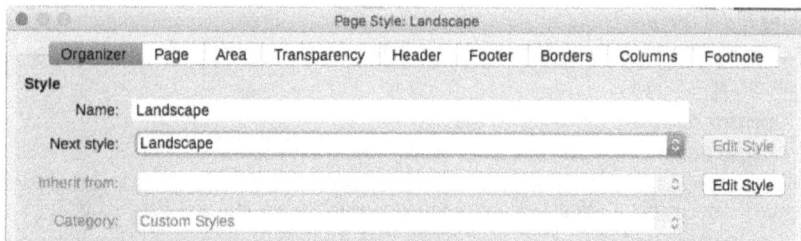

Figure 129: Set the next page style to Landscape

4) On the *Page* page of the Page Style dialog (Figure 130), make sure the Orientation is set to **Landscape**. Change the margins so that they correspond with the margins of the portrait page. That is, the portrait top margin becomes the landscape left margin, and so on.
5) Click **OK** to save the changes.

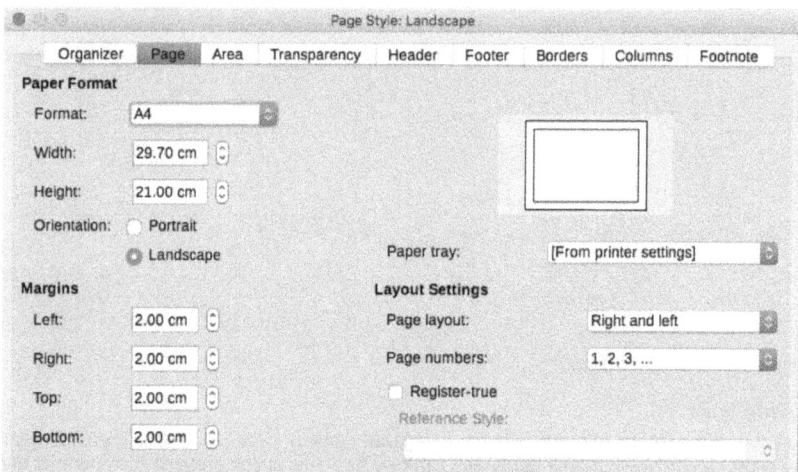

Figure 130: Set orientation and margins for a landscape page

## Inserting a landscape page into a portrait document

Now that you have defined the Landscape page style, here is how to apply it.

1) Position the cursor in the paragraph or table at the start of the page that is to be set to landscape. Right-click and choose **Paragraph** or **Table Properties**, respectively, in the context menu.
2) On the *Text Flow* page of the Paragraph dialog (Figure 131) or the Table Properties dialog (Figure 132), select **Insert** (or **Break** for a table) and **With Page Style**. Set the Page Style property to Landscape. Click **OK** to close the dialog and to apply the new page style.

Figure 131: Specifying a page break before a paragraph

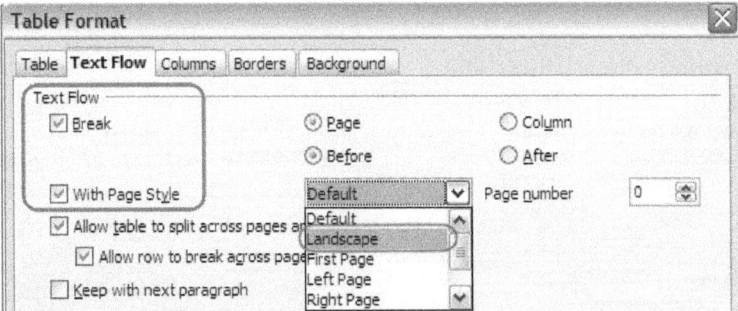

Figure 132: Specifying a page break before a table

3)  Position the cursor in the paragraph or table where the page is to return to portrait orientation and change the paragraph properties or table properties so that With Page Style is the portrait page style that was used before the Landscape page style.

4)  Click **OK** to return to the previous portrait page style.

## Portrait headers on landscape pages

When you define a header and footer on a landscape page, they will be aligned with the long side of the page. If your landscape pages are inserted between portrait pages, you might want the headers and footers to be on the short sides of the landscape pages, so the final printed product looks like the contents of the landscape pages have been rotated 90 degrees on portrait pages.

You can set up portrait headers and footers on landscape pages by using a trick involving frames. These are a bit tedious to set up, but once you have done so, you can copy and paste them to other landscape pages. This cannot be made part of the landscape page style. In the following example we want to insert a landscape page into our printed document, to have the same header and footer, and margins, as our portrait pages. We will use an A4 page size here.

To set up portrait headers and footers on landscape pages:

1)  Note the margin settings for the portrait page which is the same as the landscape page will be, that is to say, for a right landscape page, the settings from a right portrait page (see the table).

    We now need to make the landscape right and left margins 1 cm larger than the portrait top and bottom margins, respectively. This difference allows for the extra space used by the portrait header and footer (0.5 cm for the height of the header or footer and a 0.5 cm gap between the header or footer and the main text).

2)  Set the frame for the footer in the same way as for the header. Apply these margin settings in the Landscape page style.

| Portrait page (right page) | | Landscape page (right page) | |
|---|---|---|---|
| Top margin | 1.5 cm | Right margin | 2.5 cm |
| Bottom margin | 1.5 cm | Left margin | 2.5 cm |
| Left (inner) margin | 2.8 cm | Top margin | 2.8 cm |
| Right (outer) margin | 1.8 cm | Bottom margin | 1.8 cm |

3) Copy and paste the footer from the portrait page into a blank paragraph in the text. Paste or move it into the landscape page. This text will then have the Footer style so the typeface, font size, and tab settings will match.

| Instructions on how to set up a footer. | Page 1 of 2 |
|---|---|

| Instructions on how to set up a footer. | Page 1 of 2 |
|---|---|

*Figure 133: Copy the footer, paste, and select it*

4) Select the text (including the fields) you just entered. Choose **Format > Character**. On the Character dialog, choose the *Position* tab and set **Rotation / scaling** to **270 degrees** (counterclockwise). Click **OK**.

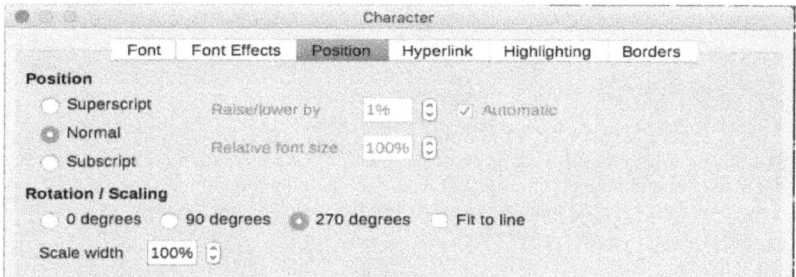

*Figure 134: Rotating the footer text 270 degrees*

5) With the text still selected, choose **Insert > Frame**. In the Frame dialog, select the *Type* tab and enter the width, height, and horizontal and vertical position for the footer. Deselect the Automatic options in Width and Height if they are selected.

   – The width is the footer height taken from the Footer page of the portrait page style dialog.

   – The frame height is obtained by simple arithmetic. The A4 page-width is 21cm, minus the sum of the top and bottom margins of 2.8cm and 1.8cm resulting in a frame height of 16.4cm.

   – The horizontal position is the portrait page bottom margin.

   – The vertical position is the landscape page top margin.

6) If your footer has a line above the text, as in this book, on the Borders page, select a right border and specify the line width and spacing to the frame's contents.

7) Click **OK** to save these settings. The footer will now appear in the required position and orientation. Any fields will update.

Because tabs have been removed, insert the cursor in the frame, at the end of the text where the tab was, and insert as many spaces using the keyboard space bar, as you require for the layout to match that on the portrait page.

Repeat these steps (using appropriate settings) to set up a portrait header on the landscape page.

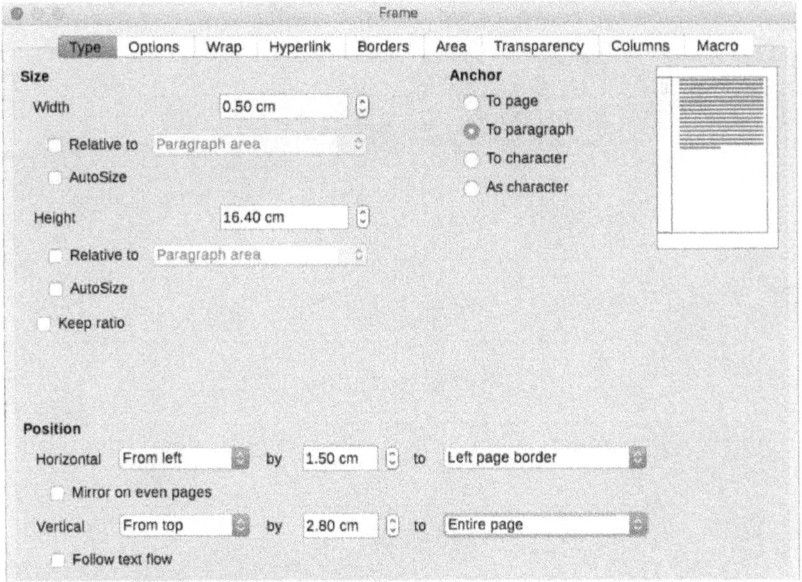

*Figure 135: Defining the size and position of the footer frame*

## Caution

Make sure to return to the paragraph in the document from which you rotated the text, and return it to 0 degrees, or any text typed in this location will rotate.

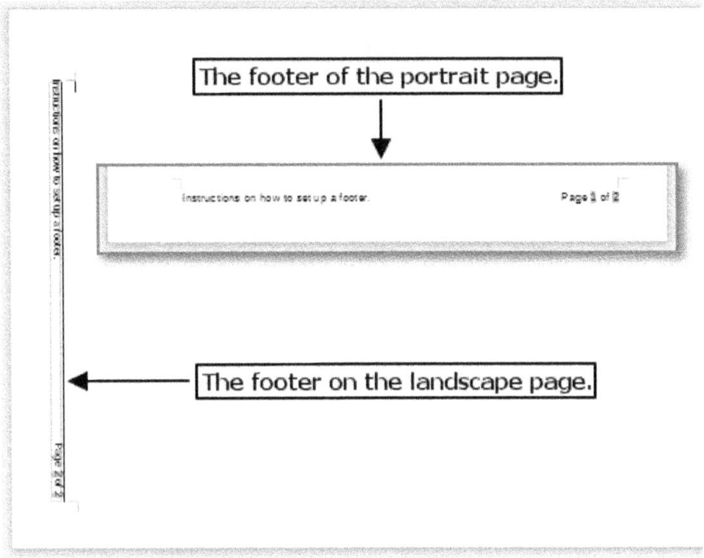

The footer of the portrait page.

Instructions on how to set up a footer.                    Page 1 of 2

The footer on the landscape page.

*Figure 136: Footers in place for both page styles*

# LibreOffice

Chapter 7
Printing, Exporting, E-mailing

# Quick printing

Click the Print icon ⊟ to send the entire document to the default printer defined for your computer.

> ⬤ **Note**
>
> You can change the action of the Print icon to send the document to the printer defined for the document instead of the default printer for the computer. Go to **Tools > Options > Load/Save > General** and select **Load printer settings with the document**.

# Controlling printing

For more control over printing, use the Print dialog (**File > Print** or *Ctrl+P*).

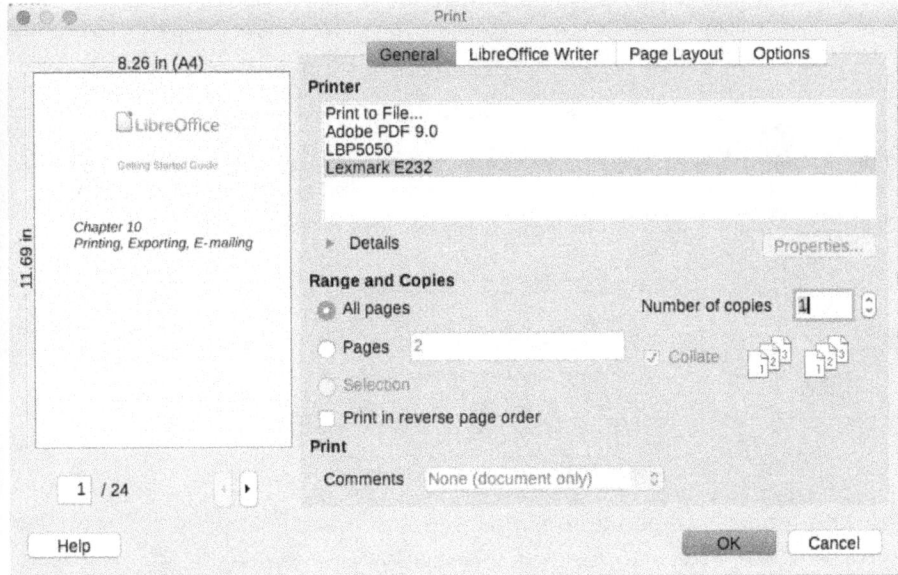

*Figure 137: The Print dialog*

> ⬤ **Note**
>
> The options selected on the Print dialog apply to this printing of this document only.
>
> To specify default printing settings for LibreOffice, go to **Tools > Options > LibreOffice > Print** and **Tools > Options > LibreOffice Writer > Print**. See Chapter 20, Setting Up Writer, for more details.

The Print dialog has four pages, from which you can choose a range of options, as described in the following sections.

## Selecting general printing options

On the *General* page of the Print dialog, you can choose:

- The printer (from the printers available). The Print to File printer is now always available and will generate a PDF file that you save on your disk.
- Which pages to print, the number of copies to print, and whether to collate multiple copies (Range and copies section)
- Whether to print any comments that are in the document, and where to print the comments.

Some selections may not be available all the time. For example, if the document contains no comments, the Print – Comments drop-down list does not work.

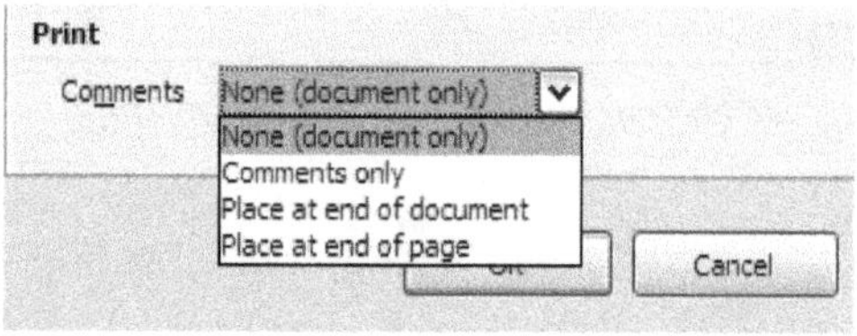

*Figure 138: Choosing whether and where to print comments*

Click the **Properties** button to display the selected printer's properties dialog, where you can choose portrait or landscape orientation, which paper tray to use, and the paper size to print on.

On the *Options* page of the Print dialog, you can choose other options for printing.

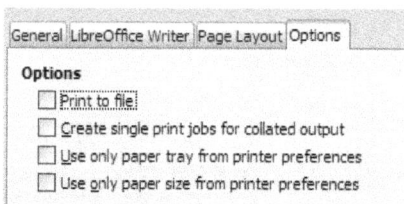

*Figure 139: General print options*

## Printing multiple pages on a single sheet of paper

You can print multiple pages of a document on one sheet of paper. To do this:

1) In the Print dialog, select the *Page Layout* tab (Figure 140).
2) In the *Layout* section, select from the drop-down list the number of pages to print per sheet. The preview panel on the left of the Print dialog shows how the printed document will look.
3) When printing more than two pages per sheet, you can choose the order in which they are printed across and down the paper. Figure 141 shows the difference.
4) In the *Page sides* section, select whether to print all pages or only some pages.
5) Click **OK**.

▶ **Tip**

> To print two pages per sheet in "facing pages" (book layout) style, print from Print Preview instead. See page 154.

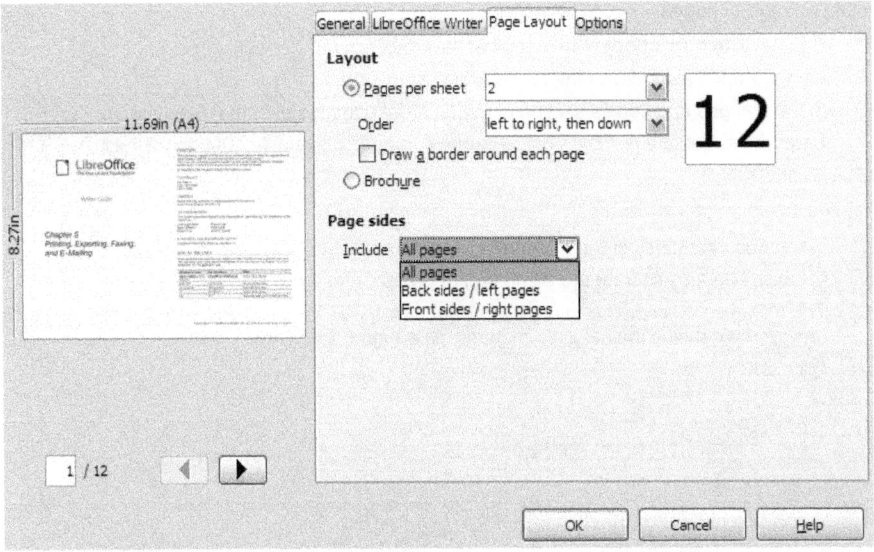

Figure 140: Printing multiple page per sheet of paper

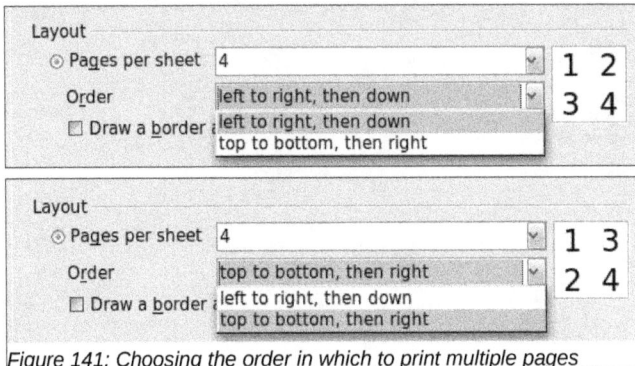

Figure 141: Choosing the order in which to print multiple pages

## Selecting what to print

In addition to printing a full document, you can choose to print individual pages, ranges of pages, or a selection of a document, as described in this section.

Printing an individual page:

1) Choose **File > Print** from the Menu bar, or press *Ctrl+P*.

2) On the Print dialog, select the page to print.

3) In the *Range and copies* section of the General page, select the **Pages** option.

4) Enter the sequence number of the page you want to print. This may differ from the page number if you have restarted page numbering within the document. The preview box changes to show the selected page.

5) Click **OK**.

Printing a range of pages:

1) Choose **File > Print** from the Menu bar, or press *Ctrl+P*.
2) On the Print dialog, select the range of pages to print.
3) In the *Ranges and copies* section of the General page, select the **Pages** option.
4) Enter the sequence numbers of the pages to print (for example, 1–4 or 1,3,7,11).
5) Click **OK**.

Printing a selection of text:

1) In the document, select the material (text and images) to print.
2) Choose **File > Print** from the menu bar, or press *Ctrl+P*.
3) The *Ranges and copies* section of the Print dialog now includes a Selection option and the preview box shows the selected material. See Figure 142.
4) Click **OK**.

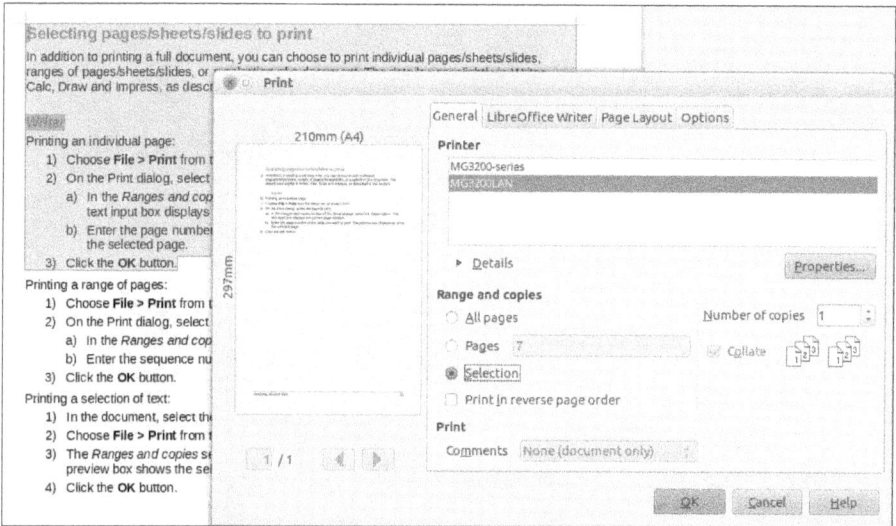

*Figure 142: Printing a selection of text*

## Printing a brochure

In Writer, you can print a document with two pages on each side of a sheet of paper, arranged so that when the printed pages are folded in half, the pages are in the correct order to form a booklet or brochure.

### ▶ Tip

Plan your document so it will look good when printed half size; choose appropriate margins, font sizes, and so on. You may need to experiment.

To print a brochure on a single-sided printer:

1) Choose **File > Print**, or press *Ctrl+P*.
2) On the *General* page of the Print dialog, click **Properties**.

---

3) Check that the printer is set to the same orientation (portrait or landscape) as specified in the page setup for your document. Usually the orientation does not matter, but it does for brochures. Click **OK** to return to the Print dialog.

4) Select the *Page layout* tab in the Print dialog.

5) Select the **Brochure** option.

6) In the *Page sides* section, select **Back sides / left pages** from the *Include* drop-down list. (See Figure 143.)

7) Click **OK**.

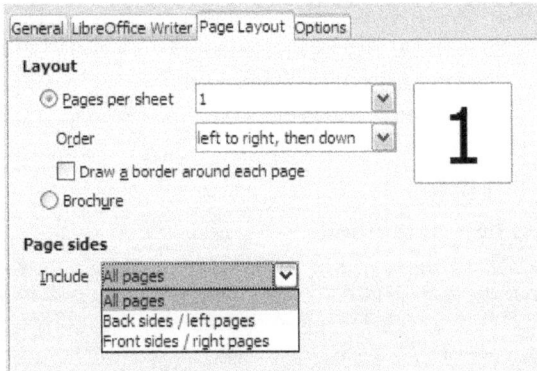

*Figure 143: Selecting which pages to print*

8) Take the printed pages out of the printer, turn the pages over, and put them back into the printer in the correct orientation to print on the blank side. You may need to experiment a bit to find out what the correct arrangement is for your printer.

9) On the Print dialog, in the *Page sides* section, select **Front sides / right pages** from the *Include* drop-down box. Click OK.

▶ **Tip**

If your printer can print double-sided automatically, choose **All pages**.

## Printing in black and white (on a color printer)

You may wish to print documents in black and white on a color printer. Several choices are available. Please note that some color printers may print in color regardless of the settings you choose.

Change the printer settings to print in black and white or grayscale:

1) Choose **File > Print**, or press *Ctrl+P*, to open the Print dialog.

2) Click **Properties** to open the Properties dialog for the printer. The available choices vary from one printer to another, but you should find options for the Color settings. See your printer's help or user manual for more information.

3) The choices for color might include black and white or grayscale. Choose the required setting.

4) Click **OK** to confirm your choice and return to the Print dialog,

5) Click **OK** to print the document.

▶ **Tip**

Grayscale is better if you have any images in the document.

Change the LibreOffice settings to print all color text and images as grayscale:

1) Choose **Tools > Options > LibreOffice > Print**.
2) Select the **Convert colors to grayscale** option. Click **OK** to save the change.
3) Open the Print dialog (**File > Print** or press *Ctrl+P*).
4) Click **OK** to print the document.

Change the LibreOffice Writer settings to print all color text as black, and all images as grayscale:

1) Choose **Tools > Options > LibreOffice Writer > Print**.
2) Under *Contents*, select the **Print text in black** option. Click **OK** to save the change.
3) Open the Print dialog (**File > Print**), or press *Ctrl+P*.
4) Click **OK** to print the document.

## Previewing pages before printing

The normal page view in Writer shows what each page will look like when printed; you can edit the pages in that view. If you are designing a document to be printed double-sided, you may want to see what facing pages look like. Writer provides two ways to do this:

- View Layout (editable view): use the Facing Pages (Book View) button on the status bar.

- Print Preview (read-only view).

To use Print Preview:

1) Choose **File > Print Preview** (or click the **Print Preview** button 🔲 on the Standard toolbar). Writer now displays the Print Preview toolbar instead of the Formatting toolbar.

*Figure 144: Page Preview toolbar*

2) Select the required preview button: Two Pages 🔲 , Book Preview 🔲 , or Multiple Pages 🔲 ▾ .

3) To print the document from this view, click the **Print** button 🔲 to open the Print dialog.

4) Choose the print options and click **OK**.

# Printing envelopes

Printing envelopes involves two steps: setup and printing.

To set up an envelope to be printed by itself or with your document:

1) Click **Insert > Envelope** from the Menu bar.
2) In the Envelope dialog, start with the *Envelope* tab. Verify, add, or edit the information in the Addressee and Sender (the "from" on the envelope) boxes.

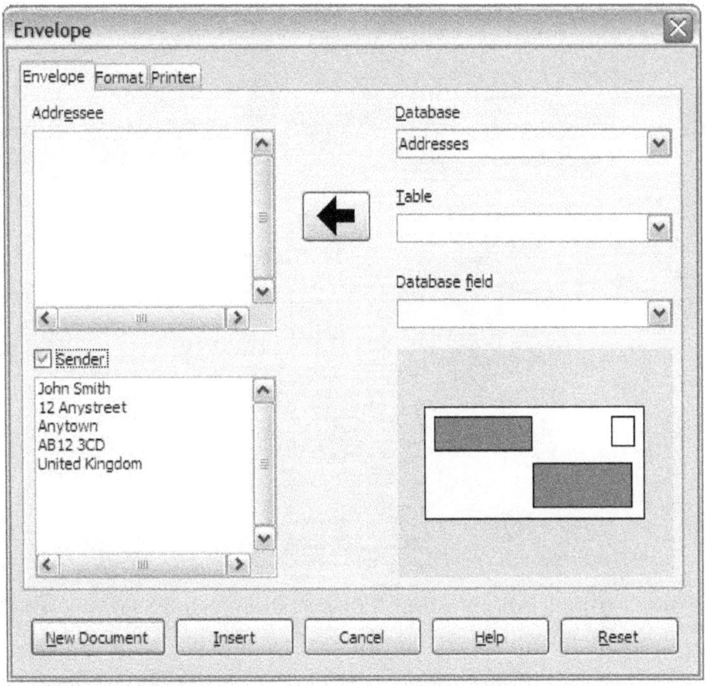

*Figure 145: Choosing addressee and sender information for an envelope*

You can type information directly into the Addressee and Sender boxes, or use the right-hand drop-down lists to select the database or table from which you can draw the envelope information, if desired. See Chapter 15, Mail Merge, for details on how to print envelopes from a database.

3) On the *Format* page (Figure 146), verify or edit the positioning of the addressee and sender information. The preview area on the lower right shows the effect of your positioning choices.

4) To format the text of these blocks, click the **Edit** buttons to the right. In the drop-down list you have two choices for each button: Character and Paragraph.

   – Select **Character** to open a Character dialog, similar to the standard Character dialog, but omitting Borders, where you can set the formatting of the text.

   – Select **Paragraph** to open a Paragraph dialog, similar to the standard Paragraph dialog, but omitting Outline & Numbering, where you to can set the paragraph's attributes.

5) In the lower left of this page, the *Size* section, choose the envelope format from the drop-down list. The width and height of the selected envelope then show in the boxes below the selected format. If you chose a pre-existing format, just verify these sizes. If you chose **User defined** in the Format list, then you can edit the sizes.

*Figure 146: Choosing positioning and size of elements for an envelope*

6) After formatting, go to the *Printer* page (Figure 147) to choose printer options such as envelope orientation and shifting. You may need to experiment a bit to see what works best for your printer.

You can also choose a different printer or alter printer setup (for example, specify the tray that holds envelopes) for this print job by clicking the **Setup** button and making selections on the Printer Setup dialog.

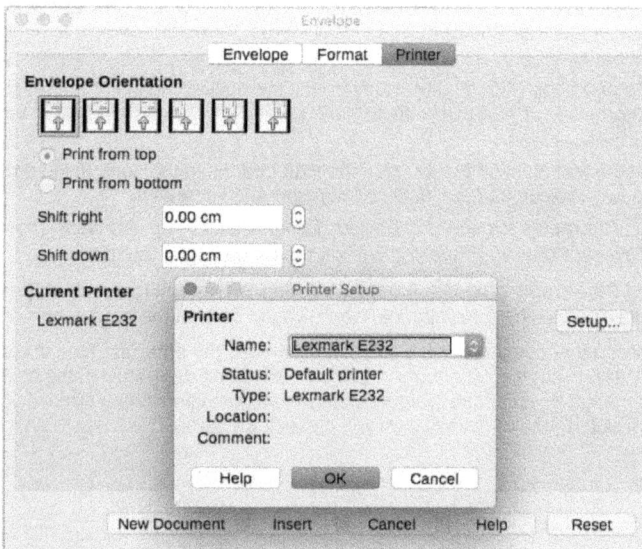

*Figure 147: Choosing printer options for an envelope*

7) When you have finished formatting and are ready to print, click either the **New Document** or **Insert** button to finish. **New Document** makes only an envelope or starts a new document with the envelope. **Insert** puts the envelope into your existing document as page 1.

To not proceed with this envelope, click **Cancel** or press the *Esc* key. You can also click **Reset** to remove your changes and return to the original settings when the dialog opened.

The document now has the envelope in the same file as the document. Save this file before you do anything else.

To print the envelope:

1) Choose **File > Print** from the menu bar.

2) On the Print dialog, under *Print range*, choose **Pages** and type 1 in the box. Click **OK** to print.

# Printing labels

Labels are commonly used for printing address lists (where each label shows a different address), but they can also be used for making multiple copies of one label only, for example return-address stickers. To print labels:

1) Choose **File > New > Labels** on the Menu bar. The Labels dialog opens.

2) On the *Labels* page, fill in your own label text in the Inscription box, or use the Database and Table drop-down lists to choose the required information, as described in Chapter 15, Mail Merge.

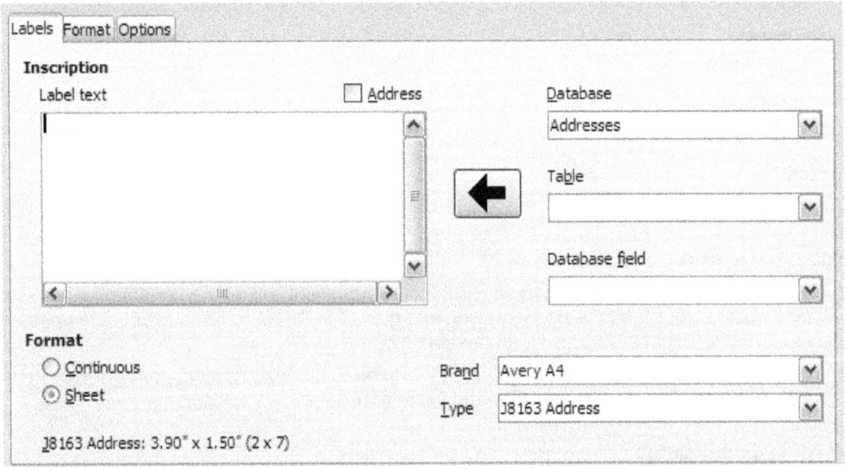

*Figure 148: Labels dialog, Labels page*

3) Select the label stock in the Brand drop-down list. The types for that brand then appear in the Type drop-down list. Select the size and type of labels required. You can also select User in the Type drop-down list and then make specific selections on the *Format* page.

4) On the *Format* page, choose the pitch, sizes, margins, columns and rows for user-defined labels, or just verify with a brand of label stock you have loaded into the printer.

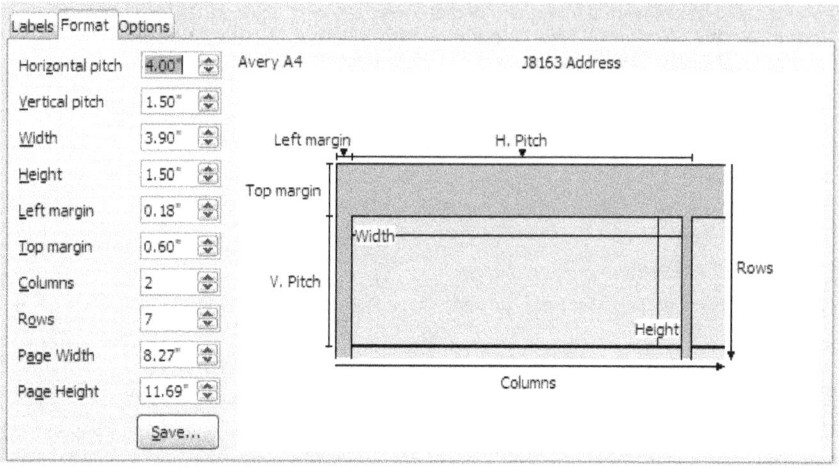

*Figure 149: Labels dialog, Format page*

5)  Click **Save** to save your new format.

6)  On the *Options* page, choose to print the entire page of labels or one single label, then select which one by the column and row. You can also change printer setup.

*Figure 150: Labels dialog, Options page*

7)  When you have finished formatting, click **New Document** to create your sheet of labels or click **Cancel** (or press the *Esc* key). You can also click **Reset** to remove your changes and return to the original settings when the dialog opened.

8)  You can print using the **Print File Directly** icon on the toolbar or by choosing **File > Print** from the Menu bar, or you can save the file to print later.

# Exporting to PDF

LibreOffice can export documents to PDF (Portable Document Format). This industry-standard file format is ideal for sending the file to someone else to view using Adobe Reader or other PDF viewers.

> **Tip**
>
> Unlike Save As, the **Export** command writes a copy of the current document in a new file with the chosen format, but keeps the current document and format open in your session.

# Quick export to PDF

Click the **Export as PDF** button ![icon] to export the entire document using the PDF settings you most recently selected in the PDF Options dialog. You are asked to enter the file name and location for the PDF, but you do not get a chance to choose a page range, the image compression, or other options.

## Controlling PDF content and quality

For more control over the content and quality of the resulting PDF, use **File > Export as PDF**. The PDF Options dialog opens. This dialog has six pages (*General, Initial View, User Interface, Links, Security*, and *Digital Signatures*). Select the appropriate settings, and then click **Export**. Then you are asked to enter the location and file name of the PDF to be created, and click **Export**.

### Note

Another choice is to use **File > Export**. This opens the Export dialog. Select the PDF file format, file name and location and click **Export**. This then opens the PDF Options dialog. Click **Export** when all the selections have been made. The only difference between the two export methods is the sequence in which steps occur.

### *General page of PDF Options dialog*

On the *General* page (Figure 151), you can choose which pages to include in the PDF, the type of compression to use for images (which affects the quality of images in the PDF), and other options.

**Range section**
- **All**: Exports the entire document.
- **Pages**: To export a range of pages, use the format 3-6 (pages 3 to 6). To export single pages, use the format 7;9;11 (pages 7, 9, and 11). You can also export a combination of page ranges and single pages, by using a format like 3-6;8;12.
- **Selection**: Exports whatever material is selected.

**Images section**
- **Lossless compression**: Images are stored without any loss of quality. Tends to make large files when used with photographs. Recommended for other kinds of images or graphics.
- **JPEG compression**: Allows for varying degrees of quality. A setting of 90% works well with photographs (small file size, little perceptible loss of quality).
- **Reduce image resolution**: Lower-DPI (dots per inch) images have lower quality. For viewing on a computer screen generally a resolution of 72dpi (for Windows) or 96dpi (GNU/Linux) is sufficient, while for printing it is generally preferable to use at least 300 or 600 dpi, depending on the capability of the printer. Higher dpi settings greatly increase the size of the exported file.

### Note

EPS (Encapsulated PostScript) images with embedded previews are exported only as previews. EPS images without embedded previews are exported as empty placeholders.

**Watermark section**
- **Sign with Watermark**: When this option is selected, a transparent overlay of the text you enter into the Watermark Text box will appear on each page of the PDF.

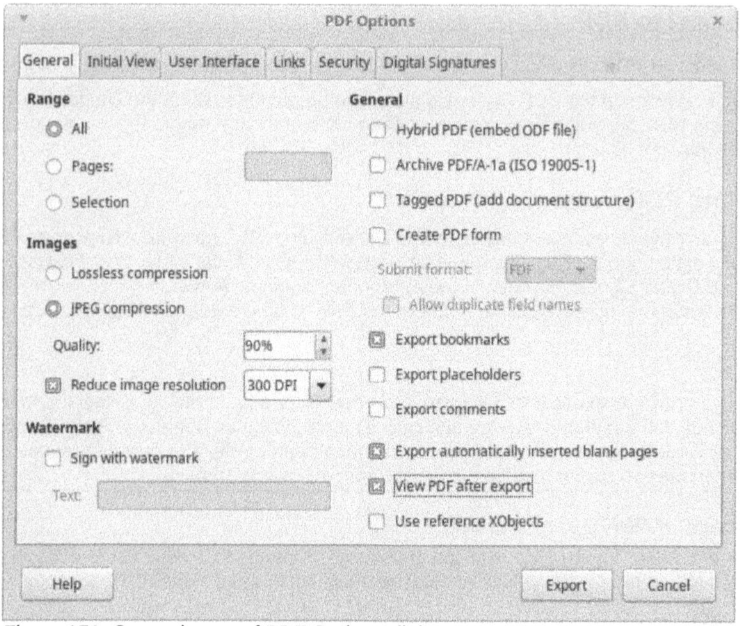

*Figure 151: General page of PDF Options dialog*

**General section**

- **Hybrid PDF (embed ODF file)**: Use this setting to export the document as a PDF file containing two file formats: PDF and ODF. In PDF viewers it behaves like a normal PDF file, and it remains fully editable in LibreOffice.

- **Archive PDF/A-1a (ISO 19005-1)**: PDF/A is an ISO standard for long-term preservation of documents, by embedding all the information necessary for faithful reproduction (such as fonts) while forbidding other elements (including forms, security, and encryption). PDF tags are written. If you select PDF/A-1a, the forbidden elements are grayed-out (not available).

- **Tagged PDF**: Tagged PDF contains information about the structure of the document's contents. This can help to display the document on devices with different screens, and when using screen reader software. Some tags that are exported are table of contents, hyperlinks, and controls. This option can increase file sizes significantly.

- **Create PDF form – Submit format**: Choose the format of submitting forms from within the PDF file. This setting overrides the control's URL property that you set in the document. There is only one common setting valid for the whole PDF document: PDF (sends the whole document), FDF (sends the control contents), HTML, and XML. Most often you will choose the PDF format.

  **Allow duplicate field names**: If enabled, the same field name can be used for multiple fields in the generated PDF file. With this option enabled, you can enter data in the first occurrence of the named field in the PDF document and all fields with the same name will carry your entry. If disabled, field names will be exported using generated unique names.

- **Export bookmarks**: Creates PDF bookmarks (a table of contents list displayed by most PDF viewers, including Adobe Reader) for all headings in the document.

- **Export placeholders**: Exports placeholder text instead of a blank placeholder.

- **Export comments**: Exports comments as PDF notes. You may not want this!

---

- **Export automatically inserted blank pages**: If selected, automatically inserted blank pages are exported to the PDF. This is best if you are printing the PDF double-sided. For example, books usually have chapters set to always start on an odd-numbered (right-hand) page. When the previous chapter ends on an odd page, LibreOffice inserts a blank page between the two odd pages. This option controls whether to export that blank page.
- **View PDF after export**: Your default PDF viewer will open and display the newly exported PDF.

### Initial View page of PDF Options dialog

On the *Initial View* page, you can choose how the PDF opens by default in a PDF viewer. The selections should be self-explanatory.

If you have Complex Text Layout enabled (in **Tools > Options > Language settings > Languages**), an additional selection is available under Continuous facing: First page is left (normally, the first page is on the right when using the Continuous facing option).

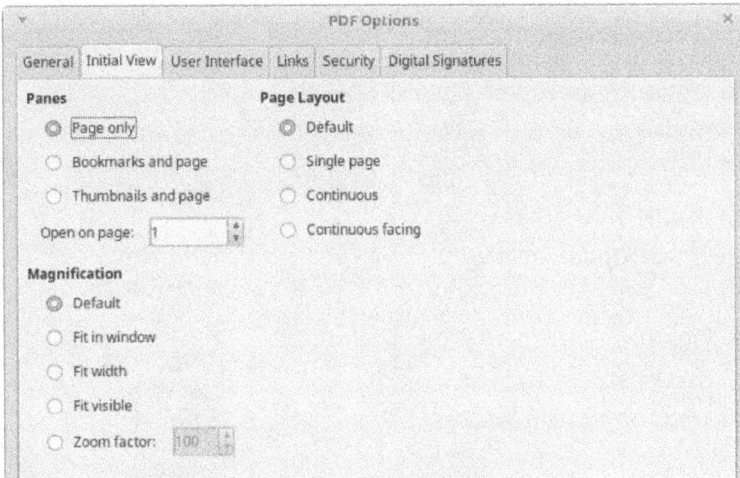

*Figure 152: Initial View page of PDF Options dialog*

### User Interface page of PDF Options dialog

On the *User Interface* page, you can choose more settings to control how a PDF viewer displays the file. Some of these choices are particularly useful when you are creating a PDF to be used as a presentation or a kiosk-type display.

**Window options section**
- **Resize window to initial page**. Causes the PDF viewer window to resize to fit the first page of the PDF.
- **Center window on screen**. Causes the PDF viewer window to be centered on the computer screen.
- **Open in full screen mode**. Causes the PDF viewer to open full-screen instead of in a smaller window.
- **Display document title**. Causes the PDF viewer to display the document's title in the title bar.

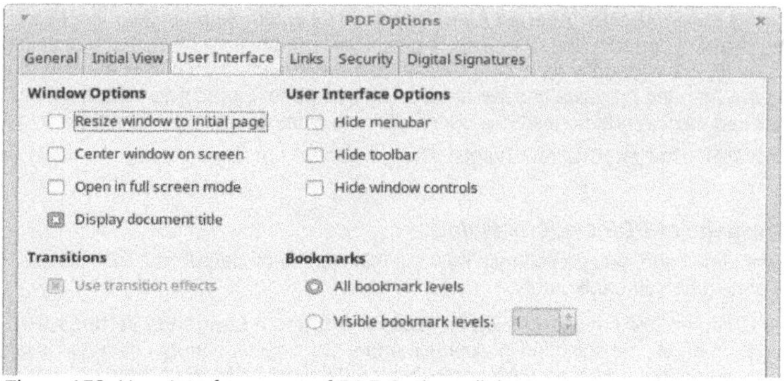

*Figure 153: User Interface page of PDF Options dialog*

**User interface options section**

- **Hide menubar**. Causes the PDF viewer to hide the menu bar.

- **Hide toolbar**. Causes the PDF viewer to hide the toolbar.

- **Hide window controls**. Causes the PDF viewer to hide other window controls.

**Bookmarks**

Select how many heading levels are displayed as bookmarks, if **Export bookmarks** is selected on the *General* page.

### Links page of PDF Options dialog

On the *Links* page, you can choose how links in documents are exported to PDF.

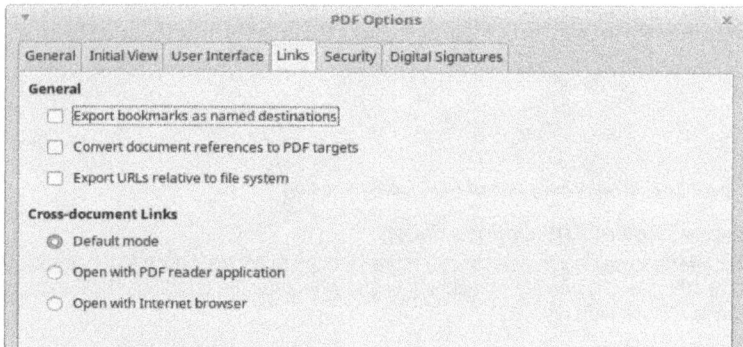

*Figure 154: Links page of PDF Options dialog*

**Export bookmarks as named destinations**

If you have defined Writer bookmarks, this option exports them as "named destinations" to which Web pages and PDF documents can link.

**Convert document references to PDF targets**

If you have defined links to other documents with OpenDocument extensions (such as .odt, .ods, and .odp), this option converts the files names to .pdf in the exported PDF document.

**Export URLs relative to the file system**

If you have defined relative links in a document, this option exports those links to the PDF.

**Cross-document links**

Set up the behavior of the PDF links to other files. Select one among the following alternatives:

*   Default mode: The PDF links will be handled as specified in your operating system.
*   Open with PDF reader application: Use the same application used to display the PDF document to open linked PDF documents.
*   Open with Internet browser: Use the default Internet browser to display linked PDF documents.

### Security page of PDF Options dialog

PDF export includes options to encrypt the PDF (so it cannot be opened without a password) and apply some digital rights management (DRM) features.

*   With an *open password* set, the PDF can only be opened with the password. Once opened, there are no restrictions on what the user can do with the document (for example, print, copy, or change it).
*   With a *permissions password* set, the PDF can be opened by anyone, but its permissions can be restricted. See Figure 155. After you set a password for permissions, the other choices on the Security page become available.
*   With *both* the open password and permission password set, the PDF can only be opened with the correct password, and its permissions can be restricted.

**Note**

Permissions settings are effective only if the user's PDF viewer respects the settings.

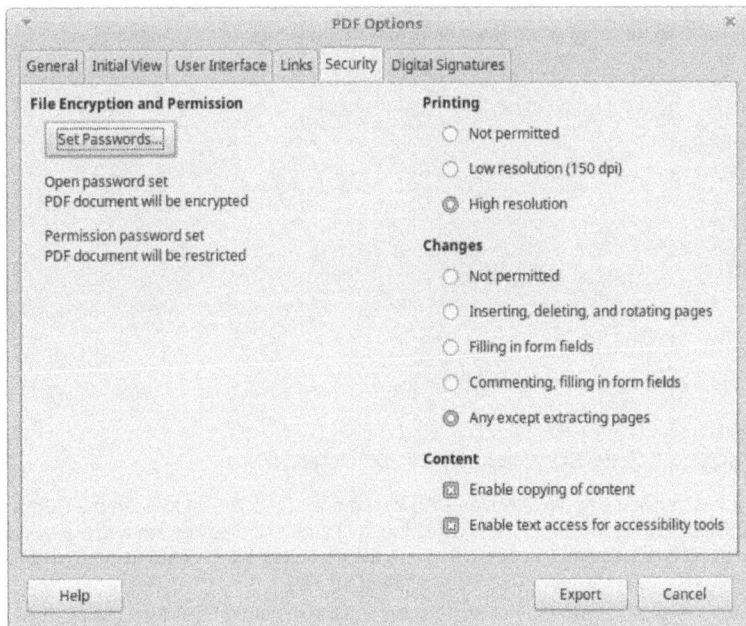

*Figure 155: Security page of PDF Options dialog with passwords set*

Figure 156 shows the pop-up dialog displayed when you click the **Set passwords** button on the *Security* page of the PDF Options dialog.

*Figure 156: Setting a password to encrypt a PDF*

### Digital Signatures page of PDF Options dialog

The *Digital Signatures* page contains the options related to exporting a digitally signed PDF.

Digital signatures are used to ensure that the PDF was really created by the original author (that is, you), and that the document has not been modified since it was signed.

The signed PDF export uses the keys and X.509 certificates already stored in your default key store location or on a smartcard. The key store to be used can be selected under **Tools > Options > LibreOffice > Security > Certificate Path**. When using a smartcard, it must already be configured for use by your key store. This is usually done during installation of the smartcard software. Details about using these features is outside the scope of this chapter.

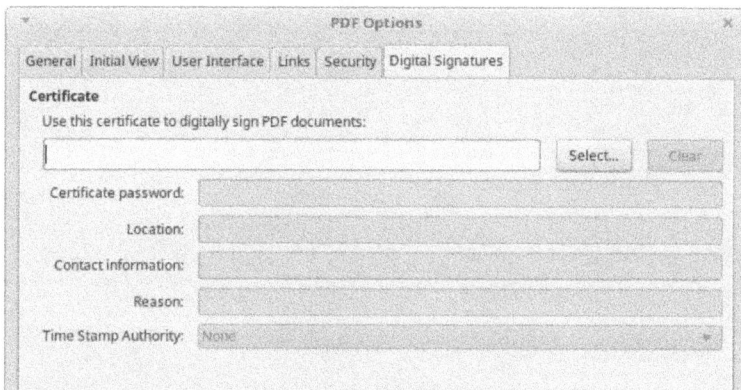

*Figure 157: Digital Signatures page of PDF Options dialog*

- Use this certificate to digitally sign PDF documents: Click Select to open the Select Certificate dialog, where all certificates found in your selected key store are displayed. If the key store is protected by a password, you are prompted for it. When using a smartcard that is protected by a PIN, you are also prompted for that.

  Select the certificate to use for digitally signing the exported PDF, then click OK. All other fields on the Digital Signatures tab are accessible only after a certificate has been selected.

- Certificate password: Enter the password used for protecting the private key associated with the selected certificate. Usually this is the key store password. If the key store password has already been entered in the Select Certificate dialog, the key store may already be unlocked and not require the password again.

  When using a smartcard, enter the PIN here. Some smartcard software will prompt you for the PIN again before signing.

- Location, Contact information, Reason: Optionally enter additional information about the digital signature that will be applied to the PDF. This information will be embedded in the appropriate PDF fields and will be visible to anyone viewing the PDF. Each or all of the three fields may be left blank.

- Time Stamp Authority: Optionally select a Time Stamping Authority (TSA) URL. During the PDF signing process, the TSA will be used to obtain a digitally signed timestamp that is then embedded in the signature. Anyone viewing the PDF can use this timestamp to verify when the document was signed.

  The list of TSA URLs that can be selected is maintained under **Tools > Options > LibreOffice > Security > TSAs**. If no TSA URL is selected (the default), the signature will not be timestamped, but will use the current time from your local computer.

## Exporting to XHTML

LibreOffice uses the term "export" for some file operations involving a change of file type. LibreOffice can export files to XHTML. Other formats may be made available through extensions.

To export to XHTML, choose **File > Export**. On the Export dialog, specify a file name for the exported document, then select the XHTML in the File format list and click the Export button.

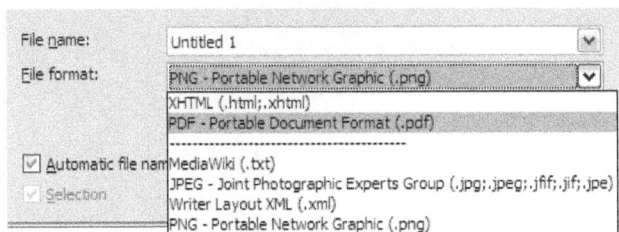

| File name: | Untitled 1 | |
|---|---|---|
| File format: | PNG - Portable Network Graphic (.png) | |
| | XHTML (.html;.xhtml) | |
| | PDF - Portable Document Format (.pdf) | |
| ☑ Automatic file nam | MediaWiki (.txt) | |
| ☑ Selection | JPEG - Joint Photographic Experts Group (.jpg;.jpeg;.jfif;.jif;.jpe) | |
| | Writer Layout XML (.xml) | |
| | PNG - Portable Network Graphic (.png) | |

*Figure 158: Export file formats*

# E-mailing Writer documents

LibreOffice provides several ways to quickly and easily send a Writer document as an e-mail attachment in one of three formats: .odt (OpenDocument Text, Writer's default format), .doc (Microsoft Word format), or .pdf.

### Note

Documents can be sent from the LibreOffice mail merge wizard only if a mail profile has been set up in **Tools > Option > LibreOffice Writer > Mail Merge E-mail**.

To send the current document in .odt format, choose:

1) **File > Send > E-mail Document**, or **File > Send > E-mail as OpenDocument Text**. Writer opens your default e-mail program. The document is attached.

2) In your e-mail program, enter the recipient, subject, and any text you want to add, then send the e-mail.

If you choose **E-mail as Microsoft Word**, Writer first creates a .doc file and then opens your e-mail program with the .doc file attached. Similarly, if you choose **E-mail as PDF**, Writer opens the PDF Options dialog where you can select the settings you want, then creates a PDF, and then opens your email program with the .pdf file attached.

## E-mailing a document to several recipients

To e-mail a document to several recipients, you can use the features in your e-mail program or you can use LibreOffice's mail merge facilities to extract email addresses from an address book.

You can use LibreOffice's mail merge to send e-mail in two ways:

- Use the Mail Merge Wizard to create the document and send it. See Chapter 15, Mail Merge, for details.

- Create the document in Writer without using the Wizard, then use the Wizard to send it. This method is described here.

To use the Mail Merge Wizard to send a previously-created Writer document:

1) Open the document in Writer. Click **Tools > Mail Merge Wizard**. On the first page of the wizard, select **Use the current document** and click **Next**.

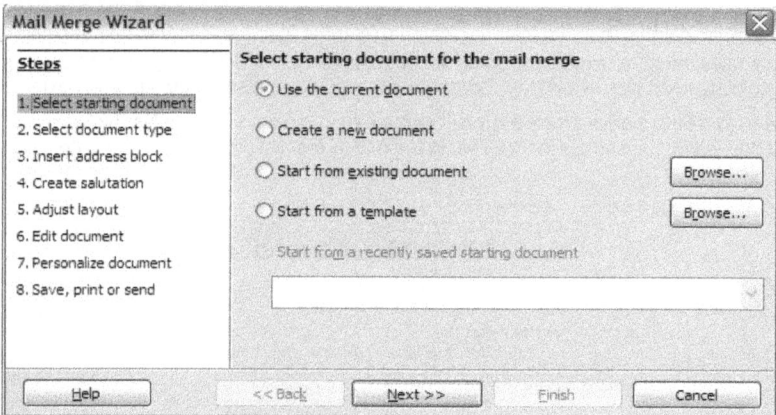

*Figure 159: Select starting document*

2) On the second page, select **E-mail message** for the type of document and click **Next**.

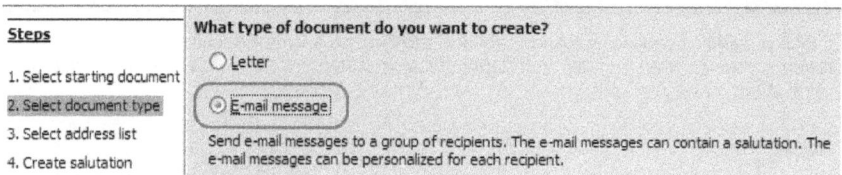

*Figure 160: Select document type*

3) On the third page, click the **Select Address List** button. Select the required address list (even if only one is shown) and then click **OK**. (If the address list you need is not shown here, you can click **Add** to find and add it to the list.)

*Figure 161: Selecting an address list*

4) Back on the *Select address list* page, click **Next**. On the *Create salutation* page, deselect the checkbox by **This document should contain a salutation**.

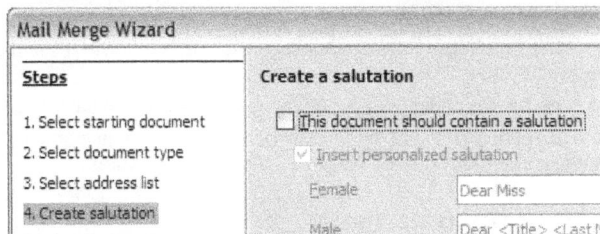

*Figure 162: Deselecting a salutation*

5) In the left-hand list, click **Step 8. Save, print or send**. LibreOffice displays a "Creating documents" message and then displays the *Save, print or send* page of the Wizard.

6) Select **Send merged document as E-Mail**. The lower part of the page changes to show e-mail settings choices.

7) Type a subject for your email and click **Send documents**. LibreOffice sends the e-mails.

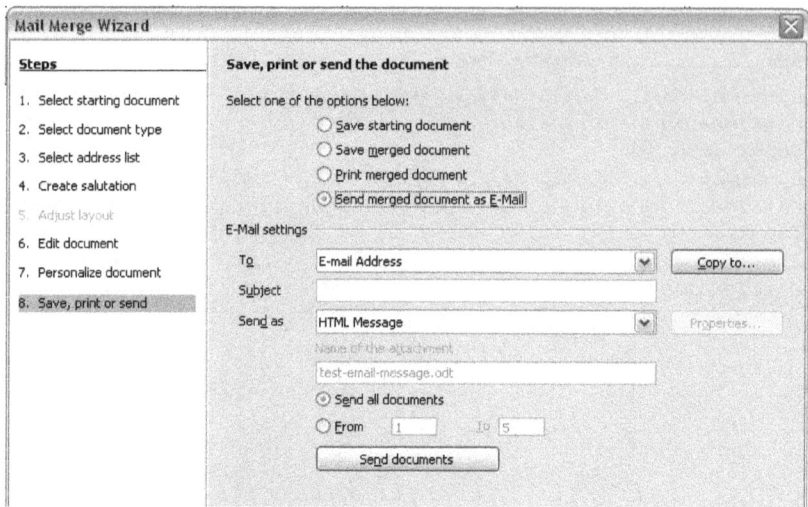

Figure 163: Sending a document as an email message

# Sending a fax

To send a fax directly from LibreOffice, you need a fax modem and a fax driver that allows applications to communicate with the fax modem.

1) Open the Print dialog (Figure 137) by choosing **File > Print** (or *Ctrl+P*) and select the fax driver in the Printer list.

2) Click **OK** to open the dialog for your fax driver, where you can select the fax recipient.

You can set up a toolbar button so that a single click sends the current document as a fax. To add a button for this purpose to a toolbar, see Chapter 21, Customizing Writer.

# Digital signing of documents

To sign a document digitally, you need a personal key, also known as a certificate. A personal key is stored on your computer as a combination of a private key, which must be kept secret, and a public key, which you add to your documents when you sign them. You can get a certificate from a certification authority, which may be a private company or a governmental institution.

When you apply a digital signature to a document, a kind of checksum is computed from the document's content plus your personal key. The checksum and your public key are stored together with the document.

When someone later opens the document on any computer with a recent version of LibreOffice, the program will compute the checksum again and compare it with the stored checksum. If both are the same, the program will signal that you see the original, unchanged document. In addition, the program can show you the public key information from the certificate. You can compare the public key with the public key that is published on the web site of the certificate authority. Whenever someone changes something in the document, this change breaks the digital signature.

On Windows operating systems, the Windows features of validating a signature are used. On Linux systems, files that are supplied by Thunderbird, Mozilla, or Firefox are used. For a more detailed description of how to get and manage a certificate, and signature validation, see "About Digital Signatures" in the LibreOffice Help.

To sign a document:

1) Choose **File > Digital Signatures**. If you have set LibreOffice to warn you when the document contains comments, you may see a message box asking whether you want to continue signing the document.

2) If you have not saved the document since the last change, a message box appears. Click **Yes** to save the file.

3) The Digital Signatures dialog opens. Click **Sign Document** to add a public key to the document.

4) In the Select Certificate dialog, select your certificate and click **OK** to return to the Digital Signatures dialog.

5) The certificate used is displayed in the dialog with an icon next to its name. This icon indicates the status of the digital signature.

   – An icon with a red seal ![seal] indicates that the document was signed and the certificate was validated.

   – An icon with a yellow caution triangle overlaying the red seal ![seal] indicates that the document is signed but that the certificate could not be validated.

   – An icon of a yellow caution triangle ![triangle] indicates an invalid digital signature.

6) Click **Close** to apply the digital signature.

A signed document shows an icon in the status bar. You can double-click the icon to view the certificate. More than one signature can be added to a document.

## Signing multiple times with same signature

In the past, LibreOffice prohibited creating multiple signatures by the same author on a document, because there was no semantic meaning of signing the same document multiple times. LibreOffice now provides a signature description, so multiple signatures from the same author are now allowed, because each signature can have a different meaning.

When you select **File > Digital Signatures**, the dialog (Figure 164) lists existing signatures together with their description (if they have any).

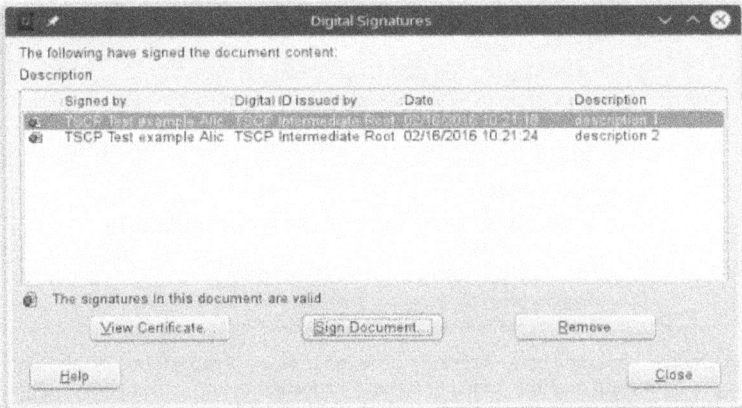

*Figure 164: Signatures of the document*

When you click the **Sign Document** button, the dialog (Figure 165) for certificate selection also asks for an optional description.

Changing an existing description invalidates the signature.

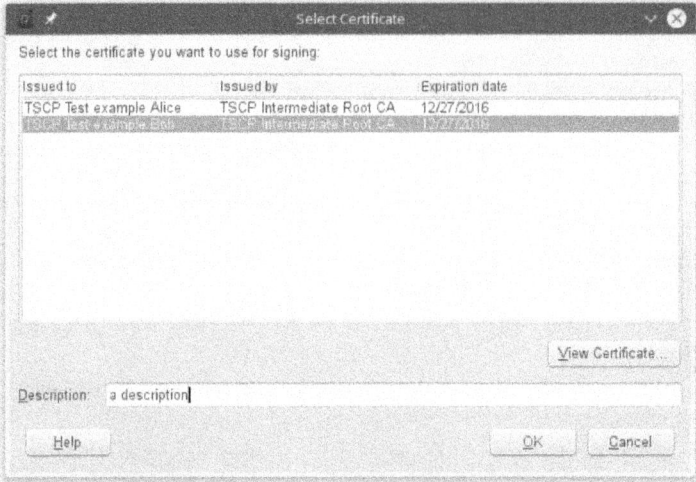

*Figure 165: Signatures can now have a description*

## Removing personal data

You may wish to ensure that personal data, versions, comments, hidden information, or recorded changes are removed from files before you send them to other people or create PDFs from them.

In **Tools > Options > LibreOffice > Security > Options**, you can set LibreOffice to remind (warn) you automatically when saving files containing certain information and optionally remove personal information.

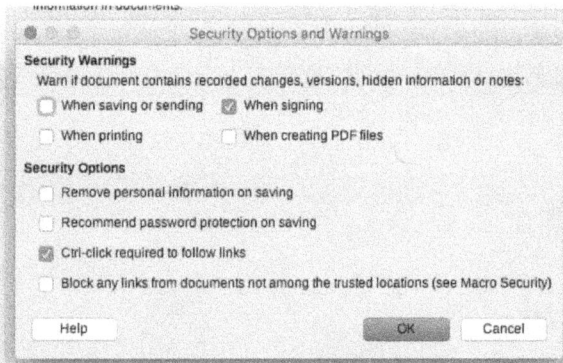

*Figure 166: Set security warnings and options*

To remove personal and some other data from a file, go to **File > Properties**. On the General tab, uncheck **Apply user data** and then click the **Reset Properties** button. This removes any names in the created and modified fields, deletes the modification and printing dates, and resets the editing time to zero, the creation date to the current date and time, and the version number to 1.

To remove version information, either (a) go to **File > Versions**, select the versions from the list and click **Delete**, or (b) use **Save As** and save the file with a different name.

# LibreOffice

*Chapter 8*
*Introduction to Styles*

# What are styles?

Most people are used to writing documents according to *physical* attributes. For example, you might specify the font family, font size, and weight (for example: Helvetica 12pt, bold).

Styles are *logical* attributes. We use styles every day. For example, there are different styles of personal computer: desktop, tablet, netbook, laptop, and so on. Each has its own distinctive set of properties. You never say "my computer is a low-weight, one-piece unit with an LCD screen attached to a rectangular casing containing the computing components and the keyboard". Instead, you would probably say that you have a laptop.

LibreOffice styles are a way to do the same thing for your document. Using styles means that you could stop saying "font size 14pt, Times New Roman, bold, centered" and start saying "title" for describing that particular font usage. In other words, styles mean that you shift the emphasis from what the text *looks like* to what the text *is*.

## Why use styles?

Styles help improve consistency in a document. They also make major formatting changes easy. For example, you might decide to change the indentation of all paragraphs or change the font of all titles. For a long document, this simple task could be prohibitive. Styles make the task easy.

## Style categories

LibreOffice Writer has six style categories:

- *Paragraph* styles affect entire paragraphs and are also used for purposes such as compiling a table of contents.
- *Character* styles affect a block of text inside a paragraph.
- *Page* styles affect page formatting (page size, margin, and the like).
- *Frame* styles affect frames and graphics.
- *List* styles affect outlines, numbered lists, and bulleted lists.
- *Table* styles affect the appearance of tables of data.

Paragraphs are the building blocks of every document: headings are paragraphs; headers, footers, and items in numbered lists are also paragraphs. Paragraph styles are, therefore, the most frequently used styles and are the ones treated in most detail in this chapter.

# The Styles and Formatting window

Styles management is primarily available through the Styles and Formatting window, located on the Sidebar (Figure 167). Here you can apply styles, modify styles, and create new styles.

To open the Styles and Formatting window, do any of the following:

- Click on the Styles and Formatting icon on the Sidebar.
- Select **Styles > Styles and Formatting** from the Menu bar.
- Press *F11* (⌘+*T* on Mac).

The first six buttons at the top of the Styles and Formatting window select the category of styles. Click on one of these buttons to display a list of styles in that category, such as paragraph or character styles.

Select the **Show Previews** option to display the styles as examples.

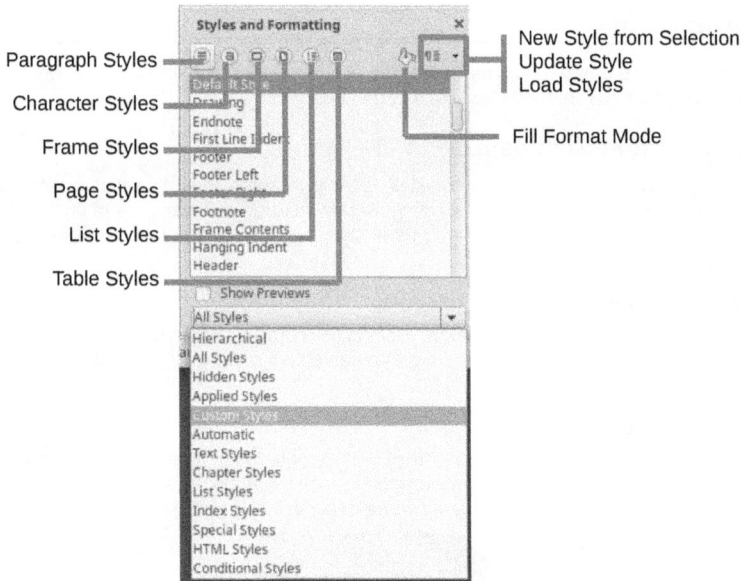

*Figure 167: The Styles and Formatting window showing paragraph styles and filter*

## Filtering the visible styles

At the bottom of the Styles and Formatting window, use the drop-down menu to select a filter for the contents of the main body of the window. Normally, you will need only a few styles in any document, so it's useful to have only these styles shown.

At the beginning of the writing process, you may want to have access to all the available styles (by selecting **All Styles**), and then to exclude some of them from use (*Ctrl+click* to select each style to be excluded and finally right-click one of these styles and select Hide from the context menu). As the document develops, it is useful to reduce the list displayed to only the styles already in use (by selecting **Applied Styles**). If you work on a document where you want to apply custom styles only, select instead **Custom Styles**. The **Hierarchical Styles** view is most useful when modifying styles as it reveals which styles are linked together. This topic is discussed in Chapter 9, Working with Styles.

In the Paragraph Styles view, the drop-down menu contains several more filtering options so you can view, for example, only Text Styles, Special Styles, and so on.

### Caution

Manual formatting (also called direct formatting) overrides styles, and you cannot get rid of the manual formatting by applying a style to it.

To remove manual formatting, select the text and choose **Format > Clear Direct Formatting** from the Menu bar, or select the text and press *Ctrl+M*.

# Applying styles

Styles can be applied easily using the Styles and Formatting window. In addition, you can apply certain styles using other methods, as explained in this section.

## Applying paragraph styles

When drafting a document, the most used style is the paragraph style. LibreOffice offers three quick alternatives to the Styles and Formatting window to apply this category of style: the *Styles menu* (with a limited selection of commonly used styles), the *Set Paragraph Style* list, and the *Clone Formatting* button.

### Using the Styles and Formatting window

Put the cursor in the paragraph and double-click on the name of the style in the Paragraph Styles section of the Styles and Formatting window. You can select more than one paragraph and apply the same style to all of them at the same time.

### Using the Styles menu

The Styles menu on the Menu bar (Figure 168) provides the most commonly used paragraph and character styles, plus quick links to create and edit styles. To apply a paragraph style, put the cursor in the paragraph and click **Styles > [name of paragraph style]** on the Menu bar.

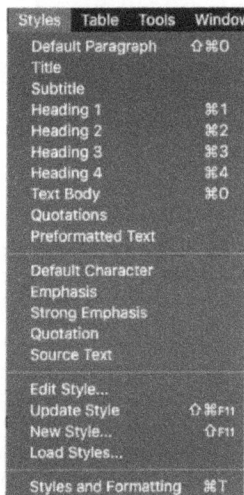

*Figure 168: The Styles menu*

**Note**

You cannot add styles to the Styles menu.

### Using the Set Paragraph Style list

When a paragraph style is in use in a document, the style name appears on the *Set Paragraph Style* list near the left end of the Formatting bar (see Figure 169).

To apply a style from this menu, put the cursor in the paragraph to change, and then click on the desired style or use the up or down arrow keys to move through the list, then press *Enter* to apply the highlighted style.

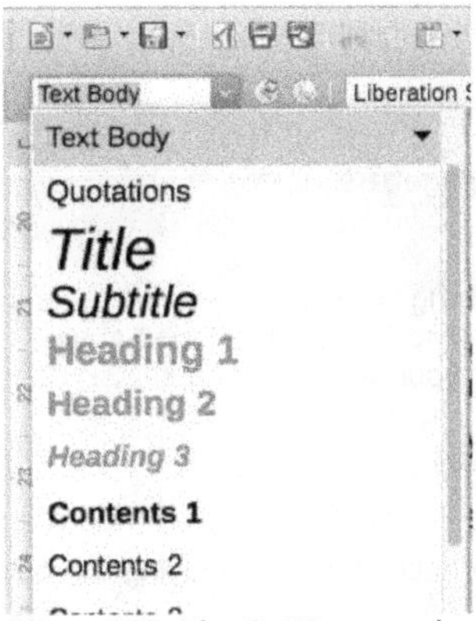

*Figure 169: The Set Paragraph Style list on the Formatting bar*

▶ **Tip**

Select **More** at the bottom of the list (not shown in illustration) to open the Styles and Formatting window.

### Using Clone Formatting

You can use *Clone Formatting* to apply a paragraph style to another paragraph or to a group of paragraphs. Table 6 shows the formatting copied as a result of a particular cursor position.

*Table 6: Formatting cloned related to cursor positioning*

| Case | Type of selection | Action |
|---|---|---|
| A | Nothing is selected, but the cursor is inside a text passage. | Copies the formatting of the paragraph and the character formatting of the next character in the text flow direction. |
| B | Text is selected. | Copies the formatting of the last selected character and of the paragraph that contains the character. |

To format a single paragraph:

1) Put the cursor in the paragraph with the formatting you want to copy. Click the **Clone Formatting** icon ( 🖌 ) on the Standard Toolbar.

   The cursor changes into an ink bottle ( 🖋 ).

2) Now click the paragraph to which you want to apply the copied style.

   If you press *Shift+Ctrl* while clicking, you exclude any character formatting wherever you select to click.

3) The paragraph is formatted and the cursor then returns to normal.

To format more than one paragraph:

1) Put the cursor in the paragraph with the formatting you want to copy. *Double-click* the **Clone Formatting** icon.

2) The cursor changes shape. Now click each of the paragraphs to which you want to apply the copied style.

   If you press *Shift+Ctrl* while clicking, you exclude any character formatting wherever you select to click.

3) The paragraphs are formatted. Click the **Clone Formatting** icon again, or press the *Esc* key, to revert to normal.

### Using Fill Format mode

See "Using Fill Format mode" on page 183.

### Using keyboard shortcuts

Some keyboard shortcuts for applying styles are predefined. For example, *Ctrl+0* applies the Text body style, *Ctrl+1* applies the Heading 1 style, and *Ctrl+2* applies the Heading 2 style. You can modify these shortcuts and create your own; see Chapter 21, Customizing Writer, for instructions.

## Applying character styles

Writer provides two ways to apply character styles, as described in this section.

You may need to remove direct formatting before applying character styles.

### Using the Styles and Formatting window

Open the Styles and Formatting window and click the second button in the top bar. The list of available character styles is displayed. To apply a character style, follow these steps:

1) Select the block of text, or put the cursor into the single word, where you wish to apply the style.
2) Double-click the appropriate character style in the Styles and Formatting window.

> **Note**
>
> To apply a character style to more than a single word, you need to select all of the text to be changed. To apply the style to a single word, you only have to place the cursor in the word. Paragraph styles are applied to the whole of the paragraph in which the cursor is placed.

### Using Clone Formatting

Clone Formatting can be used to apply character styles in much the same way as for paragraphs (see "Using Clone Formatting" on page 175).

The difference is that you must select a word that has the required formatting, and that to clone only the character style, without the underlying paragraph style, you must hold down the *Ctrl* key when applying the style.

### Removing or replacing character styles

Sometimes, you will want to remove the character style formatting from some text, or change the character style to a different style. To do this:

1) Select the text.
2) On the Styles and Formatting window, click the *Character Styles* button in the top bar.
3) Double-click the required character style.

## Applying frame styles

When you insert an object (such as a graphic) into a document, it will automatically have an invisible frame around it. Some designers like to add frame styles to introduce variety. For example, you could have one frame style for photographs and a different frame style for other graphics such as line drawings. The one for photographs might have a border with a drop shadow, while the one for drawings might have only a border.

To apply a style to a frame:

1) Select the frame.
2) Open the Styles and Formatting window.
3) Click the Frame Styles icon (the third one from the left).
4) Double-click the frame style you want.

Having applied a style to a frame, you can now modify the frame to be just how you want it. Most of a frame's design can be set in a style, but the following options must be set manually:

- *Anchoring:* how the frame is positioned in relation to the rest of the page's contents (**Format > Anchor**).
- *Arrangement:* the frame's position in a stack of objects (**Format > Arrange**).
- *Adding a hyperlink:* so that a click on the frame opens a Web page or another document (**Insert > Link**).

When a frame is selected, the Frame toolbar replaces the Formatting toolbar, and the right-click (context) menu has items for anchoring, arrangement, wrap, and alignment.

## Applying page styles

Put the cursor anywhere on the page. The applied page style is shown on the status bar.

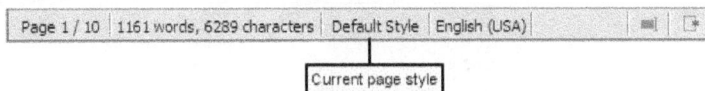

*Figure 170: The current page style is displayed on the status bar*

To apply a different style, either right-click on the style in the status bar and select a style from the context menu, or open the Styles and Formatting window, select the page style icon at the top of the window (fourth icon), and then double-click on the desired page style.

### Caution

Changing a page style may cause the style of subsequent pages to change as well. The results may not be what you want. To change the style of only one page, you may need to insert a manual page break, as described below.

As discussed in Chapter 9, Working with Styles, a correctly set up page style will, in most cases, contain information on what the page style of the next page should be. For example, when you apply a *Left* page style to a page, you can indicate in the page style settings that the next page has to apply a *Right* page style, a *First* page style could be followed by either a *Left* page style or a *Default* page style, and so on.

Another way to change the page style is to insert a manual page break and specify the style of the subsequent page. The idea is simple: you break a sequence of page styles and start a new sequence. To insert a page break, choose **Insert > Manual Break** and choose **Page break**. This section illustrates two common scenarios where page breaks are useful.

### Example: Chapters

A possible scenario: You are writing a book that is divided into chapters. Each chapter starts with a page style called *First Page*. The following pages use the *Default* page style. At the end of each (except the last) chapter, we return to the *First Page* style for the next chapter.

Figure 171 illustrates the flow of page styles when using page breaks.

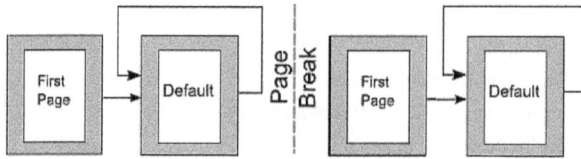
*Figure 171: Dividing a document into chapters using page styles*

At some point, you will want to start a new chapter. Follow these steps:

1) Put the cursor at the end of the chapter, on a blank line (empty paragraph) of its own.
2) Choose **Insert > Manual Break**. The Insert Break dialog (Figure 172) appears.
3) Under *Type*, choose **Page break** and under *Style*, select **First Page**.

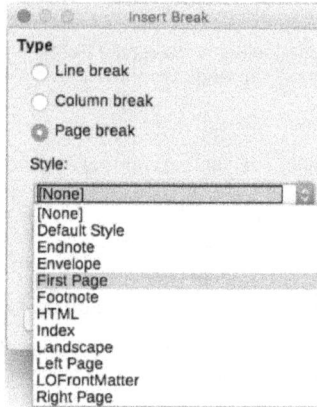
*Figure 172: Choose Page break and select the First Page style*

▶ **Tip**

You can automate these breaks by defining the paragraph style of the chapter's title (usually Heading 1) to include a page break.

### Example: Page with special formatting

Sometimes you may need to insert a page with special formatting, for example a landscape page or a page with more columns. This can also be done with page breaks. Suppose that the current page has the *Default Style* page style.

1) Choose **Insert > Manual Break**.
2) Select the desired page style (say, *Special Page*) in the Insert Break dialog.
3) Type something on this page. Then insert another page break, selecting *Default Style* again.

This concept is illustrated in Figure 173.

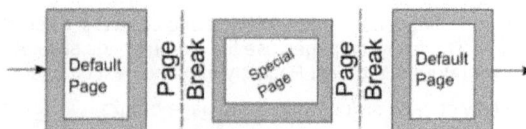
*Figure 173: Inserting a page with special formatting*

## Example: A book chapter sequence of pages

Book chapters typically start on a right-hand page, with the first page of the chapter having a different layout from the rest of the pages. The other pages in the chapter are "mirrored" for double-sided printing. For example, page numbers in the header or footer may be positioned on the outside edge of pages and in this instance a wider margin (allowing for binding) is placed on the inside edge.

Table 7 shows the properties of two page styles (Right Page and Default) set up for a typical book chapter's sequence of pages.

*Table 7: Properties of customized page styles for a book chapter*

| Page Style | Desired effect | Property: setting |
|---|---|---|
| Right Page | First page always on the right (an odd-numbered page) | Page > Page layout > Only right |
| | No header or footer | Header > Header on: Not selected |
| | Top margin of page larger than on other pages | Page > Margins > Top: 6.00cm |
| Default | Mirrored margins | Page > Page layout: Mirrored |
| | Header with page number on the top outside of the page and chapter title in the top middle center of the page | Header > Header on: Selected<br>Header > Header > Same content left/right: Not selected |

Figure 174 illustrates the transitions from the Right Page to Default page styles, with the change of header between left and right pages shown by the # symbol.

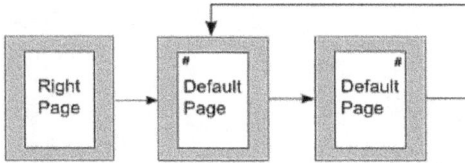

*Figure 174: Right Page and then the Default page style with different headers for alternate pages.*

**Step 1.** Set up the Right Page style.

1) On the Styles and Formatting window, click the Page Styles icon to display a list of page styles.
2) Right-click on Right Page and select **Modify** from the pop-up menu.
3) On the *Organizer* page of the Page Style: Right Page dialog, change Next Style to Default.

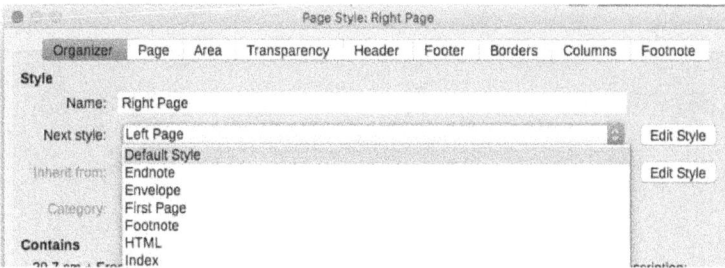

*Figure 175: Specifying the next style after the first page of a chapter*

4) On the *Page* page, specify a larger left margin for binding, and a larger top margin to move the chapter title down the page.

| Margins | | | Layout settings | |
|---------|---|---|-----------------|---|
| Left | 3.00cm | | Page layout | Only right |
| Right | 2.00cm | | Format | 1, 2, 3, ... |
| Top | 6.00cm | | ☐ Register-true | |
| Bottom | 2.50cm | | Reference Style | |

*Figure 176: Setting page margins and layout for the Right Page style*

5) On the *Header* and *Footer* pages, be sure the **Header on** and **Footer on** options are not selected. Click **OK** to save your changes.

**Step 2.** Set up the Default page style.

1) On the Styles and Formatting window, in the list of page styles, right-click on Default and select **Modify** from the pop-up menu.

2) On the *Organizer* page of the Page Style: Default dialog, be sure Next Style is set to Default.

3) On the *Page* page of the Page Style: Default dialog, select **Mirrored** for Page layout and set the Inner and Outer margins to the same width as the Left and Right margins, respectively, on the Right Page style.

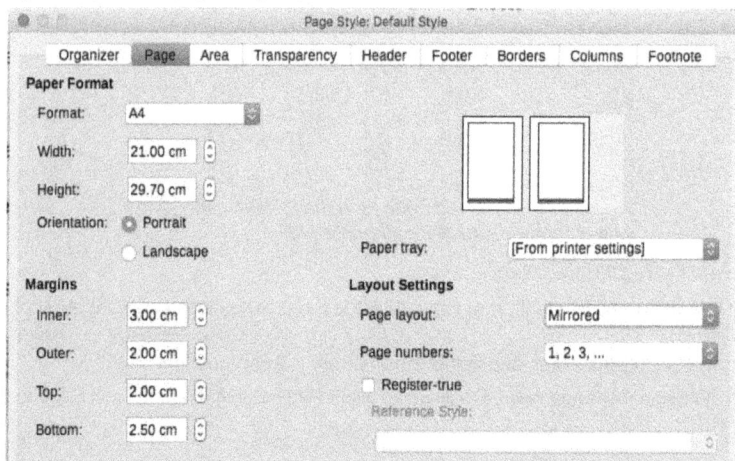

| Page Style: Default Style | | | | | | | | |
|---|---|---|---|---|---|---|---|---|
| Organizer | Page | Area | Transparency | Header | Footer | Borders | Columns | Footnote |

**Paper Format**

| | | |
|---|---|---|
| Format: | A4 | |
| Width: | 21.00 cm | |
| Height: | 29.70 cm | |
| Orientation: | ● Portrait | |
| | ○ Landscape | Paper tray: [From printer settings] |

**Margins** | **Layout Settings**

| | | | | |
|---|---|---|---|---|
| Inner: | 3.00 cm | | Page layout: | Mirrored |
| Outer: | 2.00 cm | | Page numbers: | 1, 2, 3, ... |
| Top: | 2.00 cm | | ○ Register-true | |
| Bottom: | 2.50 cm | | Reference Style: | |

*Figure 177: Setting page margins and layout for the Default page style*

4) On the *Header* page of the Page Style: Default dialog, select the **Header on** option and deselect the **Same content left/right** option. Click **OK** to save your changes.

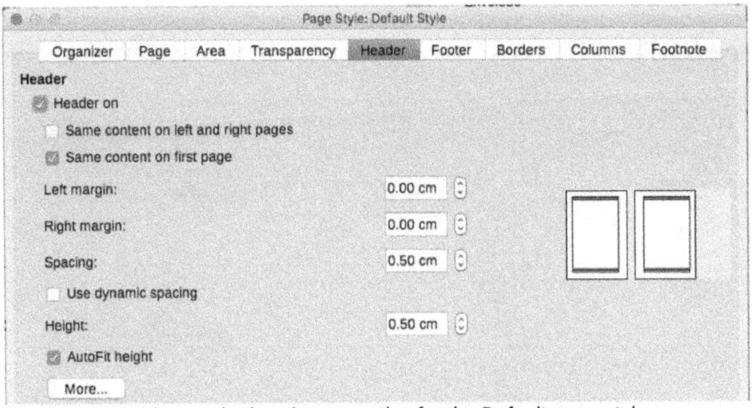

*Figure 178: Setting up the header properties for the Default page style*

**Step 3.** Set up the Heading 1 paragraph style to start on a new right-hand page.

1) In the Styles and Formatting window, on the Paragraph Styles page, right-click on Heading 1 and select **Modify**.

2) On the *Text Flow* page of the Paragraph Style dialog, in the *Breaks* section, select **Insert, With Page Style**, and **Right Page**. Click **OK** to save your changes.

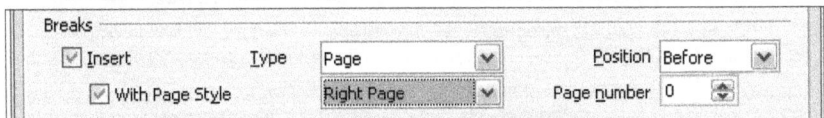

*Figure 179: Setting a paragraph style to start on a page of a selected style*

**Step 4.** Start a new chapter.

Apply the Heading 1 paragraph style to the first paragraph, which is the title of the chapter.

### Note

By default, the Heading 1 paragraph style is assigned to Outline Level 1. The assignment of paragraph styles to outline levels is done through **Tools > Chapter Numbering**.

Step 5. Set up the page headers.

1) On a left page, put the cursor in the header and insert a page number field on the left (**Insert > Fields > Page Number**).

2) Press *Tab* to put the cursor in the middle and insert a Chapter reference:

Press *Ctrl+F2* (or choose **Insert > Fields > Other** from the Menu bar) to display the Fields dialog (Figure 180).

On the Document page, for Type, select Chapter and for Format, select Chapter name. Make sure that Level is set to 1 and then click **Insert**.

3) On a right page, put the cursor in the header, press the *Tab* key, insert a Chapter reference, press *Tab* again, and insert a page number field.

4) If you need to adjust the tab stops for the header, modify the Header paragraph style. Do not manually adjust the tab stops.

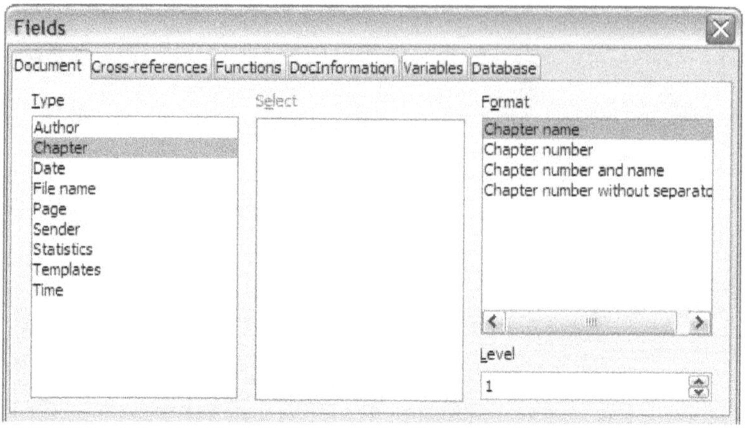

*Figure 180: Inserting a chapter title into the header of a page*

## Applying list styles

List styles define properties such as indentation, numbering style (for example, *1,2,3*; *a,b,c*; or bullets), and punctuation after the number, but they do not by themselves define properties such as font, borders, text flow, and so on. The latter are properties of paragraph styles.

If your list needs to have specific paragraph-style properties, embed the list style into paragraph styles, as explained in Chapter 9. You can then create a list by applying paragraph styles alone.

Writer has two series of predefined list styles, named *List* and *Numbering*. Each series contains five list styles, intended for the different levels of a nested list. As with any style, you can redefine the properties of these styles, for example the numbering or bullet symbol and the indentation. You can also define other list styles in these series or create your own series.

Each of the list styles predefined in Writer has four associated paragraph styles. For more information, see Chapter 9. Much more information about list styles is in Chapter 11, Lists.

If you only want to apply a list style (that is, the numbering or bullet symbol and the indentation), then place the cursor in the paragraph and double-click on the desired list style in the List Styles section of the Styles and Formatting tab in the sidebar.

List styles can have up to ten levels, used for nested lists. To switch from one level to another, use the **Promote One Level** ( ⇐ ) or **Demote One Level** ( ⇒ ) buttons on the Bullets and Numbering toolbar, or press the *Tab* key (one level down) or *Shift+Tab* keys (one level up), or right-click on the list element and select **Promote One Level** or **Demote One Level** from the context menu.

### Restarting or continuing the numbering

When creating more than one numbered list of the same type within the same chapter, Writer applies sequential numbering to all the lists. Sometimes this is what you want (for example, when placing illustrations between the numbered paragraphs), while at other times you want to restart the numbering.

To restart numbering from 1, you can do any of the following:

- Click on the Restart numbering icon on the Bullets and Numbering toolbar.
- Right-click on the first element of the list and choose Restart numbering from the context menu.

- Right-click on the first element of the list, choose Paragraph from the context menu, and go to the Outline & Numbering tab of the Paragraph dialog. In the *Numbering* section, select the options Restart at this paragraph and Start with, and set the number (see Figure 181).

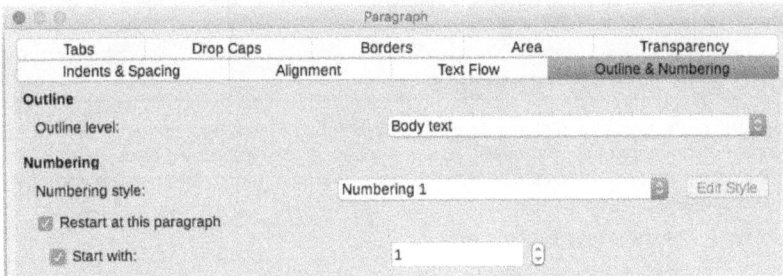

| | | | | |
|---|---|---|---|---|
| Tabs | Drop Caps | Borders | Area | Transparency |
| Indents & Spacing | Alignment | Text Flow | Outline & Numbering | |

**Outline**

Outline level:     Body text

**Numbering**

Numbering style:     Numbering 1     Edit Style

☑ Restart at this paragraph

☑ Start with:     1

*Figure 181: Restarting numbering*

If you find that the numbering does not restart as intended using the first or second method, or if you want to restart from a number greater than 1, use the third method.

When editing a document, you may want to change from restarting numbering to continuing the numbering from a previous list. To do so, right-click on the list element and choose **Continue previous numbering** from the context menu.

## Applying table styles

Table styles define properties such as the font, paragraph spacing, number of columns, borders, and background color.

To apply a table style, position the cursor anywhere in the table, go to the Styles and Formatting tab on the Sidebar, choose Table Styles, then double-click the name of a style on the list.

## Using Fill Format mode

You can use Fill Format mode to apply a style to many areas quickly without having to go back to the Styles and Formatting window and double-click each time. This method is useful for formatting scattered paragraphs, words, or other items with the same style, and it may be easier to use than making multiple selections first and then applying a style to all of them.

1) Open the Styles and Formatting window (Figure 167) and select a style.
2) Click the **Fill Format Mode** button.
3) To apply a paragraph, page, or frame style, hover the mouse over the paragraph, page, or frame and click. To apply a character style, hold down the mouse button while selecting the characters. Clicking on a word applies the character style to that word.
4) Repeat step 3 until you have made all the changes for that style.
5) To quit Fill Format mode, click the button again or press the *Esc* key.

**Caution**

When this mode is active, a right-click anywhere in the document undoes the last Fill Format action. Be careful not to accidentally right-click and undo actions you want to keep.

## Assigning styles to shortcut keys

You can configure shortcut keys to quickly assign styles in your document. Some shortcuts are predefined, such as Ctrl+1 for the *Heading 1* paragraph style and Ctrl+2 for *Heading 2*. You can modify these shortcuts and create your own. See Chapter 21, Customizing Writer, for details.

# Creating and modifying styles

Writer provides many predefined styles, but you may find that they do not fit your preferences. You can build your own library of custom styles to use in place of the predefined ones, or you can modify the existing styles. LibreOffice offers four mechanisms to modify both both predefined and custom (user-created) styles:

- Update a style from a selection.
- Load or copy styles from another document or template.
- Change a style using the Style dialog.
- Use AutoUpdate (paragraph and frame styles only).
- Use AutoFormat (table styles only). See Chapter 13, Tables.

> **Tip**
>
> Any changes made to a style are effective only in the current document. If you want to reuse modified or new styles in other documents, you need to either save the styles in a template (see Chapter 10, Working with Templates) or copy the styles into the other documents, as described in "Load Styles (from a template or document)" on page 185.

## Using New Style from Selection, Update Style, and Load Styles

Styles are part of the document properties, therefore changes made to a style or new styles you create are only available within the document they belong to. Styles always stay with a document. So, for example, if you e-mail a document to another person, the styles go with it.

If you want to reuse modified or new styles in other documents, you need to either save the styles in a template (see Chapter 10) or copy the styles into the document where you want to use them.

The last button in the toolbar of the Styles and Formatting window is a menu button that gives access to three submenu functions: *New Style from Selection*, *Update Style*, and *Load Styles*.

### New Style from Selection

Use the first function of the button to create a new style from the formatting of an object in the current document. For instance, you can change the formatting of a paragraph or frame until it appears as you like, and then you can turn that object's formatting into a new style. This procedure can save time because you do not have to remember all the formatting settings you want, as is necessary when creating a new style with the Style dialog. In addition, unlike when setting the formatting parameters in the pages of dialogs, which you will learn to do later, you can immediately see how the objects will look when formatted with the style you are creating.

Follow these steps to create a new style from a selection:

1) Change the formatting of the object (paragraph, frame, etc.) to your liking.
2) From the buttons at the top of the window, choose the category of style to create (paragraph, character, and so on).
3) In the document, select the item to save as a style.
4) Go back to the Styles and Formatting window and click the **New Style from Selection** button, then select **New Style** from the menu.

5) The Create Style dialog opens. Type a name for the new style. The list shows the names of existing custom styles of the selected type, if any. Click **OK** to save the new style.

### *Update Style (from a selection)*

Let's use paragraph styles as an example.

1) Create a new paragraph (or select an existing paragraph) and edit all the properties you want to alter in the style (such as indentation, font properties, alignment, and others).

### Caution

Make sure that there are uniform properties in this paragraph. For example, if there are two different font sizes in the paragraph which is selected to be used to update the style, that particular property will not be updated.

2) Select the paragraph by clicking anywhere in the paragraph.

3) In the Styles and Formatting window, select the style you want to update (single-click, not double-click) and then click on the **New Style from Selection** button and select **Update Style**.

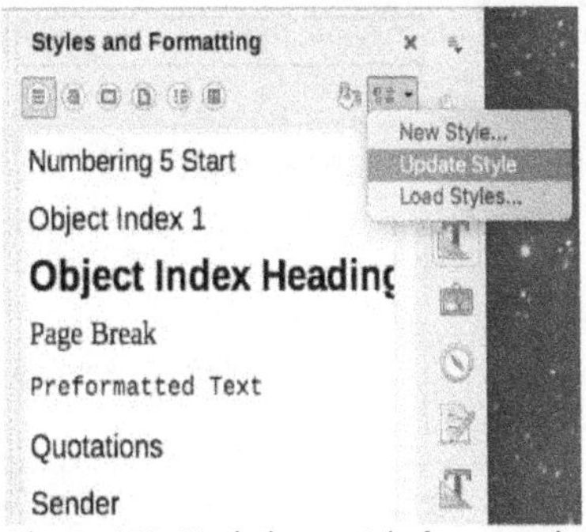

*Figure 182: Updating a style from a selection*

The procedure to update another category of style (character, page, or frame styles) is the same: select the item in question, modify it, select the style you want to update, and choose **Update Style**.

### *Load Styles (from a template or document)*

The last option under the New Style from Selection icon is used to copy styles into the current document by loading them from a template or another document. Using this method, you can copy all styles, or groups of styles, at one time.

1) Open the document to copy styles into.

2) In the Styles and Formatting window, click on the **New Style from Selection** icon and then on **Load Styles** (see Figure 182).

3) In the Load Styles dialog (Figure 183), find and select the template or document to copy styles from.

   Click the **From File** button if the styles you want are contained in a text document rather than a template. In this case, a standard file selection dialog opens up, where you can select the desired document.

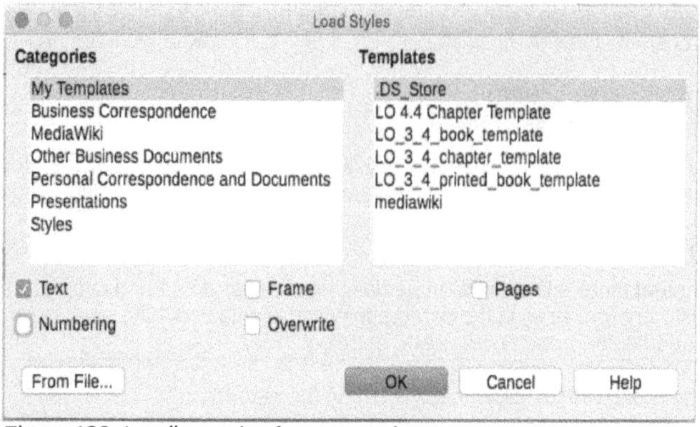

*Figure 183: Loading styles from a template*

4) Select the options for the types of styles to be copied: Text (Paragraph and Character styles), Frame, Pages, Numbering (List styles). If you select **Overwrite**, the styles being copied will replace any styles of the same names in the target document.

5) Click **OK** to copy the styles.

## Drag-and-drop a selection to create a style

Another way to create a new style is to drag-and-drop a text selection into the Styles and Formatting window.

1) Open the Styles and Formatting window.

2) Select the style category you are going to create (for example a character style) using one of the icons in the top left part of the window.

3) Select the object on which you want to base the style and drag it to the Styles and Formatting window. The cursor changes to indicate whether the operation is possible.

4) In the Create Style dialog, type a name for the new style and click **OK** to save the style.

### Note

You cannot use the drag-and-drop method to create a new page style or table style.

## Changing a style using the Style dialog

To change an existing style (but not a table style) using the Style dialog, right-click on the style in the Styles and Formatting window and select **Modify** from the pop-up menu.

The dialog displayed depends on the type of style selected. Each style's dialog has several tabs. The properties on these dialogs are described in Chapter 10.

You can click the **Help** button at any time to bring up the online help where all the options of the current page are briefly described. When you are done, click **OK** to close the dialog.

## Using AutoUpdate

On the Organizer page of the Paragraph Style and Frame Style dialogs is an AutoUpdate option. If this option is selected, then LibreOffice will apply to the style any modification made manually to a paragraph formatted with that style.

## Caution

If you are in the habit of manually overriding styles in your document, be sure that AutoUpdate is not enabled, or you will suddenly find whole sections of your document reformatting unexpectedly.

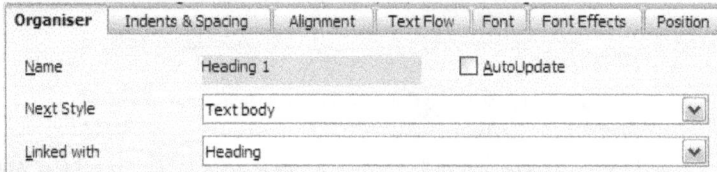

| Organiser | Indents & Spacing | Alignment | Text Flow | Font | Font Effects | Position |
|---|---|---|---|---|---|---|
| Name | Heading 1 | | ☐ AutoUpdate | | | |
| Next Style | Text body | | | | | ▼ |
| Linked with | Heading | | | | | ▼ |

*Figure 184: The Organizer page of the Paragraph Style dialog*

# Deleting styles

It is not possible to delete LibreOffice's predefined styles from a document or template, even if they are not in use. However, custom styles can be deleted.

To delete any unwanted styles, in the Styles and Formatting window select each one to be deleted (hold *Ctrl* while selecting multiple styles), and then right-click on a selected style and select **Delete** in the context menu. If the style is in use, a message appears warning you that the style is in use and asking you to verify that you really want to delete the style.

If the style is not in use, it is deleted immediately without confirmation.

## Caution

If you delete a style that is in use, all objects with that style will return to the style it was based on (inherited from) but retain some of the deleted style's formatting as manual formatting.

## Tip

If an unwanted paragraph style is in use, you can use Find & Replace to replace it with a substitute style before deleting it. See Chapter 3, Working with Text: Advanced, for more information.

# Example: creating and modifying paragraph styles

This section provides an example of a typical use of custom paragraph styles. We will create a *Poem* paragraph style and a *Poem Header* paragraph style, with the following properties:

- *Poem*: Centered, with a font size of 10pt.
- *Poem Heading*: Centered, bold, with a 12pt font size.

In addition, a *Poem Heading* style is to be followed by a *Poem* style. In other words, when you press *Enter*, the next paragraph style in the document changes to *Poem*.

## Note

You may have noticed this behavior already. After you enter a heading using a *Heading* paragraph style and press *Enter*, the next style switches to *Text body*.

## Creating the Poem paragraph style

We will use the *Default* style as a starting point.

1) In the Styles and Formatting window, click the Paragraph Styles button.
2) Right-click *Default Style* and choose **New**.

The Paragraph Style dialog opens, with the Organizer page selected. To create a custom style, you need to configure the top three entries.

| Style fields | Description |
|---|---|
| Name | The name of the style itself, like *Heading 1* or *Text body*.<br>Type the name Poem. |
| Next Style | The style of a paragraph that follows the paragraph that is in *Poem* style. When you press *Enter* while typing text in the *Poem* style, this style is automatically applied to the new paragraph.<br>Set this value to Poem. When you press *Enter*, the text of the new paragraph will remain in the *Poem* style. |
| Inherit from | If the properties of the *Poem* style are inherited from another style, say *Default Style*, then any change in *Default* will affect *Poem*.<br>For our example, this is not the behavior we want. Set this entry to – None –. This means that *Poem* is not inherited from any other style. |

Select the Custom Styles category for new styles. Do not select the AutoUpdate option.

After making these changes, your dialog should look like Figure 188.

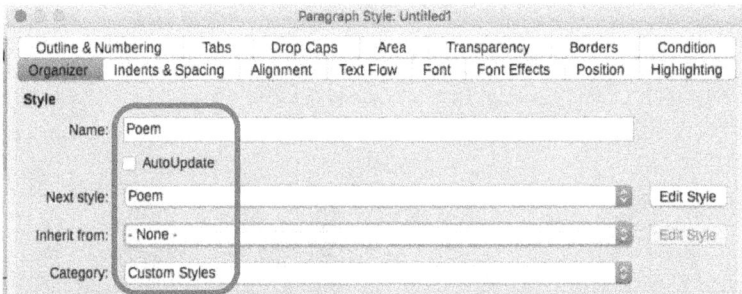

*Figure 185: Initial configuration for the Poem style. Set the first three entries as shown.*

The next step is to configure the alignment and font properties of this style.

- On the *Alignment* page, select the **Center** option.
- On the *Font* page, select the **12pt** font size.

Click **OK** to save the new *Poem* style.

## Creating the Poem Heading style

To create a new *Poem Heading* style, use the same procedure as above, with these changes:

- *Next Style*: Select *Poem*, not *Poem Heading*. When you press *Enter* while typing text in the PoemHeading style, this Poem style is automatically applied to the new paragraph.
- *Inherit from*: Heading.

The dialog should look like Figure 186.

Paragraph Style: Untitled1
Outline & Numbering
Tabs
Drop Caps
Area
Transparency
Borders
Condition
Organizer
Indents & Spacing
Alignment
Text Flow
Font
Font Effects
Position
Highlighting
Style
Name:
Poem Heading
AutoUpdate
Next style:
Poem
Edit Style
Inherit from:
Heading
Edit Style
Category:
Custom Styles


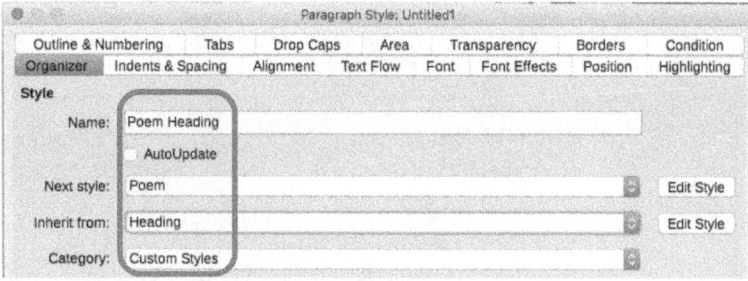

*Figure 186: Settings for the PoemHeading style*

Now set the settings of the new style:

1) On the *Alignment* page, select **Center**.
2) On the *Font* page, choose Bold and size **14pt**.

Click **OK** to save the new *PoemHeading* style.

**Sample poem**

It is a good idea to test out your new styles and see if you are happy with them. Typing a poem using the styles we have just defined should produce the results in Figure 187.

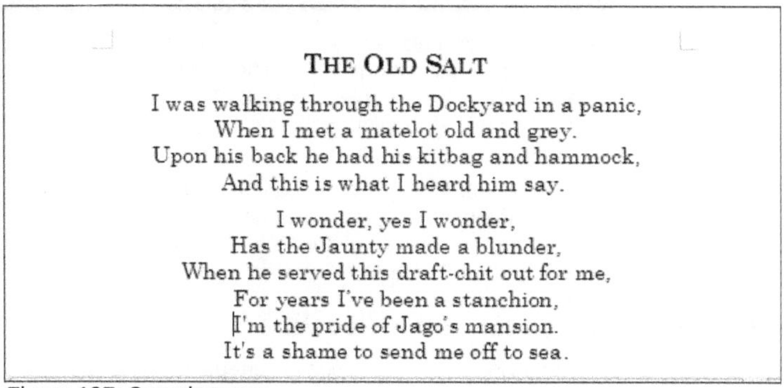

THE OLD SALT
I was walking through the Dockyard in a panic,
When I met a matelot old and grey.
Upon his back he had his kitbag and hammock,
And this is what I heard him say.
I wonder, yes I wonder,
Has the Jaunty made a blunder,
When he served this draft-chit out for me,
For years I've been a stanchion,
I'm the pride of Jago's mansion.
It's a shame to send me off to sea.


*Figure 187: Sample poem*

### *Changing the formatting of your styles*

One of the main advantages of styles is that they allow the document formatting to be changed after the content has been written. For example, suppose you have written a 100-page book of poetry. Then you (or your publisher) decide you don't like the way the poems look.

To learn about reconfiguring styles, we add an indentation to the *Poem* style instead of centering it.

First, set the *Poem* style to left alignment:

1) In the Styles and Formatting window, right-click on *Poem* and select **Modify**.
2) On the *Alignment* page, select **Left**.

Set the indentation:

1) Select the Indents & Spacing tab.
2) Under *Indent*, set the indentation before the text to **0.5in**.

Click **OK**, and you should see the text change. The poem should now look similar to Figure 188. Note in the figure that a third style has been created for the author of the poem.

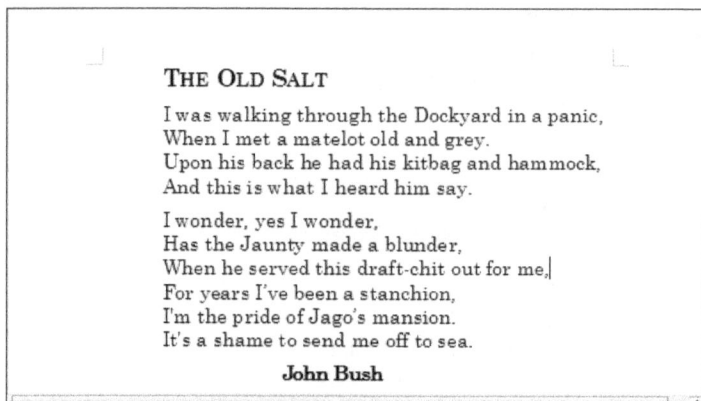

THE OLD SALT

I was walking through the Dockyard in a panic,
When I met a matelot old and grey.
Upon his back he had his kitbag and hammock,
And this is what I heard him say.

I wonder, yes I wonder,
Has the Jaunty made a blunder,
When he served this draft-chit out for me,
For years I've been a stanchion,
I'm the pride of Jago's mansion.
It's a shame to send me off to sea.

**John Bush**

*Figure 188: Final result, using three custom styles*

# Using paragraph styles to define a hierarchy of headings

Paragraph styles are the key to LibreOffice's outline numbering feature. **Tools > Chapter Numbering** defines the hierarchy of headings in a document. The default paragraph styles assigned to outline levels are the heading styles supplied with LibreOffice: *Heading 1*, *Heading 2*, and so on. However, you can substitute any styles you wish, including custom (user-defined) styles.

The headings defined using the chapter numbering feature can be used for more than the table of contents (described in Chapter 15). For example, fields are commonly used to display headings in headers and footers of pages (see Chapter 17, Fields), and Writer can send the outline to Impress to use as the basis for a presentation (see the *Impress Guide* for details).

## Choosing paragraph styles for outline levels

If you are using the default heading styles for the headings in your outline, and you do not want to use heading numbering, you do not need to do anything on the Chapter Numbering dialog. The default outline numbering scheme uses the default heading styles (Heading 1, Heading 2, and so on).

To use custom styles in place of one or more of the default heading styles:

1) Choose **Tools > Chapter Numbering** to open the Chapter Numbering dialog (Figure 189).
2) Click the number in the *Level* box corresponding to the heading for which you want to change the paragraph style.
3) In the *Numbering: Paragraph Style* section, choose from the drop-down list the paragraph style you want to assign to that heading level. In this example, you might choose My Heading 1 to replace Heading 1 and for Level 2, My Heading 2 to replace Heading 2.
4) Repeat for each numbering level that you want to change. Click **OK** when done.

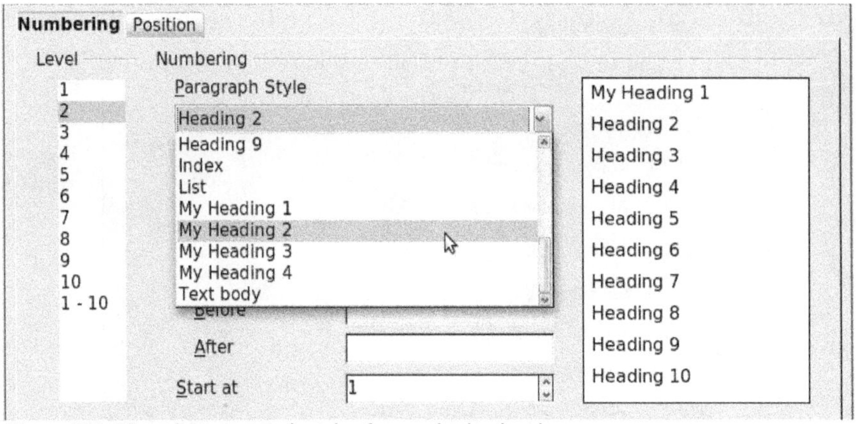

*Figure 189: Choosing paragraph styles for numbering levels*

## Assigning outline levels to other styles

In Writer, you can assign an outline level to any paragraph style. This feature enables you to create a table of contents that includes those headings along with the headings using styles listed in the Chapter Numbering dialog. For example, you might use a different sequence of styles for annexes (appendixes), but you want the appendix headings and subheadings to appear in the TOC at the same levels as the chapter headings and subheadings.

To assign an outline level to a paragraph style, go to the Outline & Numbering page for the style, and select the required outline level from the drop-down list. Click **OK** to save this change.

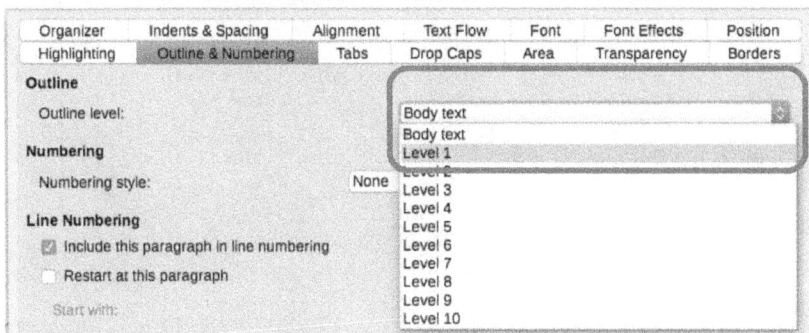

*Figure 190: Specifying an outline level for a paragraph style*

## Setting up heading numbering

If you want one or more heading levels to be numbered, many choices are available; this example defines a scheme to create headings that look like those in Figure 190.

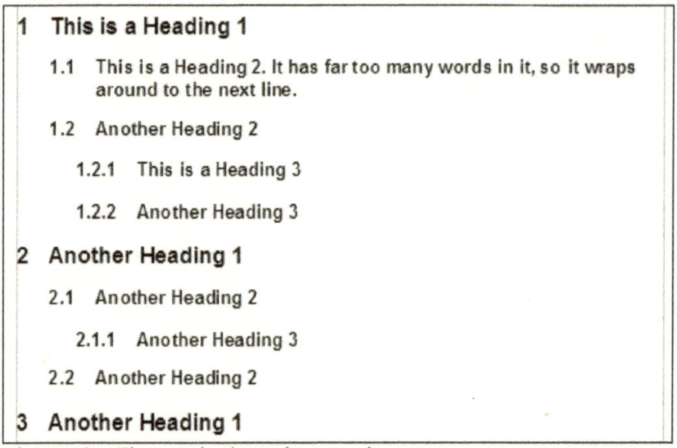

**1 This is a Heading 1**

   1.1   This is a Heading 2. It has far too many words in it, so it wraps around to the next line.

   1.2   Another Heading 2

      1.2.1   This is a Heading 3

      1.2.2   Another Heading 3

**2 Another Heading 1**

   2.1   Another Heading 2

      2.1.1   Another Heading 3

   2.2   Another Heading 2

**3 Another Heading 1**

*Figure 191: The numbering scheme to be set up*

Use the *Numbering* page of the Chapter Numbering dialog to define the numbering scheme and its appearance. Figure 192 shows the default settings.

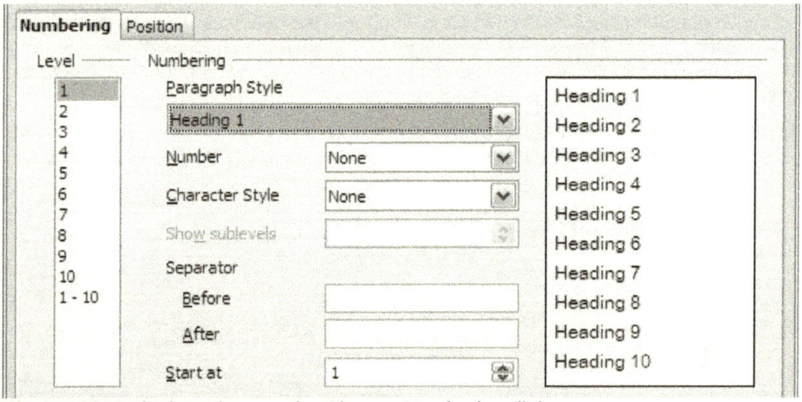

*Figure 192: Default settings on the Chapter Numbering dialog*

1) In the *Level* list, choose 1. In the *Number* list, choose 1, 2, 3, .... The result is shown in the preview box on the right in Figure 193.

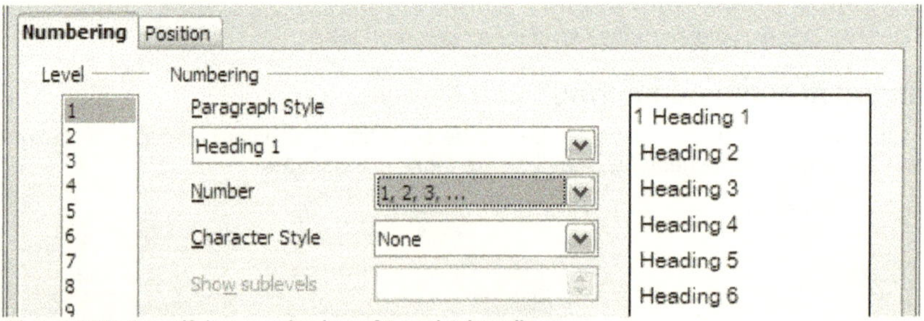

*Figure 193: Specifying numbering of Level 1 headings*

2) In the *Level* list, choose 2. In the *Number* list, choose 1, 2, 3, .... The *Show sublevels* list is now active; it should show 2 (if not, choose 2). The result is shown in Figure 194.

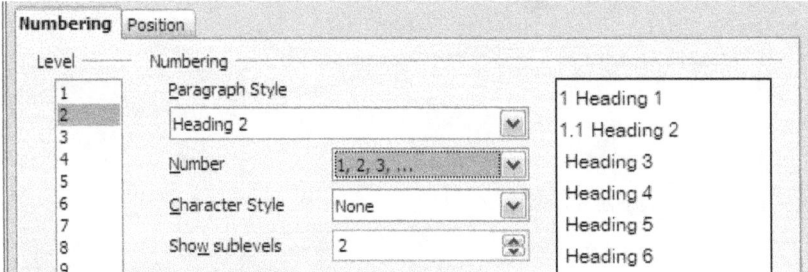
Figure 194: Specifying numbering of Level 2 headings

3) In the *Level* list, choose 3. In the *Number* list, choose 1, 2, 3, .... The *Show sublevels* list should show 3 (if not, choose 3). The result is shown in Figure 195.

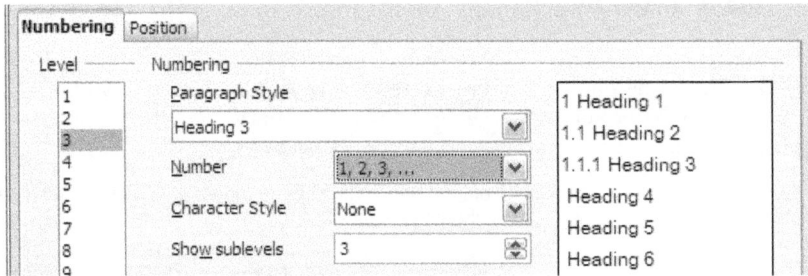
Figure 195: Specifying numbering of Level 3 headings

These choices produce the layout shown in Figure 196.

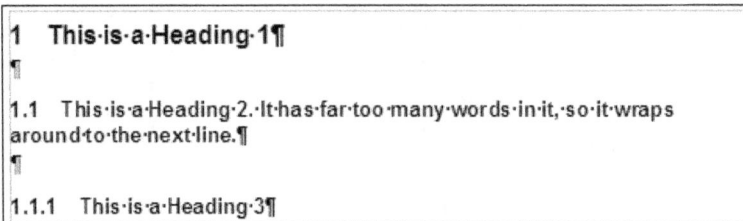
Figure 196: Results of numbering choices for headings

## Setting up the indentation of headings

Whether or not the headings are numbered, you may want to change some of their formatting. For example, you may want the second-level and third-level headings to be indented from the margin. For numbered headings, you may also want the second line of long headings to line up with the first word of the heading, not the number. For these changes, use the *Position* page of the Chapter Numbering dialog.

As an example, we will change the position and wrapping of a Heading 2:

1) In the *Level* list on the left, choose 2. Change the values for *Numbering followed by, at* and *Aligned at*, as shown in Figure 197. You may want to use a different value. This indents the entire heading but does not affect the way long headings wrap around (see Figure 198).

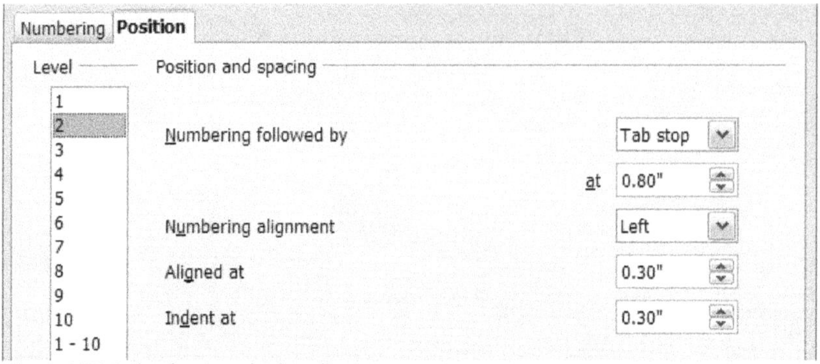

*Figure 197: Indenting Level 2 headings*

## 1    This·is·a·Heading·1¶

¶

### 1.1    This·is·a·Heading·2.·It·has·far·too·many·words·in·it,·so·it·wraps·around·to·the·next·line.¶

*Figure 198: Result of changes to indentation of Level 2 headings*

2) To change the wrapping behavior of long headings, change *Indent at* to a larger value, as shown in Figure 199. The result is shown in Figure 200.

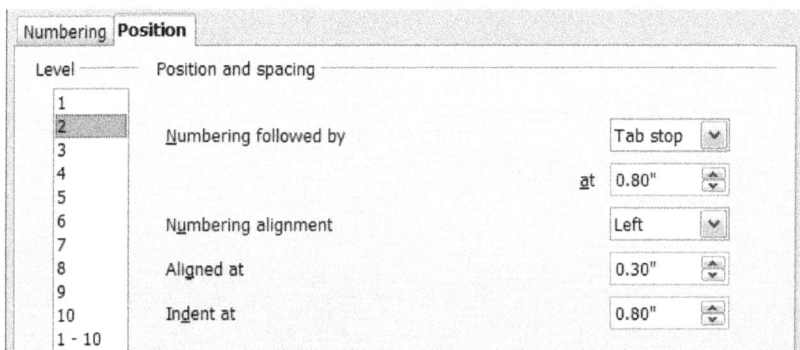

*Figure 199: Wrapping long headings*

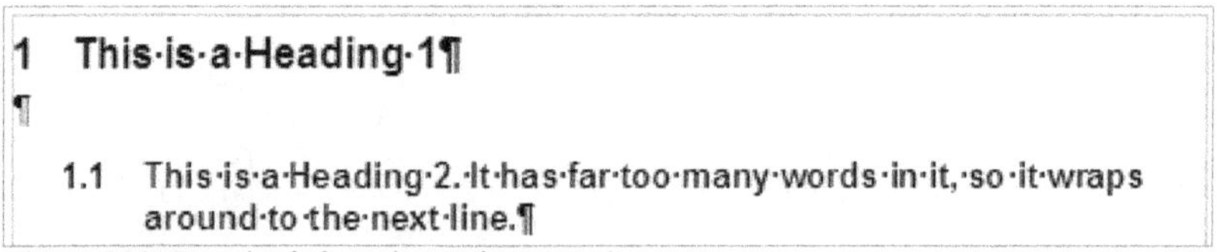

## 1    This·is·a·Heading·1¶

¶

### 1.1    This·is·a·Heading·2.·It·has·far·too·many·words·in·it,·so·it·wraps·around·to·the·next·line.¶

*Figure 200: Result of changing Indent at value*

# LibreOffice

Chapter 9
*Working with Styles*

# Introduction

Chapter 8, Introduction to Styles, describes the basics of how to use, apply, and manage styles. This chapter gives a more detailed description of how to create or modify some styles, using the many options available on the various pages of the Style dialog. It explains how these options affect the appearance of the style and how to use them efficiently.

The Style dialogs share many of the same pages as the manual formatting dialogs, so this chapter can also help you apply manual formatting (though you do not need that if you use styles).

# Creating custom (new) styles

In addition to using the predefined styles provided by LibreOffice, you can add new custom (user-defined) styles. In Chapter 8, two methods are given for creating a new style: the drag-and-drop approach and the **New Style from Selection** icon in the Styles and Formatting window.

These methods are convenient because you can check the visual effects that the style produces before creating it. However, you have a somewhat reduced amount of control on style (particularly when it comes to organizing them). The method described in this chapter, therefore, concerns the use of the Style dialog.

### Note

Table styles are created in a different way, as described in Chapter 13, Tables.

## Style dialog

Open the Styles and Formatting window. Select the category of style you want to create by clicking on the appropriate button in the top part of the Styles and Formatting window. For example, select the third button from the left to create a new frame style.

Right-click in the window and select **New** from the context menu. The dialog that is displayed depends on the type of style you selected. Many of the pages are the same as those used when applying manual formatting. Therefore, if you are familiar with manual formatting, you may already know how to use most of the options.

### Tip

The dialogs used to create a new style and to modify an existing style are mostly the same, but with one exception: conditional styles have a different dialog. See "Working with conditional paragraph styles" on page 207.

## Organizer page

The *Organizer* page, shown in Figure 201, is common to all style categories (except Table styles), with only small differences between them. Therefore, it is described only once.

Depending on the style you are creating, you will find the following fields on this page:

- **Name:** present on all the categories. Use this field to name the style you are creating.
- **AutoUpdate:** only present for paragraph and frame styles. If this option is checked, then Writer will apply any manual modification to a paragraph or frame formatted with that style to the style itself.

## Caution

If you are in the habit of manually overriding styles in your document, be sure that AutoUpdate is not enabled, or you may suddenly find whole sections of your document reformatted unexpectedly.

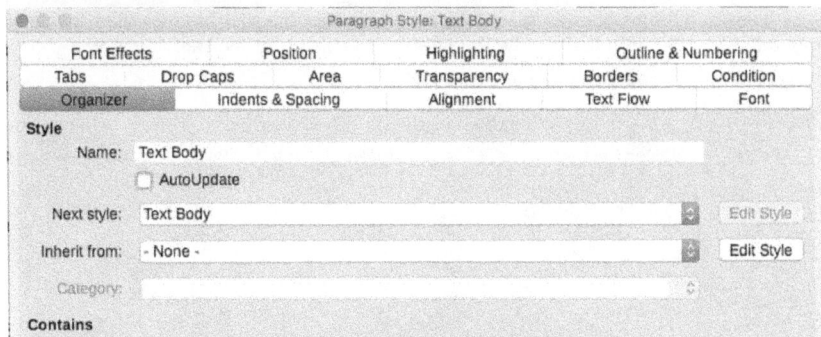

| | | | | |
|---|---|---|---|---|
| Font Effects | Position | Highlighting | Outline & Numbering | |
| Tabs | Drop Caps | Area | Transparency | Borders | Condition |
| Organizer | Indents & Spacing | Alignment | Text Flow | Font |

**Style**

Name: Text Body

☐ AutoUpdate

Next style: Text Body     Edit Style

Inherit from: - None -     Edit Style

Category:

**Contains**

*Figure 201: The Organizer page displayed when a new Paragraph style is created*

- **Next Style:** only available for paragraph and page styles. Use it to specify which style will be applied to the next element of the same type. For example, a left page style is usually followed by a right page style, a first page style followed by a left page style, a heading followed by body text, and so on.

- **Inherit from:** available for paragraph, character, and frame styles; it determines the position of the style in the hierarchy. All the starting properties of the new style are inherited (copied) from the style specified here.

- **Category:** available for all styles; use it to associate the new style with one of the categories. Note that you cannot change the category of the predefined styles. Setting this field is useful when filtering the contents of the Styles and Formatting window.

- **Contains:** shows a summary of the properties of the style.

## Style inheritance

When creating a new paragraph style or a new character style, you can use an existing style as a starting point for its settings. In this sense, LibreOffice links the styles together.

When style settings are inherited, a change in the parent style affects every style inherited from it. To see the connections between styles, switch to the Hierarchical view in the Styles and Formatting window filter. For example, every Heading style (such as Heading 1, Heading 2) is inherited from a style called Heading. This relationship is illustrated in Figure 202.

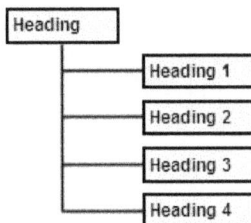

*Figure 202: Hierarchical view of inheritance in styles*

Inheritance is a method to create "families" of styles in which you can change their properties simultaneously. For example, if you decide that all the headings should be green (such as in this guide), you only need to change the font color of the parent style to achieve the desired result. However, changes made to a parameter of the parent style do not override changes previously made to the same parameter in the child styles. For example, if you changed the Heading 2 font color to green, a change of the font color of the Heading style (the parent style) to red will not affect the Heading 2 font color.

You can easily check which properties are specific to a style by looking at the *Contains* section of the Organizer page. If you want to reset the properties of a child style to that of the parent style, click the **Standard** button located at the bottom of each Paragraph and Character style dialog.

### Example: Changing a property of a parent style

Suppose that you want to change the font of not only Heading 1 or Heading 2, but all headings.

Open the Styles and Formatting window, select the *Paragraph Styles* category, right-click on **Heading**, then select **Modify** to open the Paragraph Style dialog for the Heading style.

Select the *Font* tab, then select a font and click **OK**.

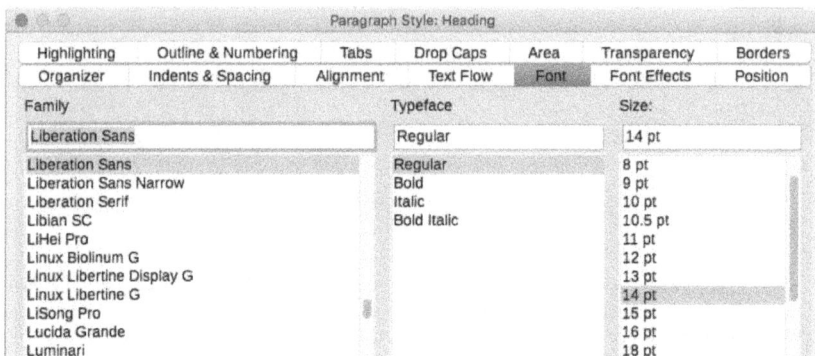

*Figure 203: Select the Heading font*

Now, the fonts of all the heading styles (Heading 1 through Heading 10) are changed in a single operation. Figure 204 shows on the left a document using the headings 1, 2 and 3 and on the right the same document after changes have been made to the Heading style.

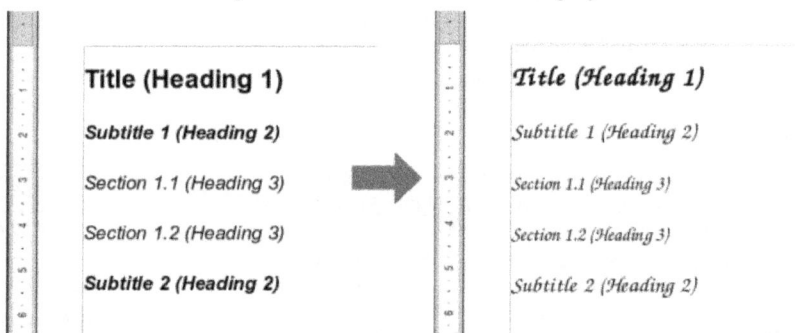

*Figure 204: Effect of changing the Heading style font*

## Working with paragraph styles

Although this section describes most of the parameters scattered over the tabbed pages shown in Figure 203, you do not need to configure them all. In most cases, you need to modify only a few attributes, particularly if you link styles or base the new style on a similar one.

# Indents & Spacing page

On the *Indents & Spacing* page (Figure 205), you can set up the parameters that affect the position of the paragraph on the page and the spacing between lines and between this paragraph and the paragraphs above and below.

Use the Indent section of the page to set up the indentation, using these parameters:

- **Before text:** controls the space in the selected unit of measurement between the left margin of the page and the leftmost part of the paragraph area. Entering a negative value results in the text starting on the left of the margin. This may be useful in situations where your left margin is quite wide, but you want the headings to be centered in the page.
- **After text:** controls the space in the selected unit of measurement between the right margin of the page and the rightmost part of the paragraph area. Entering a negative value results in the text extending into the right margin of the page.
- **First line:** enter the offset in this box (either positive or negative) of the first line of the paragraph relative to the paragraph area. A positive value increases the indentation of the first line, while a negative value makes the first line start to the left of the paragraph area.
- **Automatic:** check this box to allow Writer to automatically control the indentation of the first line. The value is calculated by Writer on the basis of the font size and other parameters.

Use the *Spacing* section of the page to determine the amount of vertical space above and below the paragraph. It is customary to include some "space above" in heading styles so that they are separated from the text body of the previous section without the need to insert empty paragraphs. Spacing between paragraphs is also normal in certain types of documents. The body text style of this guide is configured to leave some space between consecutive paragraphs.

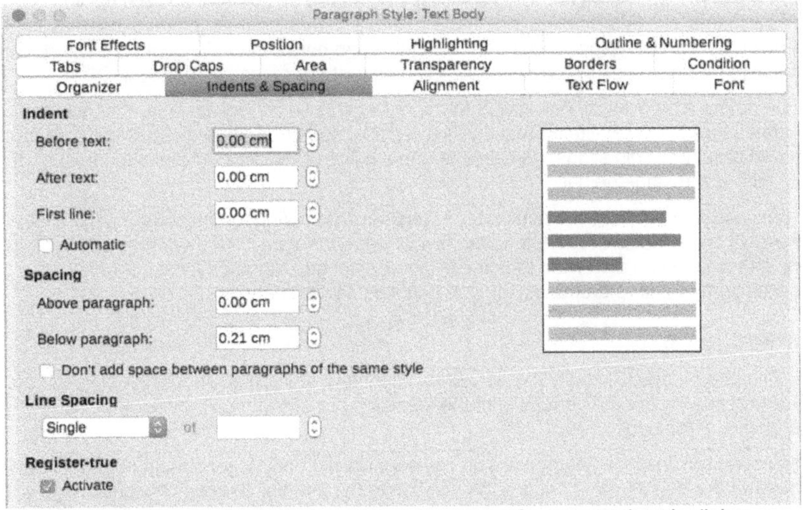

*Figure 205: Settings on the Indents and Spacing page of a paragraph style dialog*

You can select the option to remove space between paragraphs of the same style.

The spacing between paragraphs does not affect the spacing between lines, which is controlled using the drop-down box in the Line spacing section. You can select one of the following values:

- **Single:** the default setting—applies a single line spacing to the paragraph. This is calculated automatically based on the font size.

- **1.15 lines**: sets the line spacing to 1.15 lines. This small increase often improves the appearance of text without using a lot of vertical space.
- **1.5 lines**: sets the line spacing to 1.5 lines.
- **Double**: sets the line spacing to 2 lines.
- **Proportional**: this value activates the edit box next to the drop-down list where you can enter a percentage value. 100% means a single line spacing, 200% double line spacing and so on.
- **At least**: this choice activates the edit box next to the drop-down list, where you can enter the minimum value (in your selected unit of measurement) to be used for the line spacing.
- **Leading**: if this is selected, you can control the height of the vertical space between the base lines of two successive lines of text, by entering a value, which is summed with the value of single line spacing, into the edit box.
- **Fixed**: this choice activates the edit box next to the drop-down list, where you can enter the exact value of the line spacing.

▶ **Tip**

When using different font sizes in the same paragraph, the line spacing will be uneven, as Writer automatically calculates the optimal value. To obtain evenly spaced lines, select **Fixed** or **At least** in the drop-down list and a value that is large enough to create a spacing between the lines sufficient to account for the largest font size used.

The last parameter on this page is Register-true. This is a typography term used in printing; it refers to the congruent imprint of the lines within a type area on the front and the back side of book pages, newspaper pages, and magazine pages. The register-true feature make these pages easier to read by preventing gray shadows from shining through between the lines of text. The register-true term also refers to lines in adjacent text columns that are of the same height.

When you define a paragraph, Paragraph Style, or Page Style as register-true, the base lines of the affected characters are aligned to a invisible vertical page grid, regardless of font size or of the presence of graphics. This aligns the baseline of each line of text to a vertical document grid, so that each line is the same height.

To use this feature, you must first activate the Register-true option for the current page style; then the Reference style and all the styles hierarchically dependent on it will have the Activate Register-True box selected. If you also want to activate the vertical grid for other styles (or not apply it to styles dependent on the reference style), you can specifiy that here.

## Alignment page

Use the *Alignment* page to modify the horizontal alignment of the text, choosing between Left, Right, Center, and Justified. The results of the selection are shown in a preview window on the right-hand side of the page.

When selecting the Justified alignment, you can also decide how Writer should treat the last line of the paragraph. By default, Writer aligns the last line to the left, but you can choose to align it to the center or to justify it (meaning that the words on the last line will be spaced in order to occupy it fully). If you have selected to justify the last line and select the Expand single word option, then whenever the last line of a justified paragraph consists of a single word, this word is stretched by inserting spaces between characters so that it occupies the full length of the line.

The alignment page is also used to control the Text to Text vertical alignment—useful when you have mixed font sizes on the same row. Choose the element of the fonts on the line that will be aligned between Automatic, Baseline, Top, Middle, Bottom. Refer to Figure 206 for a visual representation of these reference points.

*Figure 206: Text to text vertical alignment: Baseline, Top, Middle, Bottom*

## Text flow options for paragraph styles

The *Text Flow* page (Figure 207), has three parts: Hyphenation, Breaks, and Options.

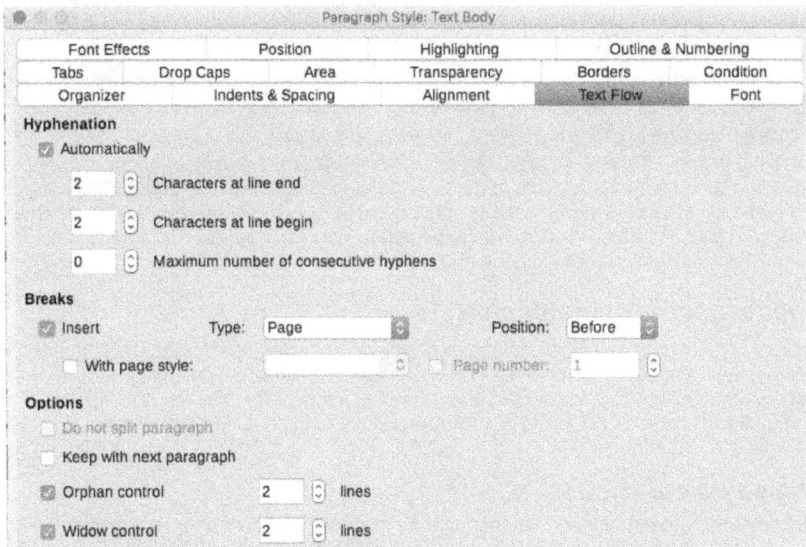

*Figure 207: The options on the Text Flow page of the Paragraph Style dialog*

With *Hyphenation* selected, three parameters are available:

- **Characters at line end**: controls the minimum number of characters to be left on a line before inserting a hyphen.
- **Characters at line begin**: controls the minimum number of characters that can be placed at the beginning of a new line following a hyphen.
- **Maximum number of consecutive hyphens**: controls the number of consecutive lines that terminate with a hyphen.

If you prefer Writer to automatically control the hyphenation, select the **Automatically** option.

In the *Breaks* section, you can require a paragraph to start on a new page or column, as well as specify the position of the break, the style of the new page, and the new page number. A typical use for this option is to ensure that the first page of a new chapter always starts on a new (usually right-hand) page.

To always start a new page with a particular style, choose the following settings:

1) In the *Breaks* section, select **Insert**. Make sure that *Type* is set to **Page** and *Position* is set to **Before**.
2) Select **With Page Style** and choose the page style from the list.
3) To continue page numbering from the previous chapter, leave **Page number** set at 0. To restart each chapter's page numbering at 1, set Page number to 1. Click **OK**.

**Note**

> If you want the first page of a new chapter to always start on a right page, make sure that the page style for the first chapter page is set for the right page only by making this selection in the **Layout settings** field on the *Page* tab of the Page Style dialog.

The *Options* section of the *Text Flow* page provides settings to control what happens when a paragraph does not fit on the bottom of a page:

- **Do not split paragraph:** If a paragraph does not fit on the bottom of one page, the entire paragraph moves to the top of the next page.
- **Keep with next paragraph:** Use for headings or the lead-in sentence to a list, to ensure that it is not the last paragraph on a page.
- **Orphan control** and **Widow control:** Widows and orphans are typographic terms. An orphan is the first line of a paragraph alone at the bottom of a page or column. A widow is the last line of a paragraph that appears alone at the top of the next page or column. Use these options to allow paragraphs to split across pages or columns but require at least two or more lines to remain together at the bottom or top of a page or column. You can specify how many lines must remain together.

## Font options for the paragraph style

Three pages of the Paragraph Style dialog are dedicated to settings controlling the appearance of the typeface: the *Font*, *Font Effects*, and *Position* pages. The use of the first two pages is straightforward. Many of the options used when creating a character style are discussed in "Creating a new character style" on page 209. Options that can be used when creating a paragraph style are described here.

### *Specifying a relative font size*

If you are creating a style based on another style (linked style), you can specify a font size relative to that other style—either as a percentage or as a plus or minus point value (–2pt or +5pt). Relative font sizes are commonly used for Web pages.

For example, the paragraph style Heading 1 is based on the paragraph style Heading. The font size of the paragraph style Heading is 14pt, and the font size of paragraph style Heading 1 is specified as 130%. Thus, the resultant font size of text in a paragraph formatted with the Heading 1 paragraph style is 14pt times 130% = 18.2pt.

To specify a percentage font size: in the Paragraph Style dialog, select the *Font* tab. In the **Size** box, enter the percentage amount followed by the symbol % (see Figure 208). Similarly, you can enter a plus or minus sign followed by the number of points to be added or subtracted from the base font size.

To change from a relative font size back to an absolute font size, enter the desired font size in points followed by the letters *pt*.

It is also possible to use a percentage font size for character styles.

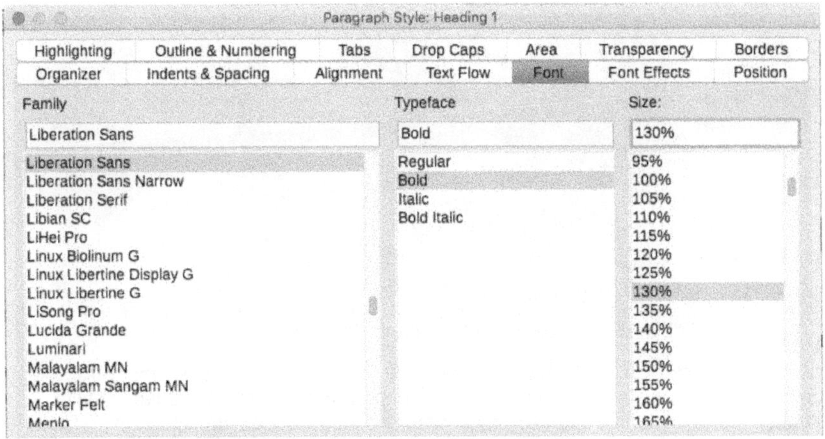

*Figure 208: Selecting a type size based on a percentage*

### Selecting a language for a paragraph style

The language selected for a document (on **Tools > Options > Language Settings > Languages**) determines the dictionary used for spell checking, thesaurus, hyphenation, the decimal and thousands delimiter used, and the default currency format.

Within the document, you can apply a separate language to any paragraph style. This setting has priority over the language of the whole document. On the *Font* page of the Paragraph Style dialog, languages with installed dictionaries are marked in the Language list by a small ABC icon (Figure 209). When checking spelling, Writer will use the correct dictionary for paragraphs with this style. If you write documents in multiple languages, you can use the linked styles to create two paragraph styles that differ only in the language option. If you then want to change some of the other properties of the paragraph style, all you need do is to change the parent style.

To insert occasional words in a different language and avoid their being picked by mistake with the check-spelling function, it is more convenient to use a character style, as discussed in "Creating a new character style" on page 209.

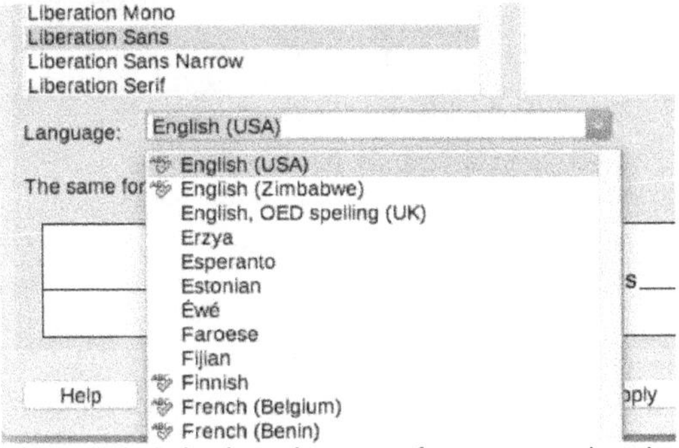

*Figure 209: Selecting a language for a paragraph style*

## Options for positioning text

The *Position* page of the Paragraph Style dialog collects all the options that affect the position of the text on the screen or printed page.

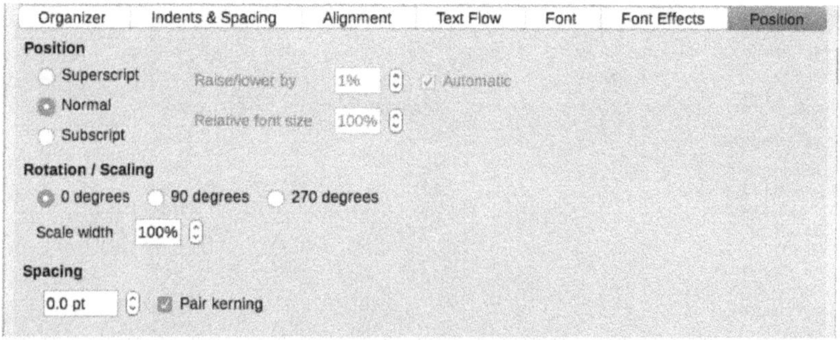
Organizer
Indents & Spacing
Alignment
Text Flow
Font
Font Effects
Position
Position
Superscript
Normal
Subscript
Raise/lower by
1%
Automatic
Relative font size
100%
Rotation / Scaling
0 degrees
90 degrees
270 degrees
Scale width
100%
Spacing
0.0 pt
Pair kerning

*Figure 210: The position page of the Paragraph Style dialog*

Use the *Position* section to control the appearance of superscripts and subscripts. However, you will normally apply superscript and subscripts to groups of characters rather than to entire paragraphs. Therefore, it is strongly recommended to change these parameters only when defining a character style and, instead, leave the default settings for the paragraph styles.

The second section of the *Position* page controls the rotation of the paragraph area. Two common uses for rotated paragraphs are:

- To put portrait headers and footers on a landscape page
- To fit headings above narrow table columns (as shown in Figure 211)

| *This is long* | *Another long heading* | *A rotated heading* | *Another heading* | *Another heading* | *Another heading* | *Another heading* |
|---|---|---|---|---|---|---|
| | | | | | | |
| | | | | | | |
| | | | | | | |

*Figure 211: A table with rotated headings*

The Scale width box controls the percentage of the font width by which to compress or stretch the rotated text horizontally; that is, from the first character to the last.

Chapter 6, Formatting Pages: Advanced, describes how to create portrait headers and footers on landscape pages by rotating characters. You can achieve the same effect by defining a separate header or footer paragraph style specifically for landscape pages.

### *Example: Rotating the text in a paragraph style*

As an example, we will apply rotated table headings to a pre-existing table.

1) Create a new paragraph style. Name it Table Heading Rotated.
2) On the *Position* page of the Paragraph Style dialog, in the *Rotation / scaling* section, select 90 degrees. Click **OK** to save the new style.
3) Select the heading row of the table and apply the new style. Any text in the cells of the heading row is now rotated.

4) If the headings are aligned to the top of the cells, you may want to change the alignment to the bottom of the cells, as shown in Figure 211. To do this, click the Bottom button on the Table toolbar or select Format > Alignment > Bottom from the main menu.

### Spacing options

Use the *Spacing* section of the Position page to control the spacing between individual characters in the paragraph. When selecting an option other than default in the drop-down menu, use the edit box to enter the value in points by which you want to expand or condense the text.

The **Pair Kerning** option (selected by default) increases or decreases the amount of space between certain pairs of letters to improve the overall appearance of the text. Kerning automatically adjusts the character spacing for specific letter combinations. Kerning is only available for certain font types and, for printed documents, only works if your printer supports it.

*Figure 212: Kerning disabled (left) and enabled (right)*

## Controlling tab stops

Although borderless tables are generally considered a much better solution to space out material across a page, in some situations tabs are sufficient to do what you need, with the added advantages of being simpler to manage and quicker to apply.

### Caution

If you need to use tabs, and you will be sending a document to other people, do not use the default tab stops. If the recipients of the document have defined default tab stops that are different from the ones you are using, the paragraph may look very different on their machines. Instead, define the tab stops explicitly in the paragraph or the paragraph style; then you can be sure that everyone will see the same layout.

To define tab stops in your paragraph style, use the Tabs page, shown in Figure 213. Here you can choose the type of tab: left, right, centered, or decimal; the character to be used as a decimal point; and the fill character—the characters that appear between the end of the text before the tab and the beginning of the text after the tab. You can also create a custom fill character by entering it in the corresponding box. Common use of a fill character is adding dots between a heading and a page number in a table of contents or underscore character when creating a form to fill in.

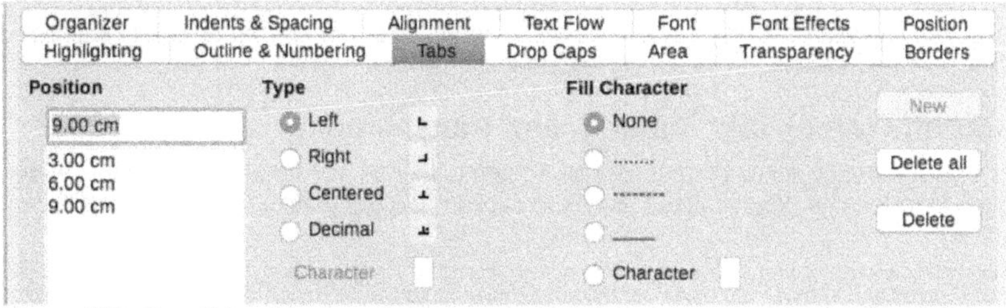

*Figure 213: Specifying tab stops for a paragraph style*

To create a new tab stop, specify its position relative to the left margin, the type of tab, and the fill character and click the New button. The new tab stop is then listed in the Position box on the left. Unfortunately, the only way to modify the position of a tab stop is to create a new one in the desired position and delete the old one using the buttons on the right-hand side of the page.

It is not possible to define tabs that exceed the page margin. In the rare cases where that may be needed, use a borderless table instead.

## Outline & Numbering page

Use the *Outline & Numbering* page to assign an outline level to any paragraph style, as described in "Assigning outline levels to other styles" in Chapter 8. This feature enables you to create a table of contents that includes those paragraphs along with the headings using styles listed in **Tools > Chapter Numbering**.

You can also use this page to associate a paragraph style with a list style. Refer to Chapter 12, Lists: Tips and Tricks, for additional information, as well as an example.

## Setting up a drop cap

If you want your paragraph to use drop caps (usually this is suitable for a first paragraph style), then you can predefine the properties in the *Drop Caps* page of the paragraph style dialog. Select the **Display drop caps** option to enable the other choices: the number of lines occupied, the number of characters to enlarge (if you want the whole first word, check the corresponding box), and the space between the drop caps and the text.

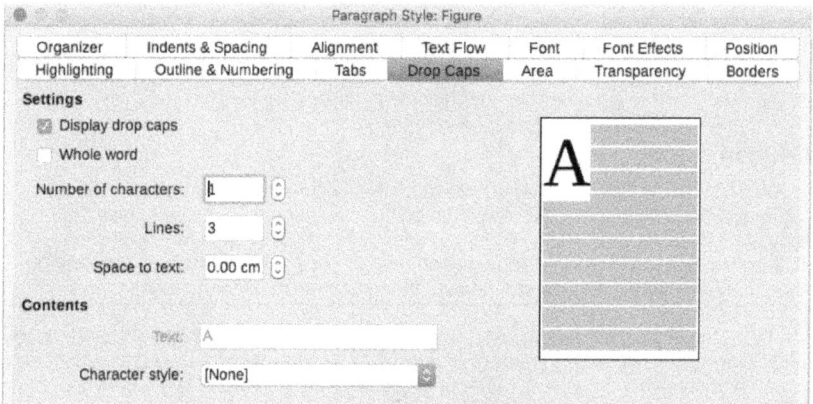

*Figure 214: Options for adding a drop cap to the paragraph style*

Drop caps use the same font and have the same properties as the rest of the paragraph; however, you can easily modify their appearance by creating a specific character style and using it. For example, you may want the drop caps to be of a different color or apply an outline effect. Select the character style you want to use in the corresponding drop-down menu.

## Background (area), highlighting, and transparency

Adding a background color or graphic to a paragraph is a good way to make it stand out without having to insert a frame. You can customize the background using the *Area* page of the Paragraph Style dialog.

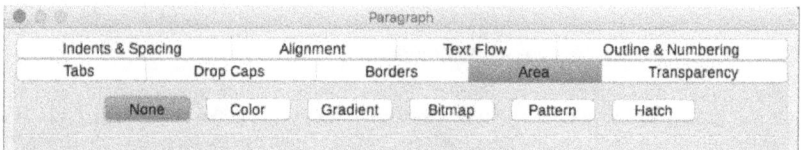

*Figure 215: Types of fill for paragraph backgrounds*

You may want to pay attention to the following points when working with the Area page:

- In case you do not find the desired color in the list of predefined ones, you can define your own by selecting **Tools > Options > LibreOffice > Colors**.
- You can use a bitmap, hatching, pattern, or gradient instead of a solid color as background.
- Different backgrounds can be selected for the paragraph area and for the text in the paragraph. Use the *Highlighting* page for the text. Figure 216 shows the difference.
- The area treatment is only applied to the paragraph area. If you have defined an indented paragraph, the space between the paragraph and the margin does not have the paragraph's background color.

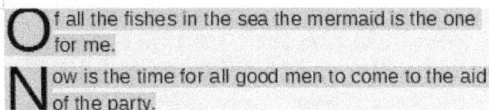

*Figure 216: Different Area and Highlighting colors*

On the *Transparency* page, you can choose the transparency options for the selected background. Values range from 0% (fully opaque) to +100% (fully transparent).

## Borders

Borders are often used to set off paragraphs from the text without using a frame, or to separate header and footer areas from the main text area (such as in this guide), and to provide decorative elements in some heading styles. Consider the following points:

- Watch out for the effects that the spacing between borders and paragraph area produces on indentations and tabulations.
- If you want the border to be drawn around multiple paragraphs, leave the **Merge with next paragraph** option at the bottom of the page selected.

See Chapter 4, Formatting Text, for more about the *Borders* page.

# Working with conditional paragraph styles

A conditional paragraph style is another way of formatting text differently in different parts of a document. In some cases, you may find it saves time to use conditional styles rather than switching between styles as you type.

Making a paragraph style conditional means it changes its formatting depending on where it is used. For example, you may want the style MyTextBody to be black by default but turn white when inside a frame with a blue background.

Probably the most common use for conditional formatting is with single-style outlining. Single-style outlining is a type of outline numbering designed with a Numbering style, rather than with **Tools > Chapter Numbering**. Instead of using different styles, it changes the number formatting whenever you press the Tab key to create a subordinate heading.

The only trouble with single-style outlining is that all levels look the same. This is where a conditional paragraph style comes in handy. Assign the paragraph style to an outline numbering style in the *Outline & Numbering* page and then open the *Condition* page. There, you can assign the levels of the outline numbering style to other paragraph styles. Then, when you press the *Tab* key while using the paragraph style, each level of the outline takes on different formatting, making single-style outlining even more convenient than it is on its own.

**Note**

Predefined styles (other than Text body) such as Default, Heading 1, and Heading 2 cannot be set to be conditional.

**Caution**

If you want to create a new style and make it conditional, you have to do it while the style window is still open for the first time. After the window closes, the *Condition* tab no longer appears in the window.

When you create a conditional style, you are saying "in this condition make this style look like that other style". For example, "When typing into a footer, make this style look like the my_footer paragraph style; when typing into a table, make this style look like the table_text paragraph style".

In addition to setting the normal (unconditional) properties of the style, you need to define which other style it will look like in different situations. You do this on the Condition page.

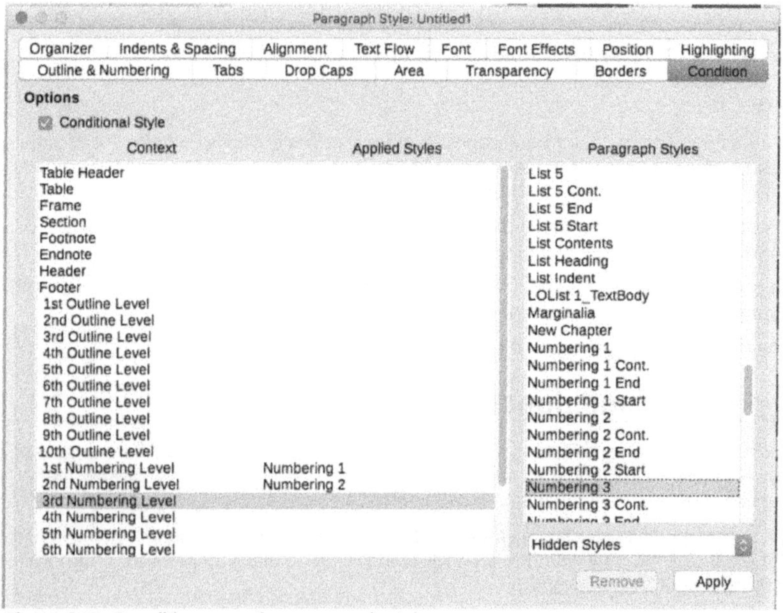

*Figure 217: Condition page for paragraph styles*

To set up a conditional paragraph style:

1) Define a new paragraph style.
2) Select all the paragraph properties for the style. Do not click OK!
3) Click the *Condition* tab.
4) Select the **Conditional Style** option.
5) Select the first condition in the Context list (left side of the dialog) and select the style you want for this condition in the Paragraph Styles list on the right-hand side.
6) Click **Apply**. The name of the paragraph style appears in the middle list.

7) Repeat steps 5 and 6 for each condition you want to have linked to a different style.

8) Click **OK**.

When the style is selected, you will see that the formatting of your text depends on the context.

# Working with character styles

Character styles complement paragraph styles and are applied to groups of characters, rather than whole paragraphs. They are mainly used when you want to change the appearance or attributes of parts of a paragraph without affecting other parts. Examples of effects that can be obtained by means of character styles are **bold** or *italic* typeface or colored words.

Two of the character styles used in this document are:

• Keystrokes use a custom KeyStroke style. For example:

To set Writer to full screen, press *Control+Shift+J*.

• Menu paths use a custom MenuPath style. For example:

To turn field shadings on or off, choose **View > Field Shadings**.

Other ways of using character styles are described elsewhere in this book. These uses include making chapter numbers, page numbers, or list numbers larger than the surrounding text and formatting hyperlinks. When inserting words in different language or words you do not want the spell checker to detect as mistakes (for example procedure names in some programming language), you can define the language to be applied in the character style's properties.

## Creating a new character style

This section illustrates the use of the Character Styles dialog. The pages used to configure the style are described in the previous section on paragraph styles.

• Use the **Organizer** page to set up the hierarchical level of the new character style (if needed) and to give it a name.

• Use the **Font** page to determine the font, style, and size for the new character style. As with paragraph styles, you can specify the font size as a percentage or as an absolute value. You can also specify the language of the text to which a certain character style is applied, so you can insert words in a different language and have them spell checked using the correct dictionary.

• Use the **Font Effects** page to set up attributes such as font color, underlining, relief, or other effects. If you frequently use hidden text, for example, it is convenient to define a character style where the Hidden option is marked. Relief effects may be appropriate for a drop cap or to give more emphasis to the chapter number or other parts of the title.

• Use the **Highlighting** page to apply a colored background to the text. This yields the same effect as using the the Highlighting tool on the Standard Toolbar.

• Use the **Borders** page to apply a border and a shadow to the text, if so desired.

• Use the **Position** page to create a subscript in case you are not satisfied with the default one or even a sub-subscript which may be useful for certain scientific publications. In the same page, you can create rotated, condensed, or expanded text.

### Note

When rotating a group of characters, you also need to specify whether the rotated text should fit in the line or if, instead, it is allowed to expand above and below the line. This property only becomes active for character styles.

# Working with frame styles

Frames are often used as containers for text or graphics. To provide consistency in the appearance of frames used for similar purposes, it is a good idea to define styles for frames. For example, you might want photographs to be enclosed in a frame with a drop-shadowed border, line drawings in a frame with a plain border, marginal notes in a frame without a border but with a shaded background, and so on.

Writer provides several predefined frame styles, which you can modify as needed, and you can define new frame styles. The technique for defining and applying frame styles is similar to that for other styles.

> **Tip**
>
> There is considerable overlap between the uses of frames and sections for some page layout purposes. You may find it useful to take a look at Chapter 6, Formatting Pages: Advanced, for information about the use of frames and sections.

## How frame styles work

When an object is added to Writer, it is automatically enclosed in a frame of a predetermined type. The frame sets how the object is placed on the page, as well as how it interacts with other elements in the document. You can edit the frame by modifying the frame style it uses or by using a manual override when a frame is added to the document.

Because frames and objects are used together, it is sometimes easy to forget they are separate elements. In some cases, such as charts, you can edit the frame and object separately.

Unlike other elements that use styles, frames can be defined only partly by their style because their use can vary so much. Several elements of frames, such as the anchor and protected elements, need to be defined manually for individual frames.

You can format a frame manually when you select **Insert > Frame**. The dialog that opens contains all the settings available when frame styles are set up, as well as some that are only available when the frame is inserted.

## Planning the styles

If you are using a mix of graphics, you may want to define two related styles, one with a border line for graphics with white backgrounds and one without a border for all other backgrounds. You also may want to design one or more frames for text only.

Otherwise, the default frame styles (listed in Table 8) cover most users' needs. The only significant addition that you might need is one or more styles for text frames.

*Table 8: Various frame styles and their uses*

| Style | Comments and Use |
|---|---|
| Formula | The frame style used for formulas. The default includes AutoSize, which adjusts the size of the frame to the formula. |
| Frame | The default frame style. |
| Graphics | The default style for graphics. The defaults include autosizing to fit the graphic, no text wrap, and a thin border around the frame. These are reasonable defaults, except for the border. Unless the background of the graphic is white and the document's background also is white, the border usually is unnecessary. |
| Labels | The default style for use with **File > New > Labels**. It seems to be used by LibreOffice automatically and is not intended for users at all. |

| Style | Comments and Use |
|---|---|
| Marginalia | A style for placing a frame beside the left margin. As the name suggests, the Marginalia style is intended for comments added in the margin of text. The style also is useful for creating sideheads—headings against the left margin, which often are used in technical documentation. See Chapter 8, Formatting Pages. |
| OLE | The default style for OLE objects and floating frames. The default places the frame at the top and center of a body of text. |
| Watermark | The default style for a watermark, a graphic placed as the background to a body of text. The default is a Through wrap, with text passing over the frame and anything in it. The graphic should be faint enough that text still is readable over top of it. |

## Creating new frame styles

You can access frame settings by selecting **New** or **Modify** in the Styles and Formatting window for a frame style.

- **Type** page: sets the size and position of the frame. One of the most useful options here is AutoSize, which automatically adjusts the frame to the object it contains. If the frame style is used automatically, then this option should be selected.

- **Options** page: sets whether the contents of the frame are printed and able to be edited in a read-only document. This page also sets the text direction, which is useful if you are using the frame for contents in a language that uses right-to-left text direction.

- **Wrap** page: sets how text is positioned in relation to the frame and how close text comes to a frame. If you want the frame contents to stand out from the paragraphs around it, set the wrap to None. This probably is the single most important page for frames.

- **Area** page: sets the background color, bitmap, hatching, gradient, or pattern. This page is useful mostly for text frames in complex page layouts, in which a text frame has an appearance different from the general background of the page.

- **Transparency** page: sets the transparency options for the selected background. Values can range from 0% (fully opaque) to +100% (fully transparent).

- **Borders** page: sets the attribute for a line around the frame, if any.

- **Columns** page: this page can be ignored unless the frame is being used for text. The page is the same as is used to set up a page style.

- **Macro** page: sets a macro to use with the frame in order to trigger an action when the user interacts with the frame. These options are useful for an on-line Writer or HTML document.

# Working with page styles

Page styles control page properties (margins, page size, header and footer, among others). However, unlike paragraphs, which can have directly applied properties, pages only have a page style and no directly applied properties.

This section describes how to create a new page style, explains the meaning of some of the options in the Page style dialog, and illustrates their usage.

## Creating a new page style

To create a new page style, open the Styles and Formatting window and click the **Page Styles** icon. Right-click anywhere in the window and select **New**.

The Page Style dialog contains nine pages.

## Organizer page

The *Organizer* page is described on page 196.

## General settings for the page style

The *Page* page of the Page Style dialog is where you can control the general settings of the page. The page consists of three sections, plus a preview area in the top right.

In the *Paper format* section, you can specify the size of the paper, choosing from one of the many predefined formats. Select **User** to define your own paper size using the Width and Height fields. Select the orientation of the paper: Portrait or Landscape. If your printer has more than one tray, you can specify the tray from which to print pages in the new page style.

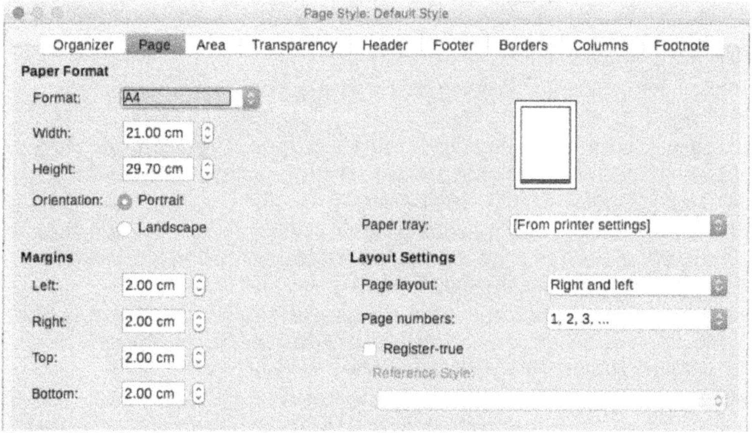

*Figure 218: The Page page for the Page Style dialog*

In the *Margins* section, specify the size of the margins in your preferred unit of measurement. If you select Mirrored for Page layout in the Layout settings section, then the names of the margins change from Left and Right to Inner and Outer.

In the *Layout settings* section, choose the desired Page layout from the four available options. Decide whether the page style being defined applies to both left and right pages (default), or applies to right or left only. Some considerations:

- If you plan to bind the printed pages using this style like a book, select a mirrored layout. Use the Format drop-down menu to determine the page numbering style to apply to this page style.
- A common practice in page layouts is to have asymmetrical page margins—both for left and right margins and for top and bottom margins. The most common scheme follows these two general rules for printed page layouts: (a) The outer margin (right margin on a right-hand page) would be wider than an inner margin (left margin on a right-hand page); (b) The bottom margin would be larger than a top margin. The rationale for an asymmetrical page layout is allowing more space for readers to place their hands while holding the books or other printed documents. See Bruce Byfield's book, *Designing with LibreOffice*, for more information. You can download a PDF free from http://designingwithlibreoffice.com.
- If you want the first page of a new chapter to always start on a right (recto) page, make sure that the page style for the first chapter page is set for the right page only by making this selection in the Layout settings field. The typical procedure for the rest of a chapter is to define a single "mirrored" page style for both left and right pages. A mirrored page can have different headers and footers. If done this way, every chapter will use two page styles.

- You can choose to define separate page styles for left and right pages, if you want the pages to be very different in appearance (for example, different margins or headers and footers only on right pages but not on left pages; imagine a book with a full-page photograph on the left pages and text on the right pages). In that case, make sure that the Next Style field for the first page style is set for a left-only page, which, in turn, is set to be followed by a right-only page style. If done this way, every chapter will use three page styles. A hypothetical case might have these page-style names: First page, Left, and Right.

If you check the **Register-true** box, Writer will create an invisible vertical grid on the page with a spacing between grid points that depends on the selected Reference Style. The vertical grid makes sure that text printed on adjacent columns, opposite pages, or even both sides of the same sheet of paper, is aligned—making it easier to read as well as being more pleasant to see.

## Area and Border pages

The *Area* and *Border* pages are described in detail in Chapter 5, Formatting Pages: Basics. Use the *Area* page to apply a background or the *Border* page to draw a border around the text area of the page (the margins). You can also add a shadow to the text area. You can choose between a solid color or a graphic image for the background and several styles of line for the borders. The page area affected by these changes does not include the area outside the margins.

If you plan to print on colored paper and want to have an idea of the final result or want to use a light color for the font, rather than changing the background, then go to **Tools > Options > LibreOffice > Applications Colors** and in the *General* section, change the Document background color. This will affect the entire page, including the area outside the margins, but the background color will not print or be exported to PDF.

## Header and Footer pages

You can associate a different header or footer with each page style. This property makes it easy to have different headers on left and right pages, to avoid headers on pages at the start of a new chapter, and so on. You can also have a different header or footer on the same page style where it is used for the first page of a document.

You can specify a different header for left or right pages even if you use a single style for both. This option is not available on the predefined *Left* and *Right* page styles or on any other page style defined to be a left or right page only.

The Header and Footer pages are described in detail in Chapter 5, Formatting Pages: Basics.

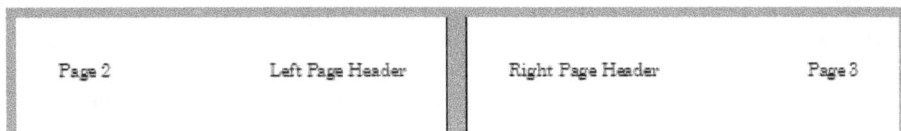

| Page 2 | Left Page Header | Right Page Header | Page 3 |

*Figure 219: Different content on left and right pages*

## Columns page

Use this page to create the desired column layout for the page style. It is described in detail in Chapter 6, Formatting Pages: Advanced.

The *Columns* page has three sections: Settings, Width and Spacing, and Separator Line. Choose the desired number of columns. If you select more than one column, the Width and Spacing section and the Separator Line section become active. You can use the predefined settings (equally spaced columns) or deselect the AutoWidth option and enter the parameters manually. When you work with multiple columns per page, you can also fine tune the position and size of a separator line between the columns.

## Footnote page

Use the *Footnote* page to adjust the appearance of the footnotes. See Chapter 5, Formatting Pages: Basics, for details.

# Working with list styles

List styles (also called numbering styles) work together with paragraph styles. They define indentation, alignment, and the numbering or bullet characters used for list items. You can define many list styles, from simple bulleted lists to complex multi-level (nested) lists.

As with other styles, the main reasons for using list styles are consistency and speeding up your work. Although you can create simple lists quickly by clicking the Numbering On/Off or Bullets On/Off icons on the Formatting toolbar, and create quite complex nested lists using the buttons on the Bullets and Numbering toolbar, the appearance of the resulting lists may not be what you want —and you might want to have more than one style of list. You can use the Bullets and Numbering choice on the Format menu to manually format the appearance of some or all of the lists, but if you later need to change their appearance, you will have a lot of manual work to do.

See Chapter 12, Lists: Tips and Tricks, for details on how list styles and paragraph styles work together.

> **Note**
>
> LibreOffice uses the terms "numbering style" and "list style" inconsistently, but they are the same thing. For example, the tooltip in the Styles and Formatting window says List Styles, but its style dialog says Numbering Style.

## Creating a new list style

The dialog to create a new list style includes six pages in addition to the usual *Organizer* page discussed on page 196.

### Bullets, Numbering Styles, and Image pages

The *Bullets*, *Numbering Style*, and *Image* pages contain predefined formatting for list item symbols (bullets or numbers). To use one of them for your style, click on the image. A thick border indicates the selection. The bullets on the *Bullets* page are font characters; those on the *Image* page are graphics.

### Outline page

Use the *Outline* page to select from eight predefined nested lists. You can also select one and use it as a starting point for your own style, customizing the list using the *Position* page and the *Customize* page, as described below.

### Position page

Use the *Position* page (Figure 220) to fine tune the indentation and spacing of the list item symbol and the text of the list item. This page is particularly effective when used in combination with the Customize page.

You can adjust the following settings for each individual level or all levels at once (to make them all the same). It is generally easier to adjust the settings in the order given below, instead of the order on the dialog. That is, start from the overall indentation for the list elements, then fix the position of the symbols, and finally adjust the alignment of the symbols.

- **Numbering followed by:** the character to follow the numbering symbol (plus any characters—for example a punctuation mark—chosen on the *Customize* page to appear after the number). Choose between a tab stop, a space, or nothing. If you select the tab stop, you can specify the position of the tab.

- **Indent at:** how much space is reserved for the numbering symbol, measured from the left page margin. The alignment of the first line of the list is also affected by any tab you may have set to follow the numbering.

- **Aligned at:** the position of the numbering symbol, measured from the left margin of the page.

- **Numbering alignment:** how the numbering (including any text before or after as set in the *Customize* page) will be aligned. The Aligned at value determines the symbol alignment.

▶ **Tip**

In normal circumstances, setting the *Numbering followed by* distance to be equal to the *Indent at* distance works well. See Figure 221 for a graphic representation of the effects of the above parameters.

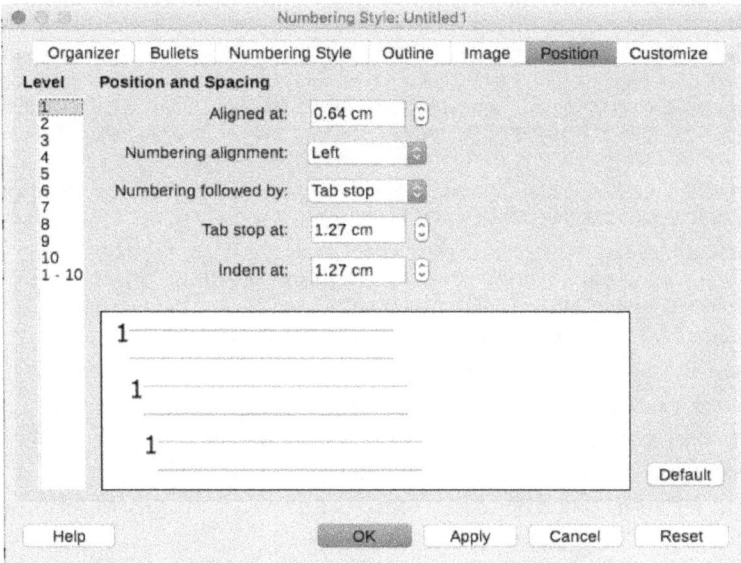

*Figure 220: Position settings for a List style*

▶ **Tip**

To fully appreciate how the Numbering alignment works, try to create a numbered list with more than ten elements and make sure that enough room has been made for numbers with two or more digits. You may also wish to right-align numbers 10 or greater, as in Figure 221.

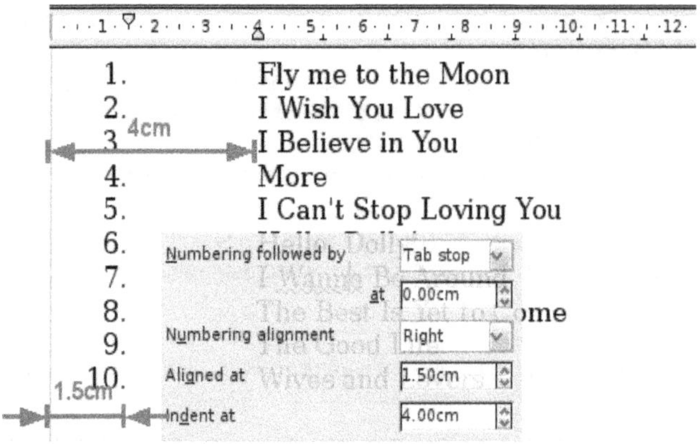

Figure 221: A numbered list of CD tracks highlighting the various elements

## Customize page

Use the *Customize* page (Figure 222) to define the style of the outline levels. The options available on this page depend on the type of marker selected for the list. First, on the left side, select the level you want to modify. To modify all ten levels at once, select 1 – 10 as the level. If you started from a predefined outline, some of the levels will already have settings.

Depending on the numbering style selected in the *Number* box (bullet, graphic, numbering), some of the following options become available on the page (not all are shown in the illustration):

- **Show sublevels:** The number of previous levels to include in the numbering style. For example, if you enter "2" and the previous level uses the "A, B, C..." numbering style, the numbering scheme for the current level becomes: "A.1".
- **Before:** any text to appear before the number (for example, Step).
- **After:** any text to appear after the number (for example, a punctuation mark).
- **Start at:** the first value of the list (for example, to start the list at 4 instead of 1).
- **Character Style:** the style to be used for the number or bullet.
- **Character** button: click to select the character for the bullet.
- **Graphics Select** button: opens a list of available graphics (Gallery) or allows the selection of a file on the hard disk to be used as the list marker.
- **Width** and **Height**: the dimensions of the graphic marker.
- **Keep ratio** option: fixes the ratio between the width and the height of the graphic marker.
- **Alignment:** the alignment of the graphic object.

The right-hand side of the dialog shows a preview of the modifications made.

If you choose the **Link Graphics** option in the *Number* list, the graphic object is linked rather than embedded in the document. The bullet will not be displayed when the document is opened on a different computer (unless the same graphic file is located in the same location on both computers) or if the graphic file used is moved to a different location on the computer.

To revert to the default values, click the **Reset** button in the bottom right corner. Finally, if you wish to use consecutive numbers regardless of the outline level, check the **Consecutive numbering** box at the bottom of the page.

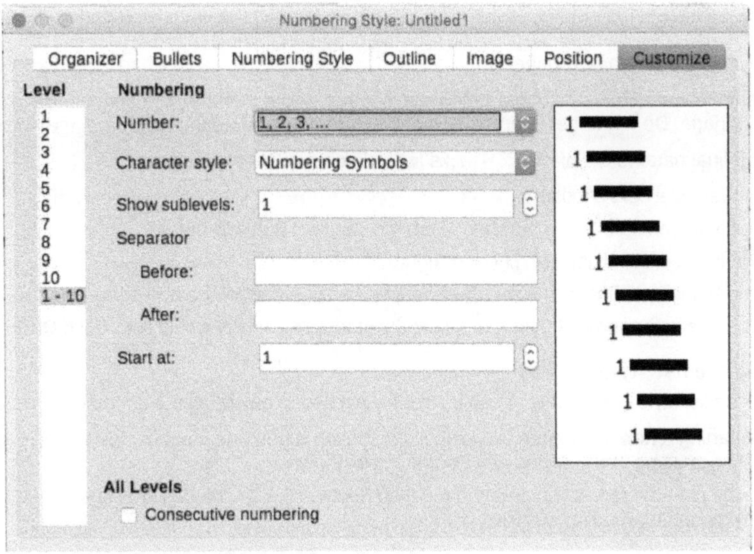

*Figure 222: The Customize page for a list style*

## Example: Creating a simple list style

In this example, we will create a numbered list that is used to number the songs on a CD. The numbers are right-aligned, and some space is left between the number and the title of the track.

As we want to reuse the same numbered list for other CDs, we will define a new list style and then apply it to the tracks list.

### Creating the CDTracks numbered list

As for the previous example, start by clicking the List Styles icon (fifth from the left) in the Styles and Formatting window. Then right-click anywhere in the list box and choose New.

The Numbering style dialog is displayed. For the CDTracks style, we need to customize fields in the Organizer, the Options, and the Position pages.

| Style fields | Description |
|---|---|
| Name | Enter CDTrack |
| Category | Custom styles will be OK for us. |

Modify the options of the *Customize* page as follows:

1)  In the Level box, choose 1.

2)  In the Number list, choose 1, 2, 3,....

3)  Leave the Before and After boxes empty.

4)  Leave the Character Style field as None.

5)  Show sublevels should be grayed out.

6)  Make sure Start at is set to 1.

7)  Do **not** select Consecutive numbering.

As discussed above, the numbered list will adopt the settings of the underlying paragraph style. If you want to use a special font, size or color for the numbering, you can create a character style and apply it in the *Customize* page.

If you want the word Track to appear before the number, add it to the Before field on the *Customize* page. Do not forget to add a space character to separate the word from the number.

Set up the final parameters of the CDTracks list style on the *Position* page.

1) In the Level box, choose 1.

2) For Numbering followed by, choose tab stop and set it at 4.0cm.

3) For Numbering alignment, choose Right.

4) For Aligned at choose 1.5cm. (this refers to the alignment of the numbers)

5) For Indent at choose 4.0cm. (This sets the indentation of the whole list.) Click **OK** to finish.

### Applying the list style

Now that the list style is available, it can be quickly applied to any list in the document:

1) If starting a new list, before pressing *Enter* to start a new line, double-click on the desired list style name in the Styles and Formatting window.

2) If you already have a list, select it and then double-click on the desired list style name in the Styles and Formatting window.

**Note**

Remember that applying a list style does not affect the characteristics of the underlying paragraph; therefore you may want to check if you are satisfied with the paragraph style before applying the list style.

If you have more than one list in a document, the second and subsequent lists with the same style continue their numbering from the previous list. To restart at 1, place the cursor anywhere in the paragraph you want numbered 1, right-click, and choose **Restart numbering**.

To stop using numbering, click the **Numbering On/Off** button on the Standard Toolbar. The final result is illustrated in Figure 221.

# LibreOffice

*Chapter 10*
*Working with Templates*

# Introduction

A template is a document model that you use to create other documents. For example, you can create a template for business reports that has your company's logo on the first page. New documents created from this template will all have your company's logo on the first page.

Templates can contain anything that regular documents can contain, such as text, graphics, a set of styles, and user-specific setup information such as measurement units, language, the default printer, and toolbar and menu customization.

All documents in LibreOffice are based on templates. If you do not specify a template when you start a new Writer document, then the document is based on the default template for text documents. If you have not specified a default template, Writer uses the blank template for text documents that is installed with LibreOffice. See "Setting a default template" on page 224.

LibreOffice supplies only a few user-selectable templates. You can add templates from other sources (see page 223) as well as creating your own templates (see page 221).

# Using a template to create a document

## Creating a document from the Templates dialog

To use a template to create a document:

1) From the Menu bar, choose **File > New > Templates**, or click on the small arrow next to the **New** icon on the Standard toolbar and select **Templates**.

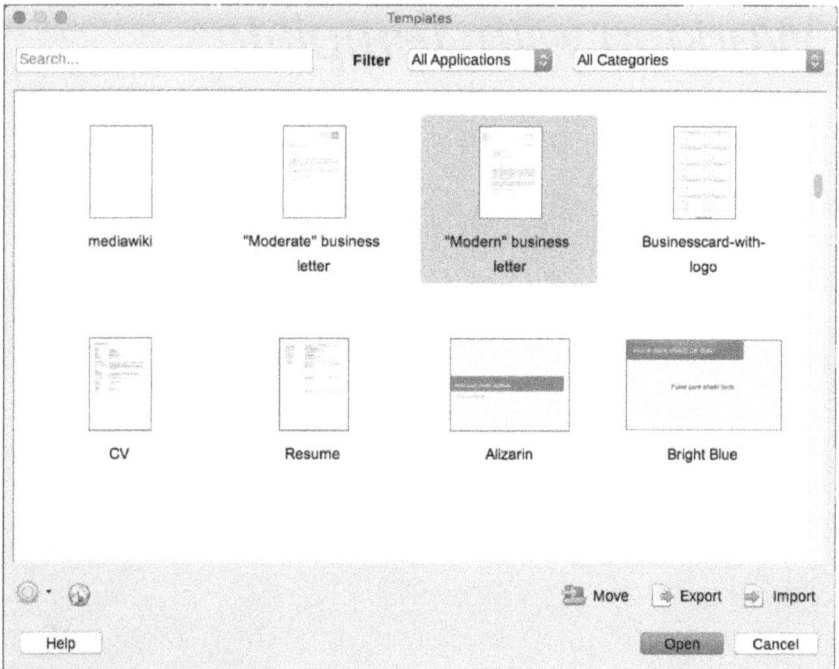

Figure 223: Templates dialog

---

2) From the Filters list at the top of the Templates dialog, select **Documents**. You can also choose a category. Templates in that folder are shown on the page.

3) Double-click on the required template. A new document based on the selected template opens in Writer. You can then edit and save the new document just as you would any other document.

The template the document is based upon is listed in **File > Properties > General**. The connection between the template and the document remains until the template is modified and, the next time that the document is opened, you choose not to update it to match the template. Or, if you copy or move the document to a different computer, which does not have a copy of that template installed, the connection is broken.

### Creating a document from a template in the Start Center

You can create a document from the template view of the Start Center, which is visible when no other document is open.

To open the Templates dialog from the Start Center, click on the **Templates** button in the left pane. The button is also a drop-down list to select the templates of a given type of document. The Manage Templates option on the list opens the Templates dialog.

## Creating a template

You can create templates in two ways: by saving a document as a template or by using a wizard.

### Creating a template from a document

In addition to formatting, any settings that can be added to or modified in a document can be saved within a template. For example, you can also save printer settings, and general behaviors set from **Tools > Options**, such as Paths and Colors.

Templates can also contain predefined text, saving you from having to type it every time you create a new document. For example, a letter template may contain your name, address, and salutation.

You can also save menu and toolbar customizations in templates; see Chapter 21, Customizing Writer, for more information.

To create a template from a document and save it to My Templates:

1) Open a new or existing document of the type you want to make into a template (text document, spreadsheet, drawing, or presentation).

2) Add any content that you want to appear in any document you create from the new template, for example company logo, copyright statement, and so on.

3) Create or modify any styles that you want to use in the new template.

4) From the Menu bar, choose **File > Templates > Save as Template**. The Save as Template dialog (Figure 224) displays the existing categories and a textbox to enter a name for the new template.

5) Select the My Templates folder.

6) Click **Save**. The template is saved and the dialog closes.

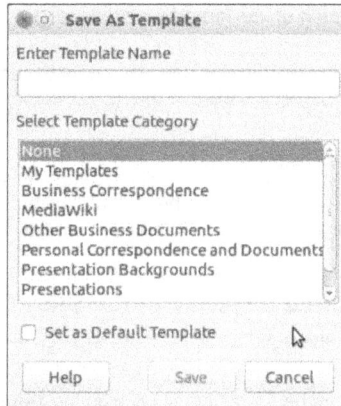

*Figure 224: Save as Template dialog*

## Creating a template using a wizard

You can use wizards to create templates for letters, faxes, and agendas, and to create presentations and Web pages.

For example, the Fax Wizard guides you through the following choices:

- Type of fax (business or personal)
- Document elements like the date, subject line (business fax), salutation, and complimentary close
- Options for sender and recipient information (business fax)
- Text to include in the footer (business fax)

To create a template using a wizard:

1) From the Menu bar, choose **File > Wizards > [type of template required]**.

2) Follow the instructions on the pages of the wizard. This process is slightly different for each type of template, but the format is very similar.

3) In the last section of the wizard, you can specify the template name which will show in the Templates dialog, and also the name and location for saving the template. The two names can be different but this may later cause confusion. The default location is your user templates folder, but you can choose a different location.

4) To set the file name or change the folder, select the **Path** button (the three dots to the right of the location). On the Save As dialog, make your selections and click **Save**.

5) Finally, you can choose whether to create a new document from the template immediately, or manually change the template, and then click Finish to save the template. For future documents, you can re-use the template created by the wizard, just like any other template.

You may need to open the Templates dialog and click Refresh on the Action menu to have any new templates appear in the listings.

## Editing a template

You can edit a template's styles and content, and then, if you wish, you can reapply the template's styles to documents that were created from that template. You cannot reapply content.

To edit a template:

1) From the Menu bar, choose **File > Templates > Manage Templates** or press *Ctrl+Shift+N*. The Templates dialog opens. You can also open the Templates dialog from the Start Center.

2) Navigate to the template that you want to edit. Click once on it to activate the file handling controls. Right-click to open the context menu and click **Edit**. The template opens in LibreOffice.

3) Edit the template as you would edit any other document. To save your changes, choose **File > Save** from the Menu bar.

## Updating a document from a changed template

If you make any changes to a template and its styles, the next time you open a document that was created from the template before the changes, a confirmation message is displayed.

To update the document:

1) Select **Update Styles** to apply the changed styles in the template to the document.

2) Select **Keep Old Styles** if you do not want to apply the changed styles in the template to the document (but see the Caution notice below).

### Caution

If you choose Keep Old Styles, the document is no longer connected to the template, even though the template is still listed under **File > Properties > General**. You can still import styles manually from the template, but to reconnect it to the template, you will have to copy it into an empty document based on the template.

# Adding templates obtained from other sources

LibreOffice refers to sources for templates as repositories. A repository can be local (a directory on your computer to which you have downloaded templates) or remote (a URL from which you can download templates).

You can get to the official template repository by using the **Browse online templates** button at the right-hand end of the Templates dialog, as shown in Figure 225, or by typing https://extensions.libreoffice.org/templates in your browser's address bar.

On other websites you may find collections of templates that have been packaged into extension (.oxt) files. These are installed a little differently, as described below.

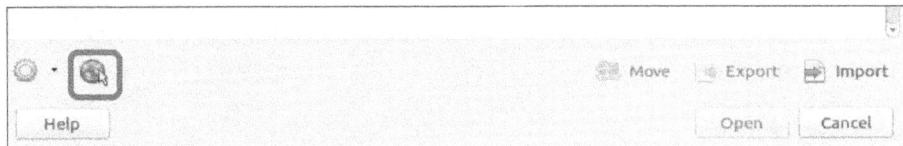

*Figure 225: Getting more templates for LibreOffice*

## Installing individual templates

To install individual templates:

1) Download the template and save it anywhere on your computer.

2) Import the template into a template folder by following the instructions in "Importing a template" on page 227.

> ► **Tip**
>
> (For advanced users) You can manually copy new templates into the template folders. The location varies with your computer's operating system. To learn where the template folders are stored on your computer, go to **Tools > Options > LibreOffice > Paths**.

## Installing collections of templates

The Extension Manager provides an easy way to install collections of templates that have been packaged as extensions. Follow these steps:

1) Download the extension package (.oxt file) and save it anywhere on your computer. If the package is in a .zip file, extract the .oxt file.

2) In LibreOffice, select **Tools > Extension Manager** from the Menu bar. In the Extension Manager dialog, click **Add** to open a file browser window.

3) Find and select the package of templates you want to install and click **Open**. The package begins installing. You may be asked to accept a license agreement.

4) When the package installation is complete, restart LibreOffice. The templates are available for use through **File > Templates > Manage Templates** and **File > New > Templates** and the extension is listed in the Extension Manager.

See Chapter 21, Customizing Writer, for more about the Extension Manager.

# Setting a default template

If you create a document by choosing **File > New > Text Document** from the Menu bar, Writer creates the document from the default template for text documents. You can, however, set a custom template to be the default. You can reset the default later, if you choose.

## Setting a template as the default

Most default settings, such as page size and page margins, can be changed in **Tools > Options**, but those changes apply only to the document you are working on. To make those changes the default settings for that document type, you need to replace the default template with a new one.

You can set any template in the Templates dialog to be the default for that document type:

1) From the Menu bar, choose **File > Templates > Manage Templates**.

2) In the Templates dialog, open the category containing the template that you want to set as the default, then select the template.

3) Right-click on the selected template and click the **Set as default** button (see Figure 226).

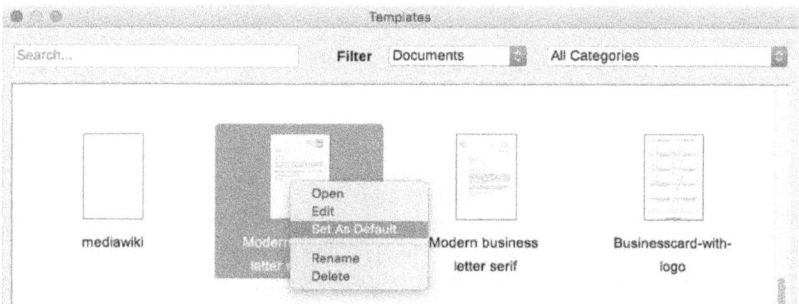

*Figure 226: Setting a template as the default template for documents*

The next time that you create a document of that type by choosing **File > New**, the document will be created from this template.

### Resetting Writer's default template as the default

To re-enable Writer's default template as the default:

1) In the Templates dialog (Figure 227), click the **Settings** icon ⬚ on the right.

2) Point to **Reset Default Template** on the drop-down menu, and click **Text Document**.

This choice does not appear unless a custom template had been set as the default, as described in the previous section.

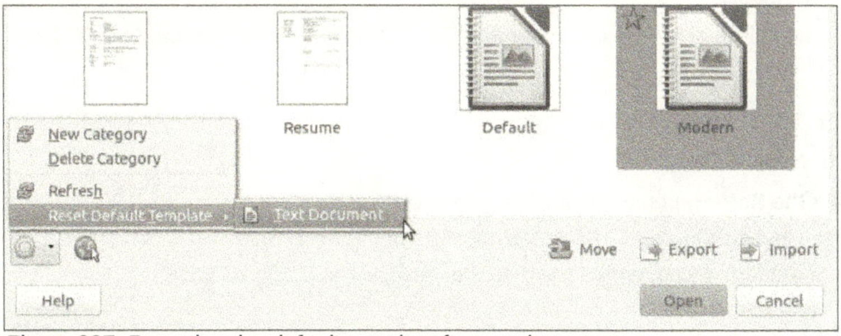

*Figure 227: Resetting the default template for text documents*

The next time that you create a document by choosing **File > New > Text Document**, the document will be created from Writer's default template.

## Associating a document with a different template

At times you might want to associate a document with a different template, or perhaps you're working with a document that did not start from a template.

One of the major advantages of using templates is the ease of updating styles in more than one document, as described in Chapter 9, Working with Styles. If you update styles in a document by loading a new set of styles from a different template (as described in Chapter 9), the document has no association with the template from which the styles were loaded—so you cannot use this method. What you need to do is associate the document with the different template.

For best results, the names of styles should be the same in the existing document and the new template. If they are not, you will need to use **Edit > Find & Replace** to replace old styles with new ones. See Chapter 2, Working with Text: Basics, for more about replacing styles.

1) Use **File > New > Templates**. In the Templates dialog, double-click the template you want to use. A new document opens, containing any text or graphics that were in the template.

2) Delete any unwanted text or graphics from this new document.

3) Open the document you want to change. (It opens in a new window.)

4) Use **Edit > Select All**, or press *Ctrl+A*, to select everything in the document.

5) Click in the blank document created in step 1. **Use Edit > Paste**, or press *Ctrl+V*, to paste the contents from the old document into the new one.

6) Update the table of contents, if there is one. Close the old file without saving. Use **File > Save As** to save this new file with the name of the file from which content was taken. When asked, confirm you wish to overwrite the old file. Or, you may prefer to save the new file under a new name and preserve the old file under its original name.

### Caution

Any changes recorded (tracked) in the document will be lost during this process. The resulting document will contain only the changed text.

# Organizing templates

Writer can only use templates that are in LibreOffice template folders. You can, however, create new LibreOffice template folders and use them to organize your templates. For example, you might have one template folder for report templates and another for letter templates. You can also import and export templates.

To begin, choose **File > Templates > Manage Templates** from the Menu bar to open the Templates dialog.

## Creating a template category

To create a template category:

1) Click the **Settings** button of the Templates dialog.
2) Click **New category** on the context menu (see Figure 228).
3) In the pop-up dialog, type a name for the new category and click **OK**.

### Note

You cannot create a sub-category inside a template category in LibreOffice.

*Figure 228: Creating a new category*

## Deleting a template category

You cannot delete template categories supplied with LibreOffice. Nor can you delete any categories added by the Extension Manager unless you first delete the extension that installed them.

However, you can delete a category that you created. Select it and click the **Delete** button. When a message box appears asking you to confirm the deletion, click **Yes**.

## Moving a template

To move a template from one template category to another, select it in the Templates dialog, and click the **Move** button in the bottom center of the dialog (see Figure 229). In the popup dialog, select the required category and click **OK**.

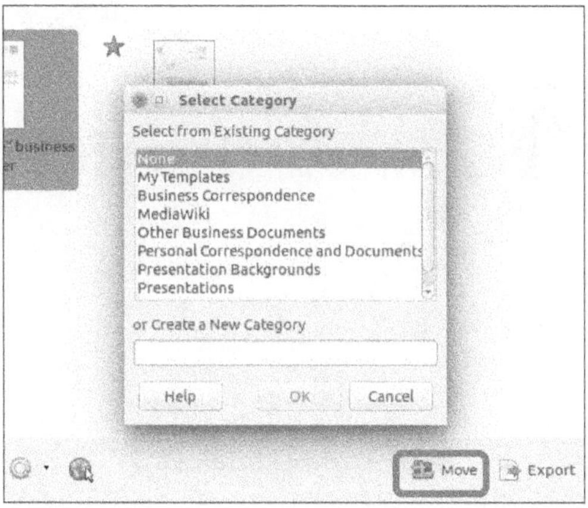

*Figure 229: Moving templates to another category*

# Deleting a template

You cannot delete templates supplied with LibreOffice. Nor can you delete any templates installed by the Extension Manager except by deleting the extension that installed them.

However, you can delete templates that you have created or imported:

1) In the Templates dialog, select the category that contains the template you want to delete.

2) Select the template to delete.

3) Right-click to open the context menu of the template and click **Delete**. A message box appears and asks you to confirm the deletion. Click **Yes**.

# Importing a template

Before you can use a template in LibreOffice, it must be in one of the folders listed for the Template path in **Tools > Options > LibreOffice > Paths**:

1) In the Templates dialog, click the Import button on the bottom right. The **Select Category** dialog appears.

2) Find and select the category where you want to import the template and click **OK**. A standard file browser window opens.

3) Find and select the template that you want to import and click **Open**. The file browser window closes and the template appears in the selected category.

# Exporting a template

To export a template from a template category to another location in your computer or network:

1) In the Templates dialog, locate the category that contains the template to export.

2) Select the template that you want to export.

3) Click the **Export** button in the bottom right of the dialog. The Save As window opens.

4) Find the folder into which you want to export the template and select **Save**.

# LibreOffice

# Chapter 11
# Images and Graphics

*Pictures, Drawing Tools, Gallery, Fontwork*

# Images (graphics) in Writer

You can add graphic and image files, including photos, drawings, and scanned images, to Writer documents. Writer can import various vector (line drawing) and raster (bitmap) file formats. The most commonly used graphic formats are GIF, JPG, PNG, and BMP.

Images in Writer are of these basic types:

- Image files, such as photos, drawings, and scanned images
- Diagrams created using LibreOffice's drawing tools
- Artwork created using clip art or Fontwork
- Charts created using LibreOffice's Chart facility

This chapter covers images, diagrams, and artwork. Instructions on how to create charts are given in Chapter 20, Spreadsheets, Charts, other Objects. For more detailed descriptions on working with drawing tools, see the *Draw Guide*.

# Creating and editing images

You might create images (also called 'pictures' in LibreOffice) using a graphics program, scan them, or download them from the Internet (make sure you have permission to use them), or use photos taken with a digital camera. Writer can import various vector (line drawing) images, and can rotate and flip such images. Writer also supports raster (bitmap) file formats, the most common of which are GIF, JPG, PNG, and BMP. See the Help for a full list.

Writer can also import SmartArt images from Microsoft Office files. For example, Writer can open a Microsoft Word file that contains SmartArt, and you can use Writer to edit the images.

Some things to consider when choosing or creating pictures include image quality and whether the picture will be printed in color or black and white (grayscale).

To edit photos and other bitmap images, use a bitmap editor. To edit line drawings, use a vector drawing program. You do not need to buy expensive programs. For many graphics, LibreOffice Draw is sufficient. Open-source (and usually no-cost) tools such as GIMP (bitmap editor) and Inkscape (vector drawing program) are excellent. These and many other programs work on Windows, MacOS, and Linux.

For best results:

- Create images that have the exact dimensions required for the document, or use an appropriate graphics package to scale photographs and large drawings to the required dimensions. Do not scale images with Writer, even though Writer has tools for doing this, because the results might not be as clear as you would like.
- Do any other required image manipulation (brightness and contrast, color balance, cropping, conversion to grayscale, and so on) in a graphics package, not in Writer, even though Writer has the tools to do a lot of these things too.
- If the document is meant for screen use only, there is no need to use high resolution images of 300 or more dpi (dots per inch). Most computer monitors work at between 72 and 96 dpi; reducing the resolution (and the file size) has no negative impact on what is displayed but does make Writer more responsive.

## Preparing images for black-and-white printing

If color images are to be printed in grayscale, check that any adjacent colors have good contrast and print dark enough. Test by printing on a black-and-white printer using a grayscale setting. Better still: change the "mode" of the image to grayscale, either in a photo editor or in Writer itself (see "Image mode" on page 235).

For example, the following diagram looks good in color. The circle is dark red and the square is dark blue. In grayscale, the difference between the two is not so clear. A third element in the diagram is a yellow arrow, which is almost invisible in grayscale.

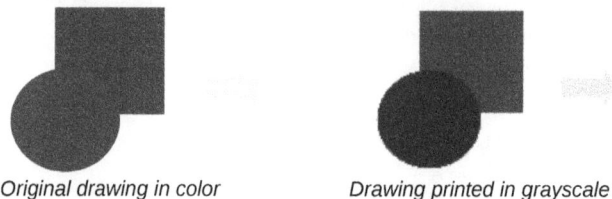

*Original drawing in color*　　　　　*Drawing printed in grayscale*

Changing the colors of the circle and the arrow improves the contrast and visibility of the resulting grayscale image.

*Original drawing in color*　　　　　*Drawing printed in grayscale*

If the document will be available in black-and-white print only, a better result can often be obtained by choosing grayscale fills, not color fills.

# Adding images to a document

Images can be added to a document in several ways: by inserting an image file, directly from a graphics program or a scanner, from a file stored on your computer, or by copying and pasting from a source being viewed on your computer.

## Inserting an image file

When the image is in a file stored on the computer, you can insert it into a LibreOffice document using either of the following methods.

### Drag and drop

1) Open a file browser window and locate the image you want to insert.
2) Drag the image into the Writer document and drop it where you want it to appear. A faint vertical line marks where the image will be dropped.

This method embeds (saves a copy of) the image file in the Writer document. To link the file instead of embedding it, hold down the *Ctrl+Shift* keys while dragging the image.

### Insert Image dialog

1) Click in the LibreOffice document where you want the image to appear.
2) Choose **Insert > Image** from the Menu bar.
3) On the Insert Image dialog, navigate to the file to be inserted, and select it.

   At the bottom of the dialog are two options, **Preview** and **Link**. Select **Preview** to view a thumbnail of the selected image on the right (as shown in the example), so you can verify that you have the correct file. See "Inserting an image file" below for the use of **Link**.
4) Click **Open.**

*Figure 230: Insert Image dialog*

**Note**

If you choose the Link option, a message box appears when you click Open. It asks if you want to embed the graphic instead. Choose Keep Link if you want the link, or Embed Graphic if you do not. To prevent this message from appearing again, deselect the option Ask when linking a graphic at the bottom of the message.

## Linking an image file

If the **Link** option in the Insert Image dialog is selected, Writer creates a link to the file containing the image instead of saving a copy of the image in the document. The result is that the image is displayed in the document, but when the document is saved, it contains only a reference to the image file—not the image itself. The document and the image remain as two separate files, and they are merged together only when you open the document again.

Linking an image has two advantages and one disadvantage:

- Advantage – You can modify the image file separately without changing the document because the link to the file remains valid, and the modified image will appear when you next open the document. This can be a big advantage if you (or someone else, perhaps a graphic artist) is updating images.

- Advantage – Linking can reduce the size of the document when it is saved, because the image file itself is not included. File size is usually not a problem on a modern computer with a reasonable amount of memory, unless the document includes many large images files; LibreOffice can handle quite large files.

- Disadvantage – If you send the document to someone else, or move it to a different computer, you must include the image files, or the recipient will not be able to see the linked images. You need to keep track of the location of the images and make sure the recipient knows where to put them on another machine, so the document can find them.

**Note**

When inserting the same image several times in the document, LibreOffice embeds in the document only one copy of the image file.

### Embedding linked images

If you originally linked the images, you can easily embed one or more of them later if you wish. To do so:

1) Open the document in LibreOffice and choose **Edit > Links**.

2) The Edit Links dialog shows all the linked files. In the Source file list, select the files you want to change from linked to embedded.

3) Click the **Break Link** button.

### Note

Going the other way, from embedded to linked, is not so easy—you must delete and reinsert each image, one at a time, selecting the **Link** option when you do so.

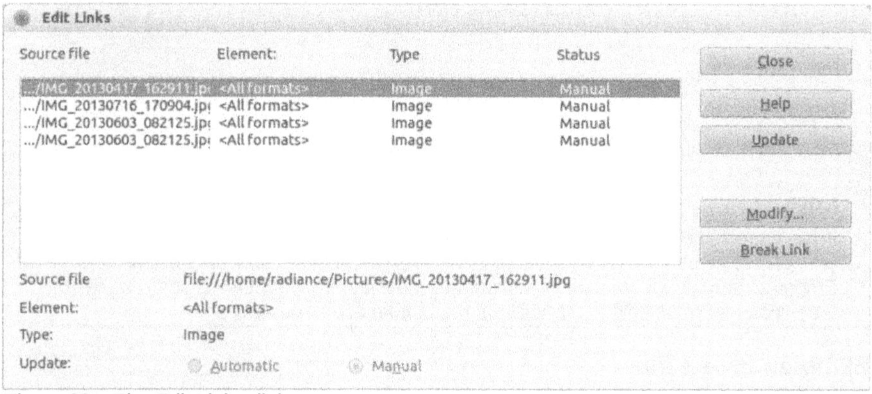

*Figure 231: The Edit Links dialog*

## Copying and pasting

Using the clipboard, you can copy images into a LibreOffice document from another LibreOffice document and from other programs. To do this:

1) Open both the source document and the target document.

2) In the source document, select the image to be copied.

3) Press *Ctrl+C* (or right-click and select **Copy** from the context menu) to copy the image to the clipboard.

4) Switch to the target document.

5) Click to place the cursor where the image is to be inserted.

6) Press *Ctrl+V* (or right-click and select **Paste** from the context menu) to insert the image.

### Caution

If the application from which the image was copied is closed before the image is pasted into the target, the image stored on the clipboard could be lost.

# Scanning

If a scanner is connected to your computer, Writer can call the scanning application and insert the scanned item into your document as an image. To start this procedure, click where you want the image to be inserted and select **Insert > Media > Scan > Select Source**.

Select the scan source from the list. This list will contain available devices. After choosing the device, select **Insert > Media > Scan > Request**. This will open the imaging software to permit you to adjust settings for picture quality, size, and other attributes. This practice is quick and easy, but may not result in a high-quality image of the correct size. You may get better results by scanning material into a graphics program and cleaning it up there before inserting the resulting image into Writer.

## Inserting an image from the Gallery

The Gallery (Figure 232) provides a convenient way to group reusable objects such as graphics and sounds that you can insert into your documents. The Gallery is available in all components of LibreOffice. See "Managing the LibreOffice Gallery" on page 253. You can copy or link an object from the Gallery into a document.

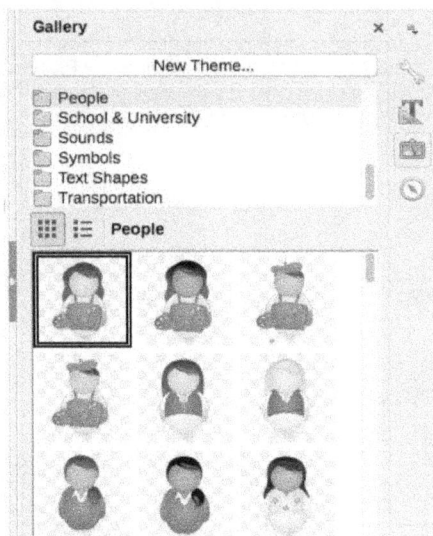

*Figure 232: The Gallery in the Sidebar*

To insert an object:

1) Click the Gallery icon in the Sidebar.
2) Select a theme.
3) Select an object with a single click.
4) Drag and drop the image into the document.

You can also right-click on the object and choose **Insert**.

To insert an object as a link, hold down the *Shift* and *Ctrl* keys and drag and drop the object into the document.

## Inserting an image as a background

To insert an image as the background to a page or paragraph, right-click on the image in the Gallery and choose **Insert as Background > Page** or **> Paragraph**.

# Modifying, handling, and positioning images

When you insert a new image, you may need to modify it to suit the document. The placement of the picture relative to the text is discussed in "Positioning images within the text" on page 241. This section describes the use of the Picture toolbar, resizing, cropping, and a workaround to rotate a picture.

Writer provides many tools for working with images. These tools are sufficient for most people's everyday requirements. However, for professional results it is generally better to use an image manipulation program such as GIMP to modify images (for example, to crop, resize, rotate, and change color values) and then insert the result into Writer. GIMP is an open-source graphics program that can be downloaded from http://www.gimp.org/downloads/.

## Using the Picture toolbar

When you insert an image or select one already present in the document, the Picture toolbar appears. You can set it to always be present (**View > Toolbars > Picture**) and choose whether to float or dock it. Picture control buttons from the Picture toolbar can also be added to the Standard toolbar. See Chapter 21, Customizing Writer, for more information.

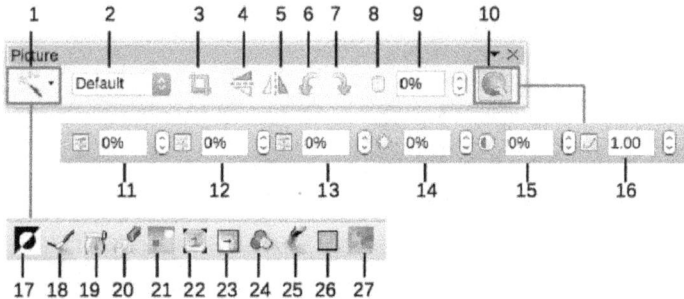

| 1 | Filter | 10 | Color | 19 | Sharpen |
|---|---|---|---|---|---|
| 2 | Image mode | 11 | Red | 20 | Remove Noise |
| 3 | Crop | 12 | Green | 21 | Solarization |
| 4 | Flip Vertically | 13 | Blue | 22 | Aging |
| 5 | Flip Horizontally | 14 | Brightness | 23 | Posterize |
| 6 | Rotate 90° Left | 15 | Contrast | 24 | Pop Art |
| 7 | Rotate 90° Right | 16 | Gamma | 25 | Charcoal Sketch |
| 8 | Frame Properties | 17 | Invert | 26 | Relief |
| 9 | Transparency | 18 | Smooth | 27 | Mosaic |

*Figure 233: Picture toolbar plus Color toolbar and Image Filter toolbar*

Two other toolbars can be opened from this one: the Image Filter toolbar, which can be torn off and placed elsewhere on the window, and the Color toolbar, which opens as a separate floating toolbar.

From these three toolbars, you can apply small corrections to the image or obtain special effects.

## Image mode

You can change color images to grayscale, to black and white, or to a watermark by selecting the image and then selecting the relevant item from the Image Mode list.

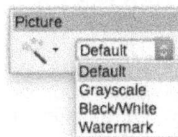

Picture

Default

Default
Grayscale
Black/White
Watermark

## Transparency

Modify the percentage value in the Transparency box on the Picture toolbar to make the image more transparent. This is particularly useful when creating a watermark or when wrapping the image in the background.

## Color

Use this toolbar to modify the individual RGB color components of the image (red, green, blue) as well as the brightness, contrast, and gamma of the image. If the result is not satisfactory, you can press *Ctrl+Z* to restore the default values.

## Flip vertically, horizontally or in 90° rotations

To flip an image vertically horizontally or rotate it by ninety degrees, select the image, and then click the relevant button.

## Image filters

Table 9 provides a short description of the available filters. The best way to understand them is to see them in action. Experiment with the different filters and filter settings, remembering that you can undo all the changes by pressing Ctrl+Z or Alt+Backspace or by selecting Edit > Undo.

*Table 9: Image filters and their effects*

| Icon | Name | Effect |
|------|------|--------|
| | Invert | Inverts the color values of a color image or the brightness values of a grayscale image. |
| | Smooth | Softens the contrast of an image. |
| | Sharpen | Increases the contrast of an image. |
| | Remove noise | Removes single pixels from an image. |
| | Solarization | Mimics the effects of too much light in a picture. A further dialog opens to adjust the parameters. |
| | Aging | Simulates the effects of time on a picture. Can be applied several times. A further dialog opens to adjust the aging level. |
| | Posterize | Makes a picture appear like a painting by reducing the number of colors used. |
| | Pop Art | Modifies the picture dramatically. |
| | Charcoal Sketch | Displays the image as a charcoal sketch. |
| | Relief | A dialog is displayed to adjust the light source that will create the shadow and, hence, the relief effect. |
| | Mosaic | Joins groups of pixels into a single area of one color. |

## Using the Formatting toolbar and Image dialog

When an image is selected, you can customize some aspects of its appearance using the tools available on the Formatting toolbar and in the dialog opened by right-clicking on the image and selecting Properties. You can, for example, create a border around the image, selecting style and color; or you can (on the Borders page of the Image dialog) add a shadow to the image.

## Cropping images

When you are only interested in a section of the image for the purpose of your document, you may wish to crop (cut off) parts of it.

### Note

If you crop an image in Writer, the image itself is not changed. Writer hides, not cuts off, part of the image. If you export the document to HTML, the original image is exported, not the cropped image.

To start cropping the image, right-click on it and select *Properties* from the context menu. In the Image dialog, select the *Crop* page.

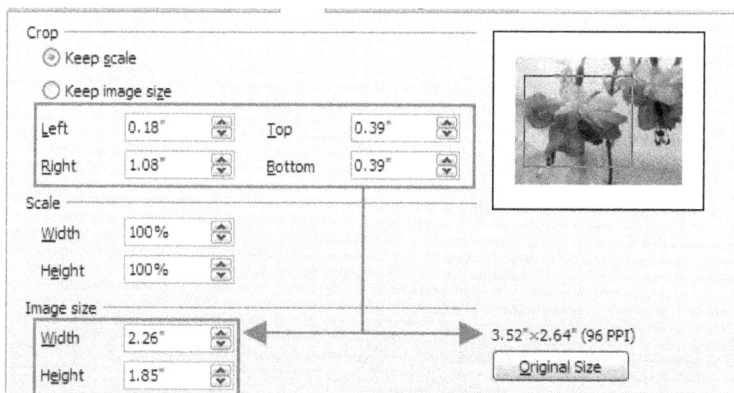

*Figure 234: Result on image size of cropping using Keep scale option*

The units of measurement shown on the Crop page are those set in **Tools > Options > LibreOffice Writer > General**.

Two options are available in the crop section for cropping an image: Keep scale and Keep image size.

Figure 234 shows that as the values in Left, Right, Top, and Bottom are altered, the boundaries of the image in the preview box change to show the crop area on the image. This results in either an image size change, or a scale change for a fixed image size (Figure 235).

The Width and Height fields under either Scale or Image size change as you enter values in the Left, Right, Top, and Bottom fields, depending on which option, Keep scale, or Keep image size, is selected.

The original image size is indicated above the Original Size button.

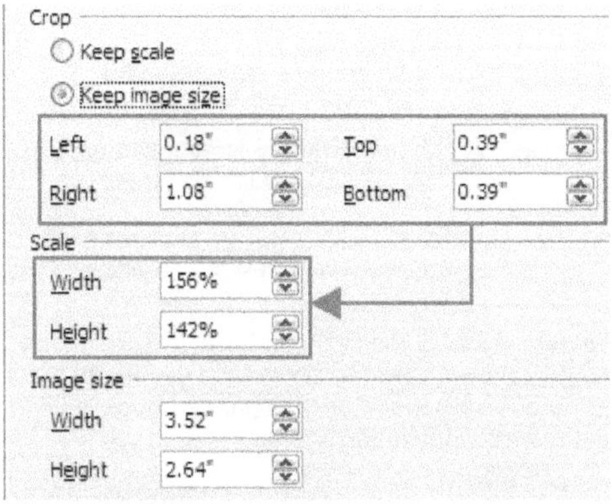

*Figure 235: Result using Keep image scale option*

# Resizing an image

To perfectly fit the image into your document, you may have to resize it. There are a number of options available in Writer to do this.

A quick and easy way to resize is by dragging the image's sizing handles:

1) Click the image, if necessary, to show the green sizing handles.

2) Position the pointer over one of the green sizing handles. The pointer changes shape, giving a graphical representation of the direction of the resizing.

3) Click and drag to resize the image.

4) Release the mouse button when satisfied with the new size.

▶ **Tip**

> The corner handles resize both the width and the height of the image simultaneously, while the other four handles resize only one dimension at a time. To retain the original proportions of the image, hold down the *Shift* key while dragging one of these handles.

For more accurate resizing of images, use either the *Crop* page (Figure 234) or the *Type* page of the Image dialog.

On the *Crop* page you can adjust the following settings:

• Scale Width and Height: specify in percentages the scaling of the image. The size of the image changes accordingly. For a symmetrical resizing, both values need to be identical.

• Image size: specify the size of the image in your preferred unit of measurement. The image enlarges or shrinks accordingly.

• Original size button: when clicked, restores the image to its original size. This will be the size resulting after any cropping was carried out.

On the *Type* page of the Image dialog, select the Relative option to toggle between percentage and actual dimension. For a symmetrical resizing, select the Keep ratio option. Clicking on the Original Size button restores the original image size, but the scale dimensions are altered if the image has been cropped.

## Rotating an image

Writer does not provide a tool for rotating an image in other than 90° increments; however, there is a simple workaround:

1) Open a new Draw or Impress document (**File > New > Drawing** or **File > New > Presentation**).
2) Insert the image you want to rotate.
3) Select the image, then in the Mode toolbar (**View > Toolbars > Mode**), select the **Rotate** icon.
4) Rotate the image as desired. Use the red handles at the corners of the image and move the mouse in the direction you wish to rotate. By default the image rotates around its center (indicated by a black cross-hair), but you can change the pivot point by moving the black cross-hair to the desired rotation center.

▶ **Tip**

To restrict the rotation angle to multiples of 15 degrees keep the *Shift* key pressed while rotating the image.

5) Select the rotated image by pressing *Ctrl+A*, then copy the image to the clipboard with *Ctrl+C*.
6) Finish by going back to the location of the Writer document where the image is to be inserted and pressing *Ctrl+V*.

## Other settings

The Image dialog (Figure 234) consists of ten pages. The *Crop* page was described on page 236; the *Type* and *Wrap* pages are explained in "Positioning images within the text" on page 241. The other pages serve the following purposes:

- Options: give the image a descriptive name (as you want it to appear in the Navigator), display alternative text when the mouse hovers over the image in a web browser, protect some of the image settings from accidental changes, and prevent the image from being printed.
- Borders: create borders around the image. The Borders dialog is the same as the one used for defining table or paragraph borders. You can also add a shadow to the image if so desired.
- Area: change the background color of the image. This setting produces the desired results only for images with a transparent color.
- Hyperlink: associate a hyperlink to the image, or create an image map (see page 251).
- Image: flip the image, and display the original location of the file in case the image is linked rather than embedded.
- Transparency: set the transparency options for the image.
- Macro: associate a macro to the image. You can choose among the predefined macros or write your own.

## Deleting an image

To delete an image, click on the image to show the green resizing handles, then press *Delete*.

## Exporting images

If you need to make complex adjustments to the image, or want to save it for use in another document, you can export it directly from the document. Right-click on the image to select it and open the context menu. Then choose **Save** to open the Image Export dialog. Depending on the original format of the image, Writer will let you save the picture in many different formats. Give a name to the image, select the desired image format in the Filter list, and click **Save**.

## Compressing images

If you insert a large image in your document and resize it to fit into the layout of the page, the complete original image is stored in the document file to preserve its content, resulting in a large document file to store or send by mail.

If you can accept some loss of quality of the image rendering, you can compress or resize the image object to reduce its data volume while preserving its display in the page layout.

Right-click to select the image and open the context menu. Then choose **Compress** to open the Compress Image dialog (Figure 236). Note that the **Calculate** button updates the image information on the dialog on each parameter set you change. Click **OK** to apply the compression settings. If the resulting image is not acceptable, press *Ctrl+Z* to undo and choose another compression setting. For more information, see the Help.

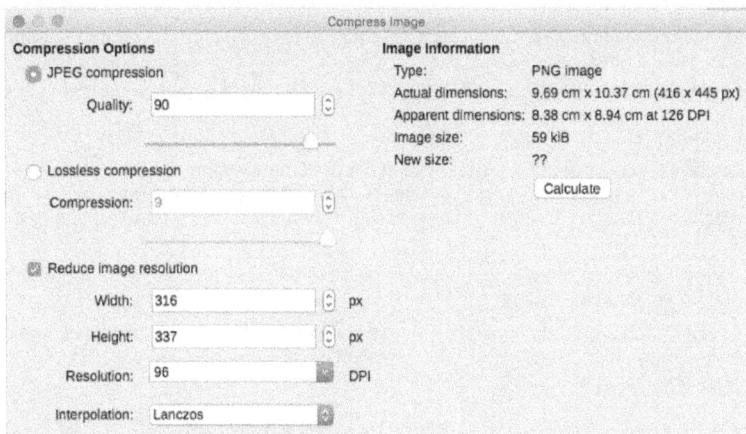

*Figure 236: Compressing an image*

# Using Writer's drawing tools

You can use Writer's drawing tools to create graphics such as simple diagrams using rectangles, circles, lines, text, and other predefined shapes. You can also group several drawing objects to make sure they maintain their relative position and proportion.

You can place the drawing objects directly on a page in your document or insert them into a frame.

You can also use the drawing tools to annotate photographs, screen captures, or other illustrations produced by other programs, but this is not recommended because:

- You cannot include images in a group with drawing objects, so they may get out of alignment in your document.
- If you convert a Writer document to another format, such as HTML, the drawing objects and the images will not remain associated; they are saved separately.

In general, if you need to create complex drawings, it is recommended you use LibreOffice Draw, which includes many more features such as layers and styles.

## Creating drawing objects

To begin using the drawing tools, display the Drawing toolbar (Figure 237) by clicking **View > Toolbars > Drawing**. This toolbar may appear at the bottom or left side of the workspace. You can move it to your preferred location and dock it, or float it and move it to a convenient place on the screen.

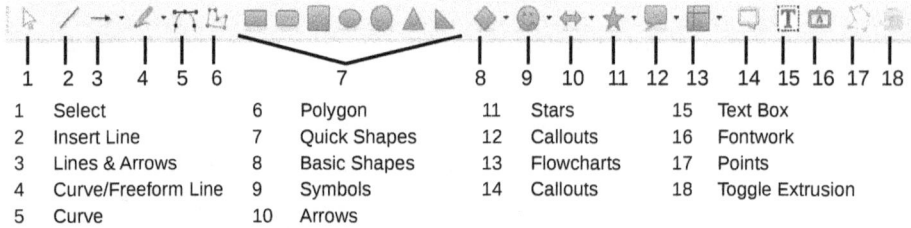

| | | | | |
|---|---|---|---|---|
| 1 | Select | 6 | Polygon | 11 | Stars | 15 | Text Box |
| 2 | Insert Line | 7 | Quick Shapes | 12 | Callouts | 16 | Fontwork |
| 3 | Lines & Arrows | 8 | Basic Shapes | 13 | Flowcharts | 17 | Points |
| 4 | Curve/Freeform Line | 9 | Symbols | 14 | Callouts | 18 | Toggle Extrusion |
| 5 | Curve | 10 | Arrows | | | | |

*Figure 237: The Drawing toolbar*

To use a drawing tool:

1) Click in the document where you want the drawing to be anchored. You can change the anchor later, if necessary.

2) Select the tool from the Drawing toolbar (Figure 237). The mouse pointer changes to a drawing-functions pointer similar to this one for a rectangle shape ( ┼□ ).

3) Move the cross-hair pointer to the place in the document where you want the image to appear and then click-and-drag to create the drawing object. Release the mouse button. The selected drawing function remains active, so you can draw another object of the same type.

4) To cancel the selected drawing function, press the *Esc* key or click the **Select** icon (the arrow) on the Drawing toolbar.

5) You can now change the properties (fill color, line type and weight, anchoring, and others) of the drawing object using either the Drawing Object Properties toolbar (Figure 238) or the choices and dialog reached by right-clicking on the drawing object.

## Setting or changing properties for drawing objects

To set the properties for a drawing object before you draw it:

1) On the Drawing toolbar (Figure 237), click the **Select** tool.

2) On the Drawing Object Properties toolbar (Figure 238), click on the icon for each property and select the value you want for that property.

3) For more control, or to define new attributes, you can click on the Area or Line icons on the toolbar to display detailed dialogs.

The default you set applies to the current document and session. It is not retained when you close the document or close Writer, and it does not apply to any other document you open. The defaults apply to all the drawing objects except text objects.

To change the properties for an existing drawing object, select the object, then continue as described above.

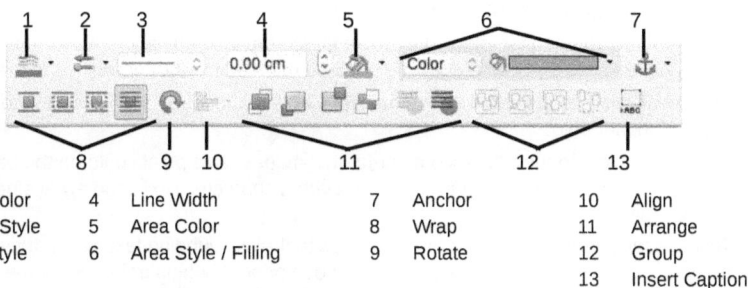

Figure 238: Drawing Object Properties toolbar

| | | | | | | |
|---|---|---|---|---|---|---|
| 1 | Line Color | 4 | Line Width | 7 | Anchor | 10 Align |
| 2 | Arrow Style | 5 | Area Color | 8 | Wrap | 11 Arrange |
| 3 | Line Style | 6 | Area Style / Filling | 9 | Rotate | 12 Group |
| | | | | | | 13 Insert Caption |

You can also specify the position and size, rotation, and slant and corner radius properties of the drawing object: right-click on the drawing object and select **Position and Size** from the context menu. Choose any properties, as required.

## Resizing a drawing object

An object is resized in a similar way to an image. Select the object, click on one of the eight handles around it and drag it to its new size. The object will be scaled up or down.

When you grab the corner handle of an object and drag it, LibreOffice will resize proportionately. If you also press the Shift key, the resizing will not keep object proportions. Conversely, if you grab one of the edges, LibreOffice will scale unproportionally in the direction perpendicular to the edge; if you also press the *Shift* key, LibreOffice will scale proportionately.

For more sophisticated control of the size of the object, choose **Format > Frame and Object > Properties** from the Menu bar. Use the *Type* tab to set the position and size independently. If the Keep ratio option is selected, then the two dimensions change so that the proportion is maintained, resulting in a scaled resizing.

## Grouping drawing objects

Grouping drawing objects makes it easier to handle several objects as a single entity, while preserving their relative sizes and positions.

To group drawing objects:

1) Select one object, then hold down the *Shift* key and select the others you want to include in the group. The bounding box expands to include all the selected objects.

2) With the objects selected, hover the mouse pointer over one of the objects and choose **Format > Group > Group** from the Menu bar or right-click and choose **Group > Group** from the context menu.

### Note

You cannot include an embedded or linked image in a group with drawing objects.

# Positioning images within the text

When you add an image to a text document, you need to choose how to position it with respect to the text and other images. The positioning of images is often rather time-consuming and may be very frustrating for both inexperienced and experienced users. As Writer is a word processor rather than a desktop publishing program, there are some limitations to the flexibility in positioning images and it takes time to get things exactly as you would like them.

Positioning of an image is controlled by four settings:

- Arrangement refers to the placement of an image on an imaginary vertical axis. Arrangement controls how images are stacked upon each other or relative to the text.
- Alignment refers to the vertical or horizontal placement of an image in relation to the chosen anchor point.
- Anchoring refers to the reference point for the images. This point could be the page, or frame where the object is, a paragraph, or even a character. An image always has an anchor point.
- Text wrapping refers to the relation of images to the surrounding text, which may wrap around the graphic on one or both sides, be overprinted behind or in front of the graphic, or treat the graphic as a separate paragraph or character.

The settings can be accessed in a number of ways, depending on the nature of the images:

1) From the Format menu, where you can find Anchor, Wrap, and Arrange (both for images and drawing objects).

2) From the context menu displayed when you right-click on the graphic; this menu also includes Alignment.

3) For images, from the Type and Wrap pages of the Image dialog. Note that you cannot control the arrangement using the dialog. To open the Image dialog, click on the image to select it and then choose **Format > Image > Properties** or right-click on the image and choose **Properties** on the context menu.

4) For drawing objects, from the Position and Size page of the Position and Size dialog. To open the dialog, right-click on the drawing object and choose Position and Size on the context menu.

5) For an embedded object (such as a Calc spreadsheet or Draw document), from the OLE-Object toolbar.

### Note

While all the positioning techniques discussed in this section apply equally to frames, contour wrapping is not possible.

## Arranging images

Arranging an image means to determine its position relative to other images or text. Arranging is only relevant when objects are overlapping. You can choose between four common settings, plus a fifth special setting for drawing objects:

**Bring to Front**
Places the image on top of any other images or text.

**Forward One**
Brings the image one level up in the stack (z-axis). Depending on the number of overlapping objects, you may need to apply this option several times to obtain the desired result.

**Back One**
Sends the image one level down in the object stack.

**Send to Back**
Sends the image to the bottom of the stack.

**To Background / To Foreground**
Only available for drawing objects; moves the drawing object behind or in front of the text respectively.

> **Tip**
>
> To select an object that is covered by other objects, press the *Tab* key to move through the objects until you reach the object you want. (*Alt+click* may also work on Windows.)

## Anchoring images

You can anchor images as a character or to a page, paragraph, or character. You can also place images in a frame and anchor the frame to a page, paragraph, or character. Which method you choose depends on what you are trying to achieve.

**To Page**
> The graphic keeps the same position in relation to the page margins. It does not move as you add or delete text or other images. This method is useful when the graphic does not need to be visually associated with a particular piece of text. It is often used when producing newsletters or other documents that are very layout intensive, or for placing logos in letterheads.

> **Caution**
>
> If you plan to use a document within a master document, do not anchor images To Page because the images will disappear from the master document. See Chapter 17, Master Documents, for more information.

**To Paragraph**
> The graphic is associated with a paragraph and moves with the paragraph. It may be placed in the margin or another location. This method is useful as an alternative to a table for placing icons beside paragraphs.

**To Character**
> The graphic is associated with a character but is not in the text sequence. It moves with the paragraph but may be placed in the margin or another location. This method is similar to anchoring to a paragraph but cannot be used with drawing objects.

**As Character**
> The graphic is placed in the document like any other character and, therefore, affects the height of the text line and the line break. The graphic moves with the paragraph as you add or delete text before the paragraph. This method is useful for keeping screen-shots in sequence in a procedure (by anchoring them as a character in a blank paragraph) or for adding a small (inline) icon in sequence in a sentence.

**To Frame**
> If the graphic has been placed in a frame, you can anchor the graphic in a fixed position inside the frame. The frame can then be anchored to the page, a paragraph, or a character, as required.

## Aligning images

Once you have established the anchor point of the graphic, you can decide the position of the graphic relative to this anchor: this is called aligning the images. Choose from six options: three for aligning the graphic horizontally (left, center, right) and three for aligning the graphic vertically (top, center, bottom). Horizontal alignment is not available for images anchored As Character.

For finer control of the alignment, use the Position options on the *Type* page of the Image dialog, shown in Figure 239.

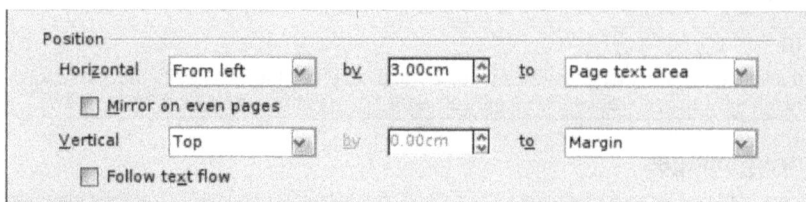

*Figure 239: Fine tuning the alignment*

For both the horizontal and vertical position, start by picking the reference point in the right hand side drop-down menu, then select in the first drop-down menu among Left, Right or Center. If you select the value From left (or From top for the vertical positioning) you can specify the amount in your selected unit of measurement. In the example in Figure 239, the upper-left corner of the image will be placed at 3 cm from the left margin of the page horizontally and on the top margin vertically.

A visual representation of the area to which the image is anchored is shown in the preview pane to the right of the page, indicated by a red bordered area. The graphic position is indicated by a green bordered area.

## Wrapping text around images

The Wrap setting determines the relation between the text and the graphic. Several choices are available from the context menu:

**No Wrap**
With this option the text is placed above and below the image but not to either side of it. This is the wrapping type used for most of the figures in this guide.

**Page Wrap or Optimal Page Wrap**
The text flows around the image. Moving the image around the page causes the text to be rearranged to fill the space to the left and right of it. Optimal Page Wrap prevents text from being placed to the side of the image if the spacing between the image and the margin is less than 2 cm.

**Wrap Through**
Superimposes the image on the text. That is, the image is in front of the text. This option must be used in conjunction with the image-transparency setting in order to make the text under the picture visible.

**In Background**
Similar to Wrap Through, but the image is placed behind the text so there may be no need to change the transparency to make the text visible.

**Note**

The No Wrap option found in the context menu of a picture is equivalent to the Wrap Off menu item in the **Format > Wrap** menu.

The wrap format is normally selected after anchoring and alignment of the image. To set the position of an image to the desired wrap format, follow these steps:

1) Select an image by clicking on it.

2) Right-click to display the context menu and move the mouse pointer to **Wrap** to display the available wrap formats. Alternatively, select **Format > Wrap** from the Menu bar.

3) Select the desired wrap format.

# Note

When anchoring an image as character, you can only adjust the distance between the image and the text, but no wrapping option is displayed.

To fine-tune the wrapping options, open the Image dialog and select the *Wrap* page.

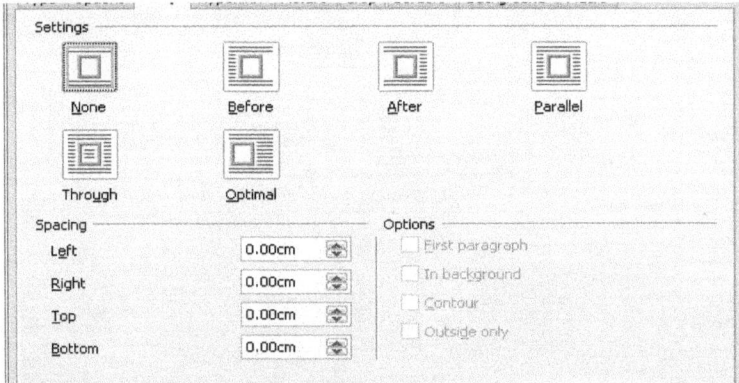

*Figure 240: The advanced wrap format options*

For images, you can open this dialog by selecting **Format > Image > Properties** from the Menu bar or right-click and select **Properties** from the context menu. For drawing objects, you can access the *Wrap* page by selecting **Format > Wrap > Edit** in the Menu bar or right-click and select **Wrap > Edit** from the context menu.

This page is divided into three sections. In the top part you can select from the wrap types mentioned above, plus two additional wrap formats that prevent the text from filling the area to the left (After) or to the right (Before) of the picture. Use the *Spacing* section of the page to adjust the spacing between the image and the text. The contents of the Options section of the page may change depending on the selected wrap format.

**First paragraph**

Check this box if you want LibreOffice to start a new paragraph after the image even if it could still wrap around the image.

**In background**

This option becomes available if Through Wrap is selected; it moves the image to the background.

**Contour**

Wraps the text around a custom contour rather than around the edge of the picture. This option is only available for Page or Optimal Page Wrap.

**Outside only**

Forces the text to wrap on the outside of the image, even if the contour contains open areas within the shape.

## Editing the contour

If you select wrapping around a drawing object, LibreOffice automatically creates a contour. The Edit Contour option is only available for image wrapping. To create a contour, right-click the image and select **Edit Contour** from the context menu, or access the Contour Editor by selecting **Format > Wrap > Contour**.

The dialog shown in Figure 241 opens with the image loaded in the main window. Use the tools to draw the region of the image you do not want to be covered by the text; this area will be shaded.

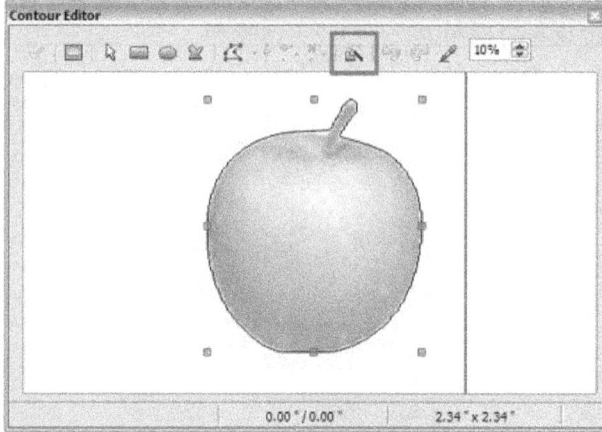

*Figure 241: The Contour Editor in action with AutoContour*

Four tools are available in the Contour Editor window: Rectangle, Ellipse, Polygon, and AutoContour. Some familiarity with drawing tools is required to create complex contours; however, in most circumstances there is no need for high accuracy. Figure 241 shows the actual contour used for "Example 2: Simple contour wrapping in action" on page 247 when using AutoContour; the shape of the line around the edge of the apple is quite acceptable.

When you are done, click on the Apply button to save the contour. If you are not satisfied with the result, you can select the contour line and press the Delete key to restart, or click the Workspace icon and then click inside the contour. You can also undo the previous steps or you can select the Edit Points button and adjust the contour shape point by point. Be aware that any of the graphic outside the contour line is not shown in the document.

### Example 1: Page wrapping

Figure 242 shows an example of page wrapping in action.

To achieve this:

1) Insert the image into the document, then anchor it to the paragraph of your choice. To move the anchor, select the image or the anchor, and move it until the anchor symbol is at the beginning of the chosen paragraph.

2) Align the image so that the left margin of the image is where you want it to be. This can be done with the mouse or using the advanced settings. The taskbar shows the location of the upper left corner and the image size.

3) Change the wrap to Page Wrap. We now wish to increase the space between the image and the text. To do this, access the Wrap page of the Picture dialog and set the gap between the image and text to 0.1" in all the boxes.

4) The last touch is to change the position so that the image has our chosen number of lines of the paragraph above it. Again, you can use the mouse to drag the image or use the advanced settings, which require a bit of trial and error. Moving with the mouse is the simplest method.

*Figure 242: Example of image with Page Wrap formatting*

## Example 2: Simple contour wrapping in action

In this example we again apply page wrapping as in Example 1, enabling this time the contour option. We will work on an image and on a drawing object as the contour option works slightly differently in each case.

The example in Figure 243 was created following the steps below.

1) Create some text.

2) Insert an image of your choice and anchor it to the first paragraph. Adjust the alignment as desired, then change the wrap type to Page Wrap.

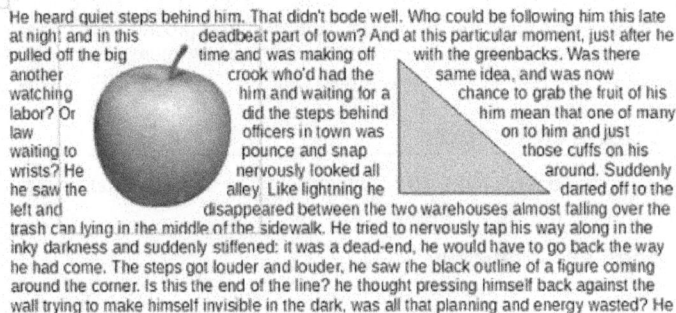

*Figure 243: Image and drawing objects with contour wrapping*

3) Right-click on the picture and select Wrap > Edit Contour from the context menu.

4) Use the technique discussed in "Editing the contour" on page 245 to create a custom contour and click Apply. If needed, adjust the spacing between the edge of the image and the text using the Wrap page of the Picture dialog.

5) Insert an AutoShape of your choice (a triangle in the example) and proceed as in step 2 above.

6) Enable the contour wrap by selecting **Format > Wrap > Contour** from the Menu bar. As discussed previously, LibreOffice automatically generates the contour. You may need to adjust the distance between the drawing object and the text using **Format > Wrap > Edit**.

### Example 3: Wrap Through and In Background

This example shows how to use an image as a watermark by wrapping the text through it and adjusting the transparency. This is not the best way to create watermarks and it is presented here only for illustration purposes. If you need to create a watermark, it is best to use a Fontworks object wrapped in the background.

Selecting the Wrap Through option for an inserted image causes the image to overlap the text, which as a result will be hidden. To make the text appear, change the transparency of the picture; although the words under the image become visible, they may be difficult to read and will appear lighter than the rest of the text.

To reproduce the example in Figure 244, create some dummy text, then insert the image of your choice. Anchor the image (to the page in the example) and select the wrap through option from the **Format > Wrap** menu or right-click on the image and select **Wrap > Wrap Through** from the context menu. Move the image into the desired position. The Picture toolbar should be displayed when the image is selected. Change the transparency to a suitable value (40% in the example) so that the text can be read.

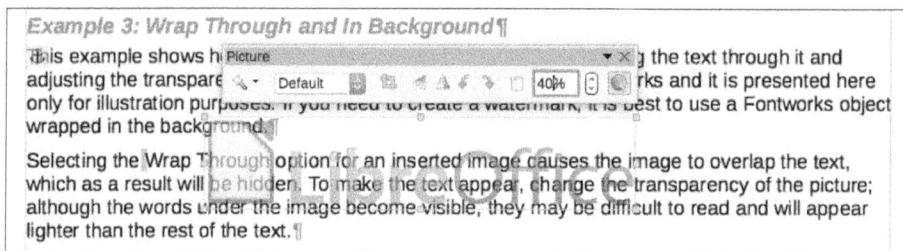

Figure 244: Transparent image added over the text

You can obtain a better result if you set an image's wrap to In Background. With this selection all the text will be clearly readable, with all characters having the same intensity, as long as the background is not too dark. You may still need to adjust the transparency of the image.

# Adding captions to images

You can add captions to images in three ways: automatically, by using the Caption dialog, or manually.

## Adding captions automatically

You can set up LibreOffice to add captions automatically whenever you insert an image, a table, or other objects into a document. You can choose which objects are captioned automatically, what the sequence name is for each caption (for example, "Table" or "Illustration"), and the position of the caption.

To set up automatic captions:

1) Click **Tools > Options > LibreOffice Writer > AutoCaption**.

2) Several choices are available at the right of the dialog for adding captions automatically. Choose which objects you want to be automatically captioned and specify the characteristics of the captions.

When you insert an image, if automatic captioning is enabled, the graphic is placed in a frame along with a caption containing the default sequence name for images: Illustration. Position the cursor in the caption area and type the text for the caption. You can change the sequence name by selecting one from the drop-down Category list or typing in your own.

A common sequence name—Figure—is not one of the names provided: <None>, Drawing, Illustration, Table, and Text. If you want the name "Figure" or any other custom name for your images, do the following:

1) Open the AutoCaption dialog, as described above.

2) In the *Add captions automatically when inserting* section, select **LibreOffice Writer Image**. This activates the Caption area in the dialog for images.

3) Under the Category drop-down list, enter the name that you want added (say, Figure), by overwriting any sequence name in the list. (Overwriting a term does not delete it from the drop-down list.) You can also set some options for the number style and for a separator between the name and the number, if desired. Click **OK** to save the changes.

## Adding captions using the Caption dialog

To add captions using the Caption dialog:

1) Insert the graphic, then either right-click it and select **Insert Caption** from the context menu, or select it and choose **Insert > Caption** from the Menu bar.

2) Under *Properties* on the Caption dialog (Figure 245), make your selections for the Category, Numbering, and Separator fields [Illustration, Arabic (1 2 3), and a colon (:), respectively, for the example in Figure 245] and type your caption text in the Caption text box at the top. Whatever text you enter for the caption appears in the box at the bottom, after the sequence name, number, and separator.

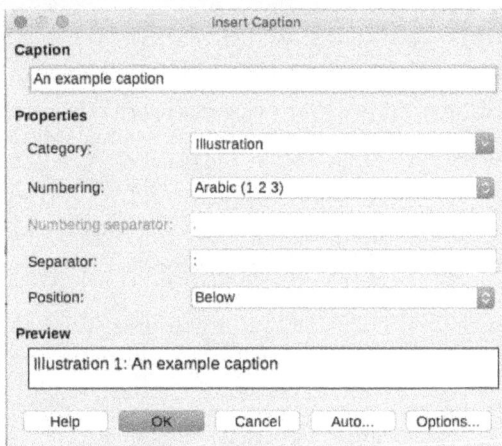

*Figure 245: Defining the caption for an illustration*

3) Click **OK**. The graphic and its caption are placed in a frame.

### ▶ Tip

In the Category box, you can type any name you want, for example Figure, if the drop-down list does not include it. Writer will create a numbering sequence using that name, as it does when using the AutoCaption feature.

### *Numbering images by chapter*

Additional options for numbering captions are available under the Options button in the Captions dialog (Figure 246). Some of these settings, which refer to the outline level, will have an effect only if you are using outline level paragraph styles on the chapter headings within your document.

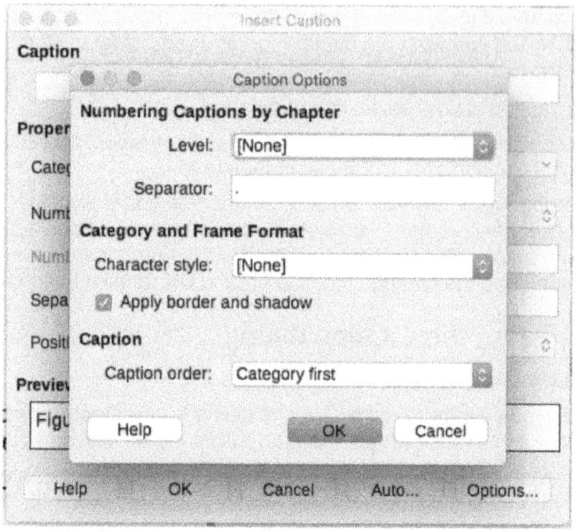

*Figure 246: Options for numbering figures*

When chapter numbering is set up, Writer will restart the caption numbering for each chapter it encounters. For example, if the last figure caption you create in chapter 1 is Figure 1.15, and the next figure caption you create is in chapter 2, the numbering will start over at Figure 2.1.

Options available to chapter numbering for captions include the following:

- Use **Level** to specify the outline level that triggers a restart of the numbering as well as how many levels of outline numbering are shown before the table number. For example, if the document uses Heading 1 style for chapters and Heading 2 style for sub-headings, if you want all the tables in a chapter (that is, between two Heading 1 paragraphs) to be numbered sequentially independently of the sub-heading they are under, select 1 as Level. If instead you want to restart the numbering at each sub-heading, select level 2.

- Use the **Separator** field to establish the separator between the chapter number and figure number.

- Use **Character style** to set a character style for the caption. This is useful if the separator of your choice is not a symbol included in the default font type of your document or if you want the caption to have a special color, size and so on.

- The **Apply border and shadow** option does not apply to table captions. LibreOffice normally wraps the objects you can add a caption to in a frame, but not for tables.

- Use **Caption order** to specify whether you want the category or numbering to appear first in the caption.

## Adding captions manually

If you need to save as *.docx files or export in other formats, you may find that captions applied as described above (either automatically or using the Caption dialog) are lost during the export.

To avoid export problems, or as another way to put captions above pictures or below them (the usual case), you can add a caption manually, in either of two ways:

- Place the graphic and its caption in separate paragraphs.
- Use a table.

### *Place the graphic and its caption in separate paragraphs*

Insert the graphic and anchor it to its paragraph as a character. Press Enter to create a new paragraph for the caption.

1) In the caption paragraph, type, for example, Figure and add a space.

2) To insert the figure number automatically, click **Insert > Fields > Other** (*Ctrl+F2*) and select the *Variables* tab.

3) Select Number range in the Type list. Select Figure in the Selection list and choose, for example, Arabic (1 2 3) in the Format drop-down list. Click the **Insert** button.

4) A number will appear after the word "Figure" in the caption. Now, type the text of the caption.

> ### Tip
>
> If you are manually adding captions to a lot of figures using this method, you might want to make an AutoText entry containing, for example, Figure and a space, the figure-number field, and an optional separator and a space after it.
>
> To ensure the picture and its caption stay together on the page, create a new paragraph style, for example Figure. If the picture is going above the caption, define the text flow of the Figure paragraph style as Keep with next paragraph and the next style as Caption. Conversely, if the caption is going above, define the Caption paragraph style as Keep with next paragraph and the next style as Figure.

### *Use a table*

Create a one-column, two-row table. Place the picture in one row and type the caption in the other row—or use two or more rows for the caption and other text. This method can be especially useful for pictures with numbered legends, such as Figure 237 on page 240.

## Creating an image map

An image map defines areas of an image (called hotspots) with hyperlinks to web addresses, other files on the computer, or parts of the same document. Hotspots are the graphic equivalent of text hyperlinks. Clicking on a hotspot causes LibreOffice to open the linked page in the appropriate program (for example, the default browser for an HTML page; LibreOffice Calc for a ODS file; a PDF viewer for a PDF file). You can create hotspots of various shapes and include several hotspots in the same image.

To use the image map editor (Figure 247):

1) In the Writer document, select the image in which you want to define the hotspots.

2) Choose **Edit > ImageMap** from the Menu bar. The ImageMap Editor (Figure 247) opens.

3) Use the tools and fields in the dialog (described below) to define the hotspots and links necessary.

4) Click the Apply icon ( ) to apply the settings.

5) When done, click the Save icon ( ) to save the image map to a file, then close the dialog.

Figure 247: The dialog to create or edit an image map

The main part of the dialog shows the image on which the hotspots are defined. A hotspot is identified by a line indicating its shape.

The toolbar at the top of the dialog contains the following tools:

- Apply button: click this button to apply the changes.
- Open, Save, and Select icons.
- Tools for drawing a hotspot shape: these tools work in exactly the same way as the corresponding tools in the Drawing toolbar.
- Edit, Move, Insert, Delete Points: advanced editing tools to manipulate the shape of a polygon hotspot. Select the Edit Points tool to activate the other tools.
- Active icon: toggles the status of a selected hotspot between active and inactive.
- Macro: associates a macro with the hotspot instead of just associating a hyperlink.
- Properties: sets the hyperlink properties and adds the Name attribute to the hyperlink.

Below the toolbar, specify for the selected hotspot:

- Address: the address pointed by the hyperlink. You can also point to an anchor in a document; to do this, write the address in this format:
  file:///<path>/document_name#anchor_name
- Text: type the text that you want to be displayed when the mouse pointer is moved over the hotspot.
- Frame: where the target of the hyperlink will open: pick among _blank (opens in a new browser window), _self (opens in the active browser window), _top or _parent.

▶ Tip

The value _self for the target frame will work just fine in the vast majority of occasions. It is therefore not recommended to use the other choices unless absolutely necessary.

# Managing the LibreOffice Gallery

Graphics in the Gallery are grouped by themes, such as Arrows, Diagrams, and People. You can create other groups or themes and add your own pictures or find extensions containing more graphics. Click on a theme to see its contents displayed in the Gallery window.

You can display the Gallery in Icon View (Figure 231) or Detailed View (Figure 248), and you can hide or show the Gallery by clicking on the Sidebar's Hide button.

### Note

> In some installations, only the My themes theme is customizable, although new themes can be added as explained in "Adding a new theme to the Gallery" on page 255. The locked themes are easily recognizable by right-clicking on them; the only available option in the context menu is Properties.

By default, the Gallery is opened in the Sidebar. You can float the Gallery as you can other Sidebar panes; see Chapter 1, Introducing Writer, for more information.

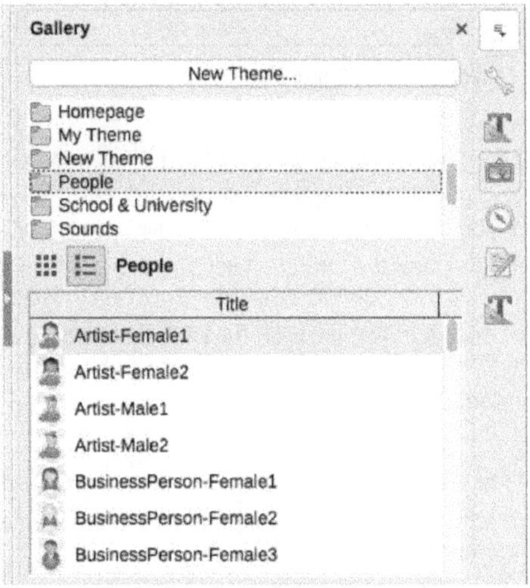

*Figure 248: Gallery in Detailed View*

## Adding objects to the Gallery

You may wish to add to the My Theme folder in the Gallery any images that you use frequently, for example, a company logo. You can then easily insert these graphics into a document later.

1) Right-click on the My Theme folder and select **Properties** from the context menu.
2) In the theme's Properties dialog, click the *Files* tab (Figure 249).

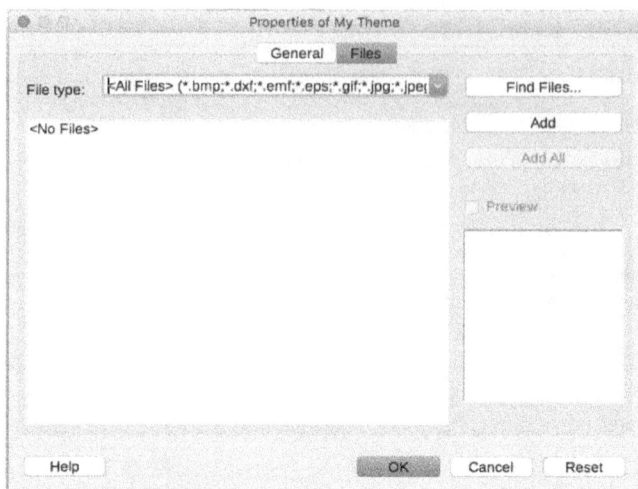

*Figure 249: Gallery Properties dialog*

To add several files at once:

1) In the Properties of My Theme dialog, click the **Find Files** button.

2) The Select path dialog (not shown) opens. You can enter the path for the file's directory in the Path text box, or you can navigate to locate the file's directory.

3) Click the **Select** button to start the search. A list of graphic files is then displayed in the Properties dialog. You can use the File type drop-down list to limit the files displayed.

4) To add all of the files shown in the list, click **Add All**. Otherwise, select the files to add and then click **Add** (hold down either the *Shift* key or the *Ctrl* key while clicking on the files).

5) Click **OK** on the Properties dialog to close it.

To add a single file:

1) In the Properties of My Theme dialog, click **Add** to open the Gallery dialog.

2) Use the navigation controls to locate the image to add to the theme. Select it and then click **Open** to add it to the theme.

3) Click **OK** on the Properties dialog to close it.

## Deleting images from the Gallery

To delete an image from a theme:

1) Right-click on the name of the image file or its thumbnail in the Gallery.

2) Click **Delete** in the context menu. A confirmation message appears; click **Yes**.

**Note**

Deleting the name of a file from the list in the Gallery does not delete the file from the hard disk or other location.

## Adding a new theme to the Gallery

To add a new theme to the Gallery:

1) Click the **New Theme** button above the list of themes (Figure 248).
2) In the Properties of New Theme dialog, click the *General* tab and type a name for the new theme.
3) Click the *Files* tab and add images to the theme, as described earlier.

## Deleting a theme from the Gallery

To delete a theme from the Gallery:

1) Go to **Insert > Media > Gallery**.
2) Select from the list of themes the theme you wish to delete.
3) Right-click on the theme, then click **Delete** on the context menu.

## Location of the Gallery and the objects in it

Graphics and other objects shown in the Gallery can be located anywhere on your computer's hard disk, on a network drive, or other removable media. When you add graphics to the Gallery, the files are not moved or copied; the location of each new object is simply added as a reference.

In a workgroup, you may have access to a shared Gallery (where you cannot change the contents unless authorized to do so) and a user Gallery, where you can add, change, or delete objects.

The location of the user Gallery is specified in **Tools > Options > LibreOffice > Paths**. You can change this location, and you can copy your gallery files (SDV) to other computers.

Gallery contents provided with LibreOffice are stored in a different location. You cannot change this location.

### Note

Gallery themes can be packed for distribution through the LibreOffice extensions framework. In that case, the location of the graphic files is determined by the extension settings. To get more gallery themes, visit the LibreOffice extensions website at http://extensions.libreoffice.org.

# Using Fontwork

With Fontwork you can create graphical text art objects to make your work more attractive. There are many different settings for text art objects (line, area, position, size, and more), so you have a large choice.

Fontwork is available with each component of LibreOffice, but you will notice small differences in the way that each component displays it.

## Creating a Fontwork object

1) Choose **Insert > FontWork** from the Menu bar. Or, click the Fontwork Gallery icon 🅰 on the Fontwork toolbar (**View > Toolbars > Fontwork**) or the Drawing toolbar (**View > Toolbars > Drawing**).
2) In the Fontwork Gallery (Figure 250), select a Fontwork style, then click **OK**. The Fontwork object will appear in your document.

*Figure 250: The Fontwork Gallery*

3) Notice the colored squares around the edge (indicating that the object is selected) and the yellow dot; these are discussed in "Moving and resizing Fontwork objects" on page 258.

Resize the object using one of the corner handles (hold down the *Shift* key to keep the sides proportional), or right-click and choose **Position and Size** from the context menu for more precise sizing.

4) Double-click the object to edit the Fontwork text (see Figure 251). Select the text and type your own text in place of the black Fontwork text that appears over the object.

*Figure 251: Editing Fontwork text*

5) Click anywhere in a free space or press *Esc* to apply your changes.

## Editing a Fontwork object

Now that the Fontwork object is created, you can edit some of its attributes. To do this, you can use the Fontwork toolbar, the Formatting toolbar, or menu options as described in this section. If the selected Fontwork object is a 3-D object, you can also use the 3D-Settings toolbar.

### Using the Fontwork toolbar

Make sure that the Fontwork toolbar, shown in Figure 252, is visible. If you do not see it, go to View > Toolbars > Fontwork. Click on the different icons to edit Fontwork objects.

*Figure 252: The floating Fontwork toolbar*

**Fontwork Shape:** Edits the shape of the selected object. You can choose from a palette of shapes.

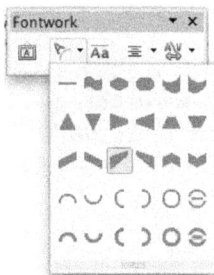

*Figure 253: Fontwork toolbar showing palette of shapes*

**Fontwork Same Letter Heights:** Changes the height of characters in the object. Toggles between normal height (some characters taller than others, for example capital letters, d, h, I and others) and all letters the same height.

*Figure 254: Left: normal letters; right: same letter heights*

**Fontwork Alignment:** Changes the alignment of characters. Choices are left align, center, right align, word justify, and stretch justify. The effects of the text alignment can only be seen if the text spans over two or more lines. In the stretch justify mode, all the lines are filled completely.

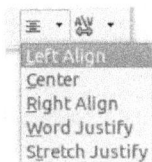

**Fontwork Character Spacing:** Changes the character spacing and kerning in the object. Select from the choices in the drop-down list.

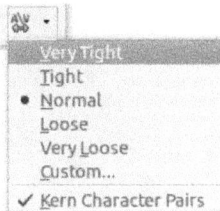

## Using the Formatting toolbar

You can customize the Fontwork object with several more attributes. Click on the object; the Formatting toolbar changes to show the options for customizing the object. These choices are the same as the ones for other drawing objects, described earlier in this chapter. See also the *Draw Guide* for details.

## Using menu options

You can use some the choices on the Format menu to anchor, align, arrange, and group selected Fontwork objects, wrap text around them, and flip them horizontally and vertically.

You can also right-click on a Fontwork object and choose many of the same options from the context menu. The context menu also provides quick access to the Line, Area, Text, and Position and Size dialogs. For more information on all of these menu options, see the *Draw Guide*.

### Using the 3D-Settings toolbar

If the selected Fontwork object is a 3-D object, you can also use the options on the 3D-Settings toolbar. You can also change a 2-D Fontwork object into a 3-D object (or change a 3-D object into a 2-D object) by clicking the Extrusion On/Off icon on the 3D-Settings toolbar. For more information, see the *Draw Guide*.

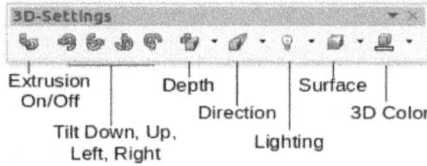

## Moving and resizing Fontwork objects

When you select a Fontwork object, eight colored squares (known as handles) appear around the edge of the object, as shown below. You can drag these handles to resize the object.

A yellow dot also appears on the object. This dot may be along an edge of the object, or it may be somewhere else; in the example on the right. If you hover the pointer over this yellow dot, the pointer turns into a hand symbol. You can drag the dot in different directions to distort the object.

Hovering the pointer over other parts of the object turns the pointer into the usual symbol for dragging the object to another part of the page.

For precise control of the location and size of the object, use the Position and Size areas of the *Type* tab in the Properties dialog.

# LibreOffice

Chapter 12
*Lists: Tips and Tricks*

# Introduction

This chapter expands on information given in Chapter 9, Working with Styles, and provides some extra examples.

In many word processors, list options are included in paragraph styles, but Writer treats them as a separate type of style.

Writer's separate list styles have two major advantages:

- The same list style can be used with multiple paragraph styles, avoiding duplication of design work.
- A paragraph's associated list style can be changed with a single selection.

▶ **Tip**

You cannot change the style used by the default toolbar buttons for lists. You can create new toolbar buttons that apply list styles to paragraphs, but a better strategy is to create paragraph styles for lists and, if you wish, create toolbar buttons for them. See Chapter 21, Customizing Writer, for information on creating toolbar buttons.

# Types of list

With list styles, you can create three types of list:

- Bullet lists: Unordered lists whose items start with a bullet, special character, dingbat, or graphic.
- Numbered lists: Ordered lists whose items start with a number, upper or lower case letters, or upper and lower case Roman numerals.
- Outline lists: Hierarchical summaries of an argument or piece of writing, in which each level has its own numbering system.

All these types of list are in common use today, especially online.

Each type of list has its own set of conventions about how they are structured and used, as described in this section.

## Bullet lists

Bullet lists are popular in technical documents, presentations, and many web sites and other online documents. Writer provides several pre-defined bullet list styles (see Figure 255), and you can select others from the Gallery or create your own bullets.

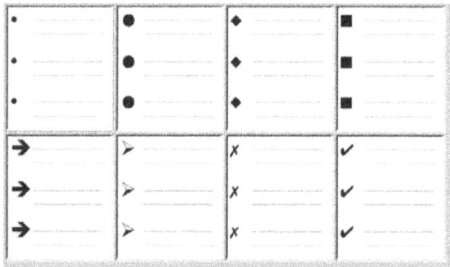

*Figure 255: Writer's pre-defined bullet types*

### *The conventions for bullet lists*

The use of bullet lists follows well-defined conventions. Bullet lists:

- Are used only when the order of the points is irrelevant. You might want to arrange points for rhetorical effect, starting with one fairly important point and ending with your strongest point, but readers do not actually need to know one point before another.
- Have three points or more. If you have two points, they both stay in the body of the text.
- Are introduced in the last sentence in the body text above them either without any punctuation, or with a colon.
- Consist of points that are all grammatical completions of the last sentence in the paragraph before them. That means that each point has a similar grammatical structure to the others. In this bullet list, for instance, each point starts with a present tense verb.
- May be sentence fragments, but should be consistent with each other. For example, they could be all nouns or participles.
- Start with a bullet on, or indented from, the left margin, then indent for the text. If they are lists within lists, then the bullet has the same indent as the text in the top level list.
- Can start with either an upper or lower case letter, so long as the convention is consistent throughout the list and the document.
- End each point with the same punctuation. No punctuation, commas, semi-colons, and periods are all valid choices. What matters is the consistency of list items and of all lists within the document.
- Are generally no more than 6–8 items long. Much longer, and the ease of reading is lost.
- Do not use an "and," "or," or any other word to introduce the last point in the list, even though that would be grammatically correct.
- Are sometimes considered too informal to use. When in doubt, avoid them.

## Numbered lists

While people number lists all the time, the convention is that numbered lists should only be used when the order of the information matters. For instance, in a procedure in a technical manual, one step might be impossible – or even dangerous – without doing another one first.

Writer provides several pre-defined numbered list styles (Figure 256), and you can define others.

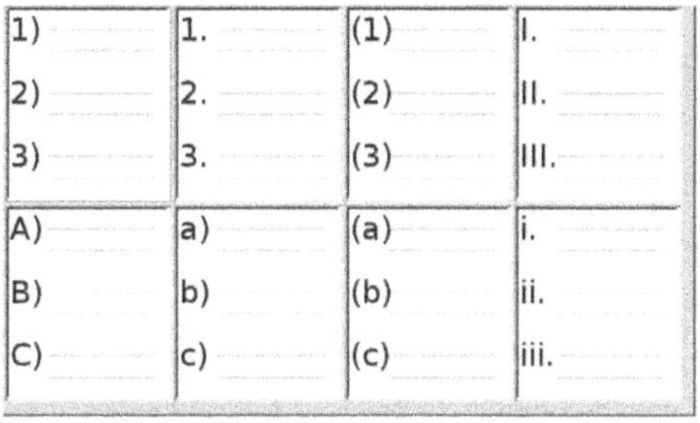

| 1) | 1. | (1) | I. |
|---|---|---|---|
| 2) | 2. | (2) | II. |
| 3) | 3. | (3) | III. |
| A) | a) | (a) | i. |
| B) | b) | (b) | ii. |
| C) | c) | (c) | iii. |

*Figure 256: Writer's pre-defined numbered lists*

### *The conventions for numbered lists*

Numbered lists have fewer conventions than bullet lists, but they do have a few:

- They are used when the order of items is important. If the order is irrelevant, use bullet lists instead.
- Like bullet lists, they are used only for three items or more. Two-step procedures stay in the body of the text.
- They are generally introduced in the body text by a summary of the overall task they describe that ends in a colon. For example, "To install the software update, follow these steps:" or, simply "To install:"
- Each step can have multiple paragraphs, most of them unnumbered, describing what happens when it is performed or the alternatives.
- The steps in a procedure should be less than a dozen (some suggest 6–8).

> ### Tip
>
> If each step has multiple paragraphs or you have more than about a dozen steps, you may need to break down the list into smaller lists or else present the points as ordinary body text.

## Outline lists

Outline lists summarize the structure of a much longer, typically unwritten document. In finished technical and legal documents, they are used in headings to make the structure obvious, although this use is becoming less common than it was a few decades ago.

Writer gives several options for outline lists (see Figure 257). List styles create an outline method that uses a single paragraph style. When such a paragraph style is in use, you change the level and the numbering by pressing the *Tab* key to descend a level, and *Shift+Tab* to ascend a level. This single style outlining is by far the quickest to apply and learn.

You can choose to use outline lists when writing a document and then, before publication, remove the letters and numbers of the outline by changing or removing the numbering style associated with the paragraph style.

| | | | |
|---|---|---|---|
| 1. | 1. | 1. | 1. |
| 1.1. | a) | (a) | 1. |
| a) | • | i. | 1. |
| • | • | A. | 1. |
| • | • | •. | 1. |
| I. | A. | 1 | ➤ |
| A. | I. | 1.1 | → |
| i. | a. | 1.1.1 | •) |
| a) | i. | 1.1.1.1 | • |
| • | • | 1.1.1.1.1 | • |

*Figure 257: Writer's pre-defined outline list styles*

### *The conventions for outline lists*

The conventions for outline lists are:

- Usually, a different numbering system is used for each level to help distinguish them.
- Levels can be ordered using Arabic numerals, upper and lower case Roman numerals, and upper and lower case letters.

- Upper case Roman numerals are usually reserved for the top level, and upper case letters are used before lower case ones. Another alternative is Arabic numbers followed by lower case letters. However, these rules are not fixed.

- In technical manuals, you used to see multiple levels in a heading (for instance, I.A.2 or 1.1.1). These headings have largely fallen out of practice except in a few specialized cases such as legal documents, for the obvious reason that they are hard to remember. Also, if each heading is indented, after two or three levels almost no space is left for text.

## Combining list and paragraph styles

Paragraph styles are essential to lists and outlining. When applying a list style, the underlying paragraph style remains unchanged. If your list must also have a certain font size, indentations, and so on, you might expect to first apply a paragraph style and then a list style (or the other way around). However, you can embed a list style in a paragraph style using the *Outline & Numbering* page of the Paragraph Style dialog, and then apply only the paragraph style to the list.

This section gives an example of combining list and paragraph styles.

1) Create a list style you want to use for the paragraph. For example: MyNumberedList.

2) Create a new paragraph style.

3) On the *Organizer* page of the Paragraph Style dialog:

   a) Give the new paragraph style a name, say NumberedParagraph.

   b) For the Next Style, choose NumberedParagraph (this will make the following paragraph also be in this style, until you choose a different style).

   c) In *Inherited from*, choose None.

4) Set up this paragraph style to your liking. Because the indentation is controlled by the List style, to avoid undesired interactions do not change the indent settings on the Indents & Spacing page. (You might want to change the spacing above and below the paragraph.)

5) On the *Outline & Numbering* page (Figure 258), choose the MyNumberedList style created in step 1. See Figure 258.

6) Click **OK** to save this style.

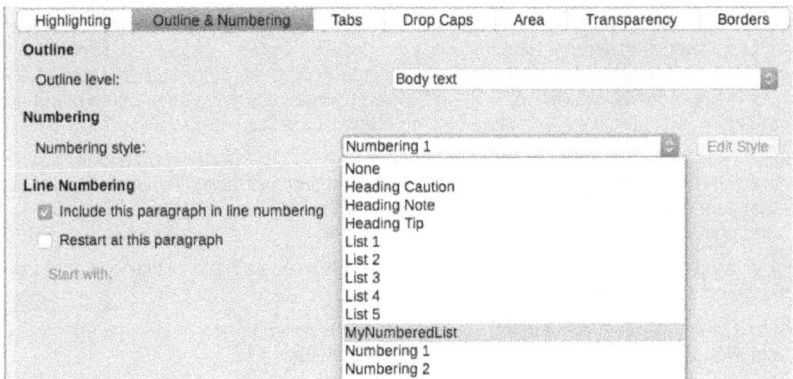

*Figure 258: Assigning a List style to a Paragraph style*

To have full control, it is common practice to define three base paragraph styles for lists: List Start for the first element of the list, List Continue for the subsequent elements of the list, and List End for the last element of the list. You could also define a paragraph style to be used for unnumbered list items (one for each nested level you intend to use) as well as an introductory style for the paragraph preceding the start of the list (to allow for keeping the introductory paragraph with the first list item, or for specifying spacing before the first list item that is different from the spacing between other paragraphs).

## Restarting paragraph numbering

To restart the numbering of any numbered list, right-click on the paragraph and select **Restart Numbering** from the context menu or use the **Restart at this paragraph** option in the *Numbering* section on the Paragraph dialog (Figure 259).

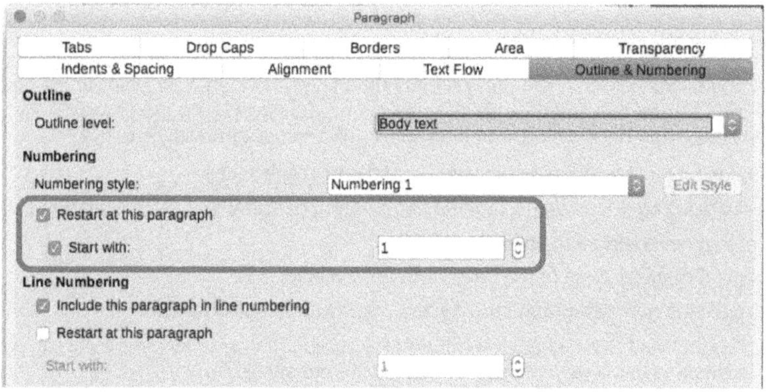

*Figure 259: Restarting paragraph numbering*

**Note**

The *Restart at this paragraph* field in the Line Numbering section of the *Outline & Numbering* tab is for line numbering, not paragraph numbering.

## Nesting lists

A nested list – a list within a list – is a numbered or bulleted list with subordinate (usually indented) numbered or bulleted lists. Rather than just a list of numbered items (1, 2, 3...), a nested list may have item 1, then indented items numbered a, b, c or i, ii, iii or some other numbering method before the main number 2. With numbering styles, you can achieve any combination of numbering formats you want. A nested list may even combine numbered items with bulleted items.

To nest a list, you have two choices. The first is to create a list style, and set up two or more list levels with different formatting choices on the *Position* and *Options* tabs. The advantage of list levels is that each level can be formatted separately, but all the levels remain connected. You can switch to the next level below by pressing the *Tab* key, or to the one above by pressing *Shift+Tab*.

The preview pane can help you set up each list level, and the customized list style is associated with a paragraph style for use.

To switch to a lower list level while using the associated paragraph style, press the *Tab* key before entering content; to switch to a higher list level, press *Shift+Tab*.

The second choice is to create two list styles, then associate each list style with a separate paragraph style.

Neither choice has any advantage over the other, since you are still dealing with the same options. However, in both cases, each nested list is typically indented more than the list level above it. Typically, too, each list level will use a different bullet style or numbering system.

Style names like *Bulleted* and *Bulleted 2* or *Nested* will help to remind you of the relation between the two paragraph styles. For convenience, use the same names for both the Paragraph and List styles, since they cannot be mixed up.

1st list style   1. Lorem ipsum dolor sit amet, consectetur adipiscing elit.

      2. Sed et urna ac lorem malesuada venenatis ut et lorem.

2nd list style    • Phasellus imperdiet lorem turpis, at egestas neque egestas nec.

      • Vestibulum a nibh ante.

      • Sed accumsan orci at turpis tempor, sit amet pulvinar ipsum vehicula.

1st list style   3. Tincidunt ac magna.

*Figure 260: Nested lists created using two separate list styles*

# Outlining with paragraph styles

LibreOffice has several ways to outline using paragraph styles. With **Tools > Chapter Numbering**, you can choose a numbering style for each paragraph style, making it part of the Outline Levels. Alternatively, you can ignore **Tools > Chapter Numbering**, and associate each Heading style with a separate list style using the Styles and Formatting window.

An even easier form of outlining is to create a single list style for outlining. You can manually set up the different levels on the list style's *Customize* tab, or you can get much the same result by selecting a pre-defined pattern from the list style's *Outline* tab instead.

To use the paragraph style, press *Enter+Tab* to add a sub-level paragraph. The sub-level paragraph automatically uses the numbering pattern of the list style. To raise the level of a paragraph style, press *Enter+Tab+Shift*.

## Creating outlines with a single paragraph style

To set up a single paragraph style for outlining:

1) Create a list style and associate it with one of the pre-defined formats on the *Outline* tab.
2) Select or make a paragraph style for outlining. You cannot use the *Heading 1-10* styles. Presumably, this restriction prevents confusion between a single paragraph style outline and the registered outline levels.
3) On the *Organizer* tab of the paragraph style, set the style to use itself as the *Next style*.
4) Assign the list style to the paragraph style using the *Numbering* field on the paragraph style's *Outline & Numbering* tab.

## Adding paragraph styles to outline levels

Outline levels are a concept used throughout LibreOffice to automate advanced features. For example, outline levels determine which paragraph styles are displayed by default in the Navigator under *Headings,* and in a table of contents.

By default, outline levels are mapped to the *Heading 1-10* paragraph styles. *Outline Level 1* is mapped to *Heading 1*, and so on. You can change these mappings, or add another paragraph style to an outline level in the *Outline level* field on the *Outline & Numbering* tab (see Figure 261).

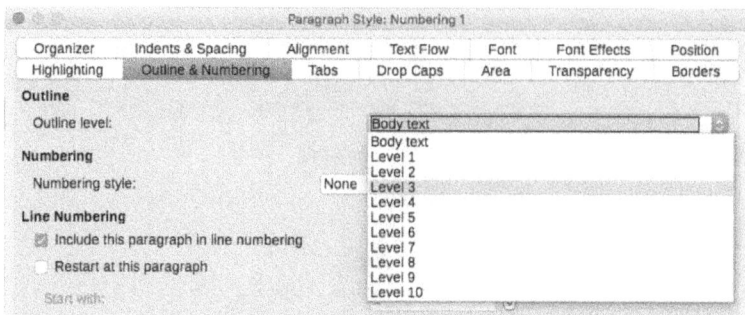

*Figure 261: Assigning a paragraph style to an outline level*

▶ **Tip**

You can assign more than one paragraph style to an outline level, but only one paragraph style displays in **Tools > Chapter Numbering**.

## Skipping a paragraph in a list

In many lists, each paragraph is a list item and is therefore numbered or bulleted. However, you sometimes need to break up a list with an unnumbered or unbulleted paragraph that gives more detail about a list item. Without such a paragraph, a list item may turn into a long paragraph, reducing the readability that is the whole point of using a list.

To create a style for such paragraphs, use the paragraph style with a list to create a linked paragraph that is mostly formatted identically except for on the *Outline & Numbering* tab, where:

- *Outline Level* is set to *Body Text*.
- *Numbering Style* is set to *None*.
- *This paragraph in line numbering* is unchecked.

If you have only a few horizontal indents, this style may be usable with multiple lists. *Body Text Indent* is a pre-defined paragraph style that you can use for this purpose.

# Naming list styles

LibreOffice uses *List 1-5* for default bullet lists, and *Numbering 1-5* for numbered lists. However, these names are too limited to remember easily. Instead, add your own styles and give them descriptive names like *Arabic Numeral Blue* or *Lower Case Indented*.

▶ **Tip**

Using the same name for both the list style and the paragraph style with which it is linked can make working with different types of styles much easier. If you use a character style to define the bullet or number, give it the same name, too.

Along with each basic paragraph style, LibreOffice also includes list styles ending in *Cont.* (Continue), *End,* and *Start.* You can use these styles to customize lists.

For example, the *Start* list style might have extra space above it to separate the list from the body text, and the *End* list style extra space below it.

The *Cont.* style is sometimes used for unnumbered paragraphs in a list that have a different format. However, the name suggests using it with a list style with the *Numbering* field set to *None* on the *Options* tab, and *(continued)* or the equivalent in the *Before* field.

The text in the *Before* field will be added automatically whenever you apply the style.

▶ **Tip**

If the paragraph has no other content than the *Before* field, you need to type a space before you press the *Enter* key. Otherwise, the paragraph disappears.

If you decide not to use these styles, you can right-click on each of them in the *Styles and Formatting* window and hide them. You can go to the *Hidden* view and unhide them later if you decide you need them after all.

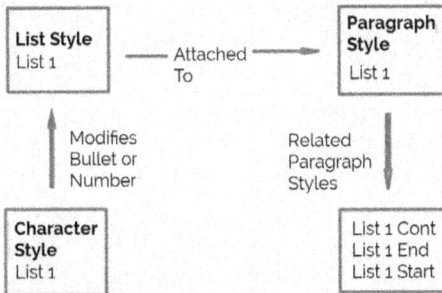

*Figure 262: Give related styles similar names and you can locate the ones you need more quickly*

# Formatting list styles

You have two ways of formatting bullets and numbers in list styles.

The quick way is to select a style from the *Bullets, Numbering Style, Outline,* or *Image* tabs for a list style. Each of these tabs give a variety of options, although not an exhaustive list.

Although the choices on the *Image* tab look old-fashioned, they can be useful; for instance, see "Example: Styling the Tips, Notes, and Cautions in this book" on page 274.

The second and more practical way is to customize bullets or numbered lists for yourself, using the *Options* and *Position* tabs. Both tabs have ten levels. This setting is mostly useful for creating a single outline numbering style, in which the numbering changes each time you press the *Tab* key (see "Outline lists," page 262).For most bulleted and numbered lists, either set the *Level* to *1*, or leave the *Level* at the default *1-10*.

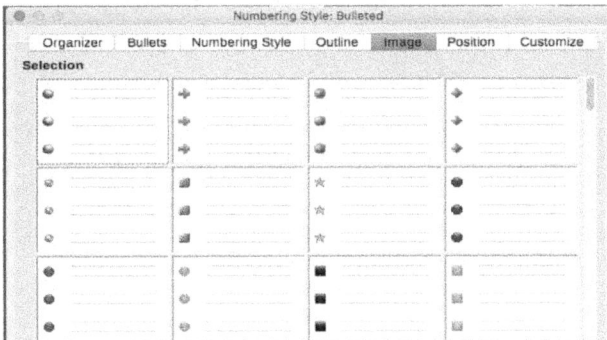

*Figure 263: The bullets on the Image tab*

If your design gets muddled, restart by clicking the *Default* button on the *Position* tab or the *Reset* button on any tab.

## Positioning bullets, numbers, and list items

The *Position* tab sets up the spacing before bullets or numbers, and between the bullet or number and the text.

When a list style is linked to a paragraph style, editing the fields on the *Position* tab in the list number dialog results in changes to the *Indent > Before text* and *Indent > First line* settings on the *Indents & Spacing* tab for the paragraph style.

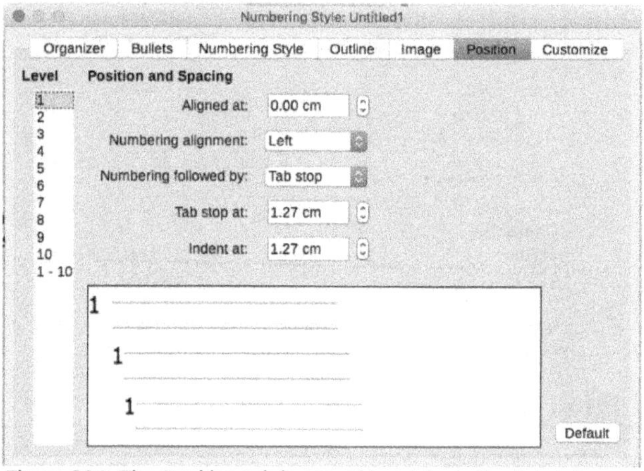

*Figure 264: The Position tab is one of two tabs in the list style dialog for customizing lists*

The reverse is also true. However, to avoid complications, make all the changes on the *Position* tab for the list style. Not only is that the logical place to look for changes on the list style, but adjusting the paragraph settings usually involves negative entries for the *First Line* field, which can complicate editing immensely.

### Understanding position fields

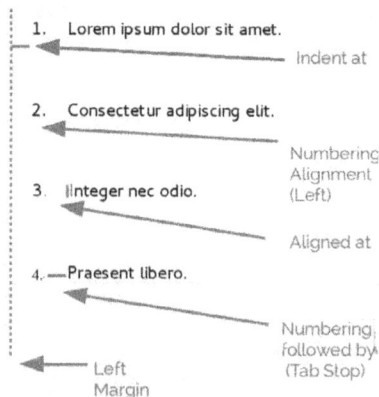

*Figure 265: Fields on the Position tab for list styles and what they refer to*

When you are defining a new list style, the important fields on the *Position* tab are:

- *Aligned at:* The vertical position for numbers, measured from the left margin. In most cases, you can leave this field at *0* (at the left margin). However, if you use any *Numbering Alignment* except *Left,* numbers set this field to another value.
- *Numbering Alignment:* How the bullet or number is aligned. Most of the time, you can leave this field at the default of *Left,* but if you are having trouble positioning text, changing the alignment to *Center* or *Right* can sometimes solve the problem, especially for lists or levels that require two-digit numbers.

| Left | Center | Right |
|---|---|---|
| 1. Lorem ipsum dolor sit amet. | 1. Lorem ipsum dolor sit amet. | 1 Lorem ipsum dolor sit amet. |
| 2. Consectetur adipiscing elit. | 2. Consectetur adipiscing elit. | 2 Consectetur adipiscing elit. |
| 3. Integer nec odio. | 3. Integer nec odio. | 3 Integer nec odio. |

*Figure 266: The dotted line is the margin in this example. If the value of the Numbering Alignment is 0, then choosing Center or Right can force the numbers into the left margin.*

- *Numbering followed by:* Sets the space between the number or bullet and the text. Although the choices include *space* or *nothing,* the choice that offers the most control is *Tab Stop.* Set the exact tab in the *at* field directly below the drop-down list.
- *Aligned at:* Sets where the numbers or bullets are on the line. In many cases, this setting is 0 points – that is, against the left margin.
- *Indent at:* Sets the start of the text. This setting should be equal or greater to the tab stop set for *Numbering followed by.*

▶ **Tip**

This setting should not be more than about two line-heights, or else the connection between the bullet or number and the text might be lost.

## Formatting ordered (numbered) lists

To create a numbered list, select a numbering style from the *Number* field on the *Customize* tab (Figure 267). The selections in the drop-down list begin with typical choices for Western European languages: Arabic, upper and lower case letters, and upper and lower case Roman numerals. Scroll down, and options for Bulgarian, Russian, Serbian, and Greek are available.

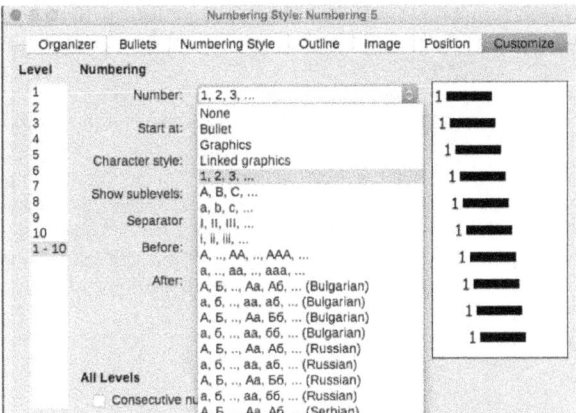

*Figure 267: Select a numbering style from the Customize tab*

### Adding characters before and after numbers

You can set up to 40 characters before or after the actual number using the *Before* and *After* fields. These characters are added automatically whenever the list style they are attached to is applied.

Common characters after a number might be a period, a parenthesis, or both. Alternatively, you might put a parenthesis both before or after the number, or text such as *Step #* in the *Before* field. In a *List Cont.* style, you might add *(Continued)* before.

More elaborately, you might set a paragraph style to start at the top of the page, then attach to it a list style with text so that the paragraph style will automatically add text.

In a numbered list, you can choose the number of outline levels in the list by adjusting the *Show sublevels* field. For example, if you decided to show three sublevels, the first use of the third sublevel would be numbered 1.1.1.

> **Note**
>
> Using the *Before, After,* and/or *Show sublevels* fields means that the settings on the *Position* tab need to be adjusted so there is enough space between the number and the text.

### Setting the character style

By default, the *Character Style* field for numbered lists is set to the *Numbering Symbol* character style, and for bulleted lists to the *Bullets* character style.

For most purposes, you probably have no reason to change these defaults. Unless modified, these character styles use the same font and font size as the *Default Style* character style, and apply to both the number and any text in the *Before* or *After* fields.

Common modifications include making the numbers or bullets larger, giving them a corporate color, making them bold, or using a condensed version of a font.

> **Note**
>
> You may need to change the text indent if you use a larger font, especially for two or three digit numbers. The line height may also need to be increased.

### Example: Formatting large list numbers

You may want to have the numbers in a larger or different font, or a different color, from the text of the list. To create this effect, follow these steps:

1) Create a new character style for the numbers, or modify an existing character style. For this example, the new style is named Numbers Large.

   On the *Font* page of the character style dialog, increase the font size. To change the color of the number, go to the Font Effect page. Click **OK** to save the new or modified character style.

2) Create a new list style, or modify an existing list style. On the *Customize* page of the numbering style dialog (Figure 268), choose the character style you created or modified. For this example, choose Numbers Large. Click **OK** to save the style.

3) Create a new paragraph style, or modify an existing paragraph style. On the *Outline & Numbering* page of the paragraph style dialog, choose the numbering style you created or modified.

4) Apply the paragraph style in the usual way to the items of the list.

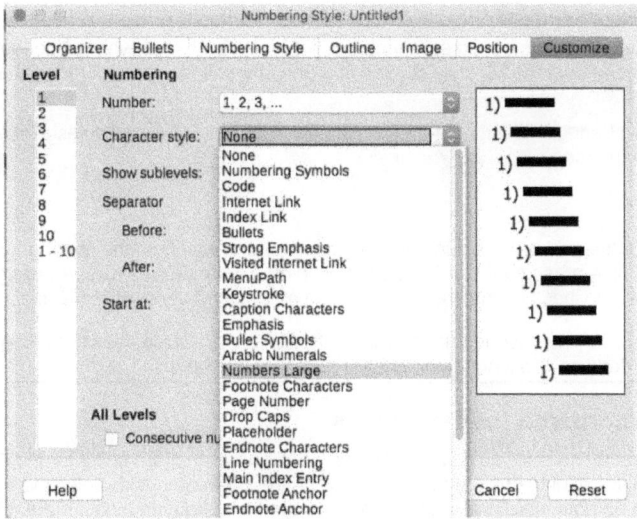

*Figure 268: Choosing the character style for the numbers of a list*

### ⚠ Caution

If you modify an existing character, list, or paragraph style, the changes will affect all lists in the document that use those styles.

### *Working with two-digit list numbers*

Numbered lists with two digits can displace list items, upsetting your carefully calculated designs by offsetting the text too much.

> 9. Lorem ipsum dolor sit amet, consectetur adipiscing elit.
>
> 10. Fusce molestie, nisl eu suscipit imperdiet nibh orci sodales erat, in scelerisque justo lacus vitæ leo

*Figure 269: Unless extra spacing is provided, the list items are displaced when the numbering enters two digits.*

You can correct this problem in several ways:

- Never have a list with more than nine items. Rewrite lists that have more, combining steps or dividing one list into two or more shorter ones. This arrangement may make your instructions easier to remember.
- Add extra space between the number and the list item using the *Indent at* field on the xxx page of the dialog. Do not add so much space that the association between numbers and list items is lost.
- Adjust the size of the numbers using the *Character Style* field on the *Customize* tab.
- Set the *Numbering Alignment* to *Right*. Watch that this change does not extend numbers into the left margin.

### Restarting a numbered list

The *Customize* tab for a numbering style includes a *Start at* field. However, notice that this field refers to the first time that the list style is used in a document. It is not a tool for re-starting the numbering.

To restart the numbering in a list, right-click on a paragraph with a list and select *Restart Numbering* from the menu.

> ▶ **Tip**
>
> People occasionally ask for numbered lists that count down from the starting number, instead of up – presumably for Top 10 lists and other countdowns. Unfortunately, LibreOffice provides no way short of a custom macro for reverse order in lists.
>
> A reverse order list must be entered manually. Since LibreOffice does not recognize reverse order lists, it will not automatically generate numbers.

## Designing unordered (bulleted) lists

The default character style for bullets is *Bullets*. It gives you a standard bullet for the Default style. However, you might want to change the symbol using the *Character* field. Selecting the *Character* field opens a dialog from which you can choose any symbol supported by the current font.

To choose a truly unusual bullet, set the character style to use a dingbat font. However, be careful: too detailed or unusual a dingbat distracts from the contents.

> ▨ **Caution**
>
> When you use an unusual character style for bullets, be sure to include the font used when you share a file.

If your design includes nested bullets – that is, bullet lists within bullet lists – you might want to create an additional list style with a name like *Bullets2*.

However, if you do use more than one bullet list style, make sure their designs are compatible. In fact, indenting the nested bullets and nothing more is enough to distinguish them from the top level bullets.

### Example: Making a checklist

Depending on the characters you choose, bulleted list styles can serve as more than unordered lists. For example, a bullet list can be made into a checklist by selecting the font or character used for the bullet.

If you want a checklist to be used with a pen, set up the list style in the usual way, using a character style that uses the OpenSymbol font that ships with LibreOffice, and assign the character *U+E00B* (a shaded open box) as the bullet (that is two zeros, not lower case "o"s). Print the list, and it is immediately ready for use. Add some corporate branding and letterhead, and the To Do list can be used in business.

If you want to use the list on the computer, create two list styles, one that uses the character U+2752, and one that uses the character U+E531 (a box with a check mark). Create the list using the first style, then tick off an item by applying the second style to it.

Depending on the purpose of the list, you can also create a third list style that uses the character U+E532 (an X mark) to indicate items that were not completed.

☐ Lorem ipsum dolor sit

☑ Etiam dictum mattis

☒ Nulla facilisi

*Figure 270: With three list styles, you can create both manual and computer-based checklists.*

## Using images as bullets

Using an image instead of a standard bullet is a convenient way to add some originality to your document. However, you are limited by the small size at which most bullets display. Mostly, you need simple images with strong contrast as a substitute bullet. Often, a black and white image will be more effective.

Images used for bullets are also a way to position an image on a page. In particular, they can be used to create tip and warning signs in a technical manual or an informal text.

In either case, select a graphic to use from *Position > Number* in the dialog for the List style.

Choosing *Graphics* embeds the picture within the document file. By contrast, *Linked graphics* only adds a link to the graphic.

▶ **Tip**

If the image is cut off, you need either to adjust the image size, or else change the line spacing to *At Least* so the top half of the characters in a line is not chopped off.

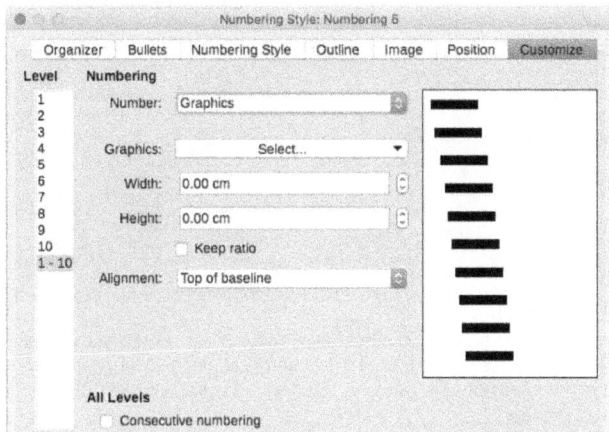

*Figure 271: The fields for using a picture as a bullet appear after you have selected Options > Number > Graphics or Linked Graphics.*

After you choose *Graphics* or *Linked graphics,* the dialog lists a set of fields for editing the bullet:

- The *Select* button opens a file manager to select the picture.

- The *Width* and *Height* fields set the size at which the picture displays. They do not affect the original picture file.

    Remember that too large a height requires changing the paragraph *Line spacing* setting to *At Least* so that the letters are not cut off at the top.

- *Keep ratio*, when selected, ensures that changing either the *Width* or *Height* field changes the other proportionally.
- *Alignment* can usually be ignored, but can help when the height of the graphic is greater than the height of the text, as in the Tips, Notes, and Cautions in this book.

### Example: Styling the Tips, Notes, and Cautions in this book

List styles can be used for more than lists. For example, the Tips, Notes, and Cautions in this book use list styles to position the graphics and text. Here is how the Tips are created and used. The others are done in the same way, but with a different logo and text.

Step 1. Create a paragraph style for the body of a tip, note, or caution.

The body of a tip, note, or caution in this book is indented under the heading and has a line under it to set it off from the main text.

1) In the Sidebar, go to Styles and Formatting > Paragraph Styles. Right-click and choose New. Name the new style Text Note.

2) On the *Indents & Spacing* page (Figure 272), specify the indentation and spacing for the body of the Tip.

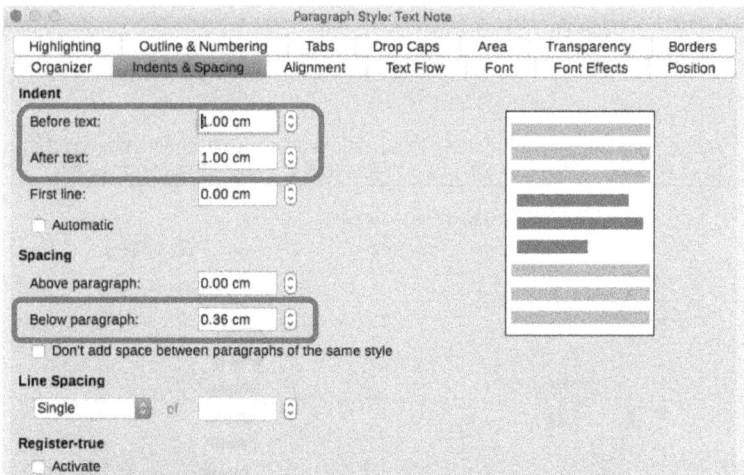

*Figure 272: Choosing indentation and spacing for the body of the Tip*

3) On the *Borders* page (Figure 273), select a bottom border, increase the thickness, and specify the spacing between the text and the border. Choose **Merge with next paragraph** to cause the border to appear under only the final paragraph if the Tip includes more than one paragraph.

4) Style the paragraph (font and so on) in the usual way.

5) Click **OK** to save the paragraph style.

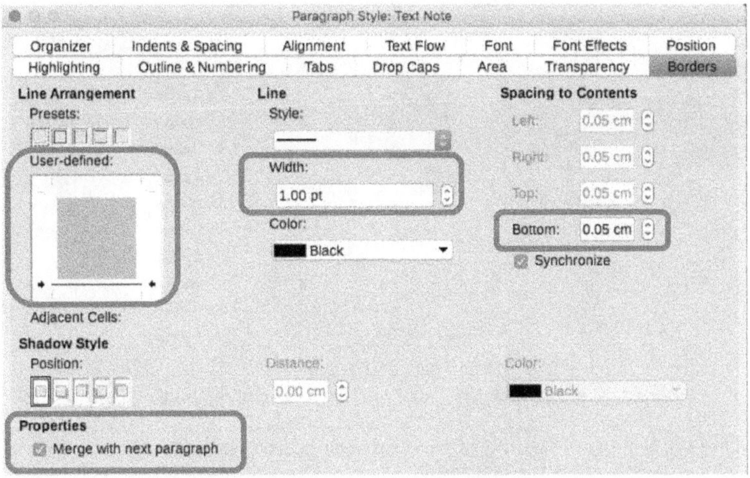

Figure 273: Defining the bottom border of the Tip body text

Step 2. Create a list style.

1) In the Sidebar, go to **Styles and Formatting > List Styles**. Right-click and choose **New**. Name the new style Heading Tip.

2) On the *Image* page (Figure 274), select an appropriate image. (Or, skip this step and select an image on the *Customize* page.)

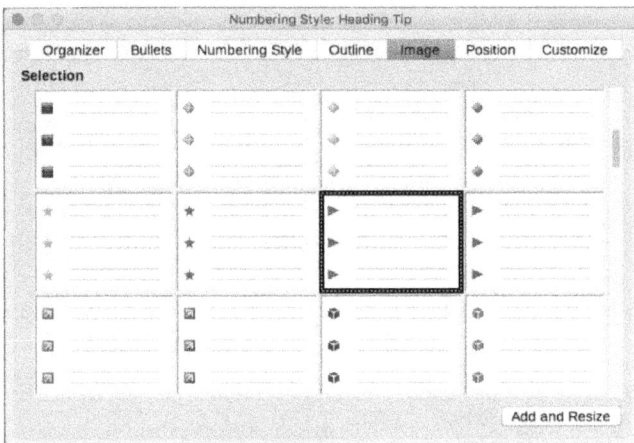

Figure 274: Selecting a bullet image

3) On the *Customize* page (Figure 275), choose **Graphics** in the Number field. Optionally, click **Select**... in the Graphics field and choose an image from a file or from the Gallery.

If the bullet image selected is too large or too small for your design, specify a width and height. You can use these fields to distort the original image.

In the Alignment field, select where you want the image to line up with the text.

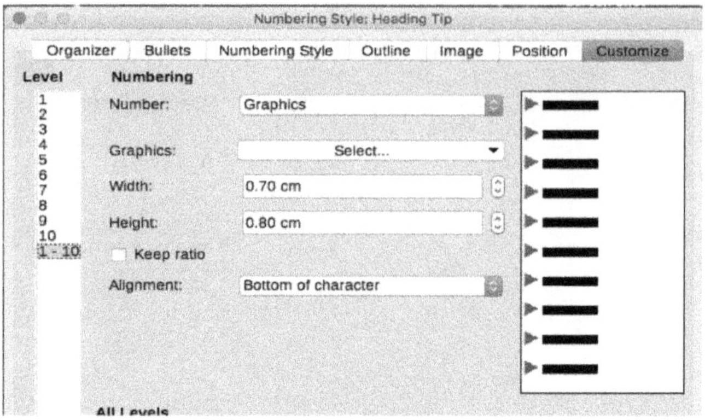

*Figure 275: Customizing the size and alignment of the bullet image*

4) On the *Position* page (Figure 276), choose settings as described in "Positioning bullets, numbers, and list items" on page 268.

5) Click **OK** to save the list style.

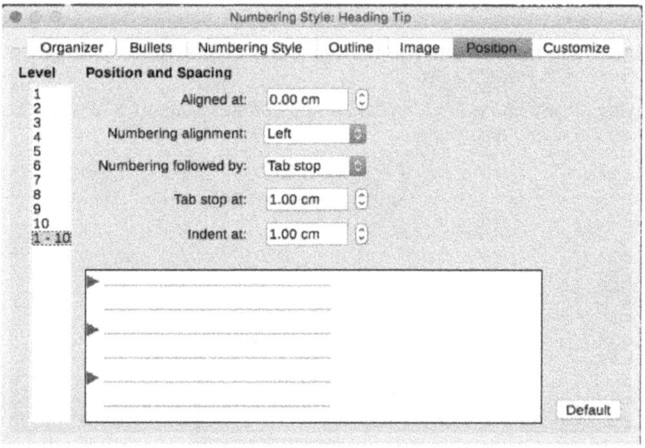

*Figure 276: Choosing position and spacing settings for the bullet image*

Step 3. Create a paragraph style for the Heading Tip and connect it to the list style.

1) In the Sidebar, go to **Styles and Formatting > Paragraph Styles**. Right-click and choose **New**. Name the new style Heading Tip.

2) On the *Organizer* page (Figure 277), specify the Next Style to be the one you created for the body of the Tip; in this case, Text Note.

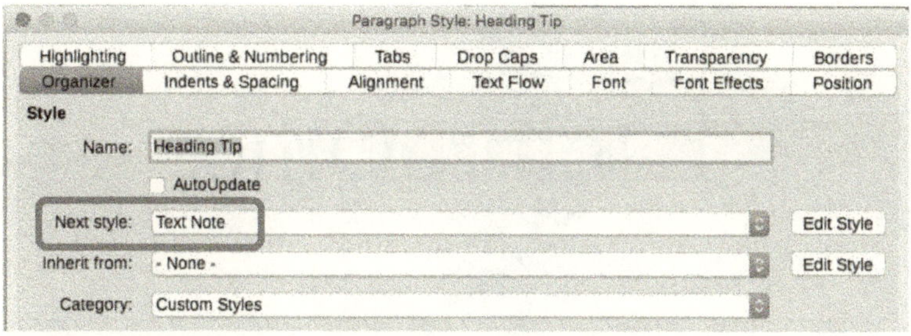

*Figure 277: Specifying the Next Style for a Heading Tip style*

3) Style the paragraph in the usual way, then go to the *Outline & Numbering* page (Figure 278). In the Numbering style field, select the list style you created. Click **OK** to save the style.

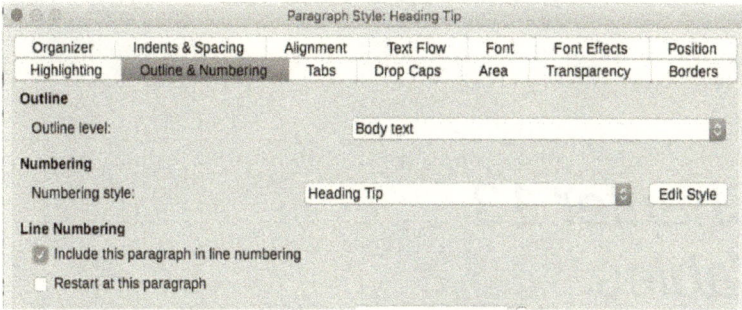

*Figure 278: Connecting the list style to the paragraph style*

Step 4. Apply the paragraph styles to the heading and text of the Tip, Note, or Caution.

1) Type the word "Tip" in a new paragraph. (You must enter at least one character or a space, or else the graphic disappears when you press *Enter*, leaving the indent but no bullet.)

2) Apply the Heading Tip paragraph style.

3) Press *Enter*. The next paragraph should automatically have the Text Note paragraph style. Type the text for the body of the tip. (If you have already typed the text, then apply the style manually.)

# LibreOffice

*Chapter 13*
*Tables*

# Introduction

Tables are a useful way to organize and present large amounts of information, for example:

- Technical, financial, or statistical reports.
- Product catalogs showing descriptions, prices, characteristics, and photographs of products.
- Bills or invoices.
- Lists of names with address, age, profession, and other information.

Tables can often be used as an alternative to spreadsheets to organize materials. A well-designed table can help readers understand better what you are saying. While you would normally use tables for text or numbers, you could put other objects, such as pictures, in cells.

Tables can also be used as a page-layout tool to position text in areas of a document instead of using several Tab characters. Another example is in headers and footers to support independent positioning of different elements, such as page number, document title, and so on. This use of tables is described in Chapter 7, Formatting Pages: Advanced.

# Creating a table

Before you insert a table into a document, it helps to have an idea of the visual result you want to obtain as well as an estimate of the number of rows and columns required. Every parameter can be changed at a later stage; however, thinking ahead can save a large amount of time as changes to fully formatted tables often require a significant effort.

## Inserting a new table

To directly insert a table with the default properties, click the **Table** icon on the Standard toolbar. On the drop-down graphic, choose the size of the table (up to fifteen rows and up to ten columns). To create the table, click on the cell that you want to be on the last row of the last column. Holding down the mouse button over the Table icon will also display the graphic.

To insert a new table using the Insert Table dialog (Figure 279), where you can specify the properties for the table, position the cursor where you want the table to appear, then use any of the following methods to open the dialog:

- Choose **Table > Insert Table** from the Menu bar.
- Press *Ctrl+F12*.
- On the Standard toolbar, click the **Insert Table** icon and select **More Options** at the bottom of the drop-down graphic.

General settings: In the Name box, you can enter a different name from the Writer-generated default for the table. This might come in handy when using the Navigator to jump quickly to a table.

In the Columns and Rows boxes, specify the number of columns and rows for the new table. You can change the size of the table later, if necessary.

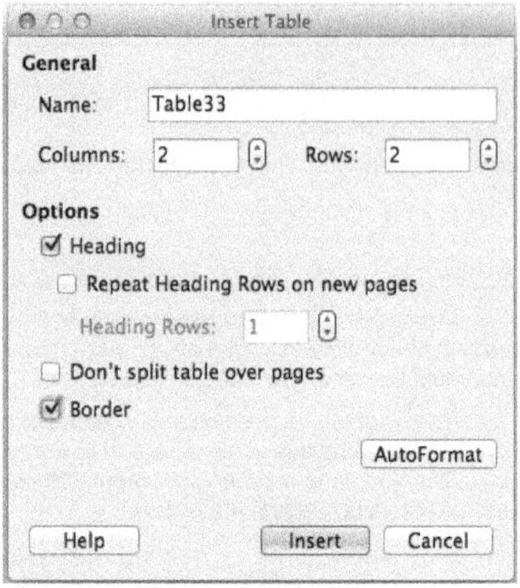

*Figure 279: The Insert Table dialog*

Under Options, set up the initial table characteristics:

- **Heading** — Enables a heading to be used in the table and defines the number of rows to be used as headings.

  The default Table Heading paragraph style is applied to the heading rows. You can edit the Table Heading paragraph style in the Styles and Formatting window to change these default settings.

  **Repeat Heading Rows on new pages** — Enables the heading rows to be repeated at the top of subsequent pages if the table spans more than one page.

  Heading Rows — Specifies the number of rows to be used for the heading. Default is 1.

- **Don't split table over pages** — Prevents the table from spanning more than one page. This can be useful if the table starts near the end of a page, and would look better if it were completely located on the following page. If the table becomes longer than would fit on one page, you will need to either deselect this option or manually split the table.

- **Border** — Surrounds each cell of the table with a border. This border can be modified or deleted later.

The **AutoFormat** button opens a dialog from which you can select one of several predefined table layouts, also known as table styles. See "Applying table styles" on page 289 for more information. Click **OK** after selecting your table layout.

After making your choices, click **Insert**. Writer creates a table as wide as the text area (from the left page margin to the right page margin), with all columns the same width and all rows the same height. You can adjust the columns and rows later to suit your needs.

## Creating nested tables

You can create tables within tables, nested to a depth limited only by imagination and practicality. Figure 280 demonstrates a simple, two-level example. The shaded table is inside a cell of the larger table. To achieve this, simply click in a cell of an existing table and use any of the methods mentioned in "Inserting a new table" above.

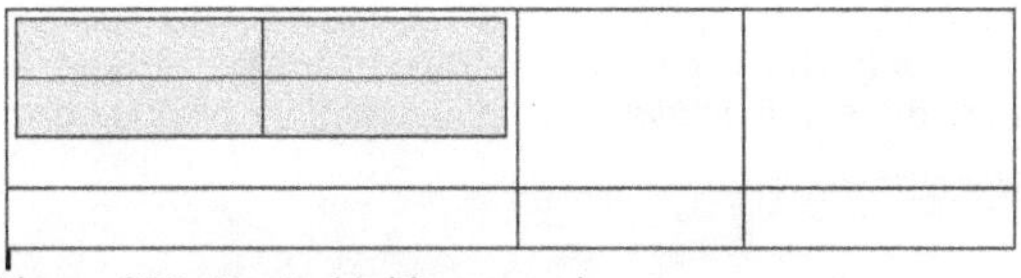

*Figure 280: Nested table example*

## Using AutoCorrect to create a table

You can also create a table by typing a series of hyphens (-) or tabs separated by plus signs. Use the plus signs to indicate column dividers, while hyphens and tabs are used to indicate the width of a column. When using tabs, the default tab setting determines the width; this setting can be changed in Tools > Options > LibreOffice Writer > General.

For example, this character sequence:

```
+-----------------+---------------+------+
```

creates a table like this:

### Note

This function can be disabled or enabled in **Tools > AutoCorrect Options**. On the *Options* page, deselect or select **Create table**.

### *Create a table from formatted text*

You can create a table from plain text by using **Table > Convert > Text to Table** on the Menu bar. The text to be converted must contain characters to indicate column separators. Paragraph marks indicate an end of a table row.

Start by editing the text, if necessary, to ensure the column separator character is in place where you want it. Select the text you want to convert and choose **Table > Convert > Text to Table** to open the dialog shown in Figure 281.

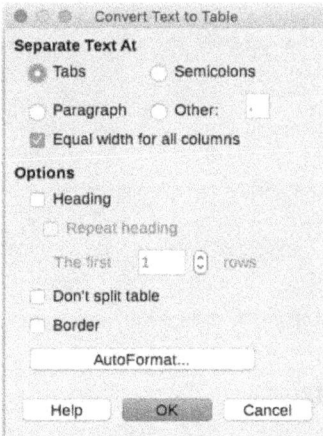

*Figure 281: Dialog for the text to table conversion*

The *Separate text at* section has four options for the separator for the columns of text. Select Other to choose the default comma (useful if you are importing a .csv file) or type any character in the box. The other options are the same as those in the Insert Table dialog shown in Figure 279.

Click **OK** to convert the text.

### Example

In this example we will convert the following text into a table.

```
Row 1 Column 1; Row 1 Column 2; Row 1 Column 3
Row 2 Column 1; Row 2 Column 2; Row 2 Column 3
```

In this case, the separator between elements is a semicolon. Select the text and choose **Table > Convert > Text to Table**. We obtain the following result.

| Row 1 Column 1 | Row 1 Column 2 | Row 1 Column 3 |
| --- | --- | --- |
| Row 2 Column 1 | Row 2 Column 2 | Row 2 Column 3 |

> **Tip**
>
> Unlike the creation of a table by other methods, conversion from text to table preserves the paragraph style and character style applied to the original text.

You can also use the Convert menu to perform the opposite operation; that is, to transform a table into plain text. This may be useful when you want to export the table contents into a different program.

To transform a table into text, place the cursor anywhere in the table, choose **Table > Convert > Table to Text** in the Menu bar, pick the preferred row separator, and click **OK** to finish.

# Formatting the table layout

Formatting a table is, generally speaking, a two-step process: formatting the table layout (the subject of this section) and formatting the table text (the subject of the next section).

Formatting the layout normally involves one or more of the following operations: adjusting the size of the table and its position on the page, adjusting sizes of rows and columns, adding or removing rows or columns, merging and splitting individual cells, changing borders and background.

## Default parameters

If you create a table using the Insert Table dialog or the Table button on the Standard toolbar, the following defaults are set:

- The cells use the Table Contents paragraph style, which, in the default template, is identical to the Default Style paragraph style.
- The default table occupies all the space from margin to margin (text area).
- The default table has thin black borders around each cell (grid).

Additionally, if you activate the Heading option, the cells in the heading row (or rows) use the Table Heading paragraph style.

## Resizing and positioning the table

Using the default settings, any newly created table will occupy the entire width of the text area. This is sometimes what you want, or you may prefer a smaller table. To quickly resize a table, first move the mouse to either the left or right edge. When the cursor changes shape into a double arrow, drag the border to the new position. This operation only changes the size of the first or last column; it does not change the alignment of the table on the page.

If you need more precise control over the size and position of the table on the page, open the Table Properties dialog by choosing **Table > Properties** or by right-clicking anywhere in the table and choosing Table Properties from the context menu.

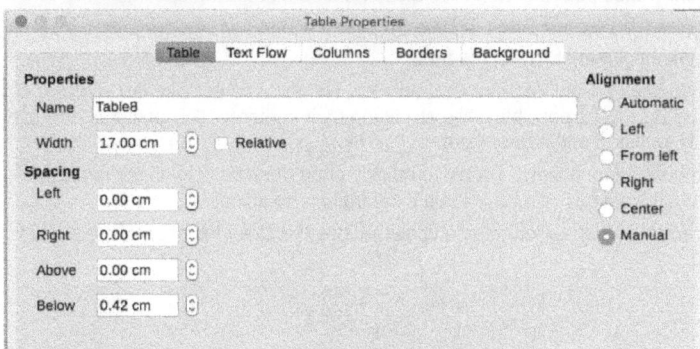

*Figure 282: The Table page of the Table Properties dialog*

On the *Table* page of the dialog (Figure 282), you can set the alignment of the table, choosing among the following options:

- **Automatic**: the default setting for a table, fills the width of the text area.
- **Left**: aligns the table with the left margin.
- **Right**: aligns the table with the right margin.
- **From Left**: lets you specify under Spacing exactly how far from the left margin the table is placed.
- **Center**: aligns the table in the middle between the left and right margins. If the table width is greater than the margin, the table will extend outside of the margins.
- **Manual**: lets you specify the distances from both left and right margins under Spacing.

Selecting an alignment option other than Automatic activates the Width field in the *Properties* section, where you can enter the desired size of the table. Select **Relative** to see the width as percentage of the text area.

In the *Spacing* section, use the Above and Below boxes to modify the separation between the text and the table. When the size of the table is less than the size of the text area, Writer will insert some values in the Left and Right boxes. You can enter values in both the Left and Right boxes if you select Manual alignment. You can enter values in the Left box when you select the From Left, Right or Center alignment. You can enter values in the Right box if you select Left alignment. Otherwise these values are not available. Note that the sum of the table width, and the values in the Left and Right boxes, should not be greater than the width of the text area.

## Resizing rows and columns

You can adjust the height of rows and the width of columns in a table in several ways.

- Move the mouse next to the edge of the cell and when a double-headed arrow appears, click and hold the left mouse button, drag the border to the desired position, and release the mouse button.

- On the horizontal ruler, column dividers are marked by a pair of thin gray lines; the vertical ruler indicates row dividers in the same way. You can resize a row or column by holding the mouse button down on the appropriate divider and dragging it to the desired location.
- Use the keyboard as described below.

Selecting **Table > Size** from the Menu bar also offers some resizing options:

- Select Column Width or Row Height to enter a dimension into the size box for each selectable column or row of the table.
- The Optimal Column Width or Optimal Row Height options make the selected columns or rows as narrow as possible while still fitting their contents. This option is only available if the table is selected and has content.
- Distribute Columns/Rows Evenly to quickly bring them back to all being the same width or height. This option is only available if the table is selected.

For greater control over the width of each column, use the *Columns* page of the Table Properties dialog.

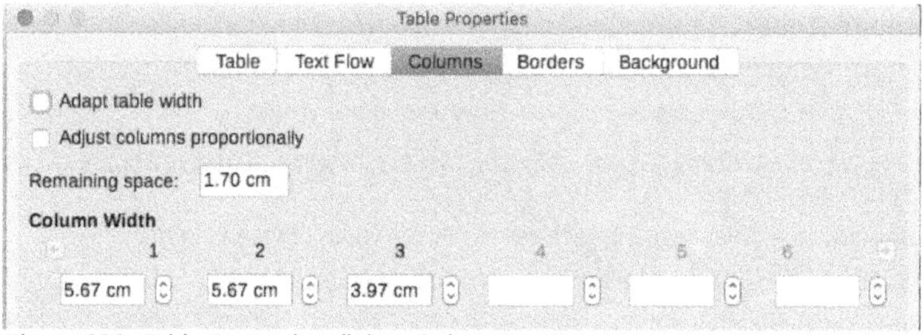

*Figure 283: Table Properties dialog: Columns page*

Right-click on the table and choose **Table Properties** from the context menu or choose **Table > Properties** from the Menu bar. On the Table Properties dialog, select the *Columns* tab.

- Adapt table width: If a table already stretches to the page margins, it cannot stretch any wider and the Adapt table width option can only be used to reduce the column width. If the table is narrower, increasing the width of a column will increase the width of the whole table. This option is not available if Automatic has been selected in the Alignment area of the Table page.

  If the table width already extends past the margins, with the Adapt table width option checked, attempting to change a column width will automatically decrease that column's size so that the table will now shrink to the page margins while keeping the size of any other column intact.

- Adjust columns proportionally results in all columns changing their widths by the same percentage when one is changed. For example, if you reduce by half the size of a column, the sizes of all the other columns will be halved. This option is not available if Automatic has been selected in the Alignment area of the Table page.

- Remaining space shows how much further the table can expand before hitting the limit of the margins. This value cannot be edited and will not be negative in the event that the table width is already larger than the space between the left and right margins.

- Under Column width, each individual column can be adjusted. If you have more than six columns, use the arrows at the right and left to view them all. With no options selected, the column to the right of the one being adjusted will automatically adjust to keep the table width constant. Adjusting the most right hand column causes the first column to adjust.

Rather than start from the Table Properties dialog, it is often more efficient to make rough adjustments to a new table using the mouse, and then fine tune the layout using the Columns page in conjunction with the Table page of the Table Properties dialog.

It is also possible to resize a table using only the keyboard. This is sometimes easier than using the mouse.

1) Place the cursor in the cell where you want to make changes.
2) Press and hold the *Alt* key while using the arrow keys.
   - The left and right arrow keys adjust the column width by moving the border on the right edge of the cell, but not past the margin.
   - The up and down arrows adjust the row height (when possible) by moving the border on the lower edge of the cell.
3) Press and hold the *Shift+Alt* keys while using the left/right arrow keys.
   - Adjusts the column width by moving the border on the left edge of the cell, but not past the margin.

To adjust the resizing parameters and behavior for keyboard handling, choose **Tools > Options > LibreOffice Writer > Table**.

Use the Row and Column values in the Move cells section to determine the amount of change produced by a single keystroke while resizing. In the Behavior of rows/columns section you can choose one of the following three strategies when resizing:

- Fixed: select this if you want the resizing to affect only the adjacent cell and not the entire table. The width of the table does not change when resizing its cells.
- Fixed, proportional: when resizing a cell with this option selected, all the other cells are also resized proportionally, but in the opposite direction so as to maintain the width of the table.
- Variable: this is the default option. Resizing a cell affects the table size. For example, when you widen a cell, the width of the table increases.

## Resizing individual cells

Place the cursor in the cell you wish to change.

1) Press and hold the *Ctrl+Alt* keys while using the left/right arrow keys.
   Resizes the current cell on its right edge, but not past the margin.
2) Press and hold the *Ctrl+Shift+Alt* keys while using the left/right arrow keys.
   Resizes the current cell on its left edge, but not past the margin.

## Inserting rows and columns

To quickly insert one row or column, do one of the following:

- Click on the Rows Above or Rows Below icons on the Table toolbar to insert one row above or below the selected one. Click on the Columns Left or Columns Right icons on the Table toolbar inserts a column to the left or right of the selected one.
- Place the cursor in the row or column before or after which you want to add new rows or columns, right-click, and choose **Insert > Rows Above/Below** or **Insert > Columns Above/Below**.

To insert any number of rows or columns:

1) Place the cursor in the row or column where you want to add new rows or columns and right-click.

2) In the context menu, choose **Insert > Rows** to display a dialog where you can select the number of rows or columns to add, and whether they appear before or after the one selected.

3) Set Number to the number of rows or columns to insert, and Position to Before or After.

4) Click **OK** to close the dialog.

The **Table > Insert > Rows** and **Table > Insert > Columns** choices from the Menu bar provide the same options.

> **Note**
>
> Regardless of how they are inserted, new rows or columns have the same formatting as the row or column where the cursor was when the insert command was issued.

You can also quickly insert a row or a column using the keyboard:

1) Place the cursor in the row or column next to the row or column you want to insert.

2) Press *Alt+Insert* to activate keyboard handling.

3) Use the arrow keys as desired to add a row or column:

   – Left to insert a new column to the left of the cell where the cursor is located.

   – Right to insert a new column to the right of the cell where the cursor is.

   – Down to insert a new row below the cell where the cursor is.

   – Up to insert a new row above the cell where the cursor is.

## Deleting rows and columns

To quickly delete one or more rows or columns, place the cursor in the row or column you want to delete and do one of the following:

- Click on the Rows or Columns icons on the Table toolbar

- Right-click and choose **Delete > Rows** or **Delete > Columns**.

- Press *Alt+Delete* on the keyboard and use the arrow keys to delete rows or columns as described above for inserting.

## Merging and splitting cells

To merge a cell or group of cells into one cell:

1) Select the cells to merge.

2) Right-click and choose **Merge Cells** in the context menu, or choose **Table > Merge Cells** from the Menu bar. Any content of the cells appears in the merged cell.

   To merge a single cell into an adjacent cell, you can also place the cursor in the cell (origin), press *Alt+Delete*, release, then hold down *Ctrl*, and then press the left or the right arrow key. Any contents in the origin cell are lost.

To split a cell into multiple cells:

1) Position the cursor inside the cell.

2) Right-click and choose **Split Cells** in the context menu, or choose **Table > Split Cells** from the Menu bar.

3) Select how to split the cell. A cell can be split either horizontally (create more rows) or vertically (create more columns), and you can specify the total number of cells to create.

To split a single cell, you can also place the cursor in an adjacent cell, press *Alt+Insert*, release, then hold down *Ctrl*, and then press the left or the right arrow key to split the cell to the left/right.

It is generally a good rule to merge and split cells after completing other layout formatting. This is because some operations such as deleting a column or a row may produce a result difficult to predict when applied to a table with merged or split cells.

## Specifying table borders

On the Table Properties dialog, select the *Borders* tab. Here you can set borders for a whole table or groups of cells within a table. In addition, you can set a shadow for the whole table.

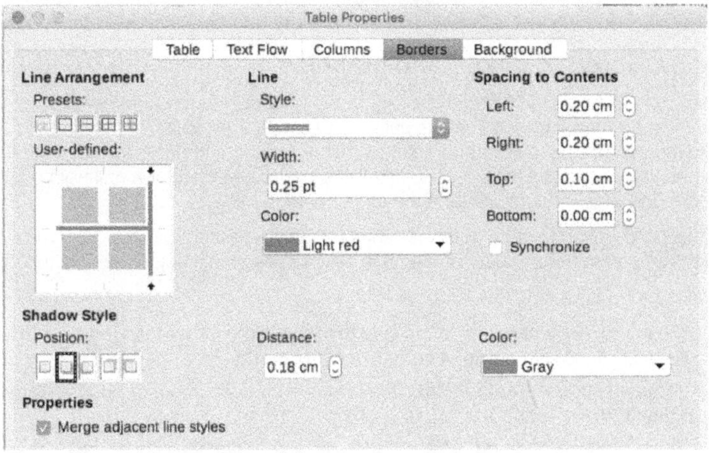

*Figure 284: Table Properties dialog: Borders page*

Borders have three components: where they go, what they look like, and how much space is left around them.

- **Line arrangement** specifies where the borders go. If a group of cells is selected, the border will be applied only to those cells. You can specify individually the style of the border for the outside edges of the selected cells as well as for the cell divisions. Writer provides five default arrangements, but you can click on the line you want to customize in the User-defined area to get exactly what you want. When multiple cells are selected, the User-defined area allows you to select the edges of the selection as well as the cell dividers.

> **Note**
>
> When the selected cells have different styles of border the User-defined area shows the border as a gray line. You can click on the gray line to choose a new border style (first click), leave the border as it is (second click) or delete the border (third click).

- **Line** specifies what the border looks like: the style, width, and color. There are a number of different styles and colors to choose from. Style, Width, and Color selections apply to those borders highlighted by a pair of black arrows in the User-defined map on the left-hand side of the dialog.
- **Spacing to contents** specifies how much space to leave between the border and the cell contents. Spaces can be specified to the left, right, above, and below. Check Synchronize to have the same spacing for all four sides. This spacing is like a padding and it is not factored in when calculating the text measurements.

- **Shadow Style** properties always apply to the whole table. A shadow has three components: where it is (position), how far from the table it is cast (distance), and what color it is.

- If **Merge adjacent line styles** is checked, two cells sharing a common border will have their borders merged, rather than being side by side or above/below each other.

> ▶ **Tip**
>
> To reset everything if you are having problems with borders, right-click in the table and choose **Table Properties** or choose **Table > Properties** from the Menu bar. On the *Borders* tab, select the **Set No Borders** icon under *Line arrangement Presets* (the box on the left).

## Selecting background colors and graphics

A table background can greatly improve the readability of data, visually highlight important parts of the table (such as the heading or a specific cell), or just make the table more appealing. You can choose between two types of background: solid color or image. The background can be applied to the whole table, to a single cell, or to a row. The background selected for a cell will be in front of the row background which in turn will hide the table background.

The row background option is quite handy when you want to create alternate color rows or assign a different background to the heading of the table. The tables in this guide use this technique.

To set the background for a cell, row, or table:

1) Place the cursor anywhere inside the cell, row, or table you want to work with. If you want to apply a background to a group of cells, select the group.

2) Right-click and choose **Table Properties** from the context menu, or choose **Table > Properties** from the Menu bar.

3) In the Table Properties dialog, select the *Background* tab (see Figure 285).

4) In the *For* section, chose whether to apply the settings to cell, row, or table.

   - **Cell**: changes apply only to the selected cells, or the cell where the cursor currently resides. Even when selecting a group of cells, the background settings are applied to each cell individually.

   - **Row**: changes affect the entire row where the cursor resides.

   - **Table**: changes will set the background for the entire table, regardless of the cursor position or selected cells.

5) In the *As selection* box, choose whether the background is a color or an image.

   To apply a color, select the color and click **OK**.

   To apply an image:

   a) Use the **Browse** button to select the image from your computer's file system.

   b) If you choose the **Link** option, changes to the image (for example, if you edit it in a different software package) are reflected in your document. However, you also need to keep the linked image file with the document file. If, for example, you email the document without the image file, the image will no longer be visible.

   c) Under *Type*, select the type of placement for the image.

      **Position**: select in the position map where the image will be displayed.

      **Area**: the image will be stretched to fill the whole area.

      **Tile**: the image will be tiled (repeated horizontally and vertically) to fill the area.

d) Select the **Preview** option to display the image in the pane on the right.

e) To apply the image, click **OK**.

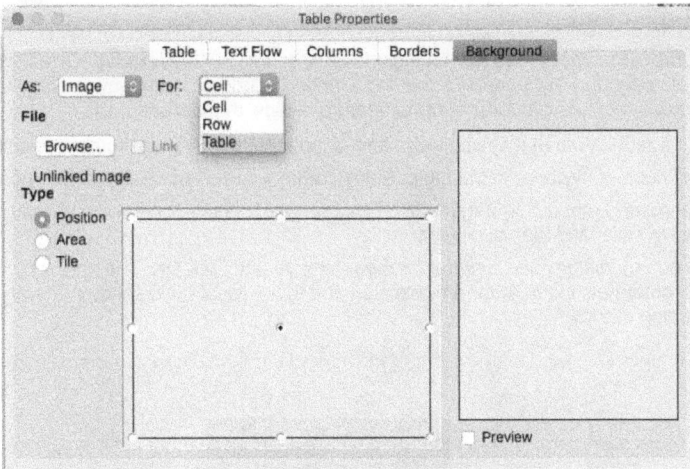

*Figure 285: Table Properties dialog: inserting a graphic background*

Figure 286 shows an example of a table set with a background image, and the first row background colored. As you can see, the row background covers the table background.

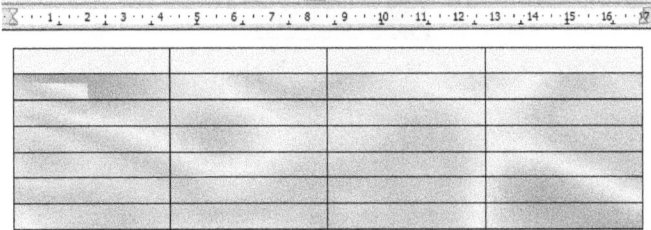

*Figure 286: Example of table with different row and table backgrounds*

## Displaying or hiding table boundaries

A table boundary is a set of pale (usually gray) lines around the cells when viewed on-screen in LibreOffice with no borders enabled. These boundaries are not printed; their only function is to help you see where the table cells are.

To display tables the same way on the screen as on the printed page, with no boundary lines, go to **Tools > Options > LibreOffice > Application Colors**. On that page, you can display or hide boundaries around text, pages headers and footers, figures, and other parts of a document, and you can choose the color of boundary lines.

**Note**

Turning boundaries off does not hide any borders that the table may have.

## Applying table styles

Using table styles, you can apply an elaborate format to your table with just a few clicks. Like other styles, table styles enable you to produce consistent looking tables in a document.

To apply a table style, go to the Table Styles page of the Styles and Formatting window in the Sidebar. Then place the cursor anywhere in the table and double-click the name of a style.

## Creating table styles

Versions of LibreOffice prior to 5.3 did not include table styles, but they did have AutoFormats for tables. Now, although the Styles and Formatting window includes a quick way to apply table styles, they are still created by using the AutoFormat feature. Follow these steps:

1) Create a table. Format it as you wish: font, alignment, borders, background, number format.

2) Put the cursor anywhere in the table. Select **Table > AutoFormat Styles** on the Menu bar.

3) On the AutoFormat dialog (Figure 287), choose which features you wish to include in the new table style, and then click **Add**.

4) In the pop-up dialog, type a name for the new style and click **OK**. The new style is added to the list of formats in the AutoFormat dialog and to the list of table styles in the Styles and Formatting window.

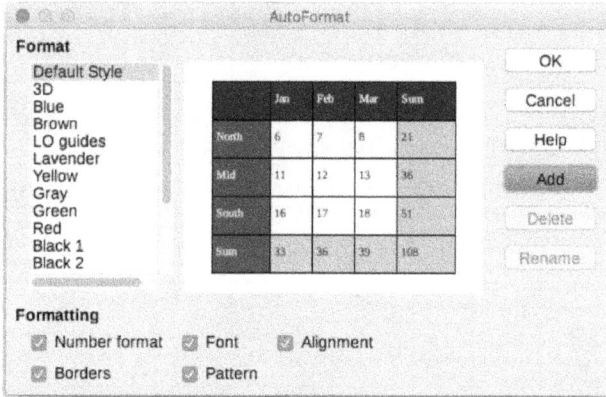

*Figure 287: Table AutoFormat dialog*

You can rename the selected table format scheme as well as decide which parts of the predefined formatting you want to apply to your table. You can selectively apply the number format, the font, the alignment, the border, or the pattern.

### Note

You cannot rename or delete the Default Style. Figure 287 shows that with Default Style selected, the **Rename** and **Delete** buttons are not available.

Table styles (autoformats) also include the following table-level properties:

- Break
- Keep with next paragraph
- Repeat heading
- Allow table to split across pages
- Allow rows to break across pages
- Merge adjacent line styles
- Table shadow

# Formatting the table text

Once the table layout is satisfactory, you can move on to formatting the text in the individual cells. You can apply manual formatting as with any other paragraph in the text, but it is highly recommended, for the sake of consistency and ease of maintenance, that you use paragraph and character styles.

In addition to paragraph and character styles, other aspects to consider when placing text in a table cell include text flow, alignment, and orientation.

You can format each cell independently of other cells, or you can simultaneously format a group of cells by selecting them before applying the desired formatting.

## Specifying text flow

On the *Text Flow page* of the Table Properties dialog (Figure 288), you can:

- Insert a page or column break either before or after the table. Use the **Text Flow: Break** option, combined with the **Page** or **Column** and the **Before** or **After** buttons. If you insert a page break before the table (that is, start the table on a new page), you can also change the page style that will go with it by selecting the **With Page Style** option and a new page style. As with any page break, you can also reset the page numbers using the **Page number** box.

- Keep a table on one page by deselecting the **Allow table to split across pages and columns** option. If this item is deselected, the next item is not active.

- Keep each row on one page by deselecting the **Allow row to break across pages and columns** option.

- Use the **Keep with next paragraph** option to keep the table and an immediately following paragraph together if you insert a page break.

- Use the **Repeat heading** option, and its associated numbers box, to select the number of table heading rows that will be repeated on each page. A complicated table may need two or three heading rows to be easily read and understood.

- Use the **Text orientation** list to select the direction for the text in the cells. Select either **Horizontal**, **Vertical**, or **Use superordinate object settings** (meaning *use the default text flow settings for the page*).

- Select the vertical alignment of the text in the table or the selected cells; the choices are to align with the top of the cell, the center of the cell, or the bottom of the cell. This alignment is in addition to the Left-Right alignment options available on the *Table* page of the Table Properties dialog.

● **Note**

A table heading row cannot span two pages, but any other row can. A one-row table (often used for page layout purposes), if set up with the default of including a heading, will not break across pages. The cure is to make sure the table is defined without a heading row.

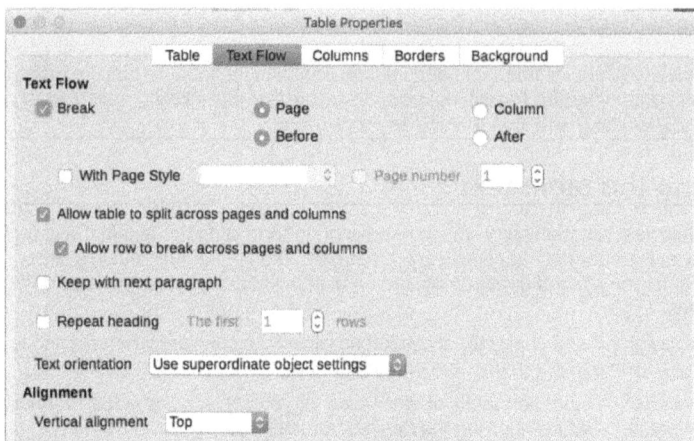

*Figure 288: Table Properties dialog: Text Flow page*

## Vertical alignment

By default, text entered into a table is aligned to the top-left of the cell. You can change the default for the entire table, as described above, or for individually selected cells.

To vertically align the text in specific cells:

1) Place the cursor in the cell you wish to change, or click and drag to select multiple cells.

2) Right-click in the selected area and click an icon on the Table toolbar: Align Top, Center Vertically, or Align Bottom.

## Number formats

The number format can be set for a whole table or group of cells. For example, cells can be set to display in a particular currency, to four decimal places, or in a particular date format.

To enable Number recognition, go to **Tools > Options > LibreOffice Writer > Table** and select the option in the *Input in Tables* section.

Number recognition specifies that numbers in a text table are recognized and formatted as numbers. If Number recognition is not selected, numbers are saved in text format and are automatically left-aligned.

To set the number format for one or more cells, select the cells, then either click the icon for one of the popular formats from the Table toolbar, or right-click and choose Number Format from the context menu. On the Format Number dialog (Figure 289), set options for various categories of numerical data.

- In the Category list, select the category you want, such as currency, date, or text.

- In the Format list, choose a format for the category you just selected.

- For some categories, such as date, you may wish to change the language using the Language list, while for other numerical categories you can use the Options section of the dialog to customize the appearance.

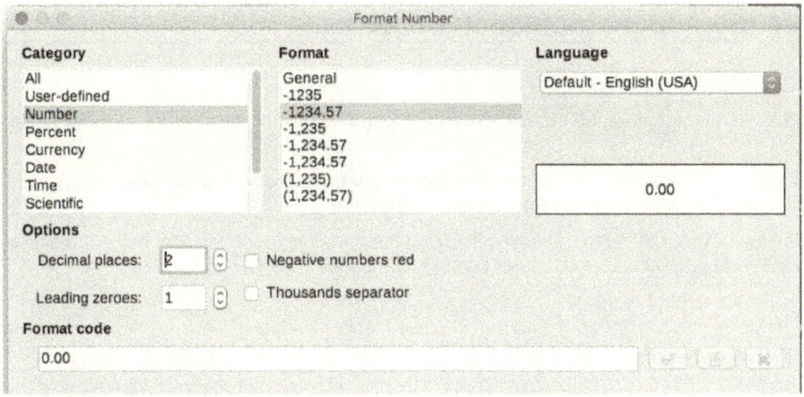

Format Number

| Category | Format | Language |
|---|---|---|
| All | General | Default - English (USA) |
| User-defined | -1235 | |
| Number | -1234.57 | |
| Percent | -1,235 | |
| Currency | -1,234.57 | |
| Date | -1,234.57 | |
| Time | (1,235) | 0.00 |
| Scientific | (1,234.57) | |

**Options**

Decimal places: 2    ☐ Negative numbers red

Leading zeroes: 1    ☐ Thousands separator

**Format code**

0.00

*Figure 289: The Format Number dialog*

▶ **Tip**

Writer displays the formatting code for the category and format selected in *Format Code* section at the bottom of the dialog. For example, if you select a date format such as 31 Dec 1999 the corresponding code is D MMM YYYY. Advanced users can easily customize this formatting code as well as create new user-defined codes.

## Rotating text in a table cell

You can rotate text in a table cell by 90 or 270 degrees. Text rotation can be useful when you have long headings for narrow columns.

- Select the text to be rotated and then choose **Format > Character**, or right-click and select **Character** from the context menu.
- On the *Position* page, in the *Rotation / Scaling* section, choose the rotation angle and click **OK**.

Figure 290 shows a sample table with rotated headings.

| This is long | Another long heading | A rotated heading | Another heading | Another heading | Another heading | Another heading |
|---|---|---|---|---|---|---|
| | | | | | | |
| | | | | | | |
| | | | | | | |

*Figure 290: A table with rotated headings*

⬤ **Note**

Text rotation within table cells can also be achieved with the use of paragraph styles, discussed in detail in Chapter 9, Working with Styles.

# Data entry and manipulation in tables

## Moving between cells

Within a table, you can use the mouse, the cursor (arrow) keys, or the *Tab* key to move between cells.

The cursor keys move the cursor one text character left or right at a time. With an empty cell, pressing the cursor key will move the cursor to the adjacent cell.

The *Tab* key moves directly to the next cell and, if the cursor is in the last cell in the table, creates a new row. Pressing *Shift+Tab* moves the cursor back a cell.

> ### ▶ Tip
>
> To enter a *Tab* character as part of the text of the cell, press the *Ctrl* and *Tab* keys at the same time.

To move to the beginning of the table, press *Ctrl+Home*. If the active cell is empty, the move is to the beginning of the table. If the cell has content, the first press goes to the beginning of the cell and the next press goes to the beginning of the table (pressing again takes you to the beginning of the document).

To move to the end of the table, press *Ctrl+End*. If the active cell is empty, the move is to the end of the table. If the cell has content, the first press goes to the end of the cell and the next press goes to the end of the table (pressing again takes you to the end of the document).

## Sorting data in a table

Just as in a spreadsheet, Writer allows data in a table to be sorted. Up to three levels of sorting can be specified (for example, sort first by age numerically, then alphabetically by name within each age).

To sort data in a table:

1) Select the table (or part of the table) to be sorted.
2) From the Menu bar, choose **Table > Sort**, or select the **Sort** icon from the Table toolbar.
3) In the Sort dialog (Figure 291):
   a) Decide whether you want to sort in the direction of rows or columns. The default sorting direction is by rows, which results in sorting the data in a column.
   b) Select up to three keys to sort on, in the correct order.
   c) For each key, select which column or row to sort on, whether the sort is Numeric or Alphanumeric and whether it is Ascending or Descending.
   d) Click **OK** to perform the sort.

> ### ⬤ Note
>
> You have to select all cells that might be affected by the sorting. For example, if you select only the cells of one column, the sort affects that column only, while the others remain unchanged. In such a case, you risk mixing the data of the rows.

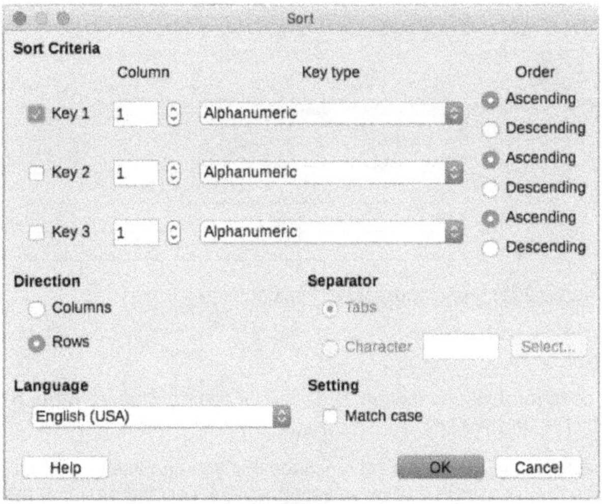

*Figure 291: Selecting criteria for sorting*

## Using spreadsheet functions in a table

In a table in a Writer document, you can use some of the mathematical functions that are normally implemented by LibreOffice Calc. For many simple functions, Writer tables can be used as basic spreadsheets.

Just as in a spreadsheet, each table cell is identified by a letter (for the column) and a number (for the row). For example, cell C4 is the cell in the third column from the left and fourth row from the top. When the cursor is in a cell, the table name and this cell reference is displayed on the status bar.

> **Tip**
>
> Basic spreadsheet functions in tables are much the same as in LibreOffice Calc. The main difference is that cell references are formatted differently. Cell A2 (first column, second row) is referred to in Calc as A2 (or $A$2 for an absolute reference). In Writer tables, it is referred to as <A2>.

For example, suppose you had two numbers in cells <B1> and <C2> and wanted to display the sum of the two in cell <A1>, as shown in Figure 292.

Do the following:

1) Click in cell <A1> and press the = key, or choose **Table > Formula** from the Menu bar, or press *F2*. The Formula bar appears automatically, near the top of the screen. In the leftmost side of the bar, you can see the coordinates of the selected cell.

2) Click in cell <B1>. The identifiers of this cell are automatically displayed in the Formula bar and inserted into cell <A1>.

3) Press the + key.

4) Click on cell <C2>. You can see the final formula = <B1>+<C2> displayed both in the selected cell and in the Object bar.

5) Press the *Enter* key, or click the green tick (check mark) on the Formula Bar, to replace the formula in the cell with the result of the calculation.

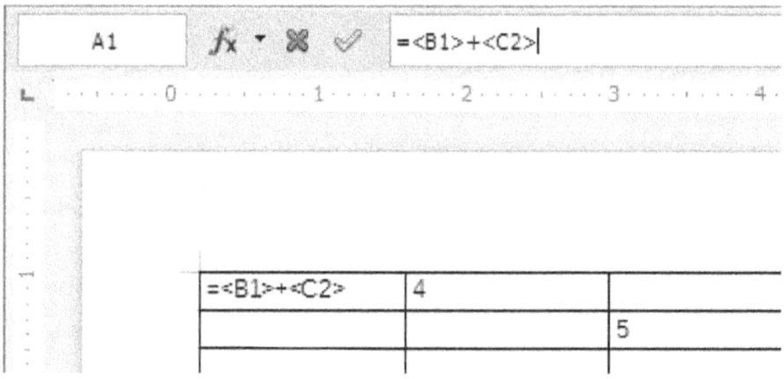

Figure 292: Using spreadsheet functions in a table

### Tip

To display a cell's formula and make it available for editing, choose **Table > Formula** from the Menu bar, or press *F2*.

To display the list of the mathematical functions that you can use in a table, display the Formula toolbar by pressing *F2* or by selecting a blank cell and pressing the = key, and then click the **Formula f(x)** icon.

In our example, this gives the result 9 in the top left cell. For summing contiguous cells, you can simply select the cells in the row, column, or the rectangle of rows and columns. Thus, for example, to add a column of numbers, do this:

1) Type an equals sign = in an empty cell.
2) Select the cells to be added together—in this case the cells from A2 to A5. The formula should be something like =<A2:A5>.
3) Press the Enter key or click the green tick (check mark) on the Formula Bar.
4) The result appears in the cell you have selected.

When using a function, you can enter the cells manually or by selecting them. Thus, to add up the four numbers that we added above (A2, A3, A4, A5), do this:

1) Type an equals sign = in an empty cell.
2) Type sum or select it from the function list f(x).
3) Select the contiguous cells to be added together. The formula should be something like =sum<A2:A5>.
4) Press the *Enter* key or click the green tick (check mark) on the Formula Bar.
5) The answer appears in the cell you have selected.

### Caution

Unlike in Calc, when inserting or deleting rows or columns of the table, formulas are not updated automatically. If you plan to use complex formulas, consider embedding a Calc spreadsheet in your Writer document. See Chapter 19, Spreadsheets, Charts, other Objects.

# Additional table operations

## Protecting cells in a table

You can protect the contents of individual cells of a text table from changes.

### Note

This protection is not intended for secure protection. It is just a switch to protect the cells against accidental changes.

To turn on cell protection:

• Place the cursor in a cell or select cells, then slick the **Protect Cells** icon on the Table toolbar or choose **Table > Protect Cells** from the Menu bar.

To tun off cell protection:

• Place the cursor in the cell or select the cells. First, if necessary, choose **Tools > Options > LibreOffice Writer > Formatting Aids** and mark **Enable cursor** in the *Protected Areas* section. Then click the **Unprotect Cells** icon on the Table toolbar or choose **Table > Unprotect Cells** from the Menu bar.

To remove protection for the entire current table or all selected tables, press *Shift+Ctrl+T*.

## Adding a caption

You can easily add a caption to any table. Writer will keep track of all your captioned tables, automatically number them, and update any links to them. The procedure is the same as for adding captions to images, described in Chapter 11.

## Cross-referencing to a table

You can insert a cross-reference to a captioned table. Clicking on the cross-reference takes the reader directly to the table. For details, see "Using automatic cross-references" in Chapter 17, Fields.

## Creating a heading row in an existing table

To create a heading row in an existing table that does not have one:

1) Select the first row in the table and from the Menu bar select **Table > Insert > Rows**.

2) In the dialog that opens, ensure the Before option is selected and click **OK**.

3) Select the new first row and then from the Styles and Formatting window, double-click the Table Heading paragraph style to apply it to the heading row.

As an alternative, you could apply a table style that does have a heading defined. (Here is where having some personalized table styles could come in very handy.) Place the cursor anywhere in the table, go to Table Styles in the Sidebar, and choose a style.

## Merging and splitting tables

One table can be split into two tables, and two tables can be merged into a single table. Tables are split only horizontally (the rows above the split point are put into one table, and the rows below into another).

To split a table:

1) Place the cursor in a cell that will be in the top row of the second table after the split (the table splits immediately above the cursor).

2) Choose **Table > Split Table** from the Menu bar.

3) A Split Table dialog opens. You can select No heading or an alternative formatting for the heading—the top row(s) of the new table.

4) Click **OK**. The table is then split into two tables separated by a blank paragraph.

**Note**

> If cells in one table include formulas using data from the other table, those cells will contain an error message: **Expression is faulty**.

To merge two tables:

1) Delete the blank paragraph between the tables. You must use the Delete key (not the Backspace key) to do this.

2) Select any cell in one of the tables.

3) Right-click and choose Merge Tables in the context menu. You can also use **Table > Merge Table** from the Menu bar.

**Tip**

> To see clearly where the paragraphs are and to delete them easily, choose **View > Formatting Marks** (*Ctrl+F10*) or click the ¶ button in the Standard toolbar.

## Deleting a table

To delete a table:

1) Click anywhere in the table.

2) Choose **Table > Delete > Table** from the Menu bar.

Or:

1) Select from the end of the paragraph before the table to the start of the paragraph after the table.

2) Press the *Delete* key or the *Backspace* key.

**Note**

> The second method also merges the paragraph after the table with the paragraph before the table, which may not be what you want.

## Copying a table

To copy a table from one part of the document and paste it into another part:

1) Click anywhere in the table.

2) From the Menu bar choose **Table > Select > Table**.

3) Press *Ctrl+C* or click the **Copy** icon on the Standard toolbar.

4) Move the cursor to the target position and click on it to fix the insertion point.

5) Press *Ctrl+V* or click the **Paste** icon in the Standard toolbar.

## Moving a table

To move a table from one part of a document to another part:

1) Click anywhere in the table.

2) From the Menu bar, choose **Table > Select > Table**.

3) Press *Ctrl+X* or click the **Cut** icon in the Standard toolbar. (This step removes the contents of the cells but leaves the empty cells, which must be removed in step 6.)

4) Move the cursor to the target position and click on it to fix the insertion point.

5) Press *Ctrl+V* or click the **Paste** icon in the Standard toolbar. (This pastes the cells and their contents and formatting.)

6) Return to the original table, click somewhere in it and then choose **Table > Delete > Table** from the Menu bar.

## Inserting a paragraph before or after a table

To insert a paragraph before a table, position the cursor before any text or other contents in the first (upper left-hand) cell and press *Enter* or *Alt+Enter*. To insert a paragraph after a table, position the cursor after any text in the last (lower right-hand) cell and press *Alt+Enter*.

### Note

Captions are paragraphs separate from the table itself. If there is a caption below a table, for example, just position the cursor at the end of the caption and press *Enter*.

## Using tables as a page layout tool

Tables may be used as a page layout tool to position text in a document instead of using tabs or spaces. For more information and tips about using tables in page layout, see Chapter 5. Formatting Pages.

### Tip

When inserting a table used for layout, you may wish to deselect the Heading and Border options (see "Inserting a new table" on page 279).

To remove the borders from an existing table, right-click on the table, choose **Table Properties** from the context menu, select the *Borders* tab, and select the icon for no borders.

# The Table menu and toolbar

All of the table commands described in this chapter are conveniently located in the Menu bar under the Table item and on the Table toolbar. When you create a table or select an existing table, the Table toolbar is displayed automatically. You can manually display it at any time by clicking **View > Toolbars > Table**. The toolbar can float over the main Writer window, or it can be docked along any edge of the main window. See Chapter 1, Introducing Writer, for more about docking and floating toolbars, and how to hide and display specific tools on a toolbar.

# LibreOffice

# Chapter 14
# Mail Merge

Form Letters, Mailing Labels, and Envelopes

# What is mail merge?

LibreOffice Writer provides very useful features to create and print:

- Multiple copies of a document to send to a list of different recipients (form letters)
- Mailing labels
- Envelopes

All these facilities, though different in application, are based around the concept of a registered data source, from which is derived the necessary variable address information.

This chapter describes the process. The steps include:

1) How to create and register a data source.
2) How to create and print form letters, mailing labels, and envelopes.
3) Optionally, how to save the output in an editable file instead of printing it directly.

## Creating and registering the data source

A data source is a database containing the name and address records (and optionally other information) from which a mailing list may be derived. Although you can create and print mailing labels and envelopes without using a data source, in most cases using one is the best approach. This chapter assumes that you are using a data source.

LibreOffice can access a wide variety of sources to create the database, including spreadsheets, text files, and databases such as MySQL, Adabas, and ODBC. If the information to be used in the mail merge is currently in a format that LibreOffice cannot access directly, you need to convert it, for example by exporting it to a comma-separated values (CSV) file.

For the following example we start with a spreadsheet with the following column (field) headers: Title, First Name, Last Name, Address, State/County, Country, Post Code, Sex, and Points. A sample of data is shown in Figure 293.

| | A | B | C | D | E | F | G | H | I |
|---|---|---|---|---|---|---|---|---|---|
| 1 | Title | First Name | Last Name | Address | State/County | Country | Post Code | Sex | Points |
| 2 | Mrs. | Alice | Azure | 1, First Avenue Average Town | Ampshire | | AA1 1AA | F | 67 |
| 3 | Mr. | Brian | Brown | 2, Bottom Lane Bilborough | Burkshire | | BB2 2BB | M | 91 |

Figure 293: Spreadsheet data example

After being created as described below, for a data source to be directly accessible from within a Writer document, it must be registered. You only need to do this once; after that, the data source is available to all components of LibreOffice.

1) From within any Writer document, or from the LibreOffice Start Center, choose **File > Wizards > Address Data Source**.
2) The choices on the first page of the wizard vary with your operating system. Select the appropriate type of external address book. In this example, it is **Other external data source**. Click **Next**.

Figure 294: Select type of external address book

3) On the next page of the Wizard, click the **Settings** button.

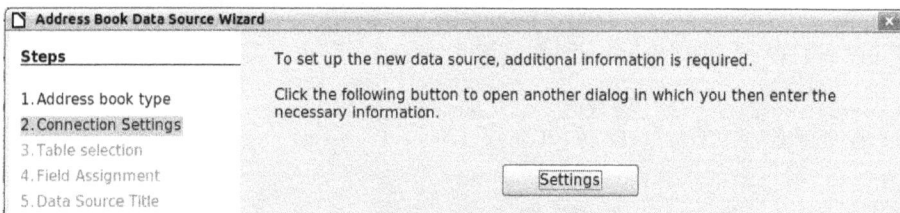

Figure 295: Starting the Settings part of the Wizard

4) In the *Data Source Properties* page, select the Database type. In our example, it is **Spreadsheet**. Click **Next**.

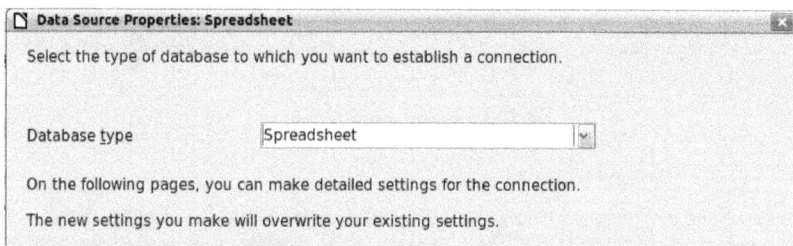

Figure 296: Selecting the database type

5) In the next dialog, click **Browse** and navigate to the spreadsheet that contains the address information. Select the spreadsheet and click **Open** to return to this dialog. At this time you may wish to test that the connection has been correctly established by clicking on the Test Connection button (not shown in illustration).

*Figure 297: Selecting the spreadsheet document*

6) Click **Finish**.

7) On the following page, click **Next**. Because this is a spreadsheet, do **not** click Field Assignment.

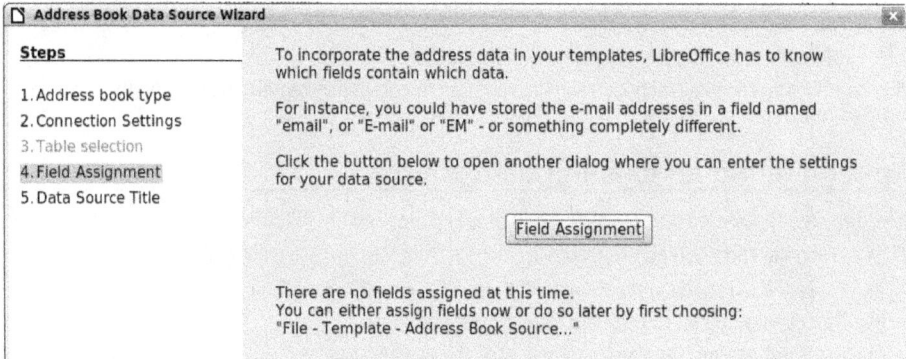

*Figure 298: Because this is a spreadsheet, do **not** click Field Assignment*

8) A database file will be created. Name the file in the path in the Location field. The default is Addresses.odb; but you may replace Addresses with another name if you wish. You may also change the name in the "Address book name" field. The name in this field is the registered name, which LibreOffice will display in data source listings. In our example, the name "Points" was used for both.

*Figure 299: Name the .odb file and the address book*

9) Click Finish. The data source is now registered.

# Deregistering a data source

To remove a registered data source from LibreOffice so it is no longer available for use, as for example an obsolete address list, do the following:

1) Open the Data sources window (by selecting **View > Data Sources** from the Menu bar, or by pressing *F4*, or by selecting the **Data Sources** icon on the Standard toolbar).
2) In the left pane, the Data source explorer, right-click a data source.
3) Select **Registered databases** from the context menu.
4) In the Registered databases dialog, select the data source to be removed.
5) Click **Delete**, then click **Yes** in the confirmation box which opens.
6) Repeat steps 4) and 5) as required.
7) Click **OK** to close the Registered databases dialog.

This does not delete the database from your system. It can be registered again using the methods outlined below.

# Re-registering an existing data source

To re-register an existing database file (.odt) of addresses, do the following:

1) Open the Data sources window.
2) In the left pane, the Data source explorer, right-click a data source.
3) Select **Registered databases** from the context menu.
4) In the Registered databases dialog, click the **New** button.
5) In the Create Database Link dialog, click the **Browse** button, and navigate to the database file location and select it. Click **Open** to return to the Create Database Link dialog.
6) Change the Registered name if required.
7) Click **OK** to exit this dialog.
8) Click **OK** to exit the Registered databases dialog.

# Creating a form letter

> **Example: Sending a letter to your customer base**
>
> A mail order company organized a campaign to assign credit points to their customers according to the quantity of goods they buy during one year.
>
> At the end of the year, they want to send a letter to each customer to show the total of credit points collected.

You can create a form letter manually, which is the simplest and most comprehensive method and is described here, or you can use the Mail Merge wizard as described in "Using the Mail Merge Wizard to create a form letter" starting on page 317. If you elect to use the wizard, pay close attention to its current limitations, as identified within its description.

1) Create a new text document: **File > New > Text Document**, or open a pre-existing form letter with **File > Open**.
2) Display the registered data sources: **View > Data sources** (or press *F4*).
3) Find the data source that you wish to use for the form letter, in this case Points. Expand the Points and Tables folders, and select Sheet1. The address data file is displayed.

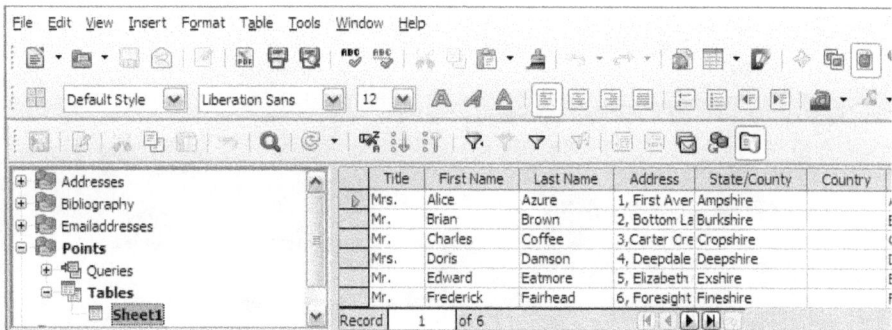

| | Title | First Name | Last Name | Address | State/County | Country |
|---|---|---|---|---|---|---|
| ⊞ 📚 Addresses | Mrs. | Alice | Azure | 1, First Aver | Ampshire | |
| ⊞ 📚 Bibliography | Mr. | Brian | Brown | 2, Bottom La | Burkshire | |
| ⊞ 📚 Emailaddresses | Mr. | Charles | Coffee | 3, Carter Cre | Cropshire | |
| ⊟ 📚 Points | Mrs. | Doris | Damson | 4, Deepdale | Deepshire | |
| ⊞ 🔍 Queries | Mr. | Edward | Eatmore | 5, Elizabeth | Exshire | |
| ⊟ 📑 Tables | Mr. | Frederick | Fairhead | 6, Foresight | Fineshire | |
| ▢ Sheet1 | Record 1 | of 6 | | | | |

*Figure 300: Selecting the data source*

4) Now create or modify the form letter by typing in the text, punctuation, line breaks, and so on that will be present in all of the letters.

   To add the mail-merge fields where needed (such as names and addresses), click in the field heading and drag it to the appropriate point in the letter.

   Note that address lines should be in individual paragraphs, not separated by line breaks as might seem preferable. The reason for this will be made clear in the next step.

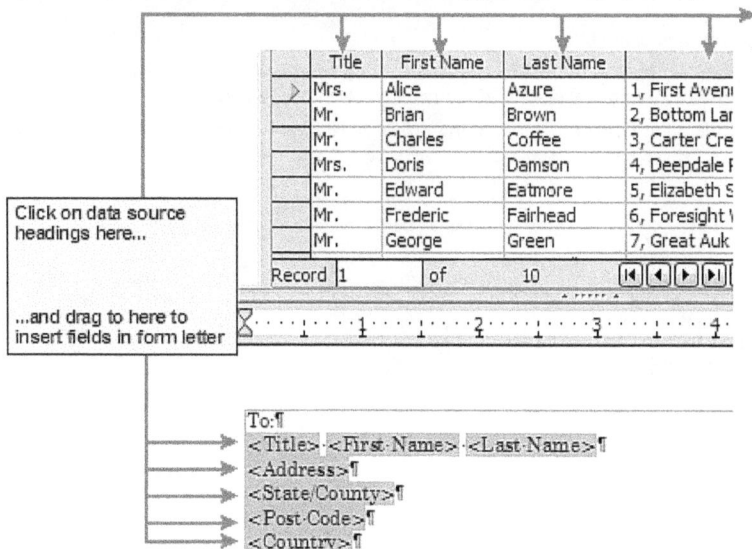

*Figure 301: Dragging fields to the body of the form letter*

5) Continue until you have composed the entire document. At this time you may wish to consider suppressing any blank lines that may appear in the resulting letters. If not, skip ahead to Step 7.

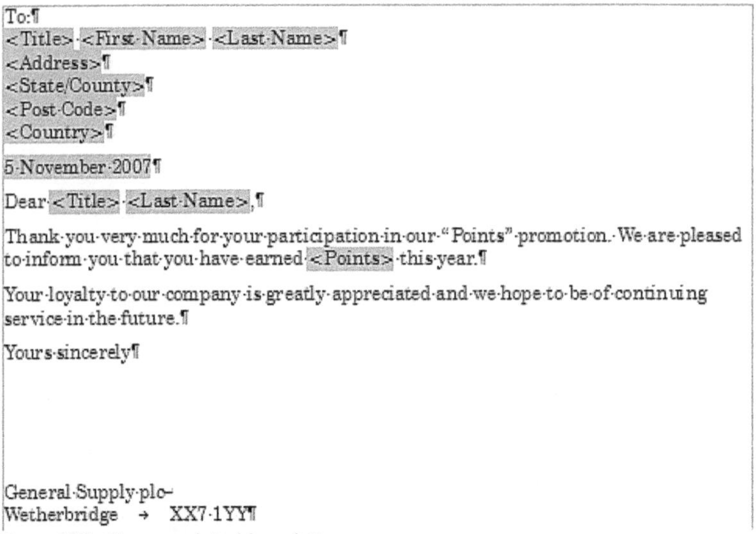

```
To:¶
<Title> <First·Name> <Last·Name>¶
<Address>¶
<State/County>¶
<Post·Code>¶
<Country>¶

5·November·2007¶

Dear·<Title>·<Last·Name>,¶

Thank·you·very·much·for·your·participation·in·our·"Points"·promotion.·We·are·pleased
to·inform·you·that·you·have·earned·<Points>·this·year.¶

Your·loyalty·to·our·company·is·greatly·appreciated·and·we·hope·to·be·of·continuing
service·in·the·future.¶

Yours·sincerely¶




General·Supply·plc-
Wetherbridge    →    XX7·1YY¶
```

*Figure 302: The completed form letter*

6) To suppress blank lines:

   a) Click at the end of the first paragraph to be suppressed if empty, and then choose **Insert > Field > More Fields** to display the Fields dialog.

   b) Select the Functions tab and then click on Hidden Paragraph in the Type column.

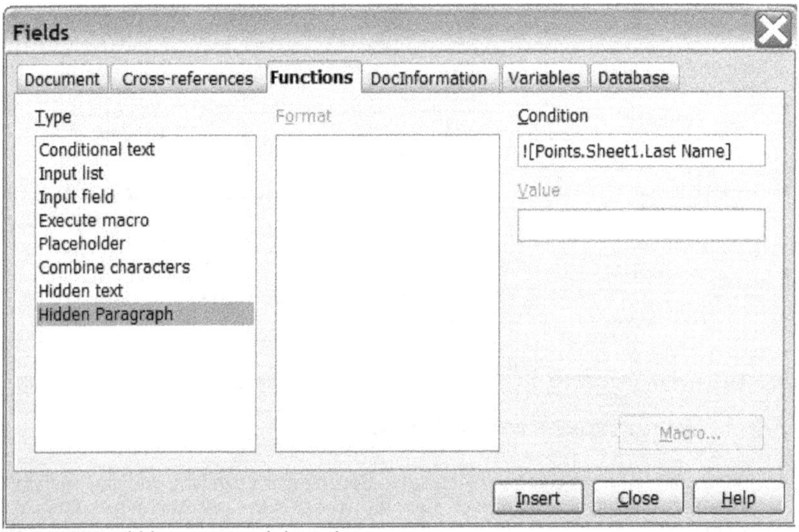

*Figure 303: Hidden paragraph insertion*

c) Now click in the Condition box and enter the details of the condition that defines a blank address field. It has the general form of:

![Database.Table.Database field]

where the '!' (NOT) character indicates the negative case and the square brackets indicate the condition.

For example, in our Points database the condition to test if the Last Name field is empty would be:

![Points.Sheet1.Last Name] as illustrated in Figure 303.

To test for multiple conditions use the operators AND and/or OR between the conditional statements, for example:

![Points.Sheet1.Title]AND![Points.Sheet1.Last Name]

d) Click **Insert**, but do not close the dialog until you have amended all the lines that should be suppressed.

7) The document is now ready to be printed.

a) Choose **File > Print** and respond with **Yes** in the message box.

Your document contains address database fields. Do you want to print a form letter?

Yes    No    Help

*Figure 304: Mail merge confirmation message*

b) In the Mail Merge dialog (Figure 305), you can choose to print all records or selected records. To select records to be printed, use *Ctrl+click* to select individual records. To select a block of records, select the first record in the block, scroll to the last record in the block, and *Shift+click* on the last record.

c) Click **OK** to send the letters directly to the printer. Or, you can save the letters to a file for further editing or formatting; see "Editing merged documents" below.

d) If you have not saved the original, prototype form letter document (template) previously, then you should do so now. Having a form letter template could greatly simplify the creation of other form letters in the future and is highly recommended.

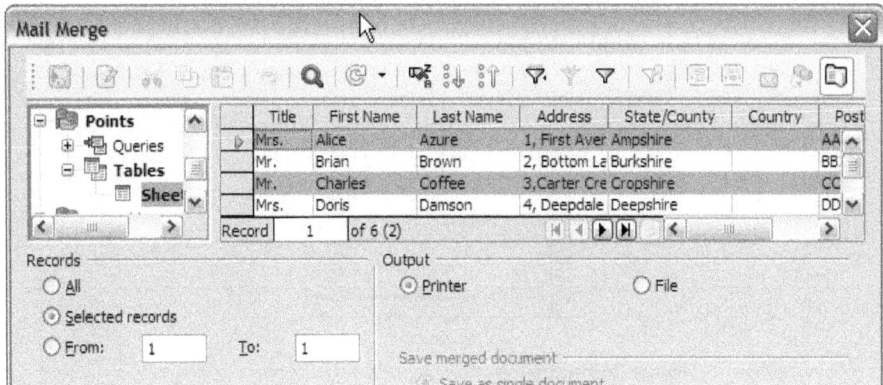

*Figure 305: The Mail Merge dialog*

# Editing merged documents

You may prefer to save the letters to a file, to allow for proofreading or some later formatting. To do this:

1) In the Mail Merge dialog (Figure 305), select **File** in the output section, instead of using the default Printer selection.

2) This changes the dialog to display the *Save merged document* section, where Save as single document is preselected. You can choose to save each letter as an individual document instead.

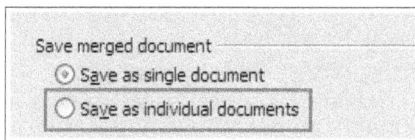

3) Click **OK**. In the Save as dialog, enter a file name for the saved letters and choose a folder in which to save them. The letters will be saved consecutively as separate pages in the single document, or numbered consecutively in individual files if saved as individual documents.

You can now open the letters and edit them individually as you would edit any other document.

# Printing mailing labels

Before beginning this process, note the brand and type of labels you intend to use.

## Preparing for printing

To prepare mailing labels for printing:

1) Choose **File > New > Labels**.

2) On the *Options* page, ensure that **Synchronize contents** is selected.

3) On the **Labels** page (Figure 307), select the Database and Table. Select the Brand of labels to be used, and then select the Type of label.

4) If you are unable to identify your label product in the list, then you can define the labels you have.

   a) Select the User setting in the Type selection box. Click on the *Format* tab of the Labels dialog. Measure on your labels those dimensions illustrated in Figure 306, and enter them into the respective boxes on the left side.

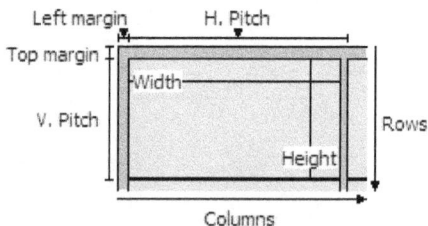

*Figure 306: Required information for label set-up*

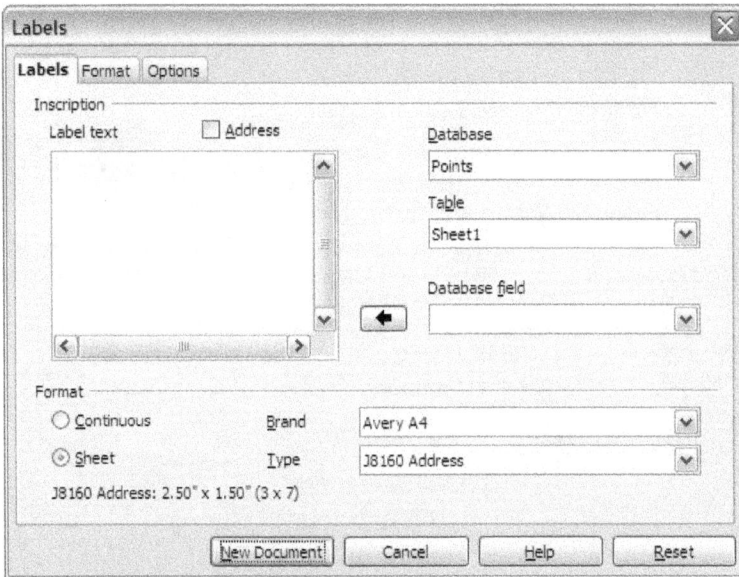

Figure 307: Select Database, Table, label Brand, and label Type

Figure 308: Specify settings, if necessary

b) You can now save your label template if you are likely to use it again. Click **Save**.

c) In the Save Label Format dialog (Figure 309), enter names for your label Brand and Type. Click **OK**.

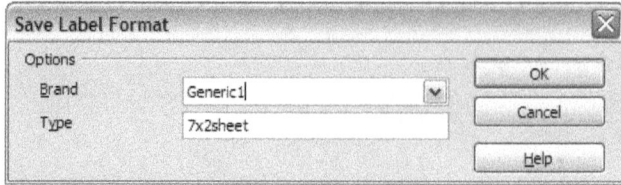

*Figure 309: Name and save the label template.*

5) Click the *Labels* tab. Click the drop-down arrow under Database field. Select the first field to be used in the label (in this example, Title). Click the left arrow button to move this field to the Label text area, as shown in Figure 310.

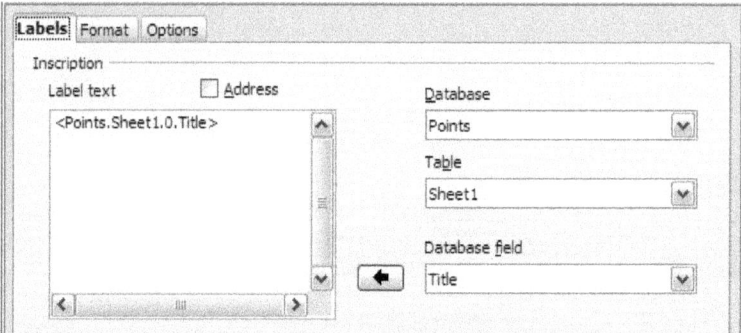

*Figure 310: Move fields from Database field list to Label text area*

6) Continue adding fields and inserting desired punctuation, spaces, and line breaks until the label is composed. Figure 311 shows the completed label.

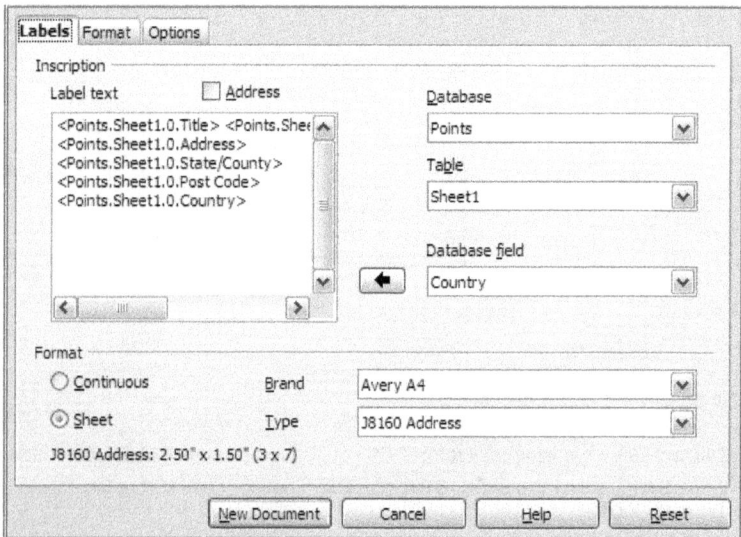

*Figure 311: The completed label*

7) Click **New Document**. You now have a new, single-page document containing a series of frames, one for each label of the selected type and filled with the data source address fields that you selected. Quite often some of the fields in your address data source will be unused, leading to blank lines in your labels. If this is not important, go to "Printing" on page 312; otherwise, continue with "Removing blank lines from labels".

## Removing blank lines from labels

1) First ensure that the label frames are showing the field contents (data source headings), rather than their underlying field names. If this is not the case, then either press *Ctrl+F9* or choose **View > Field Names** to toggle the view.

2) Next, ensure that you can see non-printing characters, such as paragraph marks, line breaks and so on. If these are not already visible, choose **View > Formatting Marks** from the Menu bar, or press *Ctrl+F10*, or click on the **Formatting Marks** icon ( ) on the Standard toolbar.

   You will now see that address field separation is created by line breaks ( ↵ ), rather than paragraphs ( ¶ ). As the suppression of blank address fields depends on hiding paragraphs, not lines, you need to replace line breaks with paragraphs as follows.

3) Click in the first label, at the end of the last data source address field in the first line of the label. Press *Delete* to remove the new line character and then press *Return* (or the *Enter* key) to insert a paragraph marker. Repeat this action for each line in the address.

   If the line spacing in the first label is not satisfactory, you may wish to correct this before proceeding, by modifying the paragraph style associated with the address. Unless you have changed it, the address uses the Default style.

### Caution

The objective of step 3) is to replace all line breaks at the end of data source address fields with paragraphs. Sometimes the address data field may be longer than the width of the label and will wrap to the next physical line: make sure that you are not misled by this into deleting and replacing anything other than line break characters.

4) Click again at the end of the first paragraph to be conditionally suppressed and then choose **Insert > Fields > More Fields**. Select the *Functions* tab and then click on Hidden Paragraph in the Type column. Now click in the Condition box and enter the details of the condition that defines a blank address field. It has the general form of:

   ![Database.Table.Database field]

   where the '!' (NOT) character indicates the negative case and the square brackets indicate the condition.

   For example, in our Points database the condition to test if the Last Name field is empty would be

   ![Points.Sheet1.Last Name] as illustrated in Figure 303.

   To test for multiple conditions, use the operators AND and/or OR between the conditional statements, for example:

   ![Points.Sheet1.Title]AND![Points.Sheet1.Last Name]

   Click Insert, but do not close the dialog until all lines have been amended.

5) Repeat for each paragraph to be conditionally suppressed, remembering to advance the cursor to the end of the line in question before changing the last element of the condition and Inserting the result.

### Caution

The last paragraph of the label address block ends with a special field, Next record:Database.Table (Next record:Points.Sheet1 in our example), and the Hidden paragraph field must be inserted before this field. This can generally be accomplished by clicking at the end of the paragraph and then using the Left Arrow key once to skip back over it.

A clue that you omitted this action is the observation that some records have been skipped and are missing from the final output.

6) Remembering that we selected **Synchronize contents** earlier, you should now be able to see a small window containing a **Synchronize Labels** button. Click on this button and the hidden paragraph fields are propagated to all the labels in your document.

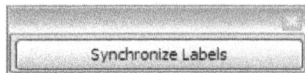

> Synchronize Labels

You now have a template suitable for future use with the same data source and type of label. If you wish to save it, use **File > Templates > Save as Template** to save it as an Open Document Text Template (.ott).

## Printing

1) Choose **File > Print.** The message shown in Figure 304 appears. Click **Yes** to print.

2) In the Mail Merge dialog (Figure 305), you can choose to print all records or selected records. To select records to be printed, use *Ctrl+click* to select individual records. To select a block of records, select the first record in the block, scroll to the last record in the block, and *Shift+click* on the last record.

3) Click **OK** to send the labels directly to the printer.

### Note

If you prefer to save the labels to a file, perhaps to allow some later editing such as changing the typeface or paragraph format, then select File in the output section of the Mail Merge dialog, noy the default Printer selection. This changes the dialog to highlight the Save merged document section, where Save as single document is preselected.

In this case, clicking OK brings up the Save as dialog, where a file name can be entered for the saved labels.

If you did not save the prototype label fields document (template) in Step 6 of the Removing blank lines from documents paragraph, then you are prompted to do so now by another Save as dialog.

In either case, whether printing or saving to file, despite there apparently being only one page of labels, the printed or saved output will be expanded to include all of the selected records from the data source.

## Editing a saved file of mailing labels

To edit a saved file of mailing labels, open the saved label file in the same way as any other Writer document. You will be prompted to update all links. Choose **No** for the following reason: The first label on the page is termed the "Master Label" and all other labels are linked to it. If you update the links, then all labels will end up containing the same data, which may not be what you want.

You can edit individual records in the normal way, by highlighting and changing the font name, for example.

However, you cannot edit all labels globally (for example, to change the font name for all records) by the technique of selecting the entire document. To achieve this result you have to edit the paragraph style associated with the label records as follows.

1) Right-click any correctly spelled word in a label record. Select **Edit Paragraph Style** from the context menu. (Note: If you click on a misspelled word, a different menu appears.)

2) Then from the Paragraph Style dialog, you can make changes to the font name, the font size, the indents, and other attributes.

# Printing envelopes

Instead of printing mailing labels, you may wish to print directly onto envelopes. By selecting **Insert > Envelope** from the Menu bar, you can select one of two methods for their production. The first is where the envelope is embedded within a letter, generally as the first page (Insert in the Envelope dialog), and the second is where the envelope is an independent document (New Document in the dialog). In each case the addressing data may be manually entered, for example by copying and pasting from the letter with which it is associated, or it may originate within an address data source.

This section assumes the use of an address data source and, for convenience, a free-standing envelope. The production of envelopes involves two steps, setup and printing.

## Setting up envelopes for printing

1) Choose **Insert > Envelope** from the Menu bar.

2) In the Envelope dialog, select the *Format* tab (Figure 312), where you can select the envelope format to use. You can then arrange the layout of the envelope to suit your requirements, together with the character and paragraph attributes to be used in the Sender and Addressee areas. These attributes are accessed using the Edit buttons to the right of the dialog, next to the word Format.

### Note

If the list of envelope formats in the Size section of this dialog does not include the size you need, choose User Defined (at the bottom of the list) and specify the envelope size using the Width and Height boxes.

### Tip

At this stage it is only possible to vary the position of the origin points (upper left corners) of the frames that will hold the Sender and Addressee information, but once the envelope has been created, full adjustment of size and position will become possible and you may wish to make some cosmetic adjustments.

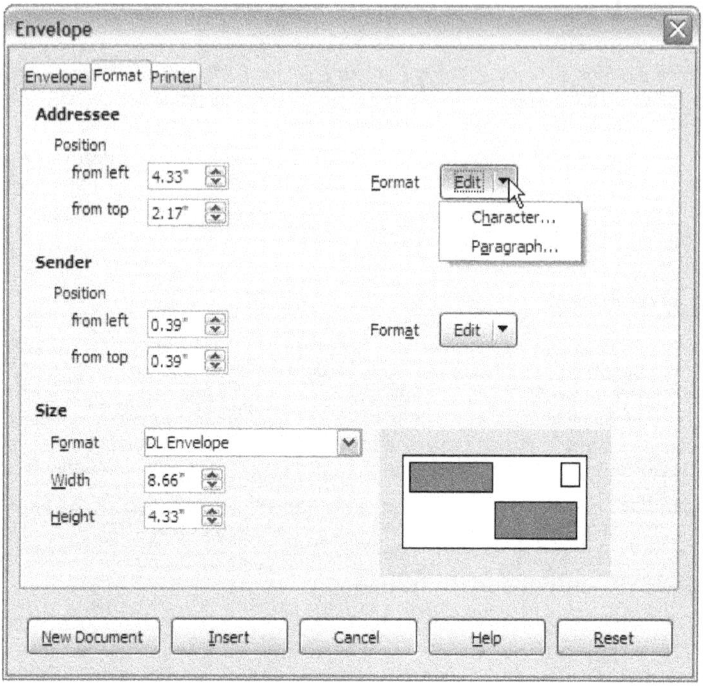

*Figure 312: Envelope formatting dialog*

3) The next step is to select the *Printer* tab (Figure 313), from where you can choose the printer you intend to use, its setup—for example, specification of the tray holding envelopes —and other printer-related options such as envelope orientation and shifting. You may need to experiment with these settings to achieve the best results with your printer.

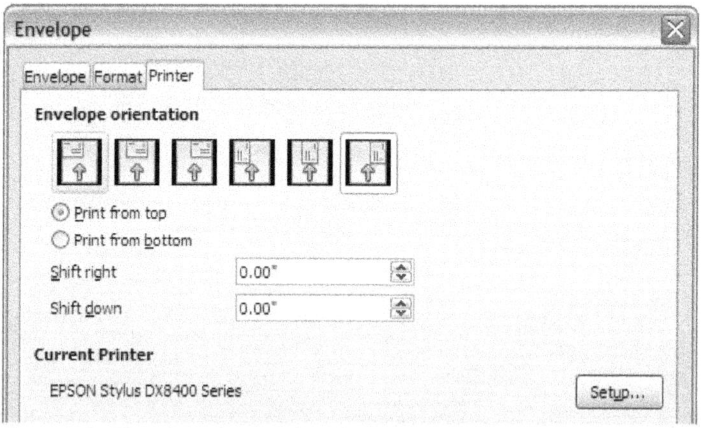

*Figure 313: Choosing printer options for an envelope*

---

4) Select the *Envelope* tab (Figure 314).

5) Choose whether or not to add Sender information to the envelope by selecting or deselecting the Sender option. If wanted, edit the information in the Sender box (Sender is the "from" on the envelope).

6) You now have the choice of creating the Addressee fields by dragging and dropping from the data source headings (as described in "Creating a form letter" on page 304, and in particular in Figure 301) or using the facilities of the Envelope tab.

7) If you prefer dragging and dropping, then click New Document, drag your data source headings into the Addressee area on your new envelope and skip to step 10), otherwise continue with the next step.

8) Verify, add, or edit the information in the Addressee box. You can use the right-hand drop-down lists to select the database and table from which you can access the Addressee information, in a similar fashion to that described for "Printing mailing labels", paragraphs 3, 4, and 5. The similarity of the method with Figures 310 and 311 will be clear.

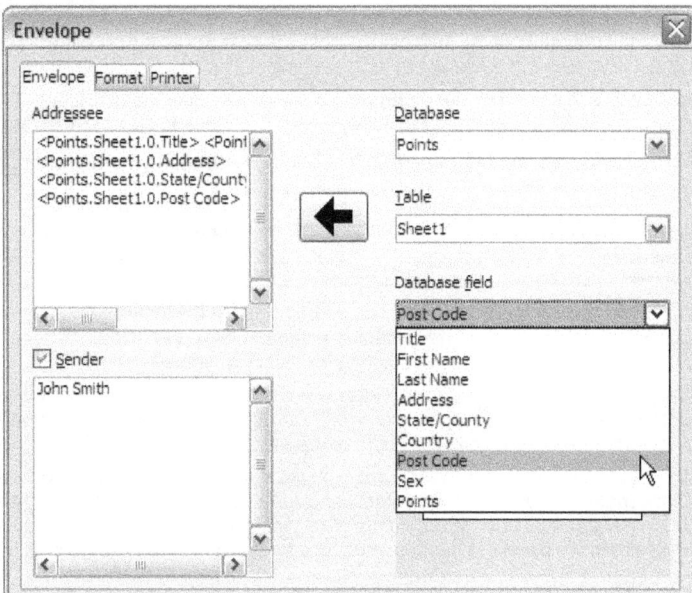

*Figure 314: Choosing addressee and sender information for envelopes*

9) When you have finished formatting, click either the **New Document** or **Insert** button to finish. As might be expected, New Document creates only the envelope template in a new document, whereas **Insert** inserts the envelope into your current document as page 1.

If you don't want to proceed with this envelope, click Cancel or press the Esc key. You can also click Reset to remove your changes and return to the original settings extant when the dialog opened.

You can now modify the placement of the frames containing the sender and addressee information, or make further changes to the character and paragraph attributes (for example, the font) or add a logo or other graphic to the envelope.

**▶ Tip**

If you frequently print envelopes from the same database onto the same size envelopes, at this point you may wish to create a template from this setup. See "Creating an envelope template" on page 317.

10) Quite often some of the fields in your address data source will be unused, leading to blank lines in your envelope Addressee area. If this is not important, you can skip the next few paragraphs and go straight to "Merging and printing the envelopes" on page 317, otherwise continue as described here.

**▶ Tip**

The following procedure is very similar to that used for a similar purpose in the section on printing mailing labels. It is reproduced here for ease of reference.

   a) First ensure that the envelope is showing the field contents (data source headings), rather than their underlying field names. If this is not the case, then either press *Ctrl+F9* or choose **View > Field Names** to toggle the view.

   b) Next, ensure that you can see non-printing characters, such as paragraph marks, line breaks and so on. If these are not already visible, choose **View > Formatting Marks** from the menu bar, or press *Ctrl+F10*, or click the **Formatting Marks** icon ( ¶ ) on the Standard toolbar.

   You will now see that address field separation is created by line breaks ( ⌐ ), rather than paragraphs ( ¶ ). As the suppression of blank address fields depends on hiding paragraphs, not lines, you need to replace line breaks with paragraphs as follows.

   c) Click at the end of the last data source address field in the first line of the envelope. Press *Delete* to remove the new line character and then press Return (or the Enter key) to insert a paragraph. Repeat this action for each line of the envelope.

   If the line spacing in the Addressee area is not satisfactory, you may wish to correct this before proceeding, by modifying the paragraph style associated with the address. Unless you have changed it, the address uses the Default style.

   d) Click again at the end of the first paragraph to be conditionally suppressed and then choose **Insert > Field > Other Fields**. Select the *Functions* tab and then click on Hidden Paragraph in the Type column. Now click in the Condition box and enter the details of the condition that defines a blank address field. It has the general form of:

   ![Database.Table.Database field]

   where the '!' (NOT) character indicates the negative case and the square brackets indicate the condition.

   For example, in our Points database the condition to test if the Last Name field is empty would be:
   ![Points.Sheet1.Last Name] as illustrated in Figure 303.

   To test for multiple conditions, use the operators AND and/or OR between the conditional statements, for example:
   ![Points.Sheet1.Title]AND![Points.Sheet1.Last Name]

   Click Insert, but do not close the dialog until all lines have been amended.

   e) Repeat for each paragraph to be conditionally suppressed, remembering to advance the cursor to the end of the line in question before changing the last element of the condition and Inserting the result.

## Merging and printing the envelopes

To merge addresses and print the envelopes:

1) Choose **File > Print**. A message box appears. Click **Yes**.

2) The Mail Merge dialog (Figure 305) appears. As with form letters and mailing labels, you can choose to print envelopes for one, several or all address records in the database.

3) Make your selections and then click **OK** to print direct to the printer. To check the envelopes before printing them, see "Editing merged documents" on page 308 for instructions.

## Creating an envelope template

When your envelope layout and fields are complete to your satisfaction, you can save the result as a template.

1) Choose **File > Templates > Save As Template**.

2) In the Templates dialog, click **Save**.

3) Enter a name in the text input box and click **OK** to save the template.

# Using the Mail Merge Wizard to create a form letter

The manual method of creating a form letter described in "Creating a form letter" on page 304 provides the most control over the result and is therefore recommended. If you prefer to use the Mail Merge wizard, the technique is described below.

Open a new document with **File > New > Text Document** and start the Mail Merge wizard using **Tools > Mail Merge Wizard**. The wizard opens, as shown in Figure 315.

## Step 1: Select starting document

The wizard gives several options for your starting document:

- Use the current document.
- Create a new document.
- Start with an existing document.
- Start from a template.

For the purposes of this example, we assume that you opened a new text document.

Select **Use the current document** and click **Next**.

*Figure 315: Select starting document*

## Step 2: Select document type

The wizard can produce letters or email messages. In this example, we are producing a letter. Select **Letter** and click **Next**.

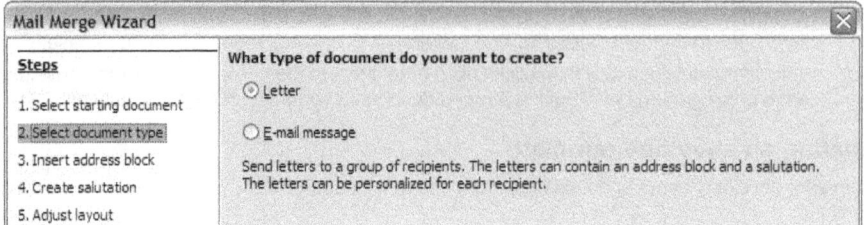

*Figure 316: Choose document type*

## Step 3: Insert address block

This is the most complex step in the wizard. In this step (Figure 317) you will do three things:

1) Tell the wizard which data source to use. The data source must be an existing file; in this example it is the "Points" spreadsheet created earlier.

2) Select the address block to use in the document. This means choosing which fields appear (for example, whether the country is included) and how they look.

3) Make sure that the fields all match correctly. This is very important. For example, the UK English version of the wizard has a field called <Surname>. If your spreadsheet has a column called "Last Name", you need to tell the wizard that <Surname> and "Last Name" are equivalent. This is described in "Matching the fields" on page 320.

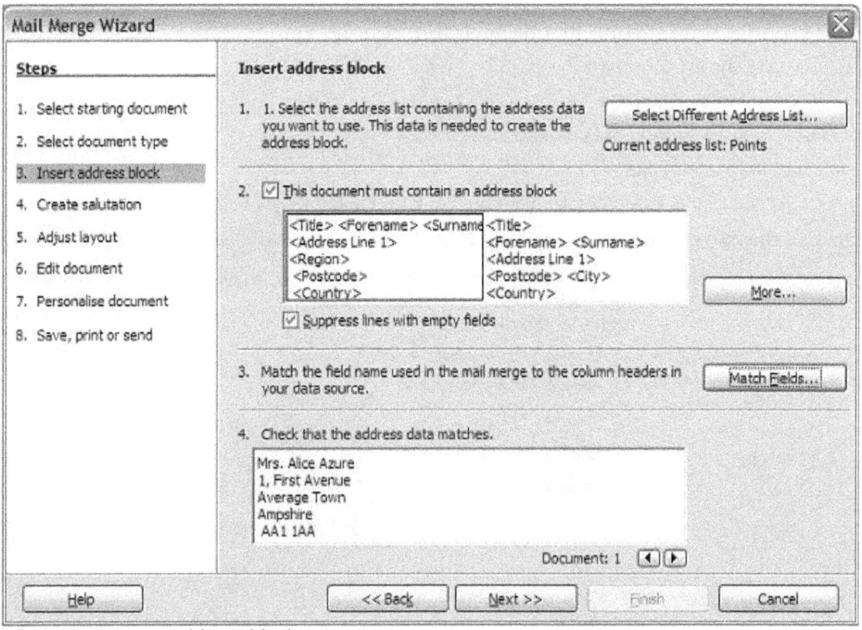

*Figure 317: Insert address block*

### Selecting the data source (address list)

1) If the current address list, identified beneath the Select Different Address List button in section 1, is not the one you wish to use, click the button to open the Select Address List dialog (Figure 318) for choosing a data source.

2) If you have not already created the address list, you may click **Create** to do so now. This step will allow you to create a .csv (Comma Separated Values) file with a new list of address records.

   If you have an address list that is not registered in LibreOffice, but which you wish to use, click Add and select the file from the location in which it is saved.

   In each of the above cases a new data source (.odb file) will be created and registered.

3) Select the address list and click OK to return to step 3 of the wizard. We retain "Points" as our address book for this example. The wizard can also exclude certain records; click Filter to choose them.

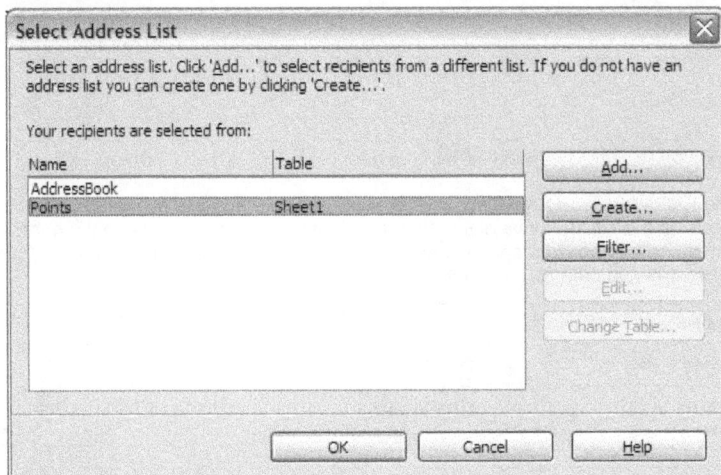
Figure 318: Select address list dialog

### Selecting the address block

1) In section 2 (shown in Figure 317), select the address block to appear on the letter, define its appearance, and choose the fields it contains. The main page gives two choices. Click **More** to open the Select Address Block dialog for more choices.

2) The Select Address Block dialog (Figure 319) displays the original two blocks plus other choices for the format of the address block (you may need to scroll down to see all of the choices). You can also optionally include or exclude the country (for example, only include the country if it is not England) in the Address block settings. The formats provided are relatively common, but they might not exactly match your preference. If this is the case, select the address block that is closest to what you want and click **Edit**, which opens the Edit Address Block dialog.

*Figure 319: Select address block*

3) In the Edit Address Block dialog, you can add or delete address elements using the arrow buttons on the left. To move elements around, use the arrow buttons on the right. For example, to add an extra space between forename and surname in Figure 320, click <Surname> and then click the right arrow button.

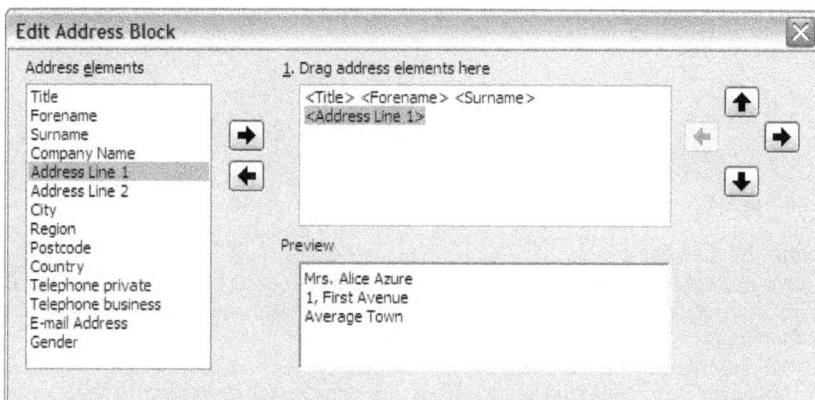

*Figure 320: Edit address block*

## Matching the fields

Finally, it is time to match the wizard's fields with the spreadsheet fields, so that items like <Surname> and "Last Name" match correctly.

1) Look at section 3 of the wizard (shown in Figure 317 on page 318). The box at the bottom displays one record at a time, using the address block format you specified. Use the right and left arrow buttons below that address box to step through the addresses, checking that they display correctly. Do not assume that all the records display correctly, just because one or two do. Check them all if you can, or at least a good proportion.

2) If the addresses do not display correctly (and they probably will not right away), click Match Fields.

The Match Fields dialog (Figure 321) has three columns:

– Address Elements are the terms the wizard uses for each field, such as <Forename> and <Surname>.

– Use the Matches to Field column to select, for each address element, the field from your data source that matches it.

– The Preview column shows what will be shown for this field from the selected address block, so you can double-check that the match is correct.

3) When you have matched all the fields, click OK to return to step 3 of the wizard. Now, when you use the arrow buttons to look at all the addresses, they should all look correct. If not, go back and change anything you're not happy with, before clicking Next to move to step 4.

Note that you will not be able to continue until you have correctly matched all the fields in your chosen address block. If you see <not yet matched> in a field position it indicates that the field in question is not correctly matched.

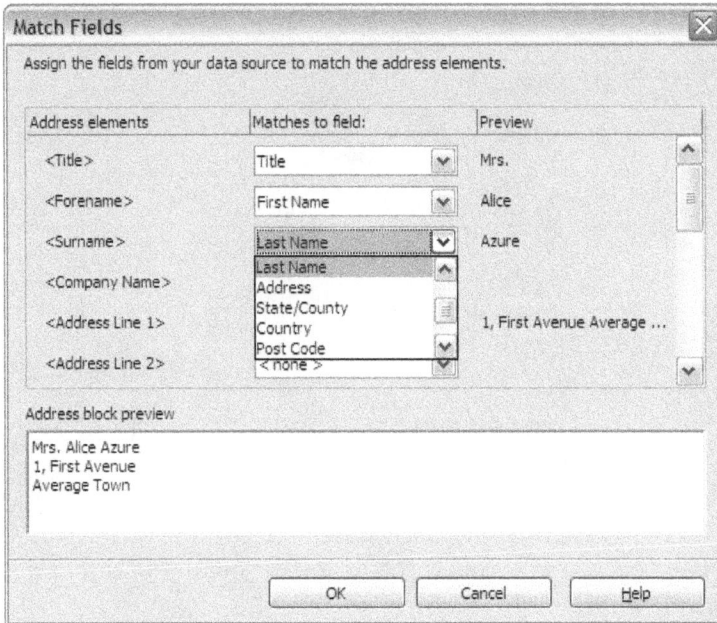

*Figure 321: Match fields dialog*

4) Notice the option for Suppress lines with empty fields in section 2 of Figure 317. Using the Wizard, you do not have to create your own conditional suppression fields.

## Step 4: Create salutation

It is possible to create just about any salutation you want in this step.

Select **This document should contain a salutation** to enable the General salutation list box. Some general texts are available in the list box, or you can enter your own text. A preview pane displays your choice.

Select **Insert personalized salutation** to enable further salutation constructs.

You can, for example, use a different greeting for men and women. To do this, Writer must have some way of knowing whether a person is male or female. In a spreadsheet, you might have a column called Gender. In the section Address list field indicating a female recipient, set the Field name to Gender and the Field value to F. The Male salutation is then printed for all men and the Female salutation for all women. Unfortunately, LibreOffice does not provide for other genders.

> **Note**
>
> You do not need to tell LibreOffice who is a male, because it assumes that all non-female records are males.

If you do not have such a column in your spreadsheet, or if you do not need to distinguish between genders in the salutation, then you can leave the Field name and Field value boxes empty and use the customized content of the Male list box for the salutation to all recipients.

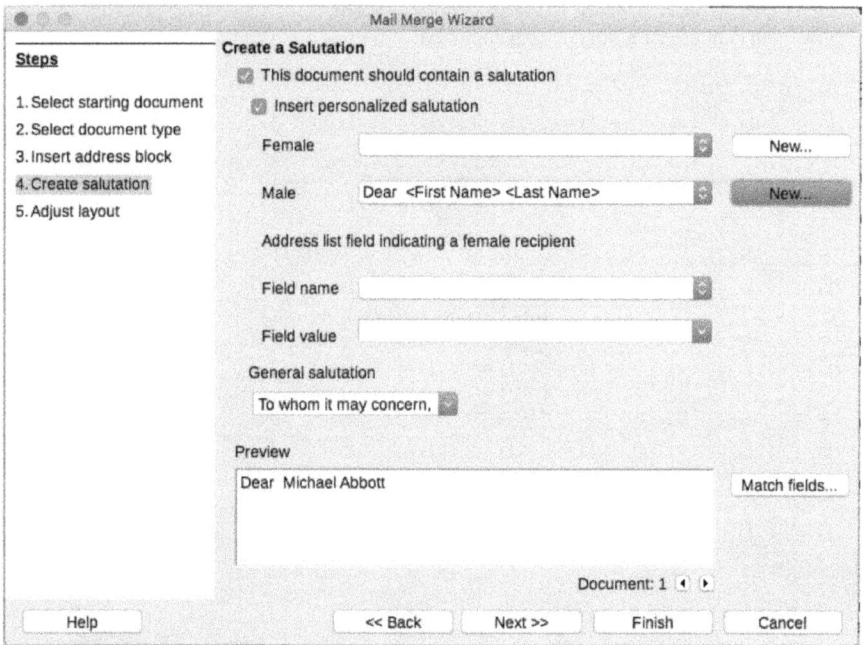

Figure 322: Create a salutation

As an example:

1) Click the **New** button alongside the Male list box. The Custom Salutation (Male Recipients) dialog opens (see Figure 323).
2) Select Salutation in the Salutation elements listings.
3) Click the arrow button to add it to box 1.
4) Open the list box choices for box 2, select an appropriate greeting or type your own text into the list box. Edit it as needed.
5) Select and move across First Name from the Salutation elements listings into box 1.
6) Type a space and then move Last Name across.

7) Finally, move Punctuation Mark across and select the comma from the choices in box 2.

8) The construct is shown in the Preview box.

9) Carry out any final editing. Click OK.

*Figure 323: Customizing the salutation*

This method allows you to use gender neutral titles such as Doctor (Dr) and Reverend (Rev), or titles such as Ms, or omit titles.

## Step 5: Adjust layout

In step 5, you can adjust the position of the address block and salutation on the page. You can place the address block anywhere on the page. The salutation is always on the left, but you can move it up and down the page. Use the buttons shown in Figure 324 to move the elements.

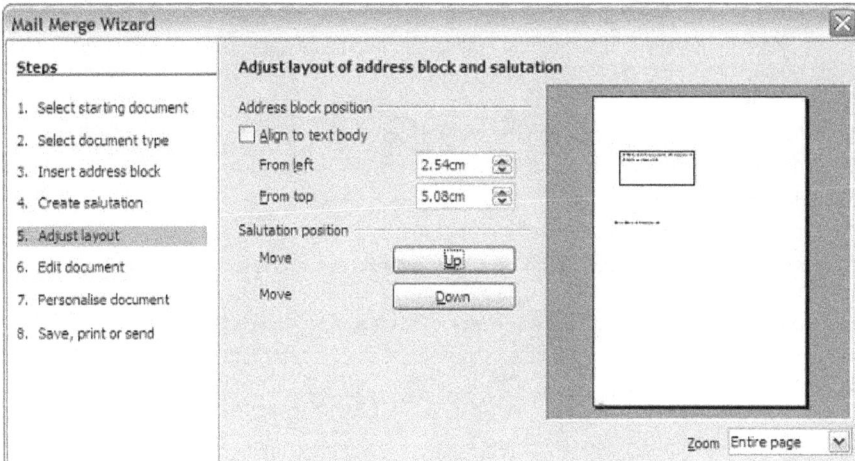

*Figure 324: Adjust layout*

## Step 6: Edit document and insert extra fields

In step 6 you have another opportunity to exclude particular recipients from the mail merge, as shown in Figure 325.

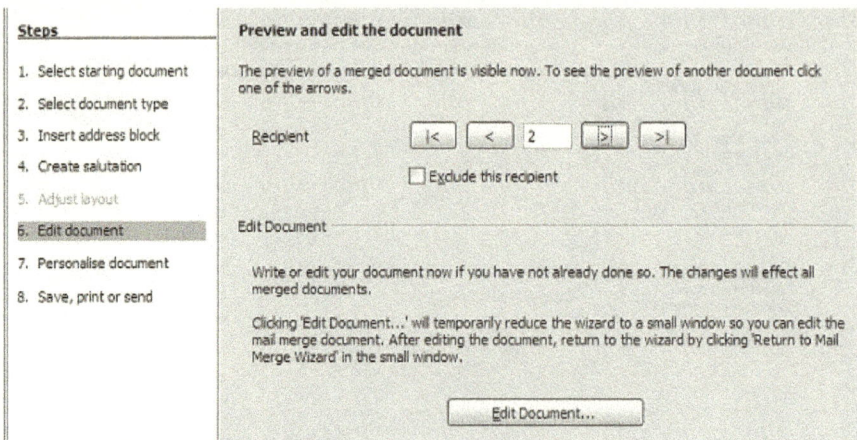

*Figure 325: Edit document*

You can also edit the body of the document. If you started with a blank document, you can write the whole letter in this step. Click Edit Document to shrink the wizard to a small window (Figure 326) so you can easily edit the letter.

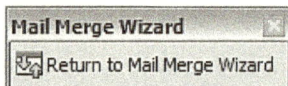

*Figure 326: Minimized mail merge wizard*

You need to perform another important task in this step. The wizard only inserts information from the name and address fields, but you may wish to add additional data. In our example, we want to tell each person how many points they had accumulated during the year; that information is in the database. To do this:

1) Click Edit Document in step 6 of the wizard.
2) Choose **Insert > Fields > Other Fields**. The Fields dialog opens.
3) Click the *Database* tab.
4) On the left hand side, select Mail merge fields.
5) Under Database selection find your data source (in this example, it is Points). Expand it to see the fields.
6) Click the field you want to insert (Points), then click Insert to insert the field.
7) You can insert any number of fields any number of times into your mail merge document.
8) Click Close when you are done.

### Note

The Database selection lists the data source you selected in step 3. All the information you need for the letter must be contained in that data source.

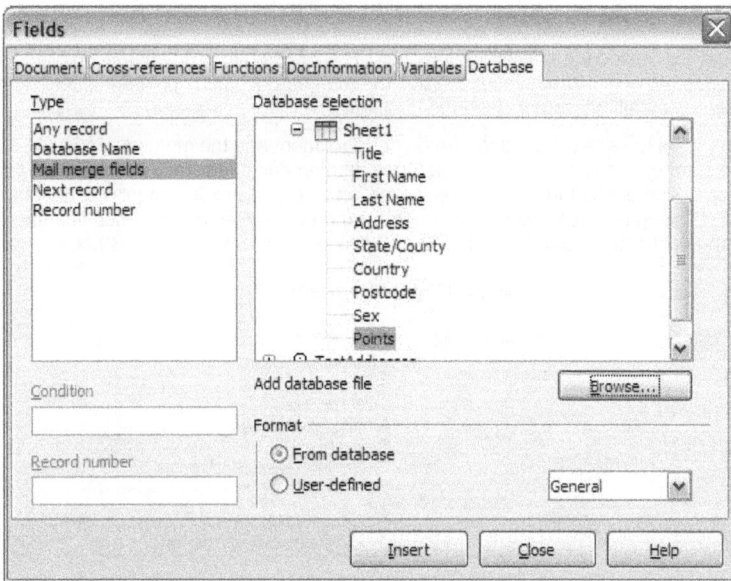

*Figure 327: Insert mail merge fields dialog*

## Step 7: Personalize documents

This step creates all your letters, one per recipient.

Clicking the Edit individual Document button here is similar to step 6. The difference is that you now edit a long file containing all of the letters, so you can make changes to a particular letter to one person. In this step of the Mail Merge wizard, click **Find** to open a dialog that allows searches within the document, perhaps for an individual addressee.

*Figure 328: Personalize document*

As with step 6, when editing the document, the wizard shrinks to a small window (Figure 326). Click on this window to expand the wizard to its full size.

## Step 8: Save, print or send

You have now completed the mail merge process. The last step is to do something with it. In step 8, you can save the original sample letter, save the merged document, print the letters right away or, if you created email messages, send them.

You probably want to save the starting (prototype) document and the merged document. To do this, select Save starting document to reveal the Save starting document section containing the Save starting document button. This button will be active only if the document has not already been saved. Clicking on this button brings up the standard Save as dialog. Once you have named and saved the document you return to the Step 8 dialog as shown in Figure 330.

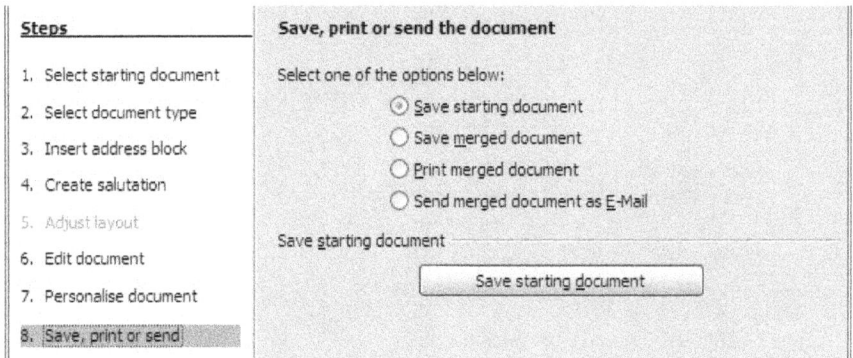

*Figure 329: Step 8: Save, print or send*

The merged document can now be saved by selecting Save merged document. This will reveal the Save merged document settings section, from which you can select to save either as one large file containing all the individual, generated letters or as a separate file for each letter.

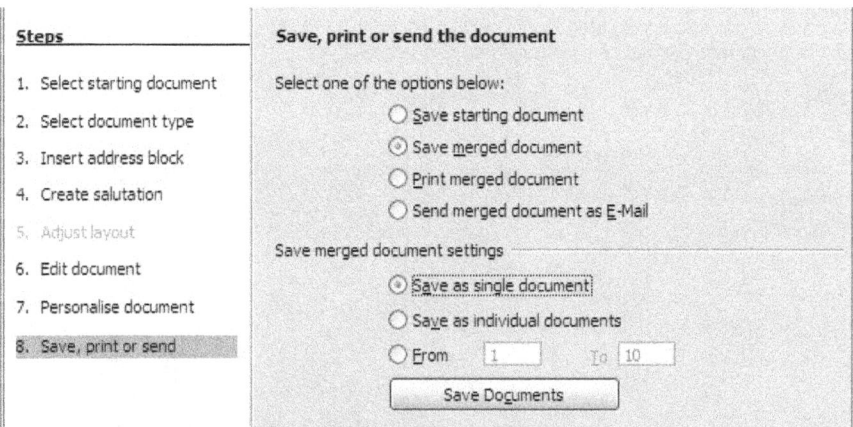

*Figure 330: Saving a merged document*

When you have saved the merged document, you can print the final letters now or later; and you can still manually check and edit the letters if necessary. If you elect to print at this stage, the dialog shown in Figure 331 appears; it should be self-explanatory.

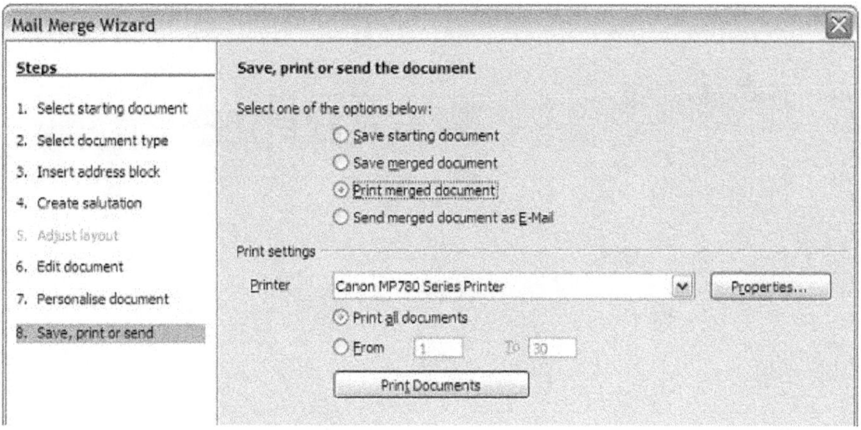

*Figure 331: Printing the merged document*

# LibreOffice

*Chapter 15*
*Tables of Contents, Indexes,*
*Bibliographies*

# Introduction

This chapter describes how to create and maintain a table of contents (TOC), an index, and a bibliography for a text document using LibreOffice Writer. To understand the instructions, you need to have a basic familiarity with Writer and styles (see Chapters 8 and 9). Some common usage examples are given.

# Tables of contents

Writer's table of contents feature lets you build an automated TOC from the headings in a document. These entries are automatically generated as hyperlinks in the table. Whenever changes are made to the text of a heading in the body of the document or the page on which the heading appears, those changes automatically appear in the table of contents when it is next updated.

Before you start, make sure that the headings are styled consistently. For example, you can use the Heading 1 style for chapter titles and the Heading 2 and Heading 3 styles for chapter subheadings.

This section shows you how to:

- Create a table of contents quickly, using the defaults.
- Customize a table of contents.

### Note

You can use any style you want for the different levels to appear in the table of contents; however, for simplicity, most of this chapter uses the default Heading [x] styles.

## Creating a table of contents quickly

Most of the time you will probably find the default table of contents (TOC) to be what you need. Inserting a default TOC is simple:

1) When you create a document, use the following paragraph styles for different heading levels (such as chapter and section headings): Heading 1, Heading 2, and Heading 3. These are what will appear in your TOC. Writer can evaluate up to ten levels of headings.

2) Click in the document where you want the TOC to appear.

3) Choose **Insert > Table of Contents and Index > Table of Contents, Index or Bibliography**.

4) Click **OK**. The result will be a typical table of contents with the entries generated as hyperlinks.

Some tips you may find useful:

- If some of your headings do not show up in the table of contents, check that the headings have been tagged with the correct paragraph style. If a whole level of headings does not show up, check the settings in **Tools > Chapter Numbering**. See "Defining a hierarchy of headings" in Chapter 8, Introduction to Styles, for more information.
- The TOC appears with a gray background. This background is there to remind you that the text is generated automatically. It is not printed and does not appear if the document is converted to a PDF. To turn off this gray background, go to **Tools > Options > LibreOffice > Application Colors**, then scroll down to the Text Document section and deselect the option for Index and table shadings.

This change may leave a gray background showing behind the dots between the headings and the page numbers, because the dots are part of a tab. To turn that shading off, go to **Tools > Options > LibreOffice Writer > Formatting Aids** and deselect the option for Tabs.

- If you cannot place the cursor in the TOC, choose **Tools > Options > LibreOffice Writer > Formatting Aids**, and then select **Enable cursor** in the *Protected Areas* section.

If you add or delete text (so that headings move to different pages) or you add, delete, or change headings, you need to update the table of contents. To do this: Right-click anywhere in the TOC and select **Update Index** from the context menu.

## Caution

If you have **Edit > Track Changes > Show** enabled when editing a document and you update the TOC, then errors may occur, as the TOC will still include any deleted headings and you may find that deleted text causes page numbering in the TOC to be wrong. To avoid this problem, be sure this option is deselected before updating a TOC.

## Customizing a table of contents

Almost every aspect of the table of contents can be customized to suit the style and requirements of your document. However, with this flexibility also comes some complexity, so it is good to have in mind the desired end result.

Start by clicking in the document where you want the table of contents to appear and choose **Insert > Table of Contents and Index > Table of Contents, Index or Bibliography** to open the Table of Contents, Index or Bibliography dialog shown in Figure 332.

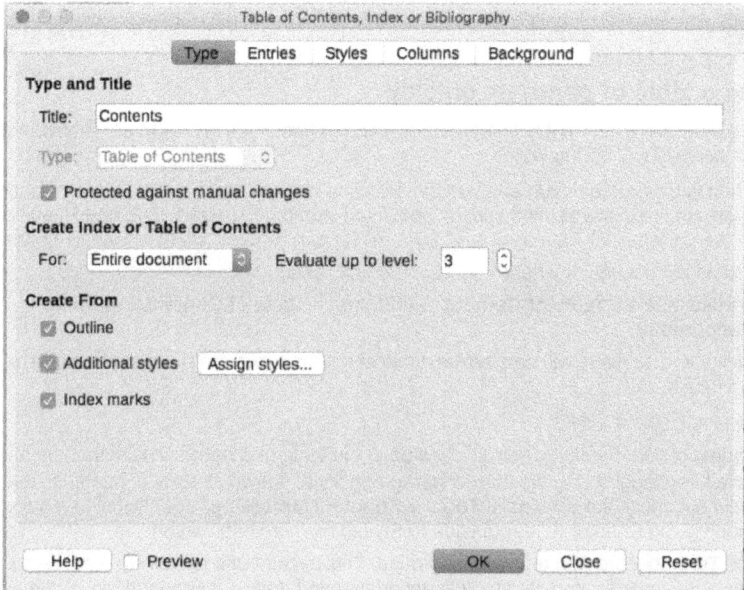

*Figure 332: Type page of Table of Contents, Index or Bibliography dialog*

You can also access this dialog at any time by right-clicking anywhere in an existing table of contents and choosing **Edit Index** from the context menu.

The Table of Contents, Index or Bibliography dialog has five pages. Each of them covers a different aspect of the TOC structure and appearance:

- Use the *Type* page to set the attributes of the TOC.
- Use the *Entries* and *Styles* pages to format the entries in the TOC.
- Use the *Columns* page to put the TOC into more than one column.
- Use the *Background* page to add color or an image to the background of the TOC.

You can display a preview box, located on the left-hand side of each page, to show as you work how the TOC will look: select the **Preview** option in the lower left-hand corner of the dialog. The illustrations in this chapter show the dialog as it appears with the preview box hidden.

**Note**

> The preview box only shows the appearance from settings made on the *Type*, *Entries*, and *Styles* pages. The other pages have their own preview panes.

After making all your changes, click **OK** to apply them. To revert to the default settings for the *Columns* and *Background* pages, select each page in turn and click the **Reset** button. The settings on the *Entries* and *Styles* pages must be reset manually; the **Reset** button has no effect.

### Type page

Use the *Type* page, pictured in Figure 332, to set the attributes of the TOC.

**Changing the title**

> To give the table of contents a different title, type it in the Title field. To delete the title, clear the Title field.

**Setting the type**

> Be sure the *Type* is set to Table of Contents.

**Note**

> You can change the type of index only when you first create it. Once you define an index type (for example, make a table of contents) you cannot change the type.

**Protecting against manual changes**

> By default, to prevent the TOC from being changed accidentally, the **Protected against manual changes** option is selected; the TOC can only be changed by using the right-click menu or the dialog. If the option is not selected, the TOC can be changed directly on the document page, just like other text. However, any manual changes will be lost when you update it.

**Choosing the scope of the table of contents**

> In the **For** drop-down list in the *Create from* area, you can select whether the TOC will cover all the headings of the document (Entire document) or just the headings of the chapter where it is inserted. Writer identifies a "chapter" as all the headings between two first level outline headings (normally Heading 1).

**Changing the number of levels included**

> Writer uses 10 levels of headings when it builds the table of contents (or the number of levels used in the document, whichever is smaller). To change the number of levels included, enter the required number in the **Evaluate up to level** box. For example, the TOC in this book includes only the first four heading levels.

**Creating a table of contents from an outline**

The third section of the *Type* page determines what Writer should use to create the TOC. The choices (not mutually exclusive) are:

- Outline

- Additional styles

- Index marks

By default Writer uses the outline levels; that is, paragraphs formatted with the paragraph styles associated with outline levels in **Tools > Chapter Numbering**.

You can change the paragraph styles included in the outline as described in "Using paragraph styles to define a hierarchy of headings" in Chapter 8, Introduction to Styles, and you can include other paragraph styles in the TOC by assigning an outline level to those styles. To do this, modify the paragraph style definition: go to the Outline & Numbering page for the style, and select the required outline level. Click **OK** to save the change.

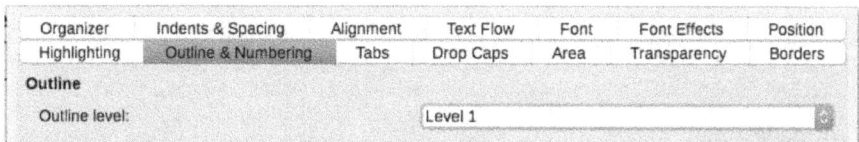

| Organizer | Indents & Spacing | Alignment | Text Flow | Font | Font Effects | Position |
|---|---|---|---|---|---|---|
| Highlighting | Outline & Numbering | Tabs | Drop Caps | Area | Transparency | Borders |

**Outline**

Outline level: Level 1

*Figure 333: Specifying an outline level on the Outline & Numbering page for a paragraph style*

**Creating from additional styles**

By selecting the **Additional Styles** option on the *Type* page, you can add more paragraph styles to the TOC. This can be useful when you want to include in the TOC the heading of an annex (appendix). If the **Outline** option is also selected, the additional styles will be included in the table of contents together with the ones defined in the outline numbering.

**Creating from index marks**

This selection adds any index entries that you have inserted into the document by using **Insert > Indexes and Tables > Entry**. Normally you would not use this selection for a table of contents. However, if you do wish to use it, be sure to select **Table of Contents** from the drop-down list in the Insert Index Entry dialog (see Figure 8) when you are entering the index entries for use in a TOC, so that Writer can distinguish between them and any index entries intended for inclusion in an alphabetic index.

## *Entries page*

Use the *Entries* page (see Figure 334) to define and format the entries in the TOC. Each outline level can be styled independently from the other levels by adding and deleting elements.

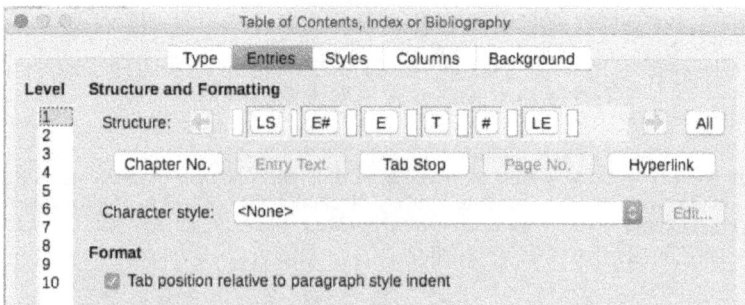

*Figure 334: Entries page of Insert Index/Table dialog*

Click on a number in the *Level* column to select the outline level whose elements you want to format. The *Structure* line contains the elements included in the entries for that level. Elements that can be added to the structure line are displayed just below the structure line, and are grayed out if they cannot be included:

- The **E#** icon represents the "chapter number", which means the heading number value assigned in **Tools > Chapter Numbering** to a heading style, not just for chapters but also for other levels of headings. See "Setting up heading numbering" in Chapter 8, Introduction to Styles.
- The **E** icon represents the chapter (or sub-chapter) text: That is the text formatted with the paragraph style used for each level.
- The **T** icon represents a tab stop.
- The **#** icon represents the page number.
- The **LS** icon represents the start of a hyperlink.
- The **LE** icon represents the end of a hyperlink.
- Each white field on the Structure line represents a blank space where you can add custom text or another element.

### Caution

In the Chapter Numbering dialog (covered in Chapter 8), if you have included any text in the **Separator Before** or **After** boxes for any given level, then that text will be part of the E# field for that level. Take care when building the structure line not to create any unwanted effects in the appearance of the TOC.

**Adding elements**

To add an element to the Structure line:

1) Click in the white field where you want to insert the element.
2) Click one of the active buttons just below the Structure line. For example, to add a tab, click the **Tab Stop** button. An icon representing the new element appears on the Structure line.
3) To add custom text, such as the word Chapter, type the text in the white field. Don't forget a trailing space.

**Changing elements**

To change an element in the Structure line, click the icon representing that element and then click a non-grayed out element in the row of buttons just below the Structure line. For example, to change a chapter number to a tab stop, click the **E#** icon on the Structure line (it shows then as being pressed) and then click the **Tab stop** button in the row of available elements. To cancel before swapping an element, click in one of the white spaces.

**Applying changes to all outline levels**

To apply the displayed structure and formatting to all outline levels, click the **All** button on the right.

**Deleting elements**

To delete an element from the Structure line, click the button representing that element and then press the *Delete* key on your keyboard. For example, to delete the default hyperlink setting, click the **LS** icon and then press the *Delete* key. Repeat this for the **LE** icon.

**Applying character styles**

You might want an element to be a bit different from the rest of the line. For example, you might want the page number to be bold. To apply a character style to an element:

1) Be sure you have previously defined a suitable character style.

2) On the Structure line, click the button representing the element to which you want to apply a style.

3) From the Character Style drop-down list, select the desired style.

To view or edit the attributes of a character style, select the style from the Character Style drop-down list and then click the **Edit** button.

> **Tip**
>
> The default character style for hyperlinks is Internet Link (such as those inserted by **Insert > Hyperlink**), which by default is underlined and shown in blue.
>
> The default hyperlinks of TOC entries are set to the Index Link character style, which may be different in appearance from the Internet Link style. If you want them to appear the same as internet links, you can select the LS icon on the Structure line and change the character style selection for TOC entries to Internet Link.
>
> You can also change the attributes for Index Link to what you want.

**Tab parameters**

Click on the Tab stop icon on the structure line to bring up two controls:

• Fill character: select from the three options the tab leader you wish to use.

• Tab stop position: Enter the distance to leave between the left page margin and the tab stop.

**Tab position relative to paragraph style indent**

When this option is selected, entries are indented according to the settings of their individual formats. Where a paragraph style specifies an indent on the left, tab stops are relative to this indent. If this option is not selected, tab stops are relative to the left margin position.

### Styles page

Use the Styles page (Figure 335) to change which paragraph style is assigned to display the text of each level in the table of contents. In most cases, the best strategy is to keep the assigned styles but change their settings as needed to make the TOC appear the way you want.

To apply a custom paragraph style to an outline level:

1) In the *Levels* list, select the outline level.

2) In the *Paragraph Styles* list, click the desired paragraph style.

3) Click the < button to apply the selected paragraph style to the selected outline level.

The style assigned to each level appears in square brackets in the *Levels* list.

To remove paragraph styling from an outline level, select the outline level in the *Levels* list, and then click the **Default** button.

To view or edit the attributes of a paragraph style, click the style in the *Paragraph Styles* list, and then click the **Edit** button.

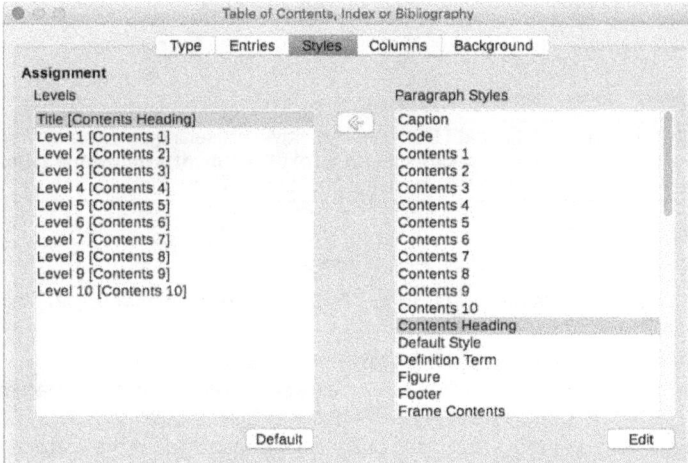

*Figure 335: Styles page of the Table of Contents, Index or Bibliography dialog*

## Note

Changes to a paragraph style will affect any text in the document that is formatted using this style, not just the format of the table of contents.

### Columns page

Use the *Columns* page to change the number of columns for the TOC. Multiple columns are more likely to be used in an index than in a TOC, so this page is described in the section on indexes. See Figure 12.

### Background page

Use the *Background* page (Figure 336) to add color or an image to the background of the TOC.

*Figure 336: Background page, showing Color choices*

**Adding color**

To add color to the background of the table of contents, select from the color grid.

> **⬤ Note**
>
> By default, the background to the TOC is shaded gray. This setting is in **Tools > Options > LibreOffice > Application Colors > Text Document > Index and table shadings**. Deselect this option to remove the gray background.

**Adding an image**

To add an image to the background of the table of contents:

1) From the **As** drop-down list, select Image. The *Background* page now displays the image options, as shown in Figure 337.

2) Click the **Browse** button. The Find images dialog opens.

3) Find the image file you want and then click the **Open** button. The selected image appears in the preview box. (If you do not see the image, select the **Preview** option.)

4) To embed the image in your document, clear the **Link** option. To link the image to the document but not embed it, select the **Link** option.

5) In the *Type* area, choose how you want the background image to appear:

   – To position the image in a specific location, select **Position** and then click the desired location in the position grid.

   – To stretch the image to fill the entire background area, select **Area**.

   – To repeat the image across the entire background area, select **Tile**.

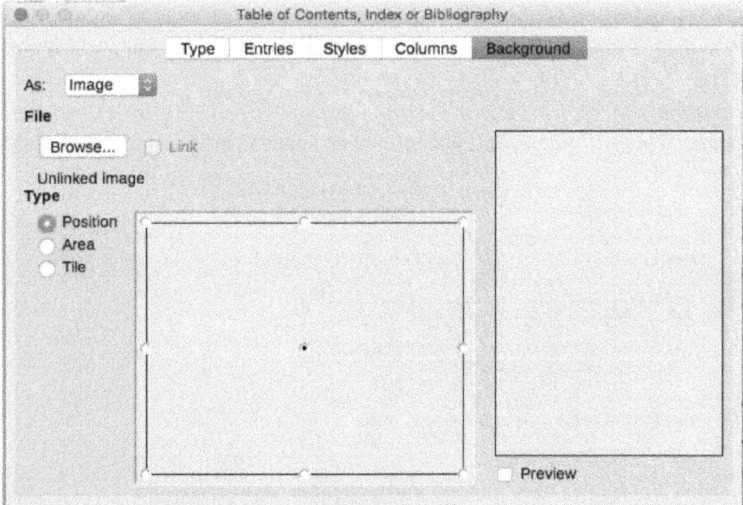

*Figure 337: Image options on the Background page*

**Deleting a color or an image**

To delete color or an image from the table background:

1) From the **As** drop-down list, select **Color**.

2) Click **No Fill** on the color grid.

## Maintaining a table of contents

This section shows you how to:

- Edit an existing TOC.
- Update a TOC when changes are made to the document.
- Delete a TOC.

### *Editing a table of contents*

To edit an existing TOC:

1) Right-click anywhere in the TOC.
2) From the context menu, choose **Edit Index**. The Table of Contents, Index or Bibliography dialog (Figure 332 on page 330) opens. You can edit and save the table as described in the previous section.

> **Tip**
>
> If you cannot click in the TOC, it is probably protected. To disable this protection, choose **Tools > Options > LibreOffice Writer > Formatting Aids**, and then select **Enable Cursor** in the *Protected areas* section. If you wish to edit the TOC without enabling the cursor, you can access it from the Navigator.

You can also access the Table of Contents, Index or Bibliography dialog from the Navigator.

1) Open the Navigator (press *F5*).
2) Click the expansion symbol (+ sign or triangle) next to Indexes.
3) Right-click on Table of Contents1 and choose Index > Edit.

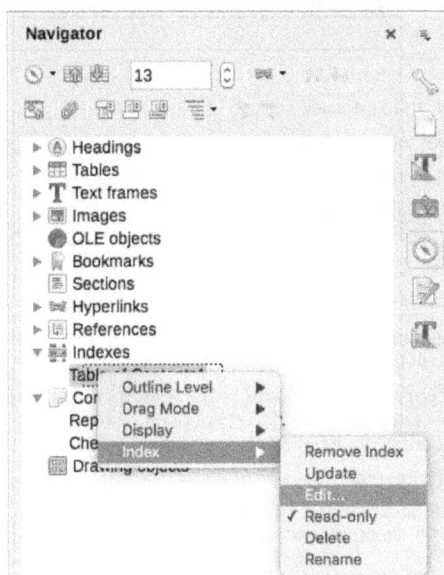

*Figure 338: Access a TOC from the Navigator*

### Updating a table of contents

Writer does not update the TOC automatically, so after any changes to the headings, you must update it manually:

1) Right-click anywhere in the TOC.

2) From the context menu, choose **Update Index**. Writer updates the TOC to reflect the changes in the document.

You can also update the index from the Navigator by expanding Indexes, right-clicking on Table of Contents1, and choosing **Index > Update**.

### Deleting a table of contents

To delete the TOC from a document:

1) Right-click anywhere in the TOC.

2) From the context menu, choose **Delete Index**. Writer deletes the TOC.

> **Caution**
>
> Writer will not prompt you to confirm the deletion.

You can also delete the index from the Navigator by selecting **Index > Delete** from the menu shown in Figure 338.

# Alphabetic indexes

An alphabetical index (referred to as an index) is a list of keywords or phrases used throughout a document that, if listed in order with page numbers, may help the reader find information quickly. Generally an index is found in the back of a book or document.

This section describes how to:

• Add index entries

• Create an alphabetic index quickly

• Customize the display of index entries

• Customize the appearance of the index

• View and edit existing index entries

## Adding index entries

Before you can create an index, you must create some index entries.

1) To add a word to the index, place the cursor anywhere in that word. If you want to add multiple words as one entry, select the entire phrase.

2) Choose **Insert > Table of Contents and Index > Index Entry** to display a dialog similar to that shown in Figure 339. When the dialog opens, the selected text appears in the Entry text input box. You can accept the word or phrase shown, or change it to whatever you want.

3) Click **Insert** to create the entry.

You may of course open the dialog before selecting text, and then select the text required. After selecting the text, click on the dialog to enter the text into the Entry text input box.

> **Note**
>
> A cursor placed immediately before the first character of a word, or immediately after the last character of a word if it is followed by a space, counts as being in that word.

See "Customizing index entries" below for an explanation of the fields on this dialog.

You can create multiple entries without closing the dialog. For each one:

1) Click at the location in the document that you want to index.
2) Click again on the dialog.
3) Change the entry if needed, and click **Insert**.
4) Repeat steps 1–3 until you have finished with the entries, then click **Close**.

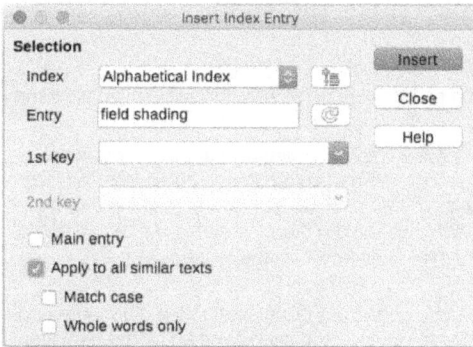

*Figure 339: Inserting an index entry*

## Note

If field shading is active (**Tools > Options > LibreOffice > Application Colors > Text Document > Field shadings**), when a selected word or phrase has been added to the index, it is shown in the text with a gray background. If the text of an index entry has been changed from the text of the word selected, the index entry is marked by a small gray rectangle at the start of that word.

## Tip

You can also open the Insert Index Entry dialog by clicking the **Entry** icon on the Insert toolbar, as shown in Figure 340.

*Figure 340: Index Entry icon on Insert toolbar*

## Creating an alphabetic index quickly

Now that you have some index entries, you can create the index.

Although indexes can be customized extensively in Writer, most of the time you need to make only a few choices.

To create an index quickly:

1) Click in the document where you want to add the index and click **Insert > Table of Contents and Index > Table of Contents, Index or Bibliography** to open the Table of Contents, Index or Bibliography dialog.

2) In the Type box on the *Type* page (Figure 341), select Alphabetical Index.

3) In the *Options* section, you may want to uncheck **Case sensitive** (so that capitalized and lower-case words are treated as the same word) and uncheck **Combine identical entries with p or pp**.

4) Click **OK**. The result will be a typical index.

Writer does not update an index automatically. If you add, delete, or change the text of index entries, you need to update the index. To do this, follow the steps outlined in "Updating a table of contents" on page 338.

## Customizing index entries

Below is a brief explanation of the fields in the Insert Index Entry dialog and how to use them.

**Index**
The type of index this entry is for. The default is Alphabetical Index, but you can use this field to create extra entries for a table of contents or user-defined indexes or lists of almost anything. For example, you might want an index containing only the scientific names of species mentioned in the text, and a separate index containing only the common names of species. See "Other types of indexes" on page 346.

**Entry**
The word or phrase to be added to the selected index. This word or phrase does not need to be in the document itself; you can add synonyms and other terms that you want to appear in the index.

**1st key**
An index key is an entry that has no associated page number and has several subentries that do have page numbers. Using keys is a useful way of grouping related topics. (See "Example of using an index key" below.)

**2nd key**
You can have up to a three-level index, where some of the first-level keys have level-2 entries that are also keys (without page numbers). This degree of index complexity is not often necessary.

**Main entry**
When the same term is indexed on several pages, often one of those pages has more important or detailed information on that topic, so you want it to be the main entry. To make the page number for the main, or most important, entry stand out, select this option and then define the character style for the page number of a main index entry to be bold, for example.

**Apply to all similar texts**
Select this option to have Writer automatically identify and mark any other word or phrase that matches the current selection. The Match case and Whole words only options become available if this option is selected. Use this option with care, as it may result in many unwanted page numbers (for minor uses of a word) being listed in the index.

### Example of using an index key

An index key is a primary entry under which subentries are grouped. For example, you might want to create a grouping similar to this:

LibreOffice
    Calc,  10
    Impress,  15
    Writer,  5

In this example, LibreOffice is the 1st key. The subentries (with the page numbers showing) are the indexed entries. To insert an index entry for the topic Writer, on the Insert Index Entry dialog (Figure 339 on page 339), type Writer in the Entry box and LibreOffice in the 1st key box.

## Customizing the appearance of an index

To customize an existing index, right-click anywhere in the index and choose Edit Index/Entry from the context menu.

The Table of Contents, Index or Bibliography dialog (Figure 341) has five pages. Any or all of them can be used to customize the appearance of an index.

- Use the *Type* page to set the attributes of the index.
- Use the *Entries* and *Styles* pages to format the entries in the index.
- Use the *Columns* page to put the index into more than one column.
- Use the *Background* page to add color or an image to the background of the index.

The preview box, located on the left-hand side of the dialog, shows as you work how the index will look. (If you do not see the preview box, select **Preview** in the lower right-hand corner of the dialog.)

After making your changes, click **OK** to save the index so it appears in your document.

### Note

The preview box only shows the appearance from settings made on the *Type*, *Entries*, and *Styles* pages. The other pages have their own preview panes.

### *Type page*

Use the *Type* page to set the basic attributes of the index.

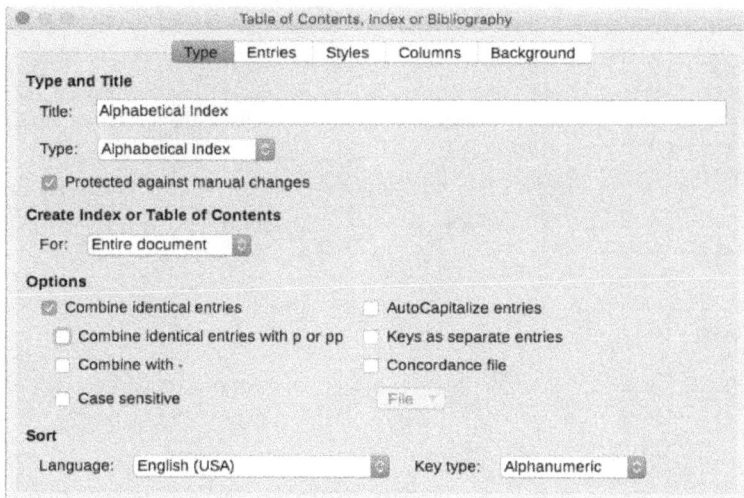

Figure 341: Type page for an alphabetic index

1) To give the Index a different title, type it in the Title field. To delete the title, clear the Title field.
2) Be sure the type of index is set to Alphabetical Index.

3) To prevent the index from being changed accidentally, select Protected against manual changes. If this option is selected, the index can only be changed using the right-click menu or the Table of Contents, Index or Bibliography dialog. If the option is not selected, the index can be changed directly on the document page, just like other text, but any manual changes to an index are lost when you update it.

4) From the drop-down list in the Create Index or Table of COntents section, select Entire document. You can also choose to create an index for just the current chapter.

5) Various other options determine how the index handles entries:

 - Combine identical entries. Defines how identical entries are dealt with. Normally each page number of an indexed word or phrase will be shown in the index; however, these can be combined using the Combine identical entries with p or pp. If you want a page range displayed, select Combine with – (which will produce something similar to 23–31). If you want different entries based on what letters are capitalized, select Case sensitive.

 - AutoCapitalize entries. Automatically capitalizes the first letter of each entry regardless of how they show within the document itself.

 - Keys as separate entries. For the keys to have their own page numbers, select this option.

 - Concordance file. Enables a list of words in an external file to be imported (select using the File button) and then used within the index. The concordance file has a special file format; for further information, refer to concordance file in Help > LibreOffice Help. Using a concordance file can speed up production of an index, but unless the words are very carefully selected and you edit the index afterwards, the resulting index can be full of entries for minor mentions of a term, making it less useful than a more selective index.

 - Sort. Defines how the entries are sorted when displayed. The only option is alphanumeric, but you can define which language alphabet will be used.

### Entries page

Use the *Entries* page to set exactly how and what will be displayed for each of the entries. The page is similar to Figure 342. Note that hyperlinking from the index to the location of entries in the text is not available.

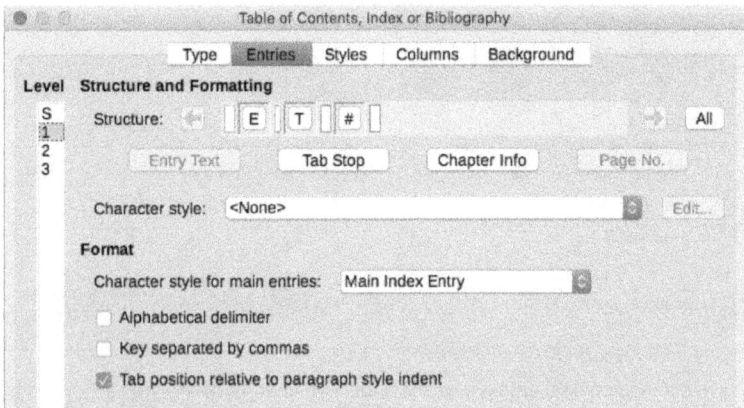

*Figure 342: Entries page for an alphabetical index*

To begin, in the Level column select the index level whose elements you want to format. Level "S" refers to the single letter headings that divide the index entries alphabetically when the Alphabetical delimiter option is selected in the Format section. (You will be able to apply your changes to all index levels later.) The Structure line displays the elements for entries in that level. Each button on the Structure line represents one element:

- The E icon represents the entry text.
- The T icon represents a tab stop.
- The # icon represents the page number.
- The CI icon represents chapter information. This is not present by default, but can be added by selecting the **Chapter info** button.

Each white field on the Structure line represents a blank space. You can add custom text if you desire.

**Adding elements**

To add an element to the Structure line:

1) Place the cursor in the white field to the left of where you want to insert the element.
2) Click one of the active buttons below the Structure line. (For example, to add a tab stop, click the **Tab stop** button.) An icon representing the new element appears on the Structure line.
3) To add custom text, click in the white space at the position you want to insert it, and type the text. Don't forget a trailing space.

**Changing elements**

To change an element in the Structure line, click the icon representing that element and then click the element that you want to substitute it for in the row of buttons just below the Structure line. For example, to change entry text to a tab stop, click the E icon on the Structure line (it shows then as being pressed) and then click the **Tab stop** button in the row of available elements.

**Deleting elements**

To delete an element from the Structure line, click the button that represents that element and then press the *Delete* key on your keyboard. For example, to delete a tab stop, click the T icon and then press the *Delete* key.

**Chapter Info**

This button inserts chapter information, such as the chapter heading and number. The information to be displayed is selected from the Chapter entry box menu. This data is determined in the Chapter Numbering dialog (**Tools > Chapter Numbering**).

**Applying character styles**

Each of the items that can be added to the Structure line may be given additional formatting. For example, you may want the page number to be a different size from the rest of the index text. To do this, apply a character style to one of the elements in the Structure line.

To apply a character style to an element:

1) On the Structure line, click the icon representing the element to which you want to apply a style.
2) Select the desired style from the Character Style drop-down list. Writer applies the style to the selected element.

To view or edit the attributes of a character style, select the style from the Character Style drop-down list and then click the **Edit** button.

**Formatting entries**

Apply additional formatting using the options in the *Format* section.

- Alphabetical delimiter. This separates the index entries into blocks that start with the same first letter, using that letter as a header. For example, if your index begins:

  apple,  4
  author, 10
  break,  2
  bus, 4

  Then selecting this option will give you:

  A

  apple,  4
  author, 10

  B

  break,  2
  bus, 4

- Key separated by commas. Arranges the entries in the index on the same line but separated by commas.
- Tab position relative to Paragraph Style indent. When checked, entries are indented according to the settings of their individual formats. Where a paragraph style with an indent on the left is in use, tab stops will be relative to this indent. If this option is not selected, tab stops will be relative to the left margin position.

### Styles, Columns and Background pages

Refer to "Styles page" on page 334 and "Background page" on page 335 for detailed information on these pages.

### Columns page

Use the Columns page (Figure 343) to change the number of columns for the index.

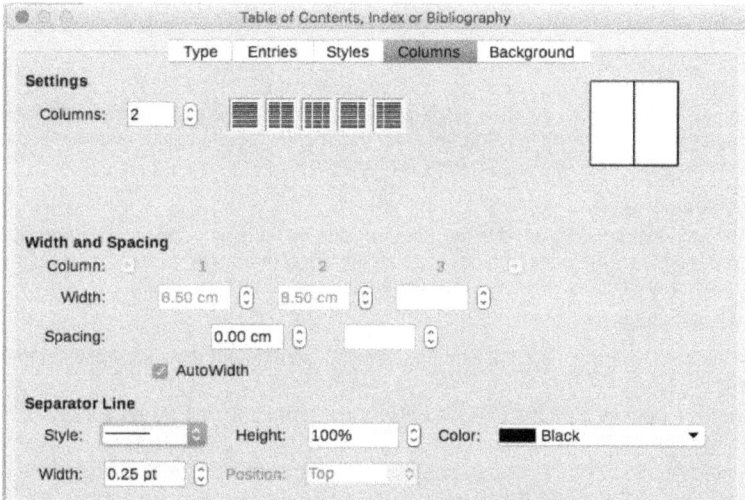

*Figure 343: Columns page of the Insert Index/Table dialog*

**Adding multiple columns**

To display the index in more than one column:

1) Either enter the number of columns desired in the box labeled Columns or select the icon representing the number of columns.

2) To evenly distribute the columns according to the page width, check the AutoWidth box. If it is unchecked, you can manually set each of the following:

   – Width of each of the columns

   – Spacing between the columns

3) You can choose to have a separator line between the columns:

   – Style: The default is None, or select from three choices of line style.

   – Width: The width (thickness) of the line. The default is 0.25pt.

   – Height: The height of the line, as a percentage of the full column height. The default is 100%

   – Position: Position of the line relative to the columns (top, centered, or bottom) if the height is less than 100%.

   – Color: Allows the color of the separator line to be set.

# Maintaining an index

To modify the appearance of an index:

1) Right-click anywhere in the index.

2) From the context menu, choose **Edit Index**. The Table of Contents, Index or Bibliography dialog opens and you can edit and save the index using the five tabs described in the previous section.

To update or delete an index, right-click anywhere in the index and select **Update Index** or **Delete Index**.

## *Viewing and editing existing index entries*

Once you have added the initial entries, you can make some amendments. You can view and edit these using the following steps:

1) Ensure that field shading is active (**View > Field Shadings** or *Ctrl+F8*), so you can locate index entries more easily.

2) Place the cursor in the field shading of an existing index entry in the body of the document, right-click, and select **Index Entry** from the content menu. In the case of a changed-text entry, the field shading is immediately before the word. Placing the cursor immediately before a word marked as a text entry will satisfy both selection criteria.

3) A dialog similar to Figure 344 appears. You can move through the various index entries using the forward and back arrow buttons. If there is more than one entry for a single word or phrase, a second row of buttons with a vertical bar at the point of the arrow head is displayed allowing you to scroll through each of these entries.

4) Make the necessary modifications or additions to the index entries, and then click **OK**.

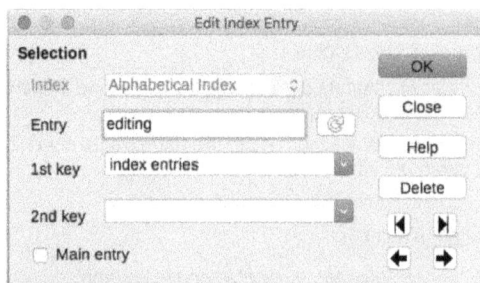

*Figure 344: Viewing and editing index entries*

# Other types of indexes

An alphabetical index is not the only type of index that you can build with Writer. Other types of indexes supplied with Writer include those for illustrations, tables, and objects, and you can even create a user-defined index. This chapter does not give examples of all the possibilities.

To create other indexes:

1) Place the cursor where you want the index created.

2) Select **Insert > Table of Contents and Index > Table of Contents, Index or Bibliography** from the Menu bar.

3) On the Table of Contents, Index or Bibliography dialog, in the Type drop-down list, select the index wanted.

4) Modify the various pages, which are similar to those discussed in previous sections.

5) Select **OK** when everything has been set.

## Example: Creating an index of figures

Creating an index (list) of figures or tables is easy if the figure captions were created using Insert > Caption or manually using a number range variable as described in Chapter 17, Fields.

1) On the Table of Contents, Index or Bibliography dialog, in the Type drop-down list, choose Illustration Index. You can change the title of the index to something else; we have used Table of Figures as our title.

2) Be sure Captions is selected in the Create from section, and choose the category of caption. The default for Category is Illustration; in our example we have used Figure for the figure captions.

(The category Figure is not supplied with LibreOffice; however, if you have defined it when creating a caption in your document, it will appear on this list. See Chapter 11, Images and Graphics, for more about creating captions.)

3) Under Display, you can choose References (to include the category, number, and caption text), Category and Number, or Caption Text. We have chosen References.

4) The other pages of this dialog are similar to those described for tables of contents.

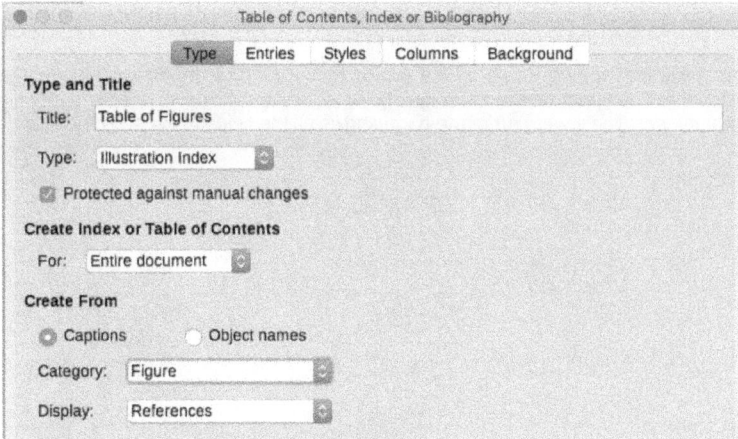

*Figure 345: Creating other types of indexes*

5) Click **OK**. The result is shown below.

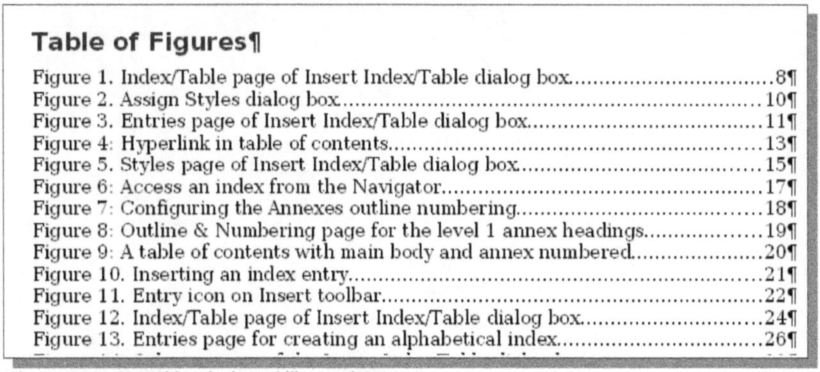

**Table of Figures¶**

Figure 1. Index/Table page of Insert Index/Table dialog box....8¶
Figure 2. Assign Styles dialog box....10¶
Figure 3. Entries page of Insert Index/Table dialog box....11¶
Figure 4: Hyperlink in table of contents....13¶
Figure 5. Styles page of Insert Index/Table dialog box....15¶
Figure 6: Access an index from the Navigator....17¶
Figure 7: Configuring the Annexes outline numbering....18¶
Figure 8: Outline & Numbering page for the level 1 annex headings....19¶
Figure 9: A table of contents with main body and annex numbered....20¶
Figure 10. Inserting an index entry....21¶
Figure 11. Entry icon on Insert toolbar....22¶
Figure 12. Index/Table page of Insert Index/Table dialog box....24¶
Figure 13. Entries page for creating an alphabetical index....26¶

*Figure 346: Resulting index of illustrations*

# Bibliographies

A bibliography is a list for displaying references used throughout a document. These references are either stored in a bibliographic database or within the document itself.

This section shows you how to:

- Create a bibliographic database; add and maintain entries.
- Add a reference into a document.
- Format the bibliography.
- Update and edit an existing bibliography.

## Creating a bibliographic database

For most of this section, the database table used is the sample one that comes with Writer. For information on creating a new table in the bibliographic database, see Chapter 8, Getting Started with Base, in the *Getting Started Guide*.

Although you can create references within the document itself, creating a bibliographic database allows reuse in other documents and saves a lot of time.

Select **Tools > Bibliography Database**. The Bibliography Database window, similar to that in Figure 347, opens. The upper part of the page shows all of the records, in a table layout similar to that of a spreadsheet. The lower part of the page shows all the fields of the selected record.

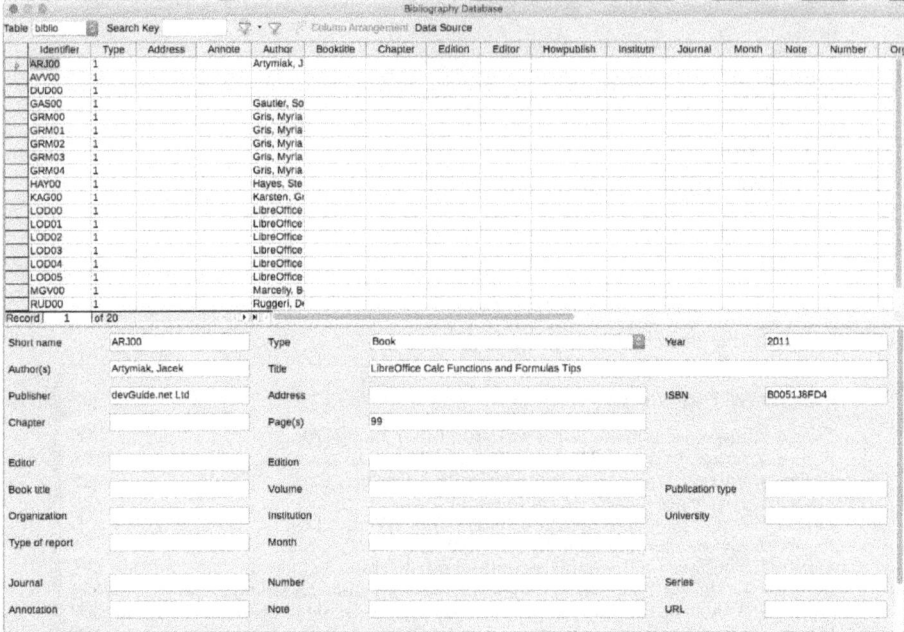

| | Bibliography Database | | | | | | | | | | | | | | |
|---|---|---|---|---|---|---|---|---|---|---|---|---|---|---|---|
| Table biblio | Search Key | | | Column Arrangement | Data Source | | | | | | | | | | |

| Identifier | Type | Address | Annote | Author | Booktitle | Chapter | Edition | Editor | Howpublish | Institutn | Journal | Month | Note | Number | Or |
|---|---|---|---|---|---|---|---|---|---|---|---|---|---|---|---|
| ARJ00 | 1 | | | Artymiak, J | | | | | | | | | | | |
| AVV00 | 1 | | | | | | | | | | | | | | |
| DUD00 | 1 | | | | | | | | | | | | | | |
| GAS00 | 1 | | | Gautier, So | | | | | | | | | | | |
| GRM00 | 1 | | | Gris, Myria | | | | | | | | | | | |
| GRM01 | 1 | | | Gris, Myria | | | | | | | | | | | |
| GRM02 | 1 | | | Gris, Myria | | | | | | | | | | | |
| GRM03 | 1 | | | Gris, Myria | | | | | | | | | | | |
| GRM04 | 1 | | | Gris, Myria | | | | | | | | | | | |
| HAY00 | 1 | | | Hayes, Ste | | | | | | | | | | | |
| KAG00 | 1 | | | Karsten, Ge | | | | | | | | | | | |
| LOD00 | 1 | | | LibreOffice | | | | | | | | | | | |
| LOD01 | 1 | | | LibreOffice | | | | | | | | | | | |
| LOD02 | 1 | | | LibreOffice | | | | | | | | | | | |
| LOD03 | 1 | | | LibreOffice | | | | | | | | | | | |
| LOD04 | 1 | | | LibreOffice | | | | | | | | | | | |
| LOD05 | 1 | | | LibreOffice | | | | | | | | | | | |
| MGV00 | 1 | | | Marcelly, B | | | | | | | | | | | |
| RUD00 | 1 | | | Ruggeri, De | | | | | | | | | | | |

Record | 1 | of 20

| | | | | |
|---|---|---|---|---|
| Short name | ARJ00 | Type | Book | Year | 2011 |
| Author(s) | Artymiak, Jacek | Title | LibreOffice Calc Functions and Formulas Tips | | |
| Publisher | devGuide.net Ltd | Address | | ISBN | B0051J8FD4 |
| Chapter | | Page(s) | 99 | | |
| Editor | | Edition | | | |
| Book title | | Volume | | Publication type | |
| Organization | | Institution | | University | |
| Type of report | | Month | | | |
| Journal | | Number | | Series | |
| Annotation | | Note | | URL | |

*Figure 347: Bibliography Database main window*

## Filtering records

To set up a filter for specific records within the bibliographic database, select **Tools > Filter** from the Bibliographic Database Menu bar, or click the Standard Filter button on the toolbar near the top of the window. On the Standard Filter dialog (Figure 348), choose the fields, conditions, and values for the filter and click **OK**.

| | Standard Filter | | |
|---|---|---|---|
| **Criteria** | | | |
| Operator | Field name | Condition | Value |
| | - none - | | |
| AND | - none - | | |
| AND | - none - | | |
| Help | | OK | Cancel |

*Figure 348: Setting up a filter for the bibliographic database*

## Changing column details

To change the details of columns in the bibliographic database, select **Edit > Column Arrangement** from the Menu bar, or click the **Column Arrangement** button on the tolbar near the top of the window (see Figure 347). On the Column Layout for Table biblio dialog (Figure 349), you can change which fields are allocated to which columns. As an example, you can select to have Author data go into the Identifier column, by changing the destination in the drop-down list. The Short name data column destination sets to None automatically, as you can't set duplicate destinations for data.

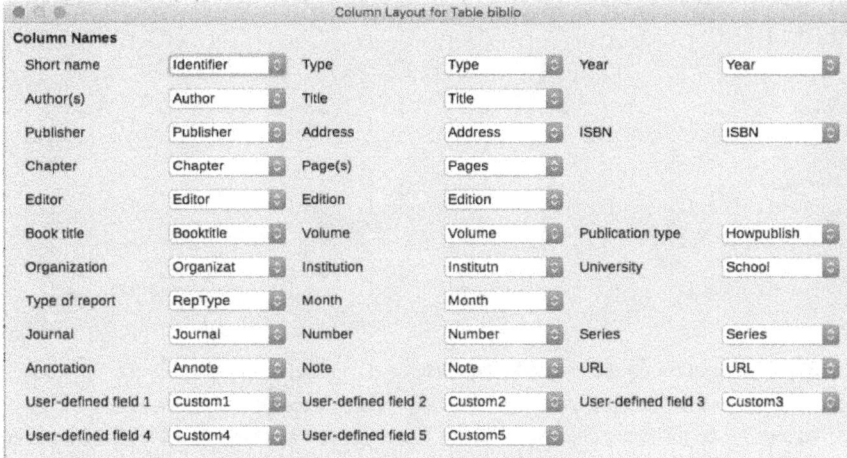

Figure 349: Changing column layout for bibliographic database

## Changing the data source

To change the data source in use (for example, if you have more than one bibliographic database for different purposes), select **Edit > Choose Data Source** from the menu bar, or click the **Data Source** button on the toolbar near the top of the window. On the Choose Data Source dialog, select a data source and click **OK**.

## Changing field details

You can make changes to the bibliography database (for example, rename fields or change the length of fields) by doing the following:

1) In the main document (not the Bibliography Database window), press *F4* or click **View > Data Sources** to open the data source window, similar to Figure 350.

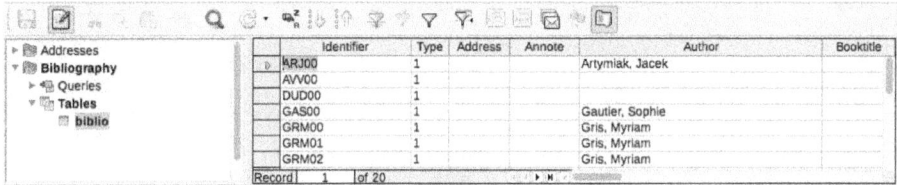

Figure 350: Data Source view of Bibliography database

2) Make sure that the Bibliography database is selected as well as the correct table. You may have to expand some levels to be able to select the correct ones.

---

3) Right-click on the table entry (biblio in the example) and select **Edit Database File** from the context menu. This opens a window similar to Figure 351, which is the main menu for Base, the database component of LibreOffice.

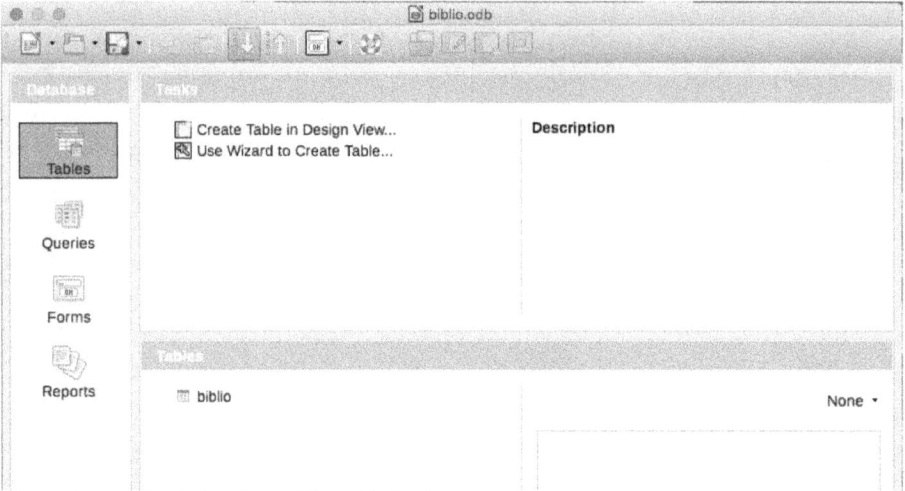

*Figure 351: Main window for working with databases*

4) If Tables (in the Database section on the left) is not selected, select it now.

5) Right-click on the biblio table name in the Tables section and select **Edit** from the context menu to display a window similar to that shown in Figure 352.

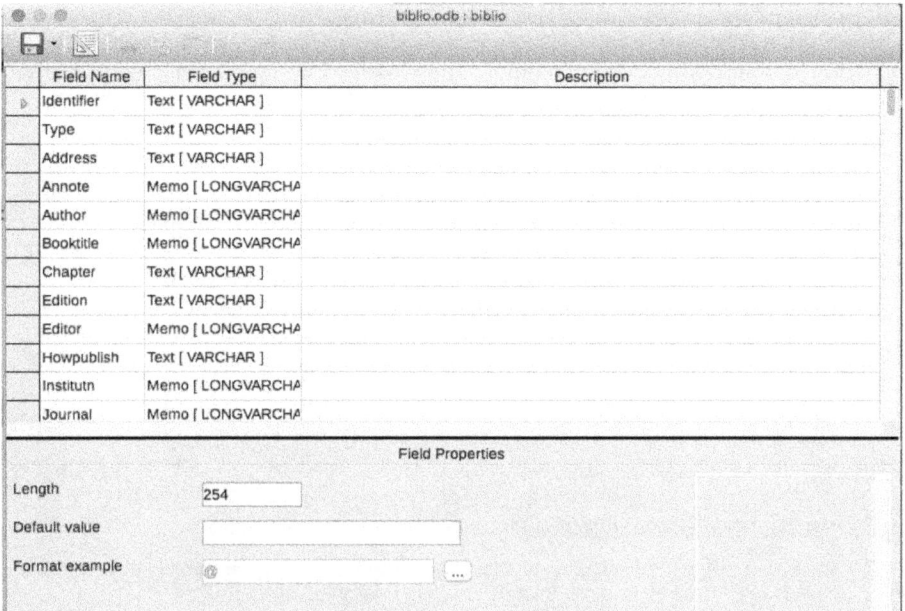

| Field Name | Field Type | Description |
|---|---|---|
| Identifier | Text [ VARCHAR ] | |
| Type | Text [ VARCHAR ] | |
| Address | Text [ VARCHAR ] | |
| Annote | Memo [ LONGVARCHA | |
| Author | Memo [ LONGVARCHA | |
| Booktitle | Memo [ LONGVARCHA | |
| Chapter | Text [ VARCHAR ] | |
| Edition | Text [ VARCHAR ] | |
| Editor | Memo [ LONGVARCHA | |
| Howpublish | Text [ VARCHAR ] | |
| Institutn | Memo [ LONGVARCHA | |
| Journal | Memo [ LONGVARCHA | |

Field Properties

Length        254

Default value

Format example

*Figure 352: Modify table properties window*

6) You can now select each of the fields. You can select the text in the Field Name cell and change the entry as required. Clicking in the Field Type cell, allows you to open a selection menu to change the data type in that cell. In the Field Properties section, the data properties can be modified. For each data field selected, an explanation of that field appears in a window to the right of the section.

7) When finished, you will be asked to confirm that you want the changes saved.

**Note**

For more information on how to use LibreOffice's database features, see Chapter 8, Getting Started with Base, in the *Getting Started Guide*.

## Adding entries to the database

Use the Bibliography Database dialog (**Tools > Bibliography Database**) to add entries to the database:

1) You can add records directly into the database using the fields in the lower section of the dialog shown in Figure 16 on page 41.

2) Select **Insert > Record** from the Menu bar of the Bibliography Database dialog, or click the **Insert Record** icon to the left of the horizontal scroll bar.

3) Enter a name for the entry in the Short Name box. Complete other fields as required. Use the *Tab* key to move between fields.

   It is best to use a unique name in the Short name field. This field is used when inserting entries into documents.

4) To complete the entry, move to the last field and press *Tab* once more.

If your document requires [Author, date] style citations, use the Short name field of the database to record the information in the required format.

## Maintaining entries in the database

To maintain entries in the database, use the Bibliography Database dialog (**Tools > Bibliography Database**). Click on the appropriate record and modify the fields as appropriate.

Modified entries are saved automatically to the database when the cursor moves off the record.

## Adding references (citations) into a document

Writer supports two methods of adding references to your document:

- From a bibliography database, such as the one built into Writer.
- Directly from the keyboard.

### Entering references from a database

To add references from the bibliographic database into a document:

1) Place the cursor where you want the reference to appear.

2) From the main menu, choose **Insert > Table of Contents and Index > Bibliography Entry**.

3) In the Insert Bibliographic Entry dialog, choose **From bibliography database** at the top of the dialog.

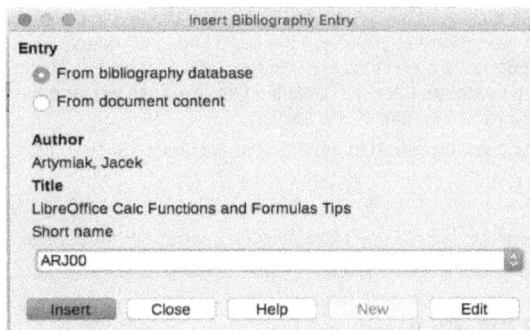
*Figure 353: Inserting bibliographic entries into a document*

4) Select the reference from the Short name drop-down list near the bottom of the dialog. The Author and Title of the selected reference are shown in the middle of the dialog, to help you verify that it is the reference you want.

5) To insert the reference into the document, click **Insert**.

6) You can keep the dialog open and insert another reference into the document; you don't need to close and reopen it.

7) When you have finished inserting all the references, click **Close**.

### Entering references from documents

You may choose to enter your bibliographic entries directly into the document, instead of from an external database. For example, you may not be working on your own computer.

Click in the document where you want to add the entry.

1) Select **Insert > Table of Contents and Index > Bibliography Entry**.

2) In the dialog that opens, select the **From document content** option.
   - Select **New**.
   - In the Define Bibliography Entry dialog, complete all the fields which are relevant to your entry. Type a unique name in the Short name text entry box, because the Insert Bibliography Entry dialog uses this entry for the citation.
   - Select a choice from the menu in the Type box to enable the OK button.
   - Click **OK** when all the fields wanted are completed.
   - Click **Insert** to add the Short name field to the document
   - Click in each location you wish to add an entry and repeat this sequence

3) Click **Close**.

To re-use an entry in your document, restart the sequence above, and then select the Short name required from the current list of entries, instead of selecting to add a new entry.

## Editing a reference

To edit a reference:

1) Right-click on the entry (the cursor then displays to the left of the entry).

2) From the context menu, select **Bibliography Entry**. The Edit Bibliography Entry dialog opens.

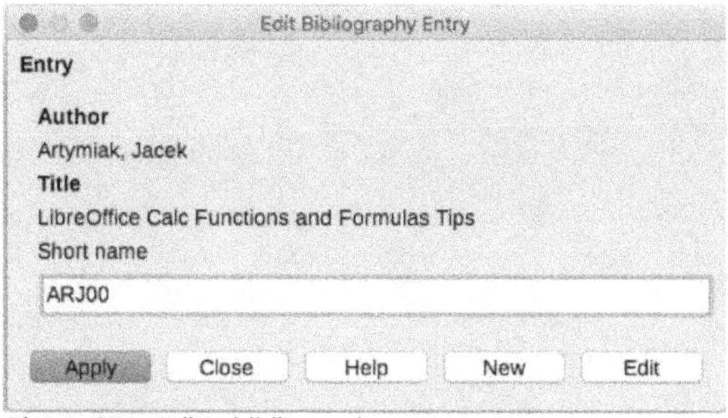

*Figure 354: Edit a bibliography entry*

3) To quickly edit only the Short name, click on the text box, alter the entry and then click **Apply**.

4) To edit more of the entry, click **Edit** to open the Define Bibliography Entry dialog.

 Make any changes required and then click **OK** to return to the dialog of Figure 354.

5) If you are satisfied with your changes, click **Apply** to accept the changes and exit the dialog.

Whatever the source of the citation, the modified references are stored in the document. If the source was a bibliography database, that database remains unmodified.

## Creating the bibliography

To create the bibliography:

1) Place the cursor at the point where you wish to insert the bibliography.

2) Select **Insert > Table of Contents and Index > Table of Contents, Index or Bibliography** and change the Type to Bibliography, to display a dialog similar to that shown in Figure 355.

The Insert Index/Table dialog has five pages.

### Index/Table page

Writer supports two ways of displaying references (citations) in the text of a document:

- Using the text recorded in the Short name field of each bibliographic entry, for example [GUR00].

- By numbering the referenced documents in the sequence they occur in the text, for example [1].

▶ **Tip**

 To specify which citation style is used in the document, use the *Type* page on the Table of Contents, Index or Bibliography dialog (Figure 355).

Formatting the bibliography involves choices made in two places:

- Table of Contents, Index or Bibliography dialog, covered in this section.

- Bibliography 1 paragraph style (see page 355).

The basic settings are selected on this page.

1) To give the bibliography a title, enter it in the Title field. (A title is not required.)

2) You can protect the bibliography from being changed accidentally, by checking Protected against manual changes. If this option is selected, the bibliography can only be changed using the right-click menu or the Table of Contents, Index or Bibliography dialog. If the option is not selected, the bibliography can be changed directly on the document page, just like other text, but any manual changes will be lost when you update the bibliography.

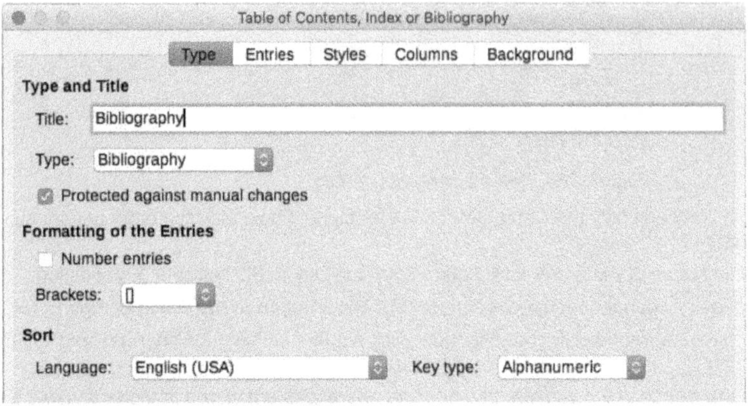

*Figure 355: Inserting a bibliography*

3) To have the bibliographic entries (citations) numbered within the body of the document (for example, [1], [2]...), select Number entries. If, however, you wish to have the Short name field contents (from the database) appear in the document, deselect this option.

4) Select the type of brackets that you want for the referenced entries shown within the body of the document.

5) Define the sorting you require. Currently only alphanumeric sorting is supported. Sorting by the sequence that entries appear in the text is done on the *Entries* page.

## Entries page

The structure of this page (see Figure 356) is similar to that for tables of contents and for indexes.

Each type of source that you use when creating your document will have its own unique works cited format. You can define how the entry will appear, based on its source, by selecting from the Type list of entries, or simply apply the same format to all entries by selecting the All button.

Each entry in the Type list has a default structure format.

The Structure of the entry is based on the fields available in the bibliographic database. The ones shown by default for Article in the Type list are:

Sh – Short name
Au – Author
Ti – Title
Ye – Year

To remove elements from the Structure line, click the element then click the Remove button.

To add an element, click in the Structure line where it is to be inserted. Select either the Tab stop, or an element in the drop-down list to the left of the Insert button, and then click Insert. The elements in the drop-down list are those fields found in the Bibliography Database.

All the elements on the Structure line can be formatted using the Character Style selection list.

To determine how entries are sorted, modify the Sort by options. To sort by the sequence that entries appear in the text, choose Document position. To sort alphanumerically, choose Content. Use Sort keys to group similar references.

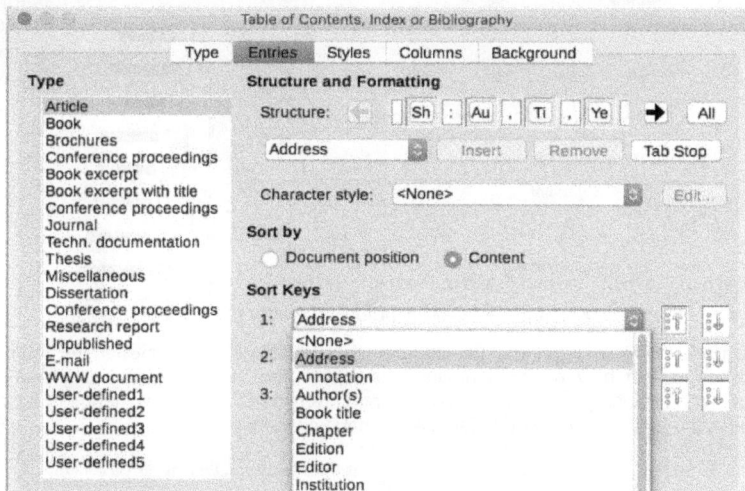

*Figure 356: Entries page for bibliographies*

### Styles, Columns and Background pages

Refer to "Styles page" on page 334, "Columns page" on page 344 and "Background page" on page 335 for detailed information on these pages.

### Generating the bibliography

To generate the bibliography so that it appears in your document, click **OK.** The dialog closes and the bibliography appears in your document.

## Defining the paragraph style for the bibliography

You can modify the Bibliography 1 paragraph style to suit your requirements. For example, to number the entries in the bibliography list, you need to define a numbering style and link that numbering style to the Bibliography 1 paragraph style. To do this:

1) On the Styles and Formatting window, click on the List Styles icon. You can either define a new list style or modify one of those supplied. In this example, we will modify the Numbering 5 style. Right-click on Numbering 5 and choose **Modify** from the context menu.

2) On the Numbering Style dialog, go to the *Customize* page. In our example we want to have the numbers enclosed in square brackets. To do this, type [ in the Before box and ] in the After box, as shown in Figure 357.

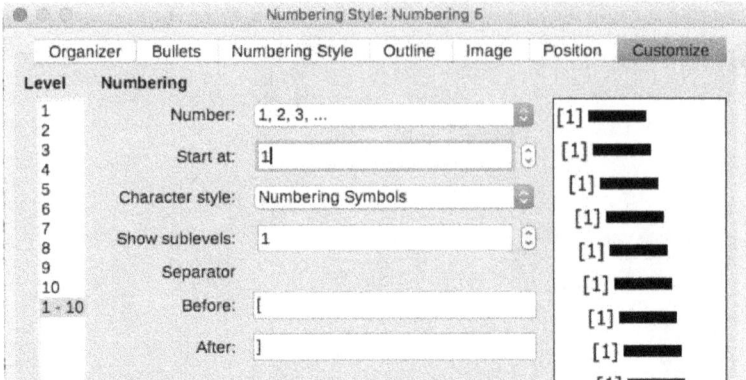

*Figure 357: Specifying square brackets before and after the number in a list*

3) Now go to the *Position* page of the Numbering style dialog (Figure 358). In the **Spacing to text** box, specify how much indentation you want for the second and following lines of any item in the bibliography list of your document. Often you will need to experiment a bit to see what is the best setting. In our example, we have chosen 1 cm.

*Figure 358: Setting the spacing between the margin and the text*

4) Click **OK** to save these settings and close the Numbering Style dialog. Return to the Styles and Formatting window, click on the Paragraph Styles icon, choose All Styles from the list at the bottom of that window, then right-click on Bibliography 1 and choose **Modify**.

5) On the Paragraph Style dialog, go to the Outline & Numbering tab and select Numbering 5 from the drop-down list. (See Figure 359.) Click **OK** to save this change to the Bibliography 1 paragraph style.

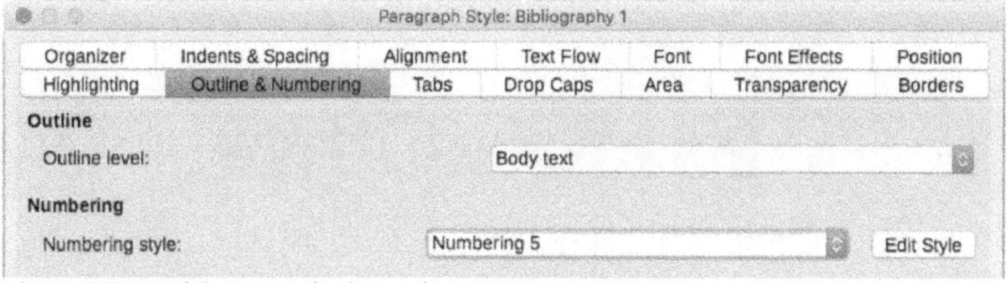

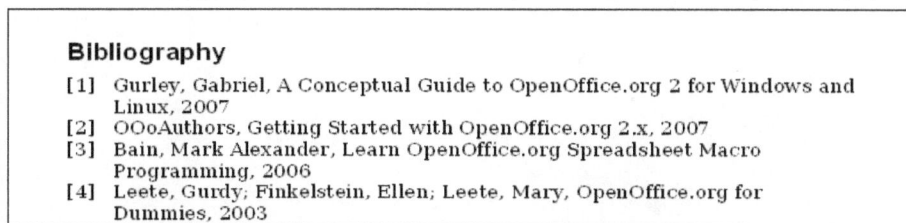

*Figure 359: Applying a numbering style to a paragraph style*

Now when you generate the bibliography, the list will look something like the one shown below for a book after removing elements from the structure line (the Short name and colon, for example).

**Bibliography**

[1] Gurley, Gabriel, A Conceptual Guide to OpenOffice.org 2 for Windows and Linux, 2007
[2] OOoAuthors, Getting Started with OpenOffice.org 2.x, 2007
[3] Bain, Mark Alexander, Learn OpenOffice.org Spreadsheet Macro Programming, 2006
[4] Leete, Gurdy; Finkelstein, Ellen; Leete, Mary, OpenOffice.org for Dummies, 2003

*Figure 360: Result of changing settings for Bibliography 1 paragraph style*

## Updating, editing, and deleting an existing bibliography

Right-click anywhere in the bibliography. From the context menu, select:

- **Update Index** to update the bibliography.
- **Edit Index** to open the Table of Contents, Index or Bibliography dialog so you can edit and save the table.
- **Delete Index** to delete the table without a confirmation request.

▶ **Tip**

If you find Writer's bibliography feature too limited, you may wish to try Zotero, which is free and open source, available for Mac, Windows, and Linux. It is reported to work well with Writer (http://www.zotero.org/).

# LibreOffice

Chapter 16
Master Documents

# Why use a master document?

A master document (.odm) is a container that joins separate text documents (.odt) into one larger document, and unifies the formatting, table of contents (TOC), bibliography, index, and other material. Master documents are typically used for producing long documents such as a book, a thesis, or a long report.

A master document is especially useful in these situations:

- When the file size or number of pages is quite large; writing, reviewing, and editing may be easier when done on subsets of the full document.
- When different people are writing different chapters or other parts of the full document.
- When files will be published as stand-alone documents as well as becoming part of a larger document. The chapters of this *Writer Guide* are an example of this usage.
- When subdocuments are used in more than one final document.

You can use several methods to create master documents. Each method has its advantages and disadvantages. Which method you choose depends on what you are trying to accomplish. The different methods are described in this chapter, along with suggestions on when to use each one.

> **Tip**
>
> A master document is not always the best method to use in any of the situations given above. You may find that an ordinary document (.odt) containing sections linked to other files may do the job just as well. For more about using sections to combine files, see Chapter 6, Formatting Pages: Advanced.

# Styles in master documents and subdocuments

A stand-alone document becomes a subdocument when it is linked into a master document. A document can be used as a subdocument in several master documents. Each master document may have different style definitions (font, type size, color, page size, margins, and so on), which affect the appearance of the final document, but the individual documents retain their original characteristics.

The relationship between styles in a master document and its subdocuments is as follows:

- Custom styles used in subdocuments, such as paragraph styles, are automatically imported into the master document.
- If more than one subdocument uses a custom style with the same name (for example, myBodyText), then only the one in the first subdocument to be linked is imported into the master document.
- If a style with the same name exists in the master document and in the subdocuments (for example, Default Style), then the style is applied as defined in the master document.
- The styles in the subdocuments are only changed in the master document, so when a subdocument is opened for editing the original styles are not affected.

> **Tip**
>
> If you use the same document template for the master document and its subdocuments, the subdocuments will look the same when they are loaded into the master document as they do when viewed as individual files. When you modify or create a style, make the change in the template (not in the master document or any of the subdocuments). Then when you reopen the master document or a subdocument, the styles will update from the template.

# Creating a master document: scenarios

Which method you choose from the three most common methods for creating a master document depends on the current state of your document:

- You have one existing document (a book) that you want to split into several subdocuments (chapters) that will be controlled by the master document.

- You have several existing documents (chapters) by one or more authors that you want to combine into one book, controlled by the master document.

- You have no existing documents but intend to write a long book containing several chapters, possibly by multiple authors.

We will look at each of these scenarios in turn.

# Splitting a document into master and subdocuments

When you have one existing document that you want to split into a master document and several subdocuments, you can have Writer split the document automatically at headings with an outline level of your choice.

Although this method is quick and easy, some cleanup work may be necessary:

- The automatically generated file names for the subdocuments are maindocnameX.odt, where X is 1, 2, 3, and so on. If you have a Preface or other "chapter" starting with a Heading 1 before Chapter 1, the file names will not directly correspond to the chapter numbers. You may wish to rename the subdocuments; see "Adding, deleting, or renaming subdocuments" on page 369.

- If the original document is associated with a template, the .odm file will also be associated with that template, but the subdocuments will not. The subdocuments will inherit the styles in the original document, but their association with the template will be lost.

How to do it:

1) Open the document and choose **File > Send > Create Master Document**.

2) On the Name and Path of Master Document dialog (Figure 361):

   a) Navigate to the folder where you want to save the master document and its subdocuments (or create a new folder).

   b) Type a name for the master document in the File name box.

   c) In the separated by: list, choose the outline level where the file should be split into subdocuments. Usually this is Outline: Level 1 for a chapter heading, but your document may be structured differently. For more information about outline levels, see "Using paragraph styles to define a hierarchy of headings" in Chapter 8, Introduction to Styles.

   d) Leave the **Automatic file name extension** option selected, and click **Save** to split the document into subdocuments and create the master document.

If you selected Outline: Level 1 and the paragraph style at that level is Heading 1, each of the subdocuments begins with a Heading 1 paragraph.

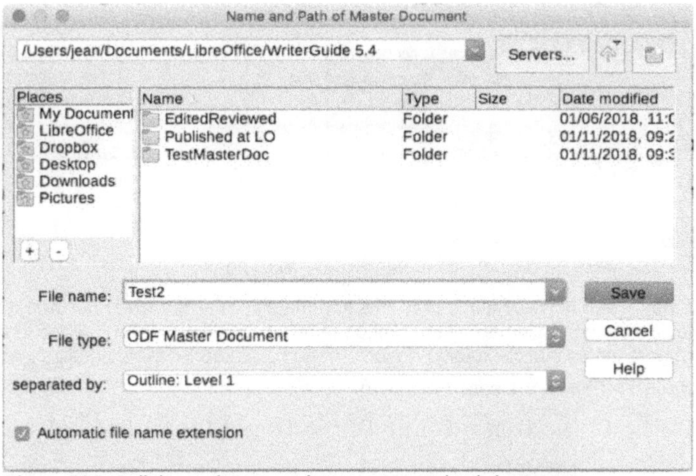

*Figure 361: Splitting a document into master and subdocuments*

## Combining several documents into a master document

When you have several existing documents, you can combine them into one document controlled by a master document.

This method works best when all of the documents were created from the same template, but you can also use it when the documents have been created from different templates. This method is especially useful when the subdocuments are created or maintained by multiple writers. For example, you might be creating an anthology of short stories, a book of symposium papers, or a set of engineering test results with a standard company title page.

We will use a book of engineering test results as an example.

▶ **Tip**

You could create a master document template (see page 374) and use it as the starting point for this method. In that case, skip steps 1 and 2 and start with step 3.

1) Open the title page document that you plan to use as the master document. To avoid creating too many subdocuments when this document is converted to a master document, have only one level 1 heading present. If there are more, temporarily change them to lower level headings and note which they are (add, for example, an asterisk at the end of each heading to remind you which have to revert to level 1 headings later).

2) Select **File > Send > Create Master Document**, name and save this master document (see "How to do it:" on page 360).

Let us assume our original document was named FrontPage with a single Level 1 heading, and that when we created the master document (.odm file) we named it TestFile.

In this case, the master document is a blank file containing only one section. Also created at the same time was a subdocument named TestFile1, which is a .odt file containing the text from the FrontPage file. When opening the .odm file and clicking **Yes** to update all links, this file is linked in to the master document to provide the original content.

The original FrontPage file is left intact in its folder.

| Places | Title | Type | Size | Date modifi |
|---|---|---|---|---|
| My Documents | FrontPage.odt | OpenDocument Text | 17.3 KB | 05/08/2013, |
| | Results1.odt | OpenDocument Text | 16.3 KB | 05/08/2013, |
| | Results2.odt | OpenDocument Text | 16.2 KB | 05/08/2013, |
| | TestFile.odm | OpenDocument Master Document | 21.4 KB | 05/08/2013, |
| | TestFile1.odt | OpenDocument Text | 8132 Bytes | 05/08/2013, |

*Figure 362: TestFile documents created from FrontPage*

3) Open the master document and click **Yes** to update links. The master document opens with the Navigator open by default (see "Using the Navigator" on page 373 and "Step 6. Insert the subdocuments into the master document" on page 366 for more detailed information).

4) Click **Insert > File** and release the button.

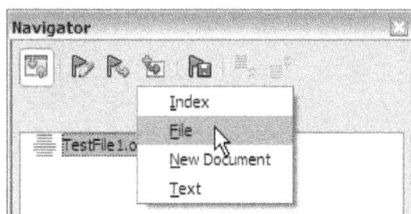

*Figure 363: Adding files to the master document*

5) Navigate to the location of the test results files (Results1.odt, Results2.odt, and so on). Select the first file to insert, Results1.odt for example, and click **Insert**. The file is inserted above the existing entry.

6) Click the **Move Up** icon to have the TestFile1 text above the Results1 text (file contents are inserted above the selected file in the master document).

7) Repeat from step 4 as often as required. It does not matter which file is highlighted in the master document when you insert the next one, just select the inserted file and use the **Move Up** or **Move Down** icons to position it as required.

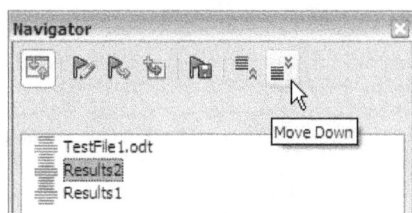

*Figure 364: Moving subdocuments*

8) To edit the master document, to perhaps add a widget serial number and a client's name, in the master document right-click TestFile1 and select **Edit** from the context menu. Add the required content to the file which opens, save and close the file (see "Editing a master document" on page 369 for more detailed information).

9) Select **Tools > Update > Links** from the Menu bar, or click **Update > Links** in the Navigator. All the edits in the master document will now show.

# Starting with no existing documents

When you start with no existing documents, you can set up everything the way you want from the beginning. Follow these steps, in the order given. Each step is explained in detail in the following subsections.

Step 1. Plan the project

Step 2. Create a template

Step 3. Create the master document

Step 4. Create subdocuments

Step 5. Add some pages to the master document

Step 6. Insert the subdocuments into the master document

Step 7. Add table of contents, bibliography, index

## Step 1. Plan the project

Although you can make changes at most steps in this process, the more you can plan before you start, the less work you will have to do to correct any problems later. Here are some things you need to plan.

**Parts of book or report required.** What pages will be in the master document and what will be in the subdocuments?

Consider as an example a book with the parts given in the table below.

| Part | Location |
|------|----------|
| Title (cover) page | In master document |
| Copyright page | In master document |
| Table of contents (TOC) | In master document |
| Preface (Foreword) | Subdocument |
| Chapters 1 to 7 | Subdocuments |
| Index | In master document |

**Page, paragraph, character, frame, and numbering styles.** Determine the styles you wish to use. See Chapter 8, Introduction to Styles, and Chapter 9, Working with Styles, for instructions on how to create or modify styles and examples of the use of styles in book design. Pay particular attention to setting up headings using styles, as described in "Using paragraph styles to define a hierarchy of headings" in Chapter 8.

**Fields and AutoText entries, as required.** See Chapter 2, Working with Text: Basics, and Chapter 17, Fields, for ideas.

**One or more templates for master and subdocuments.** If you are starting a new project, create the master document and all the subdocuments from the same template. Not using the same template can create style inconsistencies that could cause your document not to look as you expect. For example, if two subdocuments have a style with the same name that is formatted differently in each document, the master document will use the formatting from the first subdocument that was added.

**Page numbering.** In our example, the pages are numbered sequentially from the title page. (The title page style can be defined not to show the page number, but it will still count as page 1.) Therefore the first chapter begins on a higher number page, for example page 5. To create a book in which the page numbering restarts at 1 for the first chapter, you need to do some additional work. See "Restarting page numbering" on page 367.

## Step 2. Create a template

You can create a template from an existing document or template that contains some or all of the page, paragraph, character, and other styles you want for this document, or you can create the template from a blank document. For more about templates, see Chapter 10, Working with Templates.

Be sure to use **File > Save As Template** when creating the template.

▶ **Tip**

You can also create master document templates; see page 374.

## Step 3. Create the master document

It does not matter in what order you create the master and subdocuments, and you do not have to create all the subdocuments at the same time, when you are starting the project. You can add new subdocuments at any time, as you need them.

Follow this process to create the master document:

1) Open a new document from the template you created in Step 2, by choosing **File > New > Templates**, then selecting the template you created. Be sure the first page of this new document is set to the page style you want for the first page of the final document; if it is not, change it. In our example, the style for the first page is Title page.

2) If any text or page breaks came into this document from the template, delete the text. (The TOC, index, and any fields in headers and footers can stay.)

3) Click **File > Send > Create Master Document**. Save the master document in the folder for this project. We will return to this master document later. For now, you can either leave it open or close it.

⬤ **Note**

Using **File > New > Master Document** will create a master document file (.odm) associated with the default template. If your document is, or will be, based on a custom template, use the method described above.

▶ **Tip**

You can also create a master document directly from a master document template.

## Step 4. Create subdocuments

A subdocument is no different from any other text document. It becomes a subdocument only when it is linked into a master document and opened from within the master document. Some settings in the master document will override the settings in a subdocument, but only when the document is being viewed, manipulated, or printed through the master document.

Create a subdocument in the same way as you create any ordinary document:

1) Open a blank document based on the project template (very important) by choosing **File > New > Templates**, then selecting the required template.

2) Delete any unwanted text or other material that was brought in from the template, and set the first page to the page style you specified for the first page of a chapter.

3) Click **File > Save As**. Give the document a suitable name and save it in the folder for this project.

If you already have some of the chapters written, the files may not be based on the template you just created for this project. If you want to change the template attached to the existing files, use the technique described in "Associating a document with a different template" in Chapter 10, Working with Templates.

## Step 5. Add some pages to the master document

To assist you, do the following:

- Make sure paragraph marks are showing. You can set them in **Tools > Options > LibreOffice Writer > Formatting Aids**, or click the **Fomatting Marks** icon 🔲 on the Standard toolbar, or press *Ctrl+F10*.
- Show text boundaries, table boundaries, and section boundaries (**Tools > Options > LibreOffice > Application Colors**).

If your master document does not contain any required "front matter" such as a title page, copyright page, or TOC page, add them now. The example in this section uses the sequence of page styles given in "Step 1. Plan the project" on page 363.

1) Type the contents of the title page (or leave placeholders and fill in later). With the insertion point in the last blank paragraph on the page, click **Insert > Manual Break**. On the Insert Break dialog, select **Page break** and the page style for the second page (Copyright Page in our example), and leave the **Change page number** option deselected. Click **OK**.

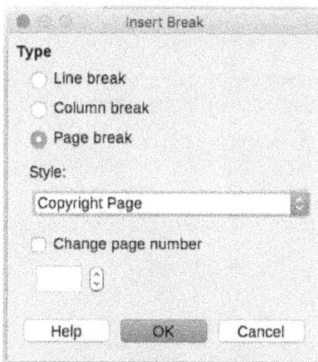

*Figure 365: Inserting a page break between the title page and the copyright page*

2) Type the contents of the copyright page (or leave placeholders). With the insertion point in the last blank paragraph on the page, insert another manual page break, this time setting the page style to Table of Contents page.

3) On the Table of Contents page, leave a blank paragraph or two or insert a TOC (**Insert > Table of Contents and Index > Table of Contents, Index or Bibliography**). The TOC will not have any contents until you add the subdocuments, but you should see a gray mark or box indicating its location. For more about inserting and formatting TOCs, see Chapter 15, Tables of Contents, Indexes, Bibliographies.

### Note

Depending on the style definitions for the first paragraph (usually a heading) on the Copyright and TOC pages, you may not need to insert manual page breaks.

## Step 6. Insert the subdocuments into the master document

Now we are ready to add the subdocuments.

▶ **Tip**

Subdocuments are inserted into a master document *before* the item highlighted in the Navigator. If you insert the last subdocument first, and then insert the other subdocuments before the last one, they will end up in the correct sequence without the necessity of moving them up or down in the list.

1) Display the Navigator (click **View > Navigator**, or press *F5*, or click the **Navigator** icon on the Sidebar.

2) Be sure the Navigator is showing the Master View (see "Using the Navigator" on page 373). If necessary, click on the **Toggle** icon at the upper left to switch between regular and master views.

3) On the Navigator, select **Text**, then click **Insert > File**.

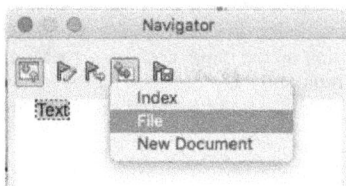

*Figure 366: Inserting a subdocument into a master document using the Navigator*

A standard file browser dialog opens. Select the required file (which you created in Step 4) and click **Insert**. This example uses 7 chapters; we will load Chapter 7 first, as suggested in the Tip above.

The inserted file is listed in the Navigator *before* the Text item, as shown in Figure 367.

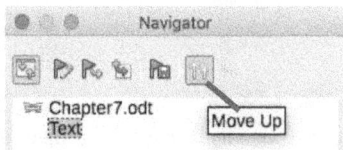

*Figure 367: Navigator after inserting one subdocument*

4) Because the Text section contains the title page and other material, highlight it and click the **Move Up** icon to move it to the top of the list.

5) Highlight the subdocument you just inserted (Chapter 7), then click **Insert > File** to insert the first subdocument; in this example, Chapter 1. Chapter 7 remains highlighted. Repeat with Chapter 1, Chapter 2, and so on until all the subdocuments have been added to the list. The Navigator will now look something like Figure 368.

6) Save the master document again.

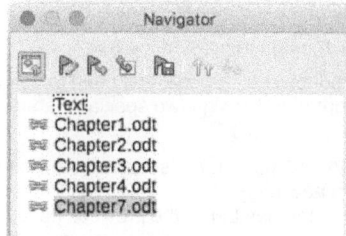

*Figure 368: The Navigator showing a series of files in a master document*

## Step 7. Add table of contents, bibliography, index

You can generate a table of contents, bibliography, or index for the book, using the master document. You must insert these items into a text section in the master document. For more about these document elements, see Chapter 15, Tables of Contents, Indexes, Bibliographies.

Put the insertion point on the page in the first text section where the table of contents is to go and choose **Insert > Table of Contents and Index > Table of Contents, Index or Bibliography** to create the table of contents.

If you do not have a Text section at the end of the master document, insert one before the last subdocument, then move it down so it is after the last subdocument. Now, if you have included bibliographic entries in your subdocuments, you can put the insertion point on the page in this last text section where the bibliography is to go and create the bibliography.

If you have included index entries in your subdocuments, put the insertion point on the page in the last text section where the index is to go and create the index.

Figure 369 shows the Navigator after addition of a TOC and index.

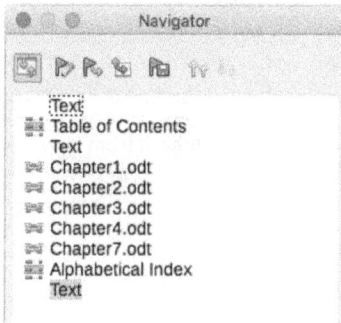

*Figure 369: Navigator showing subdocuments, table of contents, and index in a master document*

# Restarting page numbering

The example in the previous section showed a very basic collection of files with sequential page numbering. This is useful for many documents, including e-books, but a typical printed book has the following sequence of page numbers:

- No page numbers on cover page or copyright page.
- Lower-case roman numerals in the front matter, starting with i.

- Arabic numerals in the body of the document, starting with 1.
- Page numbering sequential through the rest of the book.

To set up a master document to produce such a book, you need to define a different paragraph style for the heading of the first chapter and assign two special characteristics to it.

**Example**

Each chapter may start with a Heading 1 paragraph, set up on the Text Flow page of the Paragraph Style dialog to start on a new page (Figure 370). The Page number is set to 0, with the effect that numbering continues from the number of the previous page.

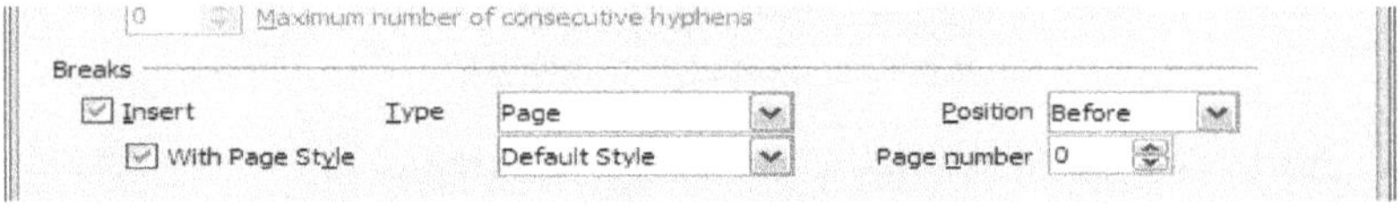

*Figure 370: Text Flow tab of Paragraph Style dialog for Heading 1*

Look on the Outline & Numbering tab (Figure 371) of this dialog to see what outline level Heading 1 is assigned to. Usually this will be Outline Level 1. The level cannot be changed here because it has been set in **Tools > Chapter Numbering**.

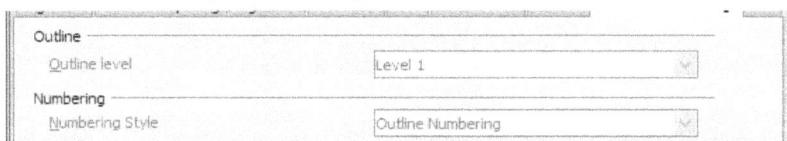

*Figure 371: Outline & Numbering tab of Paragraph Style dialog for Heading 1*

Only one paragraph style can be assigned to Outline Level 1 through **Tools > Chapter Numbering**. However, you can assign additional paragraph styles to any outline level by using the Outline & Numbering tab on the Paragraph Style dialog.

Therefore, you want to define a style called *Heading 1 Chapter 1* that is identical in appearance to *Heading 1* but has one essential difference:

1) Right-click on Heading 1 in the Paragraph Styles section of the Styles and Formatting tab in the Sidebar, and select **New**. On the *Organizer* page of the Paragraph Style dialog, name the new style, select the next style, and be sure **Inherit from** shows Heading 1.

*Figure 372: Organizer page for the new style*

2) On the *Text Flow* tab, in the *Breaks* section, select Insert, Page, Before, With Page Style, and Page number 1 (Figure 374).

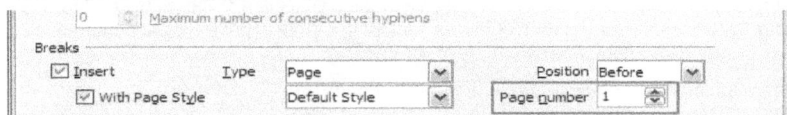

*Figure 373: Set the page number to restart at 1 for this heading style*

3) On the *Outline & Numbering* tab, set the Outline level to Level 1 (Figure 374). This ensures that the heading will appear in the Table of Contents along with the other chapter headings. (The Numbering Style for this heading is None, as it was not assigned an outline level through the Outline Numbering dialog.)

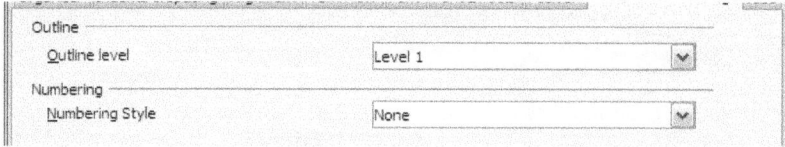

| Outline | |
|---|---|
| Outline level | Level 1 |
| Numbering | |
| Numbering Style | None |

*Figure 374: Assign the style to outline level*

4) Now, assign the new style to the first paragraph of Chapter 1, and you're done.

# Editing a master document

After creating a master document, you may want to change its appearance or contents.

## Changing the appearance of the master document

You can change the styles in the template as your project develops. Do not make changes to styles in the master document or in any of the subdocuments; make those changes in the template.

To update the master document (and all of the subdocuments) with changes to the template, open the master document. You will get two messages: first, to ask if you want to update all links; and second, if you want to apply the changed styles. Answer **Yes** to both of these messages.

## Editing subdocuments

You cannot edit a subdocument from within the master document. Instead, you must open the subdocument, either by double-clicking on it in the master document's Navigator, or by opening it from outside the master document. Then you can edit it just as you would edit any other document.

If, while editing a subdocument, you want to make changes to the styles that apply to the master document, follow the recommendations in "Changing the appearance of the master document" above.

If you change the contents of any subdocument, you need to manually update the table of contents, bibliography, and index from within the master document.

## Adding, deleting, or renaming subdocuments

To add a subdocument, follow the method described in "Step 6. Insert the subdocuments into the master document" on page 366.

To delete a subdocument, right-click on its file name in the Navigator and choose **Delete**.

If you rename a subdocument by changing its file name, the next time you update links in the master document, that subdocument will show up as a broken link (shown in red). To fix this:

1) Right-click on the broken link in the Navigator and choose **Edit link**.
2) In the Edit Sections dialog (Figure 375), select the renamed file, and edit the name of the section (which is the name shown in the Navigator).
3) Click **OK** to save the changes.

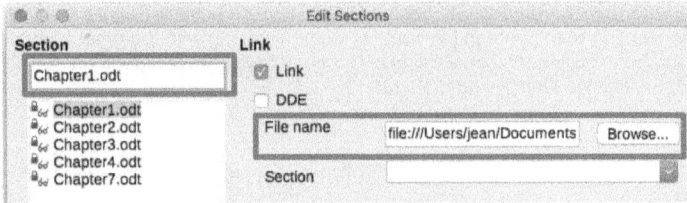

*Figure 375: Editing a link in a master document*

# Cross-referencing between subdocuments

The methods described earlier in this chapter are all most writers will need when using master documents. However, you might want to include automatically updated cross-references between subdocuments. This section describes how to do this.

The process to create cross-references between subdocuments is time consuming, but it works.

## Preparing items as targets for cross-referencing

Before you can insert a cross-reference to anything that is not automatically shown on the Cross-references tab of the Fields dialog, such as a heading, you must prepare that heading as an item to be referenced. To do this, you can either use bookmarks or set references.

### Using bookmarks

Bookmarks are listed in the Navigator and can be accessed directly from there.

To insert a bookmark:

1) Select the text you want to bookmark. Click **Insert > Bookmark**.

2) On the Insert Bookmark dialog, the larger box lists any previously defined bookmarks. Type a name for the new bookmark in the top box. Click **OK**.

*Figure 376: Inserting a bookmark*

### Setting references

When you set references, be sure to select the entire text you want to use as the reference, such as a heading or figure number. Keep a list of your names for the reference fields, and be sure each name is unique. One way to keep track of this information is to save it in a separate file.

The field names are case-sensitive. You can check the field name by holding the cursor over the referenced item. In our example (Figure 377), the heading has the field name *word count*.

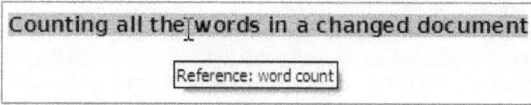

*Figure 377: Finding the field name for a heading*

Open the subdocument in which you want to set references.

1) Click **Insert > Cross-reference**.

2) On the *Cross-references* page of the Fields dialog (Figure 378), click **Set Reference** in the *Type* list. The *Selection* list now shows any references that have been defined. You can leave this page open while you set many headings as references.

3) Click in the document and highlight the text of the first heading to be used as a target for a cross-reference. Click on the Fields dialog. The text of the heading will appear in the *Value* box in the lower right of the dialog. In the *Name* box, type some text by which you can identify this heading.

4) Click **Insert**. The text you typed in the Name box now appears in the *Selection* list.

5) Repeat steps 3 and 4 as often as required, keeping a note of your references as needed.

6) Repeat for other subdocuments if wanted. Save and close.

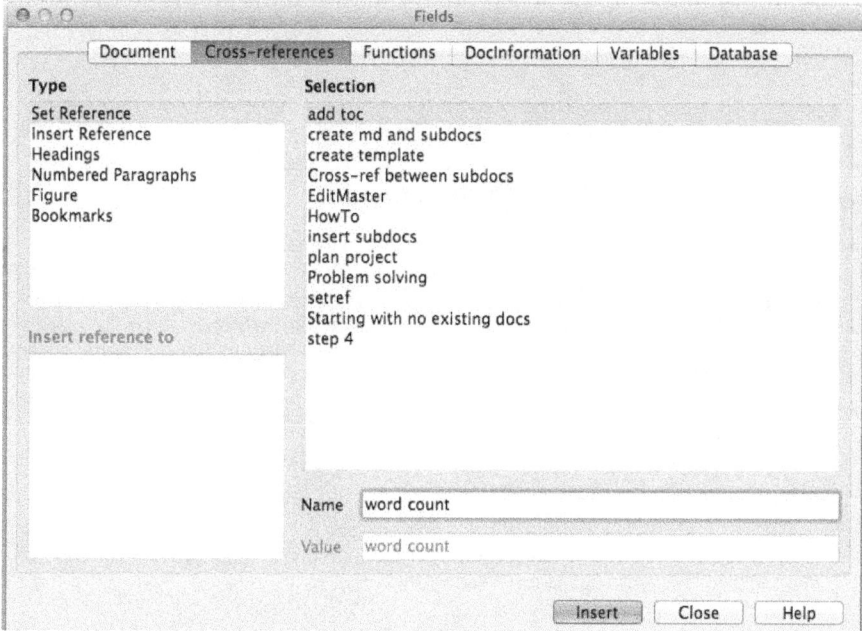

*Figure 378: Setting text to be used as a target for a cross-reference*

## Inserting the cross-references

1) Open the master document. In the Navigator, select a subdocument, right-click and choose **Edit** from the context menu. The subdocument opens for editing.

2) In the subdocument, place the cursor where you want the cross-reference to appear. Click **Insert > Cross Reference**.

3) On the *Cross-references* page of the Fields dialog (Figure 379), select **Insert Reference** in the *Type* list on the left. The *Selection* list on the right shows only the reference field names for the subdocument you are using, so ignore that list and check the list you created manually in "Setting references" above. Select **Reference** in the *Insert reference to* list.

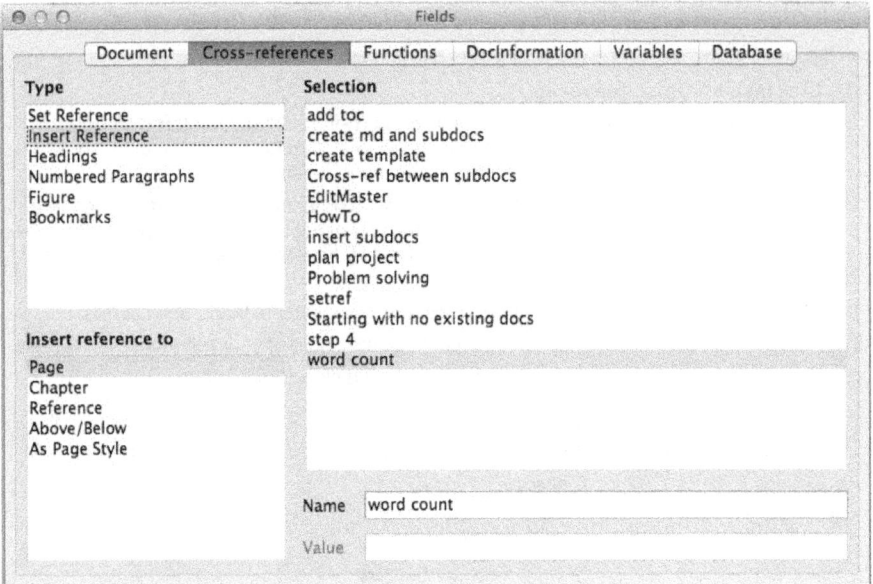

*Figure 379: Fields dialog showing manual entry of field name*

4) In the Name field in the lower right, type the name of the reference you set in the subdocument you are referring to. In our example, the name of the reference is word count.

5) Click **Insert,** type any text you want to appear between the reference and page number (such as "on page"), and then insert another reference with **Page** from the *Insert reference to* list. The cross-references will show an error as shown in Figure 380. When you hover the mouse pointer over one of these fields, you will see the field name.

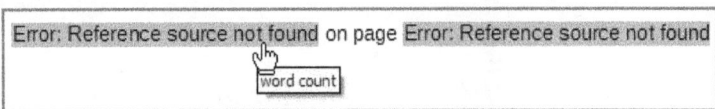

*Figure 380: Viewing the field name*

(You can turn on the display of field codes by clicking **View > Field Names.** The two error fields shown in Figure 380 now look like Figure 381.)

*Figure 381: Displaying field codes*

6) After you have inserted all the cross-references required in the subdocument, save and close it and return to the master document window.

---

Select **Tools > Update > Links** from the Menu bar, or click **Update > Links** in the Navigator. All the edits in the master document will now show. Within the master document, navigate to the page of the subdocument on which you inserted the cross-reference field. You should now see the text of the cross-reference appear in the spot where you inserted it. If it does not work, save the master document, close it, and open it again, updating the links.

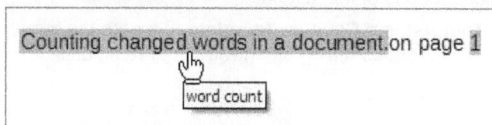

*Figure 382: Field contents visible*

This technique also works if you open a subdocument directly in step 2 (that is, not from within the master document) and insert a cross-reference field.

## Using the Navigator

The Navigator is a very useful tool that helps you move quickly to specific parts of your document. It also provides information about the content of the document and enables you to reorganize some of the content. For example, if each chapter in your final book is a separate document, then in the master document they can be reordered; the references are renumbered automatically and the table of contents and index can be updated.

In Writer, the Navigator has two distinct forms. One form is used in ordinary text documents and the other in master documents.

In an ordinary text document, the Navigator displays lists of the graphics, tables, index entries, hyperlinks, references, and other items in the document, as shown on the left hand side of Figure 383. Click the indicator (+ sign or triangle) by any list to display the contents of the list. You can double-click an entry in the Navigator and jump immediately to that place in the document.

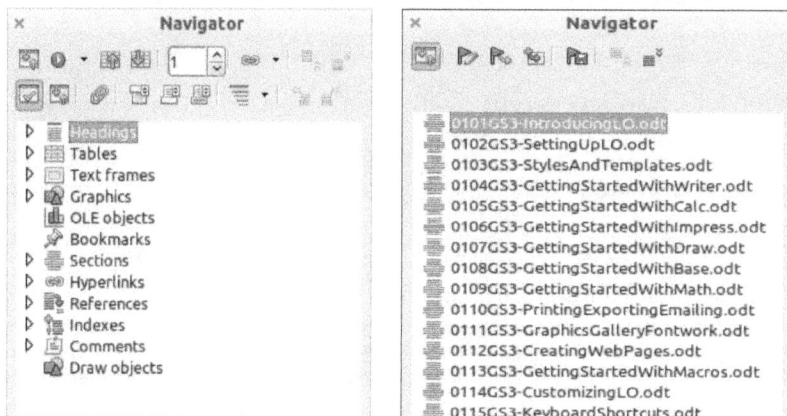

*Figure 383: The Navigator for a text document (left) and for a master document (right)*

In a master document, you can toggle between the regular and master views by clicking on the Toggle icon at the upper left. In the master view, the Navigator lists the subdocuments and text sections, as shown on the right hand side of Figure 383. The use of the Navigator in a master document is covered in more detail later in this chapter (see "Step 6. Insert the subdocuments into the master document" on page 366 and "Cross-referencing between subdocuments" on page 370).

# Creating a master document template

A master document template is created in much the same way as any other template:

1) First, create the master document using **File > Send > Create Master Document**, as described in earlier sections of this chapter.

2) Then, use **File > Templates > Save as Template** to create the template (.otm), which will then be listed in the Templates dialog along with other templates.

▶ **Tip**

Include in the name you give a master document template some indication that it's not an ordinary template.

# Creating one file from a master document and its subdocuments

Master documents are .odm files containing linked subdocuments, which are in .odt format. Although linked files are very useful when writing and editing a large document such as a book, sometimes you might need to have a copy of the entire book in one file, for example when sending it to a publisher.

To export a master document to a .odt file (without affecting the original .odm file):

1) Open the master document and update all links. Choose **File > Export** from the Menu bar.

2) On the Export dialog (Figure 384), type a name for the exported .odt file and choose ODF Text Document (.odt) from the File format list (it should be the default choice). Click **Export**. This step creates from a write-protected .odt file, with each subdocument in a separate section.

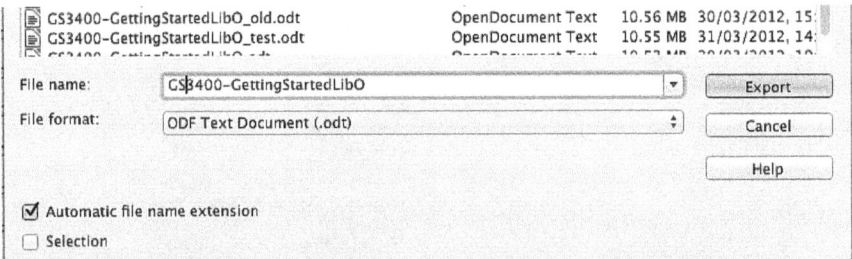

| GS3400-GettingStartedLibO_old.odt | OpenDocument Text | 10.56 MB | 30/03/2012, 15: |
| GS3400-GettingStartedLibO_test.odt | OpenDocument Text | 10.55 MB | 31/03/2012, 14: |

File name: GS3400-GettingStartedLibO        Export

File format: ODF Text Document (.odt)        Cancel

Help

☑ Automatic file name extension
☐ Selection

*Figure 384: Exporting a master document to an Open Document Text (.odt) file*

3) Close the master document and open the new .odt file, updating all links.

4) To break the links and remove the write protection, go to **Format > Sections**, select the first item in the Section list, then press *Shift+click* on the last item in the list in order to select all the items in the list. Deselect both **Link** in the *Link* section and **Protected** in the *Write protection* section.

5) Click **OK**.

6) If you wish to eliminate some or all of the sections to have a plain text document, select the sections you wish to remove, and click **Remove**. The contents of those sections remain in the document; only the section markers are removed. Click **OK**.

# Anchoring images to a page

An image (graphic) anchored "to page" in a subdocument is not displayed in the master document although it always appears correctly in the subdocument.

Because the master document reorganizes the page flow, page numbers, and cross-references when it collates all the subdocuments together, the absolute reference to a page X in a subdocument is lost in the master document. The image loses its anchor reference and simply disappears.

To avoid this problem but keep images positioned precisely on a particular page, anchor the pictures as follows:

1) Right-click on the image and choose **Properties** from the context menu.

2) On the *Type* page of the Image dialog (Figure 385), set the anchor to **To character** or **To paragraph**.

3) Under *Position*, choose suitable horizontal and vertical references to the page. Click **OK** to save the changes.

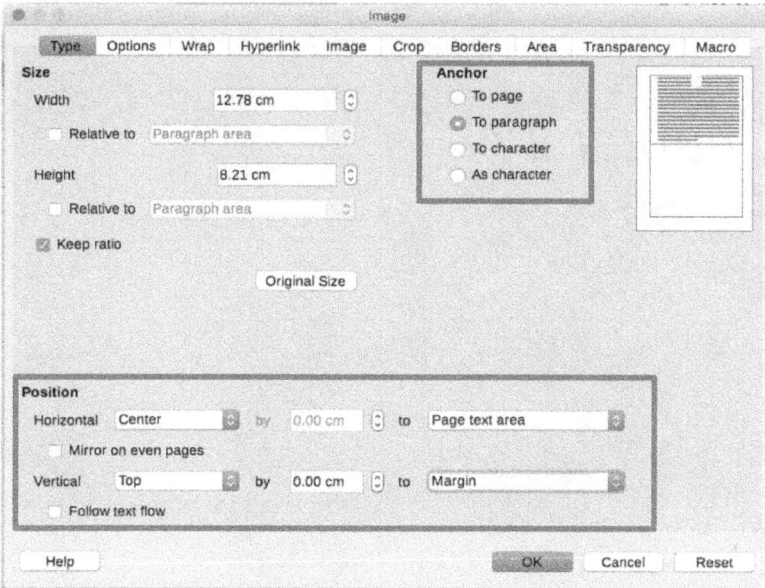

*Figure 385: Anchoring a graphic and setting its position on a page*

# LibreOffice

*Chapter 17*
*Fields*

# Introduction to fields

Fields are extremely useful in Writer. They are used for a variety of purposes; for example, data that changes (such as the current date or the total number of pages) or might change (the name of a product or book under development), user-defined numbering sequences, automatic cross-references, and conditional content (words or paragraphs that are visible or printed in some conditions but not others). Index entries are also fields.

This chapter describes some common uses of fields. A full discussion of fields and their use is beyond the scope of this book. Power users can find more details in the application Help.

▶ **Tip**

Fields have a gray background when viewed on screen, unless you have deselected the Field shadings option or changed the color of field shadings in **Tools > Options > LibreOffice > Application Colors**. This gray background does not show when you print the file or export to PDF.

To turn field shadings on or off quickly, choose **View > Field Shadings** or press *Ctrl+F8*.

# Quick and easy field entry

You can quickly insert common fields into your document by choosing **Insert > Page Number** or **Insert > Field** from the Menu bar and selecting the required field from the list.

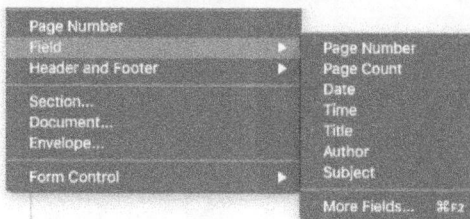

*Figure 386: Inserting common fields*

# Using document properties to hold metadata and information that changes

The Properties dialog (**File > Properties**) for a document has seven tabs. The information on the *General* page and the *Statistics* page is generated by the program. Some information (the name of the person on the Created and Modified lines of the *General* page) is derived from the User Data page in **Tools > Options > LibreOffice**. The options on the *Font* and *Security* pages are discussed elsewhere in this book. *CMIS Properties* are outside the scope of this book.

Use the *Description* and *Custom Properties* pages to hold:

• Metadata to assist in classifying, sorting, storing, and retrieving documents. Some of this metadata is exported to the closest equivalent in HTML and PDF; some fields have no equivalent and are not exported.

• Information that changes. You can store data for use in fields in your document; for example, the title of the document, contact information for a project participant, or the name of a product might change during the course of a project.

This dialog can be used in a template, where the field names can serve as reminders to writers of information they need to include.

To open the Properties dialog, choose **File > Properties**.

You can return to this dialog at any time and change the information you entered. When you do so, all of the references to that information will change wherever they appear in the document. For example, on the *Description* page (Figure 387) you might need to change the contents of the Title field from the draft title to the production title.

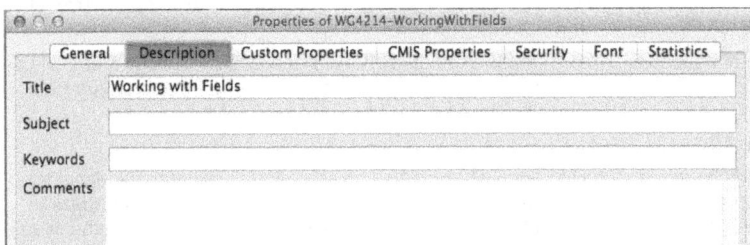

*Figure 387: The Description page of the document's Properties dialog*

Use the *Custom Properties* page (Figure 388) to store information that does not fit into the fields supplied on the other pages of this dialog.

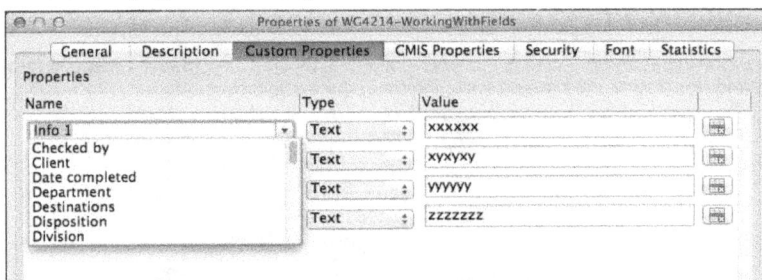

*Figure 388: Custom Properties page, showing drop-down lists of names and types*

When the *Custom Properties* page is first opened in a new document, it may be blank. If the new document is based on a template, this page may contain fields.

Click the **Add Property** button to insert a row of boxes into which you can enter your custom properties.

- The *Name* box includes a drop-down list of typical choices; scroll down to see all the choices. If none of the choices meet your needs, you can type a new name into the box.
- In the *Type* column, you can choose from Text, Date+Time, Date, Duration, Number, or Yes/no for each field. You cannot create new types.
- In the *Value* column, type or select what you want to appear in the document where this field is used. Choices may be limited to specific data types depending on the selection in the *Type* column; for example, if the *Type* selection is Date, the Value for that property is limited to a date.
- To remove a custom property, click the button at the end of the row.

▶ **Tip**

To change the format of the Date value, go to **Tools > Options > Language Settings > Languages** and change the **Locale** setting.

# Using other fields to hold information that changes

One way that people use fields is to hold information that is likely to change during the course of a project. For example, the name of a manager, a product, or even your entire company may change just before the document is due to be printed. If you have inserted the changeable information as fields, you can change the information in one place, and it will automatically change in all the places where that field occurs.

Writer provides several places where you can store the information referred to by a field. We will look at some of them here.

Seven document properties (Date, Time, Page Number, Page Count, Subject, Title, and Author) are on the **Insert > Field** menu (Figure 386). To insert one of these fields, click on it in the menu. Some of these fields get their information from the Document Properties dialog (Figure 387.)

Other document properties are on the *DocInformation* and *Document* pages of the Fields dialog (Figures 389 and 390), reached by choosing **Insert > Field > More Fields** or pressing *Ctrl+F2*. The Custom item in the Type list on the DocInformation page is derived from the Custom Properties page of the Document Properties dialog (Figure 388); it does not appear on the list if no custom properties have been defined.

Some of these items are picked up from the User Data page of the **Tools > Options > LibreOffice** dialog, so make sure the information on that page is correct.

To insert one of these fields, select it in the *Type* list and then select from the *Select* and *Format* lists if choices appear. Finally, click **Insert**.

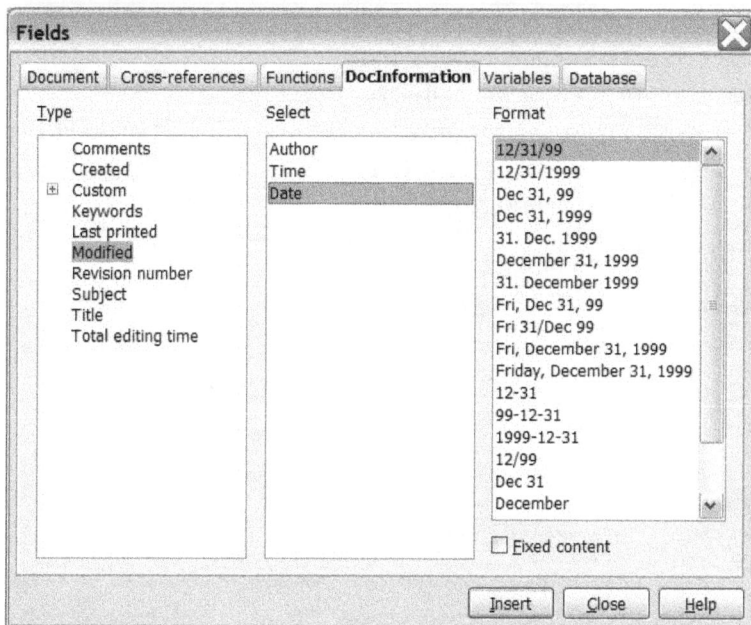

Figure 389: Inserting a Date Modified field using the DocInformation page of the Fields dialog

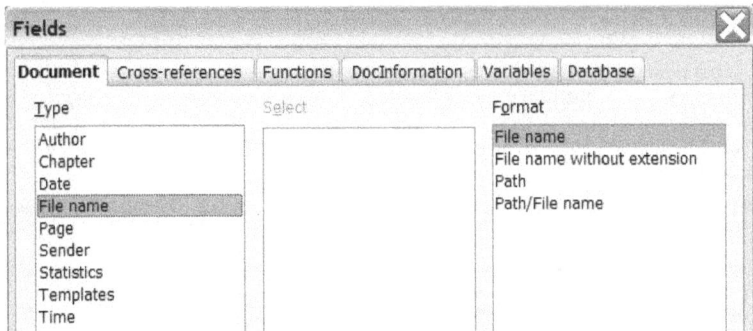

*Figure 390: Inserting a File name field using the Document page of the Fields dialog*

▶ **Tip**

Although these fields are often used to hold information that changes, you can make the content unchangeable by selecting the **Fixed content** option (visible in Figure 389, lower right) when inserting the field. If necessary, you can come back to this dialog later and deselect this option to make the field variable again.

## Using AutoText to insert often-used fields

If you use the same fields often, you will want a quick and easy way to insert them. Use AutoText for this purpose. To define an AutoText entry for a field:

1) Insert a field into your document, as described previously.

2) Select the field you inserted, and then choose **Tools > AutoText** (or press *Ctrl+F3*).

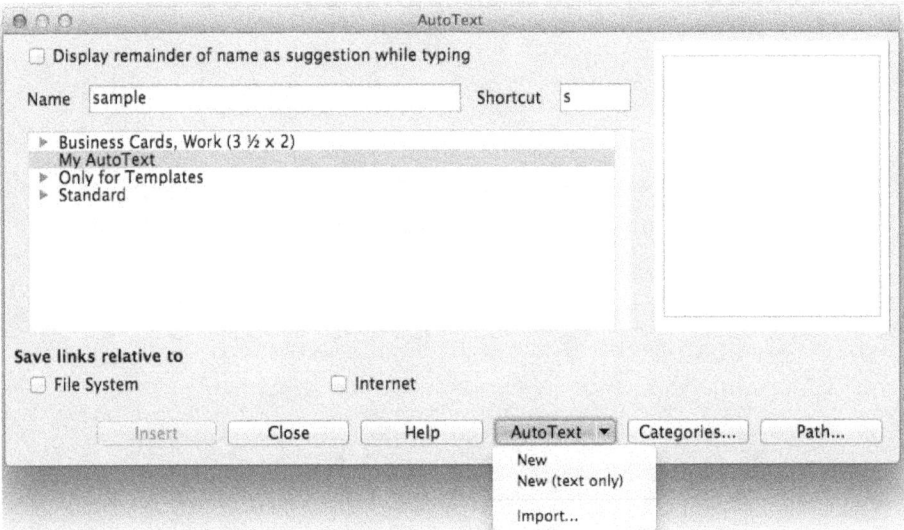

*Figure 391: Creating a new AutoText entry*

3) On the AutoText dialog, choose the group where this new entry will be stored (in this example, My AutoText), type a name for the entry, and change the suggested shortcut if you wish.

4) Click the **AutoText** button and click **New** to have the entry inserted as a field. Do not choose New (text only) because the AutoText entry will be plain text, not a field. (The New selections do not appear until you have selected a group and typed a name for the entry.) Click **Close** to close the AutoText dialog.

When you want to insert this field at the cursor position, type the shortcut and press *F3*.

# Defining your own numbering sequences

You may want to define your own numbering sequences to use in situations where you do not always want the number at the start of the paragraph or where you want more control than the built-in numbering choices give you.

This topic describes how to create and use a numbering sequence, using a number range variable field.

## Create a number range variable

To create a number range variable using Arabic (1 2 3) numbers:

1) Place the insertion point in a blank paragraph in your document.

2) Choose **Insert > Field > More Fields** or press *Ctrl+F2*, then select the *Variables* page.

3) In the *Type* list, select **Number range**. In the *Format* list, select **Arabic (1 2 3)**. Type whatever you want in the Name field. (We have used Step in this example.)

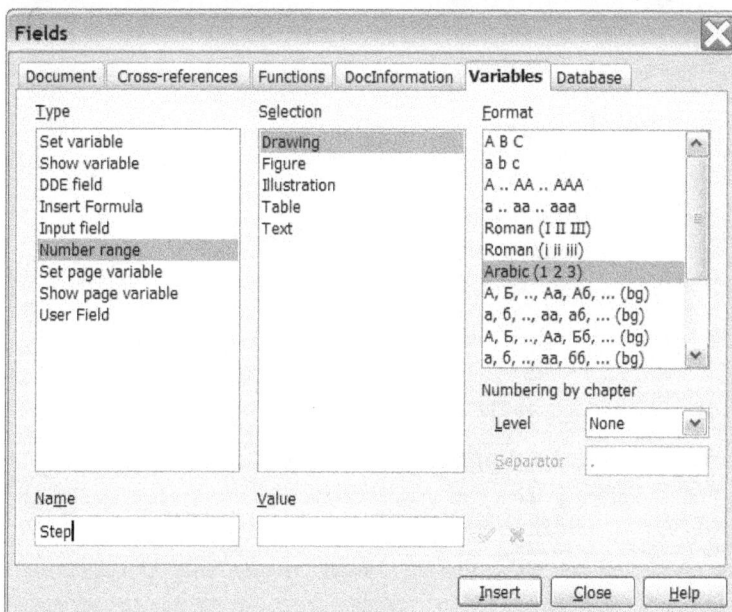

*Figure 392: Defining a number range variable*

4) Click **Insert**. The name of the variable (Step) now appears in the *Selection* list, and a number field (showing 1) appears at the insertion point in your document. The Fields dialog remains open.

5) If you click several more times on the **Insert** button in the Fields dialog, the numbers 2, 3, 4, and so on will appear in the document.

Now you may want to change the Step sequence to a different number, greater or less than the current value, so you can use the same sequence name more than once in your document (for example, to begin each set of instructions). To do that, you need to insert a new field of the same name, while instructing LibreOffice to force the value to the new choice.

1) Open the Fields dialog to the *Variables* page. Make sure the variable name Step appears in the Name box.

2) In the Value box, type 1 (we will illustrate a numbering restart here, but any number will work), as shown in Figure 393. Click **Insert**.

3) To continue with the normal sequence (that is, to have the next Step value be 2), you need to delete the contents of the Value box after inserting at step 2.

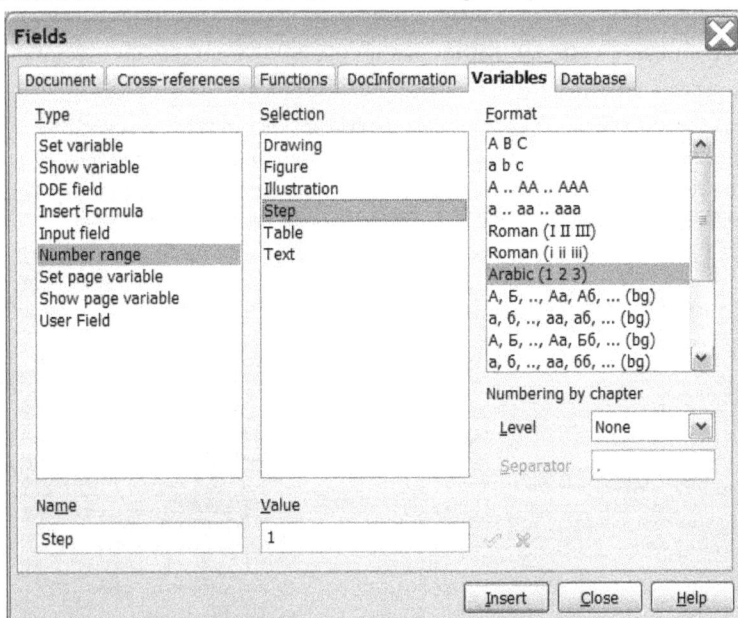

*Figure 393: Defining a field to restart a number range variable*

## Use AutoText to insert a number range field

You certainly do not want to go through all of that every time you want to put in a Step number. Instead, create two AutoText entries, one for the Step (Value=1) field (call it Step1, for example) and one for the Step = Step+1 field (StepNext). Then insert the fields in the same way you would insert any other AutoText. See "Using AutoText to insert often-used fields" on page 380.

You can create similar fields for substeps or other sequences that you want to be numbered with letters (a, b, c), Roman numerals (i, ii, iii), or some other sequence. In the Fields dialog, choose the required format in the Format list when creating the field codes.

> **Tip**
>
> If a user-defined variable is not in use in the document, the ![X] icon next to the Value box is active. You can delete the variable by clicking this icon. To remove a variable that is used in the current document, first delete from the document all fields using that variable, and then remove the variable from the list.

# Using automatic cross-references

If you type in cross-references to other parts of the document, those references can easily get out of date if you reword a heading, add or remove figures, or reorganize topics. Replace any typed cross-references with automatic ones and, when you update fields, all the references will update automatically to show the current wording or page numbers.

> **Tip**
>
> Some people use Writer's Hyperlink feature for cross-references, but it has the major disadvantage that the visible text of the hyperlink does not change if you change the text of the item to which it links. For that reason, you are advised to use cross-references in most situations.
>
> The exception is when you are creating a document to be saved as HTML; cross-references do not become hyperlinks in an HTML document.

The Cross-references page of the Fields dialog (Figure 394) lists some items, such as headings, numbered paragraphs, and bookmarks. If figure captions, table captions, user-defined number range variables, and some other items have been defined in a document, that type also appears in the list.

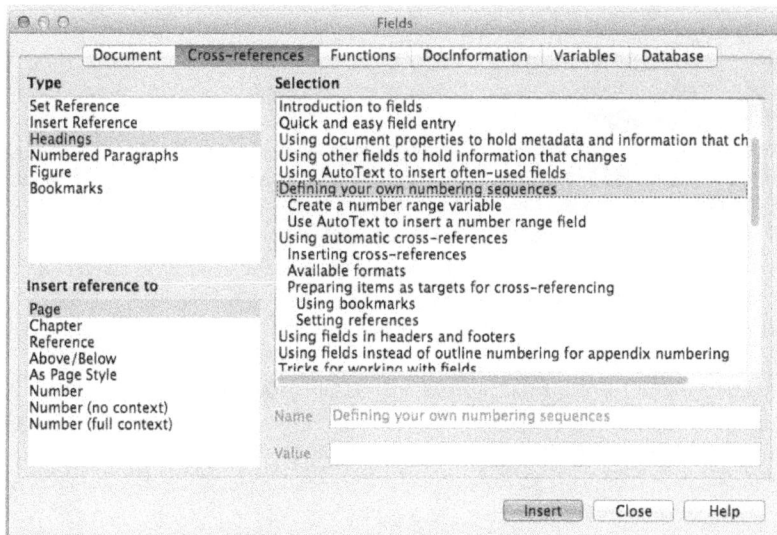

Figure 394: The Cross-references page of the Fields dialog

## Inserting cross-references

To insert a cross-reference to a heading, figure, or other item shown on the *Cross-references* page:

1) In the document, place the cursor where you want the cross-reference to appear.
2) If the Fields dialog is not open, choose **Insert > Cross Reference** or press *Ctrl+F2*. On the Cross-references page (Figure 394), in the Type list, click the type of item you are referencing (for example, Heading or Figure).
3) You can leave this page open while you insert many cross-references.
4) Click on the required item in the *Selection* list, which shows both automatically created entries (for example Headings) as well as user-defined references (for example bookmarks).
5) In the *Insert reference to* list, choose the type of reference required. The choices vary with the item being referenced.

    For headings, usually you will choose Reference (to insert the full text of the heading) or Page (to insert the number of the page the heading is on).

    For figures, you will usually choose Category and Number (to insert the word "Figure" and its number), Reference (to insert the word "Figure" with its number and the full text of the caption), Page (to insert the number of the page the figure is on), or Numbering (to insert only the figure number).
6) Click **Insert**.

For a full list of the reference formats available, and their use, consult the Help.

## Available formats

For all the types of reference, you can select one of the following formats:

- **Page:** the page number of the target.
- **Chapter:** the number of the chapter where the referenced target is located.
- **Reference:** the full text set as reference.
- **Above/Below:** the word *above* or *below* depending on the position of the field relative to the referenced target.
- **As Page Style:** similar to Page, the page number where the reference is, but using the formatting specified in the page style. This is very useful when putting a reference to a page in the front matter where roman numerals are usually employed.

For headings or numbered paragraphs, two additional options are available:

- **Number (no context)**: inserts only the number of the heading or of the numbered paragraph. For example, if referencing a numbered item 2.4, it inserts 4.
- **Number (full context):** inserts the full number including higher hierarchical levels. For example, if referencing a numbered item 2.4, the full numbering (2.4) is inserted.

For objects inserted with captions such as a table or a figure, you can choose:

- **Category and Number:** inserts both the category and number of the referenced object (for example, Figure 6). This is the most used formatting for figures and tables.
- **Caption Text:** inserts the full caption of the referenced object. For example, Figure 6: This is an example figure.
- **Numbering:** inserts the sequential number of the referenced object, without the category (for example, if referencing Table 2, the field will contain only the number 2).

# Preparing items as targets for cross-referencing

Occasionally you might want to insert a cross-reference to something that is not automatically shown on the Cross-references page: an illustration without a caption or an item in a bullet list, for example. Before you can insert a cross-reference to such an item, you must prepare the item as a target to be referenced. To do this, you can either use bookmarks or set references.

After a target has been defined, you can cross-reference to it as described on page 384.

## Using bookmarks

Bookmarks are listed in the Navigator and can be accessed directly from there. In HTML documents, bookmarks are converted to anchors that you can jump to using a hyperlink.

1) Select the text you want to bookmark, or click in the required place in the text. Choose **Insert > Bookmark**.

2) On the Insert Bookmark dialog, the larger box lists any previously defined bookmarks. Type a name for this bookmark in the top box. Click **OK**.

## Setting references

1) Choose **Insert > Cross reference** or press *Ctrl+F2*.

2) On the Cross-references page of the Fields dialog (Figure 395), select **Set Reference** in the *Type* list. The *Selection* list shows any references that have been defined. You can leave this dialog open while you set several items as references.

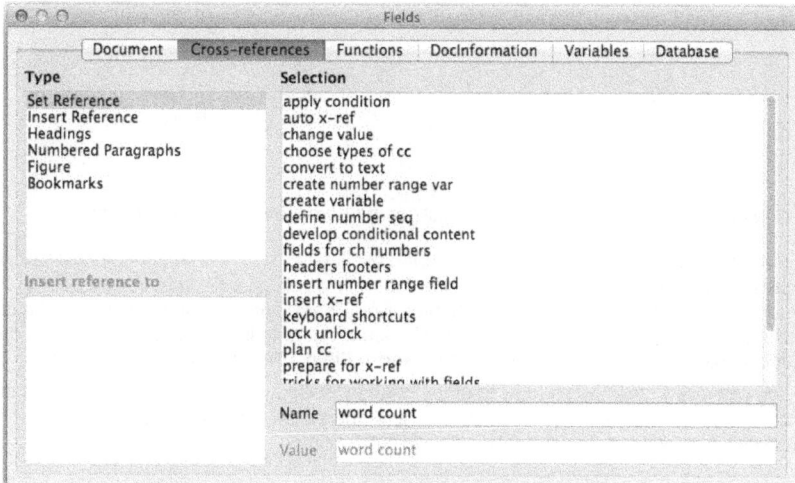

*Figure 395: Setting text to be used as a target for a cross-reference*

3) Click in the document and highlight the text of the first item to set as a target for a cross-reference. Click on the Fields dialog. The text of the item will appear in the Value box in the lower right. In the Name box, type some text by which you can identify this item.

4) Click **Insert**. The text you typed in the Name box now appears in the *Selection* list.

## Tip

See Chapter 16 for how to create cross-references to other subdocuments in a master document.

# Using fields in headers and footers

You can insert fields into headers or footers, using techniques described earlier in this chapter:

- To insert a page number, document title, author, creation date and time, current date and time, or total page count field, use Document Properties (see page 377) or choose **Insert > Field > [item]** from the Menu bar.

- To insert a cross-reference to a bookmark, heading, or other item, use **Insert > Field > More Fields > Cross-references**.

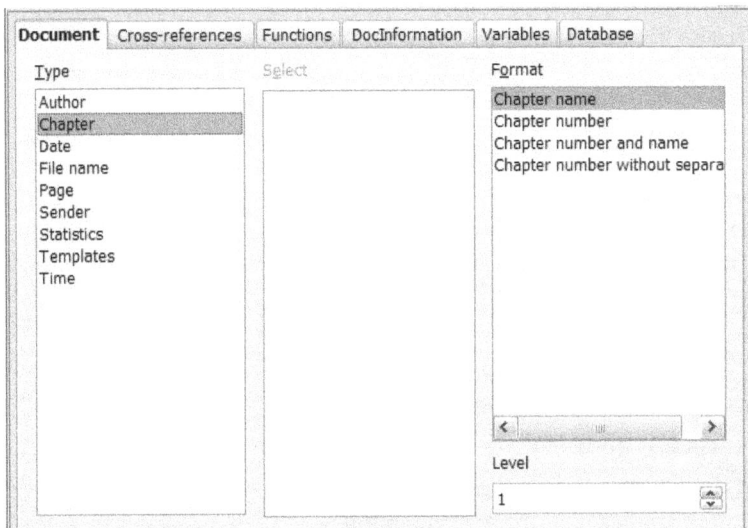

*Figure 396: Inserting the current chapter name and number into your document*

- If you have used Heading 1 for your chapter titles, you can use a Document field to insert the current chapter title, so the header or footer contents change from one chapter to the next. See Figure 396. (Writer calls chapter titles Chapter names.) If you have used outline numbering on your Heading 1, you can choose whether to include these numbers in the field (Chapter number and name). Use **Insert > Field > More Fields > Document**.

- You can insert cross-references to other heading levels by specifying a value in the Level box in the lower right of the Document page of the Fields dialog (Figure 396). That is, Level 1 = Heading 1, Level 2 = Heading 2, and so on.

> **Note**
>
> A cross-reference field in the header of a page picks up the *first* heading of that level on the page, and a field in the footer picks up the *last* heading of that level on the page.

- To include the chapter number with the page number, position the cursor just before the Page field you inserted. On the *Document* page of the Fields dialog, select **Chapter** in the *Type* column and **Chapter number without separator** in the *Format* column. Click Insert.

  Go to the header or footer where you inserted this field and type the character you want to appear between the chapter number and the page number—for example, a period or a dash.

The table of contents will not automatically pick up these chapter numbers, so you will need to make a change on the Entries page of the Table of Contents, Index or Bibliography dialog, as described in Chapter 15.

- You can add a page count to the footer; for example, Page 9 of 12. Type the word Page and a space in front of the Page field. Type a space, the word of, and a space after the Page field. Then choose **Insert > Field > Page Count**.

# Tips for working with fields

## Keyboard shortcuts for fields

Here are some handy keyboard shortcuts to use when working with fields:

| | |
|---|---|
| *Ctrl+F2* | Open the Fields dialog. |
| *Ctrl+F8* | Turn field shadings on or off. |
| *Ctrl+F9* | Show or hide field names. |
| *F9* | Update fields. |

## Fixing the contents of fields

You can specify **Fixed content** for many items on the Document and DocInformation pages so the field contents do not update. For example, you might use a field to insert the creation date of a document, and you would not want that date to change. In another place you might use a date field to show the current date, which you do want to change; in that case, deselect **Fixed content** when you insert the field.

# Developing conditional content

Conditional content is text and graphics that are included or excluded from a document depending on a condition you specify.

A simple example is a reminder letter for an overdue account. The first and second reminders might have a subject line of "Reminder Notice", but the third reminder letter might have the subject "Final Notice" and a different final paragraph.

A more complex example is a software manual for a product that comes in two versions, Pro and Lite. Both product versions have much in common, but the Pro version includes some features that are not in the Lite version. If you use conditional content, you can maintain one file containing information for both versions and print (or create online help) customized for each version. You do not have to maintain two sets of the information that is the same for both versions, so you will not forget to update both versions when something changes.

## Choose the types of conditional content to use

This section describes several Writer features that can help you design and maintain conditional content. You can use one or any combination of these features in the same document.

### Conditional text

With conditional text, you can have two alternative texts (a word, phrase, or sentence). One text will be displayed and printed if the condition you specify is met, and the other will be displayed and printed if the condition is not met. You cannot include graphics or edit the text except in the field dialog (not in the body of the document). You also cannot format part of the text (for example, bolding one word but not the others), but you can format the field to affect all of the field contents (for example, bolding all of the words). You cannot include a cross-reference or other field in the text.

**Hidden text**

With hidden text (a word, phrase, or sentence), you have only two choices: show or hide. If the condition you specify is met, the text is hidden; if the condition is not met, the text is displayed. The disadvantages are the same as for conditional text: you cannot include graphics, edit the text in the body of the document, format part of the text, or include a field.

**Hidden paragraphs**

Hidden paragraphs are like any other paragraphs, but you can specify a condition under which the paragraph is not displayed or printed. A blank paragraph can also be hidden—for example, if a database field has no content for the current record. This is very useful when merging an address into a letter: if you allow two lines for the street address and the database record uses only one line, you can prevent the blank line from appearing in your document. You can include graphics, edit the text in the body of the document, format any part of the text, and include fields.

**Hidden sections**

Hidden sections are like hidden paragraphs, but they can include more than one paragraph —for example, a heading plus one or more paragraphs. However, a section cannot contain less than a paragraph, so you cannot use this method for single words or phrases. The contents of a hidden section behave just like the contents of any other part of the document, but you can specify a condition under which the section is not displayed or printed. In addition, you can password protect a section.

## Plan your conditional content

Conditions are what programmers call *logical expressions*. You must formulate a logical expression for each condition because a condition is always either true (met) or false (not met). You can use the same condition in many places in your document, for different types of conditional content.

To make conditional content work, you need to:

1) Choose or define a variable.

2) Define a logical expression (condition) involving the selected variable.

### Choose or define a variable

You can use the following variables in your condition:

- User-defined variables
- Predefined LibreOffice variables, which use statistical values from the document properties
- User data
- Database field contents—for example from your address book

You cannot use internal variables (for example, page number, or chapter name) to formulate conditions.

The examples in this chapter use user-defined variables.

### Define a logical expression (condition) involving the variable

The condition compares a specified fixed value with the contents of a variable or database field.

To formulate a condition, use the same elements as you would to create a formula: operators, mathematical and statistical functions, number formats, variables, and constants. The possible operators, and many examples of use, are given in the Help; look in the index under *Defining Conditions* and *conditional*. You can define quite complex expressions, but in most cases a simple condition will do the job.

# Create the variable

To create the variable, you can use choices found on the *DocInformation*, *Variables*, and *Database* pages of the Fields dialog.

### DocInformation fields

"Using document properties to hold metadata and information that changes" on page 377 described how to set up a custom document property. You can use that document property as the variable in your condition statement.

### User-defined variable field

To set up a variable or user field:

1) Place the cursor where you want the field to be inserted.
2) On the Fields dialog, select the *Variables* page.

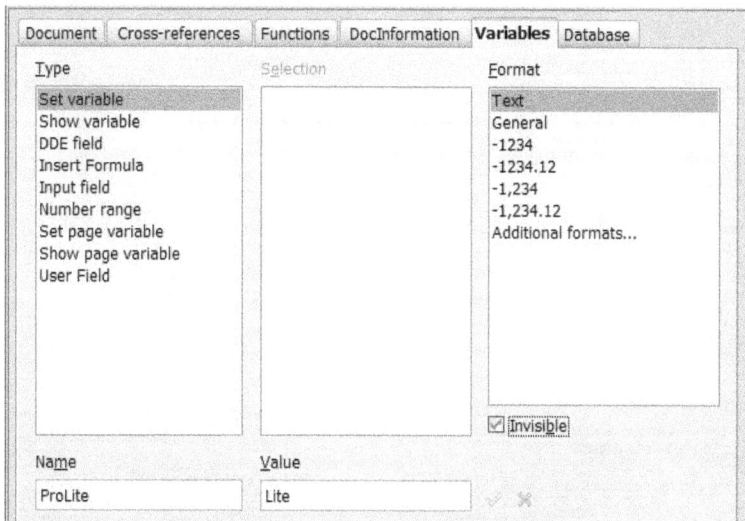

*Figure 397: Defining a variable to use with conditional content*

3) Select **Set variable** in the *Type* list and **Text** in the *Format* list. Type a name for the variable in the *Name* box, and a value in the *Value* box. I have chosen ProLite for the name (to remind me that this variable is related to the two product versions), and I set the value as Lite because I can remember "If it is the Lite version, then this text should be hidden."
4) Select **Invisible** so the field does not show in the document. Click **Insert**, then click **Close**.
5) A small gray mark will appear where you inserted the field. We will come back to this later.

▶ **Tip**

Because the gray mark is so small, you may have trouble finding it again, especially if you have other fields in the document. You may prefer to leave the variable field visible while you work, and change it to invisible just before you create final copy.

At any time, you can place the insertion point just before the field and choose **Edit > Fields** or right-click the field and choose **Fields** on the context menu. On the Edit Fields dialog (Figure 402), select or deselect **Invisible**.

## Apply the condition to the content

Now that you have defined the variable, you can use it in a condition statement. This topic describes some of the possibilities.

### Conditional text

First, let us set up some conditional text that will insert the words *Great Product Lite* into the Lite version and *Great Product Pro* into the Pro version of the manual. You would use this field whenever you want to mention the name of the product.

1) Place the cursor where you want one of these phrases to appear. (You can move or delete it later, if you wish.)

2) On the *Functions* page of the Fields dialog, select **Conditional text** in the *Type* list.

3) As shown in Figure 398, type `ProLite EQ "Lite"` in the *Condition* box, `Great Product Lite` in the *Then* box, and `Great Product Pro` in the *Else* box.

### Note

These fields are case-sensitive, and quotation marks are required around a text value such as Lite.

4) Click **Insert** to insert the field, then click **Close**. You should see *Great Product Lite* in the text.

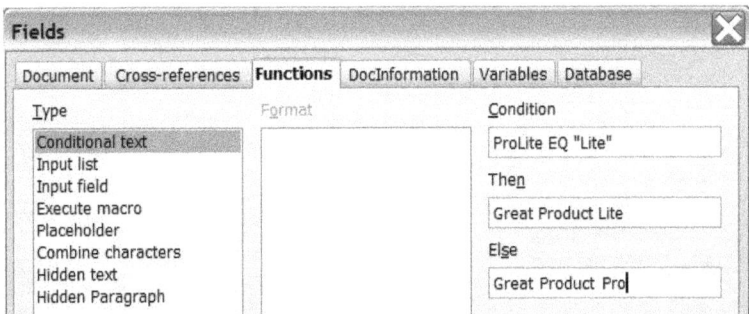

*Figure 398: Inserting conditional text*

### Tip

If you want to insert this field into your text in many places (as you probably would for a product name), create an AutoText entry for it. See "Using AutoText to insert often-used fields" on page 380 for instructions.

### Hidden text

You might use hidden text for words or short phrases that describe features of Great Product Pro that are not found in the Lite version. You can reuse the same field in several places in the document—for example, by copying and pasting it.

To create a hidden text field:

1) On the *Functions* page of the Fields dialog, select **Hidden text** in the *Type* list, as shown in Figure 399.

2) Type `ProLite EQ "Lite"` in the Condition box and type the required text in the *Hidden text* box. Remember, this is the text that is *hidden* if the condition is true.

3) Click **Insert** to create and insert the field.

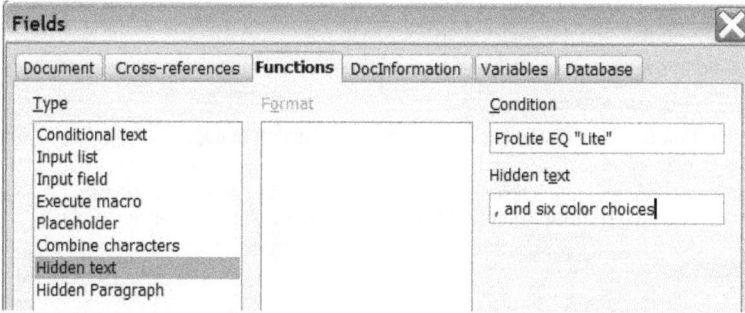

*Figure 399: Creating a condition for hidden text*

### Hidden paragraphs

A conditional paragraph is hidden if the condition is true. To hide a paragraph:

1) Click in the paragraph to be hidden.
2) On the Functions page (Figure 400) of the Fields dialog, select **Hidden paragraph** in the *Type* list.
3) For this example, type `ProLite EQ "Lite"` in the Condition box.
4) Click **Insert** to create and insert the field. If an extra paragraph mark appears, delete it.

*Figure 400: Creating a condition for a a hidden paragraph*

To show all hidden paragraphs so you can edit them, do one of the following:

- Choose **View > Hidden Paragraphs** from the menu bar, so it is checked.
- On the **Tools > Options > LibreOffice Writer > Formatting Aids** page, select the **Fields: Hidden paragraphs** option.
- Double-click in front of the variable that you used to define the condition for hiding the paragraph, and enter a different value for the variable.

### Hidden sections

A conditional section is hidden if the condition is true. To create a conditional section:

1) Select the text that you want to be included in the conditional section. (You can edit this text later, just as you can edit any other text.)
2) Choose **Insert > Section**. On the Insert Section dialog (Figure 401), select the Section tab, then select **Hide** and enter the condition in the **With Condition** box. You can also give the

section a name, if you wish (strongly recommended, so you can find it again easily if you have several sections in your document).

3) Click **Insert** to insert the section into your document.

To show a hidden section so you can edit it:

1) Choose **Format > Sections**.

2) On the Edit Sections dialog (similar to the Insert Section dialog), select the section from the list.

3) Deselect **Hide**, and then click **OK**. You can now edit the contents of the section. Afterwards, you can choose **Format > Sections** and select **Hide** to hide the section again.

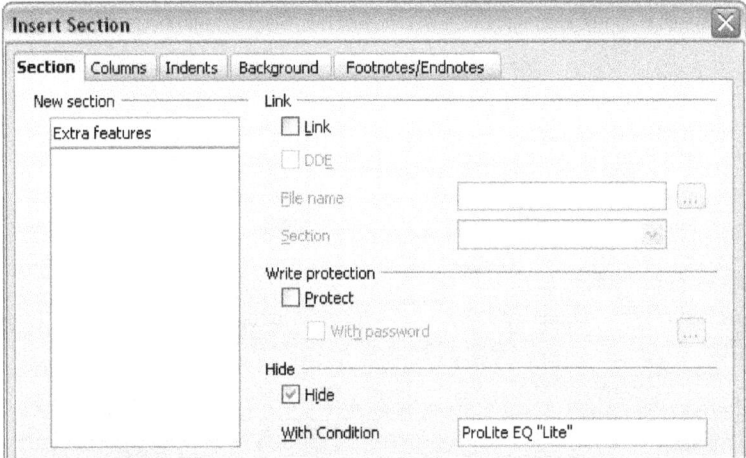

*Figure 401: Creating a section to be hidden when a specified condition is met*

To make the hidden section a normal part of the document (that is, to remove the section markers, but not the contents of the section):

1) Show the hidden section, as described above.

2) On the Edit Sections dialog, select the section from the list.

3) Click **Remove**. The contents of the section are now a normal part of the document.

## Change the value of the variable

To change the value of the variable between *Lite* and *Pro*:

1) Find the variable field you created in "Choose or define a variable" on page 388.

2) Click once just in front of this field, then right-click and click **Fields** on the context menu.

3) On the Edit Fields dialog (Figure 402), change the value of the variable to Pro.

4) If you have set fields to update automatically, all of the conditional and hidden text that uses this variable as a condition will change.

▶ **Tip**

Conditional text and hidden text can only be edited in the Edit Fields dialog.

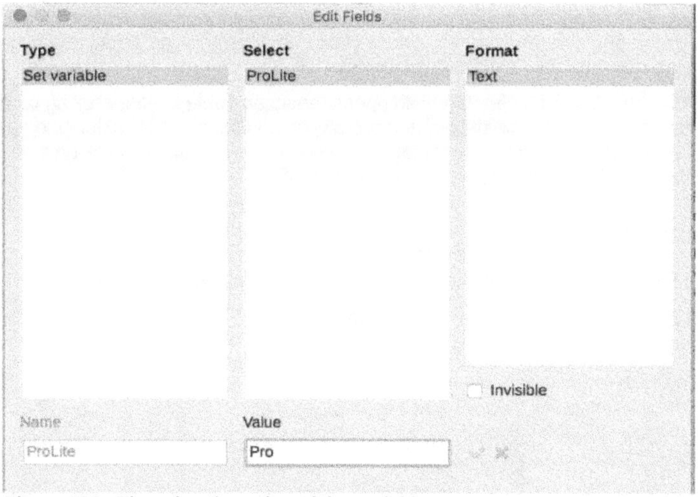

*Figure 402: Changing the value of the variable*

▶ **Tip**

To turn on automatic updating of fields, choose **Tools > Options > LibreOffice Writer > General**, and select **Fields** under Update: Automatically. Lite

# Using placeholder fields

A placeholder field prompts you to enter something (text, a table, a frame, an image, or an object).

To insert a placeholder field into a document:

1) On the *Functions* page of the Fields dialog, select **Placeholder** in the *Type* column and select what the placeholder is for in the *Format* column.

2) In the Placeholder box, type the text that you want to appear in the placeholder field.

3) In the Reference box, type the text that you want to display as a help tip when you rest the mouse pointer over the field.

Figure 403 shows the results of inserting a placeholder field for an image.

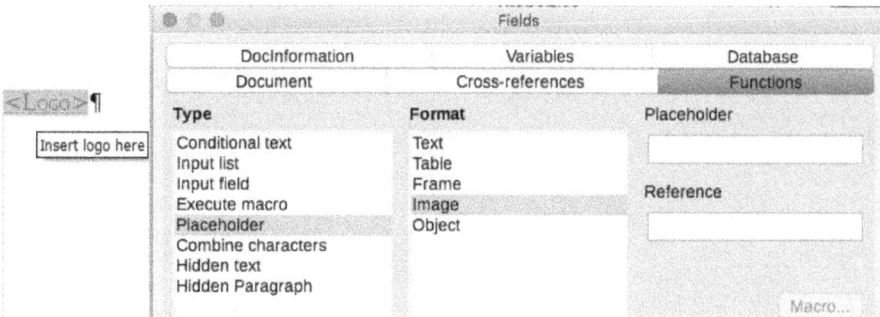

*Figure 403: Inserting a placeholder field*

Because the <Logo> field is an Image placeholder, when you click on the field in the document, the Insert Image dialog opens, prompting you to select an image. When you select an image and click **Open**, the image replaces the field in the document.

Similarly, clicking on a Table placeholder field opens the Insert Table dialog, clicking on a Frame placeholder field opens the Frame dialog, and clicking on an Object placeholder field opens the Insert OLE Object dialog. The text placeholder field is different: you simply click on it and type some text in the Placeholder box, which replaces the field.

## Using other fields

Other uses of fields, including database fields, are described in various chapters of this book.

LibreOffice provides many other fields that you may find useful, but they are too specialized to cover in this book. Please refer to the Help system for details, instructions, and examples.

# LibreOffice

*Chapter 18*
*Forms*

# Introduction to forms

This chapter covers the use of forms within Writer documents. Most of the information here also applies to forms in other LibreOffice components, but there are some differences.

The chapter presents information on using forms in four main sections: setting up a basic form, an example of creating a form, linking a form to a data source, and some advanced techniques.

LibreOffice forms cover a lot of features; not everything is included here. Notable omissions are using forms in HTML documents and writing macros to link to form controls.

# When to use forms

A standard text document displays information: a letter, report, or brochure, for example. Typically the reader may edit everything or nothing in the document. A form has sections that are not to be edited, and other sections that are designed for the reader to make changes. For example, a questionnaire has an introduction and questions (which do not change) and spaces for the reader to enter answers.

Writer provides several ways to enter information into a form, including check boxes, option buttons, text boxes, pull-down lists, and other items, collectively known as form controls.

Forms are used in three ways:

- To create a simple document for the recipient to complete, such as a questionnaire sent out to a group of people who fill it in and return it.
- To link into a database or data source and allow the user to enter information. Someone in a sales department might enter purchasers' information into a database using a form.
- To view information held in a database or data source. A librarian might call up information about books.

Using forms to access a database offers a fast and easy way to build up complex graphical front ends. Your form can include not only the fields that link up to the data source but also text, graphics, tables, drawings and other elements.

A typical way to use a simple form is:

1) You design the form, then save it.
2) You send the form to others (for example, by email).
3) They fill in the form, save it, and send it back to you.
4) You open the form and see what their answers are.

▶ **Tip**

By using a data source, or setting a form to update over the web, you can automatically gather data. However, both of those methods are more complex and are not covered in this book.

## Alternatives to using forms in Writer

LibreOffice Base provides an alternative way to access a data source. There are a lot of similarities between forms in Base and Writer, but one may be better for a particular task than the other. Base is appropriate only if the form accesses a data source; you would not use it for simple forms.

LibreOffice Calc, Impress, and Draw also support forms in much the same way that Writer does.

# Creating a simple form

This section explains how to create a simple form without any links to a data source or database and without advanced customization.

## Create a document

There is nothing special to be done when creating a document to use as a form. Create a new Writer document with **File > New > Text document**.

## Open the form toolbars

Two toolbars control form creation: Form Controls and Form Design. Select **View > Toolbars > Form Controls** and **View > Toolbars > Form Design** to show them both. The Form Controls toolbar has an icon for each of the most commonly used types of control.

You can also open the Form Design toolbar from the Form Controls toolbar. Some of the less commonly used controls are on a third toolbar—More Controls—also opened from the Form Controls toolbar.

You can dock these toolbars in different places on the Writer window, or leave them floating. Figure 404 shows the three toolbars floating. When they are floating, you can also change them from vertical to horizontal and change the number of tools on a row; to make these changes, drag a corner of the toolbar.

See "Form controls reference" on page 399 for descriptions of the tools on these toolbars.

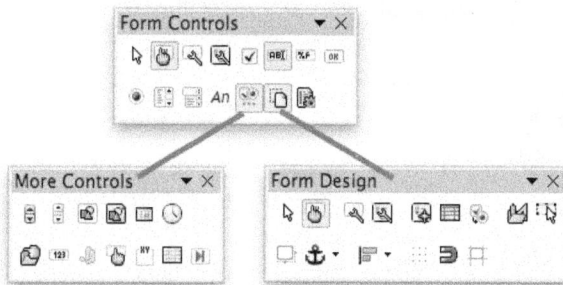

*Figure 404: The Form Control, More Controls, and Form Design Toolbars*

## Activate design mode

Click the **Design Mode On/Off** icon on the Form Controls toolbar to turn design mode on. (Click it again to turn it off.) This activates the icons for inserting form controls and selects controls for editing.

When design mode is off, the form behaves as it would for the end user. Buttons can be pressed, check boxes selected, list items selected, and so on.

## Insert form controls

1) To insert a form control into the document, click the control's icon to select it. The mouse pointer changes to look like this: ⌐□

2) Click in the document where you want the control to appear. (You can move it later.)

3) Hold the left mouse button down and drag the control to size it. Some controls have a fixed size symbol followed by the name of the control (for example, Check Box or Option Button).

4) The control icon remains active, so you can insert several controls of the same type without needing to go back to the toolbar.

5) To change to another tool, click its icon on the toolbar.

6) To stop inserting controls, click the **Select** icon on the Form Controls toolbar, or click on any of the controls you have just inserted. The mouse pointer changes back to its normal appearance.

▶ **Tip**

To make a form control square, hold down the *Shift* key when creating it. To keep the proportions of an existing control the same, hold down *Shift* when resizing it.

## Configure controls

After inserting the controls, you need to configure them to look and behave as you want. Right-click on a form control within the document and select **Control** from the context menu to open the Properties dialog for the selected control. Double-clicking on a form control also opens this dialog.

The Properties dialog has three pages: *General*, *Data*, and *Events*. For simple forms, only the *General* page is needed. Use this page to set the look and feel of the control. See "Configure form controls" on page 403 and "Form control formatting options" on page 412 for more information, and the descriptions in the Help for details. Configuration for use with a database is discussed in "Creating a form for data entry" on page 408.

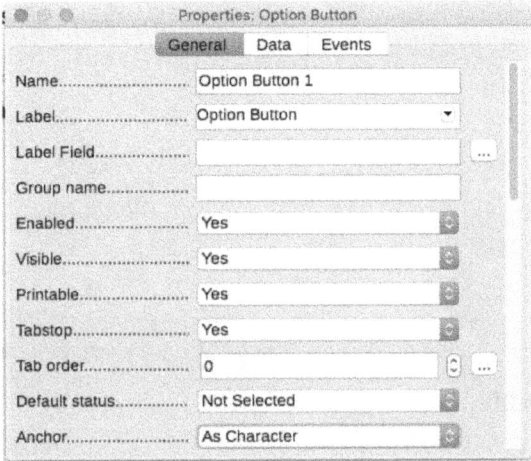

*Figure 405: Example of the Properties dialog for a form control*

The fields on this dialog vary with the type of control.

To see additional fields, use the scroll bar or enlarge the dialog.

## Use the form

To use the form, leave design mode by clicking the **Design Mode On/Off** icon to deactivate it. Save the form document.

# Form controls reference

| | | |
|---|---|---|
| ⌖ | Select | Selects a form control to perform some other action on it. |
| ✋ | Design mode on/off | Toggles between design mode on (to edit forms) and design mode off (to use forms). |
| ⚒ | Control | Launches form control properties dialog. This dialog can be kept open as different controls are selected. |
| ⚒ | Form | Launches form properties dialog, controlling properties for the form as a whole, such as which data source it connects to. |
| ☑ | Check Box | A box that can be selected or deselected on the form. You can label the box. |
| ⓐⒷⒸ | Text Box | A control to create a box into which the form's user can type any text. |
| %f | Formatted Field | A control allowing numeric formatting options. For example, you can set maximum and minimum values for the number entered, or the number type (decimal places, scientific, currency). |
| OK | Push Button | Creates a button that can be linked to a macro. The label is the name that appears on the button. |
| ◉ | Option Button | Creates an option button (also known as a radio button). When multiple buttons are grouped together, only one can be selected at a time. The easiest way to group multiple buttons is to use the Group Box icon on the More Controls toolbar, with wizards enabled. |
| ☰ | List Box | Creates a list of options as a pull-down menu that the user can choose from. If the form is linked to a data source and wizards are on, creating a list box launches the List Box Wizard.<br>If the form is not linked to a data source, turn wizards off and create an empty list box. Then in the *List Entries* field on the *General* tab, enter the options you want to appear on the list. |
| ☰ | Combo Box | As with a List Box, you set up a list of choices. In addition, a panel at the top either displays the choice made or allows the form user to type in something else. This works the same as the List Box. |
| An | Label Field | A text label. The difference between this and just typing on the page is that, as a control, you can link a label field to macros so, for example, something happens when the mouse passes over it or clicks on it. |
| ⋮⋮ | More Controls | Launches the More Controls toolbar. |
| 🗔 | Form Design | Launches the Form Design toolbar, which can also be opened with **View > Toolbars > Form Design**. |
| 🪄 | Wizards On/Off | Some form controls (List Box and Combo Box) have optional wizards. If you do not want the wizard to launch when you create one of these controls, use the Wizards On/Off icon to switch wizards off. |

| More Controls toolbar | | |
|---|---|---|
| ⬙ | Spin Button | Allows form users to choose a number by cycling through the list of numbers. You can specify maximum, minimum, default, and the step between numbers.<br>This control is not commonly used in Writer. |
| ⬙ | Scrollbar | Creates a scrollbar, with a number of options to define the exact appearance. This control is not commonly used in Writer. |
| ⬙ | Image Button | Behaves exactly like a push button, but displays as an image. Choose the image in the Graphics option on the *General* tab in the Control Properties dialog. |
| ⬙ | Image Control | Only useful when the form is connected to a data source and a field in the data source exists that can hold images. You can add new images to the database or retrieve and display images from it. |
| ⬙ | Date Field | Stores a date. You need to configure the earliest and latest dates the field will accept, the default date, and the date format. You can add a spinner. |
| ⬙ | Time Field | Works like a date field but specifies a time. |
| ⬙ | File Selection | Allows a user to select a file, either by typing the path and name directly or by clicking on a Browse button and choosing the file from a dialog. |
| 123 | Numeric Field | Displays a number. You need to specify formatting, maximum, minimum and default values. You can add a spinner. |
| ⬙ | Currency Field | Works like a numeric field; additionally you can add a currency symbol. |
| ⬙ | Pattern Field | Useful when the form links into a data source. Specify an Edit Mask to restrict what a user can enter into the field. Specify a Literal Mask to restrict which data is displayed from the data source. |
| ⬙ | Group Box | Group boxes have two different uses.<br>If wizards are on, creating a group box launches the Group Element wizard. This creates a group of options buttons (in which only one may be selected at a time). In most cases, using a group box is the best way to create a set of option buttons.<br>If wizards are off, a group box is simply a visual box to group together different controls. It has no effect on the way the controls operate. |
| ⬙ | Table Control | Table controls are only useful with a data source. If no data source is specified, you will be prompted to choose one in the Table Element Wizard. You then pick the fields to display and, when design mode is off, the data appears in the table. The table also includes controls to step through the records.<br>Records can be added, deleted, and modified in the table. |
| ⬙ | Navigation Bar | A navigation bar is the same as the Form Navigation toolbar (**View > Toolbars > Form Navigation**), but can be placed anywhere in the document and be resized. |

## Form Design toolbar

| | | |
|---|---|---|
| ⬚ | Select | Selects a form control to perform an action on it. |
| ⬚ | Design mode on/off | Toggles between design mode on (to edit forms) and design mode off (to use forms). |
| ⬚ | Control | Launches form control properties dialog. This dialog can be kept open whiles different controls are selected. |
| ⬚ | Form | Launches form properties dialog, which controls properties for the form as a whole, such as which data source it connects to. |
| ⬚ | Form Navigator | Displays all the forms and controls in the current document and allows you to edit and delete them easily. If you use the Form Navigator, give your controls names (in the properties dialog) you can tell which is which in the navigator. |
| ⬚ | Add Field | Useful only if you have specified a data source for the form. Otherwise, an empty box opens. If you have specified a data source, Add Field opens a list of all the fields in the specified table, which you can then drag and drop onto the page. The fields are placed on the page with the name of the field before them. This is a quick and easy way to create a form from a data source. |
| ⬚ | Activation Order | Allows you to specify the order in which focus shifts between controls. You can test the order by leaving design mode and using *Tab* to switch between the controls. |
| ⬚ | Open in Design Mode | Opens the current form in design mode (to edit the form rather than entering data into it). |
| ⬚ | Automatic Control Focus | If activated, focus is set to the first form control. |
| ⬚ | Position and Size | Launches the Position and Size dialog, where you can type precise values, rather than dragging the control. You can also lock the size or position, so they do not get changed accidentally. For some controls, you can rotate and set the slant and corner radius. |
| ⬚ | Change Anchor | Just as with a frame, any form control can be anchored to page, paragraph, or character and also anchored as a character (meaning that it behaves like any other character on the page). |
| ⬚ | Alignment | Disabled unless the control is anchored as a character. You can align a control in different ways, for example so the top of the control lines up with the top of the text or the bottom lines up with the bottom of the text. |
| ⬚ | Display Grid | Displays a grid of dots on the page, to help you line up controls. |
| ⬚ | Snap to Grid | When a control is brought close to a grid point or line, it will snap to the grid. This makes it is easier to line up controls. |
| ⬚ | Guides when Moving | When a control is being moved, lines extend from the control horizontally and vertically to help you position it accurately. |

# Example: a simple form

## Create the document

Open a new document (**File > New > Text Document**). It is a good idea to write down the outline of the document, without form controls, though of course it can easily be changed later.

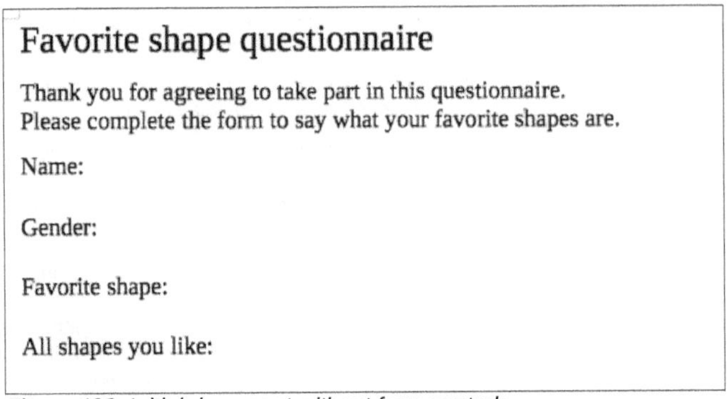

## Favorite shape questionnaire

Thank you for agreeing to take part in this questionnaire.
Please complete the form to say what your favorite shapes are.

Name:

Gender:

Favorite shape:

All shapes you like:

*Figure 406: Initial document without form controls*

## Add form controls

The next step is to add the form controls to the document. We will have four controls:

- Name is a text box.
- Gender is three option buttons: male, female, or other; user can select one.
- Favourite shape is a list of options.
- All shapes you like is a series of check boxes.

To add these controls:

1) Select **View > Toolbars > Form Controls** to open the Form Control toolbar.
2) If the tools are not active, click the **Design Mode On/Off** icon to activate them.
3) Click the **Text Box** icon, then click in the document and drag the shape of the Name text box to approximately the size you want. Drag it to line up with the Name: label.
4) Make sure **Wizards On/Off** is **off**. Click the **Option Button** icon. Click and drag to create three option buttons near the *Gender:* label in the document. We will configure these in the next section.
5) Click the **List Box** icon and draw a list box by *Favourite Shape:* in the document. This will just be an empty pane for now.
6) Click the **Check Box** icon and create four check boxes by *All shapes you like*, side by side across the page.

Your document should now look something like Figure 407.

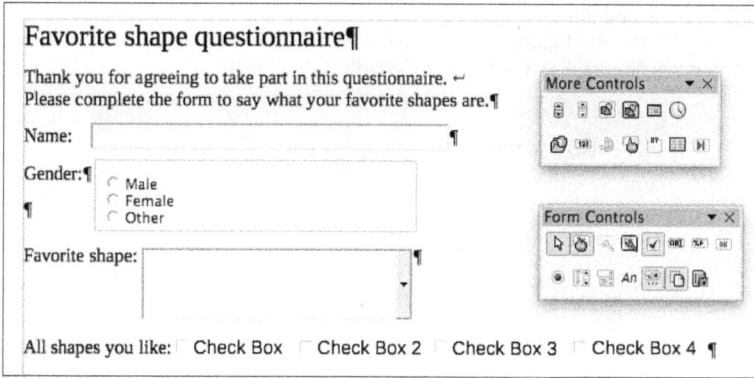

Figure 407: Document with form controls

# Configure form controls

No further configuration is required for the Name field.

For the option buttons, do this:

1)  Be sure design mode is on. Right-click on the first option button and click **Control** on the context menu. In the Properties dialog (Figure 408), on the *General* tab, type **Male** in the *Label* field and **Gender** in the *Group name* field.

2)  Repeat for the other two options, using **Female** and **Other**, respectively, for the Label and Gender for the Group name. (Grouping options allows only one to be selected at a time.)

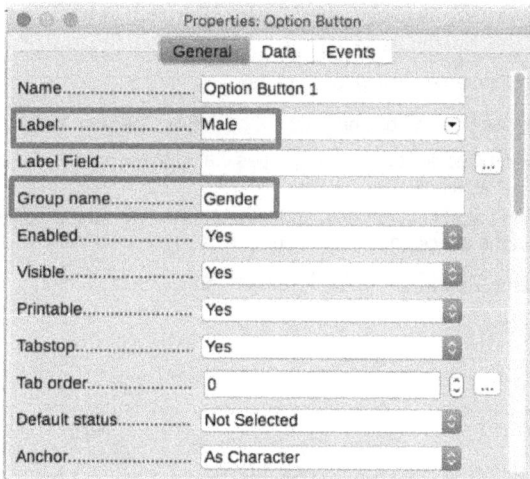

Figure 408: Specifying label and group names for an option button

To add the list of choices to the the the list box, do this:

1)  Be sure Design Mode is on and Wizards are off. Double-click on the **List Box** control to open the control's Properties dialog (Figure 409). Select the *General* tab.

2) Scroll down to find the List Entries text input box. Type the names of the shapes (Circle, Triangle, Square, Pentagon) one at a time. After each, press *Shift+Enter*. You should end up with a line saying "Circle";"Triangle";"Square";"Pentagon".

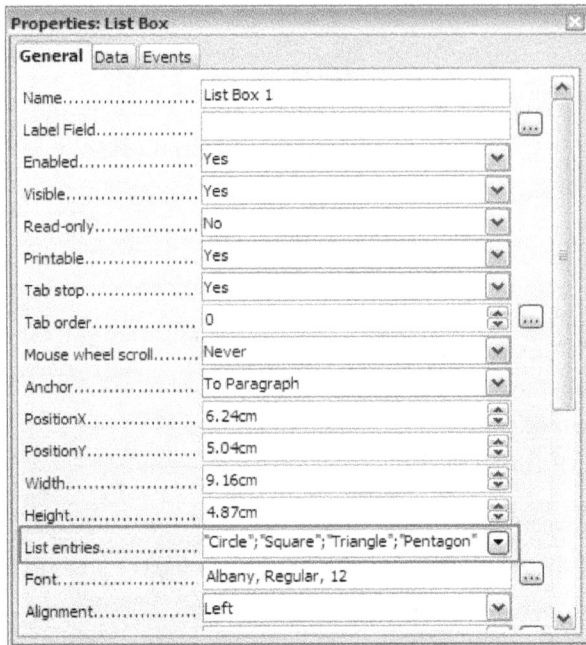

*Figure 409: Properties dialog for a list box*

To give the check boxes names (instead of Check Box, Check Box 2, and so forth):

1) Double-click on the first Check Box. The Properties dialog stays open but changes to show the properties for the check box.

2) Change the text in the Label field to Circle and press *Enter*. The cursor moves to the next line, and the label on the check box in the document changes immediately.

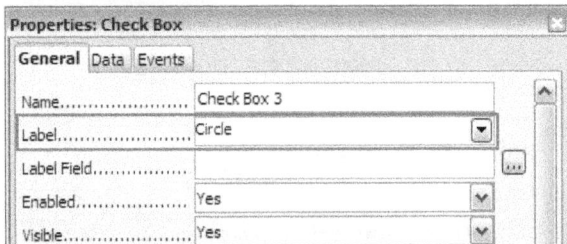

*Figure 410: Top part of Properties dialog for a check box*

3) Click on each of the other three check boxes in turn. Change the text in the Label text input box in the Properties dialog to Triangle, Square, and Pentagon in turn.

4) Close the Properties dialog.

5) Turn design mode off and close the two Controls toolbars.

You have now completed the form, which should look something like Figure 411.

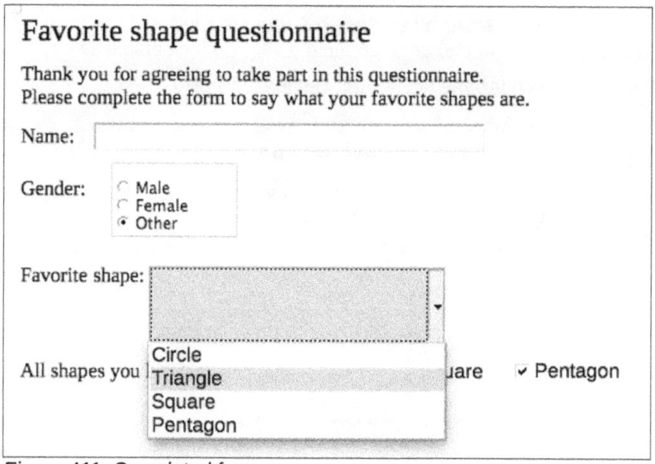

## Favorite shape questionnaire

Thank you for agreeing to take part in this questionnaire.
Please complete the form to say what your favorite shapes are.

Name:

Gender:    ○ Male
            ○ Female
            ◉ Other

Favorite shape:

All shapes you   Circle
               Triangle           uare    ☑ Pentagon
               Square
               Pentagon

*Figure 411: Completed form*

## Finishing touches

The form is complete, but you are free to make further changes to the document. If you were sending this out to other people to complete, you would probably want to make the document read-only. The effect would be that users would be able to fill in the form but not to make any other changes to the document.

To make the document read-only, select **File > Properties**, select the *Security* tab and enable **Open file read-only**.

### Note

If the document is read-only, anyone filling in the form will need to use **File > Save as** to save the document.

## Accessing data sources

The most common use for a form is as the front end of a database. You can provide a form that allows users to enter information into a contacts database and, because it is part of a Writer document, the form can contain graphics, formatting, tables, and other elements to make it look just the way you want. Modifying the form is as simple as editing a document.

LibreOffice can access numerous data sources. These include ODBC, MySQL, Oracle JDBC, spreadsheets and text files. As a general rule, databases can be accessed for read and write; other data sources (such as spreadsheets) are read-only.

### Tip

To see the list of supported data source types for your operating system, choose **File > New > Database**. On the first page of the Database Wizard (Figure 415), select **Connect to an existing database** and then open the drop-down list.

# Creating a database

Chapter 8, Getting Started with Base, in the *Getting Started Guide* covers in more detail how to create a database. Below is a short guide to creating a very simple database.

1) Select **File > New > Database** to start the Database Wizard.

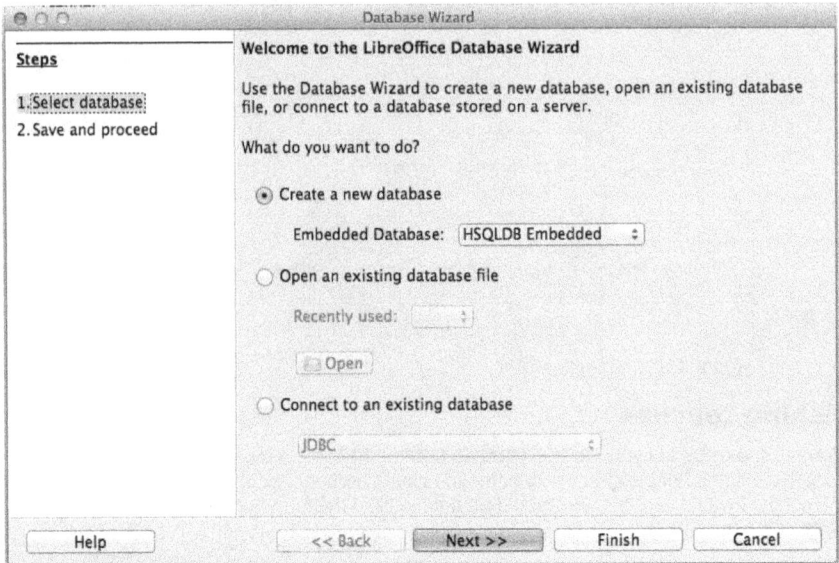

*Figure 412: Database Wizard*

2) Select **Create a new database** and click **Next >>**.

3) On the next page, select **Yes, register the database for me** and **Open the database for editing**. Registering the database means that it can be accessed from other LibreOffice components such as Writer and Calc. You need to do this if you want to link forms into it.

4) Click **Finish** and save your new database, giving it a name. Unlike creating other documents in LibreOffice, databases must be saved when you first create them.

After saving the database, you should see the main Base window (Figure 413), which contains three panels. The left-hand panel is Database, with icons for Tables, Queries, Forms and Reports.

The next step is to create a table:

1) Choose **Tables** in the left-hand column, then choose **Create Table in Design View** under *Tasks*.

2) Use the Table Design window to tell Base which fields to create. We will have three input data fields: Name, Address, and Telephone.

3) On the first line, enter under Field Name, ID, and set the Field Type to Integer [INTEGER]. In the box at the left of the line, right-click and select Primary Key, bringing up a key icon in the box. In the Field Properties at the bottom of the window is an Auto Value option; change this to Yes. Optionally, type Primary key in the Description column. See Figure 414.

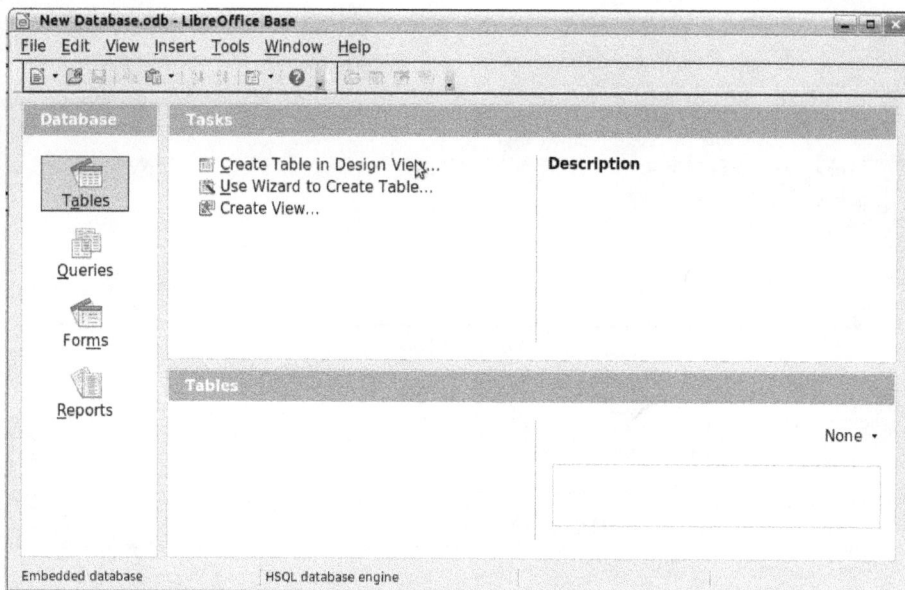
Figure 413: Main Base window

## Caution

Setting up the Primary Key field with Auto Value set to **Yes** is an important step. If this is not done, the form you create later will be much trickier to use and may generate errors for the user. It could even prevent the user from saving the records in the form. Make sure you get this step right!

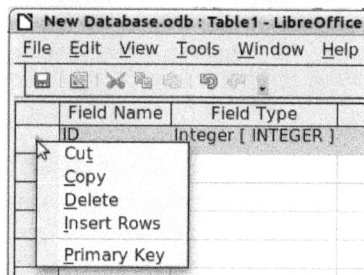
Figure 414: Setting a primary key

4)  On the next three lines, enter under Field Name Name, Address and Telephone. Accept the default Field Type of Text [VARCHAR] and leave Description blank.

5)  Save the table (**File > Save**). You will be prompted to name it. The name can be anything you like. Click **OK**.

6)  Finally, close the table design window to return to the main Base window. If **File > Save** is available, select it to save the whole database.

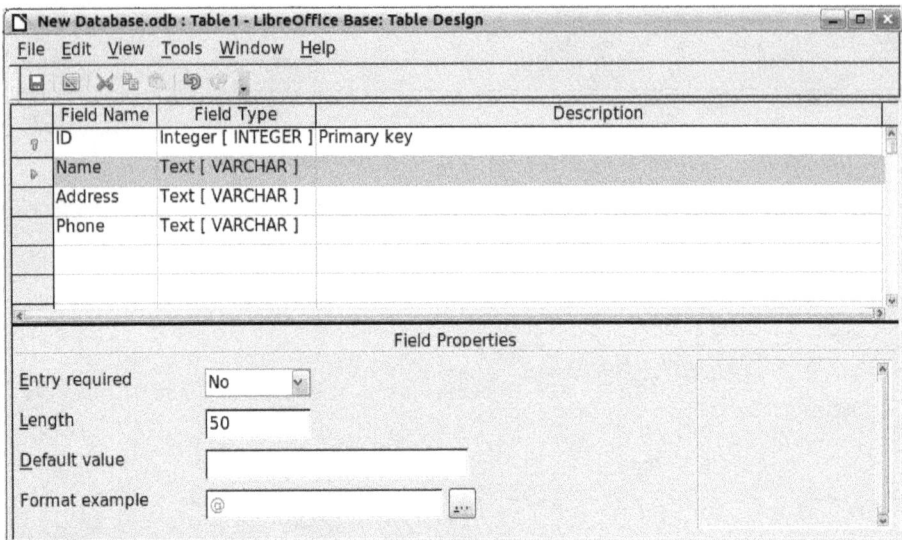

Figure 415: Database table design

## Accessing an existing data source

If you have an existing data source, such as a spreadsheet or database, you need to register it with LibreOffice. An example of registering a spreadsheet as a data source is given in Chapter 14, Mail Merge. To summarize:

1) Select **File > New > Database** to launch the Database Wizard.

2) Select **Connect to an existing database** and choose the type from the drop-down list.

3) Click **Next >>** and follow the instructions to select the database to register (the exact process varies between different types of data source).

4) In Step 3: Save and proceed, check that **Yes, register the database for me** is selected. Deselect *Open the database for editing*; you just need to register it, not edit it through Base.

### Creating a form for data entry

Once a database is registered with LibreOffice, follow these steps to link a form to the data source:

1) Create a new document in Writer (**File > New > Text Document**).

2) Design your form, without putting in the actual fields (you can always change it later).

3) Show the Form Controls toolbar (**View > Toolbars > Form Controls**).

4) Click the **Design Mode On/Off** icon to put the document into design mode, if necessary. With design mode off, most of the toolbar buttons are grayed out. If the Design Mode icon is also grayed out, click on the Select icon to activate it.

5) Click the **Text Box** icon. Click in the document and drag to create a text box for the first form field (for example, Name, if you are linking to the database created above).

6) Click the Text Box icon again and drag the mouse to draw another field. Additional fields, of any type, can be added in the same way (click and drag).

So far you have followed the same steps used before when creating your first form. Now you will link the form with the data source you registered.

1) Click the **Form** icon in the Form Controls toolbar, or right-click on any of the fields you inserted and select **Form**, to open the Form Properties dialog (Figure 416).

2) In the Form Properties dialog, choose the *Data* tab.

   – Set Data Source to be the data source you registered.

   – Set Content Type to be Table.

   – Set Content to be the name of the table you want to access.

   – Close the dialog.

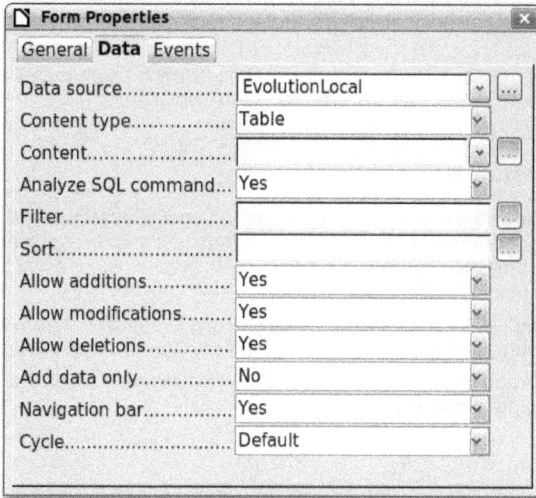

*Figure 416: Form properties, connecting to a data source*

3) For each form control in turn, click on the control to select it (so small green boxes appear around it), then launch the Properties dialog: either right-click and select **Control** or click on the **Control** icon on the Form Controls toolbar.

4) In the Properties dialog, click on the *Data* tab (Figure 417). If you set up the form correctly, the Data Field option will contain a list of the different fields in the data source (for example, Name, Address and Telephone). Select the field you want.

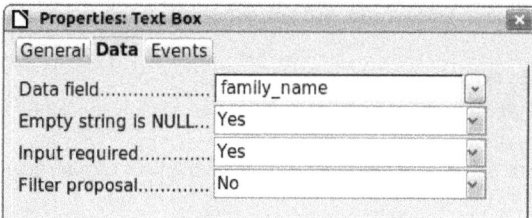

*Figure 417: Form control properties, Data tab*

5) Repeat for each control in turn until every control that should be assigned to a field has been assigned.

### Caution

If you created a database in LibreOffice Base and your Primary Key field had Auto Value set to Yes, that field does not need to be part of the form. If Auto Value was set to No, you will have to include it and have your users enter a unique value into that field whenever they make a new entry—not something that is recommended.

## Entering data into a form

Once you have created a form and tied it to a database, you want to use it to enter data into the database, or modify data already there.

1) Make sure that the form is **not** in design mode. (In the Form Controls toolbar, click the Design Mode On/Off icon. If design mode is off, most of the buttons on the toolbar will be grayed out.)

2) Make sure that the Form Navigation toolbar is on (**View > Toolbars > Form Navigation**). This toolbar normally appears at the bottom of the workspace.

*Figure 418: Form Navigation toolbar*

3) If there is existing data in the data source, use the control buttons on the Form Navigation toolbar to look at different records. You can amend data in a record by editing the values in the form. To submit the changes, press *Enter* with the cursor in the last field. The record is saved and the next record is displayed.

4) If there is no data in the form, you can start entering information by typing into the fields of the form. To submit the new record, press *Enter* with the cursor in the last field.

5) Other functions can be performed from the Form Navigation toolbar, including deleting a record and adding a new record.

### Note

If a user tries to fill in the form and receives the error "Attempt to insert null into a non-nullable column", then the form designer should go back to the database and confirm that the Primary Key field has the Auto Value set to Yes. This error will prevent the form user from saving the records.

# Advanced form customization

## Linking a macro to a form control

You can set any form control (for example, text box or button) to perform an action when triggered by some event.

To assign a macro to an event:

1) Create the macro. See Chapter 13, Getting Started with Macros, in the *Getting Started Guide*.

2) Be sure the form is in design mode. Right-click on the form control, select **Control** and click on the *Events* tab (Figure 419).

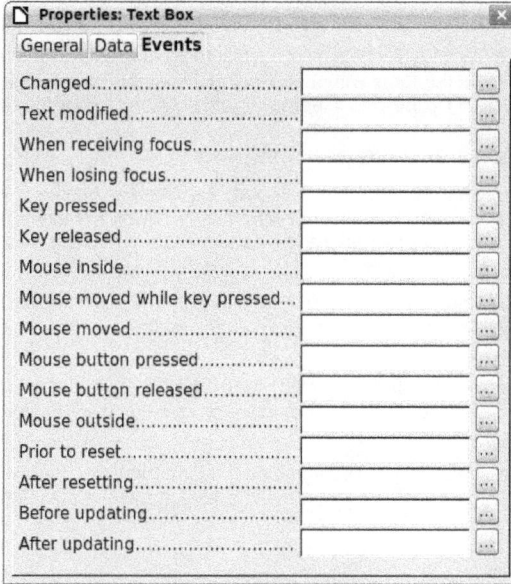

*Figure 419: Control properties, Events tab*

3) Click the browse icon by any event to open the Assign action dialog (Figure 420).

4) Click the **Macro** button and select the macro from the list in the Macro Selector dialog (not shown). You return to the Assign action dialog. Repeat as needed, then click **OK** to close the dialog.

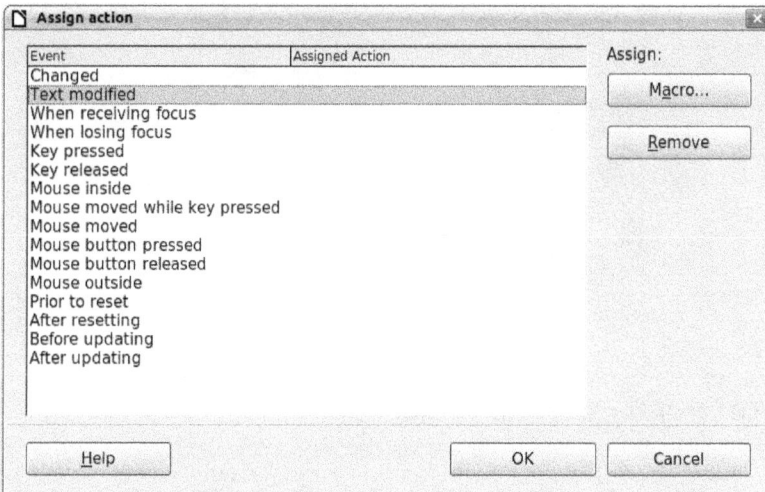

*Figure 420: Assign action dialog*

Macros can also be assigned to events relating to the form as a whole. To do this, right-click on a form control in the document, select **Form** and click on the *Events* tab.

## Read-only documents

Having created your form, you want whoever is using it to be able to access the information stored in the database, or complete the form, without changing the layout. To do this, make the document read-only by choosing **File > Properties > Security** and selecting **Open file read-only**.

## Fine-tuning database access permissions

By default, when a database is accessed from a form, any changes can be made to it: records can be added, deleted, and amended. You may not want that behavior. For example, you may want users to be able only to add new records or to be prohibited from deleting existing records.

In design mode, right-click on a form control and select Form from the context menu. On the Data tab of the Form Properties dialog are a number of options: Allow additions, Allow deletions, Allow modifications and Add data only. Set each of these to Yes or No to control the access users have to the data source.

Individual fields can also be protected. This might be useful if you wanted a user to be able to modify some parts of a record but only view others, such as a stock list where item descriptions are fixed and quantities can be modified.

To make an individual field read-only, in design mode, right-click on the form control within the document and select Control from the context menu. Select the General tab and set Read-only to Yes.

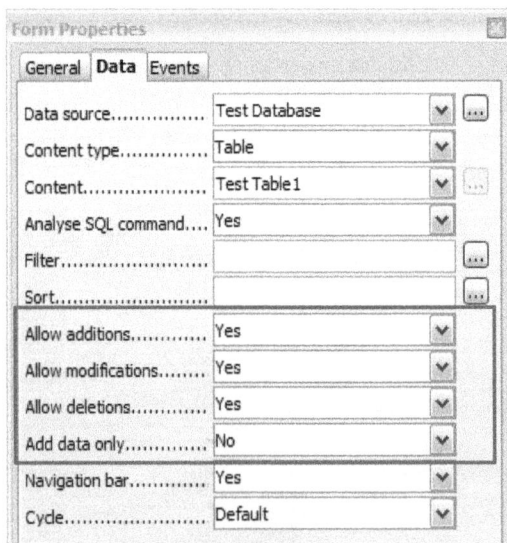

*Figure 421: Data Properties of a form*

## Form control formatting options

You can customize the way form controls look and behave in a number of ways. These are all accessed in design mode. Right-click on the form control, select **Control** from the context menu and select the *General* tab in the Properties dialog.

- Set a label for the control in the Label box (not to be confused with the box called Label Field). Some form controls, such as push buttons and option buttons, have visible labels that can be set. Others, such as text boxes, do not.

- Set whether the form control will print out if the document is printed with the Print option.

- Use the Font setting to set the font, typeface, and size for a field's label or for text typed into a field. This setting does not affect the size of check boxes or option buttons.

- For a text box, you can set the maximum text length. This is very useful when adding records into a database. Every database text field has a maximum length and, if the data entered is too long, LibreOffice displays an error message. By setting the maximum text length of the form control to be the same as that of the database field, this error can be avoided.

- You can set the default option for a form control. By default, a control is blank, or has every option unselected. You can set the control to start with a particular option or list item selected.

- For controls where a password is being entered, setting the Password character (for example to *) displays only that character, but saves what the user really types.

- You can add additional information and help text for a form control.

- Other formatting controls such as background color, 3-D look, text formatting, scroll bars, and borders allow you to further define how the control appears.

# LibreOffice

# Chapter 19
# Spreadsheets, Charts, Other Objects

# Introduction: OLE objects

Object Linking and Embedding (OLE) is a way to use information from one application (say, Calc) in another application (Writer, in this case).

Both linking and embedding insert information from one document into another document, but they store information differently. In addition, they are different from directly copying and pasting information because you can open and edit objects in the applications that created them.

An **embedded** OLE object is a *copy* of information from another document. When you embed objects, there is no link to the source document and any changes made to the source document are not reflected in the destination document. Embed objects if you want to be able to use the application that created them for editing, but you do not want the OLE object to be updated when you edit information in the source document.

A **linked** object is a *reference* to information in another document. Link objects when you want to use the same information in more than one document. Then, if you change the original information, you need to update only the links in order to update the document containing the OLE objects. You can also set links to be updated automatically. When you link an object, you need to maintain access to the source application and the linked document. If you rename or move either of them, you may need to reestablish the link.

The following types of files or documents can be inserted into a Writer document as an OLE object: spreadsheets, charts, drawings, formulas (equations), presentation.

## Inserting a new OLE object

When you insert a **new** OLE object into a document, it is embedded; that is, the object is available only in that document and can only be edited using Writer.

To insert a new OLE object into a document:

1) Click where you want to insert the object.
2) Choose **Insert > Object > OLE Object** from the Menu bar.
3) On the Insert OLE Object dialog (Figure 422), select **Create new**.
4) Select the type of object you want to create and click **OK**.
5) A new OLE object is inserted in the document in edit mode. The toolbars displayed in Writer will change, providing the necessary tools for you to create the new OLE object.

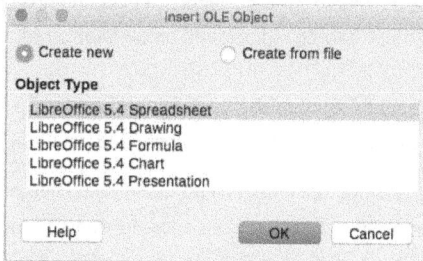

*Figure 422: Inserting a new OLE object*

### Note

Computers running Microsoft Windows show an additional option of Further Objects in the Object Type list. This option opens another dialog where you can create an OLE object using other software that is compatible with OLE and LibreOffice. This option is available for new OLE objects and OLE objects from a file.

## Inserting an OLE object from a file

When you insert an existing file (for example, a spreadsheet) into a Writer document as an OLE object, you can choose whether to embed or link the file.

1) Click where you want to insert the file and choose **Insert > Object > OLE Object** from the Menu bar.

2) On the Insert OLE Object dialog, select **Create from file**. The dialog changes to show a File text box (Figure 423).

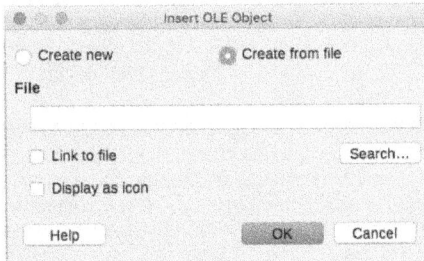

*Figure 423: Inserting an OLE object from a file*

3) Click **Search** and the Open dialog is displayed.

4) Locate the file you want to insert and click **Open**.

5) Select the **Link to file** option if you wish to insert the file as a live link so that any changes made are synchronized in both the original file and your document.

6) Select the **Display as icon** option to show an icon for the application that created the file (for example, Calc), instead of displaying the contents of the file.

7) Click **OK** to insert the file as an OLE object.

## Editing OLE objects

To edit an OLE object after it has been created or inserted from a file:

1) Double-click on the OLE object to open it in edit mode. The toolbars displayed in Writer will change to provide the tools necessary to edit the object.

2) When finished editing the object, click anywhere outside the object to cancel editing.

3) Save the Writer document. Any changes made to the OLE object are also saved.

# Spreadsheets

To include a spreadsheet in an Writer document, you can insert either an existing spreadsheet file or a new spreadsheet as an OLE object. See above for more information. You can also copy a portion of a spreadsheet into a Writer document as an OLE object; see below.

Embedding a spreadsheet into Writer includes most of the functionality of a Calc spreadsheet. Writer is capable of performing complex calculations and data analysis. However, if you plan to use complex data or formulas, it is recommended to perform those operations in a separate Calc spreadsheet and use Writer only to display the embedded spreadsheet with the results.

You may be tempted to use spreadsheets in Writer for creating complex tables or presenting data in a tabular format. However, the Table feature in Writer is often more suitable and faster to use, depending on the complexity of your data; see Chapter 13, Tables.

To copy a spreadsheet area to a Writer document:

1) Open both the Writer document and the spreadsheet.

2) Select the sheet area (cells) that you want to copy.

3) Right-click and choose **Copy** from the context menu, or press *Ctrl+C*, or drag the area into the Writer document. The sheet area is inserted as an OLE object.

When an entire spreadsheet is inserted into a document, if it contains more than one sheet and the one you want is not visible, double-click the spreadsheet, and then select a different sheet from the row of sheet tabs at the bottom.

## Resizing and moving spreadsheet objects

When resizing or moving a spreadsheet object in Writer, ignore the first row and first column (easily recognizable because of their light background color) and any horizontal and vertical scroll bars. They are only used for spreadsheet editing purposes and will not be included in the spreadsheet that appears in the document.

### Resizing

When selected, a spreadsheet object is treated like any other object. However, resizing an embedded spreadsheet also changes the spreadsheet area that is visible in the document.

To resize the area occupied by the spreadsheet:

1) Double-click the object to enter edit mode, if it is not already active. Note the selection handles visible in the border surrounding the spreadsheet object.

2) Move the mouse pointer over one of the handles. The pointer changes shape to give a visual representation of the effects applied to the area.

3) Click and hold the left mouse button and drag the handle. The corner handles move the two adjacent sides simultaneously, while the handles at the midpoint of the sides modify one dimension at a time.

### Moving

Moving a spreadsheet object to change its position within the document is the same as moving any other object in Writer:

1) Select the object so that the selection handles are displayed.

2) Move the cursor over the object until the cursor changes shape (normally a hand, but this depends on your computer setup). Be careful to not double-click on the spreadsheet object and enter into object editing mode.

3) Click and drag the object to the desired position. Release the mouse button.

## Editing a spreadsheet object

To edit a spreadsheet object, double-click on it, or select it and choose **Edit > Object > Edit** from the Menu bar, or right-click and choose **Edit** from the context menu.

You edit the object in its own frame within the Writer document, but some of the toolbars change in Writer so that you can easily edit the spreadsheet. One of the most important changes is the presence of the Formula toolbar, which contains (from left to right):

- The active cell reference or the name of a selected range of cells.

- The **Formula Wizard** icon.

- The **Sum** and **Function** icons or the **Cancel** and **Accept** icons, depending on the editing actions taken in the spreadsheet.

- A long edit box to enter or review the contents of the active cell.

If you are familiar with Calc, you will immediately recognize the tools and the menu items. See Chapter 5, Getting Started with Calc, in the *Getting Started Guide* for more information.

### Spreadsheet organization

A spreadsheet consists of pages called sheets. However, in Writer, only one sheet can be shown at any one time when a spreadsheet with multiple sheets is embedded into an Writer document. The default names for sheets are Sheet 1, Sheet 2, Sheet 3 and so on, unless the sheets have been renamed, and the sheet names are shown at the bottom of the spreadsheet area.

Each sheet is organized into cells, which are the elementary units of the spreadsheet. They are identified by a row number (shown on the left hand side) and a column letter (shown in the top row). For example, the top left cell is identified as A1, while the third cell in the second row is C2. All data elements, whether text, numbers, or formulas, are entered into a cell.

### Note

> If you have multiple sheets in your embedded spreadsheet, only the active sheet is shown on the page after exiting edit mode.

### Working with sheets

You can insert, rename, delete, etc sheets in an embedded spreadsheet. To begin, double-click on the embedded spreadsheet to open it in edit mode. When finished editing the embedded spreadsheet, click anywhere outside the border to cancel edit mode and save the changes.

#### Inserting sheets

1) Right-click on the sheet names and select **Insert > Sheet** from the context menu, or click on the plus sign to the right of the sheet names, or go to **Insert > Sheet** on the Menu bar to open the Insert Sheet dialog.

2) Select the sheet position, number of sheets to be inserted, sheet name, or which spreadsheet file to use from the options available in the Insert Sheet dialog.

3) Click **OK** to close the dialog and insert the sheet.

#### Renaming sheets

1) Click on the sheet tab you want to rename.

2) Right-click on the sheet tab and select **Rename Sheet** from the context menu, or go to **Format > Sheet > Rename** on the Menu bar.

#### Moving and copying sheets

1) Right-click on the sheet names and select **Move/Copy Sheet** from the context menu, or go to **Edit > Sheet > Move/Copy** on the Menu bar to open the Move/Copy Sheet dialog.

2) Select whether to move or copy the sheet, the sheet location and position, and a new sheet name. Click **OK** to close the dialog and move or copy the sheet.

3) Alternatively, click on the sheet tab and drag it to a new position in the embedded spreadsheet.

#### Deleting sheets

1) Right-click on the tab of the sheet you want to delete and select **Delete Sheet** from the context menu, or go to **Edit > Sheet > Delete** on the Menu bar.

2) Click **Yes** to confirm.

### Cell navigation

To move around the spreadsheet to select a cell to make it active, you can:

- Use the keyboard arrow keys.
- Position the cursor in a cell and left-click on the mouse.

- Use the *Enter* key to move one cell down and *Shift+Enter* to move one cell up.
- Use the *Tab* key to move one cell to the right and *Shift+Tab* to move one cell to the left.
- Use other keyboard shortcuts.

### Entering data

Data input into a cell can only be done when a cell is active. An active cell is easily identified by a thickened and bolder border. The cell reference (or coordinates) for the active cell is displayed at the left hand end of the Formula toolbar.

1) Select the cell to make it active and start typing. The data input is also displayed in the large text box on the Formula toolbar making the data entry easier to read.

2) Use the Formula Wizard icon $f_x$ , **Sum** icon $\Sigma$ and **Function** icon $=$ to enter data, formula or function into a cell. If the input is not a formula (for example, a text or date entry), the Sum and Function icons change to the **Cancel** icon ✖ and **Accept** icon ✓ .

3) To confirm data input into a cell either select a different cell, or press the *Enter* key, or click on the **Accept** icon.

### Formatting cell data

Writer normally recognizes the type of contents (text, number, date, time, and so on) entered into a cell and applies default formatting to it. However, if Writer wrongly recognizes the type of data you have entered into a cell:

1) Select the cell, then right-click on the cell and select **Format Cells** from the context menu, or go to **Format > Cells** on the Menu bar, or use the keyboard shortcut *Ctrl+1*.

2) In the Format Cells dialog, click on the appropriate tab to open the correct page and use the options on that page to format the cell data.

3) Click **OK** to close the dialog and save your changes.

### ▶ Tip

To force Writer to treat numbers as text (for example, telephone numbers) and to prevent Writer from removing the leading zeros or right-align them in a cell, type a single quotation mark (') before entering the number.

## Formatting spreadsheets

It may be necessary to change the formatting of a spreadsheet to match the style used in the document.

When working on an embedded spreadsheet, you can also access any cell styles created in Calc and use them. However, if you are going to use styles, it is recommended to create specific cell styles for embedded spreadsheets, as Calc cell styles may be unsuitable when working within Writer.

### Manual formatting

To manually format an embedded spreadsheet:

1) Select a cell or a range of cells. See Chapter 5, Getting Started with Calc, in the *Getting Started Guide* for more information on selecting ranges of cells.

 d) To select the whole sheet, click on the blank cell at the top left corner between the row and column indexes, or use the keyboard shortcut *Ctrl+A*.

 e) To select a column, click on the column header at the top of the spreadsheet.

 f) To select a row, click on the row header on the left hand side of the spreadsheet.

2) Right-click on a cell and select Format Cells from the context menu, or go to **Format > Cells** on the Menu bar, or use the keyboard shortcut *Ctrl+1* to open the Format Cells dialog.

3) Use the various dialog pages to format the embedded spreadsheet so that it matches the style of your document.

4) Click **OK** to close the dialog and save your changes.

5) If necessary, adjust the column width by hovering the mouse over the line separating two columns in the header row until the mouse cursor changes to a double-headed arrow; then click the left button and drag the separating line to the new position.

6) If necessary, adjust the row height by hovering the mouse over the line separating two rows in the row header until the mouse cursor changes to a double-headed arrow; then click the left button and drag the separating line to the new position.

7) When you are satisfied with the formatting changes, click outside the spreadsheet area to save your changes and cancel editing.

### Using formatting styles

When an embedded spreadsheet is in edit mode, Writer displays the available styles for a spreadsheet in the Styles and Formatting window.

If style formatting you want to use is not available, then see Chapter 8, Introduction to Styles, on how to create a style. Styles used in an embedded spreadsheet are similar to paragraph styles used in Writer.

To use styles in your embedded spreadsheet:

1) Open Styles and Formatting in the Sidebar.

2) Select data in a cell and double-click on a style in Styles and Formatting to apply that style.

### Inserting and deleting rows, columns, or cells

To insert rows, columns, or cells in an embedded spreadsheet:

1) Select the same number of rows, columns, or cells on the embedded spreadsheet that you want to insert.

2) Go to **Insert > Rows** or **Insert > Columns** or **Insert > Cells** on the Menu bar or right-click on the selection and select **Insert** from the context menu.

3) When inserting cells, select **Insert** from the Insert Cells dialog that opens and click **OK**.

To delete rows, columns, or cells from an embedded spreadsheet:

1) Highlight the number of rows, columns, or cells on the embedded spreadsheet you want to delete.

2) Go to **Edit > Delete Cells** on the Menu bar or right-click on the row or column headers and select **Delete Selected Rows** or **Delete Selected Columns** or **Delete** from the context menu.

### Merging and splitting cells

To merge multiple cells into a single cell:

1) Select the cells to be merged.

2) Go to **Format > Merge cells** on the Menu bar and select either **Merge and Center Cells** or **Merge Cells**.

3) Alternatively, right-click on the selected cells and select **Merge Cells** from the context menu.

To split a group of cells that have been merged into a single cell:

1) Select the cell that contains merged cells.
2) Go to **Format > Split Cells** or right-click on the cell and select **Split Cells** from the context menu.

# Charts

A chart is a graphical interpretation of information that is contained in a spreadsheet. More information about charts and the use of charts is described in the *Calc Guide*.

## Inserting a chart

You can add a chart to your document as an OLE object or using the tools within Writer.

To add a chart using Writer's tools, choose **Insert > Chart** on the Menu bar to insert a generic chart (Figure 424) at the cursor location. The chart is selected and the Menu bar and toolbars change to those appropriate for charts.

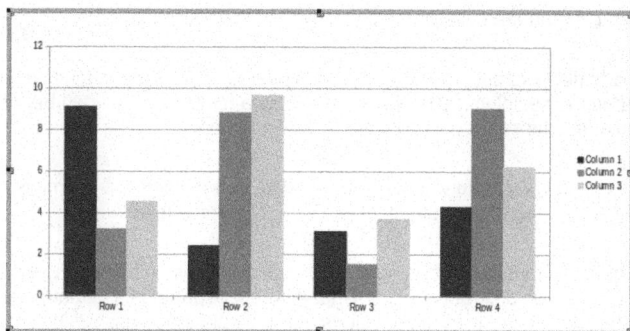

*Figure 424: Chart with sample data*

## Selecting chart type

Your data can be presented using a variety of different charts. Writer contains several chart types that will help you convey your message to your audience. See "Chart types" below.

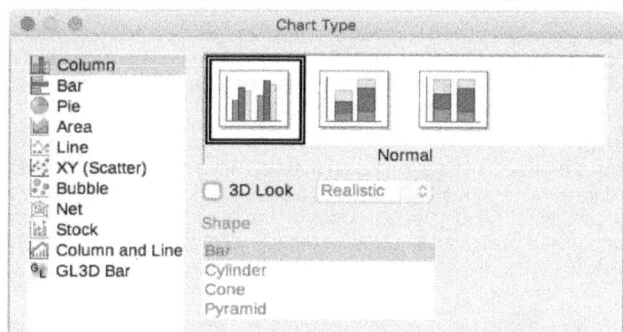

*Figure 425: Chart Type dialog showing two-dimensional charts*

1) Make sure that the chart is selected. The chart has a border and selection handles when selected.

2) Click the **Chart Type** icon on the Formatting toolbar or go to **Format > Chart Type** on the Menu bar, or right-click on the chart and select **Chart Type** from the context menu to open Chart Type dialog (Figure 425).

3) As you change selections in the left-hand list, the chart examples on the right change. Move the Chart Type dialog to one side to see the effect in the chart.

4) As you change chart types, other selections become available on the right-hand side. For example, some chart types have both 3D and 2D variants. When 3D charts are selected, more options become available for selection of shapes for the columns or bars.

5) Choose the chart characteristics you want and click **OK**. You return to the edit window.

6) Continue to format the chart, add data to the chart, or click outside the chart to return to normal view.

## Chart types

The following summary of the chart types available will help you choose a type suitable for your data. Column, bar, pie, and area charts are available as 2D or 3D types.

### Column charts

Column charts displays data that shows trends over time. This the default type of chart. It is recommended to use column charts where there is a relatively small number of data points. If you have a large time series as your data, it is recommended to use a line chart.

### Bar charts

Bar charts give an immediate visual impact for data comparison where time is not important, for example comparing the popularity of products in a marketplace.

### Pie charts

Pie charts give a comparison of proportions, for example, when comparing what different departments spent on different items or what different departments actually spent overall. They work best with a small range of values, for example six or less. Using larger range of values, the visual impact of a pie chart begins to fade.

### Area charts

Area charts are versions of line or column charts. They are useful when you want to emphasize volume of change. Area charts have a greater visual impact than a line chart, but the type of data you use does make a difference to the visual impact.

### Line charts

Line charts are time series with progression. Ideal for raw data and useful for charts with data showing trends or changes over time where you want to emphasize continuity. On line charts, the X-axis is ideal for representing time series data. 3D lines confuse the viewer, so just using a thicker line gives a better visual impact.

### Scatter or XY charts

Scatter charts are great for visualizing data that you have not had time to analyze and may be best for data where you have a constant value for comparison: for example weather data, reactions under different acidity levels, conditions at altitude, or any data which matches two numeric series. The X-axis usually plots the independent variable or control parameter (often a time series).

### Bubble charts

Bubble charts are used to represent three variables. Two variables identify the position of the center of a bubble on a Cartesian graph, while the third variable indicates the radius of the bubble.

**Net charts**

Net charts are similar to polar or radar graphs and are useful for comparing data not in time series, but show different circumstances, such as variables in a scientific experiment. The poles of the net chart are the Y-axes of other charts. Generally, between three and eight axes are best; any more and this type of chart becomes confusing.

**Stock charts**

Stock charts are specialized column graphs specifically used for stocks and shares. You can choose traditional lines, candlestick, and two-column charts. The data required for these charts is specialized with a series for opening price, closing price, and high and low prices. The X-axis represents a time series.

**Column and line charts**

Column and line charts are a combination of two other chart types. It is useful for combining two distinct, but related data series, for example sales over time (column) and the profit margin trends (line).

## Entering chart data

1) Make sure that the chart is selected and you have selected the chart type.
2) Click on the **Data Table** icon, or select **View > Data Table**, or right-click on the chart and select **Data Table** from the context menu to open the Data Table dialog (Figure 426).
3) Type or paste information into the cells within the desired rows and columns in the Data Table dialog. You can also use the icons in the top left corner of the Data Table dialog to insert, delete or move data.

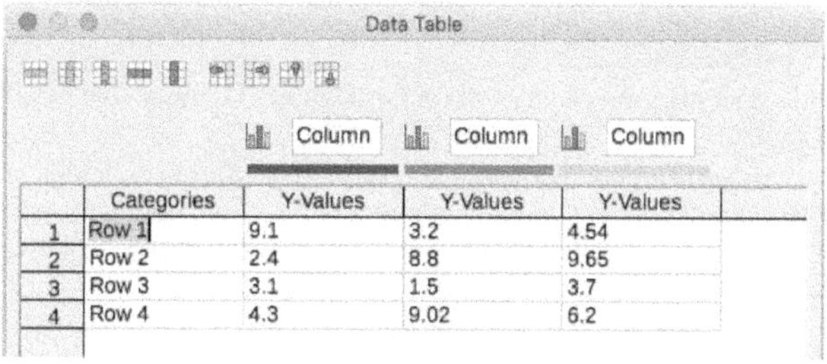

| | Categories | Y-Values | Y-Values | Y-Values |
|---|---|---|---|---|
| 1 | Row 1 | 9.1 | 3.2 | 4.54 |
| 2 | Row 2 | 2.4 | 8.8 | 9.65 |
| 3 | Row 3 | 3.1 | 1.5 | 3.7 |
| 4 | Row 4 | 4.3 | 9.02 | 6.2 |

*Figure 426: Chart Data Table dialog*

## Adding or removing chart elements

The specimen chart inserted into a document includes two elements: a chart wall and a chart legend (also known as the key). You can add or remove elements to or from a chart as follows:

1) Make sure the chart is selected and in edit mode.
2) Go to **Insert** on the Menu bar and select from the submenu an element that you want to add to the chart, or right-click on the chart wall or a chart element and select an element you want to add from the context menu. Selecting an element opens a dialog where you can specify options for the element.

**Note**

Right-clicking on a chart element will give you more options to choose from when adding elements to your chart. The number of available insert options in the context menu depends on the type of element selected.

3) To remove an element from a chart, right-click on the chart element you want to remove and select **Delete** from the context menu. The type of element selected for removal will change the delete options in the context menu.

4) Select a chart element and press the *Del* or *Backspace* (←) key to remove it from the chart.

## Chart formatting

To change the format of a selected chart:

1) Make sure the chart is selected and in edit mode.

2) Go to **Format** on the Menu bar and select from the submenu an element that you want to format, or right-click on a chart element and select a format option from the context menu. Selecting an element opens a dialog where you can specify format options for the element.

The formatting options available depend on whether the whole chart is selected or which chart element has been selected.

## Resizing and moving charts

You can resize or move a chart interactively or by using the Position and Size dialog. You can also use a combination of both methods.

### Resizing

To resize a chart interactively:

1) Click on a chart to select it. Selection handles appear around the chart.

2) To increase or decrease the height of a chart, click and drag on a selection handle at the top or bottom of the chart.

3) To increase or decrease the width of a chart, click and drag on a selection handle at the left or right of the chart.

4) To increase or decrease both the height and width of a chart at the same time , click and drag on a selection handle in one of the corners of the chart. To maintain the correct aspect ratio between height and width, hold the *Shift* key down while you click and drag.

### Moving

To move a chart interactively:

1) Click on the chart to select it. Selection handles appear around the chart.

2) Move the cursor anywhere on the chart other than on a selection handle.

3) When it changes shape, click and drag the chart to its new location.

4) Release the mouse button when the chart is in the desired position.

### Position and Size dialog

To resize or move a chart using the Position and Size dialog:

1) Click on the chart to select it.

2) Go to **Format > Position and Size** on the Menu bar, or right-click on the chart and select **Position and Size** from the context menu. For more information on using the Position and Size dialog, see Chapter 13, Images and Graphics.

## Chart elements

You can move or resize individual elements of a chart element independently of other chart elements. For example, you can move the chart legend to a different position. Pie charts allow individual wedges of the pie to be moved as well as "exploding" the entire pie.

1) Double-click the chart so that it is in edit mode.
2) Click any chart element to select it. Selection handles appear.
3) Move the cursor over the selected element and when the cursor changes shape, click and drag to move the element.
4) Release the mouse button when the element is in the desired position.

### Note

If the chart is 3D, round selection handles appear; these control the three-dimensional angle of the chart. You cannot resize or reposition the chart while the round selection handles are showing. *Shift+click* to get back to the square resizing handles. You can now resize and reposition the 3D chart.

## Changing chart area background

The chart area is the area surrounding the chart graphic and includes the (optional) main title and key.

1) Double-click the chart so that it is in edit mode.
2) Go to **Format > Chart Area** on the Menu bar, or right-click in the chart area and select **Format Chart Area**, or double-click in the chart area to open the Chart Area dialog.
3) Click on the *Area* tab and select the button corresponding to the type of background fill you want to use. The available options will change depending on the type of fill selected.
4) Make your selections and click **OK** to close the dialog and save the changes.

## Changing chart wall background

The chart wall is the area that contains the chart graphic.

1) Double-click the chart so that it is in edit mode.
2) Go to **Format > Format Selection** on the Menu bar, or right-click in the chart wall and select **Format Wall**, or double-click in the chart wall to open the Chart Wall dialog.
3) Click on the *Area* tab and proceed as above.
4) Click **OK** to close the dialog and save the changes.

# Audio and video

Although linked audio and video files are irrelevant when a Writer document is printed, if the document is opened on a computer or exported to PDF or HTML, you can play the files by clicking on the links.

## Using media files

To insert a media file into your document:

1) Choose **Insert > Media > Audio or Video** on the Menu bar to open the Insert Audio or Video dialog.
2) Select the media file to insert and click **Open** to place the object in the document.

### Tip

To see a list of audio and video file types supported by Writer, open the drop-down list of file types. This list defaults to *All audio and video files*, so you can also choose unsupported files such as .mov.

Writer only links media files and does not embed a media file into a document. Therefore if a document is moved to a different computer, any links will be broken and the media files will not play. To prevent this from happening:

1) Place any media files which are included in a document in the same folder where the document is stored.

2) Insert the media file in the document.

3) Send both the document and any media files to the computer which is to be used for the document and place both files in the same folder on that computer.

## Using the Gallery

To insert media clips directly from the Gallery:

1) Go to the Gallery in the Sidebar.

2) Browse to a theme containing media files (for example, Sounds).

3) Click on the movie or sound to be inserted and drag it into the document area.

## Media playback

The Media Playback toolbar is automatically opened when a media file is selected. The default position of the toolbar is at the bottom of the workspace, just above the Drawing toolbar. However, this toolbar can be undocked and placed anywhere. If the toolbar does not open, go to **View > Toolbars > Media Playback** on the Menu bar.

The Media Playback toolbar contains the following tools:

- Insert Audio or Video – opens the Insert Audio or Video dialog.
- Play, Pause, Stop – controls media playback.
- Repeat – if selected, media will continuously repeat playing until this tool is de-selected.
- Playback slider – selects the position to start playing from within the media file.
- Timer – displays current position of the media clip and length of media file.
- Mute – when selected, the sound will be suppressed.
- Volume slider – adjusts the volume of the media file.
- Media path – the location of the file on the computer.
- Scaling drop-down menu – only available for movies and allows scaling of the movie clip.

# Formulas

Go to **Insert > Object > Formula** on the Menu bar to create a formula (equation). A formula can also be inserted as an OLE object.

When creating or editing a formula, the Math menu becomes available.

When creating formulas, take care about font sizes used to make sure they are similar in size to fonts used in the document. To change font attributes of a Math object, go to **Format > Font Size** on the Menu bar. To change font type, use **Format > Fonts**.

For information on how to create formulas, see the *Math Guide* or Chapter 9, Getting Started with Math, in the *Getting Started Guide*.

# LibreOffice

# Chapter 20
# Setting up Writer

Choosing options to suit the way you work

# Introduction

This chapter briefly presents some of the setup options found under **Tools > Options** on the Menu bar. Additional options, and more details about the ones given here, are covered in the Help and in Chapter 2, Setting up LibreOffice, in the *Getting Started Guide*.

Several of the most relevant options are discussed in other chapters of this book, in the context of tasks where they are most applicable.

> ### Tip
>
> Many options are intended for power users and programmers. If you don't understand what an option does, leave it on the default setting unless instructions in this book recommend changing the setting.

# Choosing options that affect all LibreOffice components

This section covers some of the settings that apply to all the components of LibreOffice (Writer, Calc, Impress, Draw, Math, and Base) and that are particularly important when using Writer.

To navigate to options that govern all LibreOffice components, click **Tools > Options** and then click the marker (+ or triangle) by **LibreOffice** on the left-hand side. A list of pages drops down. Select an item in the list to display the relevant page on the right-hand side of the dialog.

> ### Tip
>
> The **Reset** button (located in the lower right of any page of the Options dialog) resets the values on that page to the values that were in place when you opened the dialog.

If you are using a version of LibreOffice other than US English, some field labels may be different from those shown in the illustrations.

## User data

Because Writer can use the name or initials stored in the *LibreOffice – User Data* page for several things, including document properties ('created by' and 'last edited by' information), the name of the author of comments and changes, and the sender address in mailing lists, you will want to ensure that the correct information appears here. If you do not want user data to be part of the document's properties, clear the box at the bottom.

## General options

Among the options on the *LibreOffice – General* page is **Open/Save dialogs – Use LibreOffice dialogs**. When this option is selected, the Open and Save dialogs supplied with LibreOffice will be used. Usually this selection is a matter of personal preference; however, a few features (such as accessing remote servers, as described in Chapter 1) require the use of LibreOffice dialogs. This book uses the LibreOffice Open and Save dialogs in illustrations.

## Memory options

The options on the *LibreOffice – Memory* page control how LibreOffice uses your computer's memory and how much memory it requires.

This page includes the option for enabling or disabling the Quickstarter, where this feature is available. It is not available on MacOS or on systems where the Quickstarter module has not been installed. For more about Quickstarter, see Chapter 1.

## View options

The options on the *LibreOffice – View* page affect how the document window looks and behaves. Set them to suit your personal preferences. For details, see the Help or Chapter 2, Setting up LibreOffice, in the *Getting Started Guide*.

## Print options

On the *LibreOffice – Print* page, set the print options to suit your default printer and your most common printing method.

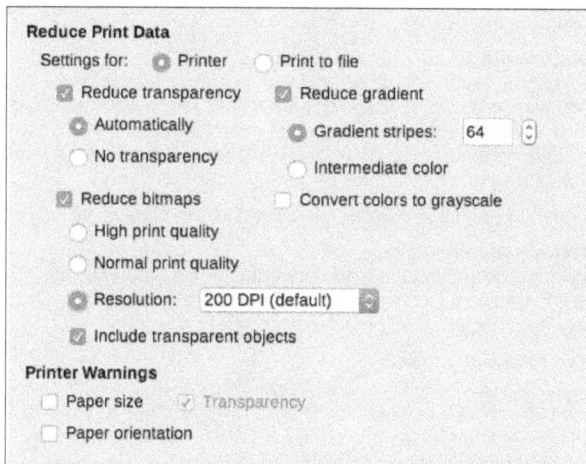

*Figure 427: Choosing general printing options to apply to all LibreOffice components*

In the *Printer warnings* section near the bottom of the page, you can choose whether to be warned if the paper size or orientation specified in your document does not match the paper size or orientation available for your printer. Having these warnings turned on can be quite helpful, particularly if you work with documents produced by people in other countries where the standard paper size is different from yours.

> **Tip**
>
> If your printouts are incorrectly placed on the page or chopped off at the top, bottom, or sides, or the printer is refusing to print, a likely cause is incorrect page size in printer settings.

## Paths options

On the *LibreOffice – Paths* page, you can change the location of files associated with, or used by, LibreOffice to suit your needs. For example, you might want to store documents by default somewhere other than My Documents.

## Fonts options

If you receive a document containing fonts that you do not have on your system, LibreOffice will use substitute fonts for those it does not find. On the *LibreOffice – Fonts* page, you can specify a font different from the one the program chooses.

> **Note**
>
> These choices do not affect the default font for your documents. To do that, you need to create a new default template for Writer documents as described in Chapter 10, Working with Templates.

## Security options

Use the *LibreOffice – Security* page to choose security options for saving documents and for opening documents that contain macros. If you need information on the options not discussed here, refer to the Help or to the *Getting Started Guide*.

### Security options and warnings

If you record changes, save multiple versions, or include hidden information or notes in your documents, and you do not want some recipients to see that information, you can set warnings to remind you to remove it, or you can have LibreOffice remove some of it automatically. Note that unless the information is removed, much of it is retained even when the file has been saved to other formats, including PDF.

Click the **Options** button to open a separate dialog with several options, including the following.

### Remove personal information on saving

Select this option to always remove user data from the file properties when saving the file. To save personal information with documents and still be able to manually remove personal information only from specific documents, do not select this option.

### Ctrl-click required to follow hyperlinks

The default behavior in LibreOffice is that using *Ctrl+click* on a hyperlink opens the linked document or website. This is because many people find writing and editing documents easier when accidental clicks on links do not activate the links. To set LibreOffice to activate hyperlinks using just an ordinary click, deselect this option.

## Application colors

Writing, editing, and (especially) page layout are often easier when you can see the page margins (text boundaries), the boundaries of tables and sections, grid lines, and other features. In addition, you might prefer to use colors that are different from LibreOffice's defaults.

On the *LibreOffice – Application colors* page (Figure 428), you can specify which user interface elements are visible and the colors used to display them.

- To show or hide items such as text boundaries, select or deselect the boxes in the *On* column next to the names of the elements.
- To change the default colors for a specific element, click the down-arrow in the *Color setting* column by the name of the element and select a color from the drop-down list.
- To save your color changes as a color scheme, click **Save**, type a name in the Scheme box, and then click **OK**.

> **Note**
>
> To change the color settings used in Track Changes mode, go to **Tools > Options > LibreOffice Writer > Changes**.

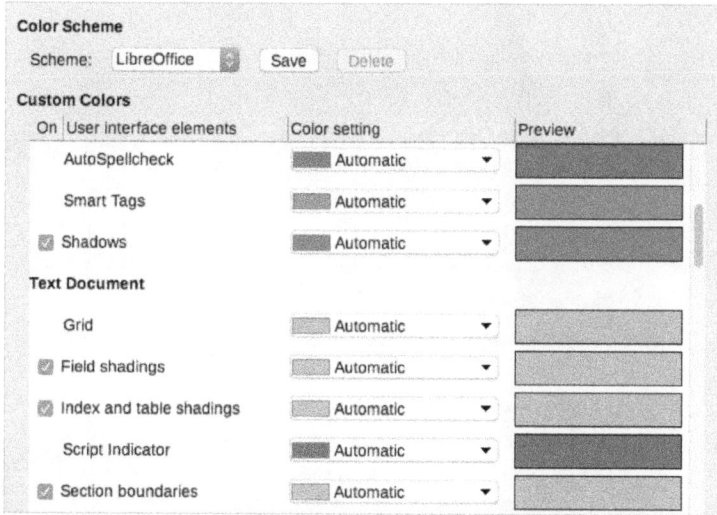

*Figure 428: Showing or hiding text, object, and table boundaries*

# Choosing options for loading and saving documents

You can set the options for loading and saving documents to suit the way you work.

If the Options dialog is not already open, click **Tools > Options**. Click the expansion symbol (+ or triangle) to the left of **Load/Save**.

## General

Most of the choices on the *Load/Save – General* page (Figure 429) are familiar to users of other office suites. Some items of interest are described below.

### Load user-specific settings with the document

When a LibreOffice document is saved, certain settings from the user's system are saved with it. When the document is opened on another user's system, it will use the settings saved from the previous user's system. Deselecting this option causes the current user's settings to override the settings previously saved with the document.

Even if you deselect this option, some settings are always loaded with the document:

- Settings available in **File > Print > Options**.

- Name of Fax.

- Spacing options for paragraphs before text tables.

- Information about automatic updating for links, field functions, and charts.

- Information about working with Asian character formats.

**Note**

The settings for any data sources linked to a document are always loaded with the document, whether or not the option *Load user-specific settings with the document* is selected.

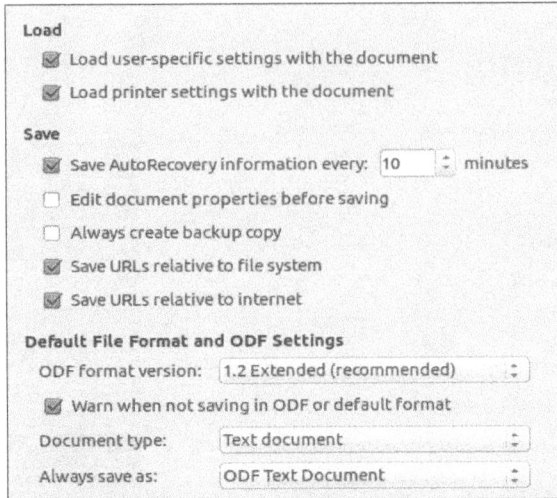
*Figure 429: Choosing Load and Save options*

### Load printer settings with the document
If this option is enabled, the printer settings of the previous user will be loaded with the document. In an office setting, this may cause a document to be printed on a distant network printer unless the printer is manually changed in the Print dialog. If disabled, the current user's default printer will be used to print the document. The current printer settings will be stored with the document whether or not this option is selected.

### Save AutoRecovery information every __ minutes
Choose whether to enable AutoRecovery and how often to save the information used by the AutoRecovery process. AutoRecovery in LibreOffice saves the information needed to restore all open documents in case of a crash. If you have this option set, recovering your document after a system crash will be easier.

### Edit document properties before saving
If this option is selected, the document's Properties dialog pops up to prompt you to enter relevant information the first time you save a new document (or whenever you use **Save As**).

### Always create backup copy
Saves the previously-saved version of a document as a backup copy in a separate folder whenever you save a document. When LibreOffice creates a new backup copy, the previous backup copy is replaced. To see or change the backup folder, go to **Tools > Options > LibreOffice > Paths**. When opening a backup file, you will be prompted to specify the program to open it with; choose LibreOffice.

► **Tip**

Authors whose work may be very lengthy should always consider enabling LibreOffice to create an automatic backup copy.

### Save URLs relative to file system / to internet
Use these options to select the default for relative addressing of URLs in the file system and on the Internet. For details, see Chapter 2, Setting up LibreOffice, in the *Getting Started Guide*.

### Default file format and ODF settings

**ODF format version:** LibreOffice by default saves documents in OpenDocument Format (ODF) version 1.2 Extended. You will rarely need to change this for compatibility when exchanging files with other people.

**Document type:** If you routinely share documents with users of Microsoft Word, you might want to change the **Always save as** option to one of the Word formats. However, you can choose a Word format when you save any individual file.

## Microsoft Office

On the *Load/Save – Microsoft Office* page, you can choose what to do when importing and exporting Microsoft Office OLE objects (linked or embedded objects or documents such as equations or spreadsheets): convert them into or from the corresponding LibreOffice OLE object or load and save them in their original format.

## HTML compatibility

Choices made on the *Load/Save – HTML Compatibility* page (not shown) affect HTML pages imported into LibreOffice and those exported from LibreOffice. See *HTML documents; HTML import and export* in the Help, and Chapter 2 in the *Getting Started Guide*, for more information.

# Choosing Writer-specific options

Settings chosen in the LibreOffice Writer section of the Options dialog determine how Writer documents look and behave while you are working on them.

If the Options dialog is not already open, choose **Tools > Options**. Click the marker (+ or triangle) by **LibreOffice Writer** on the left side of the dialog.

## General options

The choices on the *LibreOffice Writer – General* page affect the updating of links and fields, the units used for rulers and other measurements, and the default tab stop positions.

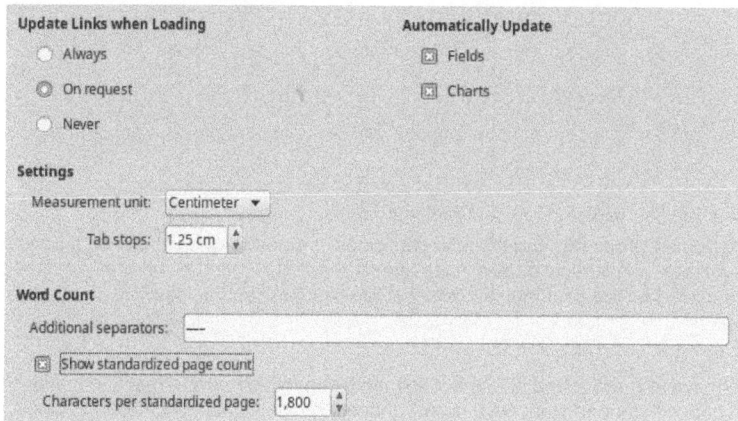

*Figure 430: Choosing general options for Writer*

**Update links when loading**

Depending on your work patterns, you may not want links to be updated when you load a document. For example, if your file links to other files on a network, you won't want those links to try to update when you are not connected to the network.

**Update fields and charts automatically**
You may not want fields or charts to update automatically while you are working, because that slows down performance.

**Settings – Tab stops**
The Tab stops setting specifies the distance the cursor travels for each press of the *Tab* key. This setting is also used for the indent distance applied by the **Increase Indent** and **Decrease Indent** buttons on the Formatting Toolbar, which affect the indentation of entire paragraphs.

▶ **Tip**

To avoid unwanted changes, do not rely on default tab settings. Rather, define your own tabs in paragraph styles or individual paragraphs (see "Defining your own tab stops and indents" in Chapter 4, Formatting Text).

**Word Count – Additional separators**
For counting words, specifies the characters that are considered to separate words, in addition to spaces, tabs, line breaks, and paragraph breaks.

**Word Count – Show standardized page count**
Editors and publishers often define a "standard" page as containing a specified number of characters or words; this field allows quick calculation of the number of these pages.

## View options

Two pages of options set the defaults for viewing Writer documents: *View* (described here) and *Formatting Aids* (described below).

*View* is a good page to check if, for example, you cannot see graphics on the screen.

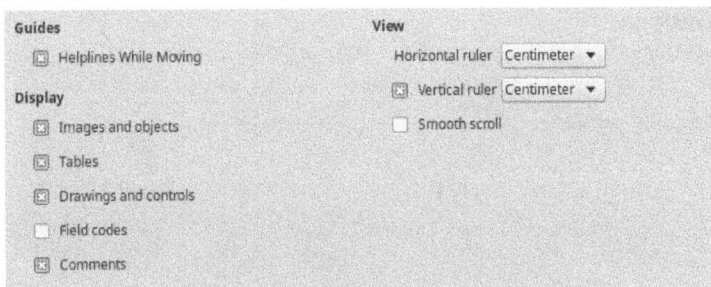

*Figure 431: Choosing View options for Writer*

Enabling **Helplines While Moving** helps to precisely position a drawing object on a page. When enabled, horizontal and vertical parallel lines appear that are the height and width of the object. These lines extend across the complete working area as the object is moved.

▶ **Tip**

If you have inserted a field but do not see the text or number you expect, uncheck Field codes here. Example: *Date (fixed)* appears on the screen when Field codes is enabled, while *21/07/17* appears when it is disabled.

## Formatting Aids options

On the *LibreOffice Writer – Formatting Aids* page (Figure 432), select the desired options.

The *Display of* options determine which symbols show when you select View > Formatting Marks from the Menu bar or the Formatting Marks icon in the Standard toolbar. Symbols such as paragraph ends and tabs can help in writing, editing, and page layout. For example, they can show if there are any blank paragraphs or if any tables or graphics are too wide and intrude into the margins of the page.

### Note

*Direct cursor* lets you enter text, images, tables, frames, and other objects in any blank area in your document. Writer then inserts blank paragraphs, tabs, spaces and so on to position the text or objects. However, this feature can lead to many formatting oddities and is incompatible with rigorous use of styles, so it should be avoided.

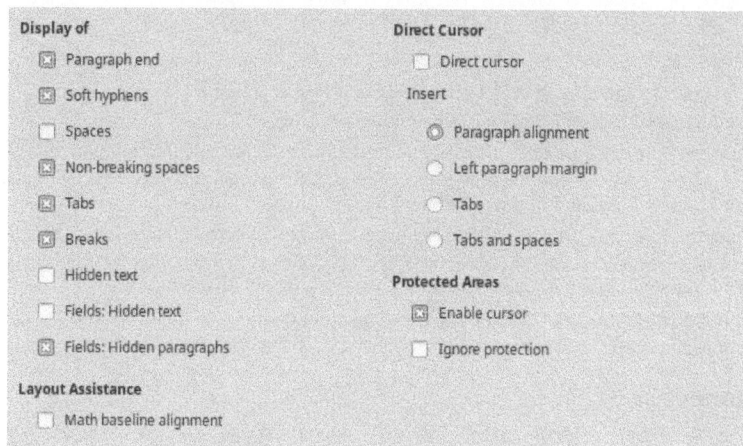

Figure 432: Choosing Formatting Aids options

## Grid options

*Snap to grid* automatically moves an object to the nearest gridlines. This can be very helpful when you are trying to align several objects such as graphics or tables.

On the *LibreOffice Writer – Grid* page, you can choose whether to enable this feature and what grid intervals to use. If the grid intervals (subdivisions) are too large, you may find that you do not have enough control in placing the objects.

## Print options

On the *LibreOffice Writer – Print* page, you can choose which items are printed with a Writer document by default. These options are in addition to the general options for all LibreOffice components on the *LibreOffice – Print* page (see page 429).

### Tip

You can override any of these defaults when printing a specific document. Click **File > Print**, then use the options on the various pages of the Print dialog.

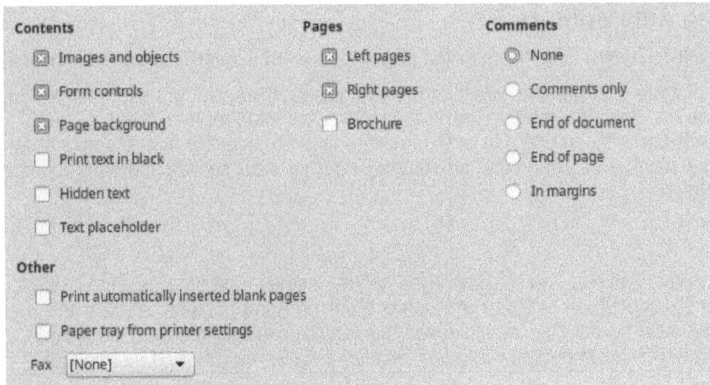

| Contents | Pages | Comments |
|---|---|---|
| ☒ Images and objects | ☒ Left pages | ○ None |
| ☒ Form controls | ☒ Right pages | ○ Comments only |
| ☒ Page background | ☐ Brochure | ○ End of document |
| ☐ Print text in black | | ○ End of page |
| ☐ Hidden text | | ○ In margins |
| ☐ Text placeholder | | |

**Other**

☐ Print automatically inserted blank pages

☐ Paper tray from printer settings

Fax [None] ▼

*Figure 433: Choosing Print options for Writer*

Some considerations:

- When you are working on drafts and you want to save printer ink or toner, you might want to deselect some of the items in the *Contents* section.
- The **Print text in black** option causes color text (but not graphics) to print as black on a color printer; on a black-and-white printer, this option causes color text to print as solid black instead of shades of gray (dithered).
- By comparison, the **Convert colors to grayscale** option on the **Options – LibreOffice – Print** page (Figure 427), prints all text and graphics as grayscale on color printers. (On black-and-white printers, color in graphics normally prints as grayscale.)
- If you are printing double-sided on a non-duplexing printer, you might choose to print only left or right pages, then turn the stack over and print the other pages.

## Table options

On the *LibreOffice Writer – Table* page (Figure 434), you can specify the default behavior of tables. See the Help or Chapter 13, Tables, for more information.

Some considerations:

- If most of your tables will require borders or headings, select those options. If most of your tables are used for page layout, deselect **Border** and **Heading**.
- Select **Do not split** to prevent tables from being split across pages.*Number recognition* can be very useful if most of your tables contain numerical data. Writer will recognize dates or currency, for example, and format the numbers appropriately. However, if you want the numbers to remain as ordinary text, this feature can be quite irritating, so you may want to deselect it.
- The *Keyboard handling* section specifies the distances that cells move when you use keyboard shortcuts to move them and the size of rows and columns inserted using keyboard shortcuts. If you don't use keyboard shortcuts for this purpose, you can ignore these settings. See the Help for more information.
- The *Behavior of rows/columns* section specifies the effects that changes to rows or columns have on adjacent rows or columns and the entire table. You might need to test these selections to fully understand the effects.

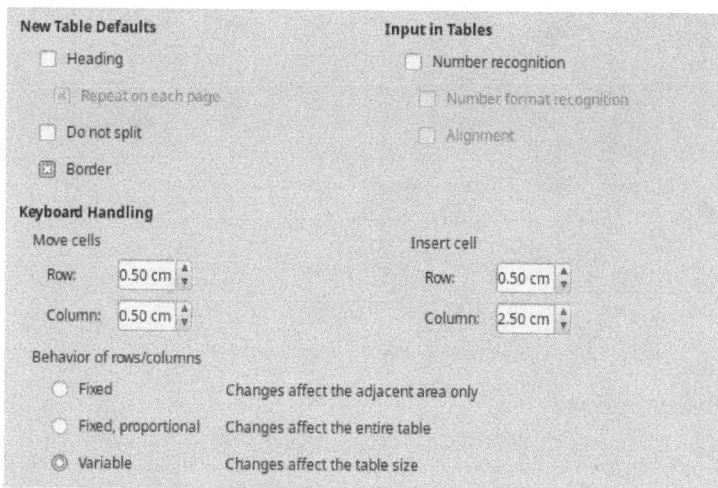

*Figure 434: Choosing default Table options*

# Changes options

If you plan to use the change-tracking feature of Writer (described in Chapter 3, Working with Text: Advanced), use the *LibreOffice Writer – Changes* page to choose the way changes to text and formatting are marked. Change bars can show wherever a change has been made to a line of text and are formatted under Lines Changed.

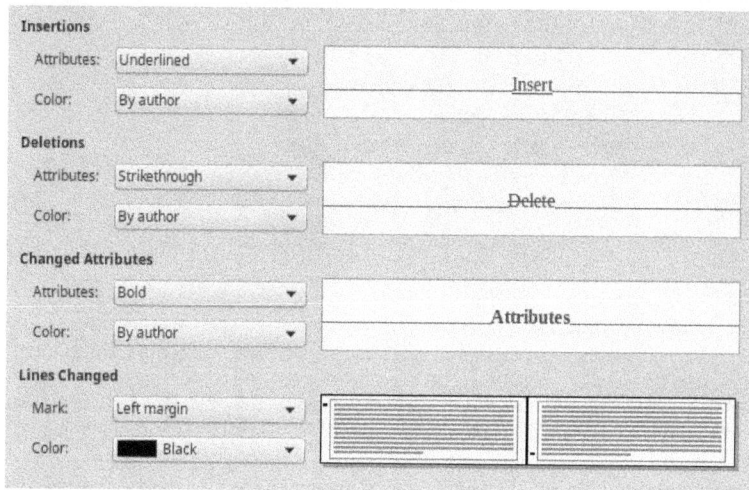

*Figure 435: Choosing options for tracking changes*

# Comparison options

The options on the *LibreOffice Writer – Comparison* page determine the level of detail used by the Compare Document feature (**Edit > Track Changes > Compare Document**), described in Chapter 3, Working with Text: Advanced.

---

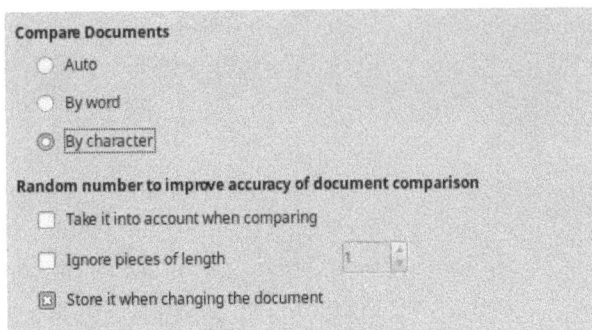

*Figure 436: Options for comparing documents*

## Compatibility options

The settings on the *LibreOffice Writer – Compatibility* page (Figure 437) are used mainly when importing documents from Microsoft Word. If you are not sure about the effects of these settings, leave them as the defaults provided by LibreOffice. For information about settings that are not described below, see the Help. All settings selected will apply only to the current document.

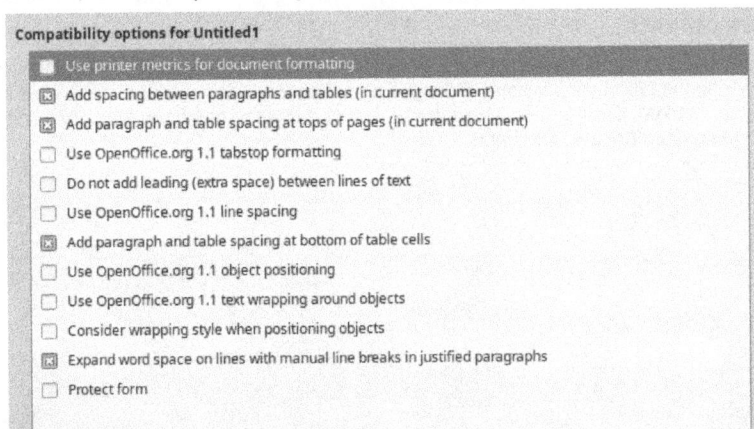

*Figure 437: Choosing compatibility options*

### Use printer metrics for document formatting

If this option is selected, the printer specified for the document determines how the document is formatted for viewing on screen. The line breaks and paragraph breaks you see on screen match those that apply when the document is printed on that printer. If this option is not selected, a printer-independent layout will be used for screen display and printing.

This setting can be useful when several people are reviewing a document that will eventually be printed on a specific printer or when the document is exported to PDF (a process that treats "Adobe PDF" as the printer).

### Add spacing between paragraphs and tables (in current document)

Paragraph spacing is treated differently in LibreOffice Writer than it is in Microsoft Word. If you have defined spacing between paragraphs or tables in LibreOffice, this spacing is added to the spacing defined in Microsoft Word.

---

If this option is selected, Microsoft Word-compatible spacing is added between paragraphs and tables in LibreOffice Writer documents.

**Add paragraph and table spacing at tops of pages (in current document)**
You can define paragraphs and tables to have space appear before (above) them. If this option is selected, any space above a paragraph will also appear if the paragraph is at the beginning of a page or column, or if the paragraph is positioned on the first page of the document, or after a manual page break.

If you import a Microsoft Word document, the spaces are automatically added during the conversion.

**Add paragraph and table spacing at bottom of table cells**
Specifies that the bottom spacing is added to a paragraph, even when it is the last paragraph in a table cell.

**Use as Default**
Click this button to use the settings on this page as the default in Writer.

## AutoCaption options

LibreOffice can automatically insert captions for tables, pictures, frames, and OLE objects in a Writer document. To set this up, use the options on the **LibreOffice Writer > AutoCaption** page. Select the object you want to be automatically captioned (**LibreOffice Writer Image** in Figure 438). With the item highlighted, specify the characteristics of the caption.

**Note**

You may not want captions for every table, for example if you use tables for layout as well as for tables of data. You can always add captions to individual tables, graphics, or other objects (*right-click* > **Insert Caption**).

The categories supplied for captions are **Drawing**, **Illustration**, **Table**, and **Text**. To use another name (for example, **Figure**) for the caption label, type the required term in the Category box.

Information about numbering captions by chapter, character styles, frame styles, and other items on the AutoCaption page is given in other chapters in this book.

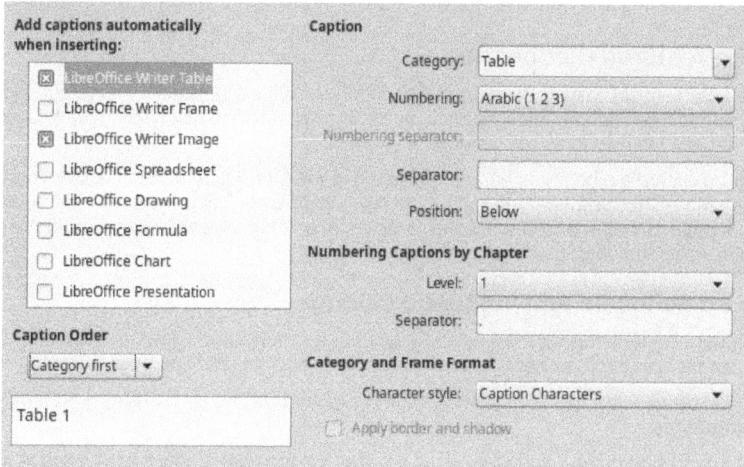

*Figure 438: Setting up automatic captions*

## Mail Merge E-mail options

Using a data source such as an address book, Writer can insert personal, address, and other information into form letters. These documents can be printed for mailing or they can be e-mailed through Writer. (See Chapter 14, Using Mail Merge, for details.)

Use the *LibreOffice Writer – Mail Merge E-mail* page to set up the user and server information for sending form letters by e-mail. If you are not sure what information to put in any of the fields, consult your e-mail program or your internet service provider.

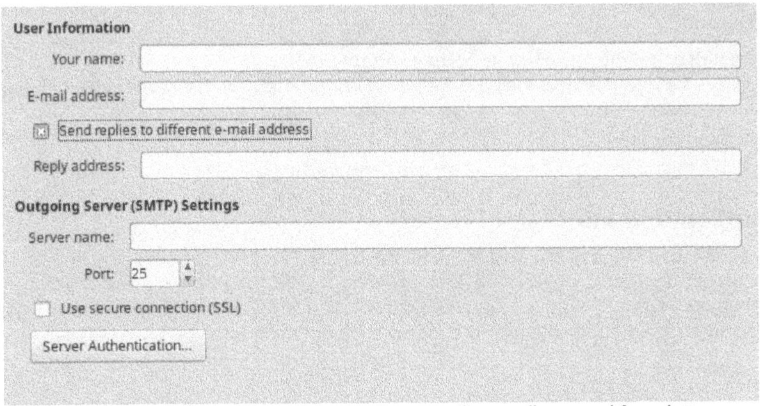

*Figure 439: Specifying settings for use when emailing mail-merged form letters*

# Choosing language settings

You may need to do several things to set the language settings you want:

- Install the required dictionaries.
- Change some locale and language settings.
- Choose spelling and grammar options.

## Install the required dictionaries

LibreOffice automatically installs many language modules with the program. A language module can contain up to three submodules: spelling dictionary, hyphenation dictionary, and thesaurus. These are usually referred to as "dictionaries" in Writer.

To add other dictionaries, be sure you are connected to the Internet, and then choose **Tools > Language > More Dictionaries Online** from the Menu bar. LibreOffice will open your default web browser to a page containing links to additional dictionaries that you can install. Follow the prompts to select and install the ones you want.

## Change some locale and language settings

You can change some details of the locale and language settings that LibreOffice uses for all documents or for specific documents. See the Help for details on all these options.

In the Options dialog, click the expansion symbol (+ sign or triangle) by **Language Settings** and choose **Languages**.

On the right-hand side of the *Language Settings – Languages* page (Figure 440), change the settings as required. In the example, English (USA) has been chosen for all the appropriate settings, but you could choose a mixture of languages. For example, if you were working in Germany, you might prefer the user interface to be in English (USA), but German (Germany) for the Locale setting, which influences settings for numbering, currency, and units of measure.

If you want the language setting to apply to the current document only, instead of being the default for all new documents, select **For the current document only**.

Changes to the system input language/keyboard normally affect text typed into a document after the change. If you do not want this to happen, select **Ignore system input language**; new text will then continue to follow the language of the document or the paragraph, not the system language.

If necessary, select the options to enable support for Asian languages (Chinese, Japanese, Korean) and support for CTL (complex text layout) languages such as Hindi, Thai, Hebrew, and Arabic. If you choose either of these options, the next time you open the Options dialog, you will see some extra pages under **Language Settings**, as shown in the right side of Figure 441. These pages (Searching in Japanese, Asian Layout, and Complex Text Layout) are not discussed here.

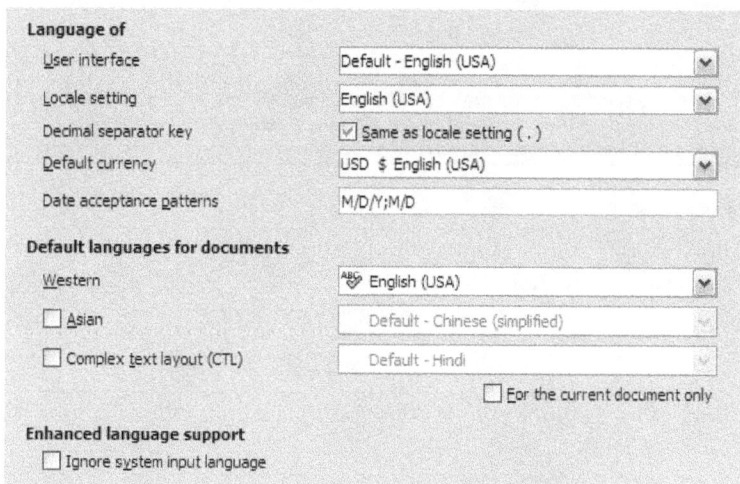

Figure 440: Choosing language options

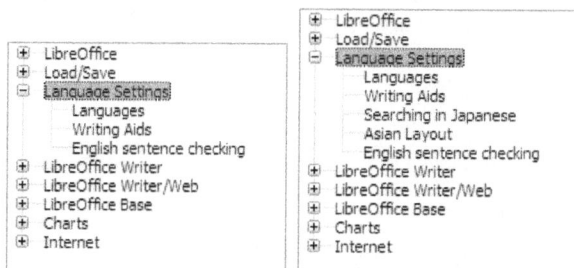

Figure 441: LibreOffice language options, with Asian language options enabled on the right side

## Sentence checking

LibreOffice can check sentences in several languages, including English, Hungarian, Russian, and Brazilian Portuguese. These checkers are enabled by default if the language is the computer's default language. The set of rules available for these sentence checkers depends on the language.

## Choose spelling and grammar options

To change the options for checking spelling and grammar, use the *Language Settings > Writing Aids* page (Figure 442). Some considerations:

- If you do not want spelling checked while you type, deselect **Check spelling as you type**. (You can over-ride this setting in a document using **Tools > Automatic Spell Checking** on the Menu bar or the **Auto Spellcheck** icon on the Standard toolbar.)

- If you want grammar to be checked as you type, you must have **Check spelling as you type** enabled too.

- **Check special regions** means that text in headers, footers, frames, and tables are also checked when checking spelling.

Here you can also select which of the user-defined (custom) dictionaries are active, add a new custom dictionary, edit dictionaries, and delete custom dictionaries. Dictionaries installed by the system cannot be deleted.

► **Tip**

When checking spelling, words marked "Add to Dictionary" are added by default to the Standard dictionary. Words marked "Ignore All" are added to the IgnoreAllList dictionary. See Chapter 2, Working with Text: Basics.

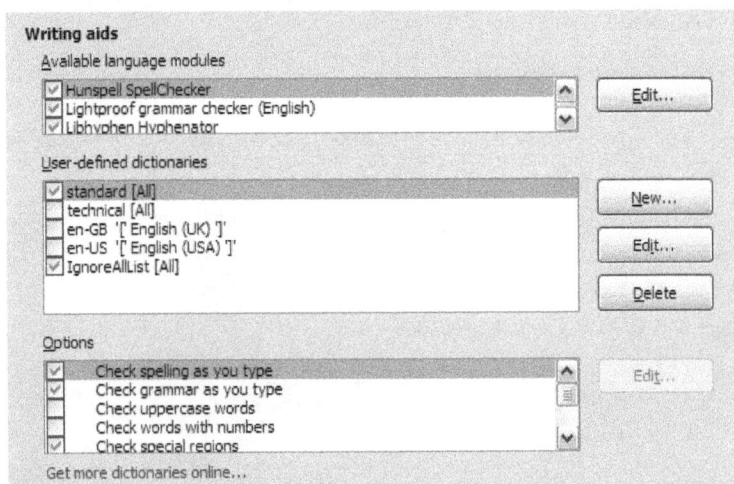

*Figure 442: Choosing languages, dictionaries, and options for checking spelling*

## English sentence checking

On the *Language Settings > English sentence checking* page, you can choose which items are checked for, reported to you, or converted automatically. This menu is also found in the English dictionaries extension installed by default by LibreOffice (select **Tools > Extension Manager**, select **English spelling dictionaries** and click the **Options** button to reveal the menu). Select which of the optional features you wish to check. These are described in Chapter 2, Working with Text: Basics.

After selecting the additional grammar checks, you must restart LibreOffice, or reload the document, for them to take effect.

# LibreOffice

*Chapter 21*
*Customizing Writer*

# Introduction

This chapter describes some common customizations that you may wish to do, in addition to the options described in Chapter 20, Setting up Writer.

You can customize menus, toolbars, and keyboard shortcuts in LibreOffice, add new menus and toolbars, and assign macros to events.

Other customizations are made easy by extensions that you can install from the LibreOffice website or from other providers.

### Note

Customizations to menus and toolbars can be saved in a template. To do so, first save them in a document and then save the document as a template as described in Chapter 10, Working with Templates.

# Customizing menu content

You can add to and rearrange menus on the Menu bar, add commands to menus, and make other changes. You can also modify context (right-click) menus in a similar way.

To customize menus:

1) Choose **Tools > Customize**.
2) On the Customize dialog, go to the *Menus* page (Figure 443) or the *Context Menus* page.

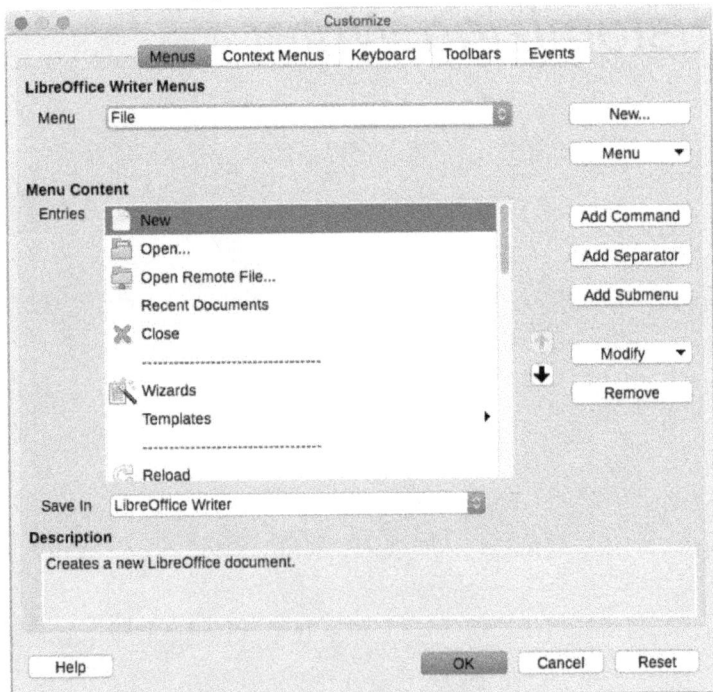

*Figure 443: The Menus page of the Customize dialog*

3) In the *LibreOffice Writer Menus* section, select from the *Menu* drop-down list the menu that you want to customize. The list includes all the main menus as well as submenus, that is menus that are contained under another menu. For example, in addition to File, Edit, View, and so on, there are File | Send, File | Templates, and others. The commands contained in the selected menu are shown in the central part of the dialog (*Menu Content*).

4) In the *Save In* drop-down list below the Menu Content box, choose whether to save this changed menu for the application (Writer) or for a selected document.

5) To customize the selected menu, click one of the buttons on the right of the *Entries* list. These actions are described in the following sections. Use the up and down arrows next to the *Entries* list to move the selected command to a different position.

6) When you have finished making all your changes, click **OK** to save them.

## Creating a new menu

On the *Menus* page of the Customize dialog, click **New** to display the New Menu dialog (Figure 444). (Not available for context menus.)

1) Type a name for the new menu in the *Menu name* box.

2) Use the up and down arrow buttons to move the new menu into the required position on the Menu bar.

3) Click **OK** to save.

The new menu now appears on the list of menus in the Customize dialog. (It will appear on the Menu bar itself after you save your customizations.)

After creating a new menu, you need to add some commands to it, as described in "Adding a command, a separator, or a submenu to a menu" on page 446.

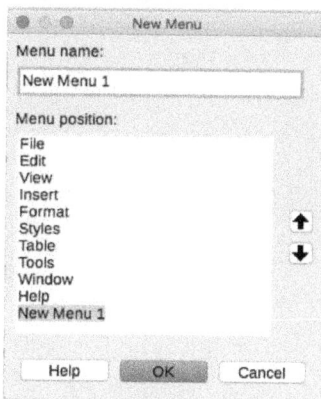

*Figure 444: Adding a new menu*

## Modifying existing menus

To modify an existing menu, select it in the *Menu* list and click the **Menu** button to drop down a list of modifications: **Move**, **Rename**, **Delete**. Not all of these modifications can be applied to all the entries in the *Menu* list. For example, **Rename** and **Delete** are not available for the supplied menus, and **Move** is not available for submenus.

To move a menu (such as File), click the **Menu** button and select **Move**. A dialog similar to the one shown in Figure 444 (but without the *Menu name* box) opens. Use the up and down arrow buttons to move the menu into the required position.

To move commands (such as Close) and submenus (such as File | Send), select the main menu item (File) in the Menu list and then, in the Menu Content section of the Customize dialog, select the command or submenu (Send) in the *Entries* list and use the arrow icons to move it up or down in the sequence. Submenus are easily identified in the *Entries* list by a small black triangle on the right hand side of the name.

To move the commands on a submenu, select the submenu in the *Menu* list and then, in the Menu Content section of the Customize dialog, select the command and use the arrow icons to move it up or down in the sequence.

To rename a custom menu, select it in the *Menu* list, click the **Menu** button, and select **Rename**.

To rename a menu item or a submenu, select the item in the *Entries* list, click the **Modify** button and select **Rename**.

### Note

Changes to the menus are not immediately displayed. Changes saved to LibreOffice Writer's menu are displayed the next time Writer is opened. Changes saved to a document's menu are displayed the next time the document is opened.

## Adding a command, a separator, or a submenu to a menu

You can add commands to both the supplied menus and menus you have created. On the Customize dialog, select the menu in the Menu list and click the **Add Command** button in the Menu Content section of the dialog. The Add Commands dialog (Figure 445) is displayed.

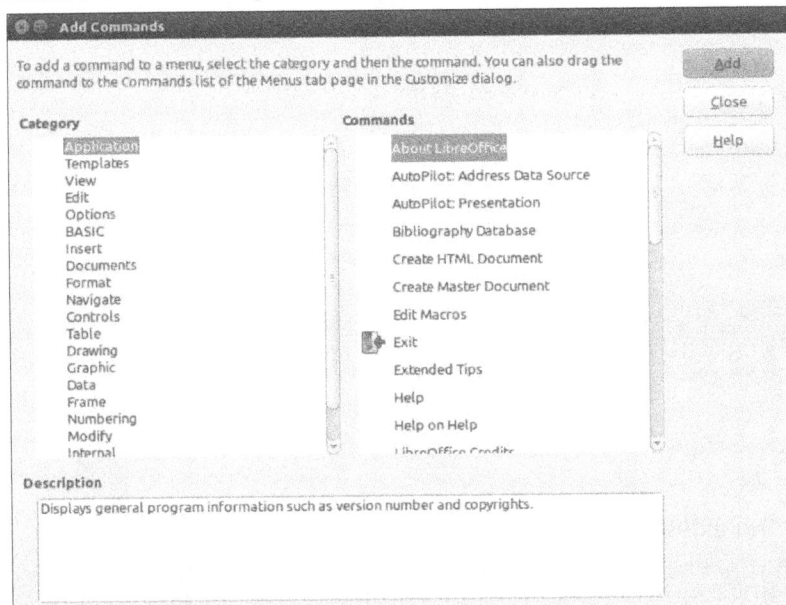

*Figure 445: Adding a command to a menu*

On the Add Commands dialog, select a category and then the command, and click **Add**. The dialog remains open, so you can select several commands. When you have finished adding commands, click **Close**. Back on the Customize dialog, you can use the up and down arrow buttons to arrange the commands in your preferred sequence.

In addition to adding commands, you can add submenus and group separators by clicking the appropriate button on the Customize dialog.

After adding a submenu, you can select it in the Menu list in the top section of the page and add commands to it. A separator line is added after the highlighted entry.

# Customizing toolbars

You can customize toolbars in several ways, including choosing which icons are visible and locking the position of a docked toolbar (as described in Chapter 1, Introducing Writer), and adding or deleting icons (commands) in the list of those available on a toolbar. You can also create new toolbars. The controls on the *Toolbars* page of the Customize dialog (Figure 446) are similar to those on the *Menus* page.

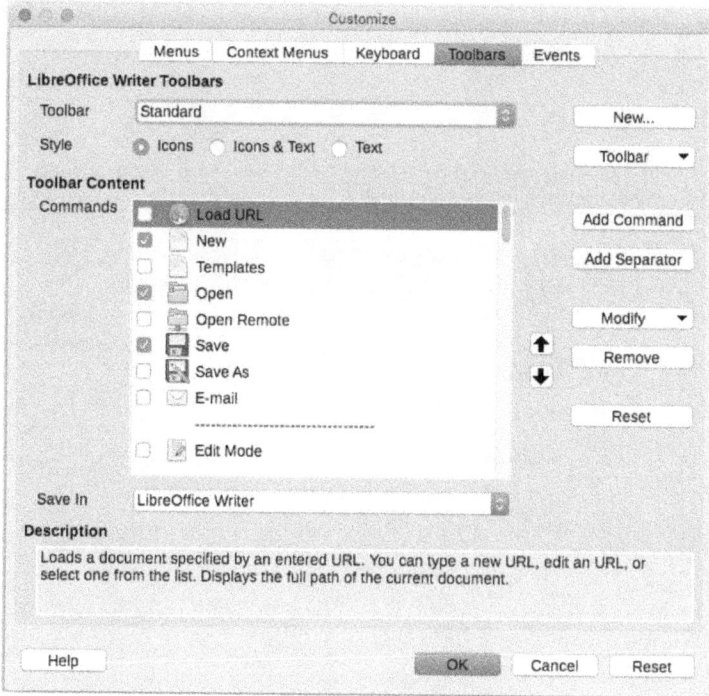

Figure 446: The Toolbars page of the Customize dialog

## Choosing icons for toolbar commands

Toolbar buttons usually have icons, not words, on them, but not all of the commands have associated icons.

To choose an icon for a command, select the command in the Toolbar Content – Commands list in the Customize dialog, and click **Modify > Change icon**. On the Change Icon dialog, scroll through the available icons, select one, and click **OK** to assign it to the command.

To use a custom icon, create it in a graphics program and import it into LibreOffice by clicking the Import button on the Change Icon dialog. Custom icons must be 16×16 in size and cannot contain more than 256 colors.

# Assigning shortcut keys

In addition to using the built-in keyboard shortcuts, you can define others. You can assign shortcuts to standard LibreOffice functions or your own macros and save them for use with Writer or with the entire LibreOffice suite.

To adapt shortcut keys to your needs, use the *Keyboard* page of the Customize dialog (Figure 447):

1) Choose whether to have the shortcut key assignment available in all components of LibreOffice or only in Writer.

2) Select the desired shortcut key in the *Shortcut keys* list at the top of the page.

3) Select the required function from the *Category* and *Function* lists.

4) Click the **Modify** button. The selection now appears in the *Keys* list on the lower right.

5) Click **OK** to accept the change.

Repeat as required.

> **Note**
>
> Shortcut keys that are grayed-out in the listing on the Customize dialog, such as *F1* and *F10*, are not available for reassignment.

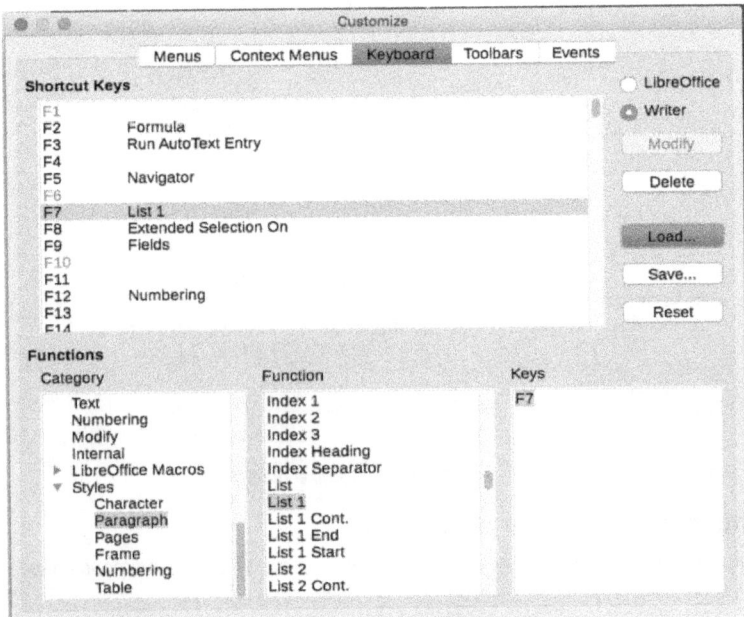

*Figure 447: Defining keyboard shortcuts for applying styles*

## Resetting the shortcut keys

To reset all of the keyboard shortcuts to their default values, click the **Reset** button near the bottom right of the Customize dialog. Use this feature with care as no confirmation dialog will be displayed; the defaults will be set without any further notice or user input.

## Saving changes to a file

Changes to the shortcut key assignments can be saved in a keyboard configuration file for use at a later time, so you can create and apply different configurations as needed. To save keyboard shortcuts to a file:

1) After making keyboard shortcut assignments, click the **Save** button on the Customize dialog (Figure 447).

2) In the Save Keyboard Configuration dialog, type a name for the keyboard configuration file in the **File name** box, or select an existing file from the list. Browse to the location where you want to save the file.

3) Click **Save**. A confirmation dialog appears if you are about to overwrite an existing file, otherwise there will be no feedback and the file will be saved.

## Loading a saved keyboard configuration

To load a saved keyboard configuration file and replace your existing configuration, click the **Load** button on the Customize dialog, and then select the configuration file from the Load Keyboard Configuration dialog.

# Assigning macros to events

In LibreOffice, when something happens, we say that an event occurred. For example, a document was opened, a key was pressed, or the mouse moved. You can associate a macro with an event, so the macro is run when the event occurs. For example, a common use is to assign the "open document" event to run a macro that performs certain setup tasks for the document.

To associate a macro with an event, use the *Events* page of the Customize dialog. For more information, see Chapter 13, Getting Started with Macros, in the *Getting Started Guide*.

# Adding functionality with extensions

An extension is a package that can be installed into LibreOffice to add new functionality.

Several extensions are shipped bundled with LibreOffice and are installed with the program. Others can be downloaded from various websites. The official extension repository is located at http://extensions.libreoffice.org/. These extensions are free of charge.

Some extensions from other sources are free of charge; others are available for a fee. Check the descriptions to see what licenses and fees apply to the ones that interest you.

## Installing extensions

Extensions can be installed in these ways:

• Directly from the *.oxt file in your system's file browser. Double-click the file.

• Directly from **Tools > Extension Manager**, as follows:

1) In LibreOffice, select **Tools > Extension Manager** from the Menu bar.

2) In the Extension Manager dialog (Figure 448), click **Add**.

3) A file browser window opens. Find and select the extension you want to install and click **Open**.

4) Users with administrator or root privileges will see a dialog where they can choose to install extensions "for all users" (shared) or "only for me" (user). Users without those privileges can install, remove, or modify extensions only for their own use.

5) The extension begins installing.

In each case, during the process you may be asked to accept a license agreement. When the installation is complete, the extension is listed in the Extension Manager dialog.

▶ **Tip**

To get extensions that are listed in the repository, you can open the Extension Manager and click the **Get more extensions online** link. You do not need to download them separately.

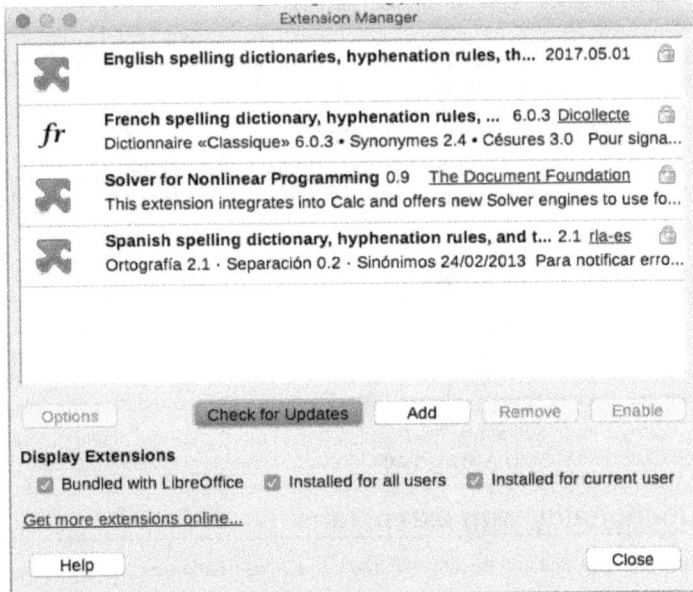

Figure 448: Using the Extension Manager